Emotions in Antiquity
(EmAnt)

Editors

Douglas Cairns (Edinburgh), Eric Cullhed (Uppsala),
Margaret Graver (Hanover, NH), Damien Nelis (Geneva),
Dennis Pausch (Dresden)

Advisory Board

Ruth R. Caston (Michigan), Thorsten Fögen (Durham),
Therese Fuhrer (Munich), Laurel Fulkerson (Florida State),
Jonas Grethlein (Heidelberg), Brooke A. Holmes (Princeton),
Christof Rapp (Munich), Ruth Scodel (Michigan),
Frisbee Sheffield (Cambridge), Teun Tieleman (Utrecht)

1

Emotions through Time

From Antiquity to Byzantium

Edited by

**Douglas Cairns, Martin Hinterberger,
Aglae Pizzone, and Matteo Zaccarini**

Mohr Siebeck

Douglas Cairns (Professor of Classics, School of History, Classics, and Archaeology, University of Edinburgh)
orcid.org/0000-0003-4408-8967

Martin Hinterberger (Professor of Byzantine Literature, Department of Byzantine and Modern Greek Studies, University of Cyprus)
orcid.org/0000-0002-4856-7132

Aglae Pizzone (Associate Professor, Department of History, University of Southern Denmark)
orcid..org/0000-0001-7765-9485

Matteo Zaccarini (Assistant Professor in Ancient History, University of Bologna at Ravenna)
orcid.org/0000-0002-4894-5607

ISBN 978-3-16-161341-8 / eISBN 978-3-16-161400-2
DOI 10.1628/978-3-16-161400-2
ISSN 2750-4689 / eISSN 2750-4700 (Emotions in Antiquity)

Die Deutsche Bibliothek lists this publication in the Deutsche Nationalbibliographie; detailed bibliographic data are available at *http://dnb.dnb.de.*

© 2022 by Mohr Siebeck, Tübingen, Germany. www.mohrsiebeck.com

This book may not be reproduced, in whole or in part, in any form (beyond that permitted by copyright law) without the publisher's written permission. This applies particularly to reproductions, translations and storage and processing in electronic systems.

The book was typeset by Martin Fischer in Tübingen, printed and bound by Hubert & Co. in Göttingen on non-aging paper.

Cover image: Church of Panagia tou Arakos, nave, south bay under dome, wall paintings, Lagoudera, Cyprus, 1192; Byzantine Institute Dumbarton Oaks fieldwork records and papers, Dumbarton Oaks, Trustees for Harvard University, Washington, D.C.

Printed in Germany.

Acknowledgements

This volume derives from a project funded by a Leverhulme Trust International Research Network grant that ran from April 2016 to March 2018 and involved partners at the University of Cyprus, the University of Edinburgh, King's College London, the University of Southern Denmark in Odense, and the University of Vienna. The editors are very grateful indeed to the Trust for the funding that made the project possible and to the network partners and their colleagues in each of the five centres who supported the project and its events. As well as meetings in Edinburgh, London, and Vienna, the network was fortunate in being able to hold one workshop in the ideal location and facilities of the Fondation Hardt, Geneva (in March 2017), and its final conference at the beautiful A. G. Leventis Gallery in Nicosia, Cyprus, from 27–9 September 2017. We are very grateful to Gary Vachicouras and his colleagues at the Fondation Hardt, to George David and Myrto Hatzaki of the Leventis Foundation, and to Loukia Loizou Hadjigavriel, Director of the A. G. Leventis Gallery, for their hospitality and assistance in making these wonderful events happen.

Three of the network partners (Cairns, Hinterberger, and Pizzone) have been involved in seeing this volume through to publication, with the indispensable assistance of Matteo Zaccarini, now of the University of Bologna. We were very sorry indeed that two partners, Lioba Theis (Vienna) and Ioannis Papadogiannakis (KCL), were, in the end, unable to submit chapters to the volume, but we should like to express our thanks here for the enormous contributions they made to making the network project both successful and convivial, as well as to the work of reviewing the chapters at an earlier stage. We are also sorry to have missed the opportunity to publish the papers of several workshop and conference participants (Toni Bierl, Inna Kupreeva, Filippomaria Pontani, Sophia Xenophontos, and Sarah Teetor): though absent from the product, they nonetheless played an important part in the process.

One of the most positive features of the Leverhulme International Network format was that it allowed us to employ a Network Facilitator, a role filled until October 2016 by Divna Manolova and thereafter by Matteo Zaccarini. Just as it was a delight to work with such efficient, committed, and companionable colleagues, so it is a huge source of satisfaction to be able to celebrate the steady progress of their academic careers on leaving the project.

VI Acknowledgements

Finally, we should like to express our thanks to the Editorial Board of the series, Emotions in Antiquity, for accommodating our volume, to Jane Burkowski for her exemplary copy-editing, to Klaus Hermannstädter and Tobias Stäbler at Mohr Siebeck for advice and support, and to Stephanie Winder for all her hard work on the Indexes.

Table of Contents

Acknowledgements V

Introduction

Douglas Cairns
A. Emotions through time? 3

Douglas Cairns
B. Emotion research in Classics 35

Martin Hinterberger and Aglae Pizzone
C. Research on emotions in the Byzantine world 41

Douglas Cairns, Martin Hinterberger, and Aglae Pizzone
D. Chapter summaries 49

Part I: Philosophy and Religion

Andrea Capra
1. Philosophy as a Chain of 'Poetic' Emotions? Plato and Beyond 59

Divna Manolova
2. Wondrous Knowledge and the Emotional Responses of Late Byzantine
Scholars to Its Acquisition 75

Petra von Gemünden
3. Methodological Issues and Issues of Content, as Exemplified
by ὀξυχολία in the *Shepherd of Hermas* 95

VIII   *Table of Contents*

Part II: Rhetorical Theory and Practice

Byron MacDougall
4. Lend a Sympathetic Ear: Rhetorical Theory and Emotion
   in Late Antique and Byzantine Homiletic 121

Aglae Pizzone
5. Emotions and λόγος ἐνδιάθετος: Πάθη in John Sikeliotes'
   Commentary on Hermogenes' *On Types of Style* 141

Floris Bernard
6. Emotional Communities in the Eleventh Century:
   Bodily Practices and Emotional Scripts 157

Jan R. Stenger
7. 'Aren't You Afraid That You Will Suffer the Same?':
   Emotive Persuasion in John Chrysostom's Preaching 179

Niels Gaul
8. Voicing and Gesturing Emotions: Remarks on Emotive Performance
   from Antiquity to the Middle Byzantine Period 201

Part III: Literature

Douglas Cairns
9. Mental Conflict from Homer to Eustathius 227

Mircea Graţian Duluş
10. *Ekphrasis* and Emotional Intensity in the *Homilies* of Philagathos
    of Cerami 247

Margaret Mullett
11. Tragic Emotions? The *Christos Paschon* 281

Martin Hinterberger
12. *Alazoneia* and *Aidōs/Aischunē* in Anna Komnene's and Niketas
    Choniates' Histories 303

Stavroula Constantinou
13. Angry Warriors in the Byzantine *War of Troy* 339

Part IV: Art and Ritual

Vicky Manolopoulou
14. Visualizing and Enacting Emotion: The Affective Capacities of the *Litē* 361

Galina Fingarova
15. Evoking Fear through the Image of the Last Judgement 383

Viktoria Räuchle
16. The Terrible Power in Giving Birth: Images of Motherhood from
    Antiquity to Byzantium 407

David Konstan
Afterword 433

Bibliography 443

Index locorum 507
Index rerum 514

Introduction

A.

Emotions through time?

Douglas Cairns

This volume (one of the outcomes of a two-year International Research Network project, funded by the Leverhulme Trust) constitutes a first step in the project of exploring the complex interactions between the emotional worlds of ancient Greece and Byzantium. The Byzantine world shaped the reception of ancient Greece for the modern; and the appropriation and reconfiguration of ancient Greek sources helped, at each historical stage and in each cultural context, to define the Byzantine world.[1] This volume's goal is thus, on the one hand, to shed new light on the Byzantine emotional universe and its impact on Medieval and early modern culture and, on the other, to illuminate ancient Greek concepts, theories, and representations of emotion by investigating their reception in Byzantium. With all due allowance for the availability of scholars and their expertise, and for the vicissitudes of the sometimes tortuous process that has led us from preliminary workshops to summative conference and thence to final publication, we have tried not to limit ourselves only to textual evidence, but to explore additional areas such as visual and material culture, performance, ritual, and the creation of affective environments.

We build on the progress that has been made to date in the investigation of the emotions in our two main disciplines, Classics and Ancient History and Byzantine studies (see Introduction B and C below). More generally, we see our work as a contribution to the growing field of emotion history, now a mature sub-discipline in which the original landmark studies have, over the past forty years, inspired a steady stream of monographs, edited collections, and articles. This is a field that has in recent years been consolidated further by the now standard proliferation of companions and handbooks and achieved a new level of institutional respectability through the establishment of dedicated research centres.[2] In venturing a contribution to this field we (clearly) believe that the

---

[1] For stimulating remarks, see Jeffreys (2014).

[2] The landmark studies are generally seen as Stearns and Stearns (1985), together with subsequent publications, such as Stearns and Stearns (1986) and Stearns (1989); Reddy (2001); Rosenwein (2006). Overviews of the field first began to appear in article form, e. g. Hitzer (2011), Matt (2011), followed by book-length surveys, such as Matt and Stearns (2014); Plamper (2015); Boddice (2018); Rosenwein and Cristiani (2018); Barclay (2020); Barclay, Crozier-de Rosa, and

history of emotions is not just a possible but also a valuable enterprise. This is not a wholly uncontroversial position, and even among those who would accept the general possibility and utility of emotion history the subject still requires a degree of definition and justification.

Scepticism regarding the possibility of emotion history is at its most forthright and extensive in Rüdiger Schnell's highly polemical (and very enjoyable) 1,052-page monograph, *Haben Gefühle eine Geschichte? Aporien einer History of Emotions*, published in 2015. Schnell has two main problems with the 'history of emotions' as an enterprise: first, it does not deliver what it promises, given that its true focus is not the inner life of subjective psychological experience, but merely the representation of such experience in the form of evaluations, classifications, concepts, standards of behaviour, or expressions – what Schnell calls 'signs' (*Zeichen*) of emotions.[3] It is these that are subject to historical change, Schnell argues, not 'the emotions themselves'.[4] Interest in the latter, Schnell argues, reflects a movement that has its roots in a contemporary and media-driven fascination (since the 1980s) with the inner life of others, with how people 'really feel'.[5] Yet subjective psychological experience, he alleges, is properly the stuff of psychology and neuroscience. Those disciplines study emotion, and need to know what it is that they are studying. We who study only representations of emotion need no such knowledge.[6] Which is fortunate, because Schnell believes that historians of emotion have set themselves the impossible task of studying not only something that cannot be accessed through the methods of historical research, but also a subject that has not been satisfactorily defined, one whose defining features are in fact constituted differently by the various disciplines that purport to study it.[7] This in effect means that historians cannot in fact decide

---

Stearns (2020). Research projects and centres include Les émotions au Moyen Age (EMMA), at Aix-Marseille and Québec; History of Emotions, at the Max Planck Institute for Human Development, Berlin; the Centre for the History of Emotions, Queen Mary University of London; and the Australian Research Council Centre of Excellence for the History of Emotions, with member institutions throughout Australia, and a journal, *Emotions: History, Culture, Society*. The Australian Centre has also given rise to a Routledge History of Emotions in Europe (Broomhall and Lynch (2019)) and a six-volume Bloomsbury series, A Cultural History of the Emotions (2019). Monograph series include Oxford University Press's Emotions of the Past (which includes titles in Classics) and Emotions in History (which so far has not), as well as Bloomsbury's History of Emotions. Specifically in Classics, the Mohr Siebeck series to which this title belongs is joined by the De Gruyter Trends in Classics sub-series on Ancient Emotions and by the Franz Steiner series, Unveiling Emotions.

[3] Schnell (2015) 17–20 and often.

[4] References to 'Gefühle an sich', 'die Gefühle selbst' (etc.) recur: e. g. Schnell (2015) 405, 456, 762, 788, 805. See, for instance, 773–4: 'Die geschichtswissenschaftliche Emotionsforschung … sieht in der Analyse von "emotion words" einen Schwerpunkt ihrer Tätigkeit. Denn sie glaubt in und mit den Worten die Emotionen selbst zu fassen.'

[5] Schnell (2015) 15–18.

[6] Schnell (2015) 20.

[7] Schnell (2015) 31; cf. 985.

A. Emotions through time? 5

what precisely it is that they profess to study.[8] 'Emotion history' means different things to different people.[9]

As a research project, therefore, 'Geschichte der Gefühle' or 'history of emotions' is to be abandoned, since *feelings* as such, i. e. subjective psychological experiences, remain inaccessible to the text-based approaches that historical disciplines must adopt. As he states in the book's conclusion (p. 967):

> Das geschichtswissenschaftliche Projekt 'Geschichte der Gefühle' ist aufzugeben, ebenso das Projekt einer 'History of emotions', sofern darunter die Geschichte von Gefühlen als subjektiven Erfahrungen bzw. als eine Geschichte des inneren Erlebens verstanden wird. Für diese Entscheidung sprechen zwei Einsichten dieses Buches. Wir kommen, erstens, an die 'tatsächlichen' Gefühle nicht heran, auch wenn dies immer wieder versucht worden ist. Noch viel weniger sind wir, zweitens, imstande, eine Geschichte dieser nicht fassbaren Gefühle zu schreiben. In einigen Studien der historischen Emotionsforschung wird offen eingeräumt, dass wir, genauso wenig wie wir wüssten, was unsere Mitmenschen – oder gar was wir selbst – fühlten, keine Auskunft geben könnten über die Gefühle unserer Vorfahren ...

Historical research, on Schnell's view, would be liberated were it to dispense with the focus on inner feelings and concentrate instead on externally observable phenomena.[10] According to him, this would still leave a great deal in the domain of emotion that we *can* study historically:

> Geschichte der emotionsrelevanten Handlungen, Gesten, Praktiken, sozialen Interaktionen (II), die Geschichte der verbalen Emotionsäußerungen (III), die Geschichte der Diskurse über Emotionen (IV), die Geschichte der Darstellungen von Emotionen und deren Funktionen (V u. VI), schließlich die Beschreibung der Veränderungen in diesen Bereichen und die Frage nach den Gründen für diese Veränderungen (VII).[11]

Schnell's vigorous polemic misses the mark in many ways. But his critique is nonetheless useful for that, as criticism almost always is. Even if it rested on no more than misapprehension it would require a more thorough justification for the enterprise of emotion history than is normally offered, and so may help clarify the aims and character of that enterprise. Schnell does, moreover, as his argument proceeds, make a number of valid points against some of the sweeping generalizations, the unsubstantiated theories of change and development, the monolithic models by which whole periods and societies are assigned a particular emotional character, and the tendency to reinvent the wheel by giving an affective inflection to quite familiar (grand) narratives of social, cultural, and intellectual history. A great deal of emotion history *is* broad-brush, over-schematic, and reductive, especially in the often undefended application of social

---

[8] Schnell (2015) 405.

[9] E.g. Schnell (2015) 808.

[10] Schnell (2015) 967–73. Cf. above, n. 3.

[11] Schnell (2015) 971–2; Roman numerals refer to the earlier chapters of the book.

constructionist premises that Schnell so doggedly assails. Yet his argument is at its most interesting, and the attempt to refute it most productive, where it in fact agrees with the suppositions of those who do believe in the history of emotions. In both these ways, answering Schnell also entails a critical examination of some of the working assumptions of the 'history of emotions' movement.

Schnell and his targets do not in fact differ greatly on the question of which aspects of affectivity or emotion lend themselves to historical study. The externally observable signs, representations, constructions, and conceptions of emotion that Schnell proposes as legitimate objects of historical enquiry are precisely what those who profess to write the history of emotions *do* focus on.[12] There is a superficial issue here, about what we mean by 'history' (and to some extent even about what we mean by 'of'), but also a crucially important one, about what we mean by 'emotion'. To take the superficial issue first: the history of phenomenon *x* is by no means confined to changes in the phenomenon itself. A history of influenza (or of Covid-19) would not focus only on the biology of viruses and their genetic mutations,[13] but would encompass also the social, political, cultural, and scientific contexts in which viruses spread and are treated, as well as the social, political, cultural, and scientific consequences of their spread and treatment. A history of Ben Nevis would not be limited to geological and other physical changes. A history of beer would not just be about hops, malted barley, and water, how beer matures or goes sour, or how it is physically processed by those who drink it. A history of the River Clyde would be more than a monotonous tale of flowing H_2O, with growing admixtures of other substances over the years. A *history of* these things would include all kinds of contextual material, from the uses of beer in a wide range of societies and social contexts to the role of the Clyde in Glasgow's development as a centre for the importation of tobacco from Virginia and as the 'workshop' of the British Empire.[14]

The clue is in the word *history* – the history of *x* is a narrative of human interactions with *x*. A 'history of' a phenomenon will never depend simply on access to phenomena as such, because, in the relevant sense, there are no phenomena as such – all phenomena must appear (φαίνεσθαι), under some aspect, to someone. History is about the record of human interaction *with* phenomena in so far as they are cognized by human beings, and so also about the social, political, and cultural implications and consequences *of* these cognized phenomena. It is precisely a matter of representations and traces. It involves a narrative of events and phenomena that is largely based on earlier narratives about those events

---

[12] To take only the most prominent examples, the Stearnses' 'emotionology', Reddy's 'emotional regimes', and Rosenwein's 'emotional communities' focus precisely on emotion norms and emotion concepts as negotiated and accommodated in the pragmatics of social interaction.

[13] See e. g. Spinney (2017), one of many works on the 'Spanish flu' of 1918–19; cf. Honigsbaum (2020) on that and subsequent pandemics.

[14] See Unger (2007) on beer; Riddell (2000) on the River Clyde.

A. Emotions through time? 7

and phenomena, as well as on the traces that those events and phenomena have left in a variety of sources and media. It is not just the emotions of the past that are gone; past events are gone too – we generally have only representations, accounts, reconstructions, and external signs. But we do not conclude on that basis that history as such is impossible. History deals not with events 'as such', but with the evidence for events. We also have evidence for emotions. Schnell clearly thinks that we can study such evidence; and to do so is largely what the targets of his criticism mean by doing emotion history. If emotion were indeed the subjective, internal, private thing that Schnell claims, historians would be acting wholly within the remit of their profession in seeking to study how people in different societies and at different times have tried to come to terms with it.

This takes us to the more substantive issue. Emotions are also events – they have an action- or event-structure of their own (one that is often described in terms of 'scripts');[15] and both emotion events themselves and the place of those events in larger event-structures lend themselves to representation in narrative terms.[16] This is true because emotions are not private, internal, subjective experiences, but physically embodied, manifested in behaviour, socially and contextually situated, and embedded in the conceptual categories of particular linguistic communities. The evidence of emotion events that survives in the historical record is evidence of emotion as such, in the true sense of the term, not of phenomena that are in some way derivative of or secondary to emotion.

An oddity of Schnell's polemic is that, though few have pursued the point with quite his tenacity, a great many of those whom he attacks do in fact agree with him that a history of emotions as such is an impossibility. A leading figure in Classical emotions research, Angelos Chaniotis, writes that 'the ancient historian cannot study what people really felt', but only 'the external stimuli that generated emotions as well as the cultural and social parameters that determined when and how emotions were represented in texts and images'.[17] A number of our contributors in the present volume are, not unreasonably, attracted by similar formulations. Schnell acknowledges that such views are widespread in

---

[15] See Schank and Abelson (1977); Abelson (1981); Fehr and Russell (1984) 482; Mandler (1984); Shaver et al. (1987); Tomkins (1987); Fischer (1991); Russell (1991a) 442–4, (1991b) 39, (2003) 150–2, 160–6; in Classics, see Kaster (2005), esp. 63; cf. Cairns (2008). As Russell writes ((1991a) 443 = (1991b) 39): 'A script is to an event what a prototype is to an object', and so script theory is a species of the prototype approach to categorization pioneered by Wittgenstein (2009) §§ 66–7, and developed in particular by E. Rosch (e.g. Rosch (1978)) and G. Lakoff (esp. Lakoff (1987)). See also below.

[16] See De Sousa (1987) 183, (1990) 438; Goldie (1999), (2012), esp. 56–75; Nussbaum (2001) 236; Voss (2004) 181–224; Mendonça (2019) 679–84. A trail was blazed in this direction by Bruner (1986); cf. Bruner (1991).

[17] Chaniotis (2012b) 94–5. See also Chaniotis and Ducrey (2013) 11. The point is virtually a founding principle of the 'history of emotions' movement: see Stearns and Stearns (1985), esp. 825–6; Matt (2014) 44.

the 'history of emotions' community, but still tasks those who make these concessions with the mistaken conviction that they are able, nonetheless, to get to 'the emotions themselves'.[18] Though such people are, on the whole (according to Schnell), social constructionists who do not generally accept that emotions are private, internal, historically invariant subjective experiences, nevertheless they are driven to accept that there are indeed inner feelings independent of language and culture and persistently fail to distinguish signs (concepts, expressions, etc.) of emotion from emotions themselves.[19] These scholars, according to Schnell, promise to do emotion history, but in fact do only the history of emotional discourse. Literary scholars who deal with emotions in the literary artefacts of the past similarly deal only with representations, not with the emotions themselves,[20] and their task is further complicated (Schnell alleges) by the possibility that emotions represented in literary texts may bear little relation to those of everyday life.[21]

A further oddity, therefore, is that Schnell regards his opponents' research as fatally compromised by the fact that emotions do not represent a single and easily definable category, yet his own critique is underpinned by a narrow and rigid sense of what emotions 'really' are – private, internal, historically invariant subjective experiences, present only in the moment, only in real-time interaction, and irrecoverable once that moment is gone. A partial explanation for this approach perhaps lies in a particular aspect of emotion history that many readers will have lived through, namely the gradual replacement of *Gefühl* by *Emotion* as the default German term for 'emotion'.[22] 'Feelings' may sound more private, more internal, than 'emotions'.[23] But though many do distinguish between feelings and emotions (or between affect and emotion),[24] and though talking about 'feelings' rather than 'emotions' perhaps raises more immediate issues regarding conceptualization, labelling, and communicability, not even the distinction between feeling and emotion makes for a private, internal world of purely subjective experience.

We should probably concede that first-person experience rests, at least to some extent, on processes that are not accessible to others. In some cases, indeed, there are aspects of these processes that are not phenomenally present to us in experience. Equally, however, many aspects of first-person experience and

---

[18] Schnell (2015) 20–3 and *passim* (e.g. 365–6, 368, 371, 395).

[19] Schnell (2015) 23–9 and often, e.g. 364–74, 403, 405, 685, 687, 788.

[20] Schnell (2015) 711–17, 731, 737, 745–6.

[21] Schnell (2015), e.g. 692–3, 710–17.

[22] Schnell (2015) 59–64 and 685–6 n. 55 discusses differences between *Gefühl* and *Emotion*, but charges historians with effacing distinctions drawn in other disciplines, while insisting that both *Gefühle* and *Emotionen* are private, internal, subjective experiences.

[23] See Schnell (2015) 59–61.

[24] See e.g. Damasio (1994). Cf. below on 'core affect' vs 'emotion'.

the processes that underpin it are intersubjectively constituted by conceptual knowledge, language, and culture. Visual perception, for example, is not just a matter of passive sensory input, but to a substantial extent also involves top-down processes such as active prediction and the application of conceptual and experiential knowledge. It may appear to us that we receive, passively, a complete and objective picture of a given visual scene, but any number of well-known experiments, common illusions, and phenomena such as change blindness and inattentional blindness indicate that, to a very large extent, what we see is what we expect to see in the light of predictions made on the basis of experience and in the light of our own subjective aims and concerns.[25] Similarly, what one sees is influenced by the conceptual structure of one's native language.[26] The performance of Russian speakers vis-à-vis English speakers, for example, in simple colour discrimination tasks is influenced by the fact that Russian has two linguistic categories for the range that English speakers call blue.[27] These hues appear together in Russian representations of the rainbow.[28] Users of English can translate the Russian terms easily, and both Russian and English speakers can see and distinguish the same hues, but the experimental evidence shows that English speakers do not process those hues precisely as Russian speakers do – reaction times differ in a way that suggests that linguistic categories influence attention, and thus that the hues in question mean something slightly different for members of the two linguistic communities. Language, on this evidence, influences the top-down aspect of vision as a rich perceptual process. As language influences perception, so it influences thought: in languages which have the relevant feature, for example, grammatical gender conditions the way that speakers think and talk about inanimate objects.[29] Though they distance themselves from earlier, more sweeping and deterministic versions of the 'Sapir–Whorf hypothesis', many linguists now contend that language permeates and influences thought in multiple ways.[30] Just as the mechanisms by which we perceive the external world are thoroughly permeated by the concepts and categories given by our experience as social and cultural beings and as users of language, so too are those by which we make sense of our own subjective experiences. A substantial body of work suggests that affect and emotion can be experienced dif-

---

[25] See e.g. Simons and Chabris (1999); Hansen et al. (2006); Zhang and Lin (2013); Vetter and Newen (2014); Barrett (2017) 59–61. Cf. Noë (2004) 49–57; Troscianko (2014) 50–3. For a recent set of essays on the cognitive penetrability of perception in general, see Zeimbekis and Raftopoulos (2015).

[26] See in general Lupyan et al. (2020).

[27] Winawer et al. (2007).

[28] Barrett (2017) 145.

[29] Boroditsky, Schmidt, and Phillips (2003).

[30] See Casasanto (2008); Deutscher (2010); Boroditsky (2012); Casasanto (2016), (2017); cf. (on Homeric psychology) Russo (2012) 25–8. For the relevance of Whorfian linguistic relativism to the psychological constructionist view of emotion, see Barrett (2006a) 37.

ferently when speakers of more than one language (or late versus early bilinguals) do not use their mother tongue,[31] indicating that use of the native language involves forms of affective processing that second and further languages do not. These indications of the influence of language on first-person experience suggest that differences in the conceptualization of emotion – e. g. where a single concept in language A maps on to more than one in language B – represent, at least to some extent, different ways both of seeing the world and of understanding oneself as an experiencer of the world.[32]

As thinkers from 'Longinus' in the first century to William James in the nineteenth have recognized,[33] emotions do not come in distinct, pre-labelled packages – all human beings are at all times in some affective state or another.[34] Every action we undertake, every state we are in feels a certain way, even if that feeling seems to us to involve a relative absence of affect. The episodes that we, in contemporary English, describe as 'emotions' are merely the peaks and troughs in this affective continuum.[35] This is what the constructionist psychologists James A. Russell and Lisa Feldman Barrett call 'core affect'.[36] As Lindquist and Barrett put it, 'Core affect is an ongoing, ever-changing, psychologically primitive state that has both hedonic and arousal-based properties',[37] that is states of core affect

---

[31] See e.g. Keysar, Hayakawa, and An (2012); Pavlenko (2012); Costa et al. (2014); Hayakawa et al. (2016); Ivaz, Costa, and Duñabeitia (2016); Shin and Kim (2017).

[32] See further below.

[33] As Longinus has it, *On the Sublime* 22.1: 'There is an indefinite multiplicity of emotions (πάθη) and no one can even say how many there are.' For the same point, see James (1890) ii.485:

> [I]f one should seek to name each particular one [of the emotions] of which the human heart is the seat, it is plain that the limit to their number would lie in the introspective vocabulary of the seeker, each race of men having found names for some shade of feeling which other races have left undiscriminated. If then we should seek to break the emotions, thus enumerated, into groups, according to their affinities, it is again plain that all sorts of groupings would be possible, according as we chose this character or that as a basis, and that all groupings would be equally real and true. The only question would be, does this grouping or that suit our purpose best?

Cf. James (1890) ii.454:

> Now the moment the genesis of an emotion is accounted for, as the arousal by an object of a lot of reflex acts which are forthwith felt, *we immediately see why there is no limit to the number of possible different emotions which may exist, and why the emotions of different individuals may vary indefinitely*, both as to their constitution and as to objects which call them forth.

For James as a believer in 'core affect' *avant la lettre*, see Barrett (2006a) 38–40.

[34] Russell and Barrett (1999) 806; Lindquist and Barrett (2008) 902; Russell and Barrett (2009) 104; Russell (2009) 1265.

[35] Cf. Barrett (2006a) 36: 'the experience of an emotion will pop out as a separate event from the ebb and flow in ongoing core affect'. Cf. Cairns (2008) 50–1; Cairns and Nelis (2017) 12.

[36] See Russell and Barrett (1999); Russell (2003); Barrett (2004); Russell (2005); Barrett (2006a), (2006b); Russell (2009); Russell and Barrett (2009); Barrett (2017) 72–7.

[37] Lindquist and Barrett (2008) 898; cf. Russell (2003) 148; Barrett (2006a) 30; Russell (2009) 1264.

exist on a continuum of valence (pleasant/good or unpleasant/bad for the subject) and arousal (how calm or agitated the subject feels). Core affect underpins a variety of states, including emotion, and differs from emotion in that it need not be labelled or interpreted. For psychological constructionists, such as Barrett and Russell,[38] it is precisely interpretation, or conceptualization, that makes the difference: core affective states are experienced as emotions when interpreted in the light of the conceptual categories of emotion that the individual has acquired through experience and socialization.[39] According to them, this is a process in which language plays a crucial role.[40] On this view, emotions are like perception (e. g. colour perception) in that they have both bottom-up and top-down aspects; in the case of emotions, the bottom-up aspect is supplied by core affect, a matter of perceiving both the world and one's own bodily states, while the top-down aspect depends on concepts and categories.[41] In making sense of the world, emotions also make sense of our experience of and responses to the world.[42] As Lisa Feldman Barrett puts it in her book-length synthesis of this approach:[43]

In every waking moment, your brain uses past experience, organized as concepts to guide your actions and give your sensations meaning. When the concepts involved are emotion concepts, your brain constructs instances of emotion ...

Emotions are not reactions to the world. You are not a passive receiver of sensory input but an active constructor of your emotions. From sensory input and past experience, your

---

[38] See Russell (2003) 151:

The proposed approach is called *psychological construction* to emphasize that the sequence of events that make up any actual emotional episode is neither fixed by biological inheritance from the human evolutionary past (as basic emotion theories have it) nor fixed by social rules or categories (as social constructionist theories have it) but is constructed anew each time to fit its specific circumstances.

The most accessible summary is Russell (2009). See also Lindquist and Barrett (2008); Barrett (2009), (2017). For precursors of this approach in earlier psychology, including William James (James (1884), (1890), (1894)) and the well-known experiments of Schachter and Singer (1962), see Barrett (2006a) 38–40, (2017) 34.

[39] See Barrett (2006a) 31: 'Core affect is the ongoing, ever-changing state that is available to be categorized during emotion conceptualization, much like the visible light spectrum is categorized in color perception and physical movements in person perception.' Plamper (2015) 263 is quite wrong to say that '"core affects" [*sic*] are ultimately basic emotions à la Tomkins and Ekman'.

[40] Barrett (2017) 84–111 and *passim*.

[41] Top-down/bottom-up: see Barrett (2006a) 35. As Russell (2009) 1270 puts it:

Perceiving oneself as having an emotion is no different in kind from other perceptions. Percepts are often compelling, but they are not simple. Nor are they infallible. Like other acts of perception, an emotional experience is not entirely 'bottom-up', not entirely data driven. A percept is the end product of a complex process involving raw data, concepts, learning, and context.

For the specific analogy with colour perception, see Barrett (2006a) 20, 27–31, 34–5, 41–2; Lindquist and Barrett (2008) 902; Barrett (2017) 84, 129, 145–6.

[42] For feelings and emotions as forms of self-perception, see Damasio (1999); Laird (2007).

[43] Barrett (2017) 31.

brain constructs meaning and prescribes action. If you didn't have concepts that represent your past experience, all your sensory inputs would just be noise. You wouldn't know what the sensations are, what caused them, nor how to behave to deal with them. With concepts, your brain makes meaning of sensation, and sometimes that meaning is an emotion.

The crucial point about this is that, while there may be more or less 'private', i. e. internal and subjective, aspects of core affect, emotions are not wholly private, internal, subjective experiences. They depend on concepts and categories that may be individually inflected (and in whose deployment individuals may be more or less sophisticated) but are not unique to any one individual. While there are unmediated aspects of subjective affective experience – perhaps ineffable or not immediately transparent even to their patients – as soon as we think and talk about such experience, it is mediated. In so far as 'the feelings themselves' are interpreted, conceptualized, and labelled as objects of our thought, they are more than purely personal. As Wittgenstein insisted, no one has a private language for subjective experience:[44] as soon as we name, categorize, talk, or think about such things, difficult though that sometimes is, we inevitably draw on the shared, intersubjective resources of the languages we speak. One's own subjective understanding of one's own emotions is inflected by what emotions are taken to be in one's language and culture. Emotions are not perceiver-independent entities to which we merely apply the labels that name them,[45] but perceiver-dependent notions which depend on intersubjective categories and on interactions between the perceiver and the world. The concepts and categories, moreover, by which we make sense of our core affective experience are, on this view, not 'classical' ones, in which membership depends on fulfilment of a limited set of necessary and sufficient conditions, but 'fuzzy' ones with indeterminate boundaries, exhibiting overlap with other categories, ambiguities regarding membership, and an internal structure that encompasses peripheral as well as prototypical cases.[46] Just as affective experience does not come in discrete chunks, ready to be labelled, so the labels that we do apply cover a range of cases with a variety of characteristics.

Subjective experience is, accordingly, thoroughly permeated by intersubjectivity. Even to reflect on how one feels at any given moment involves a process of sense-making that draws on the resources of language and culture. As William Reddy sees it, getting from feeling to expression is an act of *translation*, one that both reduces complexity and simultaneously influences how we feel.[47] Thinking about, categorizing, naming, expressing, and acting on one's feelings involve a

---

[44] Wittgenstein (2009) §§ 243–315. His views are briefly noted but dismissed by Schnell (2015) 691 n. 76; cf. 781 n. 393.

[45] See Barrett (2006a) 40, (2017) 160–3, quoting James (1890) i.195, (1894) 520.

[46] See Fehr and Russell (1984); Shaver et al. (1987); Russell (1991a), (1991b), (2003), (2009) 1267, 1275–6; Russell and Barrett (1999) 805–8; Barrett (2017) 16, 88–9; cf. n. 15 above.

[47] See Reddy (1997) 330–2; Reddy (2001) 96–111, 128–9. Schnell (2015) deals with Reddy's work throughout his book, but systematically and in detail at pp. 419–63.

A. Emotions through time? 13

process of transformation,[48] but one that is also part of the whole experience of having the emotion in question. And it need not be only a matter of language or conscious reflection: even where there is no explicit act of categorization or labelling – i.e. nothing that is actually or potentially formulated in linguistic terms – aspects of non-verbal behaviour, of expression and performance, may play the same role of transforming the inner affective experience, whatever it is, into something that is now a member of a culturally recognized emotion category.[49] The 'mess inside' does exist, but human beings are pattern-making creatures, driven to impose sense on the mess both inside and outside,[50] and our perceptions not only of the world, but also of our own internal states are thoroughly permeated by patterns drawn from the conceptual, linguistic, and social resources that shape our experience. This process of thinking and talking about emotion (and all such processes), whether we do it privately, in everyday interaction with others, or in our scholarly and scientific endeavours, does reduce complexity,[51] but this is a loss which is the price of all communication and all the ways in which we endeavour to understand ourselves and the world we live in.[52] In the case of emotion, too, the reduction in complexity is not a matter of the relation between the phenomenon and our attempts to communicate it, but

---

[48] See specifically Reddy (1997) 331–2; (2001) 102–5, 128–9. The limitation of Reddy's approach lies in its primary focus on what he calls 'emotives', statements of the sort 'I am angry', which he regards as 'instruments for directly changing, building, hiding, intensifying emotions' (Reddy (2001) 105), as 'emotional expressions' that 'are like performatives in that they do something to the world' (Reddy (2001) 111). But, as we have seen, the role of linguistic and conceptual categories in the construction of emotions as sense-making mechanisms goes much further than that. With that proviso, however, Reddy's approach is comparable at least in general terms with the psychological constructionism of Russell and Barrett: for a summary of the importance of language in that approach see Lindquist et al. (2016). Views such as his, in fact, are widely held: see e.g. Collingwood (1938) 111, cited by Colombetti (2009) 6; Solomon (2007) 127–36; Frevert (2009) 205; Scheer (2012) 212–13; Matt and Stearns (2014) 10; Matt (2014) 42–4; Plamper (2015) 32–3 (quoting Miller (1997) 31). For a critical overview of 'what language does to feelings' see Colombetti (2009).

[49] See (roughly) Reddy (2001) 106.

[50] See Boyd (2009) 87–90, with references; Barrett (2017), esp. 87–104. On emotion perception as pattern recognition (or pattern construction) see Gallagher (2020) 128–36, 149, 206. For the 'mess inside' and how we use narrative to make sense of it, see Goldie (2012).

[51] See Reddy (2001) 108 on 'emotives': 'as descriptions they always fail, because of the complexity of the personal states they describe in the first instance, and because of the effects they have on these states as they are formulated and uttered'.

[52] See Eco (1995) on Borges (1935). In so far as Schnell accepts this point at all, it is in his claim that emotion labels often designate episodes of emotional experience that in fact involve compounds of mixed emotions. See Schnell (2015) 223–6 (with references in 224 nn. 108–9); cf. pp. 236, 318. This recognizes that language can reduce the complexity of subjective experience; but it still presents subjective experience as a matter of mixed, but still reified entities. Some of those that Schnell cites in support of his contention that 'Die emotionalen Zustände eines Menschen sind weniger durch Basalemotionen als durch Mischzustände von Emotionen geprägt' (223–4), entailing a 'Differenz von tatsächlicher individueller Emotionserfahrung (Mischung mehrerer Emotionen) und soziokultureller Bezeichnungspraxis (ein einziges Emo-

14 *Douglas Cairns*

a fundamental aspect of the phenomenon as we experience it. Though one must concede (to Schnell and others) that the role, in views of this sort, of unconceptualized feelings or core affect – the mess inside – does entail an acceptance that there are *some* aspects of affective experience that are inaccessible to historical methods,[53] there is absolutely no reason to concede that raw, unmediated affect (what Russell calls 'the simplest raw (nonreflective) feelings evident in moods and emotions') is what emotion 'really' is.[54] Such feelings may be perceptible by their patient in ways that are unavailable to others, and so largely unavailable for historical analysis, but still it is not these that are the proposed subject matter of emotion history, precisely because, in so far as they are unconceptualized, they are not 'the emotions themselves' or the emotions 'as such'. Even at the level of individual subjective experience emotion is thoroughly permeated by intersubjectivity; and the fundamental relation between language and emotional experience already offers considerable scope for historical investigation of emotion in the texts and documents that are our sources.

One need not go all the way with the psychological constructionism of Barrett and Russell, and indeed most psychologists do not. There is discussion to be had about whether and if so precisely how the twin variables of valence and arousal account for the complexity of core affective states (including the possibility of mixed or ambivalent states in which positive and negative valence coexist).[55] And it remains possible to question the hard and fast distinction that Russell and Barrett draw between 'core affect' and 'emotion', which seems to sit rather uneasily with the view that both subjective experience and the perceptible world form a continuum that our concepts and categories differentiate – 'core affect' and 'emotion' themselves would seem to be labels that effect a reduction of this complexity. This might itself suggest that core affect and emotion are themselves ranges within a continuum – for example, that cases of core affect might exhibit varying degrees of cognitive and conceptual penetration of the kind that Barrett and Russell attribute to emotions, while what most people would regard as fullblown emotions, in terms of the definiteness of their eliciting conditions and the specificity of their intentionality, might still resist easy conceptualization or labelling as one of the set of phenomena that our culture typically regards as emotions.[56] We might, that is, know perfectly well how our current affective state

---

tionswort)', in fact support a position on the relation between emotion language and emotion experience that is closer to Reddy's or to Russell's and Barrett's (e. g. Kagan (2007) 111–41, 191–2).

[53] Schnell (2015) 365.

[54] Russell (2003) 148.

[55] For recent discussion bearing on these issues, see Russell (2017).

[56] Barrett (2006a) 36 writes: 'Core affect, in philosophical terms, is not intentional, not "about" anything in particular. Core affect is caused – it represents the state of the person in relation to the immediate environment (in philosophical terms, this is its intension), but "cause" and "aboutness" are not equivalent. When we identify our core affect as being about something, it becomes intentional, and the experience of emotion begins.' But if at least some states of core

arose and what its objects are, feel ourselves to be affected in a way that stands out against the background of affective experience, and yet still be unable to put a conventional name to the feeling. There may be aspects of a full-blown emotion scenario as well as of states of core affect that are difficult to express in words. One suspects that patterns of core affect may amount to what most people would call emotions, and it remains possible to believe that, though emotions have no single 'fingerprint' in the brain, in the body, or in behaviour, nonetheless there are more substantive patterns of correlation between affect, bodily changes, expression, and behaviour than psychological constructionism allows,[57] and thus that cross-cultural similarity in prototypical patterns of emotion expression and emotional response depends on more than just cross-cultural similarity in the conditions that give rise to emotion. One consequence of the hard and fast distinction between 'emotion' and 'core affect' is to separate the former from features of the latter that those of us who are not psychological constructionists might see as characteristic of emotion – features such as what seems to some an impressive degree of cross-cultural similarity in the patterns of bodily changes, symptoms, expressions, behaviour, and action that different cultures associate with what appear to be reflexes of similar types of phenomenon.

None of these doubts, however, would warrant the assumptions either that emotions or feelings are nothing more than essentially private, subjectively experienced internal causes of external expression and behaviour or that the experience of emotion – like our experience of ourselves and the world in all other respects – is not thoroughly permeated by the linguistic and cultural concepts and categories by which we make sense of the world. If that is so, then the resources – linguistic or non-linguistic – that one uses to conceptualize emotion are also available to communicate it. All forms of communication share the intersubjectivity that is the hallmark of language. Emotion is enmeshed in language in a variety of different ways, but its relation to language makes it, in all these contexts, tractable and discussable rather than something that is accessible only to the individual in question or to science.[58] As such, emotion is also accessible to the historian.

If even the first-person experience of emotion is thoroughly permeated by intersubjectivity, then there is no absolute gulf between the access that we have to our own experience and that which we have to others'. Though our experience of ourselves is in important ways unlike our experience of others,[59] neither is 100 per cent focused on private internal states. Emotions involve perceptions of the world and perceptions of our own internal states. In both respects, perception

---

affect register features of the world, they are intentional (see esp. same article, p. 38), and the distinction between core affect and emotion becomes fuzzy.

[57] For criticism along these lines, see e.g. Scherer (2009) 1334–7; Colombetti (2014) 46–9.

[58] See again Colombetti (2009).

[59] See e.g. Gallagher (2020) 118–19. The classic statement is Nagel (1974).

16 Douglas Cairns

will be as richly informed by knowledge and experience as it is in all other contexts. Thus, we can expect our perception of others' emotions as well as the perceptions of the world and of ourselves that inform our own emotions to be shaped by the linguistic and conceptual categories of the cultures we inhabit.[60] If that is the case, then, by the same token, the gulf that Schnell and others posit between the emotions of those we encounter directly in the here and now and the emotions represented in historical and literary sources also breaks down. Schnell in fact accepts that, on his own view of emotion, there is no hard and fast distinction between past and present – if emotions are the private, subjective experiences that he takes them to be, we have no access to the 'actual' emotions of anyone else at any time, even if that person is emoting, right now, before our very eyes.[61] The emotions of the long dead are not, on this view, qualitatively different. This, as Schnell recognizes, is a concession that his opponents also often make.[62]

But we should not make that concession, for it is not true that we have no access to the emotions of other people. The privacy of the mental is an extreme Cartesian standpoint that is no longer widely shared, whether at the scientific or at the popular level. Most of us believe that we can – perhaps normally, perhaps just sometimes – perceive others' emotions. We do not and cannot conduct ourselves in the world as though other people's feelings and motivations were wholly inscrutable; in operating, in fact, with quite the opposite view, our practice rests not on access to private inner states, but on context. We do not think and behave as if our responses to others' emotions depended on hidden, internal causes, nor do they. Emotions are intersubjective, interpersonal, and interactive phenomena.

Often enough, we perceive others' emotions directly, a point stressed repeatedly in the Continental phenomenological tradition.[63] As Wittgenstein puts it: 'Just try – in a real case – to doubt someone else's fear or pain!'[64] This is a point on which the psychological constructionism of Barrett and Russell agrees, at least in essentials, with the phenomenologically inspired enactivism of Shaun Gallagher.[65] According to both approaches, one perceives the emotions of others directly, but this perception is a rich process, informed by experientially formed and socially shared concepts.[66] We perceive others' facial expressions, posture, bodily movements, and actions as typical markers of the emotion concepts

---

[60] See Lindquist et al. (2006); Gendron et al. (2012); Barrett (2017) 42–7.

[61] See e.g. Schnell (2015) 971.

[62] See e.g. Schnell (2015) 967, quoted above.

[63] See e.g. Scheler (1973) 21, 232–58; Merleau-Ponty (2012) 190–2, 372. Cf. Gallagher (2005) 228; Gallagher and Zahavi (2008) 202–3; Gallagher (2012) 181–5, (2020) 122–3; Schloßberger (2020) 76–9.

[64] Wittgenstein (2009) § 303; cf. § 170; also Wittgenstein (1967) §§ 220, 225.

[65] See most recently Gallagher (2020) 128–31.

[66] Contrast Schnell (2015) 972: what we observe in everyday life is not emotion but the performance of emotion.

that our socially developed brains construct; and we do so to different degrees depending on whether we are interacting with a member of the group to which we ourselves belong or with an out-group member.[67] Neither approach holds that we merely recognize pre-given, perceiver-independent patterns strictly associated with specific emotions. Barrett, however, on occasion refers to this process using the terminology of more traditional forms of 'Theory of Mind', both 'Theory Theory' (in which we infer, more or less theoretically, others' mental states on the basis of external evidence) and 'Simulation Theory' (according to which we understand others' mental states by – somehow – simulating them ourselves). Thus, Barrett is prepared to describe the perception of others' emotions as inference or even as guesswork.[68] One reason for this, it seems, is precisely that the properties that we perceive when we perceive others' emotions are not perceiver-independent. Thus, while we think we can see (e.g.) another person's anger, the only way to be sure that such a perception is accurate would be to ask them (and be lucky enough to receive an honest and informative answer).[69] But the fact that perception might be mistaken does not mean that more than perception is involved.[70] References to inference and guesswork sit uneasily with the constructionist premise that categorization informs and takes place at the point of perception.[71] As Barrett's constructionist colleague, James A. Russell, writes, 'most of us do not hypothesise fear – we see it. We see discrete emotions in others and experience them in ourselves.'[72] Phenomenologically, the experience does not present itself as one of guessing or inferring. There is no further stage at which inference enters the picture: if perceiving another's emotions is like perceiving colours, there is – even if both forms of perception are inflected by the conceptual categories that the perceiver brings to bear – no guesswork involved. Thus any 'inference' or 'guesswork' must, on this view, be intrinsic to the rich process of perception itself rather than a matter of phenomenologically distinct, conscious processes.[73] And that is not really 'inference' or 'guesswork' at all. True, direct social perception is not infallible;[74] but that is because the properties so perceived are not perceiver-independent. Both the constructionist and the

---

[67] See Gutsell and Inzlicht (2010); Gallagher (2020) 148–54.

[68] For 'inference' or 'guesswork', see Barrett (2017) 196, 234–6, 246; cf. Barrett (2006a) 36. The underlying neural processes, however, are regularly explained in terms of 'simulation' (e.g. (2017) 28 and often).

[69] Barrett (2006a) 24: 'Verbal report, even with all of its failings, may be the only means of assessing the experience of emotion. If we want to know whether a person is experiencing an emotion, we have to ask them.' Cf. Barrett (2017) 140.

[70] See Gallagher (2020) 131–6.

[71] So Barrett (2017) 39–40, 196, 234–6, 246; cf. (2006a) 30; Gallagher (2020) 145.

[72] Russell (2009) 1274, with further explanation on p. 1275.

[73] Cf. Barrett (2017) 86. Against even that role for 'inference' at a sub-personal level, see Gallagher (2020) 134, 140–6, 151–4.

[74] See Gallagher (2020) 131–54; cf. Barrett (2017) 40.

enactivist approach therefore emphasize that, when we think we detect others' emotions, we are not speculating about undetectable internal experiences, but construing the patterns we perceive as meaningful, both as bodily movements and as contextually and socially situated events understood substantially through our own experience of the concepts and categories of the cultures in which we have grown up.[75]

But though emotions at least typically prepare us for action of some sort, there is no necessary connection between subjective emotional experience and any one single pattern, or even any very limited set of patterns, of expression or behaviour.[76] There are, indeed, prototypical associations, embedded in the emotion categories of a given culture, but these span a wide range of often heterogeneous cases.[77] One can express or act upon emotion in a large number of different ways. Or not at all.[78] And thus not all emotional experiences, perceived and categorized as such by their patient, are by any means directly perceptible by others. In some cases, whatever external indications there are may be ambiguous or misleading. Often, too, people set out to mislead. Yet emotions typically have intentional content that relates to some pattern of eliciting conditions appraised as affectively salient by the patient. They are thus situated, contextualized experiences, experiences that respond to events and situations construed in a certain way. They have, as we noted above, an event-like structure that lends itself to representation in narrative. Thus, Gallagher argues, where direct perception fails, narrative takes over, based on whatever knowledge one can bring to bear of the contexts in which emotion unfolds.[79] This belongs in general with a narrative approach to social cognition and other-understanding that is now gaining ground against traditional 'Theory of Mind' approaches.[80]

Whether or not there is any strong correlation between emotion concepts, families of emotion concepts, cross-culturally paralleled emotion concepts and specific patterns of affect, expression, and behaviour is an issue that we can leave to one side. The main point for our purposes is that emotions, i.e. the kinds of things we talk about when we use superordinate-level categories such

---

[75] See e.g. Barrett (2006a) 33.

[76] Russell (2003), esp. 150, 159, 161–2; Baumeister et al. (2007); Kagan (2007) 192; Russell (2009) 1269; Barrett (2017) 4–15, 39–40, 42–55, and *passim*. The prototype approach to emotion categories suggests that no single element of an emotion script is necessary: thus, any given instance need not involve expression or action at all; and where action and expression are involved there is no single necessary pattern.

[77] As Kagan (2007) emphasizes (*passim*), the range of prototypical emotion behaviour can also be heterogeneous across different historical periods, even within a single society.

[78] See e.g. the range of expressions and manifestations of anger in Homer, as discussed by Cairns (2003).

[79] Gallagher (2020) 81–2, 98–9, 118–19, 132, 136, 151–4, 165–74, 229–33.

[80] See Gallagher (2020), esp. part II. See also Gallagher and Hutto (2008); Hutto (2008), (2011).

as emotion (or any of its analogues in other languages) or basic-level categories such as fear (or its analogues), are not uniquely subjective, private experiences. Our first-person awareness of our own emotional experience is intersubjectively and culturally inflected, and so are our responses – our affective, interactive responses – to the emotions of others.[81] In both cases, context plays a crucially important role.[82] Categorization of emotional experience, whether one's own or someone else's, depends on a sense of contextual situatedness that is at least potentially structured in terms of narratives of antecedent cause, intentionality, and response. Emotions are not just events in the brain or body; they are also events in the world – events of which we make sense using shared linguistic and cultural categories. These are the aspects that come especially into play when it comes to attributing to others emotions that are *not* immediately apparent in their expressions or behaviour. Though the context and our knowledge and understanding of it are relevant in all cases, including those in which we directly perceive others' emotions, they take on greater significance when others are dissimulating or inscrutable.

Our understanding of our own emotions and our understanding of the emotions of others are both forged, from the beginning, in interactive situations which come to inform the emotion scripts we internalize and the narratives in which those scripts are embedded. Though there is a genuine sense in which the prototypical case of emotion is one that is being performed, by oneself or another, in the here and now, the fact that such cases are understood interactively and intersubjectively in terms of shared concepts, with their associated scripts and narratives, means that we can talk, in narrative terms, about the present and past emotions of ourselves and others in ways that reflect the narrative structure of emotion events themselves. Emotions, as experienced online, have such a structure, but they can also be recalled and narrated offline. Historical and literary sources are rich in such narratives: if the emotions that we deal with in real-time social interaction have a narrative structure, then the narrative structures of the past can preserve the evidence of past emotions, evidence that is the stuff of emotion history.

The basic position that Schnell upholds (that 'the emotion' is to be located in only one definitive aspect of a total emotion scenario) has been widely prom-

---

[81] See Gallagher (2020) 131: 'The perception of emotion is an affective perception' (with supporting evidence); cf. p. 133 and *passim*.

[82] As already demonstrated by means of the celebrated 'Kuleshov effect' (after the pioneering Soviet film director Lev Kuleshov), by which contextual cues (montage) are used to create the impression in the observer's mind that what is in fact a neutral face, identical in each different context, is emotionally expressive. For a recent account of the phenomenon from the perspective of affective neuroscience, see Calbi et al. (2019). For the role of contextual cues and knowledge in facial mimicry of emotion expressions, see Hess, Houde, and Fischer (2014).

20   Douglas Cairns

ulgated in modern emotion research, going back at least to William James.[83] Jesse
Prinz reprises the Jamesian perspective when he writes:

> Typical emotion episodes ... contain a number of components. There are thoughts, bodily
> changes, action tendencies, modulations of mental processes such as attention, and con-
> scious feelings. But which of these things *is* the emotion? Suppose we decide that winning
> a coveted prize induces 'elation'. What part of the episode does that label designate?[84]

Against those who 'pack in too much' to the concept of emotion 'by assuming
that bodily changes, propositional attitudes, action dispositions are essential
parts or preconditions for emotions',[85] Prinz in 2004 followed James in arguing
for a simpler theory of emotions as 'embodied appraisals', perceptions of bodily
change that register and prepare the organism to respond to features of the
world.[86] Against views of that sort, however, J. L. Austin long ago objected:[87]

> It seems fair to say that 'being angry' is in many respects like 'having mumps'. It is a de-
> scription of a whole pattern of events, including occasion, symptoms, feeling and mani-
> festation, and possibly other factors besides. It is as silly to ask 'What, really, is the anger
> itself?' as to attempt to fine down 'the disease' to some one chosen item ... That the man
> himself feels something which we don't (in the sense that he feels angry and we don't) is ...
> evident enough ...: but there is no call to say that 'that' ('the feeling') is the anger.

James's argument for the opposite conclusion does not withstand scrutiny:[88]

> Without the bodily states following on the perception, the latter would be purely cognitive
> in form, pale, colorless, destitute of emotional warmth. We might then see the bear, and
> judge it best to run, receive the insult and deem it right to strike, but we could not actually
> *feel* afraid or angry.

At best, this would support the claim that the bodily states arising from perception
of an emotion's eliciting conditions are necessary for emotion. It does not prove
that they are sufficient – that they and nothing else *are* the emotion. Without
the perception of the bear or the insult, what we feel might qualify as fear or
anger, but it would not be a typical case, because such cases, even as presented
by James, involve perceptions of states of affairs in the world (perceptions that
James takes to be cognitively rich), a sense of the valence of such states, forms of

---

[83] See Russell (2003) 152: 'Historically, debate centered on the question of which of the
components is the emotion. That question does not arise in the [psychological constructionist]
approach taken here.' For James's formulation, see (1884) 189–90: 'My thesis ... is that *the bodily
changes follow directly the* PERCEPTION *of the exciting fact, and that our feeling of the same
changes as they occur* IS *the emotion.*'
[84] Prinz (2004) 3.
[85] Prinz (2004) 244.
[86] For a similar neo-Jamesian view, see Laird (2007). Prinz's later work moves substantially
away from this view towards a more inclusive, enactivist theory: see e.g. Schargel and Prinz
(2017).
[87] Austin (1979) 109, quoted in Gallagher (2020) 129.
[88] James (1884) 190.

A. *Emotions through time?* 21

bodily arousal, symptoms and expressions, tendencies to action, and behaviour. Without the perception of the bear or the insult, we should have instances of fear or anger atypically unrelated to perception and appraisal; thus, those things too would appear to be as necessary for a prototypical episode of emotion as are bodily states such as trembling. When an emotion episode occurs in the absence of any perception or evaluation of particular eliciting conditions – i.e. when we feel angry or afraid but do not know why – the most likely step is that both the patient of the emotion and any observer of the episode will search for possible objects and causes.[89] This is enough to indicate that there is at least a regular correlation between the subjective experiences that we categorize as emotion and the contexts and conditions that we similarly see as aspects of emotion categories. This is one reason why appraisal theories of emotion now take account of all the dimensions that appraisals can encompass.[90] But even among those who do not follow that precise approach it is widely assumed that emotions are prototypically multidimensional: emotion concepts are categories that, as we saw, encompass families of scripts in which no single element is necessary.[91] It is noticeable, however, that one element of a prototypical emotion script generally presupposes others – appraisal is appraisal *of* a certain emotion-eliciting scenario; such scenarios are evaluated with a view to action in the light of evaluation; there is a typical relation between the affective states of arousal and the action that typically results; and so on. Even 'thin' views of emotion as internal subjective states in fact presuppose context.

James sets out to consider only 'emotions that have a distinct bodily expression' ((1884) 189) and writes that 'A purely disembodied human emotion is a nonentity' ((1884) 194). No doubt that is in some sense true. Even on the prototype approach of the psychological constructionists Russell and Barrett, according to which no single element of a script is necessary for emotion, the occurrent emotional state, involving both valence and arousal, is the typical form. But though emotion research focuses overwhelmingly on occurrent emotion, i.e. episodes that involve some form of phenomenally salient, embodied affective state, even that typical aspect of emotion is not an absolutely necessary condition for membership of the category. Just as it is common enough to feel (e.g.) sad or angry without construing any specific state of affairs as the intentional object of one's feelings, so it is perfectly possible legitimately to use emotion concepts with no reference to any occurrent affective state.

---

[89] As noted by Dewey (1895) 17–18, with specific reference to the Jamesian self-perception theory.

[90] See e.g. Scherer (2001), (2009); Sander, Grandjean, and Scherer (2018). See also a special section of *Emotion Review* 5 (2013) 119–91.

[91] See above, n. 15; cf. Russell (2003), esp. 150–1; Russell (2009) 1260. For a taxonomy of emotion theories in terms of the dimensions or aspects on which each lays most emphasis, see Scarantino (2016).

22   *Douglas Cairns*

The inclusivity of the conceptual categories to which emotion terms relate is clearly and straightforwardly demonstrated by the fact that legitimate uses of emotion terms need not refer to affective states (states of physical arousal) at all. Not only are there non-occurrent, dispositional senses of the terms in question (e.g. the fear of high places which in fact means that one never goes anywhere near a place in which one is likely to experience an occurrent episode of fear), but there are non-occurrent, non-dispositional senses that depend solely upon the distinctions inherent in the concept itself. To say 'I'm afraid I'm too busy to chat right now' simply categorizes the scenario in a certain way, as one in which I am compelled to represent my situation in a way that I represent as negative and normally to be avoided. If we consider 'fear' to be above all an occurrent affective state, then we have to take my fear (for example) that you are mistaken as derivative of, even parasitic upon, the core member of the category. But if we take 'fear' to be a category that has a range of more and less prototypical examples, then all these senses are legitimate members. Instead of saying 'I'm afraid I'm too busy to chat', I might have said 'I'm sorry; I'm too busy to chat right now'. These statements are identical in illocutionary and perlocutionary force: they both apologize, at least formally, for a refusal to engage in interaction, represent that refusal as socially undesirable and normally to be avoided, and seek, at least formally, to mitigate the interlocutor's disappointment. Neither has any necessary reference to an occurrent episode of emotion, whether fear or sorrow. They differ in that each makes use of a different emotion concept to construct and evaluate a scenario in a different way, as a future state of affairs that one represents as something one would avoid if one could or as a current state of affairs that one represents as regrettable and for which one should apologize. Without involving any bodily changes whatever each relates to elicitors, appraisals, and action tendencies that are typical elements of the relevant script.[92]

These may seem to be trivial cases; they are certainly not typical examples of the categories to which they belong. But they demonstrate that considering occurrence to be essential for emotion is to drive a wedge between legitimate members of the category in a way that makes the exclusion of non-occurrent cases inexplicable. If we see the resemblance between occurrent and non-occurrent cases we see that the distinction between them is functional only for certain purposes, that occurrence is typical, but – like all other elements of the script – not essential. Very often, in fact, legitimate uses of emotion terms (uses which thereby identify legitimate members of the relevant category) focus primarily on external aspects of the relevant script rather than on subjective internal states or feelings. A colleague who regularly diminishes other colleagues' achievements, opposes their applications for promotion or tenure, and so on, is

---

[92] For references to older, but still helpful discussions of these points, see Cairns (1993) 5–12, esp. nn. 8 and 26.

A. Emotions through time?

quite legitimately regarded as envious, jealous, or spiteful. We should like to believe that such a colleague is in fact tortured by inner feelings of malice and insecurity; but it is not necessary that this be the case in order for his or her behaviour to be qualified in those terms – the behaviour itself is enough.[93] This has implications for the historian that are certainly not trivial. When Thucydides (1.23.6) identifies the Spartans' fear (*phobos*) of the Athenians' growing power as the 'truest cause' of the Peloponnesian War it does not matter whether he thinks or means us to think that any individual Spartan or group of Spartans experienced an occurrent episode of emotion on any particular historical occasion. The Spartans' fear represents their construal of, attitude towards, and behaviour in the light of a certain set of historical developments. That construal may have been one to which historical Spartans gave voice; but Thucydides' imputation of that emotion as a cause of war is adequately justified by his understanding of the policies and actions of the Spartan state. It is a perfectly regular feature of emotion scenarios that the behavioural and evaluative aspects of the script may be much more salient than the affective, phenomenological elements.[94] James Russell is right to conclude that 'emotional episodes can be studied without reference to conscious feelings specifically of fear, anger, jealousy, and the like'.[95]

This is the case because, as typically conceived in the categories of the languages we as scholars speak and those we, as Classicists and Byzantinists, study, emotions have intentional as well as phenomenal aspects. They are typically *about* something. And, thus, context is important. Though any given case may involve the identification of no particular set of eliciting conditions, when such conditions are identified, they are integral aspects of that instantiation of the script. The same is true of action: though one *need* not act on emotion at all, when one does, the actions one takes may in themselves be indication enough that an emotion script is being enacted. The occurrence of a specific set of phenomenologically salient physical changes is not an essential feature of every case of emotion; but occurrence, with specific patterns of valence and arousal, is prototypical of emotion, and correlates with typical patterns of eliciting conditions and resulting behaviour. Equally, though one can be in an emotional state without showing any particular expression of emotion, still expression, when it occurs, is not a detachable aspect of that particular episode: where there is expression, it is one aspect of a single process.[96] (Evidence suggests, in fact, that inhibiting, even minimally, the body's expressive capacities can interfere with the processing of emotion concepts.)[97] Emotions have dimensions that extend

---

[93] Cf. Averill (1980) 137; Fehr and Russell (1984) 465.

[94] See Russell (1991b) 41–2.

[95] Russell (2003) 164.

[96] See Laird (2007) 23–48. Cf. Frevert (2009) 205; Boddice (2018) 121.

[97] See Niedenthal et al. (2009); Niedenthal, Wood, and Rychlowska (2014); cf. Oatley (2011) 112–13.

24 *Douglas Cairns*

far beyond whatever it is that happens in the head or under the skin: they involve the outward as well as the inward aspects of the body, interaction between the individual and the physical and social environments, embodied practice in roles, relationships, and institutions, as well as shared norms and concepts.[98] This means that – despite the hard and fast distinction drawn by Schnell between emotion (on the one hand) as a private, subjective, inner experience and (on the other) its expression, its performance, its causes and contexts, the external factors that constrain it, and the concepts we use to think and talk about it – there are important respects in which the ontology of emotions as phenomena depends on much more than the subjective psychophysical states with which they are prototypically correlated. We cannot separate emotion as subjective experience from the contexts, expression, behaviour, and discourse of emotion.

The fact that both *concept* and *context* are fundamental to the ontology of emotions, as experienced, practised, recognized, and understood, positively requires that emotion research should encompass historical and cross-cultural investigations and comparisons. The primacy of conceptualization has in the past been illustrated with reference to emotions such as ἀκηδία/*acedia*/*accidie*,[99] but a more striking contemporary example might be 'empathy'. The concept of empathy in English is just over 100 years old, the term having been coined in the early 1900s to calque the German term *Einfühlung*,[100] itself a comparatively recent coinage deriving from the earlier use of *sich einfühlen* in German Romanticism as way of projecting oneself or one's emotions imaginatively chiefly on to objects, works of art, and the natural world. Though its sense was still primarily aesthetic, the term *Einfühlung* was extended by Theodor Lipps, in the later years of the nineteenth century and early years of the next, to include the process by which we allegedly understand others' mental states by perceiving and simulating the movements that express them and then projecting our own feelings back on to the other.[101] In English and especially since the 1950s, empathy has since taken on a life of its own, acquiring a variety of senses, not always closely related, and making itself at home not only in a range of academic disciplines but also in

---

[98] Contrast Schell (2015) 761.

[99] See Harré and Finlay-Jones (1986). Against this whole approach, see Schnell (2015) 773–88.

[100] Independently by E. B. Titchener and J. Ward in 1908, according to the account given in Lanzoni (2018) 9, 46–67. For Titchener, empathy involved projecting human feeling – unfelt by oneself – on to the objects of perception (contrast sympathy as identifying with another); Ward saw it in terms of panpsychism and the tendency to personify the natural and physical environments.

[101] For what Rob Boddice calls the concept's 'remarkably unstable history' (Boddice (2018) 56), see Lanzoni (2018). Cf. Zahavi (2010); Coplan and Goldie (2011) xii–xxxi (and *passim* in the contributions to that volume). On *Einfühlung*, see Curtis and Koch (2009); Edwards (2013); Lanzoni (2018) 9, 21–3, 30–3, 37–44. For the extension of the term to include other-understanding, see in particular Lipps (1903) 187–202.

everyday language. Contemporary empathy is very different from what it was when the term was first coined. That developmental history in turn means that the German equivalent is now *Empathie*, not *Einfühlung*.

The naturalization of the term in English and German coexists with a proliferation of uses, senses, and theorizations on which no consensus is likely to emerge. Complaints about the imprecision and multivalence of both *Einfühlung* and empathy begin to proliferate almost as soon as the terms are coined. Susan Lanzoni reports that 'At the 1910 Fourth Congress for Experimental Psychology in Innsbruck, the phenomenologist Moritz Geiger warned that if researchers did not spell out what they meant by Einfühlung, it was not at all clear what they were talking about!'[102] Lanzoni similarly cites Theodor Reik for the view that, by 1936, empathy (in English) had 'become so rich in meanings that it [was] beginning to mean nothing at all'.[103] Though meanings have changed, their range has not narrowed: C. Daniel Batson was probably erring on the side of caution when in 2009 he identified eight 'related but distinct phenomena' called empathy.[104] A recent review starts from the premise that 'The inconsistent definition of empathy has had a negative impact on both research and practice.'[105] There are explanations which locate at least some forms of empathy in basic mechanisms of perception, motor resonance, and mirroring,[106] and others which demand higher levels of conscious reflection and processing.[107] Some accounts maintain at least something of the term's original reference to the projection of one's own emotions on to others,[108] while many think that the phenomenon in question can in some sense encompass feeling what other people feel.[109] On yet other accounts there are forms of empathy that involve very little in the way of 'feeling' at all.[110] Though it has become conventional in psychology to distinguish empathy as 'feeling with' from sympathy as 'feeling for',[111] this reflects a historical devel-

---

[102] Lanzoni (2018) 37, citing Geiger (1911). For a similar complaint by J. M. Baldwin in 1911, cf. Lanzoni (2018) 51.

[103] Lanzoni (2018) 8, citing Reik (1936) 192.

[104] Batson (2009), with bibliography for each variety.

[105] Cuff et al. (2016). Cf. e.g. Read (2019) 2: 'All this debate about empathy notwithstanding, there is little consensus about what empathy is ... Additionally, proponents and critics often use the term "empathy" to refer to different phenomena, leading to terminological confusion.' Cf. Lanzoni (2018) 252 on contemporary psychology, neuroscience, and philosophy. On the imprecision of the term, cf. Coplan and Goldie (2011) xxxi (and various of their contributors at 4, 31–2, 103, 162–3, 211, 319).

[106] E.g. Stueber (2006), (2012) on 'basic empathy'.

[107] E.g. Coplan (2011); distinctions between lower- and higher-level empathy are also common (e.g. Stueber (2006), (2012) on 'basic' and 're-enactive' empathy; De Waal (2009)).

[108] E.g. Preston and De Waal (2002) 17.

[109] E.g. Vignemont and Singer (2006) 435, on isomorphism as a requirement for empathy. For scepticism about this and related aspects of empathy, see Carroll (2011) 180–4; McFee (2011) 187–97, 201; Goldie (2011), esp. 302–3.

[110] On 'cognitive empathy' see e.g. Spaulding (2017).

[111] See e.g. Oatley (2011) 115–20.

opment by which empathy has now come to usurp functions that from the eighteenth to the twentieth centuries were regularly attributed to sympathy,[112] while sympathy's long association with pro-social, caring attitudes and actions is now, at least in popular parlance, typical of empathy (even if we still do not quite send people our empathies).[113] Though several mainstream definitions of empathy should, on the face of it, allow us to share whatever emotion the other person may be feeling, it would sound very odd to say that one empathized with another person's happiness.[114] Having taken over sympathy's reference to feeling what others feel, empathy, in everyday speech, is beginning to usurp its later role as a form of compassion; and yet there are formulations that would predicate some kind of empathy not only of those whose distress makes them less likely to support others in their sufferings,[115] but also of those whose understanding of others' pain is a source of pleasure.[116]

In all this, there is variation between language-users, between theoretical positions, between disciplines, and between technical and non-technical applications. This is not just a matter of a single label being applied over time to a variety of discrete and generally accepted phenomena. Though people clearly do have some understanding of others' feelings, feel bad when they feel bad, and try to support them when they do, the application of the term empathy, even its popular senses, to such scenarios typically brings with it a wider set of associations. What one takes the phenomena to be will often depend on how one explains human beings' ability to understand others' feelings and mental states and the mechanisms that one supposes to underpin that ability (or those abilities). In some cases, the alleged phenomena postulated by proponents of particular conceptualizations of empathy (such as the ability in some sense to share other people's first-person experience and subjective mental states) are, at least in the opinion of their opponents, chimerical. Empathy has from the beginning been a creature of discourse, at first technical and then popular, and the phenomena to which the label is applied are substantially constructed by the explicit or implicit assumptions that the relevant discourse entails. Attempts to pin it down as a phenomenon in scholarly and scientific contexts are regularly constrained not or not only by the alleged nature of the mechanisms involved but

---

[112] On 'sympathy' in David Hume and Adam Smith, see Batson (2009) 5; Coplan and Goldie (2011) x–xi, with contributors at pp. 32 (Alvin Goldman), 103 (Murray Smith), 212 (Jesse Prinz), 233 (Martin Hoffman), 281 (Heather Battaly), 323 (Adam Morton).

[113] Cf. Batson (2009) 8. He adds: 'Both empathy and sympathy (the term with which empathy is most often contrasted) have been used in a variety of ways. Indeed, with remarkable consistency exactly the same state that some scholars have labeled empathy others have labeled sympathy. I have discerned no clear basis – either historical or logical – for favoring one labeling scheme over another.'

[114] Cf. Boddice (2018) 56.

[115] See Hoffman (1978), (2011) 251; Engelen and Röttger-Rössler (2012) 4.

[116] Bischof-Köhler (2012) 45–6; Breithaupt (2015a), (2015b).

by intuitions derived from the term's usage in many of the contexts in which it is now at home.[117] This is not to claim that none of the scenarios to which the term empathy may be applied is possible. Nor is it to claim that empathy 'does not exist'. But it does involve the claim that empathy is not an essence. It is not a label for a distinct psychological event or a single interpersonal scenario, but a complex, non-classical category with a wide range of more and less prototypical members and a particular history in which its senses have developed and mutated. If empathy is listening to others, being attuned to their feelings, trying to understand their perspective rather than imposing one's own, caring about them, and being as supportive as one can be, then hurray for empathy. But if this or something like it is empathy's current prototype, we need to be aware that this has not always been the case, that it will most probably not continue to be the case, and that the current vogue for the term and the various scenarios with which it is associated is to a substantial extent a matter of fashion, both in ordinary speech and in scientific discourse.

The power of popular and scientific discourse to combine in influencing the history of emotion concepts can be observed in action in the current interest in establishing and exploring the parameters (conceptual, evaluative, phenomenological, physiological, expressive, situational, etc.) of the experiences and scenarios that speakers of English include in the vague concept of being 'moved' or 'touched'. A number of recent studies suggest that this is indeed a distinct affective category with its own conceptual structure, one that has linguistic analogues in a wide range of cultures.[118] This process of identification and analysis, however, is not like discovering an unknown planet or a hitherto unclassified species of lichen. It is a matter of academic discourse probing the emotion concepts recognized, to varying extents, in the popular discourse of different human cultures.

Labels, as aspects of conceptualization, do matter, and they matter especially, though not only, for historians. The historical perspective here is also a comparative one: historical research on a concept such as empathy requires us to be mindful of differences in the usage and meaning of the term at different periods. This comparative perspective is central when it comes to studying emotion in cultures which use or used languages other than our own. We saw above how language conditions one's experience of the world and how one makes sense of that experience. Findings with regard to the influence of language on processes such as colour perception suggest analogues in the ways that members of different cultures perform, experience, and understand emotion. What dif-

---

[117] See e.g. Gallagher (2020) 174–84.

[118] See e.g. Zickfeld et al. (2019); Fiske (2019); for a list of further publications, see http://kamamutalab.org (accessed 12 March 2021). Cf. Deonna (2011); Cova and Deonna (2014); Menninghaus et al. (2015); Cullhed (2020).

ference might it make, for example, that speakers of ancient Greek had one concept, *aidōs*, that covers scripts that in English are associated with shame on the one hand (focusing primarily on one's own honour, though also encompassing one's sense of oneself as a social being) and with respect on the other (focusing primarily on the honour of other people, as recognized through one's own attitudes and behaviour)? According to a recent book by the philosopher Richard Gaskin, not very much difference at all.[119] For Gaskin, our ability to *translate* a term in another language that has no direct equivalent in our own allows us also to *experience* the world as users of that term in that language experience it. In my 1993 book on the subject I upheld the view that 'To recognize that we feel respect where a Greek might feel *aidōs* provides no warrant for the claim that we experience *aidōs*', concluding that 'Neither as a whole nor in part is the experience of *aidōs* as such available to those who do not conceptualize emotional experience in the same way as did native speakers of ancient Greek.'[120] Gaskin, by contrast, argues that, because we translate *aidōs* using different English terms in different contexts, *aidōs* is 'not one' and '*not* uniform, [but] embodies a multiplicity of sub-concepts', so that 'it *will* be possible for modern English speakers to feel *aidōs*'.[121] No serious philologist would deny that we can translate virtually all words in other languages into contextually adequate terms in English. But it is a big claim to argue that English has succeeded where ancient Greek has failed in picking out a genuine multiplicity of concepts, and an even bigger one to argue that someone who labels her experience as respect in English feels what a speaker of ancient Greek felt in calling her experience *aidōs*. The argument is not that a speaker of ancient Greek cannot distinguish more than one sense of *aidōs* – that is clearly not the case.[122] Rather it is that, just as we can never share *exactly* the perspective of another human being, so we do not *precisely* share the perspective of those whose languages make different distinctions from our own. To do so one would have to be able not only to translate the source language into the target, but also to use that language as a native speaker does.[123] The opportunity to do that, by inhabiting ancient Greek culture and interacting, at a native level of linguistic competence, with native speakers of ancient Greek, is now beyond our grasp. Not even the greatest of modern philologists have come anywhere close to using ancient Greek as native speakers once did. We remember that even near-native competence in another language still makes for

---

[119] See Gaskin (2018) 218–19. For a critical discussion, see Cairns (2020a).

[120] Cairns (1993) 9–10 n. 21; cf. the simpler formulation of von Erffa (1937) 9: *aidōs* is 'eine eigene Kraft, für die uns das Wort fehlt'.

[121] Gaskin (2018) 218.

[122] See Cairns (1993) 1–4, 13–14. Cf. Cairns and Fulkerson (2015), 11–20. See also Cairns (2008).

[123] See Barrett (2017) 141–2.

differences in the experience and performance of emotion.[124] *Aidōs* is not uniform, if that means that it has only one sense; but neither is it simply 'a multiplicity of sub-concepts'. The encapsulation of both shame and respect in a single concept recognizes a genuine fact about the world (the mutual entanglement of self-esteem, the esteem we receive from others, and the respect we owe others) that English speakers must laboriously reconstruct.[125] This is an altogether more complex phenomenon than that of English speakers' ability to experience an emotion (such as *Schadenfreude*) that is unnamed in their language but named in another, because in that case the mapping is straightforwardly between single scripts in each of the two cultures.

Yet this is not to deny the possibility of translation. Translation succeeds when it is contextually appropriate. To translate emotion terms in a contextually appropriate manner we need a developed understanding of the various scripts with which the emotion terms of both source and target languages are associated.[126] These scripts are themselves aspects of the relevant emotion concepts. Thus, though *aidōs*, shame, and respect are different concepts, comparison between *aidōs*, on the one hand, and shame and respect on the other is eminently possible and constitutes a fruitful way of establishing substantial common ground between ancient Greek and modern English concepts: *aidōs* is not wholly coextensive with any English term that we may use to translate it, but the category does encompass scripts that are aspects of familiar English-language categories. The common ground that comparative conceptual analysis establishes does not warrant either the false exoticism that sees partial congruence as radical difference or the unwarranted assumption that we are all just the same, really.

Where the emotion concepts of different cultures are not wholly congruent in the scripts that they cover, still the scripts, as aspects of those concepts, may be directly comparable. Thus, though English has one term, pride, that covers innocent and positively evaluated forms of pleasure in the achievements and excellences of oneself and one's own, especially when recognized by others (cf. French *fierté*), as well as various negatively evaluated ways of thinking too highly of oneself (cf. French *orgeuil*), while ancient Greek has several terms for the pride that goes before a fall, but none that unequivocally labels the positive sense of pride, this does not allow us to conclude that the scripts associated with positive

---

[124] See above, pp. 9–10.

[125] For the recognition of the interplay of esteem for others, the esteem of others, and self-esteem in Latin, see Kaster (2005) 13–65; cf. Cairns and Fulkerson (2015) 17–19. For other languages, see Cairns (1993) 13–14 n. 28 (with further references); cf. Russell (1991a) 430, 432. The underlying sociological truth of the interplay between seeking and conferring recognition is widely recognized by thinkers from Hegel to Honneth, and central to the notions of face, demeanour, and deference in the work of Erving Goffman (e.g. Goffman (1967)); cf. Brown and Levinson (1987).

[126] Cf., once more, Cairns (2008).

pride in English go unrecognized – or even, in fact, that they go unlabelled –
in ancient Greek society, much less that the forms of behaviour that the scripts
encompass did not exist in that society.[127] Though there is no Greek noun that
answers directly to English pride, positive and negative, or to the positive kind
of pride designated by the French *fierté*, Greek recognizes the scripts associated
with positive pride by means of verbs such as *agallomai*,[128] *kallōpizomai*,[129] and
kallunomai,[130] as well as by various locutions denoting the pleasure one takes
in one's (or one's family's) achievement, especially as recognized by others.[131]
Similarly, the noun *zēlotupia* (jealousy) is of comparatively late coinage and
is not found in fifth-century sources. Thus, it is not available as a label for the
motivation of Medea in Euripides' tragedy, first produced in 431 BC. And in fact
the terms most prominently predicated of Medea's feelings towards the husband
who jilted her for another all designate forms of anger.[132] But this does not mean
that we cannot also see her motivation in terms of what we call jealousy: both
Medea herself and Jason emphasize her resentment of the fact that Jason has
rejected her as a sexual partner in favour of another's bed;[133] Medea's possessive-
ness with regard to Jason is clear;[134] and it is equally clear that there is no love lost
between her and Jason's new wife, whose death she brings about in a grotesquely
macabre fashion (much to her own satisfaction).[135] The view that anger is an
aspect of jealousy as the latter is understood in English is a common one; though
often expressed in terms of the essentialist view that 'basic emotions' are used

---

[127] See Cairns (2022).

[128] E.g. Hdt. 1.143.3: unlike the majority of the Ionians, who are ashamed to be so called,
the twelve cities that founded the Panionium at Mycale positively glory in the nomenclature;
4.64.2: Scythian warriors glory in the scalps of their dead opponents which, when affixed to
their horses' bridles, testify to their prowess in battle. Cf. Thuc. 2.63.1: Athenians' pride in their
empire; 3.62.1: the Plataeans' pride in not having Medized, the reproach they level against the
Thebans; and 3.82.7: 'the majority, villains that they are, are more readily called clever than the
stupid are called good; they pride themselves in the former, but are ashamed of the latter (καὶ
τῷ μὲν αἰσχύνονται, ἐπὶ δὲ τῷ ἀγάλλονται)'.

[129] Of Protagoras' pleasure in others' admiration at Plato, *Protagoras* 317c.

[130] As when Socrates in Plato's *Apology* (20c) denies that he possesses the ability to teach civic
virtue, but if he did, it is something he would glory in.

[131] E.g. *Od.* 11.538–40: the ghost of Achilles is overjoyed to hear from Odysseus of his son's
achievements; Hdt. 1.31.4: the mother of Cleobis and Biton is 'overjoyed at their deed and the
fame that it had brought them'; Soph. *OT* 1070: Oedipus interprets Jocasta's pleas as shame at
the prospect that he will be proved to be low-born (1062–3), and proposes to leave her to rejoice
in her wealthy origins. Cf. Xen. *Mem.* 2.1.19 on the satisfaction that comes when one's efforts
prove successful and one becomes the object of one's own and others' admiration – here both
euphrainesthai and *heauton agasthai* adumbrate the notion of pride.

[132] For Medea's anger as *orgē*, see 176–7, 446–7, 520, 615, 870–1, 909; as *cholos*, 93–4, 98–9,
171–2, 588–90, 898, 1265–6; as *thumos*, 106–8, 271, 878–9, 883.

[133] Eur. *Med.* 263–6, 555–6, 568–73, 1338, 1367–8.

[134] Not least through her emphatic use of the possessive adjective 'my' in referring to the proposed victims of her revenge at 375 – 'father, daughter, and *my husband*'.

[135] For her pleasure in the gruesome details, see 1125–35.

A. Emotions through time?

as building blocks to construct more complex examples,[136] it is compatible with the position that there is an overlap between anger and jealousy in terms of the scripts and scenarios to which the terms relate. Thus, while it undoubtedly matters that Medea's motivation is labelled using 'anger' terminology rather than specifically designated by a close equivalent to the English-language notion of jealousy,[137] there can, given the right context, be considerable overlap, in both pragmatic and conceptual terms, between the emic account of Medea's actions in terms of *orgē, cholos*, and *thumos*, and the etic interpretation of her behaviour as motivated by jealousy.[138] Labels do matter, but they do not by any means constitute the totality of a concept, especially when we are dealing with concepts that have the event-like structure that emotions do. When our searches reveal an absence of labels, we still need to search further before we can establish that such absences point to radical differences between societies and their mentalities; and if we are going to compare cultures at all we need a certain level of abstraction from details and specificities if meaningful points of comparison are ever going to emerge. The absence of a label is not necessarily the total absence of the concept or of the forms of experience that the concept structures: there is no one-to-one relation between either labels and concepts or labels and experience. What makes Medea's anger, in this case, a form of what we call jealousy is not primarily a matter of how the experiences are labelled. Nor is it a matter of specific bodily changes or symptoms. It may, partly, be a matter of the way the agent appraises the situation; but a difference in appraisal between anger that counts as jealousy and anger that does not is above all a consequence of the difference in the eliciting conditions, in the scenario that the appraisal construes, i.e. in the context. This shows, once again, that emotions are not just subjective, internal feelings or states of mind. They are also implicated in the relations between people, in the external conditions in which they arise and which give rise to them, and in the actions that we take in a given emotional scenario.[139] They have many dimensions, all of which are aspects of the concepts that human beings use when they enact them and when they interpret them. Their specificity can depend on features of the context beyond the skull and the skin, on aspects of pragmatics, performance, and situation, not just on labels. Just as there is no sharp antithesis between inner and outer, emotion and expression, emotion and representation,

---

[136] For jealousy in American English as an 'amalgam of more basic emotions', including anger, cf. Stearns (1989) xi. Cf. (on German *Eifersucht*) Schnell (2015), 224–6. The view that (some, many, most) emotions are 'compounds' of other emotions is common (see the references in Schnell (2015) 224 nn. 108–9).

[137] As emphasized by Konstan (2006b) 230–4; cf. 57–9.

[138] For jealousy in Greek before *zēlotupia*, see Pizzocaro (1994); Cairns (2008) 53–6; Sanders (2014) 130–42; Sissa (2018) 9–33; Cairns (2021) 22–6.

[139] Cf. Russell (2003) 164: 'the meaning of such concepts depends on their role in a larger system of meaning. Jealousy, for instance, is also a node in a network that includes social conventions, moral rules, role obligations, and so on.'

there is no question of Schnell's distinction between *Gefühle an sich* and every other aspect of an emotion scenario. The *Gefühle*, as we have seen, are never really *an sich* – they are implicated in context, in social interaction, in narrative, in language, in shared forms of thought (such as metaphor), and in culture.

This means that we, as Byzantinists, Classicists, or historians of ideas and culture, are in a fortunate position. Many of the skills we use on an everyday basis – the understanding that translation is about ideas, not words; the knowledge that the ideas one translates must be understood in contextually situated terms; the sense that terms and concepts change over time; the sensitivity to narrative cues about the motives of characters in the diegetic, mimetic, and mixed genres of ancient and Byzantine literature – turn out to be essential if we are to use our textual sources as material for the history of emotions. Because emotions are by no means only features of some private inner world, we have plenty of scope for investigating them by means of texts that afford us no direct access to such worlds, either because their authors and the individual figures that populate them are long dead or because, *qua* dramatic or narrative fictions, they never possessed private inner lives in the first place. The narrative fictions of the past mirror the narrative structure of emotions; in so far as emotions are event-like in form and script-like in concept, we have access to the emotions of individuals represented in any text that has even a minimal narrative form – from the epic narratives of Homer to the sketches of the conditions, appraisals, and behaviour patterns associated with individual emotions in Aristotle's *Rhetoric*.

We have, in our ancient and Byzantine sources, a wide array of texts of various kinds that represent, elicit, and theorize emotions, and these theorizations, in particular, are of inestimable benefit in guiding our approaches to the representations we study. Rich as our texts are in representations, they provide, in their turn, contextual information by which we can reconstruct the affective qualities to which their ancient audiences responded. With the help of those texts, we can also begin to explore the affective qualities of other contexts for emotion and other emotion elicitors, such as the objects and artefacts that survive from the cultures we study or the remains of the physical spaces in which emotions were experienced and enacted. There is thus plenty of scope for histories not just of the signs of emotion, but of emotions themselves, because emotions are primarily concepts, concepts by which individuals and cultures make sense of their worlds and themselves. It is, *pace* Schnell,[140] not a fault that emotion history follows so closely in the footsteps of conceptual and intellectual history (or of social history, gender history, etc.). It is a culture's concepts and categories of emotion that tie the elements of emotion scripts together, that form the link between certain patterns of eliciting conditions, appraisals, subjectively experienced bodily states, externally perceptible facial and bodily movements, and kinds of action. As

---

[140] See Schnell (2015) 876–965.

Matt and Stearns observe, 'By studying feelings, historians are uncovering the worldviews and the most fundamental assumptions about life, culture, and personality that people in the past carried in their heads.'[141] Historians of many traditions and approaches have always studied these things. What the history of emotions adds to traditional approaches is an additional level of attention to and emphasis on affective concepts and phenomena as such. Emotion history is an evolving field, not just in the sense that one project builds incrementally on or takes a critical stance towards another, but also in that all its practitioners are feeling their way through obscure and difficult terrain, attempting to use the results of one difficult enterprise – an understanding of human emotion in all its complex ramifications – as a means of progress in another – the process of trying to understand the lives, experiences, motives, and perspectives of historical individuals and communities. It turns out that we do, after all, have to have as full an understanding as we can achieve of what emotions might be before we can begin to study their history. For all of us, no matter how long we have engaged in these tasks, this involves many false steps and false starts. If we fail, we hope that at least we fail better.

---

[141] Matt and Stearns (2014) 2.

B.

Emotion research in Classics

Douglas Cairns

The history of emotion is now a mature sub-discipline of the study of ancient Greece.[1] This is entirely fitting, since it is the Greeks who gave us the earliest theories of emotion and indeed, according to David Konstan (e.g. in this volume) the concept of emotion itself. A constant point of reference here is provided by Aristotle's work on the *pathē* of the soul, especially in the *De anima* and the *Rhetoric*:[2] William Fortenbaugh's 1975 book on Aristotle was the first work in Hellenic studies to emphasize the cognitive-evaluative approach to emotion which was prominent in the spate of monographs and edited collections that from the 1990s onwards began to deal with emotion and the emotions in ancient Greek society and thought,[3] while Aristotle's approach to emotion serves as an organizing principle in the most prominent general introduction to the subject in ancient Greece, David Konstan's 2006 volume on *The Emotions of the Ancient Greeks*. The central strength of these works has been their focus on the ancient emotional lexicon and the construction, conceptualization, and valorization of emotion in ancient Greek authors, genres, philosophical schools, and societies,

---

[1] For overviews of the field, see Chaniotis (2012c); Cairns and Nelis (2017) 7–18; Cairns (2019b) 5–9; Chaniotis (2021) 10–12.

[2] See Fortenbaugh (2002 [1975]); Cooper (1996); Frede (1996); Leighton (1996); Nussbaum (1996); Striker (1996); Konstan (2006); Rapp (2008); Krewet (2011); see also Morel (2016) on the physiology of emotion in the *De motu*. On emotion in Hellenistic ethics and psychology, see Annas (1992); Nussbaum (1994); Sihvola and Engberg-Pedersen (1998); Gill (2010b); cf. Fitzgerald (2008). On the Stoics, see Graver (2007); cf. Krewet (2013); on the Epicureans, see Annas (1989); Fowler (1997); Procopé (1998); Armstrong (2008). On emotion in ancient philosophy in general, see Krajczynski and Rapp (2009); cf. Cairns (2019b) 9–13.

[3] Monographs: e.g. Cairns (1993); Harris (2001); Konstan (2001); Zaborowski (2002); Sternberg (2006); Konstan (2006b); Graver (2007); Konstan (2010b); Kalimtzis (2012); Munteanu (2012); Campeggiani (2013); Fulkerson (2013); Sanders (2014); Spatharas (2019). Edited collections: e.g. Braund and Most (2003a); Konstan and Rutter (2003); Sternberg (2005); Fitzgerald (2008); Munteanu (2011); Chaniotis (2012d); Chaniotis and Ducrey (2013); Sanders et al. (2013); Sanders and Johncock (2015): Caston and Kaster (2016); Lateiner and Spatharas (2017); Cairns and Nelis (2017); Kazantzidis and Spatharas (2018); Cairns (2019a); Bettenworth and Hammerstaedt (2020); Candiotto and Renaut (2020); Chaniotis (2021); cf. the numerous papers on Greek topics in Boehm, Ferrary, and Franchet d'Espèrey (2016). See also the monographs by the philosophers Bernard Williams (1993) and Martha Nussbaum (1994), (2001).

with particular regard to the semantics and history of ancient emotional concepts and the interaction between emotions and moral and social norms.

Not only philosophy, however, but literature too has loomed large in these discussions, especially because literary sources provide unparalleled evidence for the complex dynamics of emotional episodes in multifaceted depictions of more or less realistic forms of social interaction.[4] Genres such as epic and drama have been studied for the multiple, polyphonic perspectives they provide on characters' motivation and on the eliciting conditions of their emotions, all of which can guide our interpretation both of explicit ascriptions and of implicit representations, but a wide range of other genres, too, rely similarly on narrative constructions of characteristic affective scenarios as contexts for their representations of and appeals to emotion. In a very real sense, the manifold forms of dramatic enactment and narrative representation of emotion in literature reflect the paradigmatic scenarios of emotion in the wider culture. Drama and narrative are valuable sources especially for their particular role in developing an audience's inventory of scripts, paradigm scenarios, and the range of affective responses that they evoke.[5] This process can be one of extending and deepening the reader's, auditor's or spectator's powers of imagination and perspective-taking, but it can also be a matter of codification and normalization: stories recur to typical patterns, serving to crystallize the paradigmatic cases and the norms by which audiences respond emotionally to those cases. The condensation of such complexes of thought and feeling in typical and traditional forms and genres helps make a particular ethical or emotional perspective tangible, tractable, and transferable.[6] The encapsulation of traditional norms, with their associated ways of feeling, in a traditional artistic form encourages a symbiotic replication both of the form and of the response that it evokes; it helps define the repertoire of both artists and audience. If literary representations of agency are successful, then we have good evidence of affectivity in action in the cultures we study – in the agents represented in literary artefacts, in their interaction with other agents and with internal audiences, and in the appeal to the emotions of external audiences.[7] This is one reason why Hellenists have been right to make such extensive use of literary evidence in their contributions to the historical study of emotion, and why literary sources still provide much of the evidence and subject matter for emotion research in contemporary Hellenic studies.

The emotional texture and affective character of literary works also figure prominently in contemporary emotion research.[8] But a further feature of this

---

[4] See (most recently) Konstan (2019b); Scodel and Caston (2019); Cairns (2021).

[5] See Cairns (2014a), esp. 103–9; cf. Cairns (2017b) 53–78, with references in n. 69; Munteanu (2017).

[6] See further Colombetti (2009). Cf. Cairns (2014a).

[7] See Scodel and Caston (2019).

[8] See e.g. Oatley (2011), (2012).

strand of research is its focus on the emotional responses of readers and audiences.[9] Here, the concerns of modern emotion research and those of ancient poetics, aesthetics, and rhetoric coalesce in seeing emotion as a salient element in readers' and audiences' engagement with texts, performances, and narratives and in the techniques by which those texts (etc.) succeed in fostering that engagement. The emotion-eliciting power, the affective quality, of texts is not just a matter of the depiction of emotion in the text.[10] The mechanisms by which texts exert this power, however, as well as the nature of the responses that these mechanisms elicit, are matters of controversy; this is an area where the centuries' worth of implicit and explicit testimony that classical literature and classical literary theory have to offer can still make a contribution to contemporary debate, not only in applying modern theory to ancient sources or in bringing our literary-theoretical approaches into contact with the cognitive and affective sciences,[11] but also in using the richness of ancient theory to interrogate modern assumptions.[12] For the same reasons, work on the affective aspects of ancient Greek aesthetics and poetics can provide useful points of comparison and impetus for analogous approaches to Byzantine studies.

Thus, approaches to emotion that have become established in the last thirty years or so of research in ancient Greek studies, rooted as they are in language and its deployment in (above all) literary and philosophical texts, have much to offer as contributions to debate beyond Classics. recent developments in Hellenic studies (fostered especially by Angelos Chaniotis's now completed Oxford project on the Social and Cultural Construction of Emotions)[13] have in addition brought about a widening of the field, its focus, and its source base, with greater attention to sources for the expression, performance, and context of emotion, especially in non-literary texts and material culture.[14] In one respect, this represents a move away from elite and culturally authoritative texts to other forms of textual evidence – e.g. letters, wills, and petitions;[15] inscriptions set up by private individuals;[16] and inscriptions, both religious and secular, commissioned by communities of various kinds.[17] But the broadening of the source

---

[9] For recent discussions, see Cairns (2017b); Halliwell (2017); Scodel and Caston (2019).

[10] See Halliwell (2017).

[11] See the bibliography on 'cognitive Classics' created by Felix Budelmann and Katharine Earnshaw at https://cognitiveclassics.blogs.sas.ac.uk/cognitive-classics-bibliography/ (accessed 22 March 2021), and cf. Cairns (2018).

[12] See Cairns (2017a); Halliwell (2017).

[13] The core project publications are Chaniotis (2012d); Chaniotis and Ducrey (2013); Chaniotis (2021).

[14] See esp. Chaniotis (2012c) 24–7, with the input of other contributors at (2012d) 37–150, 177–355, 389–430. Cf. more recently Chaniotis and Steel (2019); Foxhall (2019); Naiden (2019); Räuchle (2019); Frankfurter (2021).

[15] Kotsifou (2012a), (2012b), (2012c); Palme (2021); cf. Tait (2021).

[16] Chaniotis (2012a); Salvo (2012), (2016).

[17] Chaniotis (2012a), (2012b); Martzavou (2012a), (2012b); Chaniotis (2015).

base also encompasses a shift of focus on to non-textual forms of evidence – to visual and material culture. Visual culture, in particular, is an area in which great opportunities exist, but also considerable obstacles. In principle, sources such as vase-painting and sculpture might be thought to afford direct access to the physical expression of emotion in gesture and body language.[18] But we have no unmediated access to the non-verbal expression of ancient emotions: to link the depiction of non-verbal behaviour in ancient art to ancient concepts of emotion we typically require warrant from linguistic (and especially narrative) sources,[19] together with as much contextual information (e.g. about the identity and status of the individuals depicted, the relation between their depiction and ancient norms of self-presentation, proxemics, and emotional display, and so on) as can reasonably be obtained, as well as a thorough understanding of the iconography of the wider corpus to which the depiction belongs. Though progress is being made,[20] works which in the past attempted to survey this field systematically are now outdated and inadequate,[21] and coverage remains in many respects sporadic.[22]

Angelos Chaniotis' 2017 study of the multiple ways in which the dedication of a statue provides evidence for aspects of ancient affectivity indicates another fruitful approach in this connection, in so far as it represents a growing tendency to consider the products of the visual arts not just in their own right, as evidence for the depiction of emotion, but (as far as possible) in their wider original context, as functional objects in specific physical and cultural settings: statues not only represent emotional experience, but also express emotional commitment and elicit emotional responses.[23] This piece complements earlier work on the emotional dimensions of sanctuaries and other locations for ritual performance.[24] Epigraphic texts, dedications, religious architecture, and the con-

---

[18] See Räuchle (2019).

[19] See Chaniotis (2012c) 18, 27; Masséglia (2012a) 137–9, (2012c), (2015).

[20] See especially the recent contributions of Masséglia (2012c), (2013), (2015); Bobou (2013).

[21] Sittl (1890); Neumann (1965). On body language in general (chiefly in literary sources), see Bremmer and Roodenburg (1991); Lateiner (1995); Boegehold (1999); Fögen (2001); Llewellyn-Jones (2003); Cairns (2005); Catoni (2008). Among works on emotion expression in particular, one might single out Halliwell (2008) (on laughter); on tears, see the chapters in Fögen (2009). On both laughter and tears in ancient and Byzantine Greek cultures, see now Alexiou and Cairns (2017).

[22] As well as the works cited above, note Davies (1994), (2005); McNiven (2000a), (2000b) (and his unpublished 1982 dissertation); Franzoni (2006). See also Kenner (1960) on laughter and tears in Greek art. One area in which the emotionality of ancient visual culture has been more systematically explored is that of grief and mourning: see e.g. Shapiro (1991); Huber (2001); Oakley (2004). This belongs with a long-standing tradition of studies of lamentation (e.g. Alexiou (2002 [1974]); Holst-Warhaft (1992); Schauer (2002); Dué (2002), (2006); Suter (2008)) and funerary customs more generally (e.g. Vermeule (1979); Garland (1985); Loraux (1998 [1990]); Seaford (1994); Engels (1998); Derderian (2001)).

[23] See Chaniotis (2017a).

[24] See Chaniotis (2011), (2012a).

figuration of the site more generally all contribute to the creation of a shared space for emotional experience and emotional performance, a locus for the enactment of the emotions – awe, fear, wonder, respect, hope, gratitude, and so on – on which religious experience depends.[25] Such an orientation reflects the turn towards materiality in archaeology and ancient history more broadly, a concern that is also manifest in studies that focus more generally on the affective implications of human beings' interaction with objects and artefacts (and one that we take up below with reference to Byzantine studies).[26]

Yet consideration of the embodied aspects of ancient emotion need not, by any means, restrict itself to material evidence. The literary texts that have dominated the study of ancient Greek emotions to date also have a great deal to offer those who wish to investigate the concrete physicality of ancient emotions as aspects of the ways in which embodied human beings interact with the world and the objects that it contains. This is partly a consequence of the fact that literary sources are rich in representations of the objects, artefacts, spaces, symptoms, movements, postures, and gestures through which emotions can be expressed, symbolized, constructed, and elicited.[27] But, equally, there is no absolute gulf between the material and the linguistic, the physical and the mental, in the study of emotion. Metonymies and metaphors drawn from the experience of emotion itself (especially from its symptoms and physical expressions), from other aspects of embodied experience, and from our interaction with the physical and social environments more generally not only play a fundamental role in the formation and extension of emotion concepts, but also afford us at least a degree of access to a linguistic community's shared representations of the phenomenology of emotion. Thus, the ancient experience of emotion is not completely inaccessible to us, at least in so far as we can study shared cultural models of emotion phenomenology through their representation in the intersubjective medium of language, and especially as they are represented in metaphor. Almost always, these metaphors will be conventional, or at least not unique to individuals; by definition, they will reflect not unmediated, pre-reflective subjective experience as such, but shared models of the forms that subjective experience was expected to take. Scholars are beginning to explore what metaphor can tell us about the conceptualization and experience of emotion in ancient Greek societies.[28] To say 'I shudder' rather than merely 'I am afraid' is to give a more vivid and immediate sense of the emotion as a holistic, embodied experience; to present the onset of grief as the feeling of being suddenly enveloped in a cloud or a garment presents

---

[25] Cf. e.g. Masséglia (2012b).

[26] See e.g. Masséglia (2012a), (2012b); Bourbou 2013. For an overview, see Canevaro (2019).

[27] Cf. the works cited above on body language, and Mueller (2016); Canevaro (2018).

[28] See Cairns (2013a), (2013b), (2014b), (2016a), (2016b), (2016c), (2017c). See also Cánovas (2011); Horn (2016a) on erotic metaphors. More broadly, see Horn (2016b), (2018); Zanker (2019).

an individual's emotion in terms of a shared cultural model of what that emotion is supposed to feel like (and links it to the visible expression of the emotion in body language and dress).[29] When Achilles wishes that anger (*cholos*) would disappear from the world, that anger that is sweeter than liquid honey and expands like smoke in a man's chest (*Il.* 18.107–110), he is, to be sure, telling us what anger has felt like to him, but he does so in a way that draws on his culture's metaphorical models of emotional experience (e.g. as the movement of gases and fluids in a container), so that his description is meaningful also in terms of the conceptual schemas that the poem's audiences use to articulate their own subjective experiences. Similarities between these schemas and those that are found in other (including modern) societies will at least partly reflect the constraints that actual physiology, symptomatology, and other features of human embodiment place on metaphors and metonymies that depend on embodiment.

This volume itself highlights the need for a comparative aspect in historical approaches to emotion – inevitable, given that none of us belongs to any of the past cultures that we study. In bringing this comparative and historicizing impetus to bear, Classicists and Byzantinists are already in a position to supply perspectives that are too often overlooked in other branches of emotion research. We do this well when we interrogate to the best of our abilities the linguistic, social, and cultural habits that inform our own and our own societies' views about emotion and activate these when we study the emotional cultures of the past. But this dyadic approach to comparison cries out to be expanded, as it is, for example, when Classicists deploy their knowledge of both the ancient cultures that they study,[30] Rome as well as Greece – an obvious cultural interface that should be a much more regular focus of investigation – or when Byzantinists bring their sources into relation with those deriving from Western Mediaeval cultures. Other comparators readily suggest themselves: conferences and workshops have begun to examine similarities and differences between Greek and Arabic, Greek and Chinese classical traditions.[31] Our perspectives, in this volume, on the interface between ancient Greek and Byzantine affectivity represent a step in a wider set of interlocking dialogues.

---

[29] See Cairns (2013a), (2017b) on shudders (*phrikē*), and (2016a) on clouds and garments.

[30] See the essays collected in Cairns and Fulkerson (2015). For other recent studies that also engineer an explicit confrontation between the affective worlds of Greek and Roman societies, cf. Konstan (2010) and Fulkerson (2013).

[31] For the former project, see the working papers at https://archive.nyu.edu/handle/2451/33 966 (accessed 12 October 2021). For ancient Greek and Chinese emotions in an intellectual-historical context, involving also discussions of Mediaeval, Early Modern, and Modern Europe, see https://emma.hypotheses.org/histoire-intellectuelle-des-emotions (accessed 12 October 2021), now published as Boquet and Nagy (2016). Two volumes on ancient Greek and classical Chinese conceptions of emotion(s) are in preparation – Konstan (forthcoming) and Cairns and Virág (forthcoming).

C.

Research on emotions in the Byzantine world

Martin Hinterberger and Aglae Pizzone

In Byzantine life and thought, emotions were widely recognized as important factors of human life, in particular and explicitly as an essential part of religious life and as a driving force in history. This obvious importance notwithstanding and despite sporadic efforts undertaken by individual scholars in the past, emotion studies within the framework of Byzantine studies are still in an embryonic state. It is revealing that the word 'Byzantium' never occurs in the recently published *Routledge History of Emotions in Europe: 1100–1700*,[1] despite the significant contribution of Medievalists to the volume and its theoretical underpinnings. In what follows, we shall try nevertheless to draw the broad outlines of this very short history of Byzantine emotion studies and to point out fruitful fields of current and future research.

Within Byzantine studies, research on emotions was initially taken up in an effort to understand otherwise unintelligible aspects of Byzantine culture. In his pioneering study Henry Maguire (1977) for the first time systematically analysed in detail the depiction of emotion which had been accepted as a genuine quality of Byzantine art already before. Not only did he identify specific gestures as an expression of sorrow and mourning, but he also observed historical developments in the techniques by which Byzantine artists expressed this emotion. Envy and its ubiquitous presence in Byzantine literature sparked Martin Hinterberger's engagement with emotion studies.[2] The Byzantines were fascinated by *phthonos* because it reflected more than any other emotion their utterly competitive society and because the concept was linked to an irrational fear, inherited from Antiquity, of an envious superhuman power that in the Christian context became largely identified with the Devil.

Until recently, the exploration of Byzantine emotions has often been the collateral result of research undertaken in adjacent fields. Significant incentives for the exploration of Byzantine emotions were provided by closely related disciplines such as religious studies, Late Antique studies, or Classics and Medieval

---

[1] Broomhall and Lynch (2019).
[2] Hinterberger (2010b), (2013a), (2013b).

studies, from where the interest in emotions, but more importantly related methodology spilled over into Byzantine studies.

Thus, for example, Angelos Chaniotis's very successful research project extends up to the Byzantine area.[3] Because of its overlap with Late Antiquity but also due to its pre-eminent significance for the formation of Christianity, the Early Byzantine period has enjoyed much more scholarly interest than later centuries. The realms of religious and patristic studies in particular have produced substantial scholarship on certain emotions and/or certain influential authors among the fathers of the Church.[4] In this context, certain emotions have enjoyed particular scholarly interest because of their appeal to modern concerns or because of their utter strangeness in comparison with today's Western (European/American) emotional cultures. Thus, *akēdia* was investigated as a forerunner of modern depression, or the importance of tears and emotions as connected to Byzantine religiosity, and compunction in particular was highlighted.[5] Since other emotions connected to religion, particularly when conceptualized as sins, always enjoyed a significant interest, research on the Church Fathers' understanding of central emotions has proved one of the most fruitful fields of study so far (see more details below).

The tight connection between emotion and religion has produced a shift of focus towards the affective dimension of liturgical and cultic practices. Once again, specific 'liturgical emotions' have taken the centre stage in attracting detailed treatment. Derek Krueger (2017) has explored the construction and generation of liturgical joy in and through the *Paschal Kanon*, designed to instil elation in the congregation after Christ's resurrection. By looking at liturgy as a 'theatre for the formation of emotions', Krueger considers the *Kanon* as a tool to shape emotional communities.[6] His analysis has broader implications. Liturgical texts in general might fruitfully be construed as emotional speech acts, aimed at directing the performance of the emotion in the congregation. By pointing to the hymn's journey from urban Jerusalem to Constantinople, moreover, Krueger's analysis leads to the question of whether or not and, if so, how geographical dislocation impacted on the pragmatic/affective value of a given text. Spatial and geographical questions are in fact key to gaining a fuller understanding of the Byzantine emotional landscape.

Along similar lines, Mellas ((2018) and (2020)) has investigated compunction as embodied in the liturgical performance of the *Kontakion* of Romanos the melodist and the *Great Kanon* of Andrew of Crete. Mellas points out that, besides dictating the emotional tone to the congregation, liturgy also served another

---

[3] E.g. Chaniotis (2012d).
[4] See the overview given in Papadogiannakis (2017b).
[5] E.g. Jehl (2005); Hunt (2004); Giannouli (2009), (2013); Mellas (2017).
[6] Rosenwein (2006).

C. Research on emotions in the Byzantine world

purpose. It transformed the emotions, repositioning them in an eschatological dimension. This aspect automatically raises the issue of temporality, which is crucial when dealing with emotions in the religious and cultic sphere. As anyone interested in the affective sciences knows, time is one of the key factors in the definition of 'emotions', as opposed, for instance, to 'moods'.[7] However, emotional temporality is firmly grounded in punctual, historical time. The question prompted by Mellas's analysis, i.e. what are the beliefs regarding what happens when we reach the end of time or we transition to eternity, is still in need of comprehensive exploration.

The congregation as emotional community finds its natural place also in the study of homiletics, as demonstrated by the work of Papadogiannakis (2019) on Chrysostom and Tsironi (2011) on Marian homilies. The latter, in particular, shows how emotions and the senses were employed by iconophile homilists to stress and reaffirm the human nature of the incarnated Christ. From this perspective, given the importance of incarnation and material substance in Christian theology and ritual, it is even more surprising that such a crucial aspect of embodiment as the emotions has not received more attention in Byzantine studies.

Apart from the sporadic and individual endeavours mentioned above, efforts to coordinate and unite research on emotions and to create a field of emotion studies within Byzantine studies were successfully undertaken only during the second decade of the twenty-first century. After a workshop on Emotions in the framework of the 21st International Congress of Byzantine Studies (London 2006) which produced no tangible results, the institutionalization of Byzantine emotion studies was considerably enhanced by the Dumbarton Oaks Symposium in 2014. At this meeting of various scholars of Byzantium interested in emotions, it became particularly clear that for the investigation of emotions, Byzantine studies had to consult and join forces with disciplines further developed in this field. The exchange of ideas between classicists and Byzantinists on a collective level had already been ushered in with the occasion of the A. G. Leventis Conference on Greek Laughter and Tears: Antiquity and After (Edinburgh 2013).[8] In the framework of the Leverhulme project from which the present volume has resulted, for the first time Classicists and Byzantinists, both historians of literature and art historians, joined forces for a concerted approach to Byzantine emotions, focusing on the continuation of emotions of the Classical world. The novel interest in emotions has been highlighted by the dedication of a special session of the Patristic Studies Congress at Oxford in 2015 to this subject.[9] More recently, motivated by the continuous progress of gender studies, Byzantine

---

[7] Scherer (2005).
[8] Alexiou and Cairns (2017).
[9] See Vinzent and Papadogiannakis (2017).

emotions were explored as connected to the gendered role of women, men, and eunuchs in Byzantine society.[10]

The focus on gender, a crucial societal aspect, can also be seen as the natural development of a new attention to the experiential dimension, which was first encouraged and explicitly theorized by Byzantine archaeologists, in particular by Marc Jackson and Claire Nesbitt during the 44th Spring Symposium held in April 2011 in Newcastle. Emotions feature prominently in the volume resulting from the symposium,[11] which goes under the telling title *Experiencing Byzantium*. Methodologically, the editors were inspired by the work of Harris and Sørensen (2010), two prehistoric archaeologists who have advocated the inclusion of the emotional dimension in the analysis of material and archaeological records. Harris and Sørensen rely on a loose definition of emotion as 'being moved' and aim to bridge the internal and the expressive by collapsing 'the discursive awareness of the mental and the bodily, of the felt and the expressed, thus unifying the feeling of being sad and the tears rolling down the cheek'. From this perspective, objects create 'affective fields', that is a 'relationship between agents, where something or somebody is stimulating an emotional response in a causal set of events'. Archaeology, by studying objects and their function – so Harris and Sørensen argue – must therefore also take into account these affective fields, which are integral to the experience of users engaging with the materiality of those objects. The same goes for materials as such and architectural spaces, which, according to the authors, create a given emotional 'atmosphere' mediated by the people inhabiting or experiencing them. Building on these premises, Vicky Manolopoulou, in her chapter in Nesbitt and Jackson's volume,[12] addresses explicitly the affective attunement created in the populace by the Constantinopolitan processions, showing how their emotional response resulted from the interaction of bodily practices, architectural setting, urban geography, and verbal representation of divine emotions through the litanies.

Such attention to the materiality entailed by the verbal has opened up fruitful avenues of research. It has made room for a new sensitivity to the emotional impact of the phonic fabric of language, beyond the written dimension. Vessela Valiavitcharska's monograph on *Rhetoric and Rhythm in Byzantium* (2013), which was published the same year as Nesbitt and Jackson's edited volume, testifies to this new interest, as it focuses on both the sensorial and emotional aspects of uttered speeches. This is surely a most productive avenue, still in need of being explored, as we shall see in the next section.

---

[10] Constantinou and Meyer (2019).
[11] Nesbitt and Jackson (2013).
[12] Manolopoulou (2013).

C. Research on emotions in the Byzantine world

What should and could be done in the future

Despite the burgeoning interest, Byzantine emotions constitute a largely unexplored and unmapped landscape, as we have already mentioned. Based on the overview provided above and particularly on the results of our Leverhulme project the following areas of research appear as especially rewarding.

A first issue pertains to the very definition of the individual emotions as theorized and perceived by the Byzantines. Some among them are still barely known even by name (e. g. *diathesis* 'loving affection', *sobarotēs* 'arrogance', or *hupolēpsis* 'loyal attachment/friendship');[13] others, though known, have never been investigated (at least not consistently: e. g. disgust). In order to survey this vast *terra incognita* and to obtain a clearer, if not comprehensive, picture, special studies on specific emotions in given periods or authors are needed. Only after such studies will it be possible to compile a reliable and less provisional catalogue of emotions and their related terminology. The next step would be a repertoire of emotion-related concepts, so as to develop a proper *Begriffsgeschichte* of Byzantine emotions.

In order to properly map out such a varied landscape it is necessary to factor in both the engagement of Byzantine emotional culture with the past (the Byzantines reading the ancients, and writing in classicizing language) and with neighbouring cultures, as well as local and diachronic variations within the empire itself.

As far as the first point is concerned, the ancient linguistic/textual heritage is of special importance for understanding Byzantine emotions. On the one hand – and this does not apply to the emotions alone – the Byzantines read and understood the ancients from their own point of view and experience and generally regarded ancient texts and ideas as belonging to their own time with (almost) no understanding of the specific historical circumstances that conditioned them. This means that frequently the Byzantines' approach to Antiquity is an anachronistic one and that they read Byzantine emotions into ancient texts. Moreover, the tension between old and new acquires even more importance and interest, because many Byzantine authors used a classicizing language, based on schooling and reading experience, for writing literature and expressing contemporary concepts. Consequently, the practical use of this classicizing/atticizing language was heavily influenced by classical texts and their emotional vocabulary, but also by their emotional concepts. It is often not easy to understand what contemporary idea lies behind the classicizing guise. The question of how Byzantine authors applied emotional terminology when writing in classicizing language and thus using classicizing emotional terms is particularly challenging. How might the gap between an antiquated terminology and lived emotional experi-

---

[13] Cf. Hinterberger (2022).

ence be bridged? Could Byzantines talk about their emotions in such a highly elaborated linguistic medium apparently remote from daily life? If so, how did they learn to do so? When it comes to secular literature, the abundant Byzantine exegetical activity on foundational texts narrating or theorizing emotions, such as Homer, Aristophanes, Aristotle, or Hermogenes, becomes a gold mine of material for assessing perceptions of rupture and continuity.

Because of its fundamental impact on subsequent developments, the transformation of ancient Greek emotions into Byzantine Christian ones is of special interest for the field. This transformation, which goes together with a re-evaluation of the emotions, can be observed and analysed particularly well in connection with the work of those famous fourth-century intellectuals who were Christians but heavily imbued with the ancient cultural heritage and informed by their still (partly or even largely) non-Christian environment. To a considerable extent, the so-called Church Fathers incorporated in their work, and transmitted to future Christian generations, not only the literary heritage of the ancient world, but also ancient emotional concepts, theories, and vocabulary in a slightly adapted manner. Since some emotions were severely condemned as sins, Christian preachers made efforts to remind their flock of the disastrous results of succumbing to these emotions. In this respect, both Basil of Caesarea's and John Chrysostom's numerous homilies are particularly rich and therefore have been investigated as sources for the history of emotions not only recently[14] but also in the past,[15] yet much more work is still to be done.

Characteristically, excerpts concerning emotions from various works of Basil and Chrysostom constituted the basis of related chapters in thematic collections of excerpts that came into being during the tenth century and enjoyed broad dissemination in the following centuries. It is of special interest that in the so-called sacro-profane florilegia it is again excerpts from these two authors that form the core of entries on specific emotions of religious relevance.[16] In these entries, Basil and Chrysostom appear along with other Christian authorities, but also classical writers. These chapters on emotions (i.e. collections of excerpts from older texts) thus constitute a peculiar mixture of ancient and Early Byzantine concepts whose internal consistency is not self-evident and has to be examined from case to case. Again, as above, we observe a tension between the present and the past, the new and the old. Despite their complex content and origin, these chapters on emotions provide a promising starting point for a *Begriffsgeschichte* of Byzantine emotions, particularly when their study takes into consideration Byzantine theoretical writings on emotions, usually practised as part of theological-anthropological treatises, the only area where the theorization of

---

[14] See various articles in Vinzent and Papadogiannakis (2017).
[15] E.g. Nikolaou (1969); Durand (1993).
[16] Hinterberger (2013a) 84–100.

emotions takes place. Thus, the Early Byzantine intellectuals, the ancient conceptual heritage, and their use by later Byzantine generations are fields where emotional *Begriffsgeschichte* has still much work to do. The need for and the obvious profit gained from *Begriffsgeschichte* seem to be evident in the case of political concepts and influential ideas. It is high time that corresponding research were done on emotions too, although they will often turn out to be less neatly conceptualized than we would wish.

Starting from the Early Byzantine period when the Graeco-Roman world still was united, a comparative investigation into the development of emotions/ emotional concepts in the subsequently separated East and West seems to be another promising field of research. Are the slow process of drifting apart and the final rift between the East and the West reflected in emotional culture too (cf. Hinterberger in this volume)? In this and other respects, Byzantine emotion studies stand greatly to profit from a closer collaboration with Medieval studies. As we have seen above, space is an important factor to be considered. The cultural geography of the empire was as varied as the physical one. Even though notions of centre and periphery have been recently challenged,[17] it remains true that many parts of the empire were constantly exposed to influences from other cultures. Equally, as we have seen in the case of the *Paschal Kanon*, texts and practices affecting communal emotional regimes would both travel across and radiate out of the empire, further impacting on neighbouring cultures – Armenia and Georgia come immediately to mind. The capital itself was home to diverse communities. Even a central and centralized charitable institution such as the Imperial Orphanage, revamped, as it were, by Alexios I Komnenos and offering free tuition, would host and train children and young men from different regions and religious backgrounds. How did the experience of dislocation affect their engagement with both Christian emotions and the affective concepts drawn from classicizing learning? And do we have the tools to answer such questions in the first place?

Finally, emotions are central to discourses of social normativity. Even though some initial steps in this direction have been done,[18] an enormous amount of work needs to be carried out, in close connection with the *Begriffsgeschichte* illustrated above, in order to understand the correlation between different social strata, their moral and aesthetic values, and specific emotional expressions. In this case too, transitions and changes within the ruling elites need to be taken into account. Just to give a blatant example, the emotional repertoire of frontier aristocracy and Constantinopolitan urban elites could hardly have been the same. Finally, *Begriffsgeschichte* should proceed hand in hand with research inspired

---

[17] Eastmond (2008).
[18] Bernard (forthcoming).

by the new attention to phenomenology,[19] highlighted above. Concepts and ideas are more often than not transmitted and enacted through embodied behaviour. Such behaviour, in turn, does not happen in a void, but is integrated into the environment. Attention should therefore be devoted to how the physical environment and the interaction with physical objects shape the affective engagement of individual and communities. Visuality was first to be considered, as we have seen, but soundscapes, which are currently beginning to be investigated should also be taken into account,[20] as should the impact of music on emotional communities.[21] However, a number of very practical obstacles need to be overcome in this area, such as our still insufficient understanding of Byzantine musical notation. When it comes to interactions with the environment, the application of Latour's actor-network theory[22] as well as of Brown's thing theory[23] have invited a new understanding of the role of materiality in cultic and viewing practices. Such approaches have been pioneering in pointing out the shortcomings of a predominantly disembodied approach to our visual and textual sources. What needs to be done now is to refine the relevant theoretical and epistemological framework by integrating the perspectives emerging from both emotion research and cognitive studies, especially in terms of embodied, situated, and extended cognition, so as to overcome the pitfalls of more impressionistic approaches.[24]

---

[19] See e. g. Pentcheva (2011).
[20] Grünbart (forthcoming).
[21] Mellas (2018).
[22] Peers (2015).
[23] Cox Miller (2012); Peers (2020).
[24] For an attempt see Pizzone (2021).

D.

Chapter summaries

Douglas Cairns, Martin Hinterberger, and Aglae Pizzone

Our first section of chapters deals with emotions in philosophical and religious thought from Antiquity to Byzantium. In his chapter, ANDREA CAPRA considers links between emotion and physical movement in Plato and his interpreters, focusing especially on the poetic aspects of philosophy as an inspirational, mimetic, and psychagogic process. Taking his cue from the magnet simile in Plato's *Ion*, depicting a chain of emotions binding together Muse, poet, performer, and audience, Capra argues that Plato worked out this image in and against the rhapsodic tradition, which construed epic poetry as a chain of wisdom, turning it instead into an *emotional* chain. This seems to open a gap between poetry and philosophy, but in the *Symposium*, Plato applies the same model of communication to philosophy, which suggests that Socrates' 'envy' of Ion is not wholly ironic. Philosophical communication is modelled on the highly emotional paradigm provided by rhapsodic poetry as discussed in the *Ion*, with the crucial difference that philosophical chains instil a salutary sense of shame, an emotion that has pride of place in Plato's discussion of poetry because it helps inhibit more dangerous emotions. The second part of the chapter turns to later instances of the image that draw more or less directly on Plato. Both Plotinus and Proclus reinterpret the image in ways that reveal a palpable anxiety regarding Plato's emotional model. In the Christian tradition, the chain of Paul becomes a metaphor for the emotional and sapiential ties that bind Christ, Paul, John Chrysostom, and the faithful. What has been referred to as John's 'love hermeneutics' is in fact closer to Socrates' erotic emotions as described in the *Symposium*. John's inspiration was a major influence on Byzantine culture, both literary and iconographic, and is paralleled by Psellos' account of Gregory of Nazianzos' inspiration, which he construes as a stream of wisdom that draws from supernatural sources and affects Gregory's imitators. Psellos' discussion demonstrably echoes Plato's *Symposium* and provides yet another example of the chain image. The study of Plato's ambivalent 'chain' across time proves to be a powerful means of exploring the boundaries between wisdom and emotion in different contexts and traditions.

DIVNA MANOLOVA tackles the entanglements between wonder, awe, perplexity, and reason, looking at intellectual exploration, discovery, and surprise.

She investigates the philosophical paradigms of wonder advanced by Plato and Aristotle, in *Theaetetus* 155c–d and *Metaphysics* 983a11–21, investigating their reception in late Byzantium. She is interested in particular in the wonder elicited by mechanics in non-practitioners, where science shows its sensory aspect. To this end she engages with several passages from Theodore Metochites' *Semeioseis* devoted to *thauma, phantasia, pathos,* to harmonics, and to astronomy, as well as with Nikephoros Gregoras' 34th letter, which conveys a more pessimistic view of the possibility of achieving knowledge of the Creation. A close reading of these texts against the framework of Plato's and Aristotle's theories brings Manolova to explore the broader questions of whether 'intellectually curious' might be a suitable label for Byzantine science in general, or, on the contrary, whether wonder and awe were emotional responses generated only by engagement with divine and imperial power.

In the *Shepherd of Hermas*, a Christian apocalyptic text of the first half of the second century that enjoyed great popularity, the emotion of *oxucholia* ('anger', 'angry temper', or 'irascibility') plays a significant role. PETRA VON GEMÜNDEN undertakes an in-depth analysis of the key concept of *oxucholia*, approaching it from four different angles: linguistic semantics, image semantics, discourse analysis, and form criticism. *Oxucholia* is conceptualized as the opposite of *makrothumia*, 'patience', 'endurance'. It enters the human being, conceived as a vessel, from the outside, as something that is originally alien to the Christian. Yet it can also ascend to the heart from within. *Oxucholia*'s presence in the human being drives away the Holy Spirit, and therefore it is strictly to be avoided. A heightened awareness of human sinfulness and of a limited possibility for repentance seems to be the reason for the significance of *oxucholia* in this particular text.

In the next group of chapters, the focus shifts to ancient and Byzantine rhetorical theory and practice. In his contribution BYRON MACDOUGALL explores the construction of sympathy in Byzantine rhetoric from Gregory of Nazianzos to Pseudo-Dionysius the Areopagite, Andrew of Crete, and Photius, looking at their theoretical and doctrinal underpinning in Plato, Aristotle, and Dionysius of Halicarnassus. Sympathy is defined as the sharing of *pathos* between the subject of discourse, the producer of discourse, and the audience. The case study is represented by homilies and festal orations. MacDougall shows that *pathos* is functional to the construction of meaning through a dynamic of reception that builds on both the audience's previous knowledge and their recollection. Although the rhetor's *ēthos* is fundamental in eliciting *pathos* in the audience, sympathy is only a temporary disposition, fostered through reading or, in the case of the Byzantine audiences explored by MacDougall, through the liturgical experience and the homilist's performance. The latter presents his own association with and assimilation to the subject of *pathos*, provoking a comparable reaction in the audience. Significantly and most importantly, sympathy through *mimēsis* paves the way for *katharsis* and then *theōsis*, allowing the Christian listener to approach spiritual perfection.

AGLAE PIZZONE's starting point is the centrality of the emotions in rhetorical theory from Aristotle onwards. In studying the story of Byzantine emotions, it is important to see how eleventh-century rhetoricians theorized and understood the linguistic expression of emotions as well as their ethical relevance within the framework of a Christian rhetoric. To this end, Pizzone explores the treatment of *pathē* in the first fully Christian rhetorical theory composed by John Sikeliotes (second half of the tenth century AD). Sikeliotes gave rhetorical theory based on Hermogenes a Christian outlook by adducing examples from *the* Christian orator, Gregory of Nazianzos, thus replacing Demosthenes as the paragon of rhetoric. Pizzone investigates the discursive definition of *pathē* provided by Sikeliotes, looking first at some aspects of his philosophy of language. *Pathē* are discussed by Sikeliotes mostly in connection with *methodos*, or approach, one of the eight components (*ideai*) through which speech is created according to Hermogenes. *Pathē*, as movements of the soul, are seen as the equivalent of *approach* specifically when Sikeliotes discusses *endiathetos logos*. Therefore, the crucial concept of *endiathetos logos*, or inner speech/dialogue, one of the fundaments of rhetorical theory, must be explored, as must the difference between *logos prophorikos* and *logos endiathetos*. In Sikeliotes' commentary of Hermogenes' *On Styles*, *endiathetos logos* is presented as an utterance that is spontaneous and sincere, expressing *pathē*, or emotions (particularly fear, pity, sorrow, and astonishment). Therefore, if emotions are seen not just as a powerful tool to manipulate the audience, but as ontologically connected with innate and truthful speech, their ethical value becomes unquestionable. Emotions in fact characterize the most preferable and best possible discursive type from a quintessentially Christian point of view. Pizzone concludes that the rhetorical expression of affective states is not just functional to persuasion and manipulation, but is part of the broader task of rhetoric as conceptualized by Sikeliotes, that is, the reproduction and reorganization through language of every aspect of reality.

Building on Rosenwein's notion of 'emotional community' and on Bourdieu's concept of *habitus*, FLORIS BERNARD looks at emotions as socially experienced and displayed ('scripted') within different social groups. To do so he uses two clusters of texts belonging to the period 990–1070: Psellos' funeral orations for his pupils and Symeon the New Theologian's textual corpus. Using semantic analysis so as to have a more granular approach to the emotional palette, Bernard shows that the evaluation of emotions is neither monolithic nor dichotomic (secular/religious), but inherently context-bound. In Psellos' orations we see the ethical and aesthetic world of a close-knit group of urban gentlemen, who appreciate a bodily and facial display of emotions inspired by moderation and grace. Bernard shows that, even within the same group, there might be slight differences, corresponding to differences of status or hierarchy; however, the shared aesthetic and ethical values seem to be fairly constant throughout the life of the pupils to whom the eulogies are dedicated. Bernard also explores the meaning of *pathos* in Symeon, showing how the semantics of the word point to worldly passions alone rather than to emotion in the broader contemporary sense. The monk of Symeon is far from emotionless, but his emotional regime is inspired by compunction. The body plays its part here too, as tears and moderate laughter are both considered strategies to reach spiritual *apatheia*.

The homilies and writings of John Chrysostom (*ca.* AD 349–407) frequently discuss the nature of human emotions, in particular of negative experiences such as anger, fear, and envy, and give advice on the right method for dealing with them. More often than not, Chrysostom criticizes his audience for being carried away by passions that are at odds with Christian ethics and therefore should be avoided. Consequently, recent scholarship has focused on his theorization of emotions, including its medical background, and his therapeutic approach to curing the soul of pernicious passions. JAN STENGER takes a different route by looking at the ways in which Chrysostom employs emotive rhetoric in order to reshape his audience's emotional fabric. The analysis of selected homilies shows that the preacher makes use of a range of emotive techniques and evokes powerful dramas of emotions which at the same time stir up strong feelings in his listeners and make them aware of the moral component of their emotions. Stenger argues that, engendering empathy and love in his listeners, Chrysostom aimed at welding the congregation into an emotional community.

NIELS GAUL's chapter offers a *longue durée* perspective on the performative (extra-textual) means by which rhetors from antiquity through the Middle Ages sought to arouse emotions in their audiences, be this by means of voice, gestures, props, or *mise en scène*. While ancient oratory and theatre have until recently been analysed as largely separate spheres, more recently the focus has shifted to performative features and crossover from theatre into law-court rhetoric (perhaps most prominently so in the figure of Aeschines as a trained actor). In a sense, such theatrical elements in ancient oratory culminated in the physical move of Deuterosophistic rhetoric into theatrical spaces; whence the Late Antique and especially Byzantine practice of identifying instances of rhetorical performance, regardless of setting, as *theatra*. By drawing on evidence from ancient rhetorical theory (Aristotle, Hermogenes) as well as exemplary descriptions of performances embedded in ancient, Deuterosophistic, and Byzantine rhetorical texts, and paying particular attention to aspects of voice, the chapter distils the shifting attitudes to how emotions should be managed and manipulated in the context of rhetorical performances: as a preliminary result it would appear that under the influence of Christianity, the Byzantine ideal of voicing emotions came closer to the Classical ideal than to the post-Classical/Second Sophistic one, regardless of the latter's linguistic and stylistic model function.

D. Chapter summaries 53

Our third section contains a series of essays on Byzantine literature and its ancient background and on Byzantine approaches to ancient models. Douglas Cairns analyses the representation of mental conflict in Homer as dialogue between the person and his or her *thumos*, but with a special focus on the exceptional presentation of the phenomenon in terms of the dialogue between Odysseus and his heart (*kradiē*) at *Odyssey* 20.13–21, where the heart is, moreover, presented as barking like a dog. Though the relation between a person and his or her 'psychic organs' has been seen in the past as involving independent sub-personal agents that detract from the agency of the subject (and from Homer's concept of agency itself), neither the Homeric poems nor their later interpreters provide any warrant for such interpretations. A robust notion of personal agency persists in all relevant passages and in all later interpretations and appropriations, whatever model of the personality they work with. The twelfth-century rhetorician and churchman Eustathius of Thessalonica in particular is consistently correct in interpreting such scenes functionally, in terms of what they contribute to the characterization of the speaker and its situational appropriateness. Eustathius is alert to the use of figurative language and interprets that language in functional terms – the relevant locutions represent ways of talking about personal agency. Eustathius' comments thus offer an interpretation of the phenomenology and representation of motivational conflict in Homer that should command our continued respect.

Mircea Graţian Duluş's chapter takes us to the Norman Kingdom of Sicily, dealing as it does with the representation and elicitation of the emotions in the homilies of Philagathos of Cerami. The contribution focuses on the ecphrastic qualities and vividness of Philagathos' homiletic production and investigates the role of *mimēsis* and 'staging' in the preacher's rhetoric. Duluş shows that besides traditional Christian authorities, Philagathos also relies on authors belonging to the Second and Third Sophistic, from Lucian of Samosata to Synesius and the orators of the School of Gaza. In particular, the chapter successfully argues that the ancient novel – especially Achilles Tatius and Heliodorus – plays a central role in Philagathos' work when it comes to the representation of wantonness, bereavement, and mixed emotions. Such emotions have the goal of allowing the listener to re-actualize the biblical event in his mind through vividness, thus leading to a form of Christian *mimēsis*.

Margaret Mullett discusses *Christos Paschon*, the conventional name of an anonymous Byzantine tragedy, dating to the twelfth century, that relates Christ's death on the cross and his resurrection. Quite characteristically in terms of the Byzantine attitude towards ancient literature, about half of the lines are quotations from Euripides. Following the tripartite structure of the text (crucifixion, burial, resurrection), Margaret Mullett presents the wide range of strong emotions involved (fear, joy, envy, and hope are the most important ones) and asks how audiences were expected to react emotionally. Furthermore, she investigates the frequency of emotion terms in the *Christos Paschon* and compares numbers with two contemporary texts by Nikephoros Basilakes and Nikolaos Mesarites, the latter's emotional trajectories showing various similarities with *Christos Paschon*, although Mesarites' text is emotionally even more charged. The Theotokos is the play's protagonist, and almost half of the text is presented as spoken by her. In the examination of the interaction of *Christos Paschon* with Euripides' plays, Mullett points to the fact that the majority of the emotion-laden passages borrowed from Euripides come from *Medea, Hippolytus, Bacchae*, and *Rhesus*, all plays featuring strong women. Mullett further demonstrates that the reused passages were carefully chosen, that this is an intentional and conscious selection of words or passages.

MARTIN HINTERBERGER surveys Byzantine terminology for and attitudes towards shame and arrogance, particularly in twelfth- and thirteenth-century historiography, considering their ancient Greek analogues and origins (where these exist), their semantic changes over time, and the changes in social norms that accompany semantic change. The classical terms for shame, *aidōs* and *aischunē*, disappear in Byzantine contexts, except in classicizing authors; some authors use them interchangeably, others with differences of reference and nuance, following ancient associations of *aidōs* especially with women and the tendency of some authors to see *aidōs* as prospective and *aischunē* as retrospective shame. The already wide ancient repertoire of terms for pride broadens further, as Christian morality intensifies ancient condemnation of excessive self-assertion, and *huperēphania* ('pride') and *kenodoxia* ('vanity') in particular emerge as major vices and *alazoneia* (ancient 'boastfulness') comes to take on many of the connotations (of self-satisfied superiority and excessive self-esteem) of ancient *hubris*. The embodied aspect of the emotions and dispositions involved – their symptoms, expressions, etc. – are prominent in Byzantine accounts, and embodiment is further reflected in the ways in which the metaphorical nature of many of the terms employed (with their connotations of size, height, elevation, etc.) is mirrored in their association with non-verbal behaviour and demeanour, so that references to the gaze, facial expression (especially the use of the brows), and posture often serve as metonyms for the attitudes in question.

STAVROULA CONSTANTINOU investigates the presentation and construction of anger in the *War of Troy*, a reworking in vernacular Greek of Benoît de Saint-Maure's *Roman de Troie*. Taking her cue from the prominent role of emotions in characterizing the protagonists of the work, Constantinou shows that the *War of Troy* has its own emotional trajectory, distinct from Benoît's 'original'. Anger is particularly relevant because it is both genre-specific (as a feature of epic) and gender-specific (as a male characteristic). Constantinou shows that the warrior's anger conforms, in its essentials, to Aristotle's account of the emotion and at the same time is depicted as a collective experience, forging a community, in Rosenwein's sense. The anonymous poet skilfully navigates such conventions,

D. Chapter summaries 55

by choosing a well-defined vocabulary within the semantic area of *cholē*, or bile, which entails a widespread medical understanding of the bodily basis of anger. The case studies of Achilles and Hector show that rhetoric and characterization are tightly tied to this semantic choice, as both the discourse of anger and its acting out on the part of the heroes are shaped by its physiology.

The volume's fourth and final section turns to artistic representation and ritual performance. *Litē* ('supplication') is the Byzantine term used for supplicatory processions that took place at critical moments in both cities and villages. In her chapter, VICKY MANOLOPOULOU seeks to show how processions, as part of the Byzantine rite, played an essential role in shaping ideas about the relation between human and divine emotion and how the commemoration of natural disasters of the past triggered emotional responses in the participants, thus forging emotional communities. The analysis focuses on processions that took place in Constantinople in commemoration of events of the distant past (predominantly earthquakes of the Early Byzantine period), but also on funerary and festive processions. In the first part of the chapter Manolopoulou examines processions as a collective way of enacting emotion and argues that they contributed to forming and communicating ideas about divine and human emotion (in particular human fear and repentance on the one hand and divine wrath, but also God's 'love of mankind' or *philanthrōpia*, on the other). The second part highlights the performative dimension of the procession, the affective properties of its various components, and their role in the collective enactment and experience of emotion.

In her chapter, GALINA FINGAROVA brings visual representation and text closely into dialogue, examining the emotional impact on the beholder of depictions of the Last Judgement, a pictorial topic that had developed over the seventh and eighth centuries in the Byzantine world. Fingarova begins her investigation with the analysis of two textual sources (the *Oratio adversus Constantinum Cabalinum* and the *Chronicle of Theophanes Continuatus*) that highlight fear as response to the depiction of the Last Judgement. This textual material is juxtaposed with the standard depiction of the Last Judgement as preserved in various monuments. A short overview of the history of the representation of the afterlife and judgement in pre- and early Christian times is followed by a meticulous exploration and interpretation of the Last Judgement's iconography. Fingarova demonstrates that fear was induced primarily by the representation of disorder (*ataxia*) in the painting. This interpretation is corroborated by epigrams that explain the visual language of such depictions. The location of the depiction within the architectural setting of the church building is equally important, and its relation to donor portraits is also explored.

VIKTORIA RÄUCHLE explores the presentation of maternal feelings in literary and artistic sources from Greek Antiquity to Byzantium. Drawing on the distinction between *pathos* and *ēthos*, Räuchle argues that, in Classical Athens, the intense emotion that might be associated with maternal affection as a natural and fundamentally embodied imperative was in artistic representation overlaid by a thick layer of behavioural norms and artistic conventions, so that we see not maternal *pathos* but a maternal *ēthos* governed by the cultural imperative of *sophrosunē*, or (emotional) self-restraint. For viewers used to these display rules, however, even subtle references to maternal affect and corporality functioned as trigger for more intense emotion reactions on the part of the viewer. Roman and Byzantine art adopted, adapted, and transformed these artistic strategies. While the Romans represented nursing divinities of various kinds, maternal qualities play no significant role in the representation of Roman matrons. The images in question do not depict maternal affection but serve as metaphors for fertility and prosperity. Christian art adopts many motifs from ancient iconography, but their semantic content is transformed by means of a new religious symbolism. Mortal women are rarely shown as mothers, and the majority of maternal images are of the Theotokos herself. Even then, however, the corporeal aspect of motherhood is not prominent; only Coptic Egypt provides images that portray Theotokos as Galaktotrophousa. From Greek Antiquity to early Byzantium, the exemplary mother is portrayed in a restrained manner that highlights the virtues of moderation and self-restraint.

DAVID KONSTAN provides an afterword to the volume, drawing together many of the central points made in the individual chapters, but also reflects more generally on issues of continuity and change in emotion language and emotion concepts from ancient Greece to Byzantium, via ancient Rome. Byzantine writers, he argues, even when influenced by or commenting on Aristotle – the 'inventor' of the concept of emotion – move away from the focus on ethics that is characteristic of the Aristotelian approach and instead offer accounts that place more emphasis on phenomenology and valence, a phenomenon that Konstan illustrates with reference to the non-moral shame of demons in Symeon Metaphrastes' *Menologion*.

Part I: Philosophy and Religion

1

Philosophy as a Chain of 'Poetic' Emotions?
Plato and Beyond

Andrea Capra

Introduction

Plato's stance on mimesis was a considerable reason for anxieties among Byzantine intellectuals, and in fact, to this day, it has never ceased to trigger heated discussion. In this chapter, I would like to highlight a problem that strikes me as especially relevant for the subject of this book: while condemning poetic emotions, Plato conceptualizes the discourse of philosophy as an ultimately emotional practice, firmly rooted in the poetic tradition. I will make three interrelated points, designed to clarify the problem and to highlight its potential relevance to Neoplatonism and its Byzantine reception. First, I will examine the *Ion* and suggest that while the idea of a chain binding the Muse, the rhapsode, and the audience was probably available to Plato, he turned it into a highly *emotional* affair: the *motion* of the soul resulting from being exposed to poetry is the closest we get to a 'Platonic' definition of *emotion*. Second, I will argue that Plato's *Symposium* resorts to a very similar, and equally emotional, model to describe philosophy – or at least philosophical communication. Plato negotiates the boundaries of philosophy through a careful balance of analogies with, and differences from, poetry as described in the *Ion*. As a result, philosophy turns out to be both rational and deeply emotional, with an emphasis on shame as an emotion conducive to virtue. Thirdly, and finally, I will suggest a few areas of later thought, both Late Antique and Byzantine, to which Plato's model might be relevant: Plotinus, Proclus, and especially Psellos will be my focus here. Along with his Neoplatonic predecessors, Psellos echoes, while at the same time censoring, Plato's 'emotional' Socrates, possibly as a reaction against an emotional strand of the Christian tradition, which, paradoxically, is perhaps closer to Plato's 'emotional' approach than the tradition known as 'Neoplatonic'.

1.1. Philosophy's ambivalent *zēlos* for poetry:
Plato's *Ion* and poetic (e)motions

A good starting point to show why there is good reason to go back to Plato in the context of a volume devoted to Byzantine emotions is found in Stratis Papaioannou's masterful book on Psellos and Byzantine rhetoric.[1] He recalls how Plato's fierce criticism of mimesis 'instigated the fundamental anxiety over material aesthetics and discursive performance', something that affects the entire Greek and Byzantine tradition. Platonic mimesis, however, is ambivalent to the extent that Plato, while fiercely criticizing the notion of mimesis and the poets, was himself the practitioner of a 'highly aestheticized discourse'. He concludes by saying that such an ambivalence was bound to loom large in the Byzantine world, to the point that mimesis ended up acquiring a positive meaning:

> Tellingly, *mimesis* and its cognates – a ubiquitously used word-stem –, are employed in early Byzantine discourse in a reversed, positive, ethical meaning. To imitate is, in most cases, understood as the praiseworthy emulation of models of virtue. Simultaneously, mimesis as valued discursive representation formed the basis of rhetorical performance and philosophical reading practices.

Papaioannou is very cautious in making generalizations, yet even his sensible account, which rests on the apparent contradiction between Plato's anti-poetic stance and his poetic practice, is open to qualifications. In fact, Plato's very stance on mimesis is *in itself* a thorny and ambivalent question. It is worth mentioning that in the *Apology* Socrates positively promotes the mimesis of his own philosophical persona, and the discussion of mimesis found in *Republic* 3 can be interpreted precisely along the same lines, that is as an invitation to 'imitate' as much as possible noble characters such as Socrates.[2] The discussion of mimesis found in *Republic* 10, too, is far from straightforward. I am of course referring to Plato's 'mirror' argument, which is customarily cited as proof that Plato regarded artistic imitation as twice removed from truth. In fact, I agree with Stephen Halliwell – and I have developed elsewhere further arguments confirming his unorthodox view – that this is in essence an *ad hominem* argument, designed to deflate the pretensions of realism of contemporary 'artists'.[3]

Needless to say, each of these problems would require a long and intricate discussion of its own. One general point, however, should not be too controversial: not only is Plato's affair with poetry a highly complex and ambiguous one; what is more, it is integral to Plato's philosophical writing and cannot be explained

---

[1] Papaioannou (2013) 89–90.

[2] Cf. *Ap.* 24c. Cf. Blondell (2002) 86 and Erler (2011). In *Letter 7*, that is in his own voice, Plato calls Socrates 'the most righteous man of his time' (δικαιότατον ... τῶν τότε, 324e), which closely parallels the *Phaedo*'s concluding praise of Socrates at 118a.

[3] Cf. Halliwell (2002), chapter 4, and, further, Capra (2017).

1. Philosophy as a Chain of 'Poetic' Emotions? Plato and Beyond

solely as a discrepancy between theory and practice. This can be seen and argued for from various viewpoints, for example at the level of the metaphors that inform a dialogue. As Douglas Cairns puts it in his article on *psychē* and *thumos* in Homer and Plato, throughout the *Republic* 'Plato uses a wide range of techniques that might be regarded as poetic, while all the time dissociating his account from poetic models. The *Republic*, in a sense, is Plato's epic. Its psychology constitutes, at least to some extent, a system, as does Homer's. In both cases ... these are systems built on metaphor.'[4] Another entry point is provided by two amazingly dissonant statements found in the *Republic* and *Laws* respectively:

ὦ Ἀδείμαντε, **οὐκ ἐσμὲν ποιηταὶ** ἐγώ τε καὶ σὺ ἐν τῷ παρόντι, ἀλλ' οἰκισταὶ πόλεως· οἰκισταῖς δὲ τοὺς μὲν τύπους προσήκει εἰδέναι ἐν οἷς δεῖ μυθολογεῖν τοὺς ποιητάς, παρ' οὓς ἐὰν ποιῶσιν οὐκ ἐπιτρεπτέον, οὐ μὴν αὐτοῖς γε ποιητέον μύθους. (Pl. *Resp.* 378e–379a)

Adeimantus, *we are not poets*, you and I at present, but founders of a state. And to founders it pertains to know the patterns on which poets must compose their fables and from which their poems must not be allowed to deviate; but the founders are not required themselves to compose fables. (Trans. Shorey (1930))

ποιηταὶ μὲν οὖν ὑμεῖς, **ποιηταὶ δὲ καὶ ἡμεῖς ἐσμεν** τῶν αὐτῶν, ὑμῖν **ἀντίτεχνοί τε καὶ ἀνταγωνισταὶ** τοῦ καλλίστου δράματος, ὃ δὴ νόμος ἀληθὴς μόνος ἀποτελεῖν πέφυκεν, ὡς ἡ παρ' ἡμῶν ἐστιν ἐλπίς. (Pl. *Leg.* 816b–c)

You are poets, but *we are also poets* on the same subjects. *We rival you as creators and performers* of the most beautiful drama, which by nature, according to our hope, can only result from true law. (My translation)

The contexts are similar, as both passages lay the foundation for a new city, yet Plato seems to toy with his audience by evading any clear commitment on a very crucial question, namely whether the dialogues are the new poetry for the just city or they provide only the guidelines for it. Leaving aside this problem, another question arises: what does it mean for someone to be a poet or for a text to be poetic?

To cut a long story short, we can say that Plato would agree with Aristotle on two fundamental requirements: first, there can be no poetry without *muthos*,[5] though *muthos* is of course an elusive notion,[6] one that acquires a new meaning

---

[4] Cairns (2014b).

[5] Not only is *muthos* integral to Plato's discussion of poetry in the *Republic*, but the *Phaedo* devises a kind of poetics in miniature, when Socrates states that *muthos* is crucial for the very definition of poetry. As I have shown elsewhere (Capra 2014, Conclusions), this is closely echoed at the beginning of Aristotle's *Poetics*. Compare *Poet.* 1, 1447a9–10: πῶς δεῖ συνίστασθαι τοὺς μύθους εἰ μέλλει καλῶς ἕξειν ἡ ποίησις ('how *muthoi*, if poetry has to be fine, should be composed') with *Phd.* 61b: ἐννοήσας ὅτι τὸν ποιητὴν δέοι, εἴπερ μέλλοι ποιητὴς εἶναι, ποιεῖν μύθους ('seeing that the poet, if he has to be a poet, should make *muthoi*').

[6] For *muthos* in Plato cf. e.g. P. Murray (1999).

62 *Andrea Capra*

in the *Poetics*;[7] second, and related, poetry is meant to arouse emotions. Let us focus on the second point and look at the *Ion* for a moment.[8] The dialogue opens with an interesting mention of *zēlos*, that is 'a competitive emulousness or admiration for others which has as its opposite contempt':[9]

καὶ μὴν πολλάκις γε **ἐζήλωσα** ὑμᾶς τοὺς ῥαψῳδούς, ὦ Ἴων, τῆς τέχνης· τὸ γὰρ ἅμα μὲν τὸ σῶμα κεκοσμῆσθαι ἀεὶ πρέπον ὑμῶν εἶναι τῇ τέχνῃ καὶ ὡς καλλίστοις φαίνεσθαι, ἅμα δὲ ἀναγκαῖον εἶναι ἔν τε ἄλλοις ποιηταῖς διατρίβειν πολλοῖς καὶ ἀγαθοῖς καὶ δὴ καὶ μάλιστα ἐν Ὁμήρῳ, τῷ ἀρίστῳ καὶ θειοτάτῳ τῶν ποιητῶν, καὶ τὴν τούτου διάνοιαν ἐκμανθάνειν, μὴ μόνον τὰ ἔπη, **ζηλωτόν** ἐστιν. οὐ γὰρ ἂν γένοιτό ποτε ἀγαθὸς ῥαψῳδός, εἰ μὴ συνείη τὰ λεγόμενα ὑπὸ τοῦ ποιητοῦ. τὸν γὰρ ῥαψῳδὸν ἑρμηνέα δεῖ τοῦ ποιητοῦ τῆς διανοί-ας γίγνεσθαι τοῖς ἀκούουσι· τοῦτο δὲ καλῶς ποιεῖν μὴ γιγνώσκοντα ὅτι λέγει ὁ ποιητὴς ἀδύνατον. ταῦτα οὖν πάντα ἄξια **ζηλοῦσθαι**. (Pl. *Ion* 530b–c)

I often *experience zēlos* for the profession of a rhapsode, Ion; for you have always to wear fine clothes, and to look as beautiful as you can is a part of your art. Then, again, you are obliged to be continually in the company of many good poets; and especially of Homer, who is the best and most divine of them; and to understand him, and not merely learn his words by rote, is a thing *that can induce zēlos*. And no man can be a rhapsode who does not understand the meaning of the poet. For the rhapsode ought to interpret the mind of the poet to his hearers, but how can he interpret him well unless he knows what he means? All this is *worthy of zēlos*. (Trans. Jowett (1892), modified)

Socrates emphatically says he envies/emulates rhapsodes and their profession. However ironic, the very mention of this emotion may point to the fact that Plato – to borrow again Cairns's words – intends to create a new 'system' designed to supersede the 'system' of poetry.[10] Yet emotions take centre stage only a bit later in the dialogue, when Socrates resorts to the famous magnet simile:

ἔστι γὰρ τοῦτο τέχνη μὲν οὐκ ὂν παρὰ σοὶ περὶ Ὁμήρου εὖ λέγειν, ὃ νυνδὴ ἔλεγον, θεία δὲ **δύναμις ἥ σε κινεῖ**, ὥσπερ ἐν τῇ λίθῳ ἣν Εὐριπίδης μὲν Μαγνῆτιν ὠνόμασεν, οἱ δὲ πολ-λοὶ Ἡρακλείαν. καὶ γὰρ αὕτη ἡ λίθος οὐ μόνον αὐτοὺς τοὺς δακτυλίους ἄγει τοὺς σιδη-ροῦς, ἀλλὰ καὶ δύναμιν ἐντίθησι τοῖς δακτυλίοις ὥστ' αὖ δύνασθαι ταὐτὸν τοῦτο ποιεῖν ὅπερ ἡ λίθος, ἄλλους ἄγειν δακτυλίους, ὥστ' ἐνίοτε ὁρμαθὸς μακρὸς πάνυ σιδηρίων καὶ δακτυλίων ἐξ ἀλλήλων ἤρτηται. (Pl. *Ion* 533d–e)

The gift which you possess of speaking excellently about Homer is not an art, but, as I was just saying, an inspiration; there is *a divine force moving you*, like that contained in

---

[7] The novelty is signalled by the phrase 'I define *muthos*' (λέγω γὰρ μῦθον, *Poet.* 6, 1450a4). The new meaning, which is surely related to the anti-Platonic idea that poetry imitates actions rather than characters, seems to be by and large unparalleled and has been construed as proto-narratological. Cf. e.g. Zimmermann (2009). Fusillo (1986) cautiously compares Aristotelian *muthos* and narratological *récit*, and rightly stresses how the meaning of the word oscillates in the *Poetics* from the least to the most specific, as in Aristotle's explicit 'definition'. In essence, Aristotle's new meaning closely parallels his biological thought. See Capra (2020).

[8] Needless to say, the emotional nature of poetry takes centre stage in *Republic* 10 as well, and provides an explicit ground for banning it from the ideal city.

[9] This is how Aristotle's use of the term is rendered by Konstan (2006a) 140.

[10] Cairns (2014b).

1. Philosophy as a Chain of 'Poetic' Emotions? Plato and Beyond   63

the stone which Euripides calls a magnet, but which is commonly known as the stone of Heraclea. This stone not only attracts iron rings, but also imparts to them a similar power of attracting other rings; and sometimes you may see a number of pieces of iron and rings suspended from one another so as to form quite a long chain. (Trans. Jowett (1892), slightly modified)

As we will see, the simile implies, quite literally, that poetry sets the soul in 'motion'. A few lines later, the idea is reinforced by three celebrated images that complement the magnet simile: the Muse, the poet, the rhapsode, and the audience share an impulse towards movement, which is described in terms of corybantism (κορυβαντιῶντες, 534a and 536c), Bacchic frenzy (βακχεύουσι ... ὥσπερ αἱ βάκχαι, 534a), and religious possession (κατέχω, 533e, and ten more instances in what follows).

Is it legitimate to construe the soul's *motion* in terms of *emotions*? This much is suggested, I think, by Socrates' description of Ion's performances, which elicit a strong emotional reaction from the audience:

{ΣΩ.} ὅταν εὖ εἴπῃς ἔπη καὶ **ἐκπλήξῃς** μάλιστα τοὺς θεωμένους ... τότε πότερον ἔμφρων εἶ ἢ ἔξω σαυτοῦ γίγνῃ καὶ παρὰ τοῖς πράγμασιν οἴεταί σου εἶναι ἡ ψυχὴ οἷς λέγεις ἐνθου-σιάζουσα, ἢ ἐν Ἰθάκῃ οὖσιν ἢ ἐν Τροίᾳ ἢ ὅπως ἂν καὶ τὰ ἔπη ἔχῃ;
{ΙΩΝ.} ὡς ἐναργές μοι τοῦτο, ὦ Σώκρατες, τὸ τεκμήριον εἶπες· οὐ γάρ σε ἀποκρυψάμενος ἐρῶ. ἐγὼ γὰρ ὅταν ἐλεινόν τι λέγω, **δακρύων ἐμπίμπλανταί μου οἱ ὀφθαλμοί·** ὅταν τε **φοβερὸν** ἢ δεινόν, ὀρθαὶ αἱ τρίχες ἵστανται ὑπὸ **φόβου** καὶ ἡ **καρδία πηδᾷ.**
{ΣΩ.} τί οὖν; φῶμεν, ὦ Ἴων, ἔμφρονα εἶναι τότε τοῦτον τὸν ἄνθρωπον, ὃς ἂν κεκοσμη-μένος ἐσθῆτι ποικίλῃ καὶ χρυσοῖσι στεφάνοις **κλάῃ** τ’ ἐν θυσίαις καὶ ἑορταῖς, μηδὲν ἀπο-λωλεκὼς τούτων, ἢ **φοβῆται** πλέον ἢ ἐν δισμυρίοις ἀνθρώποις ἑστηκὼς φιλίοις, μηδενὸς ἀποδύοντος μηδὲ ἀδικοῦντος; (Pl. *Ion* 535b–d)

Socrates: When you *unhinge* the audience in the recitation of some striking passage ... are you in your right mind? Are you not beside yourself and does not your soul in an ecstasy seem to be among the persons or places of which you are speaking, whether they are in Ithaca or in Troy or whatever may be the scene of the poem?
Ion: That proof strikes home to me, Socrates. For I must frankly confess that at the tale of *pity, my eyes are filled with tears,* and when I speak of *horrors,* my hair stands on end and *my heart leaps.*
Socrates: Well, Ion, and what are we to say of a man who at a sacrifice or festival, when he is dressed in holiday attire and has golden crowns upon his head, of which nobody has robbed him, appears *sweeping* or *fearful* in the presence of more than twenty thousand friendly faces, when there is no one despoiling or wronging him;– is he in his right mind or is he not? (Trans. Jowett (1892), modified)

Fear and pity are vividly described along with their symptoms, which include eyes overflowing with tears and palpitations.[11] In what follows, Socrates con-cludes his argument by turning once again to the soul and its movement:

---

[11] Ion's attitude is in fact ambitious. Though supposedly overwhelmed by 'poetic' emotion, he is lucid enough to check the emotional response of the audience, which will ultimately deter-mine the degree of success of his performance (535e). In other words, it is unclear to what extent

64   *Andrea Capra*

ὦν σύ, ὦ῀Ιων, εἶς εἶ καὶ κατέχῃ ἐξ Ὁμήρου, καὶ ἐπειδὰν μέν τις ἄλλου του ποιητοῦ ᾄδῃ, καθεύδεις τε καὶ ἀπορεῖς ὅτι λέγῃς, ἐπειδὰν δὲ τούτου τοῦ ποιητοῦ φθέγξηταί τις μέλος, εὐθὺς ἐγρήγορας καὶ **ὀρχεῖταί σου ἡ ψυχὴ** καὶ εὐπορεῖς ὅτι λέγῃς (Pl. *Ion* 536b–c).

Of whom, Ion, you are one, and are possessed by Homer; and when any one repeats the words of another poet you go to sleep, and know not what to say; but when any one recites a strain of Homer you wake up in a moment, and *your soul dances* within you, and you have plenty to say. (Trans. Jowett (1892), slightly modified)

As we have seen, *motion* seems to resemble *emotion* closely: this is possibly the closest we get to a 'Platonic' definition of what we moderns call 'emotions'.[12] What are we to make of the image? Scholars often point out, rightly, that Homeric bards as described in the *Odyssey*, not to mention later poets, are not as passive as Plato suggests and that there is little evidence for a pre-Platonic view of poetry as Bacchic frenzy.[13] In Greek culture poets are usually described as authoritative men of wisdom rather than as the recipients of an emotional force. At the same time, the idea of the poet as 'prophet' of the Muses who reports their words and knowledge to his audiences was surely available to Plato – it is in fact the assumption that informs the prologue of the *Ion*, before the 'emotional turn' emerges – and, to some extent, promoted by the poets themselves.[14]

1.2. Just like poetry? Plato and the emotional discourse of philosophy

Plato may have inherited the idea of a poetic chain, which is implicit in the traditional relationship between the Muses, the poets or rhapsodes, and their audiences and is referred to at the beginning of the *Ion* as quoted above. However, he replaced wisdom with turbulence and emotions. This may look like a rather straightforward move, designed to oust poetry from the realm of wisdom so as to make room for philosophy and rational thought. Yet things are considerably

---

he actually experiences the emotions that he is able to elicit. Such an ambiguity resurfaces more than once in later theorists such as Aristotle and Horace: see Halliwell (2017).

[12] As noted by Konstan (2006a) 145, 'there is no clear evidence that, for Plato, the term πάθος has as its specific referent what we think of as the emotions; on the occasions when it seems to coincide with the modern notion, it would appear to do so simply cause the term is so capacious that these phenomena too, in the appropriate text, come under its umbrella'.

[13] See e.g. Murray (1996) 7: 'Greek poetry before Plato abounds with allusions to the idea of poetic inspiration … But despite the poet's dependence on the Muse, it is never suggested that he is merely the unconscious instrument of the divine: poetry is presented both as a gift of the Muses and as a product of the poet's own invention. His gift may be inexplicable, but it is not irrational.'

[14] Cf. the texts collected and discussed in Lanata (1963), to which one may add Simonides 11 West (i.e. the so-called Plataea elegy, where Homer receives the 'whole truth' from the Muses and, apparently, passes it on to others.

1. Philosophy as a Chain of 'Poetic' Emotions? Plato and Beyond 65

more complex. Let us remember the 'symptoms' of poetry as described in the *Ion*, namely magnetism, possession, and Bacchic frenzy: at first sight, nothing could be more remote from philosophy. Unsurprisingly, Ion is usually viewed as a quintessentially non-philosophic character: a helpless and gullible fellow, he yields all too easily to Socrates' mocking questions. On second thoughts, however, he cannot be explained away so easily. On the whole, scholars have failed to notice that the symptoms of Ion's madness strikingly overlap with the effect brought about by Socrates' own words in the heart of his followers.[15] I am thinking here of Alcibiades' famous description in the *Symposium*, when he compares Socrates to a mesmerizing Silenus, who can captivate the soul of his listeners through his magic:[16]

Σωκράτη δ᾽ ἐγὼ ἐπαινεῖν, ὦ ἄνδρες, οὕτως ἐπιχειρήσω, δι᾽ εἰκόνων. οὗτος μὲν οὖν ἴσως οἰήσεται ἐπὶ τὰ γελοιότερα, ἔσται δ᾽ ἡ εἰκὼν τοῦ ἀληθοῦς ἕνεκα, οὐ τοῦ γελοίου. φημὶ γὰρ δὴ ὁμοιότατον αὐτὸν εἶναι τοῖς σιληνοῖς τούτοις τοῖς ἐν τοῖς ἑρμογλυφείοις καθημέ-νοις, οὕστινας ἐργάζονται οἱ δημιουργοὶ **σύριγγας ἢ αὐλοὺς ἔχοντας** (Pl. *Symp.* 215a–b).

And now, my boys, I shall praise Socrates in a figure which will appear to him to be a caricature, and yet I speak, not to make fun of him, but only for the truth's sake. I say, that he is exactly like the busts of Silenus, which are set up in the statuaries, shops, *holding pipes and flutes* in their mouths. (Trans. Jowett (1892))

On mentioning the 'flutes' (*auloi*), as well as Olympus' melodies a few lines later,[17] Alcibiades is evoking Bacchic and enthusiastic music, one that typically involved chains of delirious dancers. It comes as no surprise, then, that Socrates' *words* induce a kind of possession:

σὺ δ᾽ ἐκείνου τοσοῦτον μόνον διαφέρεις, ὅτι **ἄνευ ὀργάνων ψιλοῖς λόγοις ταὐτὸν τοῦ-το ποιεῖς.** ἡμεῖς γοῦν ὅταν μέν του ἄλλου ἀκούωμεν λέγοντος καὶ πάνυ ἀγαθοῦ ῥήτορος ἄλλους λόγους, οὐδὲν μέλει ὡς ἔπος εἰπεῖν οὐδενί· ἐπειδὰν δὲ σοῦ τις ἀκούῃ ἢ τῶν σῶν λόγων ἄλλου λέγοντος, κἂν πάνυ φαῦλος ᾖ ὁ λέγων, ἐάντε γυνὴ ἀκούῃ ἐάντε ἀνὴρ ἐάν-τε μειράκιον, **ἐκπεπληγμένοι ἐσμὲν καὶ κατεχόμεθα.** ἐγὼ γοῦν, ὦ ἄνδρες, εἰ μὴ ἔμελλον

---

[15] A remarkable exception is a 'Note to Plato's *Symposium*' found in Giuliano (2005) 216–18. Only a passing remark is found in Asmis (1992) 347 and Crotty (2009) xix. My own arguments are found in Capra (2014), chapter 3.

[16] Unsurprisingly, some scholars (e. g. Nightingale (1995) 120) have questioned the reliability of Alcibiades' account on the ground of his dubious moral credentials. Yet his description of an 'emotion chain' resulting from Socrates' *logoi* is validated by the very structure of the *Symposium*, which is famously complicated and amounts to a third-degree narrative (see below). A majority of scholars, in fact, believe that Alcibiades' description ultimately reflects Plato's (see e. g. Brisson (1998) 51–4 and Zanker (1995) 32–9). Another question is the relationship of Alcibiades' speech to Socrates': see Destrée (2012) for a concise discussion of the main interpretative approaches. More recent discussions are found in Tulli and Erler (2016).

[17] Pl. *Symp.* 215c: 'For the melodies of Olympus are derived from Marsyas who taught them, and these, whether they are played by a great master or by a miserable flute-girl, have a power which no others have; they alone possess the soul and reveal the wants of those who have need of gods and mysteries, because they are divine. But you produce the same effect with your words only, and do not require the flute' (trans. Jowett (1892)).

66   Andrea Capra

κομιδῇ δόξειν μεθύειν, εἶπον ὀμόσας ἂν ὑμῖν οἷα δὴ πέπονθα αὐτὸς ὑπὸ τῶν τούτου λόγων καὶ πάσχω ἔτι καὶ νυνί. ὅταν γὰρ ἀκούω, πολύ μοι μᾶλλον ἢ **τῶν κορυβαντιώντων**
ἤ τε **καρδία πηδᾷ** καὶ **δάκρυα ἐκχεῖται** ὑπὸ τῶν λόγων τῶν τούτου, ὁρῶ δὲ καὶ ἄλλους
παμπόλλους τὰ αὐτὰ πάσχοντας (Pl. *Symp.* 215d–e).

But *you produce the same effect with your words only, with no instrument*; that is the difference between you and him. When we hear any other speaker, even a very good one,
he produces absolutely no effect upon us, or not much, whereas the mere fragments of
you and your words, even at second-hand, and however imperfectly repeated, we – man,
woman, and child who comes within hearing of them – are *unhinged and possessed*. And
if I were not afraid that you would think me hopelessly drunk, I would have sworn as well
as spoken to the influence which they have always had and still have over me. For *my heart
leaps* more than that of any *Corybantian reveller*, and *my eyes rain tears* when I hear them,
and I see so many others who are affected in the same way. (Trans. Jowett (1892))

Just like Homer, Socrates is unique in that he is able to spark frenzy among his listeners, and the symptoms are just the same: ecstasy, palpitations, tears, corybantism and Bacchic frenzy:

Unhinged mind:	ἐκπλήξης ~ ἐκπεπληγμένοι
Palpitations:	καρδία πηδᾷ ~ καρδία πηδᾷ
Tears:	δακρύων ... οἱ ὀφθαλμοί ~ δάκρυα ἐκχεῖται
Possession:	κατεχόμενοι ~ κατεχόμεθα
Corybantism:	κορυβαντιῶντες ~ κορυβαντιώντων
Bacchic frenzy	βακχεία ~ βακχεύουσι

More importantly, it is not Socrates' own voice that brings about such symptoms;
quite the contrary: the same effect is produced when someone repeats (i.e. imitates) his speeches at second hand, and even if she does so imperfectly. As a
consequence, Socrates' words result in a magic chain of speeches. Remarkably,
this is foreshadowed by the very structure of the *Symposium*, which features a
famously complex narrative frame. What we hear is the narration of a narration
of a narration, actually a third-degree narrative.

The philosophical core of the *Symposium* was originally an exposition by the
priestess Diotima, designed to persuade Socrates. Socrates, in turn, retells the
story during a symposium, and then Aristodemus reports it to Apollodorus, who
eventually tells the story once more for the benefit of a group of friends.[18] Now,

---

[18] Things are actually even more complicated: taking one's cue from philology, one may describe this process of storytelling as an 'open' and 'ramified' 'recension'. The 'text' that Plato pre-
tends to reproduce is the one reported by Apollodorus to a group of friends, but Apollodorus
has integrated some details that are 'validated' by Socrates himself. Moreover, the 'textual
tradition' has a competing branch, culminating in Glaucon (intriguingly, Glaucon was himself
an author of Socratic dialogues, and it is probably no coincidence that Apollodorus refers to
his version of the story as unreliable). Halperin (1992) convincingly interprets the *Symposium*'s
narrative structure in terms of what he calls 'the erotics of narrativity'. However, he detects a
deep ambiguity in the *Symposium* in so far as 'Plato would seem to have used the *Symposium*'s
dialogic to dramatize both the defeat and the excessive triumph of the erotic Doctrine officially

1. Philosophy as a Chain of 'Poetic' Emotions? Plato and Beyond

all of these people are more or less philosophically talented, and yet Socrates' speeches never lose their magic.[19] As a consequence, what we have is precisely the chain of speeches described by Alcibiades, which in many ways, once again, parallels the *Ion*:

MUSE	SOCRATES (DIOTIMA?)
⇓	⇓
POET ('First link')	ARISTODEMUS ('First link')
⇓	⇓
RHAPSODE ('Second link')	APOLLODORUS ('Second link')
⇓	⇓
AUDIENCE ('Third link')	AUDIENCE ('Third link')

The intermediators of this storytelling are Socrates' fans, who are prone to the kind of magic possession so well epitomized by Alcibiades' image of mesmerizing Silenus.

Let us spell out the consequences of the similarities between Homeric and Socratic symptoms and emotions. Apparently, Plato's dialogues and poetry share the same genetic features: through poetic enthusiasm, a chain of accounts is produced, resulting in a series of multiple and subsequent appropriations.[20] The analogy results in a strikingly similar set of symptoms, and still, in a sense, Socratic discourse brings about opposite effects: poetry results in self-satisfaction and instils, for example, the dangerous presumption of knowing, as is clear with Ion;[21] on the contrary, the very same symptoms, as induced by Socrates' words, convey the recognition of one's ignorance:

πέπονθα δὲ πρὸς τοῦτον μόνον ἀνθρώπων, ὃ οὐκ ἄν τις οἴοιτο ἐν ἐμοὶ ἐνεῖναι, τὸ αἰσχύ-νεσθαι ὁντινοῦν· ἐγὼ δὲ τοῦτον μόνον **αἰσχύνομαι**. σύνοιδα γὰρ ἐμαυτῷ ἀντιλέγειν μὲν οὐ δυναμένῳ ὡς οὐ δεῖ ποιεῖν ἃ οὗτος κελεύει, ἐπειδὰν δὲ ἀπέλθω, ἡττημένῳ τῆς τιμῆς τῆς ὑπὸ τῶν πολλῶν. δραπετεύω οὖν αὐτὸν καὶ φεύγω, καὶ ὅταν ἴδω, **αἰσχύνομαι** τὰ ὡμο-λογημένα (Pl. *Symp.* 216a–b).

And he is the only person who ever *made me feel ashamed*, which you might think not to be in my nature, and there is no one else who does the same. For I know that I cannot an-swer him or say that I ought not to do as he bids, but when I leave his presence the love

---

sanctioned by the dialogue' (114). In my view a mixture of success and failure is part of Plato's depiction of Socrates, as Socrates makes very clear when he presents himself as a half-success-ful midwife in the *Theaetetus* (cf. 150d–151a).

[19] Blondell (2002) 106–12 makes the interesting point that the narrators of the *Symposium* are meant to remind us of the danger of idolizing Socrates.

[20] The *Parmenides* provides a useful contrastive comparison: the transmission of Eleatic discourse is depicted as strictly 'unilineal', with no 'contagious' ramifications. In fact, Eleatic discourse turns out to be *apo*treptic as much as Socratic *logoi* are *pro*treptic, and those who are exposed to it, like Antiphon in the prologue of the dialogue, end up turning their back to philosophy. Cf. Capra and Martinelli Tempesta (2011).

[21] Plato was of course no less opposed to the other traditional claim of poetry, namely its abil-ity to provide consolation. Cf. Munteanu (2017) 92–5.

68   *Andrea Capra*

of popularity gets the better of me. And therefore I run away and fly from him, and when I see him *I am ashamed* of what I have confessed to him. (Trans. Jowett (1892), slightly modified)

This recalls the amusing image of the *Meno*, when Socrates is compared to an electric ray: like Homer's, Socrates' words are 'electric', but their effects are just the opposite (79e–80c). More interestingly for our purposes, the passage highlights the emotion of shame.[22] This is no coincidence, especially in the light of Plato's discussion of poetry in *Republic* 2 and 3. Censorship of poetry is designed to promote motionless and emotionless guardians by discouraging fear and elation: in Socrates' view, terror resulting from tragic stories instils cowardice and laughter instils damaging over-elation.[23] In this context, the one emotion that meets Socrates' approval is shame, in that it helps restrain the outbursts of other more dangerous emotions.[24] Shame, then, works, paradoxically, as an anti-emotional emotion, or as a homeopathic treatment conducive to virtue.[25]

Another telling difference is that when Diotima and Socrates replace the Muse as the magnet at the head of the chain, the flux of energy stays strong, untouched by the progressive weakening that is typical of poetic chains. Socratic chains retain their power, no doubt because their 'links' take an active role in the transmission of Socratic *logoi*, and to this extent they differ from the passive reception of poetry, which is surely a crucial target of Plato's criticism. Plato, then, proves deeply faithful to poetic tradition, while at the same time deeply transforming it: the dialogues can be viewed as poetry not because they feature embellishments, quotations, or other superficially poetic features, but in that their very genesis and process are conceptualized along recognizably 'emotional' or 'kinaesthetic' lines.[26]

---

[22] Given that Socrates' *logoi* in the *Symposium* are often thought to adumbrate Plato's own *Sōkratikoi logoi*, i.e. the dialogues (cf. e.g. Capra (2014) 178–9, with added bibliography), one wonders whether the *Symposium* resembles other works of Greek literature that function as 'emotional scripts feeding back into, recalibrating, and extending the emotional repertoires and capacities of their audiences' (Cairns and Nelis (2017) 11). More specifically, it may be argued that shame is integral to Socratic elenchus, something that involves both the internal audience (i.e. spectators who, in Plato's dialogues, listen to Socrates as he refutes his interlocutors) and the audience of Plato's dialogues in so far as they were recited or even, perhaps, performed (cf. e.g. Candiotto (2015)).

[23] In so far as he is mainly interested in the effects of poetry on society at large rather than on the intrinsic quality of poetry, Plato's approach can be broadly defined as 'sociological'. Cf. Cerri (1991).

[24] On the role of *aischunē* and *aidōs* as allies of reason in the *Republic* and elsewhere in Plato, cf. Cairns (1993) 381–3.

[25] 388d, 396c, 396d. Aristotle's discussion of shame in the *Nicomachean Ethics* (1128b10–35, on which cf. Cairns and Fulkerson (2015) 14–16) provides an interestingly different view, in that he clearly distinguishes *aidōs/aischunē* from virtue. In *Republic*, Platonic anger can play a similarly restraining, and therefore positive, role, though on the whole Plato would have disagreed, no less than Seneca, with Aristotle's endorsement of interpersonal anger. Cf. Trabattoni (2020).

[26] This point can be extended to the *Phaedrus*, as I have done in Capra (2014), chapter 3. For

1. Philosophy as a Chain of 'Poetic' Emotions? Plato and Beyond 69

1.3. From Plato's emotional chains to Neoplatonic 'radiance'

As I mentioned at the outset, my aim is to work out a radical reading of the ambiguity that was later to cause anxieties to both Late Antique and Byzantine writers. I have argued that Plato conceptualizes the discourse of philosophy in the same way he conceptualizes poetry, namely as an emotional form of communication consisting in an 'emotion chain' to be contrasted with the 'wisdom chain' ascribed to poets. If that is true, then the next step would be to see how that resonates with later authors. Such an enterprise far exceeds my competences and would of course require a book-length study. Accordingly, I will limit myself to few suggestions, which, in turn, raise further questions.

The first suggestion revolves around *ekplēxis* (and its cognate verb *ekplēttō*), a key term in both the *Ion* and the *Symposium* as well as in later traditions relevant to the consumption of poetry.[27] As one would expect, its Platonic usage bears very negative connotations in that *ekplēxis* overwhelms and blots out human rationality.[28] As we have seen, however, the *Symposium* represents an important exception, in that *ekplēxis* is used to describe the effects of Socrates' *logoi*. This may help explain why Plotinus, when rephrasing these passages, is very cautious and feels the need to qualify the term:

ἀλλὰ δεῖ ἰδόντας μὲν εἶναι ᾧ ψυχὴ τὰ τοιαῦτα βλέπει, ἰδόντας δὲ ἡσθῆναι καὶ ἔκπληξιν λαβεῖν καὶ πτοηθῆναι πολλῷ μᾶλλον ἢ ἐν τοῖς πρόσθεν, ἅτε ἀληθινῶν ἤδη ἐφαπτομένους. Ταῦτα γὰρ δεῖ τὰ πάθη γενέσθαι περὶ τὸ ὅ τι ἂν ᾖ καλόν, θάμβος καὶ ἔκπληξιν ἡδεῖαν καὶ πόθον καὶ ἔρωτα καὶ πτόησιν μεθ᾽ ἡδονῆς. Ἔστι δὲ ταῦτα παθεῖν καὶ πάσχουσιν αἱ ψυχαὶ καὶ περὶ τὰ μὴ ὁρώμενα πᾶσαι μέν, ὡς εἰπεῖν, μᾶλλον μέντοι αἱ τούτων ἐρωτικώτεραι, ὥσπερ καὶ ἐπὶ τῶν σωμάτων πάντες μὲν ὁρῶσι, κεντοῦνται δ᾽ οὐκ ἴσα, ἀλλ᾽ εἰσὶν οἳ μάλιστα, οἳ καὶ λέγονται ἐρασταί (Plotinus, 1.6.4).

Such vision is for those only who see with the Soul's sight – and at the vision, they will rejoice, and awe will fall upon them and an *ekplēxis* deeper than all the rest could ever stir, for now they are moving in the realm of Truth. This is the spirit that Beauty must ever induce, wonderment and a *sweet ekplēxis*, longing and love and a trembling that is all delight. For the unseen all this may be felt as for the seen; and this the Souls feel for it, every soul in some degree, but those the more deeply that are the more truly apt to this higher love – just as all take delight in the beauty of the body but all are not stung as sharply, and those only that feel the keener wound are known as Lovers. (Trans. MacKenna and Page (1957), slightly modified)

---

the term 'kinaesthetic' as applied to choral poetry in the context of the ideal city of the *Laws*, cf. Jackson (2016), with added bibliography.

[27] Cf. e.g. Pace (2010) and Manolova, this volume. Pace discusses the meaning of the word in pre-Platonic texts.

[28] LSJ *s.v.* II render *ekplēxis* as 'mental disturbance', and the 'Platonic' definition of *ekplēxis* is 'fear caused by the expectation of something bad' (*Definitions* 415e, ἔκπληξις φόβος ἐπὶ προσδοκίᾳ κακοῦ).

70 *Andrea Capra*

By describing the blessed vision of beauty as 'sweet *eklēxis*', Plotinus seems to be conflating Diotima's *scala amoris* with Alcibiades' praise of Socrates. So the question arises: can Plotinus' *ekstasis* and *hypostaseis* be construed as somehow analogous to the poetic chain of the *Ion* and the *Symposium*? This would involve, presumably, a process whereby ordinary emotions are eventually kept at bay, thus privileging Diotima's 'ascetic' strand as opposed to the strongly emotional character of Alcibiades' account.

My second suggestion takes its cue from the *Timaeus-Critias*, which presents us, again, with a chain of poetic accounts. The story is found in the Egyptian archives, then it is related to Solon, then to Critias the elder, then to Critias the younger, who promises to deliver it in the *Timaeus-Critias*, though the dialogue famously breaks down just as the story begins with the quintessentially epic scene of the divine assembly. In fact, Plato resorts to a distinctively rhapsodic vocabulary when describing this chain of accounts.[29] The Atlantis story projects the ideal city outlined in the *Republic* on to a mythological past. Was this an 'emotion chain' or a 'wisdom chain'? While Plato's text is silent on this point, Proclus' reading is surely relevant to the subject of emotions:

ἐπεὶ καὶ τοῦτο δεῖ μὴ παρέργως ἰδεῖν, ὅτι τρὶς τῆς πολιτείας ταύτης ῥηθείσης, ἐν Πειραιεῖ μὲν ἀγωνιστικῶς, ἐν δὲ τοῖς πρὸς Τίμαιον τῇ τρίτῃ μετ' ἐκείνην ἄνευ προσώπων συνοπτικῶς, ἐν δὲ τῇ μέσῃ διηγηματικῶς, τά τε πρόσωπα καὶ τὰ πράγματα τῆς διηγήσεως ἐχούσης, ἀλλ' ἐν τάξει μᾶλλον ἢ τῆς πρὸ αὐτῆς, οὔθ' ἡ πρώτη προσᾴδειν ἔδοξεν οὔθ' ἡ τρίτη τοῖς περὶ πολιτείας οὕτω λόγοις ὡς ἡ μέση. μιμεῖται γὰρ **ἡ μὲν ψυχῆς ἔτι πρὸς τὰ πάθη μαχομένης ζωήν**, ἡ δὲ παντελῶς εἰς θεωρίαν ἀνηγμένης καὶ ἀπεκδυσαμένης τὴν μνήμην τῶν ἀγώνων ἐκείνων, ἡ δὲ μέση τούτων ἠρεμούσης μὲν ἤδη, μεμνημένης δὲ ὅμως ὧν ἤθλησεν καταστέλλουσα τὸν πολὺν ὄχλον τῶν ἀλόγων εἰδῶν (Proclus, *In Remp.* 1.16.2–13 Kroll).

This point, too, we must consider as relevant. This *politeia* has been recounted three times: the first time in the Piraeus as a struggle; the third time, after that one, as a tale offered to Timaeus with no characters, in the form of a synopsis; and the second time, preceding the third, by providing the characters and the facts proper of a narrative, though in a more orderly way with respect to the first one. As a result, neither the first nor the third one proved suitable enough for a discussion of the *politeia. For the first one does no more than imitate the life of a soul that is still struggling against the pathē*; the third one imitates the life of a soul that has fully attained contemplation and bears no memory of those struggles; the middle one imitates the life of a soul that has already put some distance between itself and those struggles, but can still remember the battle she had to endure in the process of restraining the vast amount of irrational forms. (My translation)

Proclus interprets the sequence of accounts in terms of an increasing detachment from *pathē*. So a second question arises: can we construe these *pathē* as emotions? Can we call Proclus' reading anti-emotional and, ultimately, anti-Socratic, at least as regards Alcibiades' portrait of the philosopher?

---

[29] See Nagy (2002) and Capra (2010).

1. Philosophy as a Chain of 'Poetic' Emotions? Plato and Beyond

To answer these questions in any conclusive way would require an in-depth study of some of the main features of Neoplatonism. It would require a full-scale comparison between Plato's 'chains' and of the phenomenon of 'radiance', which, as is well known, ubiquitously informs Neoplatonic thought. A prima facie difference is that, unlike Socratic possession, Plotinian *ekstasis* is by and large an (e)motionless affair, and that the very notion of radiance entails a progressive weakening that is at odds with Plato's emphasis on the persistent and indefectible force of Socrates' words. It would be interesting to see both what the two metaphors entail and how they, more or less consciously, shape and condition philosophical thought, all the more so because, while both images have Platonic credentials, Neoplatonists tend to develop the latter at the expense of the former. Such a study is of course beyond the scope of this chapter, yet it may be worthwhile to note at least how they influence the way thinkers are represented.

Alcibiades' portrait of Socrates as a satyr in the *Symposium* matched a statue placed in the Academy's *Mouseion*, which is where Plato's dialogues were probably delivered, as a foundational move.[30] The indefectible rational-cum-emotional power of Socrates' words was thus further propelled by the inspiring image of the ugly-yet-handsome master. Things could hardly be more different when we move to Plotinus and Proclus as described by their 'biographers' Porphyrius and Marinus of Neapolis.[31] Unlike Socrates, both Plotinus and Proclus are consistently described as both calm *and* calm-inspiring characters.[32] Unlike Socrates, both are distinctly good-looking. Most importantly, portraying them is out of the question: although he was 'lovely to see' and 'his countenance radiated light', Plotinus refuses to have a portrait done of himself, which would be an 'image of the image';[33] Proclus' body, in turn, 'produced a radiance which it is scarcely possible to convey in words', let alone through images, so that 'none of those who drew him could catch his likeness'.[34] Both biographers link their masters to Apollo Musagetes, but in both cases the resulting image is that of a fully intellectual 'dance', stripped of any emotional force. All in all, both Porphyrius and Marinus give us a distinctly anti-Socratic account of their masters, one that is closely connected with the demise of emotional chains in favour of ineffable 'radiance'.

With its ups and downs, the influence of Neoplatonic thought on Byzantine culture is a remarkable and far-reaching phenomenon, as is shown, at the most basic level, by the very preservation of such a (relatively) vast corpus of texts. Among the many examples one could linger on, I will single out a remarkable passage by Psellos, whose work shows a constant engagement with both Plato

---

[30] Cf. Capra (2018) with added bibliography.
[31] See Edwards (2000). The English translations of the *Lives* come from this volume.
[32] Porph. *Plot.* 9.
[33] Porph. *Plot.* 1; cf. *Plot.* 13.
[34] Marin. *Procl.* 3.

72 *Andrea Capra*

and Neoplatonism as well as a special predilection for Proclus.[35] Psellos' 'Platonic' aesthetics thus provide an ideal conclusion for the present chapter in the form of a final suggestion. The passage I have in mind revolves around the holy *logos* as a fluid stream that is passed on in a form that resembles Plato's chains. Here is how Psellos describes the supernatural influence of the Theologian, that is of Gregory of Nazianzus:

εἰ μὲν οὖν ὁ μέγας ἐκεῖνος ἀνήρ, ὥσπερ τὰς τῆς φιλοσοφίας ἀρχὰς ἄνωθεν εἴληφε, πρὸς τὰς ἀσωμάτους καὶ θείας ἰδέας τὸν νοῦν ἀγαγὼν καὶ ἀπὸ τῆς ἑνιαίας πηγῆς τοὺς τῆς γνώσεως αὐτῷ ἀπομερισάμενος ὀχετούς, οὕτω δὴ καὶ τὸ τῶν λόγων κάλλος καὶ κράτος ἐκεῖθέν ποθεν ἀπορρήτως παρέσπασε καὶ τοῖς ἑαυτοῦ συγγράμμασι κατὰ λόγους μουσικῆς κρείττονος συνέκρασε, καινὸν τοῦτ᾽ ἂν εἴη τὸ νόημα, καὶ ταῖς ἀπηριθμημέναις πηγαῖς ἐκ τοῦ οὐρανοῦ συνναέτω καὶ **λόγου πηγήν ἀφ᾽ ἧς ἐκεῖνος μετὰ τῶν ἄλλων εἰς κόρον σπασάμενος τοὺς ποταμοὺς ἡμῖν τῆς λογικῆς ἐπέχεε χάριτος,** εἰ δ᾽ οὐδὲν ὅ τι μὴ θεῖον ἐκεῖσέ ἐστιν, τὰ δ᾽ ἄλλα κάλλη ἐκείνων μιμήματα ἐκ τῶν ψυχικῶν ἀρχῶν προερχόμενα, καὶ οὕτως ὁ θαυμάσιος οὗτος ἀνὴρ τὸ ὑπὲρ φύσιν ἀπενεγκάμενος φαίνεται. ὁ γὰρ μηδεὶς τῶν πάντων ἀφ᾽ ἑαυτοῦ μηδὲ πρὸς τὰς ἐπὶ μέρους ἀρετὰς ἔσχηκεν, οὗτος μὴ κατὰ ζῆλον ἀρχαίων, ἀλλ᾽ ἀπὸ τῆς οἰκείας πηγῆς ὁμοῦ τε πάντα ἀναστομώσας καὶ πρὸς μίαν διαυλωνίσας **λογικὴν σύριγγα** καὶ ἕν τὸ πλῆθος πεποιηκὼς καὶ τῇ ὑπάτῃ τὴν μέσην παρασυνάψας καὶ ταύτην τῇ ὑπερβολαιᾳ, εἶτα δὴ νοερῶς πλήξας καὶ τοιοῦτον μέλος ᾄσας τῷ βίῳ, οἷον οὐδὲ **τὸν κύκνον** φασίν, ὁπότε μέλλοι, ὡς μῦθος, παρὰ τὸν οἰκεῖον θεὸν ἀποδημεῖν, τὴν φύσιν ὑπερεφώνησεν (*Discourse Improvised by the Hypertimos Psellos to the Bestarches Pothos Who asked Him to Write about the Style of the Theologian, 27–45*).

That great man had received the first principles of philosophy from above, by uplifting his mind toward the incorporeal and divine forms and taking a portion of the streams of knowledge from that unitary source. One might then suppose that he also seized the beauty and power of his discourse in an ineffable way from some heavenly source and mixed it with his writings according to harmonies of a superior music. This would be a novel idea and one would then have to add to the heavenly sources, which have already been enumerated, a source also for discourse. *From this source, along with the others, Gregory drew his fill and poured the rivers of his discursive charm over us.* If, however, only divine things exist in heaven and all other kinds of beauty are imitations of those heavenly things and flow from first principles in the soul or in nature, even so this amazing man appears to have obtained what is beyond nature. Gregory achieved that which no one had ever achieved on his own account, not even with regard to particular virtues. Without emulating the ancients, he opened up each and every stream from a source within himself, channeled them into *one discursive set of pipes*, turned the multitude into one, attached the highest to the middle and this in turn to the lowest, then struck up a spiritual tune and sang during his life such a melody as not even *the swan* sings, when, as the story goes, it is about to migrate toward its own god. With all this, Gregory out-voiced nature. (Trans. Papaioannou (2013))

---

[35] This emerges clearly, for example, in a recently published anthology on Psellos 'aesthetics'. Cf. Barber and Papaioannou (2017), e.g. 102: 'Psellos seems indebted to Neoplatonic hermeneutics, especially Proklos, who, in his commentary on the *Republic* for instance, presented Plato as the summit of ideal style.'

1. Philosophy as a Chain of 'Poetic' Emotions? Plato and Beyond 73

Stratis Papaioannou notes that the *Discourse* 'is filled with comparisons between Gregory and earlier Greek rhetors' and 'Plato is the most mentioned among them (eight times by name)'.[36] This makes it all the more likely that the reference to the god-seeking swan echoes Socrates' 'swan song' in Plato's *Phaedo*. The chain of accounts from a divine source is built along a by now familiar pattern, and I would like to highlight a striking detail. This is the pipes made of *logoi* (*syrinx logikē*). This, it seems to me, is an unequivocal reference to the *Symposium*, where Socrates, unlike the satyr Marsyas, exerts the magic of his *logoi* without resorting to actual pipes. Psellos must have had Plato's chain in mind, yet, remarkably, he erases all emotions from the picture only to highlight the role of *logos*.

Indeed, Psellos' one-sided appropriation of the *Symposium* speaks volumes not only about Plato's 'looming over the entire Greek tradition of discursive theory', but also about the Byzantine – and modern for that matter – difficulty in coming to terms with the emotional side of Plato's thought.[37] From this point of view Plotinus, Proclus, and Psellos would seem to follow a similar pattern, and one may be tempted to build a consistent narrative out of the examples I have put forth. But this, in all probability, would be a wrong move, or at least a one-sided one. While echoing and somehow censoring Alcibiades' 'emotional' Socrates, Psellos is quite possibly reacting against an emotional strand of the Christian tradition. In fact, 'sympathy' and emotions are often crucial in the triangle formed by author, audience, and subject. In particular, John Chrysostom often refers to emotional chains in a way that has been compared with, if not traced back to, the *Ion*, and this tradition was well alive in later times.[38]

Plato's shoulders are broad enough to bear the burden of Christian *sympatheia* as well as the quintessentially Neoplatonic fascination for ascetic radiance. The ambivalent reception of Alcibiades' (and Plato's?) 'emotional' portrait of Socrates, as well as the ongoing opposition between 'emotion' and 'wisdom' chains, is a fascinating story, one that still remains to be written.

---

[36] Papaioannou (2013) 66.

[37] In all probability, Psellos is also reacting to an emotional strand of the Christian tradition. In fact, 'sympathy' and emotions are often crucial in the triangle formed by author, audience, and subject, and Jan Stenger has shown very well how John Chrysostom's preaching aims at forging an *emotional* community (cf. Stenger, this volume, pp. 165, 189, 198–9).

[38] Margaret Mitchell refers to this phenomenon as 'love hermeneutics': 'Chrysostom's mimetic portraiture is generated by a magnetic force that keeps the wheel of his "love hermeneutics" with Paul turning. This perspective has much in common with the hermeneutics of inspiration set out long before him by Plato in *Ion*.' This tradition was further developed in the familiar scene of Paul's icon inspiring John. An amazing image from a twelfth-century manuscript containing three works by John Chrysostom turns the scene into a public affair, whereby the *logos* passes in relay from Paul to John and eventually to what looks like a highly emotional audience (Milan, Biblioteca Ambrosiana, Cod. A 172 sup., fol. 263v). As she puts it, 'the scroll of Chrysostom's Homilies now cascades off the front of the pulpit, turning from parchment into a fountain of living water from which a host of clergy and the faithful drink' (Mitchell (2000) 437).

2

Wondrous Knowledge and the Emotional Responses of Late Byzantine Scholars to Its Acquisition[*]

Divna Manolova

'As theorized by medieval and early modern intellectuals, wonder was a cognitive passion, as much about knowing as about feeling. To register wonder was to register a breached boundary, a classification subverted.'[1]

Introduction

This chapter focuses on wonder (τὸ θαυμάζειν), an emotion that is often related to awe (ἄγη, θάμβος, σέβας) and perplexity (ἀπορία). Rather than discussing wonder in an aesthetic or religious framework, I explore its role in the process of cognition and especially in relation to attaining new knowledge. In this context, wonder relates to intellectual curiosity and exploration, to the joy and surprise of discovery and the hope that there is even more to discover. It is also related to admiration, as for instance in the admiration the already acquired wisdom inspires in those who witness it. The cognitive dimension of wonder also borders puzzlement and perplexity, and thus it may be interpreted at least in two

---

[*] My thanks go to the members of the *Emotions through Time: From Antiquity to Byzantium* international network and in particular to Douglas Cairns, Niels Gaul, Martin Hinterberger, and Aglae Pizzone who helped me develop the concept behind the present chapter. I am also grateful to the members of the audience at the international conference *Emotions through Time* in Cyprus, 27–9 September 2017, and to the anonymous reviewers who provided me with feedback and suggestions for improvement. I owe very special thanks to Matteo Zaccarini for his patience; to Michael Deckard who asked me about the relation between *thauma* and curiosity in the intellectual world of the Byzantines long before I started considering it in the context of the present chapter; and finally, to Rosa María Rodríguez Porto who read, thought and encouraged me until the final editing was done. This chapter was written as part of the project UMO-2015/19/P/HS2/02739, generously supported by the National Science Centre, Poland. This project has received funding from the European Union's Horizon 2020 research and innovation programme under the Marie Skłodowska-Curie grant agreement No 665778. The process of revising this contribution and submitting it for publication was generously supported by a postdoctoral fellowship at the Centre for Medieval Literature (University of Southern Denmark and University of York).

[1] Daston and Park (1998) 14.

ways, namely as inciting further intellectual activity or as stunning and shocking both mind and body so as to render any further cognitive process impossible. While both interpretative lines can be found in Byzantine intellectual culture, the present chapter focuses on the former, namely wonder as the type of affective and cognitive experience that initiates or is the culmination of philosophical enquiry.

My contribution derives its roots and inspiration from the conceptual framework of the Emotions through Time project, whose objective was to explore 'the continuities and discontinuities in theorizing, inducing and enacting emotions in ancient and medieval Greek texts, artefacts and spaces'.[2] Thus, in order to pursue diachronically my principal research question – regarding the relationship between (i) the role of sense perception and especially of sight and seeing and (ii) the experience of wonder in (iii) the act/process of knowing the *kosmos* – I have structured the exposition as a cross between a thought experiment and a 'proof of concept' exercise in two parts. Section 2.1, '*Thauma* and *theōria*', delineates the conceptual framework of the emotion of wonder (τὸ θαυμάζειν) and its cognitive dimension as employed in ancient and Late Antique Greek philosophy and mechanics.[3] Section 2.2, '*Thauma* and *aisthēsis*', carries over the research question into a Byzantine setting and seeks to find (dis)continuities through the detailed case study of Theodore Metochites (d. 1332) and two of his philosophical essays on perception.

In what follows, I start by discussing the cognitive dimension of wonder in relation to *theōria* and philosophizing as found in Plato and Aristotle (Section 2.1.1). The purpose of delineating these two main paradigms regarding philosophical wonder is to set them as a backdrop to my enquiry into ideas of philosophical wonder in late Byzantium (Section 2.2). In other words, I examine whether (and how) the Platonic and the Aristotelian concepts of wonder were received by Late Byzantine scholars. Philosophy, however, is not the single disciplinary focus of my enquiry. In the first section of the present chapter I discuss *thauma* and *theōria*, wonder and contemplation, in relation to the aims of both philosophy and mechanics, whereas in the second, my focus moves towards the mathematical sciences and especially to astronomy.

The setting of philosophical wondering and puzzlement does not presuppose that everyone engaged in the philosophical enquiry is both its 'maker' and its recipient. The case of mechanics, however, splits the parties engaged in two categories; thus, while a mechanical device presents no wonder to the practitioner who has engineered it and knows the cause of its operations, the

---

[2] A detailed description of the project, its scope, and methodology is available here: https://emotions.shca.ed.ac.uk/our-process/ (last accessed 7 September 2021).

[3] On the integration of cognition and emotion in the brain as well as on the danger of dichotomization of the two concepts, see Pessoa (2013). For an approach to affectivity that goes beyond the study of brain processes and takes into account the whole of the living body as well as the lived experience in order to study the mind, see Colombetti (2014).

2. Wondrous Knowledge and the Emotional Responses

audience, which is not necessarily initiated in the theory of mechanics, appears to be the sole target and subject of the wonder-making. Thus, the case of mechanics offers an alternative association of wonder and (practical) knowledge with an emphasis on display and sensory perception (Section 2.1.2). I conclude with a case study that unites both the cognitive and the affective perspectives on wonder; namely, I examine a letter and two Late Byzantine philosophical essays that tackle the subject of perception and *pathos* and focus specifically on the contemplation of the heavenly phenomena and the associated emotional and epistemic responses.

2.1. *Thauma* and *theōria*

2.1.1. Philosophy

The two most celebrated ancient Greek passages that posit wonder (τὸ θαυμά-ζειν) as the beginning of philosophy are Socrates' words in Plato's *Theaetetus* 155c–d and Aristotle's discussion in *Metaphysics* 1, 983a11–21. The literature on both is vast, and it is not my purpose here to review it. Instead, I shall bring in a sample of scholarly treatments that have acknowledged wonder as the beginning of philosophy as an affective as well as an epistemic *pathos*. As I discuss the sources, first, I focus, in particular, on those elements of Aristotle's discussion that invoke the experience of wonder in relation to mechanics (automata) and the exploration of the heavenly phenomena, both topics I turn to in the following sections of the present chapter. Second, in developing my argumentation I stage the Aristotelian position as a backdrop or counterpart to the Late Byzantine treatments of philosophical wonder exemplified by the case study of Theodore Metochites' essays.

Socrates in the *Theaetetus* identifies τὸ θαυμάζειν as the *pathos* of the philosopher and its *archē*,[4] and Aristotle seemingly restates the Platonic premise reaffirming that the experience of wonder is why people begin to philosophize. Aristotle, however, discusses the act of wondering not in terms of a philosophical experience, *pathos*, or even a state or a disposition, but rather as the impetus initiating the philosophical enquiry which is motivated by the existence of paradoxes and difficulties, such as, for instance, the movements of the heavenly bodies:

That it is not a science of production is clear even from the history of the earliest philosophers. For it is owing to their wonder that men both now begin and at first began to philosophize; they wondered originally at the obvious difficulties, then advanced little by little and stated difficulties about the greater matters, e.g. about the phenomena of

---

[4] Pl. *Tht.* 155d1–5: {ΣΩ.} Θεόδωρος γάρ, ὦ φίλε, φαίνεται οὐ κακῶς τοπάζειν περὶ τῆς φύσεώς σου. μάλα γὰρ φιλοσόφου τοῦτο τὸ πάθος, τὸ θαυμάζειν· οὐ γὰρ ἄλλη ἀρχὴ φιλοσοφίας ἢ αὕτη, καὶ ἔοικεν ὁ τὴν Ἶριν Θαύμαντος ἔκγονον φήσας οὐ κακῶς γενεαλογεῖν.

78   *Divna Manolova*

the moon and those of the sun and the stars, and about the genesis of the universe. And a man who is puzzled and wonders thinks himself ignorant (whence even the lover of myth is in a sense a lover of wisdom, for myth is composed of wonders); therefore since they philosophized in order to escape from ignorance, evidently they were pursuing science in order to know, and not for any utilitarian end.[5]

Thus, this philosophy is aporetic, that is, stimulated by an ἀπορία or difficulty, perplexity, puzzlement, or in other words, intellectual predicament and challenge underline the philosophical activity. So described, philosophy aims at achieving knowledge, and thus at transitioning from the initial state of wondering due to ignorance regarding the causes behind a given phenomenon to the opposite state of knowing them, and thus to lacking any reason to experience puzzlement and wonder:

Yet the acquisition of it must in a sense end in something which is the opposite of our original inquiries. For all men begin, as we said, by wondering that the matter is so (as in the case of automatic marionettes or the solstices or the incommensurability of the diagonal of a square with the side; for it seems wonderful to all men who have not yet perceived the explanation that there is a thing which cannot be measured even by the smallest unit). But we must end in the contrary and, according to the proverb, the better state, as is the case in these instances when men learn the cause; for there is nothing which would surprise a geometer so much as if the diagonal turned out to be commensurable.[6]

According to Nightingale's interpretation of this well-known discussion in *Metaphysics*,

the philosopher 'escapes' from perplexity and ignorance by acquiring knowledge or, to put it in his words, by 'theorizing the causes' (983a14–15). To 'theorize' or 'see' the cause of something perplexing is to move from a state of wonder to a state of certainty. Philosophy, then, begins in wonder and ends in *theōria*.[7]

---

[5] Trans. W. D. Ross in Barnes (1984); Arist. *Metaph.* 1, 982b11–21: ὅτι δ' οὐ ποιητική, δῆλον καὶ ἐκ τῶν πρώτων φιλοσοφησάντων· διὰ γὰρ τὸ θαυμάζειν οἱ ἄνθρωποι καὶ νῦν καὶ τὸ πρῶτον ἤρξαντο φιλοσοφεῖν, ἐξ ἀρχῆς μὲν τὰ πρόχειρα τῶν ἀτόπων θαυμάσαντες, εἶτα κατὰ μικρὸν οὕτω προϊόντες καὶ περὶ τῶν μειζόνων διαπορήσαντες, οἷον περί τε τῶν τῆς σελήνης παθημάτων καὶ τῶν περὶ τὸν ἥλιον καὶ ἄστρα καὶ περὶ τῆς τοῦ παντὸς γενέσεως. ὁ δ' ἀπορῶν καὶ θαυμάζων οἴεται ἀγνοεῖν (διὸ καὶ ὁ φιλόμυθος φιλόσοφός πώς ἐστιν· ὁ γὰρ μῦθος σύγκειται ἐκ θαυμασίων)· ὥστ' εἴπερ διὰ τὸ φεύγειν τὴν ἄγνοιαν ἐφιλοσόφησαν, φανερὸν ὅτι διὰ τὸ εἰδέναι τὸ ἐπίστασθαι ἐδίωκον καὶ οὐ χρήσεώς τινος ἕνεκεν.

[6] Trans. W. D. Ross in Barnes (1984); Arist. *Metaph.* 1, 983a11–21: δεῖ μέντοι πως καταστῆναι τὴν κτῆσιν αὐτῆς εἰς τοὐναντίον ἡμῖν τῶν ἐξ ἀρχῆς ζητήσεων. ἄρχονται μὲν γάρ, ὥσπερ εἴπομεν, ἀπὸ τοῦ θαυμάζειν πάντες εἰ οὕτως ἔχει, καθάπερ περὶ τῶν θαυμάτων ταὐτόματα τοῖς μήπω τεθεωρηκόσι τὴν αἰτίαν ἢ περὶ τὰς τοῦ ἡλίου τροπὰς ἢ τὴν τῆς διαμέτρου ἀσυμμετρίαν (θαυμαστὸν γὰρ εἶναι δοκεῖ πᾶσι τοῖς μήπω τεθεωρηκόσι τὴν αἰτίαν εἴ τι τῷ ἐλαχίστῳ μὴ μετρεῖται)· δεῖ δὲ εἰς τοὐναντίον καὶ τὸ ἄμεινον κατὰ τὴν παροιμίαν ἀποτελευτῆσαι, καθάπερ καὶ ἐν τούτοις ὅταν μάθωσιν· οὐθὲν γὰρ ἂν οὕτως θαυμάσειεν ἀνὴρ γεωμετρικὸς ὡς εἰ γένοιτο ἡ διάμετρος μετρητή.

[7] Nightingale (2001) 43.

2. Wondrous Knowledge and the Emotional Responses

Lev Kenaan has also emphasized the moving away from the initial perplexity and wonder that, in Aristotle's understanding, results in the philosophical enquiry.[8] While she does not explore the relationship between wonder and seeing epitomized by *theōria* to the same extent as Nightingale, Lev Kenaan posits a series of questions concerning the nature of philosophical wonder as an affective experience:

> In returning to Aristotle's understanding of wonder, it is interesting to notice that very little is said about the affective dimension of wonder, its being as a mood or as an actual experience. If wonder is philosophy's essential mood, how does the philosopher experience it? How exactly is wonder transformed into reflection, philosophical thought or speech? How is a philosopher born? Aristotle leaves these questions unanswered.[9]

True enough, awe, perplexity, wonder, and curiosity are not included in Aristotle's lists of emotions in, for instance, the *Nicomachean Ethics* (1105b20–5) and the second book of his *Rhetoric*.[10] Thus, while Plato identifies wonder as not only philosophy's *archē*, but also the *pathos* of the philosopher, Aristotle does not seem to concern himself with the affective experience of wonder, nor does he suggest that wonder should be present throughout the philosophical enquiry.[11] Epistemic wonder in the Aristotelian framework is related to puzzlement and initial ignorance. The observation of an automaton or of the heavenly phenomena, or initial lack of explanation of a geometrical construct, can generate puzzlement and surprise which arise from observing either perceptually through the senses or intellectually through contemplation an occurrence whose cause is unknown to us. The nature of this cognitive input, an input that is new for the observer, presents an *aporia*, inspires wonder, and provokes curiosity, namely the desire to identify and understand its causes and what it is. Understanding and attaining knowledge of the cause, therefore, should eliminate the feeling of wonder born out of perplexity, as long as nothing remains unexplored regarding the observed or contemplated occurrence.

Lev Kenaan's dissatisfaction with Aristotle's lack of engagement with philosophical wonder as a process involving the soul's emotions might appear unjustified and anachronistic. Similarly, the reader may discard the guiding research question of my enquiry as irrelevant: to suppose that the Late Byzantine material engages with the questions Aristotle left unanswered regarding the emotion of wonder and the role it plays in producing a 'scientific' understanding of the natural world is not only an unfair way of approaching said material but also a hypothesis built on false premises.

---

[8] Lev Kenaan (2011) 18.

[9] Lev Kenaan (2011) 19.

[10] See also Arist. *Eth. Eud.* 1220b–1221b and *De an.* 403a16–19.

[11] See note 22 below for the peculiar case of zoology as discussed by Aristotle in *Parts of Animals* 644b22–645a37.

One of the methods I employ in this chapter is to juxtapose two culturally distinct and historically distanced moments in the pre-Modern tradition of philosophical (in the widest sense) treatment of wonder in relation to cognition as found in Greek written thought. It is beyond doubt that while Palaiologan scholars such as George Pachymeres, Theodore Metochites, and Nikephoros Gregoras work in and engage with the intellectual tradition of Plato and Aristotle, it is also undeniable that the societal roles of philosophy and the philosopher in Classical Athens and in Late Medieval Constantinople are very different. If we accept, however, that a question about the nature of philosophical wonder is, in essence, a question about the epistemic relationship between humanity and the *kosmos* or what is beyond its boundaries, then, in my opinion, the juxtaposition of the Aristotelian with the Palaiologan is justified and a useful tool to think with. The characteristic and intense awareness of the Late Byzantine scholars of the pre-existing intellectual tradition, moreover, a tradition that was considered authentic, a legacy, and a privilege, as it did not require translation and rediscovery through intermediaries, is precisely what justifies the juxtaposition and renders the question about the (dis)continuity of pre-Modern Greek thought on wonder more complex than a matter pertaining strictly to the mechanisms of reception.[12]

With this framework in mind, the present contribution enquires into whether the association of wonder with philosophizing was a theoretical premise the Byzantines inherited from Plato and Aristotle and subsequently engaged with. In other words, could we speak of the Byzantine philosophical and scientific thought as 'intellectually curious' and one that either began in wonder or kept 'wondering' at the phenomena? Does Byzantine intellectual culture continue exploring the relationship between humanity and the *kosmos* through the complex epistemic framework formed by sense perception, imagination, contemplation, and concept formation, and is the role wonder and awe play in the process of cognition a matter of discussion in Byzantium?[13] Before turning to Byzantium, however, I will first complete my discussion of *thauma* and *theōria* by introducing ancient and Hellenistic mechanics as the counterpart of philosophy with respect to their competing claims on philosophical wonder.

---

[12] The Byzantine commentary practice is illustrative in this context. On what we have called its 'genealogical embeddedness', see Van den Berg and Manolova (forthcoming).

[13] Even though the scope of the present contribution is limited to a discussion of philosophical wonder, it is worthwhile suggesting that Late Byzantine fiction and, in particular, the three early Palaiologan vernacular romances provide a pertinent and productive *comparandum* concerning the construction of spaces for the marvellous. As demonstrated by Cupane (2014), the early Palaiologan romances introduce a number of innovations in setting the amazing and the astonishing by creating 'a marvelous space in its own right' for the first time in Byzantine literature. Thus, it seems to me worthwhile exploring if the novelty introduced by the Palaiologan romances is paralleled by a similar development in Palaiologan philosophy broadly understood. Also of note are Cupane's observations concerning the interplay between two sets of vocabularies, namely the terminology of amazement and the terminology of fear.

2. Wondrous Knowledge and the Emotional Responses 81

2.1.2. Mechanics

The type of philosophizing and the knowledge it leads to discussed by Aristotle in *Metaphysics* 1 are described as knowledge for the sake of knowing (διὰ τὸ εἰδέναι τὸ ἐπίστασθαι), a knowledge that has no practical purpose. Wonder, knowledge or lack thereof, and philosophy, however, have also been the subject of mechanics, starting with the earliest known Greek work dedicated to the subject. The *Mechanics* is transmitted as part of the Aristotelian corpus, but its authenticity has been continuously debated in scholarship since the nineteenth century.[14] The treatise does not seem to have been a mainstream text in Byzantium, and its earliest surviving manuscripts date to the fourteenth century.[15] It is in this same period that George Pachymeres (d. *ca.* 1310) produced his paraphrase of the pseudo-Aristotelian work.[16]

The *Mechanics* invokes an association with wonder already in its preface:

One wonders, firstly, by phenomena which occur in accordance with nature but of which we do not know the cause, and secondly by those which are produced by art despite nature for the benefit of mankind. For nature often operates contrary to human interest; for she always follows the same course without deviation, whereas human interest is always changing. Whenever, therefore, we have to do something contrary to nature, the difficulty of it causes us perplexity and we stand in need of art. Wherefore, we call the kind of art which helps us in such perplexities the art of mechanics.[17]

The first type of wonder, namely that which is rooted in our ignorance of the cause of a natural phenomenon, we have already encountered in Aristotle's *Metaphysics*. The second type of wonder, however, is caused by those products of *technē* which go against nature, perplex us, and yet are for our own benefit.

---

[14] Winter (2007) has argued for attributing the *Mechanical Problems* to Archytas of Tarentum. Counterarguments and a useful summary of the discussion so far were presented by McLaughlin (2013), while Bodnár (2011) has raised doubts as to the most commonly accepted attribution of the text's authorship, to Strato. For a comprehensive discussion of the text and its manuscript transmission, see Van Leeuwen (2016).

[15] Van Leeuwen (2016) 25.

[16] Despite its apparent lack of success in Byzantium, the *Mechanics* would become a very influential text by the seventeenth century. Notably, however, the *Mechanics*' popularity in Byzantium increases in precisely the period the present chapter is concerned with. It was copied either as part of collections of Aristotle's corpus or with works on related subject matter. An interesting example of the latter case is the fourteenth-century codex Paris, Bibliothèque nationale de France, Graecus 2507, where the *Mechanics* is transmitted together with works on astronomy and astrology.

[17] Trans. E. S. Forster in Barnes (1984), revised; [Arist.] *Mech.* 847a10–18: θαυμάζεται τῶν μὲν κατὰ φύσιν συμβαινόντων, ὅσων ἀγνοεῖται τὸ αἴτιον, τῶν δὲ παρὰ φύσιν, ὅσα γίνεται διὰ τέχνην πρὸς τὸ συμφέρον τοῖς ἀνθρώποις. ἐν πολλοῖς γὰρ ἡ φύσις ὑπεναντίον πρὸς τὸ χρήσιμον ἡμῖν ποιεῖ· ἡ μὲν γὰρ φύσις ἀεὶ τὸν αὐτὸν ἔχει τρόπον καὶ ἁπλῶς, τὸ δὲ χρήσιμον μεταβάλλει πολλαχῶς. ὅταν οὖν δέῃ τι παρὰ φύσιν πρᾶξαι, διὰ τὸ χαλεπὸν ἀπορίαν παρέχει καὶ δεῖται τέχνης. διὸ καὶ καλοῦμεν τῆς τέχνης τὸ πρὸς τὰς τοιαύτας ἀπορίας βοηθοῦν μέρος μηχανήν.

82   *Divna Manolova*

This type of wonder is the one that is born in *aporia* and thus parallels the philosophical wonder discussed above.

Wonder is more explicitly posited as the contested ground between the philosophers and the practitioners by Hero of Alexandria in his treatment of wonder in relation to mechanics and catoptrics. As argued by Tybjerg (2003), many of the mechanical devices described by Hero (fl. first century AD) were specifically intended to incite wonder. The association of mechanical knowledge (which is in Aristotelian terms productive, necessary, and useful and thus of lower status than any theoretical type of intellectual activity) with wonder-making was, according to Tybjerg, one of Hero's strategies in elevating the status of mechanics vis-à-vis philosophy: 'For through the combination of air, fire, water and earth and combining three of four principles, varied arrangements can be actualized; these on the one hand provide the most necessary needs of this life and, on the other, display some stunning wonder.'[18]

The preface of a different work of Hero, namely his *Belopoeica*, also exalts this branch of mechanics above the achievements of philosophy. The advantage of the discipline of mechanics, however, is not related to its association with wonder, but rather to its solutions regarding achieving tranquillity, or ἀταρα-ξία, a task that, according to Hero, otherwise forms the most essential part of the philosophers' occupations.[19]

Indeed, in addition to the Platonic and Aristotelian conceptions of philosophical wonder, one also ought to consider, as part of the tradition that associates wonder with philosophy and the acquisition of knowledge, that strand which relates it to the perplexity induced by the experience of wonder that can prevent the mind from performing its higher cognitive functions and can render the philosopher numbed, paralysed.[20] Instead of provoking and motivating philosophical thinking, the affective experience can preclude it instead. Correspondingly, the ideal philosopher could be the one who remains unmoved and unperturbed, thus upholding the principles of ἀθαυμαστία (as in Strabo), ἀπά-θεια (as in Stoic ethics), and ἀταραξία (as in Epicurus). According to Eustratius of Nicaea, a twelfth-century Byzantine author of a commentary of Aristotle's

---

[18] Trans. Tybjerg (2003); Hero of Alexandria, *Pneumatics* 1, p. 2, lines 15–20: διὰ γὰρ συμ-πλοκῆς ἀέρος καὶ πυρὸς καὶ ὕδατος καὶ γῆς καὶ τῶν τριῶν στοιχείων ἢ καὶ τῶν τεσσάρων συμπλεκομένων ποικίλαι διαθέσεις ἐνεργοῦνται, αἱ μὲν ἀναγκαιοτάτας τῷ βίῳ τούτῳ χρείας παρέχουσαι, αἱ δὲ ἐκπληκτικόν τινα θαυμασμὸν ἐπιδεικνύμεναι. While not rejecting directly Tybjerg's interpretation, Berryman has expressed a modified view that while wonder certainly plays a role in mechanics, it is in relation to its 'display value' rather than to its underlining theory. See Berryman (2009) 52–3.

[19] Hero, *Belopoeica* 71.1–73.11. See also Berryman (2009) 142 and especially Cuomo (2002) 174–7.

[20] Beagon (2011) 80–1. See also Lev Kenaan (2011) 20: 'Wonder does not leave the spectator calm or indifferent. The appearance of wonder touches us in a manner that forces the beholder to respond emotionally and intellectually.'

Nicomachean Ethics, for instance, one should aim rather for moderation in one's emotions (μετριοπάθεια), the latter leading to happiness (εὐδαιμονία). Achieving ἀπάθεια, however, brings one even further, namely to felicity (μακαριότης).[21]

In sum, according to the Aristotelian conception of first philosophy as a theoretical activity that pursues no practical aims, philosophy is born in wonder and puzzlement and ends in lack of ignorance, hence, in the absence of wonder.[22] From the Aristotelian position follow two 'movements of opposition'. As part of the first, the practitioners conceptually appropriated wonder for themselves (as in the case of Hero), in order to exalt the arts (*technai*) above philosophy. Even in terms of achieving tranquillity, mechanics, according to Hero, was more successful and efficient than philosophy. The wonder experienced in the context of mechanics, however, is not necessarily the same type of wonder referred to by the philosophers. Indeed, they are both epistemic types of puzzlement. While the scholar who constructed the automaton knows the cause of its movements and thus experiences no wonder, the observer does, thanks to their lack of knowledge of the underlying principles of the automaton, but the emotion, while born of perplexity, is not necessarily philosophical.

In the second 'movement of opposition', the mathematicians (Hero of Alexandria and Ptolemy) compare theology (in the Aristotelian sense), physics, and the mathematical sciences (all branches of theoretical philosophy) and reserve the supreme epistemological status for harmonics and astronomy. Evans and Carman argue for the mutual influence,[23] or in the words of Feke, 'a conversational relationship', between mechanics and astronomy in the time of Hero and possibly even in that of Ptolemy. Further, Feke underlines the similarities in both Hero's and Ptolemy's epistemological programmes in terms of singling out the primacy of mathematics over philosophy in view of the former's demonstrative

---

[21] For a more detailed discussion of Eustratius' position, see O'Meara (2017) 176–7. For the sources of the relevant portion of Eustratius' commentary, see Trizio (2016). See also its respective review by Karamanolis (2019), in which he remarks that the association of the ideas concerning emotional moderation and happiness could be found already in Hellenistic thinkers such as Antiochus of Ascalon.

[22] The study of the biological world, however, seems to be treated differently. As pointed out by Nightingale (2004) 261, it is interesting that in *Parts of Animals* 644b22–645a37, while arguing the case for the value of zoological enquiry, Aristotle also claims that 'wonder attends the theoretical investigation of animals'. Nightingale then argues (262) that 'the wonder that Aristotle refers to here is aesthetic rather than reverential, though it does have similarities to Platonic wonder'. For her analysis, see Nightingale (2004) 261–5 and especially 264, where she states that 'whatever the natural philosopher's experience of wonder is, it is not the *aporia* that precedes *theoria* (as in *Metaphysics* I), but rather a disposition that accompanies *theoria*'. For an alternative, though related, interpretation see Thein (2014), who also distinguishes two registers of Aristotelian wonder, a poetic and a scientific one. Finally, for a discussion of the twelfth-century commentary on *Parts of Animals* by Michael of Ephesus and of his usage of τὸ θαυμάσιον, see the interpretation of Arabatzis (2012).

[23] Evans and Carman (2013).

method.[24] No wonder is involved here – only the end of the cognitive process. In other words, within the Aristotelian framework, it is the mathematical sciences that can successfully eliminate wonder and puzzlement by achieving certainty. It is precisely the epistemic status of mathematics and of astronomy, in particular, which provides a parallel with and a bridge towards the Late Byzantine material and the case study of Theodore Metochites' *Semeioseis gnomikai*, or *Sententious Remarks*, which concludes the present chapter.

Before I embark on an examination of a selection of Metochites' philosophical essays, however, I shall end this section with a few words of justification of my decision to include mechanics when discussing philosophical wonder. My working hypothesis at present is that ancient and Late Antique mechanics' claim over epistemic wonder in opposition and in competition with philosophy constitutes a pivotal moment in the history of the two sciences. First, it opens the door for branches of knowledge other than metaphysics, e.g. mathematical astronomy, to position themselves as equally capable of inciting wonder and therefore of motivating the pursuit of knowledge and certainty. Second, even though mechanics falls into the domain of practical knowledge, it is, at the same time, deeply engaged with and reliant on the theoretical (geometrical) treatments of vision and movement. Thus, it should not be surprising that, as Acerbi points out, in the circle of the sixth-century Byzantine architects Isidore of Miletus and Anthemius of Tralles, mechanics was studied together with optics.[25] Similarly, engaging with both vision and motion, the astronomy of Ptolemy's *Almagest* provides a mathematical explanation of observed and dated phenomena spanning a period of more than 800 years and accompanied by Ptolemy's own observations. In other words, its methodology employs the collection and analysis of visual data concerning regularly moving celestial objects.[26] It is precisely this suspended dialectic of perception and contemplation inherent in the astronomical knowledge and its epistemic status that I shall address next as I move towards the discussion of several Late Byzantine examples.

2.2. *Thauma* and *aisthēsis*

The discussion of wonder as well as that of the related awe, perplexity, and curiosity as both cognitive and affective states can relate to a sensory experience,

---

[24] Ptolemy argues that out of the theoretical disciplines only the mathematical sciences (astronomy and harmonics) are epistemologically successful, as they lead to certain knowledge, whereas theology and physics, as practised by the philosophers, are conjectural and rely on the help of the mathematical sciences. See Feke (2014). On ancient views on celestial mechanics in relation to philosophical considerations of causality in nature, see Berryman (2009) 177–9.

[25] Acerbi (2020) 153.

[26] Goldstein (1997).

2. Wondrous Knowledge and the Emotional Responses 85

namely hearing or seeing something for the first time or experiencing what is being perceived as new.[27] This would clearly be the case with the wonder the observer experiences when presented with the workings of machines and automata. Similarly, we have already seen in Aristotle's *Metaphysics* 1, 982b11–21 that the first philosophers wondered at nothing else but the observable manifestations of celestial mechanics, namely the phenomena related to the movements of the moon, sun, and stars. The case of wonder incited by the observation of a perceptible phenomenon adduces an epistemological problem to the discussion of philosophical wonder; namely, it forces us to consider the reliability of the information obtained through sense perception that occasioned the initial puzzlement. In other words, in an epistemological framework which sees the faculty of sense perception as limited and/or fallible – and indeed, such is, generally speaking, the Neoplatonic epistemology inherited by the Byzantine philosophical discourse – the cognitive process which starts or culminates in wonder, the latter being dependent on perception, could be questioned or lead to questionable results given that the erring nature of the senses could alter and even misguide our interaction with the observed. A letter penned by Theodore Metochites' student Nikephoros Gregoras (d. *ca.* 1360) presents a pertinent example. *Letter* 34 offers a rather pessimistic view regarding our ability to achieve certain knowledge of creation. Addressed to a certain Maximos Magistros, it showcases two instances of experiencing wonder I have not discussed so far.

The first is occasioned by the contemplation of the world as a divine creation, and what is wonder-inciting about it is the world's arrangement. The cosmos, however, is perceived not as a harmonious and ever-revolving system, but as a chaotic and disorderly universe. In particular, Gregoras compares it to the so-called *kukeōn*, a drink made from barley, grated cheese, and wine. Gregoras' reference to a *kukeōn* must have reminded his addressee(s) of the familiar use of this simile in Heraclitus' fragment 125 DK. The predominant interpretation of the latter understands *kukeōn* as a metaphor for the cosmos, and the process of stirring needed for the barley and cheese to dissolve in the wine as a metaphor for the ordered cosmic rotatory movement. Similarly, Gregoras is employing the image of the *kukeōn* as a simile for the cosmos. The latter amazes us with its instability and confusion, and what results from this particular puzzlement is not philosophy, but its impossibility, unless philosophizing is understood as the continuous and traumatic wonder at the impossibility of achieving certainty:

Or how would <the Creator> not lead <us> to marvel because he neither made the movement of things in the world unmoveable, nor the unsteady steady, nor even more the movement being moved in a uniform fashion, nor the unstable uniformly unstable, but having mixed it up beyond all measure and having made it as if it were a barley-drink, then he gave the present life to those who labour to suffer a never-ending toil and to undergo

---

[27] Lev Kenaan (2011) 23.

86 *Divna Manolova*

endless hardships in order to grasp so many things that there would never be anything determined that would seem understood? For if the things which come into being move for eternity towards generation and corruption in identical manner, then the change would be unchangeable and the movement unmoveable and the unstable stable. And now all is mixed and as if some mist has spread over us who want to see clearly. And indeed, we neither know, nor shall know at any point with certainty what kind of things the things which come into being are then.[28]

What is truly marvellous, however, continues Gregoras, is rather the divine providence that harmonizes creation despite its deficiencies. This type of wonder is of a different order – that is, not only is it not occasioned by a sensory experience, but it is also said to be beyond the comprehension of the intellect:

On the one hand, thanks to such issues, it would be considered and discussed by others that the process of generation happens spontaneously, though perhaps not by me. Yet, on the other, due to them, to wonder at the providence which administers everything beyond the intellect, even if to no one else among all people ... this would much rather be something in accordance with my mind.[29]

One finds the relationship between the incitement or experience of wonder and perception unpacked and significantly more elaborated in the writings of Gregoras' mentor Theodore Metochites (d. 1332) and, more precisely, in his *Semeioseis gnomikai*, or *Sententious Remarks*, a collection of 120 reflective pieces on various topics, among them Plato and Aristotle, mathematics, physics, and logic, moral questions, Roman and Byzantine history, the nature and beauty of creation.[30]

In *Sem.* 31, *That Those Who Are in the Body Do Not Have a Perfect Apprehension of Reality*, Metochites outlines an epistemological framework which interrelates *pathos*, *phantasia*, and *thauma*:

---

[28] Trans. Manolova; Nikephoros Gregoras, *Letter* 34, ed. Leone, lines 50–61: ἢ ποῦ οὐκ ἂν ἐλαύνοι θαύματος, ὅτε μήτ᾽ ἀκίνητον τὴν κίνησιν τῶν ἐν κόσμῳ κατεσκευάκει οὔτε τὸ ἄστατον στάσιμον οὔτε μὴν ἔθ᾽ ὁμοίως τὴν κίνησιν κινουμένην οὔτε τὸ ἄστατον ὁμοίως ἄστατον, ἀλλ᾽ ὑπὲρ πάντα λόγον ἀνακερασάμενος καὶ οἷόν τινα πεποιηκὼς κυκεῶνα, τοῖς τὸν παρόντα τρίβουσιν ἔπειτα δέδωκε βίον πονεῖν κάματον ἀκάματον καὶ ἀνήνυτα μοχθεῖν καὶ καταλαμβάνειν ὁπόσα μή ποτ᾽ ἂν σχοίη πεπηγὸς οὐδὲν ὃ ἂν κατειλῆφθαι δοκοίη· εἰ γάρ τοι τὰ γιγνόμενα κατὰ ταὐτὸν ἐς τὸ ἀεὶ διεγίγνετο πρός τε γένεσιν καὶ φθοράν, ἀμετάβλητος ἂν ἦν ἡ μεταβολὴ καὶ ἀκίνητος ἡ κίνησις καὶ τὸ ἄστατον στάσιμον. νῦν δ᾽ ἀναμὶξ πάντα καὶ ὥσπερ ἀχλύς τις διορᾶν βουλομένοις ἡμῖν κατακέχυται. καὶ οὐ μέντ᾽ ἂν οὔτ᾽ ἴσμεν οὔτε ποτ᾽ εἰσόμεθα ἅττα ποτέ ἐστιν ἀσφαλῶς τὰ γιγνόμενα.

[29] Trans. Manolova; Nikephoros Gregoras, *Letter* 34, ed. Leone, lines 45–9: τὸ μὲν οὖν διὰ τὰ τοιαῦτα αὐτοματίζειν τὴν φορὰν τῆς γενέσεως ἄλλοις μὲν ἂν εἴη πεφροντισμένον καὶ εἰρημένον, ἐμοὶ δ᾽ οὐκ ἂν δήπου· τό γε μὴν ἐκ τούτων τὴν τὰ πάνθ᾽ ὑπὲρ νοῦν διοικοῦσαν θαυμάζειν πρόνοιαν, τοῦτο δ᾽ οὖν εἰ μή τῳ δὴ τῶν πάντων ἄλλῳ, ... καὶ τοῦτο δ᾽ ἔμοιγε καὶ μάλα δήπου κατὰ νοῦν. For another scholarly treatment of the same letter and a discussion of Byzantine views on scepticism see Demetracopoulos (2015), esp. 351–427. On Metochites' position on scepticism, see Bydén (2002).

[30] The first eighty-one essays are available in a modern critical edition accompanied by English translation and a commentary. See Hult (2002), (2016); Wahlgren (2018).

2. Wondrous Knowledge and the Emotional Responses   87

But as regards our understanding of human affairs, or rather regarding an accurate investigation of reality in general, the corporeal world and material bonds are a great hindrance and obstruction, since the intellect does not operate completely unattached and discretely, by itself, but in the bonds of the body. Even if it strives to do so it cannot detach itself from perceiving with the senses or from a kind of imaginative wonderment, so to speak, that belongs to and accompanies [such perception], and is somehow immaterial and with a separate existence, but not beyond the matter of sense-perception. For in imagination we live, in a way, separated from the body and the use of it, but the intellect's activity in the imagination does not take place entirely outside the corporeal. Therefore, too, this kind of intellect both is and is known as 'passible', since it is united with the body and what belongs to the body in which it can act, and cannot function uninfluenced by the affections of the body and material perception. This being so, and since, when we are stirred towards some activity or contemplation (whatever it may be) while we are still in the body, we are unable to achieve [anything] or act otherwise than to proceed in association with our imagination, and with the almost entirely corporeal function of life – under these circumstances, how could the [intellect's] activities be unerring, that is, certain and unimpeded, and its contemplation free from flaws?[31]

This complex passage indicates where, according to Metochites, wonder sits in the context of the human cognitive capacities and why. Due to the unbreakable bond between body and soul, Metochites postulates a type of intellect he refers to as *pathētikos*, or passible. This type of intellect is still an intellect, but it is, however, united with the body, and thus is influenced by what the body experiences.[32] The passible intellect is also what *phantasia*, wonder-making, and sense perception link to. Since the *pathētikos nous* acts within both *phantasia* and the body, it follows, according to Metochites, that this type of intellect is bound to err in terms of cognition. At the same time, wonder seems to be formed within the passible intellect and through the senses; thus, it would follow that *thauma* in this case is both an epistemic state experienced by the intellect and an affective one experienced by none other than the *pathētikos nous*, thus involving sense

---

[31] Trans. Hult (2016); Theodore Metochites, *Sem.* 31.1.1–5; ed. Hult (2016) 38, lines 9–24: περὶ δ᾽ [sic] τὰς καταλήψεις δὲ τῶν ἀνθρωπίνων πραγμάτων, μᾶλλον δὲ καὶ καθόλου περὶ τὴν τῶν ὄντων ἀπλανῆ θεωρίαν, μέγα δὴ προσίσταται καὶ ἐπιπροσθεῖ τὰ σωματικὰ τάδε καὶ τῆς ὕλης ὁ δεσμός, ὅτι δὴ μὴ καθάπαξ ὁ νοῦς ἀσυνδύαστος ἐνεργεῖ καθ᾽ ἑαυτὸν ἀπόλυτος, ἀλλ᾽ ἐν δεσμοῖς ἀμέλει τοῖσδε τοῦ σώματος, καὶ τῆς αἰσθήσεως οὐκ ἔχει τέμνεσθαι, ἂν ὅσ᾽ ἐπείγοιτο, καὶ τῆς ἐπ᾽ αὐτῇ καὶ μετ᾽ αὐτὴν φαντασίας, θαυματοποιοῦ τινος ὡς ἐρεῖν, ἀΰλου μέν πως καὶ ἰδίας ζωῆς, οὐκ ἔξω δὲ τῆς ὕλης αὐτῆς. ζῶμεν γὰρ κατ᾽ αὐτὴν ἰδίᾳ πως τοῦ σώματος καὶ τῆς κατ᾽ αὐτὸ χρήσεως, οὐκ ἔξω δὲ καθάπαξ τῶν σωματικῶν ὁ νοῦς ἐνεργεῖ, ὅσα κατ᾽ αὐτὴν ἐνεργεῖ. ταῦτ᾽ ἄρα καὶ νοῦς οὗτος καὶ ἔστι καὶ καλεῖται παθητικός, διὰ τὸ κοινωνεῖν τῷ σώματι καὶ τοῖς τοῦ σώματος ἐν οἷς ἔχει δρᾶν, καὶ οὐκ ἀμιγῶς τῶν ἐκ τοῦ σώματος παθῶν καὶ τῆς ἐνύλου ἐπαφῆς ταῖς ἐνεργείαις χρῆσθαι. ὅτε δὲ ταῦθ᾽ οὕτως ἔχει, καὶ νοερῶς κινούμενοι πρὸς ἐνέργειαν καὶ θεωρίαν ἥντινα δὴ πάντως ἔτ᾽ ἐν τῷ σώματι μένοντες, οὐκ ἔχομεν ἀνύτειν οὐδ᾽ ἄλλως χρῆσθαι ὅτι μὴ μετὰ φαντασίας ἰόντες, καὶ ὡς ἔπος εἰπεῖν τῆς ἐνσωμάτου χρήσεως καὶ ζωῆς, πῶς ἂν εἴη λοιπὸν ἔπειτ᾽ ἀπλανὴς εἴτουν ἀσφαλὴς καὶ ἀπρόσκοπος ἡ ἐνέργεια καὶ ἄνοσον τὸ τῆς θεωρίας χρῆμα;

[32] For a discussion of Metochites' views on epistemology and perception, see Bydén (2003) 318–26.

88   Divna Manolova

perception and *phantasia*. However, the question as to whether here wonder remains the beginning or culmination of philosophizing I leave unanswered at present.[33]

Next, I will analyse two sets of examples taken from Metochites' *Semeioseis* which treat the disciplines of harmonics and astronomy, respectively. Both these disciplines offer knowledge of the universe based on the principles of mathematics, and both are conceptually related to a type of sensory experience, an acoustic and an optic one respectively.

In *Sem.* 13, *On Plato and the Mathematical Part of Wisdom and Especially on Harmonics*, Metochites introduces the subject of musical theory and offers an account of the history of this particular branch of science along the lines of traditional heurematography; namely, he focuses on both the discovery of harmonics and on the historical developments that brought it to perfection.[34] It is within this context that we also learn that discovering a certain form of knowledge is what makes one an object of wonder:

> For the scientific study of music was begun by Pythagoras, who also himself became an admirable guide in this subject for the Hellenes, being, through his supreme acumen, perspicacity, and expert thoroughness, the first to distinguish, by means of acoustic perception and judgement and guidance to the mind, the divisions of the ratios of numbers, and the harmony inherent in reality and structured by fixed definitions that are absolutely unassailable and assist in the discovery of certain knowledge. This is truly most wondrous ...[35]

Pythagoras is admirable (θαυμάσιος) because he was the first to achieve something (πρῶτος), and what he did is nothing other than that which is most wondrous (θαυμασιώτατον). What he accomplished in the field of harmonics indeed led to the discovery of scientific knowledge (ἐπιστήμη). Instead of the intellect alone, his starting point was, however, according to Metochites, auditory perception (ἀκουστικὴ αἴσθησις) which was then, in turn, guided by the mind.

The emphasis on auditory perception as Pythagoras' starting point in inventing harmonics is reiterated throughout the essay.[36] The epistemic value of the

---

[33] For an eleventh-century Byzantine discussion by the rhetorician John Sikeliotes of the Aristotelian concept of *pathētikos nous* which treats it as identical to *phantasia* see Roilos (2014) 11; (2018) 180–1. On Sikeliotes, see also Pizzone in this volume.

[34] Zhmud (2006) 12–13.

[35] Trans. Hult (2002), with minor revisions; Theodore Metochites, *Sem.* 13.2.1–3; ed. Hult (2002) 128, lines 7–14: μουσικῶν γὰρ λόγων ἤρξατο μὲν Πυθαγόρας καὶ θαυμάσιος ἐν τούτοις ἡγεμὼν τοῖς Ἕλλησιν αὐτὸς γέγονε, πρῶτος φιλοκρινήσας ὑπ' ἄκρας ἀγχινοίας καὶ περινοίας καὶ γνωστικῆς ἐπιμελείας τὰς ἐκ τῆς ἀκουστικῆς αἰσθήσεως καὶ κρίσεως καὶ χειραγωγίας εἰς νοῦν διαιρέσεις τῶν ἐν ἀριθμοῖς λόγων καὶ τὸ σύμφυτον τοῖς οὖσιν ἐμμελὲς καὶ ἡρμοσμένον ὅροις τακτοῖς καθάπαξ τὸ ἀσάλευτον ἔχουσι καὶ μεγάλης ἐπιστήμης εὕρεσιν χορηγοῦσι, πρᾶγμα θαυμασιώτατον ὡς ἀληθῶς ...

[36] See for instance Theodore Metochites, *Sem.* 13.2.9–10; ed. Hult (2002) 130, lines 8–15: ἀλλὰ πολὺς ὡς ἀληθῶς ἀνὴρ ἐκεῖνος ὁ Πυθαγόρας καὶ θαυμάζειν μάλιστ' εἰ δή τις ἄξιος, ἀπὸ τῆς ἀκουστικῆς ταύτης ἐντεύξεως καὶ πείρας καὶ χρήσεως ... καταδιελόμενος καὶ καταριθμήσας καὶ ὁρισάμενος πήχεσι καὶ θριγγοῖς ἀσαλεύτοις τὰ ἐν τῇ φωνῇ καὶ τοῖς ἤχοις μήκη, ὁποσαοῦν

2. Wondrous Knowledge and the Emotional Responses

information derived through the sensory experience of sound is justified earlier by Metochites in *Sem.* 13.2.7–8, as he states that 'the sense of hearing seems somehow to be already from the beginning an immaterial indication of an immaterial investigation and knowledge. For we are not able, as in the case of sight, to "see" well-defined weights and lengths of hearing and sound, or divisions and measurements easy to use without effort.'[37] Metochites, however, does not relate the acoustic experience to the formation of wonder. The latter will be the case with astronomy and the observation of the heavenly phenomena.

Adopting a prototype-based approach to the emotion of awe, Keltner and Haidt propose that the two features central and present in all clear cases are vastness and accommodation:

> Vastness refers to anything that is experienced as being much larger than the self, or the self's ordinary level of experience or frame of reference ... Accommodation refers to the Piagetian process of adjusting mental structures that cannot assimilate a new experience ... We propose that prototypical awe involves a challenge to or negation of mental structures when they fail to make sense of an experience of something vast.[38]

The most common examples of encountering vastness and, as a consequence, experiencing wonder, awe, and even reverence are those of the contemplation of the sky and the heavenly bodies and that of the ocean.[39] It is thus not coincidental, in my opinion, that when Theodore Metochites includes in his *Semeioseis* a subgroup of essays (*Sem.* 42–5)[40] that deal with the role of perception and, specifically, with that of sight, he starts with a discussion of the case of observing creation in general (*Sem.* 42) and continues with the contemplation of the heavenly phenomena (*Sem.* 43) and of the sea (*Sem.* 44).[41]

ἕκαστα, καὶ τὰς διαθέσεις αὐτῶν πρὸς ἄλληλα ... ('But Pythagoras was truly a great man, worthy indeed of admiration, who from this acoustic encounter, experience, and use ... dissected and counted and defined with certain lengths and boundaries, down to the finest and most minute quantities of the voice and sounds, the size of each and what relations they have to each other ...' (trans. Hult (2002) 131).

[37] Trans. Hult (2002); Theodore Metochites, *Sem.* 13.2.7–8; ed. Hult (2002) 130, lines 3–8: ἀλλ' ἔοικεν ὥσπερ εἶναι τρόπον τινὰ ἄϋλον ἀΰλου θεωρίας καὶ καταληπτικῆς ἕξεως καὶ τελευτῆς ὑπόδειγμα τὴν ἀρχήν· οὐ γὰρ δὴ παραπλησίως ἔχομεν, ὡς ἂν δῆτ' ἐπὶ τῆς ὁράσεως αὐτῆς, σταθμούς τινας καὶ πήχεις ἀκοῆς καὶ φωνῆς εὐορίστους συνιδεῖν, καὶ διαιρέσεις καὶ μέτρα ῥᾷστ' ἄπονα χρῆσθαι.

[38] Keltner and Haidt (2003) 303–4.

[39] Although, as suggested to me by Claudia Rapp, the desert is another type of vastness extremely relevant in the Byzantine context.

[40] For a discussion of those essays in the context of Metochites' epistemological views, see Bydén (2003) 321–6.

[41] While not structurally belonging to the same subunit, *Sem.* 51, *That the Body and That Which Appertains to It Is a Great Hindrance to the Soul in Its Proper Intellectual Activity*, should read alongside *Sem.* 42–5, as it discusses the limitations of the soul's cognitive capacities and especially of *phantasia* due to its reliance on sense perception and, by extension, on body and matter. Cf. *Sem.* 56, *That It Is Always Possible, No Matter How One Is Faring, to Raise Oneself by Reasonable Mental Edification to the Level of Great Success*, esp. *Sem.* 56.1.3–4; 162, lines 2–8,

2.2.1. Theodore Metochites, Sem. 42, That It Is Extremely Pleasant for Human Beings to Behold Creation

The type of seeing referred to by Metochites in *Sem*. 42 is denoted as ἐποπτεία, that is, a contemplation but also a watchful, providential care, thus denoting an intense gaze that is analogous to the divine in its engagement with its object. In its Byzantine usage ἐποπτεία also involves monitoring and inspection. There is no sight (θέαμα) more pleasant than contemplating creation, claims Metochites, and the process results in relaxation and delight of the soul. For the soul is by nature contemplative (φιλοθεάμων) and in love with using the senses, but most of all with sight, which occupies a privileged position as the most perfect among them (*Sem*. 42.1.2). It is the sights of creation that are the best objects of human observation, as the human soul is also the most noble. To be precise, it is the rational part of the soul whose proper use is contemplation (θεωρία), and the latter may involve data collected through sense perception (*Sem*. 42.1.3). Thus, Metochites addresses the topic of contemplating creation, but distinguishes between different senses and different parts of the soul, as well as between humankind and the rest of the living beings. The premise of the passage remains unchanged: the best object of contemplation is creation. That is true whether the observer is human or not. Two distinctions follow. First, the same excellent object can be viewed by at least two different types of observers, the human and the non-human. The human observer is the better of these, thanks to their rational soul, hence the second distinction, namely, between the various senses, which can bring the objects of contemplation to the best possible observer and to the best part of their soul, which will be contemplating them. Among all the senses, sight is the most perfect, a traditional claim that Metochites does not bother to justify. Thus, Metochites has identified the best possible scenario of contemplation, or ἐποπτεία: it involves the most superior sense of the best possible observer, who possesses the most noble soul and has directed his or her gaze towards the best possible sight, namely creation:

---

in which Metochites expresses a surprisingly hopeful thesis answering to his *Sem*. 51, as it were: ἐπεὶ δ' ὅμως οὐκ αἰσθήσει μόνον καὶ τοῖς σωματικοῖς ζῶμεν, ἀλλὰ καὶ διανοίᾳ καὶ τῷ λογίζε-σθαι, εἰ μὴ παντάπασι δυστυχής ἐστι βίος καὶ βοσκηματώδης, καὶ μηδὲν ἧττον – ὅτι μὴ καὶ πλεῖον ἔστιν ἴσως ἐνίοις – ἐντεῦθεν κατὰ τὰ λογικὰ πράγματα τῆς ζωῆς ἡμῶν τὸ μέρος ἔξεστιν οἶμαι λοιπὸν ἐντεῦθεν συνδιατίθεσθαι τοῖς λογισμοῖς εἰς τὸ βιοῦν ἐν ῥᾳστώνῃ καὶ καθ' ἡδονὴν ὅπως ποτ' ἄρ' ἐχόντων τῶν κατὰ τὸν βίον ἡμῖν, εἴτ' ἐν εὐπλοίᾳ τῇ φαινομένῃ καὶ τύχης δή τι-νος χάρισιν, εἴτε καὶ μή· ('Yet, since we are living not only by sense-perception and the things of the body, but also by thought and reasoning if our lives are not altogether wretched and brutish; and since therefore the part of our lives that has to do with rational things is no lesser (and for some people perhaps even greater), it is possible, I think, because of this to compose oneself by means of reasoning to live in ease and pleasure no matter what one's circumstances in life may be, whether or not we are sailing with a wind that is apparently fair, and are favoured by some Fortune' (trans. Hult (2016) 163).

2. Wondrous Knowledge and the Emotional Responses 91

But what I especially wanted [to say was] that it is very pleasant, and immediately instils and brings great comfort to the heart whenever one lets the eye roam in free contemplation over the whole beauty of perceptible things ... revelling delightedly in all the feast and wonders of generable nature ...[42]

This overall perceptual-cognitive situation, however, is assessed in terms of emotional response; namely, not only it is something extremely pleasant to do, but it also affects the soul's disposition in a specific way, bringing relaxation and enjoyment:

and delighting, with ineffable joy and a mood innocent of and untroubled by voluptuousness, the emotional and irrational part of the soul, which we must necessarily use, and which we should not, and cannot eradicate from our nature, but must use [only] for what is appropriate, things that do not entail any penalty or reprisal.[43]

2.2.2. Theodore Metochites, Sem. 43, That It Is Very Pleasant to Behold the Sky and the Heavenly Bodies

In the following essay (*Sem.* 43) Metochites moves to one case of beholding a part of creation, namely the contemplation of the heavenly bodies. This brief text evokes two Platonic dialogues dealing with astronomy, namely the *Timaeus* and the *Epinomis*, the latter being traditionally attributed to Plato in Byzantium. Thus, the theoretical background it builds on refers, first, to another narrative concerning the origins of philosophy (*Ti.* 47a–c). According to the latter, philosophy is occasioned and motivated by the vision of the sun, moon, and stars. Second, the *Epinomis* links *theōria* and wonder with astronomy, instead of philosophy, emphasizing the former's superiority due to its mathematical foundation.[44] This view is echoed in Metochites' *Brief Introduction to Astronomy* 1.5, where, after establishing the importance and pre-eminence of astronomy by referring to the *Epinomis*, Metochites concludes that 'the heavens with the diverse and most beautiful arrangements of the stars and the wonderful passages and movements are indeed among the most significant sights for the intellect'.[45] Continuing the discursive setting of *Sem.* 42, Metochites again renders the experience of

---

[42] Trans. Hult (2016); Theodore Metochites, *Sem.* 42.2.1, 3; ed. Hult (2016) 96, lines 23–6; 98, line 1: μάλιστα δ᾽ ὅπερ ἠβουλόμην, ὡς ἡδὺ πάνυ τοι, καὶ μεγάλην ἐνίησι καὶ φέρει τῇ καρδίᾳ ῥαστώνην αὐτίκα αὐτόθεν, ὁπότε τις τὸν ὀφθαλμὸν ἀπόλυτον ἐπόπτην ἀφίησιν ἐπὶ πάσης τῆς τῶν αἰσθητῶν καλλονῆς καὶ πάντα τῇ ὄψει κατατρέχει τὰ τῆς κτίσεως θεάματα ... ἀλλ᾽ ἅπασαν τὴν τῆς γενητῆς φύσεως ἑορτὴν καὶ θαυματοποιίαν κάλλιστ᾽ ἐμπανηγυρίζων ...

[43] Trans. Hult (2016); Theodore Metochites, *Sem.* 42.2.4; ed. Hult (2016) 98, lines 5–8: καὶ τέρπων ἀμυθήτῳ γλυκυθυμίᾳ καὶ τρυφῆς ἀμέμπτῳ καὶ ἀκύμονι διαθέσει τὸ παθητικὸν τῆς ψυχῆς καὶ ἄλογον, ᾧ πᾶσα ἀνάγκη χρῆσθαι, καὶ οὐκ ἐκκοπτέον ἡμῖν οὐδ᾽ οἷόν τε τῆς φύσεως, χρηστέον δὲ ἐν προσήκουσι καὶ οἷς μὴ ζημία τις, μὴ νέμεσις ἕπεται.

[44] For further analysis, see Nightingale (2004) 180–6.

[45] Trans. Paschos and Simelidis (2017); Theodore Metochites, *Introduction to Astronomy* 1.5, 42, lines 34–7: τὸν γάρ τοι οὐρανόν, καὶ τὰς ἐν αὐτῷ ποικίλας τὲ καὶ καλλίστας διακοσμήσεις, καὶ θαυμασίας τῶν ἐν αὐτῷ ἄστρων ἁπάσας διεξόδους τὲ καὶ κινήσεις, εἶναι θέαμα τῷ

92   *Divna Manolova*

observing the heavens through an affective and an aesthetic vocabulary, emphasizing, on the one hand, the beautiful and radiant subject matter, and, on the
other, the pleasure, wonder, and joy it brings to the observer:

But heaven itself and the beautiful sights and spectacles that sparkle in it with all kinds
of radiance – who can express the great pleasure it gives to those who look at it, and how,
when the sky is clear, each sight everywhere brings not only wonder but also joy to the
roaming eyes, not only inspiration but also a mood that gladdens and sweetens the heart?[46]

The heavenly bodies and their movements are a beautiful sight that brings
pleasure when looked upon.[47] The observation and the beauty of its object
incite wonder which brings enjoyment and inspiration, which are, in turn, accompanied by a certain disposition of the heart, namely gladness and sweetness.
Here Metochites evokes a powerful sensory and affective experience and a situation which involves primarily the eyes and the heart. The intellect, however,
also plays a role in this experience of *thauma* and *theiasmos*:

For the heavenly phenomena do not partake of such dignity and wonder without partaking
of beauty; nor, on the other hand, does the sight of them exalt the eyes and especially the
soul within, and charm and soften it to ineffable pleasure without immediately amazing
the intellect, and by necessity prevailing upon those who gaze at them, because of the awe
[that they inspire], to adopt the humble frame of mind that seems to be appropriate to
exalted and awesome things.[48]

In addition to the eyes and the soul, which experience *thambos* and pleasure, it is
the intellect that is amazed and in a state of *ekplēxis* or astonishment. Metochites
continues by saying that the observation of the heavenly phenomena incites in
the viewer the desire to examine them (καὶ τὰ μὲν ἄλλ᾽ ἐῶ καὶ ὅσην αὐτόθεν
πράττεται τῶν ὁρώντων ξυναίσθησιν καὶ λογισμῶν κίνησιν κατὰ πόθον τῆς αὐτῶν ζητήσεως), thus indicating how wonder leads to the desire for knowledge, a
statement in keeping with the Platonic and Aristotelian frameworks I discussed
at the beginning of this chapter.

τῶν ἀξιολόγων ὄντως πραγμάτων θεωρῷ νῷ. I provide a detailed discussion of this treatise in
a forthcoming monograph.

[46] Trans. Hult (2016); Theodore Metochites, *Sem.* 43.1.1; ed. Hult (2016) 98, lines 19–23: Οὐ-
ρανὸς δ᾽ αὐτὸς καὶ τὰ κατ᾽ αὐτὸν ἀστράπτοντα αἴγλῃ πάσῃ κάλλη καὶ θεάματα, τίς ἐρεῖ ὅσην
ἐμπαρέχεται τοῖς ἐφορωμένοις τὴν ἡδονὴν καὶ ὅσην ἄρ᾽ ἐν αἰθρίας ὥρᾳ τοῖς περιχορεύουσιν
ὀφθαλμοῖς αὐτὰ πάνθ᾽ ἕκαστα πάντοθεν σὺν τῷ θαύματι τὴν τέρψιν καὶ μετὰ τοῦ θειασμοῦ
τὴν ἱλαρύνουσαν καὶ καταγλυκαίνουσαν τῇ καρδίᾳ διάθεσιν;

[47] Cf. the experience associated with the observation of the heavens recorded in the so-called
'Ptolemy' epigram (*Anth. Pal.* 9.577). I thank Ioannis Papadogiannakis for this suggestion.

[48] Trans. Hult (2016); Theodore Metochites, *Sem.* 43.1.2–3; ed. Hult (2016) 98, line 23–100,
line 2: οὐ γὰρ ἀξιώματος μὲν καὶ θάμβους μέτεστι καὶ πάνυ τοι πλεῖστον τοῖς φαινομένοις,
ὥρας δ᾽ οὔ, οὐδ᾽ ἀγάλλει μὲν τοὺς ὀφθαλμοὺς ὁρώμενα καὶ τὴν ψυχὴν αὐτὴν μάλιστ᾽ ἔσω καὶ
θέλγει καὶ διυγραίνει ταύτην εἰς ἡδονὴν οἵαν ἄρρητον, οὐκ ἐκπλήττει δέ γε τὸν νοῦν αὐτόθεν
καὶ σωφρόνως ἔχειν κατὰ πᾶσαν ἀνάγκην πείθει τοῖς ἐποπτεύουσιν ὑπὸ τοῦ θαύματος, ὡς ἄρ᾽
ἔοικεν ἐπὶ τῶν μεγίστων καὶ ὑπερφυῶν δή τινων ἐμπρέπειν.

2. Wondrous Knowledge and the Emotional Responses 93

Further, Metochites points out that it is peculiar to the nature of humankind to look up, and to do so is to use the faculty of perception in the most pleasurable way. Discussing perception or, in other words, the impressions that creation leaves on our senses, prepares the ground for Metochites to continue by discussing *pathē*, or how we experience the sensory input we receive. Thus, in *Sem.* 43, Metochites offers his own definition of what the *pathē*, or the emotions, are:

For on the whole the emotions and experiences of the senses are what one feels; and experience through the senses is by nature [better] suited to transmit [such things] to the heart than reports and outlines of arguments, which are not naturally suited for description, and show the mind things that belong to material perception and are cognisable together with matter, and simply cannot be detached from it.[49]

The same line of reasoning is further developed in *Sem.* 60, *That It Is Doubtful Whether People Experience Any Serenity at All in Their Thoughts*, in which Metochites further emphasizes our inability to live without *pathē* due to our bodily existence. Nevertheless, he allows for the possibility of redirecting the emotional aspects of the soul towards what's best, but deems it truly worthy of wonder.[50]

Conclusions

The history of philosophical wonder in the Byzantine tradition remains to be written. Approaching the study of wonder as an affective and cognitive experience is yet another unexplored chapter that my enquiry has barely tackled. The brief survey of the philosophical framework Greek Medieval culture inherited from its ancient and Hellenistic predecessors demonstrates the importance of wonder in staking a claim on behalf of one of the core disciplines the pre-Modern mind employed to make sense of the world and the experience of living in it. Philosophy, mechanics, mathematics, and astronomy were promoted at various times to occupy the position of a 'science' *par excellence*, the one true and infallible method of attaining knowledge. Wonder was a part of the equation either as the beginning or the culmination of the cognitive process of enquiry, or alternatively the absence of wonder and perplexity was taken to ensure the

---

[49] Trans. Hult (2016); Theodore Metochites, *Sem.* 43.2.7; ed. Hult (2016) 102, lines 8–12: ὅτι γε δὴ καὶ καθόλου τὰ τῶν αἰσθήσεων πάθη καὶ πεῖραι πεφύκασι παραδιδόναι ταῖς καρδίαις ἢ λόγων ἀνιστορήσεις καὶ τύποι, μὴ χαρακτηρίζειν πεφυκότες καὶ προδεικνύειν εὖ μάλα τῷ νῷ ἃ τῆς ὑλικῆς ἐστιν ἐπαφῆς καὶ μετὰ τῆς ὕλης γνώριμα καὶ ταύτης καθάπαξ οὐκ ἔχει τέμνεσθαι.

[50] Theodore Metochites, *Sem.* 60.6.2; ed. Hult (2016) 218, lines 19–24: οὐ γὰρ κρίνομεν καὶ νοοῦμεν μόνον, ἀλλὰ καὶ πάσχομεν τῇ ψυχῇ καὶ συνδιατιθέμεθα τοῖς τοῦ σώματος. καὶ μακάριον καὶ ὄντως θαυμάζειν ἄξιον, εἴ τις ἐν ὀλίγοις ἥττηται κομιδῇ καὶ τρέπειν τὰ παθητικὰ τῆς ψυχῆς οἷός τέ ἐστιν ἔνθα βέλτιστ' ἔχει· μὴ γὰρ ἔτ' ἐνθάδε καθάπαξ ἀπαθῶς ἄγεσθαι, μήποτ' οὐχ' οἷόν τέ ἐστιν, ἀλλ' ἔξω τῆς φύσεως.

certainty of the results. The early Palaiologan thinkers Theodore Metochites and Nikephoros Gregoras also engaged with the experience of wonder. They did so invariably in connection with the role of perception in the acquisition of knowledge of the natural world, thus implicitly interpreting the act of marvelling – either at the beauty of the heavens or at the chaotic nature of the world below – as *pathos*, that is, an embodied intellectual experience triggered by the senses and facilitated by *phantasia*.

3

Methodological Issues and Issues of Content, as Exemplified by ὀξυχολία in the *Shepherd of Hermas**

Petra von Gemünden

Introduction

It is in Hermas, *Mandata* 5, that, for the first time in the biblical tradition and in the Classical literature that has come down to us, ὀξυχολία (angry temper, ill temper) becomes a leading concept that is discussed in a section of its own. This fact prompts me to take a closer look at a text to which scholars pay very little attention, and at the section on ὀξυχολία and the concept(s) linked to this emotion. I shall attempt to show here that emotions must be seen in the context of a comprehensive interpretation of the world and of life. Hermas expects an eschatological change to the whole world and demands repentance (μετάνοια) as an individual change to personal life.

The *Shepherd of Hermas* is a text with a strongly Jewish-Christian character,[1] written in the first half of the second century.[2] It is well attested in the East in particular,[3] and it enjoyed great popularity in Christian circles in both East and

---

* A previous version of this article has been published in Japanese in *Seisho Gaku Ronshu* 50 (2019) 73–111. For the English translation I wish to express my gratitude to Dr Brian McNeil and Julia Albrecht; also to the peer reviewers for improvements and further suggestions, as well as to Prof. Dr G. Theißen. To avoid confusion, *Shepherd of Hermas* in italics refers to the book, whereas Shepherd of Hermas in roman refers to the person.

[1] The only quotation in the *Shepherd of Hermas* (in Herm. Vis. 2.3.4) is a quotation from Eldad and Modad (cf. Num. 11:26), a (lost) Jewish apocalypse; the origin of the Doctrine of the Two Spirits is Jewish (Leutzsch (1998) 134); the name 'Christ' does not appear in the *Shepherd of Hermas*. It is interesting that the antithesis of ὀξυχολία in Herm. *Mand.* 5 – the μακροθυμία – is not a Greek, but a Jewish virtue (Spanneut (1976) 254).

[2] Osiek (2000) 1788. Pratscher (2011) dates the *Shepherd of Hermas* back to approx. AD 100–25; see also Gokey (1961) 121, who dates the *Shepherd of Hermas* to about AD 140. Generally, the origin of the *Shepherd of Hermas* is located in central Italy, and more precisely in Rome (cf. Herm. *Vis.* 1.1.1 and the Muratorian Canon, cf. Vielhauer (1975) 523; Brox (1991) 22–3; Osiek (1999) 18; Markschies (2006); Hellholm (2009) 249). By contrast, Hahnemann (1992) 34–72 proposes an eastern origin. Peterson (1959) 274–5, 282, argues for a provenance in an Palestinian ascetic milieu because of the strong Jewish influence which can be seen in the Commandments and Parables.

[3] Peterson (1959) 282 (reception by the Christian ascetics in Egypt and Mesopotamia?); Hellholm (2009) 249.

West.[4] It is clear that it was regarded as quasi-canonical for a long time. This is indicated by quotations from the *Shepherd of Hermas* and allusions to it in Irenaeus of Lyon[5] and Clement of Alexandria,[6] as well as by its mention in the Muratorian Canon.[7] The text was in fact read publicly in the worship of some communities.[8] At the end of the Codex Sinaiticus – a fourth-century manuscript of the entire Bible[9] – we find the *Shepherd of Hermas* included.[10]

Its author belonged to the 'common people' with 'limited literary education'.[11] He presents a '"lay theology"', which presumably corresponds more to the thinking of a wide circle of people in the Roman community than to the theology of educated Christians'.[12] The *Shepherd* is 'the first relatively coherent presentation of moral teaching in early Christian literature',[13] and it brings 'moral ... instruction and psychological ... theory' into connection with each other.[14] Within the author's moral teaching, emotions such as ὀξυχολία are very significant. This is what makes the text particularly interesting for us.[15]

Four methodological approaches will be employed and presented:[16] (1) linguistic semantics concerning the word ὀξυχολία, (2) image semantics concerning biomorphic and technomorphic images in relation to ὀξυχολία, (3) discourse analysis for the mythologizing framework of understanding of ὀξυχολία, (4) context analysis concerning the whole book and (5) form criticism, which shows how the apocalyptic genre is changed: the revelation of eschatological realities becomes a revelation of internal processes.

---

[4] Moreschini and Norelli (2000) 204.

[5] Irenaeus, *Haer.* 4.20.2 and *passim*.

[6] Cf. e.g. Clement of Alexandria, *Strom.* 6.131.2–4.

[7] Lines 73–7.

[8] Markschies (2006); Osiek (1999) 5 with n. 50. This is clear, although the Muratorian Canon recommends 'only' the private reading of the *Shepherd of Hermas* (line 77), not the public reading in the liturgy (lines 78–80).

[9] א (01), London, British Library, Add. 43725. One page of the *Shepherd of Hermas* was discovered in Saint Catherine's Monastery in 1975.

[10] Aland and Aland (1989) 117.

[11] Osiek (1999) 21.

[12] Markschies (2006).

[13] Löhr (2016) 292.

[14] Löhr (2016) 293.

[15] Besides this, the text is also significant for us as only a few Christian texts that can be dated to the first half of the second century have survived.

[16] For these approaches see von Gemünden (2009) 17–22, 24–6, 29–31.

3. Methodological Issues and Issues of Content 97

3.1. Linguistic semantics (Wortsemantik)

In Jewish-Christian literature, the antithetical concept to μακροθυμία (patience, endurance)[17] is usually ὀργή or θυμός.[18] It is striking that μακροθυμία is contrasted in the *Shepherd of Hermas* with ὀξυχολία (angry temper,[19] ill temper,[20] bad temper[21], irascibility[22]). As Bartelink points out,[23] ὀξυχολία is attested for the first time in Classical literature in the *Shepherd of Hermas*.[24] It is a composite noun formed from ὀξύς (quick, sharp, acute) and χολή (gall, bile)[25] or χόλος (generally in the sense of bitter anger, wrath).[26] The latter terms occur very frequently in Classical literature in connection with anger or to mean 'anger'; χόλος mostly has the meaning 'bitter anger, wrath'.[27] The intensifying combination with ὀξύς to form ὀξυχολία is not attested earlier in the Classical texts that have survived, but it is possible that this apparent novelty is due to the limitation of the sources to which we have access. As the adjective ὀξύχολος is already attested earlier,[28] it may not be new at all, in which case Hermas would be using an already existing term.[29] What we can definitely hold on to is that ὀξυχολία occurs in the *Shepherd of Hermas* for the first time, and in particular that it is

---

[17] Lake (1970) 87 n. 1 remarks: 'μακροθυμία is a little more than "long suffering" and almost equals courage'. 'Courage' is the translation that Osiek (1999) 118 prefers. In Herm. *Vis.* 1.2.3 (= 2.3), Hermas is called 'the forbearing, long-suffering (μακρόθυμος) ...'.

[18] See also the antithesis ἀνὴρ θυμώδης – [ἀνὴρ] μακρόθυμος in Prov. 15:18; T. Dan 6:8 contrasts wrath (θυμός) and falsehood with truth and μακροθυμία.

[19] For this translation see Holmes (2007) 517–23, 535.

[20] For this translation see Snyder (1968) 74–5; Lake (1970) 87–99, 111–15. (Lake remarks on p. 87 n. 1: 'literally "quickness to wrath", but this phrase does not convey in English the bad sense which Hermas obviously implies').

[21] For this translation see Osiek (1999) 118.

[22] For this translation see Ehrman (2003) 255–65.

[23] Bartelink (1952) 47–8.

[24] Herm. *Mand.* 10.3 (= 41.3) also has the verb ὀξυχολεῖν, which is cognate with ὀξυχολία. ὀξύχολος ('quick to anger') is found in Herm. *Mand.* 5.2 (= 34.7); also Solon 13.25–6 West (sixth century BC): οὐδ᾽ ἐφ᾽ ἑκάστῳ ὥσπερ θνητὸς ἀνὴρ γίγνεται ὀξύχολος – 'nor is he quick to anger in each case as a mortal man would be'; Soph. *Ant.* 955 ('the quickly angered (ὀξύχολος) son of Dryas', transl. Lloyd-Jones (1994) 91); [τὸ] ὀξύχολον, Luc. *Fug.* 19 (of those who imitate the true philosophers). In Prov. 14:17; 26:20 [AS²], however, we find the concept ὀξύθυμος; in Ar. *Vesp.* 501, ὀξυθυμέω.

[25] LSJ, *s. v.*

[26] LSJ, *s. v.*; for a more detailed discussion see below.

[27] LSJ, *s. v.*; Passow (2008) 2480: 'Zorn, Hass, Groll, Grimm'.

[28] See above.

[29] *If* the noun ὀξυχολία is in fact a neologism, the evidence can be interpreted in various ways: (a) the new noun points to something that was already known; (b) it points to a reality that existed earlier, but is now better known and/or more precisely evaluated; (c) on the other hand, the new noun could also change the perception and interpretation of the reality, and thereby also the assessment of this reality and people's conduct.

98 *Petra von Gemünden*

employed there very frequently: it figures there as a leading key concept in a paraenetic text.[30]

But why did Hermas use ὀξυχολία so frequently? Why is it a key concept for him? This seems to be closely connected to Hermas' awareness of Christians' failures.[31] They contradicted the Early Christian conviction that Christians should be free of sin: in Judaism, it is always possible to 'repent',[32] but Christians at that time held that there was only one single 'repentance', at conversion and baptism, where the evil spirits 'resident in the nonbaptized are driven away'.[33] Hermas formulates this view as follows, when he says to the Shepherd: 'I have heard, sir, from some teachers that there is no second repentance beyond the one given when we went down into the water and received remission of our former sins.' The Shepherd replies: 'You have heard correctly, for that is so. For he who has received remission of sin ought never to sin again, but to live in purity.'[34] The logical consequence of the presupposition that the human being does not sin after baptism is the impossibility of further repentance after baptism.[35] This ethical rigorism strongly intensified the requirements of self-control and self-transparency in Christian circles, with the result – as Hermas is forced to observe when he looks at his own self – that Christians fail to live up to these intensified demands. The fact that Christians continue to sin, despite their baptism, causes Hermas pain. A letter sent from heaven tells him about a *unique, temporally limited* possibility of a second repentance for Christians and enjoins him to make this known to the community (*Vis.* 2.2.3–6).[36] This can lead to a keener sensitivity to sins, and thus also to psychological perceptions and reflections. These find expression in the commands of the *Shepherd of Hermas* with regard to ὀξυχολία (angry temper), φόβος (fear), διψυχία (doubt), and λύπη (sadness).[37]

---

[30] Cf. Herm. *Mand.* 6.1 (= 33.2); 5.1 (= 3.3) (thrice); 6.1 (= 33.6) (twice); 5.1 (= 33.7); 5.2 (= 34.1); 5.2 (= 34.4); 5.2 (= 34.8) (twice); 6.2 (= 36.5); 10.1 (= 40.1–2); 10.2 (= 41.3); 10.2 (= 41.4) (twice), see also Herm. *Sim.* 9.15 (= 92.3). In contrast to this we find for example θυμός and ὀργή used only once for a human being in the *Sheperd of Hermas*: Herm. *Mand.* 5.2 (= 34.4); ὀργή for the Lord: Herm. *Vis.* 3.6 (= 14.1); 4.2 (= 23.6); for the pastor: Herm. *Mand.* 12.4 (= 47.1); ὀργίζω refers always to God (Herm. *Vis.* 1.1 (= 1.6); 1.3 (= 3.1) (twice)).

[31] Löhr (2016) 292–3.

[32] See especially the prophets' exhortations to repentance, Deuteronomistic texts, and the Books of Chronicles.

[33] Osiek (1999) 125, and Clement of Alexandria, *Exc.* 77.1 (Sagnard (1970): ἀποτασσομένων ἡμῶν ταῖς Ἀρχαῖς: '[In baptism] we renounce the evil powers' (trans. Osiek (1999) 125 n. 21)). See also Kelly (1985) 40–4, 48, 74–5.

[34] Both quotations are from Herm. *Mand.* 4.3.1–2 (= 31–2). Translations of the *Shepherd* – unless otherwise indicated – are by Lake (1970).

[35] See Heb. 6:4–8; 10:26–31; 12:16–17; 1 John 3:6.

[36] Accordingly, his book is completely oriented to a penitential paraenesis (Vielhauer (1975) 520). Gokey (1961) 121 calls it a 'sermon on penance'.

[37] See above. The unique possibility of a second penance is to be understood as a 'compromise between the rigorism that flowed from the imminent expectation [of the end of time] and the reality of the church' (Vielhauer (1975) 520, trans. B. McNeil).

3. *Methodological Issues and Issues of Content* 99

The *Shepherd* returns repeatedly to the theme of self-control[38] and to that which undermines self-control, namely, sexual and aggressive impulses.[39]

3.2. Image semantics (Bildsemantik)

3.2.1. Biomorphic images and associations

As we have seen, the word ὀξυχολία is a composite formed from ὀξύς (quick, sharp, acute) and χολή or χόλος.

3.2.1.1.

Χολή can mean, in the biblical tradition:[40] (a) the gall bladder or the liver, as in the book of Tobit[41] and in the Testaments of Reuben[42] and Naphtali;[43] (b) an intensely bitter (organic) substance with an unpleasant taste,[44] for example, gall/bile as the fluid secreted by the liver,[45] a poison,[46] or wormwood.[47] The meaning

---

[38] See the beginning and the end of the section on ὀξυχολία (Herm. *Mand.* 5): πάντων τῶν πονηρῶν ἔργων **κατακυριεύσεις** (Herm. *Mand.* 5.1.1 (= 33.1)). ἐὰν γὰρ ταύτης τῆς ἐντολῆς **κυριεύσῃς** ... ἰσχυροῦ ἐν αὐταῖς (*sc.* ἐντολαῖς) καὶ ἐνδυναμοῦ (Herm. *Mand.* 5.2.8 (= 34.8); emphasis in the Greek text added).

[39] Cf. the sexual impulses of Hermas when he sees his former owner Rhoda rising out of the Tiber after her bath. It is only in prayer (in a vision) that he becomes aware of his sin (see Herm. *Vis.* 1.1–2 (= 1.1–2)); see below and also von Gemünden (2007) 262–7. Cf. also those Christians who lead superficial lives in tranquillity – ὀξυχολία can sneak into their 'emptiness' without at first being noticed (Herm. *Mand.* 5.2.2 (= 34.2)). It is – as we will see below – interesting to note that these sexual and aggressive impulses are unconscious at the outset, and are not perceived: Hermas writes (as to the literary form) an apocalyse, but contrary to what the form leads us to expect, he does not present a revelation of future and unknown eschatological events, but new insights on emotions by pointing also to their inconscient parts.

[40] Cf. Bauer (1988) 1761–2.

[41] Tob. 6:6–8 (... τὸ ἧπαρ καὶ ἡ καρδία καὶ ἡ χολὴ τοῦ ἰχθύος) and 11:4–11.

[42] In T. Rub. 3:4 the spirit of strife has its seat in the liver and gall bladder (ἐν τῷ ἥπατι καὶ τῇ χολῇ).

[43] In T. Naph. 2:8b (into which a medical onomasticon is incorporated), we read: 'a *liver* for wrath' (ἧπαρ πρὸς θυμόν), a *'gall bladder* for bitterness (χολὴν πρὸς πικρία)'.

[44] So Bauer (1988) 1761.

[45] See Job 16:14 (16:13[LXX]): 'They surrounded me with spears, / hurling them into my kidneys, without sparing; / they poured out my gall [χολή ← מְרֵרָה] on the ground.' Translations of the LXX here and in the following are by Pietersma and Wright (2007). χολή is envisaged as a liquid in Jer 8:14[LXX] and 9:14[LXX]: ὕδωρ χολῆς.

[46] Hebrew (a) רֹאשׁ (see Gesenius (1915) 738; cf. II ראשׁ: 'eine Giftpflanze Deut 29:17, die schnell sproßt und schön blüht Hos 10:4, bitter ist Ps 69:22; Thr 3:5'. 'Zuweilen für: Gift ... Giftwasser Jer 8:14; 9:14; 23:15, Schlangengift ... Hi 20:16, das Recht in Gift verwandeln Am 6:12)'. Ps. 68(69):22(21)[LXX]: 'And they gave gall as my food (ἔδωκαν εἰς τὸ βρῶμά μου χολὴν)' (it is possible that Matt. 27:34 alludes to Ps. 68:22; see Bauer (1988) 1861). (b) מְרֵרָה, cf. Gesenius (1915) 464: 'Gift ..., v. Schlangengift', Job 20:14–15 מְרֹרָה derived from מרר which means 'to be or become bitter' (Gesenius (1915) 463–4). The LXX version reads in Job 20:14 only: '... the venom (χολή) of an asp'. In relation to Deut. 32:32–3 ('their grape is the grape of gall (σταφυλὴ χολῆς

(b) 'bitter organic substance' is the more obvious, since the bile that is secreted by the liver is extremely bitter.[48] It is interesting to note that in T. Naph. 2:8 God created 'the liver for anger (ἥπαρ πρὸς θυμόν), the gall bladder for bitterness (χολὴν πρὸς πικρίαν)'.[49] Although it is the liver, not the gall bladder, that is connected with anger here,[50] the liver secretes first the gall/bile, and secondly the bitterness (πικρία), which is directly connected with the gall bladder. In Herm. *Mand.* 5.2.8 (= 34.8) and 6.2.5 (= 36.5), this is linked to ὀξυχολία,[51] and it occurs in the chain of aggressive emotions in context with ὀξυχολία.[52]

In the pagan tradition, χολή means 'gall', but also 'bitter hate, wrath'.[53]

← רֹאשׁ) and its bunches of grapes are those of bitterness (βότρυς πικρίας ← מְרֹרָה)' (Deut. 32:32–3 in Philo, *Somn.* 2.191)), Philo, *Somn.* 2.191 speaks of the negative character of the vine and the intoxicating drink of irrationality, and observes that the intoxicating drink of irrationality (ἀφροσύνη) produces bitterness (τὸ πικρόν), wickedness, rage (τὸ ἀκρόχολον), wrath (τὸ περίθυμον), etc.; see also Philo, *Ebr.* 222 (מְרֹרָה also means 'gall'; see Job 20:25, Gesenius (1915) 424).

[47] Hebrew לַעֲנָה, cf. Bauer (1988) 1761: 'Wermut'; see Prov. 5:3–4, where we find – as in Hermas(!) – the antithesis between honey and wormwood. It figures in Prov. 5:3–4 in the warning against the woman who is not one's wife: 'Pay no attention to a worthless woman, / for honey drips from the lips … Later, however, you will find it more bitter than gall (χολή ←לַעֲנָה) / and sharper than a two-edged dagger.' Lam. 3 also shows the close connection between 'poison' and 'wormwood'. In the immediate context, poison (רֹאשׁ) und 'wormwood' (לַעֲנָה) are both translated by χολή: Lam. 3:19–20: 'bitterness (πικρία) and gall (χολή ← רֹאשׁ) my soul will remember …'; Lam. 3:15: 'he has fed me with bitterness (πικρία); he has made me drunk with gall (χολή ← לַעֲנָה).' Lang (2014) is not sure whether לַעֲנָה really means 'wormwood', or whether it rather stands, 'übertragen', for bitterness.

[48] Thus, Job 20:14[MT] says about the digestion and the secretion of the liver: 'His bread in his intestines (*me'îm*) is transformed, / becomes the gall of vipers [*merorah*] in his interior (*qæræb*)' (cf. trans. from Wolff (2010) 111; I have added *merorah* = מְרֹרָה).

[49] Trans. Kee (1983). In T. Rub. 3:4, the spirit of strife has its seat in the liver and the gall bladder (ἐν τῷ ἥπατι καὶ τῇ χολῇ). What Collins (1971) 27 says with regard to the Hebrew poets may perhaps also apply to the T. 12 Patr.: 'It is not obvious that the Hebrew poets had clear and precise ideas on the *functional* anatomy of the human abdomen.' (According to *Spec. Leg.* 1.218, however, Philo appears to have had more precise ideas). On the Babylonian idea of the liver as the seat of wrath, see Dhorme (1923) 130; Eppel (1930) 117–18; for the Greek view, see also Menge (1984) 320.

[50] In antiquity, the human liver was regarded as the 'siège des passions violentes, surtout de la colère et de l'amour'; see Lesêtre (1988) 2297. According to Lam. 2:11[MT] the liver has a fluid apperance: 'my liver is poured out on the ground / because of the fall of the daughter of my people' (see the translation by Schroer and Staubli (1998) 77). The LXX, however, reads not 'my liver is poured out on the ground', but 'my honour (δόξα) was poured out on the ground'.

[51] Herm. *Mand.* 5.2.8 (= 34.8): 'stand against irascibility (ὀξυχολία) and bitterness (πικρία)' (trans. Ehrman (2003) 261); Herm. *Mand.* 6.2.5 (= 36.5): 'When any irascibility (ὀξυχολία) or bitterness (πικρία) should fall on you, realize that he [*sc.* the angel of wickedness] is in you' (trans. Ehrman (2003)). The angel of wickedness is characterized as 'irascible, bitter, and senseless' (ὀξύχολος …, πικρὸς καὶ ἄφρων) in Herm. *Mand.* 6.2.4 (= 36.4), trans. Ehrman (2003).

[52] Herm. *Mand.* 5.2.4 (= 34.4); see below.

[53] The adjective can mean 'full of gall, bilious (Hp., Pl., Arist.)', but also 'wrathful (Luc.)'; see Beekes (2009) 1642.

3. Methodological Issues and Issues of Content

3.2.1.2

Χόλος[54] is in the Septuagint always a translation of קֶצֶף (qṣp, wrath).[55] קֶצֶף is mostly translated in the Septuagint by ὀργή.[56] This can be taken as a clear indication that the Alexandrian translators saw χόλος as an expression for 'anger'.[57] Also in the pagan tradition, χόλος means 'anger, hatred, rancour, fury'.[58] Exceptionally there might also be the additional meaning 'gall, bile',[59] used in a metaphorical sense to designate 'anger': in Hom. *Il.* 16.203 χόλος means 'gall', if χόλῳ is understood as *dativus instrumentalis*:[60] 'surely it was on gall (χόλος) that your mother reared you [*sc.* hard son of Peleus]'.[61] But an understanding of it as *dativus finalis* is also possible – in that case the meaning 'anger' for χόλος fits well.[62]

In any case, χολή and χόλος have the same etymological root χολ-. Anger and bitterness are associatively and probably etymologically connected with an organ or an organic liquid – the gall bladder (bile) or the secretion of the liver – the gall (bile).

We can therefore conclude that although the earliest attestation of the concept of ὀξυχολία is in Hermas, this concept is linked at least associatively to one particular concept of the body,[63] which can connect the gall bladder (or the liver,

---

[54] Rehkopf (1989) 311 proposes the translation 'Galle'.

[55] Thus in Prov. 16:28 (S); Eccles. 5:16; 2 Macc. 3:28 (A); 3 Macc. 5:1.20 (cf. Hatch and Redpath (2005) 1472). We read in Prov. 16:28[LXX] (Sinaiticus †), without any correspondence in the Masoretic Text (= MT), of 'a crooked man': he spreads evil (MT: he kindles strife) and 'kindles a torch of wrath (of deceit) for the evil ones' – καὶ λαμπτῆρα χόλου (AB δόλου) πυρσεύσει κακοῖς (Sinaiticus †: χόλου). Χόλος can designate, properly speaking, the gall bladder, but then above all wrath. Since the text goes on to speak of the separation of friends by a perverted man (ἀνὴρ σκολιός), Prov. 16:28[LXX] probably has in mind the (more common) meaning, namely 'wrath'.

[56] Sauer (2004) 666.

[57] Muraoka (2009) 734 understands χόλος in the LXX in the sense of 'bitter anger'. Χόλος occurs alongside anger in 3 Macc. 5:1 (ὀργή), in Eccles. 5:16(17) (θυμός) and in Wis. 18:21–2 (θυμός).

[58] See Passow (2008) 2480: 'Gewöhnlich übertragen Zorn, Hass, Groll, Grimm'.

[59] So for example Passow (2008) 2480 (with reference to Hom. *Il.* 16.203, cf. *Il.* 2.241); Pape (1954) 1363; Bailly (1950) 2144; LSJ *s. v.*, 1997; Montanari (2015) 2366; O'Sullivan (2010) 1228.

[60] So Brügger (2016) 97: '"hat dich mit Galle aufgezogen" (statt mit Muttermilch)'. Brügger (2016) 97–8 also refers to the ancient custom that nursing mothers wean their babies by coating their nipples with bitter substances (amongst others bile).

[61] Trans. Murray (1999 [1924]).

[62] '... hat dich für den Zorn aufgezogen'; see Brügger (2016) 97, cf. Hom. *Il.* 16.206. For Cairns (2016a) 26, χόλος 'is not primarily seen in terms of physiological processes; its conceptualization is fundamentally metaphorical'. With regard to the formulation δριμὺς χόλος in Hom. *Il.* 18.322, Konstan (2006b) 51 states that 'the adjective "bitter" (*drimus*) suggests the root meaning of *kholos* as "bile"'.

[63] It was the neurologist Sir Henry Head who first defined the 'body schema'. Subsequently it was expanded by Schilder, who added the psychological dimension to the body-image concept; see Schilder (1923), (1950); Tiemersma (1989); Röhricht (2015) 237–47. If we follow the further

which itself secrets gall/bile), on the one hand, and anger (or one of its preceding forms or its consequences), on the other hand.[64]

This applies likewise to what is said about the heart (καρδία) into which the ὀξυχολία makes its surreptitious entry[65] and then provokes, on utterly trivial grounds, a bitterness (πικρία) that stands at the beginning of a chain of aggressive emotions that culminate in fury (μῆνις):[66] 'But ἡ ὀξυχολία is first of all foolish, fickle and senseless. And then from senselessness comes bitterness, from bitterness anger, from anger wrath, and from wrath rage.'[67] In this catena, Hermas sees irrationality (ἀφροσύνη) at the inception of the chain; this is in keeping with Old Testament Jewish and New Testament anthropology, where the heart is not only the locus of feelings, but *above all* also a locus of knowledge and insight.[68] In other words, the development that leads to fury (μῆνις) has its starting point in irrationality.[69]

---

conceptual differentiation of Gallagher (2005), we should speak in our case of a 'body image': cf. Gallagher (2005) 17–30, esp. 30.

[64] Cf. Pape (1954) 1363: 'Galle ... bes. als Ursache des Zornes, Hasses'.

[65] Herm. *Mand.* 5.2.2 (= 34.2).

[66] Εἶτα ἐκ τῆς ἀφροσύνης γίνεται πικρία, ἐκ δὲ τῆς πικρίας θυμός, ἐκ δὲ τοῦ θυμοῦ ὀργή, ἐκ δὲ τῆς ὀργῆς μῆνις (Herm. *Mand.* 5.2.4 (= 34.4)). This catena takes over Stoic ideas: see Leutzsch (1998) 452 n. 123. Wrzol (1923) 404 sees the endeavour 'psychologische Zusammenhänge zwischen den Lastern zu finden', in other words 'Lasterreihen stets das darauffolgende Laster psychologisch aus dem vorhergehenden abzuleiten', as 'typisch für die gesamte Urliteratur über die Hauptlaster'. Wrzol considers Herm. *Mand.* 5.2.4 a source for John Cassian 5.11.7 and Evagrius, *De octo vit. cog.* 6.

[67] Trans. Ehrman (2003) 259.

[68] On the Old Testament, see Schroer and Staubli (1998) 47: 'Das Herz ist ... in Israel nicht primär der Sitz der Gefühle', it is 'vor allem der Sitz der Vernunft und des Verstandes'; Lauha (1983) 50 notes: 'das Lexem לב [ist] ganz überwiegend (in über 95% der Fälle) mit der Schilderung des emotionalen, intellektuellen und religiös-ethischen Lebens des Menschen verbunden' (see pp. 49–50); Stolz (2004) 862–3 (the heart as the seat of knowledge and insight); and below. On the New Testament, see Behm (2000) 614–15. In pagan Greek too, καρδία is the seat both of the emotions (e. g. anger: Hom. *Il.* 9.646) and of the ability to think (e. g. 21.441), as well as of will and of decisions (10.244); see Behm (2000) 611.

[69] Similarly, in Philo, *Somn.* 2.192, irrationality is at the beginning of a catena with concepts of anger. This recalls the evaluation of irrationality (ἀφροσύνη) in antique philosophy (Aristotle, Stoics). In contrast to these philosophers, Hermas understands ἀφροσύνη – in conformity with the Old Testament and Jewish tradition – (Herm. *Sim.* 9.15.3 (= 92.3); cf. 1QS 4:10) as the fundamentally false orientation of the human being (cf. Zeller (1992) 446): for ἀφροσύνη as sin cf. Ps. 37:6[LXX], 68:6; Prov. 5:5.23; etc., see Leutzsch (1998) 491 n. 358.

It is interesting to note that in Hermas, people seem to be completely unaware of the risk they face: they lead a 'tranquil life' in full normality – and it is precisely then that the ὀξυχολία sneaks in (Herm. *Mand.* 5.2.2 (= 34.2)). Hermas describes the slow process of becoming conscious of desire as the 'ascending of the desire in the heart' (Herm. *Vis.* 1.1/8 (= 1/8)). On this, see von Gemünden (2007) 262–7.

3. Methodological Issues and Issues of Content 103

3.2.2. The use of the technomorphic 'vessel' image

The *Shepherd of Hermas* sees the body as a vessel (σκεῦος).[70] The Holy Spirit (πνεῦμα τὸ ἅγιον) dwells in this vessel,[71] but he can be driven out by ὀξυχολία,[72] which then dwells in the human being in place of the Holy Spirit. The 'vessel' was indeed widespread as a metaphor for the human being or the human body in the ancient Near East (among the Babylonians and in the Old Testament) but also in the Hellenistic context,[73] in which Hermas stands and is to be situated.[74] It may be connected to anthropomorphic pottery that could express and subsequently also imprint the concept of the body.[75] The vessel image for the body or the human being – as well as anthropomorphic pottery – is not astonishing, as human beings (as cognitive linguists like to emphasize) 'share a great deal of bodily experience'.[76]

As far as I know, it is in the *Shepherd of Hermas* that the metaphor of the vessel is employed for the first time *argumentatively* in a twofold manner *in connection with anger*, or more precisely with ὀξυχολία. On the basis of the idea that the Holy Spirit dwells in the patient (μακρόθυμος) human being (who is pictured as

---

[70] Hermas compares the human being to a vessel, to pots and jars, in several passages; see Brox (1991) 550; Snyder (1968) 74 n. *ad* 43.5. On the body (or a human being) as a σκεῦος (vessel), in which a spirit dwells or two spirits struggle, see T. Naph. 2:2, 8:6; the Christian magical prayer (which cannot be dated precisely) in Pradel (1907) 9 (= 261), lines 11–12 (on this, see Maurer (1990) 368 n. 61; Pradel (1907)); 4 Ezra 7:88; Mart. Is. 2:1; Luke 11:24–6; 2 Cor. 4:7 (human bodies as ὀστράκινα σκεύη); 1 Thess. 4:4 (σκεῦος here can mean either the wife or the body). 1 Pet. 3:7 calls the wife the 'weaker vessel', which implies that the husband is the stronger vessel; bGit 52a (?). Σκεῦος as vessel of the spirit: Barn. 7:3; 11:9. On the idea of the woman as a vessel (כְּלִי), see also 4Q416, 2 2:21 and on this, Rothstein 2007; see Elgvin (1997); see also Smith (2001), and Schreiber (2014) 216–18, who opts for the meaning of σκεῦος as human body.

[71] κατοικεῖν: see the excursus on the metaphor of 'dwelling' in Hermas in Brox (1991) 549. The text addresses Christians, δούλους τοῦ θεοῦ; see e.g. Herm. *Mand.* 5.2.1 and Fuchs (1931) 26: 'Ὀξυχολία [wird] im Bereich christlichen Lebens verstanden.'

[72] Herm. *Mand.* 5.1.2 (= 33.2).

[73] Texts in Plümacher (1992) 598. According to Maurer, however, its use in the pagan context is not very developed: see Maurer (1990) 359, lines 18–26.

[74] This, of course, does not exclude the fact that the vessel image for the body is much more widespread.

[75] Anthropomorphic pottery/glasses are widespread (Richter (1967)), but for the first and second centuries AD most of the Roman Imperial artefacts of this sort have been found in the North of Africa and north of the Alps. See also Roose (2005) 241 fig. 5; Zanker (1989) 46 fig. 31; 47 fig. 32; and, for Roman Britain, Braithwaite (1984). For the rare artefacts in the Levant, verifiable only from the Chalcolithic until the Iron Age, see Staubli (2015) 259–60. In methodological terms, the approach via artefacts would be an iconographic approach.

[76] Kövecses (2008) 68. But this universal bodily basis of all human beings is, as Kövecses states, '*not* utilized in the same way or to the same extent in different languages and varieties' (Kövecses (2008) 68), and 'the assumption of a "body-based constructionism" … is highly debated' (Kipfer (2017) 16 n. 76; Geeraerts (2015) 20–1; Trim (2015) 101–2). This is to be taken in consideration for further studies. See, with regard to the (non-)connection of the vessel image (for the human body) to emotions in the Hebrew Bible, Wagner (2006b) 98; cf. also Wagner (2006a) 66, and (differently) Kruger (2009) 256–8; Basson (2009) 123–4.

104   *Petra von Gemünden*

a vessel), the Shepherd admonishes Hermas that if ὀξυχολία, the angry temper, arrives, (a) there is no longer any place in this human vessel for the Holy Spirit, and (b) the purity that is very important in the Jewish tradition no longer exists, and the Holy Spirit will therefore flee.

It is clear that the human vessel is constructed for the Holy Spirit,[77] and only for him. The πνεῦμα τὸ ἅγιον is 'pure' (καθαρόν) in the one who is patient (μακρόθυμος). It is bright,[78] it lives in a broad space, and it exults and rejoices together with the vessel.[79] But if any ὀξυχολία comes in (ἐὰν δὲ ὀξυχολία τις προσέλθῃ),[80] there is a problem of space, and the Holy Spirit feels 'cramped' (στενοχωρεῖται) – or, as Osiek vividly translates the text, '[he] feels claustrophobic'.[81] Obviously, the Holy Spirit and the ὀξυχολία are both thought of as possessing a spatial extension. But there is a problem even greater than the problem of space: namely, that after the ὀξυχολία enters, the vessel is no longer pure.[82] And this means that the Holy Spirit no longer has a pure place in which he can serve the Lord.[83] An angry temper and cultic veneration are mutually exclusive. Choked and besmirched by the wicked spirit (πονηρὸν πνεῦμα) or by the angry temper (ὀξυχολία), the Holy Spirit attempts to leave.[84] But the focus remains on the human being when the Shepherd tells Hermas: 'If therefore both spirits dwell in the same place it is unprofitable and evil for that man in whom they dwell.'[85] The Shepherd explains this by varying the image of the vessel (σκεῦος) with that of a pot (κεράμιον) with honey (μέλι),[86] into which a very small quantity of wormwood (ἀψίνθιον) is poured. Here too, the starting point is positive: there is honey in the pot. It is only *subsequently* that a small quantity of wormwood is poured into it.[87] This interpretation emphasizes that patience (μακροθυμία) surpasses even honey in sweetness and usefulness, whereas ὀξυχολία is bitter and useless.[88] The image focuses on the contrast between 'much' and 'little' on

---

[77] We hear later of the 'just' spirit (Herm. *Mand.* 6.2.7 (= 34.7)).

[78] Literally: 'not darkened'.

[79] Herm. *Mand.* 6.1.2 (= 33.2): ἀγαλλιάσεται καὶ εὐφρανθήσεται.

[80] Herm. *Mand.* 6.1.3–4 (= 33.3–4), trans. cf. Osiek (1999) 117. At Herm. *Mand.* 6.1.3 (= 33.3), the ὀξυχολία is described in generalized terms as πονηρὸν πνεῦμα.

[81] Osiek (1999) 117.

[82] See Osiek (1999) 119 n. 11: 'Not the good spirit (grammatically possible) but the place is defiled by the evil spirit of bad temper.'

[83] On anger as an obstacle to cultic praxis see also Matt. 5:23–4.

[84] This last motif is not found in this form in the New Testament. Weinel (1899) 158 discusses whether the Letter to the Hebrews in the New Testament 'als entfernte Möglichkeit ... der Verlust des Geistes vorschwebt'. Osiek (1999) 119 affirms: 'What is surprising and without adequate precedent is the lack of competitiveness on the part of the good spirit.'

[85] Herm. *Mand.* 6.1.4 (= 33.4).

[86] Dibelius (1992) 515 and Joly (1968) 165 n. 5 identify the Jewish tradition and the New Testament as background. Geffcken (1908) 43 thinks rather of 'Moralien aus griechisch heidnischer Schule'.

[87] Cf. Herm. *Mand.* 6.1.2 (= 33.2): the Holy Spirit lives in the human being who is patient.

[88] Herm. *Mand.* 6.1.6 (= 33.6).

3. Methodological Issues and Issues of Content

the one hand, and between the (sweet) honey and the (bitter) wormwood on the other. It also contains the element of besmirching[89] and emphasizes that even a tiny amount of wormwood makes the honey bitter and useless for its master (δεσπότης).[90] A mixture of μακροθυμία and ὀξυχολία besmirches the former and makes the power of its prayer useless for God.[91] This shows that the *Shepherd of Hermas* cannot approve of a mixture. It aims at an 'either/or': the ὀξυχολία ought not to penetrate the human being (as a vessel) at all. The starting point is always positive: there is honey in the vessel, and the Holy Spirit is in the believer. Hermas has in mind here not the human being as such, but the Christian.

The Shepherd's exposition of the ways in which ὀξυχολία works[92] makes it clear that the decisive point for him is the continuous positive filling up of the vessel: if the believers are full of faith (because God's power is with them (μετ' αὐτῶν)), the ὀξυχολία has no room to enter.[93] Those who are completely empty (ἀπόκενοι) and those who doubt (δίψυχοι) are in danger.[94] The empty space arises when the Holy Spirit, who is described as a 'gentle spirit' (τρυφερὸν πνεῦμα),[95] in contrast to the wicked spirit (envisaged as 'hard'),[96] leaves the human being,[97] who will then be filled with wicked spirits.[98] According to the Shepherd, the worst of these is ὀξυχολία.[99]

The image of the vessel in the *Shepherd of Hermas* thematizes, *first*, the relationship between the inside and the outside, and demarcates the human being vis-à-vis wicked invaders from outside. It is linked to the mythical idea of two contrary entities, the Holy Spirit and the ὀξυχολία with its negative connotations (or analogous entities); I shall return to this below.

We find the vessel metaphor for the human being only rarely in the Old Testament wisdom literature, as in the Book of Proverbs;[100] nor do we find in wisdom literature mythical entities (spirits) outside the human being that have an

---

[89] μιαίνεται in Herm. *Mand.* 6.1.6 (= 33.6).

[90] Herm. *Mand.* 6.1.5 (= 33.5).

[91] Herm. *Mand.* 6.1.6 (= 33.6).

[92] Herm. *Mand.* 6.2.1–8 (= 34.1–8).

[93] According to Herm. *Mand.* 5.2.3 (= 34.3) μακροθυμία dwells with them.

[94] Herm. *Mand.* 5.2.1 (= 34.1), the idea that emptiness is a problem for the Christian, is also behind the recommendation to remember his own wife, who is to be protected from ἐπιθυμία and (as a consequence) from πορνεία (Herm. *Mand.* 4.1.1 (= 29.1)).

[95] Herm. *Mand.* 5.2.6 (= 34.6); cf. the τρυφερὸν ὄν in Herm. *Mand.* 5.1.3 (= 33.3). Cf. Herm. *Mand.* 6.2.3 (= 36.3) on the angel of justice (he is 'τρυφερός ... καὶ αἰσχυντερὸς καὶ ἡσύχιος').

[96] Cf. the μετὰ σκληρότητος in Herm. *Mand.* 5.2.6 (= 34.6) in regard to the evil spirit.

[97] Because he is not accustomed to living with the evil spirit; cf. Herm. *Mand.* 5.2.6 (= 34.6).

[98] Herm. *Mand.* 5.2.7 (= 34.7). Cf. Matt. 12:43–5; Luke 11:24–6. The presence of many (impure) spirits in a human being is also presupposed in Mark 5:8–9; cf. also 1QH 3:18 (1QS 3:14).

[99] Herm. *Mand.* 5.2.8 (= 34.8).

[100] The metaphor of the human being as a vessel is found only marginally in the sapiential literature, e. g. in Ecclus. 27:5(6).

impact on him, seeking to penetrate him and dwell in him.[101] In the Book of Proverbs (as in the Egyptian sapiential writings), the human being is summoned indirectly, by means of antithetical models such as the wise man and the fool,[102] to exercise an independent (autodynamic) *control* of anger.

Secondly, the image of the vessel thematizes the act of 'dwelling' inside it, and is thus closely linked to the *image of dwelling* (κατοικεῖν, κτλ.).[103] It is presented in its (a) quantitative, (b) qualitative, and (c) social aspects.

(a) The quantitative aspect: the πνεῦμα τὸ ἅγιον rejoices with the vessel when it is alone in it.[104] It lives 'in a broad space',[105] and thus has sufficient room – something that is extremely positive, when we bear in mind the cramped housing conditions of the population at large. If ὀξυχολία or other wicked spirits arrive, there is too little space: 'the vessel cannot contain them all, but overflows (ὑπερπλεονάζει)'.[106] The Holy Spirit suffers under the cramped conditions (στενοχωρεῖται).[107]

(b) The qualitative aspect: (i) As a 'gentle spirit' (τρυφερὸν πνεῦμα),[108] the Holy Spirit is unaccustomed to dwelling together with the evil spirit, or with hardness (μετὰ σκληρότητος).[109] It therefore departs from the human being in whom it dwells.[110] (ii) The cultic impurity is worse than the problem of space, because the 'vessel' has a cultic function. The Holy Spirit is besmirched through the wicked spirit (πονηρὸν πνεῦμα) or through the angry temper (ὀξυχολία),[111] so that it no longer has any place where it can serve the Lord.[112] The pot of honey has become 'bitter' and 'useless' for its owner.[113]

---

[101] In Proverbs, wine and others' example can have a negative influence on a person.

[102] Or the hot-tempered one and the cool one.

[103] On κατοικεῖν etc., cf. the excursus on the metaphor of 'dwelling' in Hermas in Brox (1991) 549. *Ad* κατοικεῖν + ἐν see Herm. *Mand.* 3.1 (= 28.1): 'Love the truth ..., so that the spirit that God made to live in this flesh may be recognized as true by everyone; in this way the Lord who dwells in you (δοξασθήσεται ὁ κύριος ὁ ἐν σοὶ κατοικῶν) will be glorified', trans. Ehrman (2003); cf. also Herm. *Sim.* 5.7.1 (= 60.1); 9.32.2 (= 109.2); *Mand.* 9.1.6 (= 40.6). Behind the exhortation in Herm. *Mand.* 4.1.1 (= 29.1) not to sin and always to remember one's own wife there lies the idea that the container must be filled positively, so that the negative desire has no possibility of penetrating the human being.

[104] Herm. *Mand.* 5.1.2 (= 33.2).

[105] Herm. *Mand.* 5.1.2 (= 33.2).

[106] Herm. *Mand.* 5.2.5 (= 34.5), trans. Osiek (1999) 118. The formulation that the vessel 'cannot contain the spirits [with a negative connotation]' suggests that the spirits are considered here – as the gall (bile) sometimes is – as a liquid.

[107] Herm. *Mand.* 5.1.3 (= 33.3). Similarly Herm. *Mand.* 10.2.6 (= 41.6).

[108] Herm. *Mand.* 5.2.6 (= 34.6): cf. the τρυφερὸν ὂν in Herm. *Mand.* 5.1.3 (= 33.3). Cf. Herm. *Mand.* 6.2.3 (= 36.3) about the angel of justice (he is 'τρυφερός ... καὶ ἡσύχιος').

[109] Herm. *Mand.* 5.2.6 (= 34.6).

[110] Herm. *Mand.* 5.2.6–7 (= 34.6–7).

[111] Herm. *Mand.* 5.1.3 (= 33.3).

[112] Herm. *Mand.* 5.1.3 (= 33.3): μὴ ἔχον τόπον λειτουργῆσαι τῷ κυρίῳ.

[113] Herm. *Mand.* 5.1.5 (= 33.5).

3. Methodological Issues and Issues of Content 107

(c) The social aspect: the presence of different or antithetical 'dwellers' in the vessel leads to unaccustomed contact and strong frictions. The Holy Spirit, which is called gentle, suffers under this. 'He seeks to live with gentleness and quiet',[114] in other words, with two virtues that are the opposite of anger, namely, πραότης and ἡσυχία.[115]

3.2.3. The use of the image of the garment

The image of the garment is in the *Shepherd of Hermas* not as pronounced as the image of the vessel. It is found in the positive injunction to 'put on' (ἔνδυσαι) μακροθυμία (the opposite of ὀξυχολία).[116] Although this is in direct proximity to the image of the vessel, we should note that the vessel encloses the Holy Spirit (or, if things go wrong, only the ὀξυχολία), whereas here it is the μακροθυμία that encases the Christian. This may not pose a problem, since the metaphorical use of 'garment' is supported by the tradition of metaphors: Hellenistic Judaism – which is indebted to the Old Testament[117] and Greek metaphorical usage – knows the 'putting on' of virtues (and vices),[118] and this metaphor recurs frequently in the New Testament in the baptismal paraenesis.[119] Baptism is the ritual expression of μετάνοια (conversion) being of central importance for its ethical consequences.[120]

3.3. Discourse analysis[121]

The affirmations in the *Shepherd of Hermas* about ὀξυχολία are marked by two opposing mythical entities: on the one hand, the Holy Spirit who dwells in the

---

[114] Herm. *Mand.* 5.2.6 (= 34.6).

[115] Herm. *Mand.* 5.2.6 (= 34.6).

[116] Herm. *Mand.* 5.2.8 (= 34.8). ἐνδύω is linked above all with positive realities in the *Shepherd of Hermas*; cf. the combination of ἐνδύω with strength (Herm. *Vis.* 3.12.2 (= 20.2)), faith (Herm. *Vis.* 4.1.8 (= 22.8); *Mand.* 9.7.10 (= 39.7.10)); cheerfulness (Herm. *Mand.* 9.3.1.4 (= 42.1.4)); truth (Herm. *Mand.* 11 (= 43.4)); 'the good and holy desire (ἐπιθυμία)' (Herm. *Mand.* 12.1 (= 44.1)); see also below *ad* Herm. *Sim.* 6.5.3 (= 65.3). Kehl (1984) has assembled texts that make it clear that the metaphor of clothing 'stets ethisch verstanden wurde' (p. 214). The antithesis at Herm. *Mand.* 5.2.8 (= 34.8) between ἀπέχου and ἔνδυσαι is also found at Herm. *Mand.* 2.3–4 (= 27.3–4) in relation to slander and σεμνότης.

[117] Clothed in righteousness: Isa. 11:5; 61:10; 64:5; see also Eph. 6:14, Rev. 19:8; Herm. *Sim.* 6.1.4 (= 61.4).

[118] In the LXX, ἐνδύω is used positively with regard to clothing oneself in 'ethisch-religiösen Eigenschaften', but it is also used negatively (see Oepke (1935) 320, lines 6–16). On the garment of virtue or of vice etc. in antiquity, cf. Ecclus. 27:8(9); Philo, *Fug.* 110 (on the garment of virtue); Strack and Billerbeck (1922–56) 2.301; Dahl (2000) 396 n. 45; Brox (1991) 271, 550; Galinier (2012). For much older uses of 'garment' metaphors see Cairns (1996), (2016a).

[119] See Col. 3:10; Eph. 4:24 (putting on the καινός or νέος ἄνθρωπος). (On clothing oneself with Christ see Gal. 3:27).

[120] See above, below, and Osiek (1999) 28.

[121] On the theory see Luther (2015), esp. 23–47.

108 *Petra von Gemünden*

human being, and on the other hand, the ὀξυχολία that attempts to enter into the human being.[122] The mythical opposition can be expressed variously: in Herm. *Mand.* 5.1.3 (= 33.3), the Lord (κύριος) opposes the Devil (διάβολος),[123] whereas in Herm. *Mand.* 5.2.5–6.7 (= 34.5–36.7), the holy or righteous spirit (πνεύματος τοῦ δικαίου) is opposed by several evil spirits. The *Shepherd of Hermas* maintains here a Doctrine of the Two Spirits, where the spirit with the negative connotations can be further differentiated hierarchically, with ὀξυχολία as the chief spirit, to which other emotions are subordinate.[124] This is completely untypical of the Old Testament, where we do not find any fully developed demonology, but it is found in Early Judaism in the Doctrine of the Two Spirits in the Community Rule in Qumran (1QS 3:13–4:26),[125] where the antithesis is between the spirit of truth and the spirit of iniquity,[126] or the prince of light and the angel of darkness,[127] with the spirits who are associated with them.[128] This means that there are two antithetical ways which impose a choice.[129] Human virtues and vices are associated with these spiritual powers, which are envisaged in personal terms. For example, there is (as in the *Shepherd of Hermas*) a contrast between the virtue of patience (אורך אפים) and the vice of angry temper[130] (אפים קצור).[131] The former of these ought to predominate in the human being, but an absolute absence of anger is not put forward as an ideal.[132]

A Doctrine of the Two Spirits also influences the so-called Testaments of the Twelve Patriarchs. This text is hard to classify, because either a Jewish compiler in the second or third century AD made extensive use of Jewish material,[133] or

---

[122] In Herm. *Mand.* 5.2.8 (= 34.8) the ὀξυχολία is called the most evil spirit (πονηροτάτου πνεύματος).

[123] The former dwells in the μακροθυμία, the latter in the ὀξυχολία.

[124] Cf. Herm. *Mand.* 5.2.5.7–8 (= 34.5.7–8).

[125] The majority of scholars hold that the Doctrine of the Two Spirits in 1QS 3:13–4:26 is originally an independent, pre-Essene text (Stegemann (1988) 128; Frey (1997) 295–6; (2001) 160; Lange (1995) 126–32). The Community Rule itself is dated between 100 and 75 BC.

[126] 1QS 3:18–19.

[127] The spirit of truth and the spirit of wickedness seem to be identical with the prince of light and the angel of darkness.

[128] 1QS 3:20–4:1.

[129] For the Two Ways doctrine see also 1QS 4:2.

[130] Qimron and Charlesworth (1994) 17 translate: 'fury'.

[131] 1QS 4:3, 4:10.

[132] In 1QS 4:3b slowness to anger is on the positive side; in 1QS 4:9b, 4:10 quickness to anger is on the negative side. This is in keeping with the idea of creation in relation to the two spirits: according to 1QS 3:18, *both* are created by God.

[133] This is the thesis of De Jonge (1975), subsequently somewhat modified: see for example De Jonge (1960), (1962), and Hollander and De Jonge (1985) 83–5 (provenance in the second half of the second century in Christian circles; it is possible 'that especially the christological and eschatological passages were subjected to later additions and revisions in the period between the beginning of the third century and the origin of the archetype of the present tradition' (p. 85). It may perhaps not be the work of one single author, but the outcome of a shared undertaking (p. 85)). De Jonge's hypothesis repristinates the consensus that reigned be-

3. Methodological Issues and Issues of Content

109

else Christian interpolations or revisions have been made to a Jewish text with basic material that may go back to the second century BC.[134] In T. Dan, the spirit of anger (τὸ πνεῦμα τοῦ θυμοῦ)[135] is contrasted with patience (μακροθυμία).[136] The former is associated with Satan in T. Dan.[137]

The new element in Hermas is that the spirits are obviously thought of as possessing a spatial extension, and that this is 'analysed' argumentatively in the new combination with the vessel metaphor.[138] Hermas aims at establishing a rigorous 'either/or': it is only the tender Holy Spirit that ought to be in the human person, because there is room only for it. The purity required for the worship of God is present only when the Holy Spirit *alone* is in the vessel (and the ὀξυχολία is not present too). Qumran and the Testaments of the Twelve Patriarchs see this differently. In the Doctrine of the Two Spirits in Qumran, the human being, with his virtues (and vices), ought to be *predominantly* in the realm of the spirit of truth, or of the prince of light.[139] Thanks to the concept of creation, anger is not viewed *in absolutely negative terms* in Qumran or in the Testaments of the Twelve Patriarchs.[140] In the *Shepherd of Hermas*, the alternative is exclusive and reflects the antithetical logic of conversion (μετάνοια).

---

fore the publication of Schnapp (1884). On the history of research, see Becker (1970) 129–58; Slingerland (1977). Very few scholars have accepted the thesis of De Jonge: e.g. Milik (1955) 405–6; Daniélou (1957) 77–8; Carmignac (1957) 32–4; Burrows (1958) 179; and the overview in Philonenko (1960) 3 n. 12.

[134] This was the thesis of the editor of the first printed Greek text of the T. 12 Patr., J. E. Grabe (see Slingerland (1977) 5; Küchler (1979) 432 with n. 7). Via Schnapp (1884) (he opts for interpolations) and Charles (1908) (he opts for a redaction), this has become the thesis accepted by the great majority of scholars (although they diverge greatly in the details); see e.g. Aschermann (1955) 1–4; Becker (1970) 129–41, 152–4, 373–7; (1980) 16; Michel (1973) 42; and Caquot and Philonenko (1987) lxxvii, who take the following position: 'la tradition textuelle ... n'établit pas la matérialité de remodelages étendus ou de larges interpolations dont l'origine chrétienne serait assurée'.

[135] T. Dan 1:8 (at 1:7 it is described as one of the spirits of Beliar); T. Dan 2:4 and *passim*.

[136] According to T. Gad 4:6–7, the spirit of love works together in forbearance (μακροθυμία) with the law of God.

[137] Cf. the application of the metaphor (κατα)κυριεύει in T. Dan 3:2 to θυμός, and in T. Dan 4:7 to Beliar.

[138] The predominant tendency in Qumran and the T. 12 Patr. is to ascribe spheres of governance to the spirits. The use of the vessel metaphor is less pronounced in connection with the two spririts. The vessel metaphor is found only to a small extent; cf. 1QS 4:20–1; T. Dan 5:1, the Lord dwells (κατοικήσῃ) 'in you'.

[139] Although the two spirits are deployed in the world 'in equal parts' (1QS 4:25), they are present in each individual human being in differing proportions. From the physiognomic-astrological text 4Q 186, which survives only fragmentarily, one can infer that the human being consists of nine parts; the 'good' and the 'wicked' spirit can be present in each individual in a different admixture – but the uneven number permits an unambiguous ascription to one or the other spirit.

[140] See 1QS 4:25; T. Naph. 2:8, T. Sim. 2:5.

110 *Petra von Gemünden*

If we take one step back and look at our analysis of the images, the obvious conclusion is that ὀξυχολία in the *Shepherd of Hermas* is *not* inherent in the Christian:[141] the human body is a vessel made only in order that the Holy Spirit may dwell in it. The human being is *only* a vessel for the Holy Spirit. The vessel is not intended for the ὀξυχολία that makes its way in from the outside. If both are in the vessel, 'it is unfortunate and evil for that person in whom they live',[142] and 'the vessel cannot contain them, but overflows'.[143]

The discourse analysis has shown the importance of the Doctrine of the Two Spirits. It links the mythical figure of the Devil with ὀξυχολία.[144] The Christian must avoid it.[145]

The results of the analysis of the images and of the discourse therefore suggest that the ὀξυχολία is presented *not* as something in the human being (more precisely: in the Christian), but as something alien that comes from the outside, as something originally not suitable for the Christian. And in fact, with one insignificant exception,[146] the *Shepherd of Hermas* does not speak about *the* irascible person, nor about *the* gentle person. This suggests the conclusion that Hermas sees the ὀξυχολία not as a disposition, but as something interpreted in demonological terms as coming from the outside, as something that is originally alien to the Christian. We must, however, differentiate this picture when we turn to context analysis.

3.4. Context analysis

The book is divided by the author himself into five ὁράσεις (*Visiones*), twelve ἐντολαί (*Mandata*) and ten παραβολαί (*Similitudines*).[147] In the narrative framework, Hermas sees his former owner Rhoda bathing in the Tiber. He helps her out of the river. 'Seeing her beauty', Hermas then says: 'I thought in my heart: "How happy I would be if I had such a wife, both in regard to beauty and manner."'[148] We then read the short statement: 'I wanted only this, nothing more.'[149] After some time, Hermas is taken hold of by the Spirit as he walks, and is carried off. When he is deep in prayer, Rhoda appears to him in a vision and gives him the heavenly message that God is angry with him, because he has

---

[141] Hermas always envisages not the human being in general, but Christians.
[142] Herm. *Mand.* 5.1.4 (= 33.4), trans. Holmes (2007) 517.
[143] Herm. *Mand.* 5.2.5 (= 34.5), trans. Holmes (2007) 521.
[144] Cf. Herm. *Mand.* 5.1.3 (= 33.3): 'the Lord dwells in patience, but the devil in irascibility (ὀξυχολία)' (trans. Ehrman (2003)).
[145] Herm. *Mand.* 5.2.8 (= 34.8).
[146] Herm. *Mand.* 5.2.7 (= 34.7).
[147] Herm. *Vis.* 5.5–7 (= 25.5–7).
[148] Herm. *Vis.* 1.1.2 (= 1.2), trans. Osiek (1999) 41.
[149] Herm. *Vis.* 1.1.2 (= 1.2), trans. Osiek (1999) 41.

3. Methodological Issues and Issues of Content

sinned against her.[150] Hermas does not understand this, and asks several questions. Then Rhoda tells him: 'The evil desire ascended in your heart. Do you not think it is an evil thing if an evil desire ascends in the heart of a just man?'[151] And she declares: 'It is a sin, a great one.'[152] She exhorts him 'to pray to God, who will heal' his 'sins'.[153] It is interesting here that Hermas, who is described in this text as 'self-controlled' (ἐγκρατής), as one 'who abstains from every evil desire (ἀπεχόμενος πάσης ἐπιθυμίας πονηρᾶς) and is full of all sincerity and great innocence',[154] this 'exemplary Christian',[155] was initially unaware of his ἐπιθυμία – it is only in prayer and in the confrontation in his vision that he becomes clearly aware of 'unconscious' emotion.

The theme of μετάνοια (repentance, conversion)[156] dominates the next visions.[157] In the last vision (*Vis.* 5), the Shepherd appears to Hermas, who recognizes him as 'the angel of repentance'. He tells Hermas to write down his commandments and parables,[158] which constitute the rest of the book.

A number of the commandments concern emotions: *Mand.* 5 deals with patience and the emotion of irascibility (angry temper) (μακροθυμία and ὀξυχολία), *Mand.* 7 with fear (φόβος),[159] and *Mand.* 10 with sadness (λύπη). The importance of the commandment about μακροθυμία and ὀξυχολία can be seen in the following words: 'if you master it [*sc.* this commandment] you will be able to guard the other commandments, which I am about to give you'.[160]

The first commandment (Herm. *Mand.* 1) specifies the fundamentals: faith (in a creator God) and the fear of God, with continence as its consequence.[161] The second (*Mand.* 2) presents the virtues of ἁπλότης (simplicity) and ἀκακία (innocence); it exhorts to personal integrity and warns against slander. The third (*Mand.* 3) demands that one love truth – in reaction to this, Hermas weeps because of his lies.[162] The Shepherd explains to him that 'a bad conscience must

---

[150] Herm. *Vis.* 1.1.6 (= 1.6).

[151] Herm. *Vis.* 1.1.8 (= 1.8), trans. Osiek (1999) 41. Snyder (1968) 29 explains: 'phrases like "rise up in your heart" … to refer to volition and consciousness indicate the Jewish vocabulary of the author (cf. Isa. 65:17; Jer. 3:16)'; see also below.

[152] Herm. *Vis.* 1.1.8 (= 1.8), trans. Osiek (1999) 41.

[153] Herm. *Vis.* 1.1.9 (= 1.9).

[154] Herm. *Vis.* 1.2.4 (= 2.4), trans. Holmes (2007).

[155] Brox (1991) 88.

[156] Osiek (1999) 29 prefers to translate not with 'repentance', but with 'conversion' – since 'conversion' better expresses a really 'profound change of heart' (Osiek (1999) 30).

[157] An old woman (the Church) appears to Hermas there. Thanks to the repentance initiated by Hermas, she is renewed and becomes younger and younger.

[158] Herm. *Vis.* 5.5–6 (= 25.5–6); see also Vielhauer (1975) 516.

[159] Herm. *Mand.* 9 (= 39.1–12) deals with doubt (διψυχία), which Hermas apparently sees as on the same level as the emotions mentioned in the context. For διψυχία see Nürnberger (2019), esp. 590–1.

[160] Herm. *Mand.* 5.2.8 (= 34.8), trans. Ehrman (2003) 261.

[161] These 'basics' are repeated in Herm. *Mand.* 6.1.1 (= 35.1).

[162] He is anxious lest he might not be saved (Herm. *Mand.* 3.3 (= 28.3)).

112 *Petra von Gemünden*

not dwell with the spirit of truth,[163] nor must sadness overtake a reverent and truthful spirit'.[164] Finally, in *Mand.* 4 (which precedes the Mandate on irascibility (ὀξυχολία)), we read the exhortation to chastity (ἁγνεία), where Hermas is admonished: 'let no thought [var. desire][165] ascend in your heart about another man's wife or about fornication (πορνεία), or about some such similar evil thing' (*Mand.* 4.1 (= 29)).[166] And the Shepherd insists: 'If this notion (ἐνθύμησις)[167] should ascend in your heart (ἐπὶ τὴν καρδίαν σου ἀναβῇ), you will sin, and if another such wicked idea [evil desire] should arise [ascend], you commit a sin ...'[168] This formulation takes up a formulation in the introductory vision, where the πονηρὰ ἐπιθυμία has ascended in the heart of Hermas.[169] In what follows, this formulation will be important for us.[170]

In *Mand.* 6–8, the commandment about faith, fear, and continence that is formulated in *Mand.* 1 (1.2 = 26.2) is taken up and commented upon,[171] and the two kinds of faith (6), the two kinds of fear (7), and the two kinds of continence (8) are discussed.[172] *Mand.* 9 thematizes διψυχία,[173] and *Mand.* 10 thematizes λύπη.[174] In *Mand.* 10.1.1 (= 40.1), sadness (λύπη) is called the 'sister of double-mindedness (διψυχία) and an angry temper (ὀξυχολία)'.[175] Finally, *Mand.* 11 takes up the theme of true and false prophecy, and *Mand.* 12 speaks of evil desire and good and holy desire (ἐπιθυμία).

It is interesting that the expression ἀναβαίνω ἐπὶ (or εἰς) τὴν καρδίαν (cf. אָלְתָה עַל לֵב), which is employed in the *Visiones* and the *Mandata* of Hermas with the (usually unconscious, but later entering into consciousness) ἐπιθυμία for a woman, is found in *Mand.* 6.2 (= 36) in the context of ὀξύχολος and πικρός,[176] or of ὀξυχολία and πικρία.[177] Hermas presents here a dualistic doctrine of two angels: an angel of righteousness and an angel of wickedness are with the human

---

[163] 'Bad conscience' = the 'coherence between ... self-image and ... public honor'; see Osiek (1999) 108.

[164] Herm. *Mand.* 3.4 (= 28.4), trans. Osiek (1999) 107.

[165] In MS L² (cf. ed. Leutzsch (1998)).

[166] Trans. Holmes (2007) 509, slightly altered. Cf. the translation of Weinel (1924): 'nicht soll in deinem Herzen die böse Begierde aufsteigen ...'.

[167] Brox (1991) 201.204 translates ἐνθύμησις with 'Verlangen'.

[168] Herm. *Mand.* 4.1.2 (= 29.2), trans. following Ehrman (2003). The formulation ἀναβαίνω ἐπὶ (or εἰς) τὴν καρδίαν is an Old Testament idiom, which is 'most likely' 'ursemitisch' (Weiss (1910) 58), a Semitism (Bauer (1988) 98); Dibelius (1923) 427. See also below *ad* אָלְתָה עַל לֵב.

[169] Herm. *Vis.* 1.8 (= 1.8); cf. trans. of Osiek (1999) 41.

[170] Note also Herm. *Mand.* 4.3 (= 29.3).

[171] Dibelius (1992) 497.

[172] See Vielhauer (1975) 516.

[173] Holmes (2007) 531–5: 'double-mindedness'; cf. Nürnberger (2019) 377.590–1.

[174] Holmes (2007) 535: 'grief'; Leutzsch (1998) 225: 'die Traurigkeit'.

[175] Trans. Holmes (2007) 535; cf. Nürnberger (2019) 590–1. Sadness too (not only ὀξυχολία) drives away the Holy Spirit; cf. Herm. *Mand.* 10.2.1 (= 41.1).

[176] Herm. *Mand.* 6.2.4 (= 36.4).

[177] Herm. *Mand.* 6.2.5 (= 36.5).

3. Methodological Issues and Issues of Content

being (μετὰ τοῦ ἀνθρώπου).[178] The description of the former angel displays traits of the Holy Spirit[179] and of μακροθυμία.[180] The latter is qualified as ὀξύχολος (ill-tempered), πικρός (bitter) and ἄφρων (senseless).[181] It is interesting that Hermas now asks how he can recognize the modes of working (ἐνεργείας) of these two angels, who dwell with him (Πῶς ... γνώσομαι).[182] The catalogue of virtues that characterize the angel of righteousness and the catalogue of vices that characterize the angel of wickedness both conclude with the expression ταῦτα οὖν ὅταν ἐπὶ τὴν καρδίαν σου ἀναβῇ, γίνωσκε ὅτι ὁ ἄγγελος τῆς πονηρίας ἐστὶν ἐν σοί.[183] The expression ἀναβαίνειν ἐπὶ τὴν καρδίαν – an idiom behind which stands the Hebrew expression אָלָה עַל לֵב[184] – describes an ascending movement to the heart, the inner dimension of the human,[185] the location of the centre of the person.[186] It is the seat of the emotions and feelings,[187] but also (and *above*

---

[178] Herm. *Mand.* 6.2.1 (= 36.1): μετὰ τοῦ ἀνθρώπου ('with a person', of both angels); *Mand.* 6.2.2: μετ' ἐμοῦ ('with me', of both angels); according to Herm. *Mand.* 6.2.5 (= 36.5), however, the ὀξυχολία is *in* (ἐν) the human being.

[179] Τρυφερός in Herm. *Mand.* 5.1.3 (= 33.3) of the Holy Spirit in the vessel which is characterized as 'delicate'; cf. Herm. *Mand.* 5.2.6 (= 34.6). Πραΰς and ἡσύχιος likewise evoke the Holy Spirit, since he strives in Herm. *Mand.* 5.2.6 (= 34.6) to dwell with πραότητος καὶ ἡσυχίας.

[180] Herm. *Mand.* 5.2.3 (= 34.3) πραεῖα καὶ ἡσύχιος are associated with μακροθυμία, forbearance.

[181] Herm. *Mand.* 6.2.4–5 (= 36.4–5): 'He [*sc.* the angel of wickedness] is irascible (ὀξύχολος), bitter (πικρός), and senseless (ἄφρων)' (trans. Ehrman (2003)); cf. Herm. *Mand.* 5.2.8 (= 34.8), where ὀξυχολία is paratactically alongside πικρία. The adjective ἄφρων (senseless) is associated with ὀξυχολία at Herm. *Mand.* 5.2.3 (= 34.4). In the same passage, ἀφροσύνη heads the sequence of filiations that culminates in fury (μῆνις).

[182] Herm. *Mand.* 6.2.2 (= 36.2). The numerous cognitive concepts in *Mand.* 6.2 make clear that recognition is obviously very important. Hermas is the first Christian text which treats the topic of the *discretio spirituum*; see Switek (1972) 38–9; Gokey (1961) 123.

[183] Cf. Herm. *Mand.* 6.2.3 (= 36.3), ταῦτα πάντα ὅταν εἰς τὴν καρδίαν σου ἀναβῇ, γίνωσκε ὅτι ὁ ἄγγελος τῆς δικαιοσύνης μετὰ σοῦ ἐστι; Herm. *Mand.* 6.2.4 (= 36.4) (a μετά or an ἐν is missing here, since we read only γνῶθι αὐτὸν ἀπὸ τῶν ἔργων αὐτοῦ); see also Herm. *Mand.* 6.2.5 (= 36.5) (μετὰ σοῦ).

[184] Cf. Blass–Debrunner–Rehkopf, 18th ed. (= BDR¹⁸) § 4.8 (treated under the heading 'ungriechische Elemente', 'Semitismen'); Hilhorst (1976) 159. For this expression, cf. 4 Kgdms 12:5; Jer. 3:16; 51:21; Isa. 65:16(17); WisCairGen 6.9 (trans. Berger (1989)); Luke 24:38; Acts 7:23; (Isa. 65:16 quoted in 1 Cor. 2:9); Physiologus 14 (trans. Schönberger (2001)). It is not found in the T. 12 Patr.

[185] This is the case in the Old Testament, Early Jewish tradition, and very predominantly in the New Testament; see Wehrle and Kampling (1995) 140.

[186] According to Wehrle and Kampling (1995) 140, the understanding of the heart as the 'central organ', which is customary in the Greek cultural sphere, is found only in Luke, not elsewhere in the New Testament; in other New Testament passages, it signifies 'the interior of the human being'. On the heart in the Hebrew-Jewish world of ideas, cf. Bauer and Felber (1988) 1098; Wolff (2010) 68–95 (the passages discussed by Wolff there show clearly that, in contradiction to what his heading to *leb(ab)*, 'der vernünftige Mensch', suggests, (ב)לב clearly goes beyond the heart as the seat of the understanding. On the heart in the world of Greek and especially of Roman ideas, see Bauer and Felber (1988).

[187] On the Old Testament, see Wehrle and Kampling (1995) 138: the seat of pain, of joy, fear, despair, and courage; on the New Testament, see Wehrle and Kampling (1995) 140: 'Ort der

114   *Petra von Gemünden*

all) of the understanding or the act of knowing[188] and of the will.[189] This expression seems to be describing here a becoming aware, a becoming conscious – the movement to coming to know something that was or is in the human being, but of which he or she was previously unaware (or not fully aware).[190] The Shepherd guides Hermas to recognize that ὀξυχολία, which initially is located outside, is something that already exists deep within his inner being. It is probably not by chance that this happens precisely in the instruction 'about faith'.[191] The image of 'ascending to the heart' may be further strengthened by the association that the liver and the gall are located anatomically under the heart – which in Semitic thought is the organ of knowledge.[192] The spatial association in the vivid metaphor of ἀναβαίνειν ἐπὶ [εἰς] τὴν καρδίαν may occasionally be rather weak, as if it meant merely that a thought occurs to the human being.[193] But if that is indeed the case, this verb once again becomes a metaphor in Hermas (remeta-

---

Affekte, Begierden und Leidenschaften' such as joy (Acts 2:26), fear (John 14:1–27), suffering (2 Cor. 2:4; Acts 21:13), desire (Rom. 10:6).

[188] Thus above all in the Old Testament, cf. Exod. 7:23; 1 Sam. 4:20; 21:13; cf. the heart as 'Bereich wichtiger intellektueller Fähigkeiten wie der Einsicht' (Deut. 8:5; Job 17:4, Prov. 2:2) and of the ability 'eine Sache kritisch zu beurteilen' (Josh. 14:7; Judg. 5:15–16; Eccles. 2:1, 3, 15), as well as the seat of remembering (of recognizing) (Deut. 4:9; Isa. 33:18; 65:17; Jer. 3:16); cf. Wehrle and Kampling (1995) 138–9. See Baumgärtel (2000) 610 (the heart as the seat of intellectual functions); Schellenberg (2007) (the heart 'als Erkenntnisorgan'); cf. also WisCairGen 16.2 (understanding and recognizing) (trans. Berger (1989)). Constantinou in this volume shows that in the *War of Troy* 2130–5 we read ἀνέβαινε χολὴ πρὸς τὸ κεφάλι and not to the heart as in Hermas.

[189] Cf. in the Old Testament, 2 Sam. 7:3; 1 Kgs 8:17; Isa. 10:7, and Wehrle and Kampling (1995) 139; in the New Testament, 1 Cor. 4:5; 7:37; 2 Cor. 9:7, and Wehrle and Kampling (1995) 140. In the pagan sphere: Verg. *Aen.* 6.675; Stat. *Theb.* 5.37.

[190] This notion is also observable in Jer. 3:16–17: 'they say no more, "The ark of the covenant of Yahweh"; neither shall it come to mind: neither shall they remember it (וְלֹא יַעֲלֶה עַל־לֵב וְלֹא יִזְכְּרוּ־בוֹ)' (transl. Driver (1908); cf. LXX: οὐκ ἀναβήσεται ἐπὶ καρδίαν, οὐκ ὀνομασθήσεται ... We can conclude: the ark of the covenant of Yahweh is forgotten. When it becomes conscient again and is remembered (note the *parallelismus membrorum* עָלָה עַל לֵב / זכר !) it ascends in the children of the Israel. The idea of 'remembering' is also found in the *schᵉma* Deut. 6:4–9 (not only outside – maybe by an amulet), but also inside by a movement which aims at the heart: וְהָיוּ הַדְּבָרִים הָאֵלֶּה אֲשֶׁר אָנֹכִי מְצַוְּךָ הַיּוֹם עַל־לְבָבֶךָ (Deut. 6:6). We also read of a becoming conscious and its consequences in Ezech. 38:10 (עַל־לְבָבֶךָ) (בַּיּוֹם הַהוּא יַעֲלוּ דְבָרִים עַל־לְבָבֶךָ), 'On that day, thoughts will come into your mind, and you will devise an evil scheme' (NRV). For Hermas, see Theißen (2007) 103–4.

[191] The chapter on the two angels is introduced by 'Now hear ... about faith'. See also Herm. *Vis.* 1.1.4–8 (= 1.8).

[192] For Hermas, the main focus lies on getting to recognize the angel of wickedness and his attributes. There is clearly more detail in what he writes here, and it is only the section on the angel of wickedness that is explicitly introduced by Hermas' question about how he is to recognize (νοέω) him.

[193] See the translation 'in den Sinn kommen' for the Hebrew in Gesenius (1915) 375. For the Greek see Bauer (1988) 819: 'es steigt jmdm. auf = er denkt an etwas' (with reference to Acts 7:23; 1 Cor. 2:9).

3. Methodological Issues and Issues of Content

phorization):[194] ἀναβαίνειν is then unambiguously a movement from below to above, as in the parable of the building of the tower.[195]

An observation confirms that ὀξυχολία – despite first appearances (the metaphor of the human being filled by the Holy Spirit, the one into whom ὀξυχολία seeks to penetrate) – not only enters into the human being from the outside,[196] but is again present in him or her: namely, that we can see a sliding transition from the outside to the inside in the case of the angel of wickedness.[197] Initially, he was located outside,[198] but a little later on in the section, he is *in* (ἐν) the human being.[199]

3.5. Form 'criticism'

Form criticism offers a fourth methodological approach to the investigation of the emotions in the *Shepherd of Hermas*. In form and in style, this text is an apocalypse,[200] and it presupposes a rich apocalyptic Jewish literature, which gives glimpses of the heavenly world in revelatory visions and words, thereby regulating what happens both in the earthly world that is passing away and in a future world.

The two best-known early Christian apocalypses, the Revelation of John and the *Shepherd of Hermas*, have one special characteristic that distinguishes them from their Jewish predecessors: they do not claim to have been written by authoritative figures of the past, such as Enoch, Abraham, Moses, or Ezra,[201] but by persons of the present day. These persons are known by name and are given a specific location, John on Patmos and Hermas in Rome.[202] This signals

---

[194] For the phenomenon of 'remetaphorization' see Weinrich (1976). For the spatial association it is interesting that BDR[18] § 4.8 (p. 6) emphasizes, with regard to ἀναβαίνειν ἐπὶ τὴν καρδίαν: 'Der Semit denkt in Bildreden anschaulich.'

[195] Herm. *Sim.* 9.3.3 (= 80.3): 'The six men ordered stones to come up (ἀναβαίνειν) out of a great depth (ἐκ βυθοῦ) ...'. This movement is also to be observed in Jer. 3:16–17.

[196] Herm. *Mand.* 6.2.3 (= 36.3) of the angel of righteousness; Herm. *Mand.* 6.2.4 (= 36.4) of the angel of wickedness.

[197] And the angel of righteousness. In this context the remark of Niebuhr may be helpful: 'Diese Unterscheidung [einer "psychologischen", "dämonologischen" oder "mythologischen" Geistanschauung] trägt neuzeitliche Kategorien in die antiken Vorstellungen ein' (Niebuhr (1987) 90).

[198] 'With a person', Herm. *Mand.* 6.2.1 (= 36.1).

[199] Herm. *Mand.* 6.2.5 (= 36.5) ('recognize that he is in you (ἐν σοί)'). In the T. 12 Patr., we find an oscillation between inside and outside. The boundaries between the inside and the outside of a human being were more blurred in antiquity than in our days: see Berger (1991) §§ 3–6.

[200] Vielhauer (1975) 518. For Vielhauer, the apocalyptic form includes the 'Ich-Stil, das Erlebnis von Visionen und Entrückungen, das Auftreten von angeli interpretes, [den] Himmelsbrief, die Allegoresen und ... die Paränese'.

[201] Cf. the intertestamental apocalypses that bear these names.

[202] For the location in Rome, see above.

that revelation takes place in the present. The decisive instance in history is something that is happening here and now.

There are two differences of emphasis that distinguish the *Shepherd of Hermas* from the Revelation of John. Hermas does not describe any events of the end times,[203] and his text centres not on the conflict between the community and the Roman Empire as the Revelation of John does,[204] but on internal problems within the community concerning moral behaviour – a theme that the Revelation of John likewise takes up in the seven Letters to the Churches. The moral problems move to centre stage in Hermas. Instead of glimpses of heaven, he offers glimpses of the social life of Christians in the community, and insights into the inner life of the Christians that reach even into the unconscious. Instead of a revelation of what lies beyond this world in heaven, we have a revelation of what lies within. This too signals something important: the decisive locus of life lies within the human being, where cosmic powers, good and evil spirits, God, and Satan struggle for supremacy.

One could perhaps attempt to posit a link between this special characteristic of Hermas and one of the special characteristics in his use of metaphors. The vessel metaphor emphasizes the border between the internal life and that which is outside. The breaching of this border takes place as a revelation.

It is certain that the choice of an apocalypse form (that is to say, of a revelatory genre) signals Hermas' consciousness that he is making known something new in the sphere of his tradition, even if he does in fact reproduce many individual traditions. In this genre, introspection takes place via revelation.

Conclusion

The key concept of ὀξυχολία is found for the first time in the biblical tradition and in ancient literature in Hermas. In Hermas, *Mandata* 5 it becomes a leading concept in the moral-psychological interpretation of the human being. This emotion[205] is presented in the context of a comprehensive interpretation of the world and of the life of the Christian. Hermas has in mind not the human being per se, but only the Christian, when he presents the human being technomorphically in *Mand.* 5 (and 6) as a vessel made exclusively for the Holy Spirit and with a limited capacity. Ὀξυχολία makes its way into this vessel from outside,

---

[203] Although we find apocalyptic images in Herm. *Vis.* 4 (= 25), they 'dienen ... aber keiner apokalyptischen Schilderung', but are 'enteschatologisiert' and 'individualisierend umgedeutet' (Vielhauer (1975) 519).

[204] The whore of Babylon (Rev. 17–18) personifies Rome or the Roman Empire.

[205] For the possibilities in terminological differentiation between 'Emotion' and 'Affekt' see Inselmann (2012) 14, and between emotions on the one hand, and passions and affections on the other, see Lasater (2017) 529–30.

3. Methodological Issues and Issues of Content

like an alien disturber of the peace, and thereby ultimately drives away the Holy Spirit. At the same time, emotions are localized on the inside: they ascend from the depths into the centre of the personality, which is designated by the biomorphic metaphor of the 'heart' (which was originally a metonymy). It is in this way that (sexual) desire (ἐπιθυμία) ascends within the Christian Hermas. It is only subsequently, in prayer, that he becomes conscious of his ἐπιθυμία. But it is also the 'angel of wickedness', who is above all ὀξύχολος and πικρός, who ascends into the heart and thus becomes recognizable (perceptible). It is possible that the biomorphic metaphor of the gall bladder (χολή) is activated (or remetaphorized) in ὀξυχολία: aggressive impulses ascend from the gall bladder into the heart.[206] In the *Shepherd of Hermas*, therefore, it is clear that emotions have their origin outside, and that they can also be present inside – less consciously.[207] Their dynamic autonomy is embodied in the spirits (that is, in mythical realities).[208] The human being stands between two contrary spirits who make it clear that this situation requires a decision. One has the freedom to choose which of the angels one will follow.[209] The Christian has already rejected the evil spirit in the baptismal *abrenuntiatio*, and he or she now has a second chance to repent.[210] This is the message of Hermas, which the *Shepherd of Hermas* communicates in the form of an apocalypse. Normally, it is the hidden secrets of heaven that are revealed in an apocalypse, but here it is the hidden emotional processes inside the human being that are revealed.

Unlike Philo or 4 Maccabees, Hermas' text displays very little concrete interaction with ancient *theories* about the emotions. This may be because Hermas, unlike Philo of Alexandria, belongs to the lower classes. He gives us an insight into the conceptual world of simple, poorly educated people,[211] of whom we otherwise have scarcely any literary traces. However, Hermas takes for granted notions of anger that were common in antiquity.

---

[206] Cf. Nemesius of Emesa (cited by Constantinou, this volume, p. 346): 'Anger is the boiling of the blood in the region of the heart [= Arist, *DA*] arising from an evaporation of bile (χολή) or from turbidity. That is why it is called bile (χολή) and also anger (χόλος)' (Nemesius, *On the Nature of Man* 20, trans. Sharples and Van der Eijk (2008) 141). Nemesius of Emesa was a bishop and physician in the late fourth century (Sharples and Van der Eijk (2008) 1; Crislip (2011) 298).

[207] This is because the negative emotions have sneaked unnoticed (back) into the Christian and dwell in him or her (again). This would presuppose an idea that is, however, attested only at a later date (the earliest evidence is probably Clement of Alexandria, *Exc.* 77.1: '[in baptism] we renounce the evil powers'): namely, that the evil spirits in the human being were expelled at baptism (exorcism); see Osiek (1999) 125. An original 'both/and' is improbable.

[208] See (taking up modern diction): Schenk (1886) 7.

[209] One could indeed understand Herm. *Mand.* 6.2.7b–8 (= 36.7b–8) in a determinist sense (the person is under the influence of the angel of wickedness or of the right angel), but according to Herm. *Mand.* 6.2.9 (= 36.9), the human being has the freedom to choose – to follow 'the angel of right but stay away from the angel of evil' (trans. Osiek (1999) 122–3).

[210] Μετάνοια is for most scholars 'the major theme or concern' in the *Shepherd of Hermas*; so Osiek (1999) 28; see also above.

[211] See Barnard (1966) 163.

Part II: Rhetorical Theory and Practice

4

Lend a Sympathetic Ear

Rhetorical Theory and Emotion
in Late Antique and Byzantine Homiletic*

Byron MacDougall

Introduction

When I speak about God, I experience trembling in both my mind and my tongue, and I pray that you also experience this same praiseworthy and blessed *pathos*.

Gregory of Nazianzus addressed this prayer to his audience in Constantinople during the Feast of Epiphany in early January 381.[1] How might this Cappadocian Father, who would become the most popular author in subsequent centuries in Byzantium, have imagined his audience as coming to share in his own *pathos*?[2] What would his extensive rhetorical training in Athens have had to say on the question?[3] The theme of this chapter is not *pathos* in rhetorical theory and Byzantine homiletic per se, nor rhetorical techniques for the production of *pathos* in general, but the sharing of *pathos* between the subject of discourse, the producer of discourse, and the audience, a dynamic which for the moment I shall call 'sympathy'. One might consider this a 'chain' of sympathy, adapting

---

* I would like to express my warm gratitude to Douglas Cairns and the members of the Emotions through Time network for inviting me to participate in this project, to audiences in Vienna and Nicosia for their feedback and collegiality, and to Matteo Zaccarini and the anonymous readers for their helpful suggestions. I am grateful as well to the Institut für Byzantinistik und Neogräzistik at the University of Vienna and Princeton University's Seeger Center for Hellenic Studies, where research for this chapter was made possible.

[1] Gregory of Nazianzus, *Or.* 39.11: φρίττων καὶ γλῶσσαν καὶ διάνοιαν, ὅταν περὶ Θεοῦ φθέγγωμαι, καὶ ὑμῖν ταὐτὸ τοῦτο συνευχόμενος τὸ ἐπαίνετον πάθος καὶ μακάριον. I use the text of Moreschini (1990). Unless otherwise noted, translations throughout are my own. For the date of this and related orations and Gregory's short-lived but influential tenure as bishop of the Nicene community in Constantinople, see Moreschini (1990) 16–22.

[2] For Gregory as the most popular author in Byzantium see Noret (1983); for the Byzantine reception in general see Papaioannou (2013) 56–63.

[3] For Gregory's rhetorical training in Athens and his teaching both there and upon returning home to Cappadocia, see Elm (2012) 150–3. For Gregory's lifelong engagement with teaching and literary circles, see McLynn (2006).

the famous metaphor from Plato's *Ion* of magnetized links of inspiration.[4] Here, however, it may be more helpful to think not of a chain but a triangle, any one of whose sides has the potential to feature more or less prominently in a given scenario. However artificial this image may be, for the purposes of the present discussion it has the conceptual advantage of making more explicit the direct link between the audience and the subject. That is, it helps remind us that contributing to the production of *pathos* in the audience is not only the discourse of the speaker, but also what the audience knows of and associates with the subject.

Another important preliminary point to tackle is one of terminology, namely the question of whether to use the English word 'sympathy' or one of the other terms that have previously been employed to describe the phenomena depicted in some of the passages we will examine. For example, one of the most famous ancient descriptions of the sharing of *pathos* between subject, performer, and audience, namely an account put in the mouth of Socrates in Book 10 of the *Republic* and which we will meet in greater detail later on, has been discussed in English in a variety of ways that not only employ the term 'sympathy' but also 'identification', 'emotional involvement', 'engagement', and 'fellow feeling'.[5] It is important to note that the word 'empathy' in this case is best avoided, as it is a term that is difficult to define and which in some of the scholarly literature is used in a variety of different ways.[6] Furthermore, concepts like emotional contagion or infection will not be effective here, since a theory that relies for its explanatory power solely on automatic, physiological processes necessarily elides the inherent role in these passages of the audience's cognitive faculties in the production of the shared emotion, whether through the recollection of events in a narrative or the formation of mental images.[7] In what follows, then, the English

---

[4] For the chain metaphor see Pl. *Ion* 532b–536b; for a discussion of the passage and how it resonates with other Platonic dialogues see especially Capra (2014) 94–7.

[5] *Resp.* 605d. See Heath (1987) 15, who cites 'identification' as a traditional interpretation and opts instead for emotional involvement or engagement; for 'sympathy' and 'fellow feeling' see Halliwell (2002) 78.

[6] For the slipperiness of the word 'empathy' and a discussion of the various ways it has been used, see Carroll (2011) 163–4 as well as Cairns (forthcoming) at note 29: 'But empathy is a very tricky concept. It has both scientific and popular senses, which overlap very imperfectly. And since there is no general agreement over the definition of either sense, but each is in its own ways both vague and elastic, the potential for equivocation is extremely high.'

[7] For the failures of the so-called 'infection model' to explain emotional reactions of audiences, see Carroll (2011) 167; for criticism of the invocation of 'emotional contagion' to explain how ancient theorists conceptualized the sharing of *pathos* between speaker and audience, see especially Cairns (forthcoming), commenting on Arist. *Rh.* 3, 1408a15–23 (quoted below): 'The listener does not simply catch, automatically or unconsciously, the emotion performed by the speaker. Rather, the listener makes an inference: the speaker creates a structured scenario which encompasses the eliciting conditions of an emotional script, and the listener may well be so disposed, on the basis of an evaluation of that scenario, to respond with the desired emotion.'

word 'sympathy' will be used as a natural placeholder to refer to the three-way sharing of *pathos* between subject, performer, and audience.

This chapter will begin by surveying select ancient theoretical discussions on the relationship between the performance of *pathos* and the subject of the text that is performed or experienced (Sections 1–3). Then, I will turn to examples of how this relationship plays out in practice in Late Antique and Byzantine homilies and festal orations (Sections 4–7). In the final section, I explore one example of the real role in religious life played by rhetorical sympathy, namely with respect to the Christian doctrine of *theōsis* or deification (Section 8).

4.1. Aristotle and Plato

One of the most famous relevant passages in the theoretical tradition features in Aristotle's *Rhetoric*. It should be noted that although he uses the related verb συνομοπαθεῖν, Aristotle himself does not use the Greek noun *sumpatheia* (συμπάθεια). As Fortenbaugh reminds us, the noun does not appear at all in the *Corpus Aristotelicum* except in the *Problems*.[8] The 'sympathy' that interests us is the *pathos* that members of an audience feel together with a speaker who speaks 'with *pathos*'.

πιθανοῖ δὲ τὸ πρᾶγμα καὶ ἡ οἰκεῖα λέξις· παραλογίζεταί τε γὰρ ἡ ψυχὴ ὡς ἀληθῶς λέγοντος, ὅτι ἐπὶ τοῖς τοιούτοις οὕτως ἔχουσιν, ὥστ᾽ οἴονται, εἰ καὶ μὴ οὕτως ἔχει ὡς ὁ λέγων, τὰ πράγματα οὕτως ἔχειν, καὶ συνομοπαθεῖ ὁ ἀκούων ἀεὶ τῷ παθητικῶς λέγοντι, κἂν μηθὲν λέγῃ.[9]

A fitting style also adds persuasiveness to the subject; for the soul of the listener reasons falsely, as if the speaker is speaking the truth, because under similar conditions they themselves are in such a state, so that they think, even if things are not as the speaker says, that they really are so, and the listener always experiences the same *pathos* as the speaker who speaks with *pathos*, even if the speaker says nothing.

The observation Aristotle makes here becomes a familiar motif: an audience experiences *pathos* together with a rhetor who speaks with *pathos* appropriate to the subject matter. Note also that the 'fitting style' and the *pathos* performed by the speaker do not suffice on their own to induce the audience to share in the feeling of *pathos*. As Douglas Cairns has emphasized, the inferential capacities of the audience play a critical role inasmuch as they conclude that the *pathos* performed by the speaker is consistent with the story he is selling.[10] Again, this is the third leg of the sympathetic triangle, which reminds us that in these passages we are not dealing with one-way emotional infection or contagion between the performer and the audience.

---

[8] Fortenbaugh (2017) 126 and 141, who notes furthermore that it is not attested at all in any Peripatetic source of the Hellenistic period.

[9] Arist. *Rh.* 3, 1408a19–23; I use here the edition of Dufour and Wartelle (1973).

[10] For discussion see especially Cairns (forthcoming).

124   *Byron MacDougall*

In the passage quoted above, Aristotle expands upon what for him and his audience is already an accepted truism. The sharing of *pathos* between subject, performer, and audience had been the object of some attention, having been prominently examined by Plato, especially with respect to poetry. The two most famous Platonic passages that bear on this theme have already been mentioned above, namely the magnetic chain of poetic inspiration in the *Ion* and Socrates' comments on poetic performance in Book 10 of the *Republic*. Plato's language in the latter explicitly addresses the sharing of *pathos*:

… ἀκροώμενοι Ὁμήρου ἢ ἄλλου τινὸς τῶν τραγῳδοποιῶν μιμουμένου τινὰ τῶν ἡρώων ἐν πένθει ὄντα καὶ μακρὰν ῥῆσιν ἀποτείνοντα ἐν τοῖς ὀδυρμοῖς ἢ καὶ ᾄδοντάς τε καὶ κοπτομένους, οἶσθ᾽ ὅτι χαίρομέν τε καὶ ἐνδόντες ἡμᾶς αὐτοὺς ἑπόμεθα συμπάσχοντες …[11]

… [the best of us] when listening to Homer or another of the tragedians imitating a hero in grief and delivering a long speech in their mourning or lamenting and striking themselves in the breast, you know that we enjoy giving ourselves over to it, and we follow along experiencing *pathos* together with him …

Note in particular how the audience is described here as συμπάσχοντες: they 'experience *pathos* together' with the performer.[12] Although this chapter focuses primarily on the communication of *pathos* in the post-Classical homiletic tradition, the diachronic presence of these themes in reflections on the theory of language and rhetoric deserves emphasis. The sympathy or shared *pathos* that is conceived of as existing potentially among subject, speaker, and audience becomes a principle that remains present in the rhetorical tradition, and that is available for adaptation as a recognizable motif. In what follows, we turn to a Greek writer living in the Augustan era to show the continuing interest in rhetorically shared *pathos* in subsequent theoretical discussions.

4.2. Dionysius of Halicarnassus

The treatise on the rhetorical style of Demosthenes by Dionysius of Halicarnassus offers a good example of how the sympathy between the subject of discourse, the producer of discourse, and the audience can be manipulated as a recognizable motif. Dionysius describes here the different feelings he experiences when reading the works of Isocrates and Demosthenes:

ἐγὼ γοῦν ὃ πρὸς ἀμφοτέρας πάσχω τὰς λέξεις ἐρῶ· οἴομαι δὲ κοινόν τι πάθος ἁπάντων ἐρεῖν καὶ οὐκ ἐμὸν ἴδιον μόνου. ὅταν μέν τινα τῶν Ἰσοκράτους ἀναγινώσκω λόγων, εἴτε

---

[11] 605c9–d4. I use the edition of Slings (2003).

[12] For this passage see for example Halliwell (2002) 78: 'Unlike the earlier model of self-likening [discussed in *Republic* 3], it makes room for at least a subconscious degree of mental dissociation between the hearer and the poetic character, positing "sympathy" or "fellow feeling" (*sumpaschein*, 605d4) where it is more appropriate to speak of identification in the case of book 3's arguments.' See also Halliwell (2002) 80–1 for the range of experiences that Plato seems to be evoking in the *Republic*.

4. Lend a Sympathetic Ear 125

τῶν πρὸς τὰ δικαστήρια καὶ τὰς ἐκκλησίας γεγραμμένων ἢ τῶν <πρὸς τὰς πανηγύρεις> τὰ ἤθη σπουδαῖος γίνομαι καὶ πολὺ τὸ εὐσταθὲς ἔχω τῆς γνώμης, ὥσπερ οἱ τῶν σπονδείων αὐλημάτων ἢ τῶν Δωρίων τε καὶ ἐναρμονίων μελῶν ἀκροώμενοι. ὅταν δὲ Δημοσθένους τινὰ λάβω λόγους, ἐνθουσιῶ τε καὶ δεῦρο κἀκεῖσε ἄγομαι, πάθος ἕτερον ἐξ ἑτέρου μεταλαμβάνων, ἀπιστῶν, ἀγωνιῶν, δεδιώς, καταφρονῶν, μισῶν, ἐλεῶν, εὐνοῶν, ὀργιζόμενος, φθονῶν, ἅπαντα τὰ πάθη μεταλαμβάνων, ὅσα κρατεῖν πέφυκεν ἀνθρωπίνης γνώμης ...

I will describe what I feel (πάσχω) with respect to both styles. I imagine though that I will be describing the common *pathos* of everyone and one that does not belong to me alone. When I read one of Isocrates' speeches, whether written for delivery in the courtroom or the assemblies or the festivals, I become earnest and virtuous in my character (τὰ ἤθη) and possess great stability and soundness in my thoughts, just like what happens when people listen to flute music in spondaic rhythm or Doric and harmonic melodies. When I read one of the orations of Demosthenes, I am inspired and led this way and that, receiving one *pathos* one another: I feel disbelief, I agonize, I am afraid, I feel contempt and hate, pity and goodwill, I grow angry, feel envy, taking up all the *pathē* that are accustomed to take control over human thought ...[13]

There are two main developments in the background for Dionysius here. One has to do with the Aristotelian division of the types of rhetorical proof into demonstration or *logos*, the performed character or *ēthos* of the speaker, and the emotion or *pathos* produced in the audience.[14] These three Aristotelian types of proof become more and more associated with a developing tripartite categorization of discursive style. In Cicero's system, for example, demonstration is characteristic of the low style whose familiar function is to *docere* or teach; *ēthos* is characteristic of the middle style whose function is variously to *delectare* (please) or *conciliare* (reconcile); and *pathos* is characteristic of the grand style, whose object is to *flectere* (bend) or *permovere* (move).[15]

Like Cicero, Dionysius also inherits the familiar tripartite division of rhetoric, and in his various treatises on rhetoric and rhetorical style he associates different styles with model orators from the Attic canon that exemplify those styles, though his chosen representatives as well as the classification of styles themselves vary from work to work.[16] In the passage quoted above, Dionysius selects Iso-

---

[13] Dion. Hal. *Dem.* 21.3–22.2; I use here the edition of Aujac (1988) 91–2.

[14] For the three types of rhetorical *pisteis* or 'proofs' see Arist. *Rh.* 1356a and Kennedy (1994) 20.

[15] For Cicero and Dionysius and the rhetorical styles characterized respectively by *ēthos* and *pathos* see especially Gill (1984) 155–6; for Cicero's tripartite division of style in the *Orator* 75–99 see Kennedy (1994) 156; for Cicero following Aristotle on the three modes of persuasion in his earlier treatise *On the Orator* see Kennedy (1994) 142–4: 'Most important is the discussion of the three functions of the orator, later known as the *officia oratoris*: to win over the audience's sympathy; to prove what is true, and to stir the emotions to the desired action ... this is Cicero's version of the three Aristotelian modes of persuasion: ethos, logos, and pathos' (142).

[16] See Kennedy (1994) 164–5. In his several treatises Dionysius presents various classifications of rhetorical style as well as various schemes of which Attic orator best models which rhetorical

crates as representative of the rhetorical style characterized by *ēthos*. We should note especially how Dionysius says that when reading Isocrates he 'become<s> earnest and virtuous in <his> character (τὰ ἤθη)'. Demosthenes on the other hand is representative of the grand style marked by *pathos*, and Dionysius accordingly says that when he reads Demosthenes he 'receive<s> one *pathos* after another'. In describing his own responses to reading Isocrates and Demosthenes, Dionysius allows the *ēthos* or rhetorical character presented by Isocrates to become the *ēthos* that he himself as reader experiences, just as the *pathos* performed by Demosthenes becomes the *pathos* that he himself feels in turn. Christopher Gill has called attention to the innovation of Dionysius here in extending '*ēthos* to an effect produced in the listener', as opposed to the rhetor's self-presentation.[17] This is particularly important for our purposes, as it means that Dionysius has *ēthos* work in the same way that *pathos* does, that is through sympathy: the audience experiences not just the *pathos* but also the *ēthos* performed by the speaker. Thus, some scholars have discussed later treatments of *ēthos* as if it were what I might call a decaf *pathos*, a spectrum of *pathē* in a softer colour palette, one comprising feelings less intense than fear, contempt, hate, pity, or anger.[18] I am interested in the importance of this step, because it seems to allow the idea of rhetorically shared *pathos* to be extended to a much wider range of what we would call emotions. An *ēthos* is something that is experienced temporarily, something that happens to the audience, so that it can function, in rhetorical theory at least, like *pathos*.

In developing this point, it will be helpful to adduce here a pair of definitions from an important text in the Byzantine rhetorical tradition, the commentary by John of Sardis (ninth century) on the *Progymnasmata* of Aphthonius.[19] Though John himself belongs to a later period, the material he has gathered for his commentary reflects the older tradition, and the definitions he gives offer a representative take on the difference between *pathos* and *ēthos*:[20]

πάθος δέ ἐστι πρόσκαιρος κατάστασις ψυχῆς σφοδροτέραν ὁρμὴν ἢ ἀφορμὴν κινοῦσα. καὶ ἄλλως· πάθος ἐστὶ **ψυχῆς διάθεσις** ἀπό τινος συμβαίνοντος κινουμένη, οἶον ὀργή, λύπη, οἶκτος, ἔρως καὶ τὰ τοιαῦτα. (206.26–207.3)

Pathos is a temporary state of the soul that stirs up a more intense urge either towards or against something. And it has also been defined otherwise: *pathos* is a *disposition of the*

---

style or virtue; for a survey of the accounts presented in the individual essays see Aujac (1988) 24–33.

[17] Gill (1984) 158.

[18] This aspect of *ēthos* has been much discussed in work on Cicero. See for example Solmsen (1941) 179, who notes that Ciceronian *ēthos* 'denotes the *leniores affectus*, a lesser degree of *pathos*'; see also Kennedy (1994) 144: 'Cicero regards ethos as consisting in presentation of the gentler emotions ... it conciliates and charms the audience and is essentially good natured, a lower level of dramatic intensity than the raging fire of pathos ...'.

[19] I cite the edition of Rabe (1927).

[20] For John's method as a commentator and a philologist see Alpers (2013).

soul, a disposition that has been stirred up by something that has happened, for example anger, grief, pity, desire, and the like.

ἦθος δὲ ἐνταῦθα τὴν τῆς ψυχῆς διάθεσιν ὀνομάζουσιν ... ἦθος γάρ ἐστι ποιότης ψυχῆς ἀπεσκιρρωμένη καὶ δυσαπόβλητος, τουτέστι παγία καὶ εἰς ἕξιν ἐλθοῦσα. (200.18)

By *ēthos* they mean here the *disposition of the soul* ... For *ēthos* is a quality of the soul that has become hardened and difficult to get rid of, that is it is set and has come to be a state.

The phrases highlighted above demonstrate an important point: both *ēthos* and *pathos* are conceptualized as dispositions of the soul, only that the former is a disposition of a longer duration, a disposition that is approaching what we would call a trait. Thus, *ēthos* differs from *pathos* in that the latter is temporary whereas the former is stable, but in passages like Dionysius' experience of the *ēthos* of Isocrates, the whole point is that Dionysius experiences that particular disposition *temporarily*. In other words, Isocrates himself might have presented an unchanging *ēthos*, but a reader like Dionysius is induced by Isocrates' presentation of his *ēthos* to experience a temporary feeling that recalls Isocrates' *ēthos* in response. When Dionysius describes how he feels 'earnest' in character when reading Isocrates, like someone listening to music with spondaic rhythms or in the Doric mode, that feeling of solemnity and purposefulness behaves as if it were a *pathos*, i.e., a temporary state or disposition of the soul. Moreover, it is something that we might recognize as an emotion.

The theoretical themes that we have surveyed so far – including both the rhetorical communication of *pathos* and an expanded understanding of *ēthos* to include emotional effects produced in the audience – will continue to feature prominently as we turn to the Christian tradition and the theoretical pronouncements of a practising homilist, Gregory of Nazianzus. A noted student of the Classical rhetorical tradition in general as well as a keen reader of Dionysius of Halicarnassus in particular, Gregory will describe his reading-induced responses in ways that closely recall Dionysius' account of his own emotional responses to the *pathos* of Demosthenes and the *ēthos* of Isocrates. As an authoritative cultural figure for the subsequent tradition, Gregory will shape how Byzantine rhetors understand rhetorical sympathy.

4.3. Gregory of Nazianzus reading Basil and the Book of Lamentations

In the following passages Gregory describes his own experiences as a reader of texts, in the first case those of his friend and fellow Cappadocian, Basil the Great, and in the second the Book of Lamentations from the Septuagint, a text traditionally attributed to the Prophet Jeremiah. Papaioannou has shown how in these passages we find a Christian analogue to Dionysius describing his reaction to reading Demosthenes:[21]

---

[21] See Papaioannou (2006).

128   *Byron MacDougall*

ὅταν ἀθλητῶν ἐγκωμίοις προσομιλήσω, περιφρονῶ τὸ σῶμα καὶ σύνειμι τοῖς ἐπαινουμένοις καὶ πρὸς τὴν ἄθλησιν διεγείρομαι. ὅταν ἠθικοῖς λόγοις καὶ πρακτικοῖς, καθαίρομαι
ψυχὴν καὶ σῶμα, καὶ ναὸς Θεοῦ γίνομαι δεκτικός, καὶ ὄργανον κρουόμενον Πνεύματι καὶ
θείας ὑμνῳδὸν δόξης τε καὶ δυνάμεως· τούτῳ μεθαρμόζομαι καὶ ῥυθμίζομαι καὶ ἄλλος ἐξ
ἄλλου γίνομαι, τὴν θείαν ἀλλοίωσιν ἀλλοιούμενος.[22]

Whenever I read his encomia of the martyrs, I despise my body and join together with
those praised and am roused to the contest. When I read his ethical and ascetic treatises,
I am purified in soul and body, and I become a temple that receives God, and an instrument played by the Spirit, singing hymns of divine glory and power. Through him I
am modulated in tune and rhythm, and from one person I become another, undergoing
the divine change.

We find a similar dynamic at work in Gregory's account of his experience reading the Book of Lamentations:[23]

ἐγὼ γοῦν ὁσάκις ἂν ταύτην ἀναλάβω τὴν Βίβλον καὶ τοῖς θρηνοῖς συγγένωμαι ... ἐγκό-
πτομαι τὴν φωνὴν καὶ συγχέομαι δάκρυσι, καὶ οἷον ὑπ᾽ ὄψιν μοι τὸ πάθος ἔρχεται καὶ
συνθρήνω τῷ θρηνήσαντι ...

As for me, whenever I take up this book and join in converse with the Lamentations ...
my voice breaks, and I dissolve in tears, and it is as if what they are suffering comes to my
sight, and I lament together with the one who made the lament ...

Part of Gregory's formulation here – 'it is as if what they are suffering comes
to my sight' (ὑπ᾽ ὄψιν μοι τὸ πάθος ἔρχεται) – opens a window on to a set of
themes related to theoretical discussions of how language can turn audiences
into spectators and make them see the things described. These include *enargeia*,
the quality of vividness in language; the faculty of *phantasia*, which within this
discourse refers to the cognitive faculty that produces mental images; and *ekphrasis*, a rhetorical exercise as well as any kind of descriptive language in general
that brings what is depicted 'to the sight' of the audience.[24] It is characteristic
of the dense texture of Gregory's language that he weaves together here the
motifs of vivid, 'enargetic' language and the discourse of rhetorical sympathy.
Papaioannou has emphasized the close relationship between these passages and
Dionysius' discussion of Demosthenes, and indeed of the strong influence of
Dionysius on Gregory in general, who in one of his letters refers by name to the
former's essay on the style of Lysias.[25] Gregory functions as a key node in the
transmission of ideas regarding the role of *pathos* in rhetoric from theorists like
Dionysius to the subsequent Byzantine tradition.

---

[22] *Or.* 43.67. I cite here the edition of Bernardi (1992).

[23] *Or.* 6.18. I cite here the edition of Calvet-Sebasti (1995).

[24] The bibliography on these interrelated themes is extensive; for *enargeia* in Byzantine
rhetorical culture see Papaioannou (2011); for *phantasia* and the making of mental images in
Gregory and the other Church Fathers see Pizzone (2011); for *ekphrasis*, the *progymnasmata*,
and the production of language characterized by *enargeia* see especially Webb (2009).

[25] Papaioannou (2006) 68–70. For Gregory citing the essay on Lysias see *Ep.* 180 to Eudoxius.

4. Lend a Sympathetic Ear
129

For a good demonstration of Gregory's role in transmitting the discourse of rhetorical sympathy to Byzantium, we can turn to a passage in the eleventh-century polymath Michael Psellos that functions, to refer again to the *Ion*'s metaphor, as a third link in a magnetic chain of *literary* inspiration that stretches from Dionysius on Demosthenes to Gregory on Basil to Psellos on Gregory himself. The passage in question is an excerpt from Psellos' essay on Gregory's rhetorical style, in which he describes his experience reading Gregory. Thus, it is a counterpart to Gregory's own assessment of Basil's texts, with Psellos here playing the role of Gregory and Gregory that of Basil.[26] Psellos characterizes Gregory as follows:

τὸν ἀκροάτην καταπλήττων, καὶ ποτὲ μὲν θαυμάζειν ποιῶν, ποτὲ δὲ κροτεῖν καὶ ἐν ῥυθ-μῷ χορείαν ἀνελίττειν καὶ συμπεπονθέναι τοῖς πράγμασιν.

Gregory astonishes his audience, sometimes making them wonder, sometimes making them applaud and dance in rhythm and feel *pathos* together with the subject matter.

According to Psellos, Gregory's language makes his audience 'feel *pathos* together' with the subject matter of his discourse. We should take note of the word he uses here, *sumpeponthenai* (συμπεπονθέναι), from the verb *sumpaschein* (συμπάσχειν). This is a word we have seen already, in fact in the famous passage from Book 10 of Plato's *Republic*. There Socrates describes how when listening to a performance in poetry of a hero experiencing great *pathos*, we follow along experiencing *pathos* – *sumpaschontes* (συμπάσχοντες) – with the performer who is channelling the emotion of the hero from Homer or tragedy.[27] Emphasized both here in Psellos and in the *Republic* is that leg of the sympathetic triangle between the audience and the subject, that of the audience 'experiencing something together with the subject'. Gregory himself recedes into the background, like the Homeric rhapsode who mediates *pathos* between the subject of the poem and the audience. We will find this to be a recurring dynamic when we turn to examples from the homiletic tradition.

4.4. *Gregory of Nazianzus,* On the Holy Lights

The preceding selections from the Ancient, Late Antique, and Byzantine periods offer a glimpse of how rhetorical sympathy was conceptualized in theoretical discussions, especially with respect to how readers responded to their texts. In the passages that follow, we turn to how this principle played out in practice and how it was applied in homilies that were experienced not only by readers but

---

[26] Michael Psellos, *Discourse Improvised to the Bestarches Pothos* 41, using the text of Levy (1912). Papaioannou has recently published an English translation and discussion of this essay by Psellos, both of which have been very useful to me; see Barber and Papaioannou (2017) 118–48.

[27] See above n. 12.

130   *Byron MacDougall*

also by liturgical audiences. We will continue to see 'readers responding to texts', in the sense that the homilists (and, in one case, the depiction of a homilist) will frequently be describing and performing their reactions to the narrative or subject of the liturgical occasion in question. However, they will be performing those emotionally inflected responses before live liturgical audiences, who in turn can be presented as reacting both to the liturgical occasion and to the homilist's performance. Thus, in what follows we will be able to observe what connections can be drawn between the theoretical discussions sketched above in outline and fundamental concerns of the Byzantine homiletic tradition.

Our first example is a representative passage from the festal orations of Gregory of Nazianzus, which were delivered, in something approximating the state in which they have been transmitted, during Gregory's tenure as bishop of the Nicene community in Constantinople from 379 to the spring of 381.[28] The oration *On the Holy Lights* (εἰς τὰ Φῶτα) celebrates Epiphany, Christ's baptism, and expounds upon the significance of baptism for the Christian community. In the following passage, Gregory begins by referring to the oration he had given a few days before (*Or.* 38) for the Nativity:

τῇ μὲν οὖν γεννήσει τὰ εἰκότα προεορτάσαμεν, ἐγώ τε ὁ τῆς ἑορτῆς ἔξαρχος, καὶ ὑμεῖς, καὶ πᾶν ὅσον ἐγκόσμιόν τε καὶ ὑπερκόσμιον. μετὰ ἀστέρος ἐδράμομεν, καὶ μετὰ Μάγων προσεκυνήσαμεν, μετὰ ποιμένων περιελλάμφθημεν, καὶ μετὰ ἀγγέλων ἐδοξάσαμεν, μετὰ Συμεὼν ἐνηγκαλισάμεθα, καὶ μετὰ Ἄννης ἀνθωμολογησάμεθα, τῆς γεραιᾶς καὶ σώφρονος ... νυνὶ δὲ πρᾶξις ἄλλη Χριστοῦ, καὶ ἄλλο μυστήριον. οὐ δύναμαι κατέχειν τὴν ἡδονήν, ἔνθεος γίνομαι, μικροῦ καί, ὡς Ἰωάννης, εὐαγγελίζομαι, εἰ καὶ μὴ πρόδρομος, ἀλλ' ἀπὸ τῆς ἐρημίας. Χριστὸς φωτίζεται, συναναστράψωμεν· Χριστὸς βαπτίζεται, συγκατέλθωμεν, ἵνα καὶ συνανέλθωμεν.[29]

And so we celebrated in advance in a fitting fashion for His birth, myself as leader of the festival, together with you and everything of this world and above it. We ran with the star, we worshipped with the Magi, and we were illuminated with the shepherds, and we proclaimed His glory with the angels, with Simeon we embraced him, with Anna, the aged and chaste, we confessed ... Now another deed of Christ, and another mystery. I cannot contain my pleasure, and I become filled with God, and I all but proclaim the Gospel, like John – if I am not a forerunner, I am still from the desert – Christ is illuminated, let us shine out together with him; Christ is baptized, let us descend together with him, so that we may also ascend together with him.

Passages like this deservedly play an important role in scholarly discussions of *anamnēsis* or 'remembrance' through the liturgy of events in Christ's life and the salvation narrative.[30] Here our focus is instead on how Gregory's performance of this material – or the experience of his audience and readership – may have been conceptualized when read against the background of the rhetorical tradition.

---

[28] See above n. 1.
[29] *Or.* 39.14, citing the edition of Moreschini (1990).
[30] See for example Harrison (2006).

Gregory alludes first to the main events in the Nativity narrative that featured during the previous festival: the Magi following the Star of Bethlehem, the heavenly host appearing to the shepherds keeping watch over their flocks by night, and the presentation of Jesus in the temple where he is received by Simeon and the prophetess Anna (Luke 2:23–35) – and we would note that the audience themselves are expected to fill in the gaps in Gregory's allusive narrative through their own familiarity with the biblical texts. The festival at hand is to celebrate John's baptism of Jesus on the banks of the Jordan, and just as Gregory and his audience are imagined as having participated together with the subjects of the previous celebration (with the Magi, the Shepherds, etc.), so now they are to experience together with Christ the events of his baptism – they are to shine out together, descend together, and rise up together with him (συναναστράψω-μεν, συγκατέλθωμεν, συνανέλθωμεν). We should compare Gregory's self-presentation of how he reacts to the subjects of the Epiphany narrative here, where he 'cannot contain his pleasure' and 'becomes filled with God' (οὐ δύναμαι κα-τέχειν τὴν ἡδονήν, ἔνθεος γίνομαι) with how he reacts to the various subjects of Basil's texts in *Or.* 43 and 'becomes a temple of God' (ναὸς Θεοῦ γίνομαι). We should further compare how Gregory uses the phrase ἔνθεος γίνομαι ('I become filled with God') to describe his reaction to the Epiphany narrative with the close etymological parallel in the term 'enthusiasm' (ἐνθουσιῶ) in Dionysius' account of his experience reading Demosthenes. Finally, note how in the oration on the Holy Lights Gregory takes on the persona of John ('I all but proclaim the Gospel, like John') just as he assimilates himself to the persona of Jeremiah in *Or.* 6 when he describes his experiences reading the Book of Lamentations.[31] Gregory presents himself as participating in the *pathos* experienced by the subjects of his orations, and presents his audience as receiving that *pathos* – we might say he primes his audience to receive that *pathos* – in turn through him. His treatment of rhetorical sympathy in passages from his festal homilies such as the one quoted above offers a template for subsequent Byzantine homilists to imitate, and we will observe the widespread adaptation of that template in the passages that follow.

4.5. Pseudo-Dionysius the Areopagite

We turn now not to a homilist proper but to the literary depiction of a homilist in action. The treatise *On Divine Names* by Pseudo-Dionysius the Areopagite includes a famous scene in which the narrator 'Dionysius', the assumed persona of the unknown author, recounts an occasion when he, his teacher, and the apostles, including Peter and James, 'gathered at the spectacle of the life-giving body, the vessel of God.' The scene is one of a few passages of the Dionysian corpus that contribute to the development of the author's fictional biblical persona as

---

[31] See above n. 23.

132   *Byron MacDougall*

Dionysius the Areopagite, who appears in Acts 17:34 during Paul's visit to Athens and becomes one of his most celebrated converts. The scene in *On Divine Names* belongs to an extended passage in praise of 'Dionysius'' teacher, a (likewise fictional) character named Hierotheus.

Scholarship on this scene is dominated by the question of whether the scene refers to the Dormition of Mary – already in the mid-sixth century this interpretation was floated, and it remains widely accepted today[32] – or if it instead depicts the celebration of the Eucharist,[33] or even if it is one of several proposed literary ciphers in which the characters stand in for groups of historical individuals in various different Christian[34] or pagan[35] contexts. I agree that the passage depicts the Dormition, but whether this is the Dormition itself or some other scenario has no bearing on the main argument that follows: to understand the character of Hierotheus, the teacher of Dionysius, we need to turn to rhetorical passages like the ones we have covered so far to see how the scene is informed by the image of a rhetor experiencing 'sympathy' with the subject of his own discourse. Dionysius presents the scene as follows:

ἐπεὶ καὶ παρ' αὐτοῖς τοῖς θεολήπτοις ἡμῶν ἱεράρχαις, ἡνίκα καὶ ἡμεῖς, ὡς οἶσθα, καὶ αὐτὸς καὶ πολλοὶ τῶν ἱερῶν ἡμῶν ἀδελφῶν ἐπὶ τὴν θέαν τοῦ ζωαρχικοῦ καὶ θεοδόχου σώματος συνεληλύθαμεν, παρῆν δὲ καὶ ὁ ἀδελφόθεος Ἰάκωβος καὶ Πέτρος, ἡ κορυφαία καὶ πρεσβυτάτη τῶν θεολόγων ἀκρότης, εἶτα ἐδόκει μετὰ τὴν θέαν ὑμνῆσαι τοὺς ἱεράρχας ἅπαντας, ὡς ἕκαστος ἦν ἱκανός, τὴν ἀπειροδύναμον ἀγαθότητα τῆς θεαρχικῆς ἀσθενείας, πάντων ἐκράτει μετὰ τοὺς θεολόγους, ὡς οἶσθα, τῶν ἄλλων ἱερομυστῶν **ὅλος ἐκδημῶν, ὅλος ἐξιστάμενος ἑαυτοῦ καὶ τὴν πρὸς τὰ ὑμνούμενα κοινωνίαν πάσχων** καὶ πρὸς πάντων, ὧν ἠκούετο καὶ ἑωρᾶτο καὶ ἐγιγνώσκετο καὶ οὐκ ἐγιγνώσκετο, θεόληπτος εἶναι καὶ θεῖος ὑμνολόγος κρινόμενος.[36]

When both [Hierotheus] and I, as you know, and many of our holy brothers assembled together at the spectacle of the life-beginning and God-receiving body, and when James the brother of God as well as Peter, the pinnacle and most senior eminence of the theologians, were also present among our divinely inspired hierarchs themselves, at that time it was decided that after the spectacle all the hierarchs would hymn, each as he was able, the boundless goodness of the thearchic meekness; after the theologians Hierotheus

---

[32] See Rorem and Lamoreaux (1998) 199–200 (on a sixth-century scholion by John of Scythopolis on the phrase τοῦ ζωαρχικοῦ that tentatively identifies it with the Virgin). An understanding of this scene as referring to the Dormition is the standard interpretation, especially in the Orthodox tradition; see for example Golitzin (2013) 34. For the possible significance of this scene as one of the early witnesses to the Dormition tradition, see Shoemaker (2003) 29–30, who notes tentatively that the scene 'appears to be the Virgin's Dormition' (29).

[33] See Shoemaker (2003) 29 for discussion on how the Assumptionist scholar Martin Jugie argued that the scene and in particular the phrase θεοδόχου σώματος refer not to the Virgin but to the Eucharist; see Jugie (1944) 99–101.

[34] For the scene as a cipher for the Council of Chalcedon see Perczel (2009) 29; (2012); for another interpretation of the scene as a Christian cipher but of an opposing Christological bent see Lourié (2010).

[35] See for example Mazzucchi (2006) and Lankila (2017).

[36] *On Divine Names* 3.2, 141.4–14, citing the edition of Suchla (1990).

surpassed, as you know, all the other holy initiates, *sojourning abroad with his whole being, and standing completely outside of himself and experiencing association with the things he was praising*, and he was judged by everyone who heard and saw and knew him – or did not know him – as inspired by God and a divine author of hymns.

Hierotheus – a fascinating character in his own right who even inspired 'fan fiction' in Syriac[37] – distinguishes himself 'at the sight of the life-giving and god-receiving body', i.e. the Dormition of the Virgin itself. As the spectators begin to hymn 'the boundless goodness of the thearchic meekness', Dionysius notes that his teacher Hierotheus surpassed them all, 'going abroad with his whole being, and standing completely outside of himself and experiencing association with the things he was praising'.

Several scholars associate Hierotheus' activity with the celebration of the Eucharist, claiming for example that Hierotheus 'has an extraordinary experience, often characterized as "mystical" but in fact identifiable as liturgical', and specifically associating the phrase 'experiencing communion with the things praised' with overtly Eucharistic language used elsewhere by Pseudo-Dionysius.[38] It is true that the word *koinōnia* (κοινωνία) can certainly refer to the Eucharist, and in fact does so in other passages in the Dionysian corpus. However, unlike the instances in the *Ecclesiastical Hierarchy*, which clearly refer to a priest handling the materials of the Eucharist and sharing them with the other celebrants, there is no mention here of Hierotheus reacting to anything other than his own words. His behaviour here is coloured not by Eucharistic but by rhetorical considerations. Hierotheus gives a rhetorical performance of *theōria*, that is a contemplation of the spectacle at hand and its meaning, and in experiencing *pathos* in common with what he is praising he is adhering to principles of rhetorical theory with a long history behind them. When Hierotheus 'experienc[es] association with the things he was praising' (τὴν πρὸς τὰ ὑμνούμενα κοινωνίαν πάσχων), we should not imagine *communion* with the Eucharist, but the *communication* of rhetorically induced *pathos*.

This is the cultural background against which we should read Dionysius' description of his master's inspired ecstasy while performing a hymn. The models for Hierotheus 'experiencing association with the things he was praising' are figures like Gregory of Nazianzus channelling the Lamentations of Jeremiah,

---

[37] For the character of Hierotheus see Sheldon-Williams (1966). One of the earliest Syriac witnesses to the Dionysian corpus is, as Perczel (2009) 27 describes, 'a baffling treatise on mystical theology allegedly authored by Dionysius' own mysterious teacher', a sixth-century theological text known as the 'Book of Holy Hierotheus'. Finally, because one of the fictional treatises that the narrator Dionysius attributes to his teacher is called the *Elements of Theology*, the possibility of a connection or even identification with Proclus of Athens himself has remained a temptation; see Rorem (1993) 143.

[38] Luibhead and Rorem (1987) 70 n. 131. For the same interpretation see also Stang (2012) 163 n. 67.

that is rhetors as they depict themselves as mediators of *pathos*. Hierotheus becomes 'inspired', and he experiences *pathos* in accordance with the subjects of the oration he performs: τὴν πρὸς τὰ ὑμνούμενα κοινωνίαν πάσχων. As I hope to show by comparing the passage from *On Divine Names* with a later Byzantine text that engages closely with Hierotheus, it is the figure of the 'sympathetic' reader and rhetor that we should see in the teacher of Dionysius as he performs hymns and 'experiences association with the things he praises'.

4.6. Andrew of Crete

Although the concerns of the rhetorical tradition that lie behind the figure of Hierotheus have largely been obscured by interest in this scene's alleged Eucharistic flavour, this has not always been the case. In fact, I would argue that one of the earlier chapters in the Byzantine reception of Pseudo-Dionysius identifies and engages with precisely the theme of rhetorical sympathy that I have tried to show is at work in the scene from *On Divine Names*. We turn now to the first of three homilies by Andrew of Crete (*ca.* 650–725) on the Dormition of Mary, which were presumably delivered in sequence over the course of a single festal celebration.[39] Together they represent one of the most focused and sustained Byzantine literary reactions to Dionysius, as the entire trilogy uses the passage quoted above from *On Divine Names* as a text for discussion. In the first homily Andrew introduces the figure of Dionysius himself and presents our passage as an account of the Dormition; in the second homily he quotes the passage in its entirety and then provides a commentary on the meaning of the passage and the scene that is being described; and in the third homily he attempts to replicate the sort of hymn that Hierotheus delivered.[40] The following passage comes from the first homily, in which Andrew confronts the difficulty of describing the Dormition scene:[41]

καὶ τίς ἂν τῶν ἐκεῖσε τελεσθέντων τοὺς λόγους διερμηνεύσειε; τίς κατ᾽ ἀξίαν τῷ μυστηρίῳ **συνεπαρθείη**; τίς πτερώσει τὸν νοῦν ὡς **συναναπτῆναι** τῷ θαύματι, καὶ **τὴν πρὸς αὐτὸ παθεῖν κοινωνίαν**;

---

[39] For summaries of Andrew's life and works, see Daley (1998) 15–18, with translation of Andrew's homilies on the Dormition at pp. 103–52. For background on Andrew see also Cunningham (1998).

[40] We might note here that for Andrew and his audience, this part of the oration, which consists of a speech put in the mouth of Hierotheus himself, in effect functions like a particular exercise in the rhetorical curriculum known as the *ēthopoiia*. In this exercise, the writer composes a speech that attempts to reproduce the *ēthos* or character of a given person in a given scenario. The speech that Andrew puts in the mouth of Hierotheus is equivalent to an *ēthopoiia* composed in response to the prompt, 'what would Hierotheus have said on seeing the Dormition of the Mother of God?' For *ēthopoiia* as well as the other rhetorical exercises or *progymnasmata* of the rhetorical curriculum see Kennedy (2003).

[41] Andrew of Crete, *On the Dormition of Mary* 1 (*PG* 97.1088B). The homily is erroneously printed second in the Migne edition.

4. Lend a Sympathetic Ear

And who could expound the words of what was there brought to accomplishment? Who could be *raised on high together* in fitting accordance with the mystery? Who could give wings to their mind to *soar up together* with the miracle, and *experience the association* with it?

For Andrew, the ideal rhetor is capable of 'experiencing association' (τὴν πρὸς αὐτὸ παθεῖν κοινωνίαν) with his awe-inspiring subject; he is 'raised up together with the mystery' and 'soars together with the miracle' (τῷ μυστηρίῳ συνεπαρθείη, συναναπτῆναι τῷ θαύματι). To be compared with these phrases are the other examples we have surveyed of a performer or reader experiencing *pathos* together with the subject of the discourse: Gregory's phrase σύνειμι τοῖς ἐπαινουμένοις on 'feeling present together' with the subjects of Basil's encomia; Gregory's similar expression συνθρήνω τῷ θρηνήσαντι on 'lamenting together' with the author of Lamentations; and Psellos 'feeling *pathos* together' with Gregory's subject matter (συμπεπονθέναι τοῖς πράγμασιν). Andrew's description of how the model rhetor should 'experience association with the miracle' he is describing (τὴν πρὸς αὐτὸ παθεῖν κοινωνίαν) is drawn from Dionysius' own description of how Hierotheus 'experienc[ed] association with the things he was praising' (τὴν πρὸς τὰ ὑμνούμενα κοινωνίαν πάσχων). In other words, both Andrew of Crete and Pseudo-Dionysius conceive of their model rhetor as communicating *pathos* via sympathy that the rhetor himself experiences with his own subject.

4.7. Photius

Having seen the role played by rhetorical sympathy in the homilies of Gregory and Andrew as well as in the depiction of Hierotheus by Pseudo-Dionysius, we will encounter much that is familiar in the following passage from the Palm Sunday homily of Patriarch Photius:

> ὅτε, τῶν παίδων ὡσαννὰ ἐν τοῖς ὑψίστοις ἀναβοώντων, ἡ ἐκκλησία σαλπίσει καὶ τῆς λαμπρᾶς ἐκείνης καὶ θεοπρεπεστάτης φωνῆς ταῖς ἀκοαῖς τὸν ἦχον ἑλκύσω, **μετάρσιος ὅλος γίνομαι τῇ προθυμίᾳ** (δεινὸν γὰρ ἡ χαρὰ χρῆμα καινοποιῆσαι τὴν φύσιν καὶ πόθος οὐκ οἶδε μένειν καιροῦ προσκαλοῦντος) καὶ λογισμῶν θειοτέρων θειοτέρῳ δρόμῳ περιέρχομαι τὴν Βηθανίαν καὶ χεῖρας κροτῶ [καὶ] χορεύων καὶ **συναγελάζομαι** σκιρτῶν τοῖς νηπίοις, τὸν ἐπινίκιον ὕμνον **συγκαταρτιζόμενος** αὐτοῖς τῷ δεσπότῃ, ὡσαννὰ ἐν τοῖς ὑψίστοις, εὐλογημένος ὁ ἐρχόμενος ἐν ὀνόματι Κυρίου.[42]

> When, as the children cry out, 'Hosanna in the highest', the Church sounds her clarion call, and I draw into my ears that splendid and most God-becoming sound, *I am altogether transported with zeal*, (for joy is a mighty thing to renew nature, and desire knows not how to wait when time bids); and I go about Bethany in the course of godly thought, and I clap my hands and dance, and *leaping I join the troop of infants*, and *fashion with them* a victorious anthem for the Lord: 'Hosanna in the highest. Blessed is he that cometh in the name of the Lord.'[43]

---

[42] Photius, *Hom.* 8.1 in the edition of Laourdas (1959).
[43] For the translation I use here Mango (1958).

136   *Byron MacDougall*

Again, much of Photius' language will by now sound familiar. As he recounts Christ's entry into Jerusalem on Palm Sunday, Photius is compelled to clap and dance (κροτῶ ... χορεύων), just as we saw that earlier Psellos was brought to clap and dance on reading Gregory (κροτεῖν καὶ ἐν ῥυθμῷ χορείαν ἀνελίττειν); Photius describes his own ecstasy (μετάρσιος ὅλος γίνομαι) in a way that recalls the ecstasy experienced by Hierotheus in his hymn performance (ὅλος ἐκδημῶν, ὅλος ἐξιστάμενος ἑαυτοῦ). Finally, Photius presents himself as joining together with the subjects of the Palm Sunday narrative in celebrating Christ's entry into Jerusalem, and we should again associate this rhetorical move with previous passages. Thus, we can compare how Photius assimilates himself to the characters of his narrative, joyfully 'joining together with the troop of infants' and 'fashioning with them' a garland of triumphal song (συναγελάζομαι, συγκαταρτιζόμενος), with our earlier examples of how rhetor and audience participate in the *pathos* of an oration's subjects. These include not only Gregory on reading Basil and Lamentations, and Psellos on reading Gregory, but also Gregory describing what he and his audience are to do when celebrating Epiphany and the Baptism of Christ: 'let us shine out together with him, let us descend together with him, let us rise up together with him' (συναναστράψωμεν, συγκατέλθωμεν, συνανέλθωμεν). The dynamic of rhetorical sympathy is presented as enabling homilist and audience to participate emotionally in key moments of the salvation narrative. Moreover, since certain emotions, such as fear and awe, feature prominently in theological discussions of the soul's progress towards God, rhetorical sympathy is conceived of as playing an active role in crucial aspects of religious life, as we shall see in what follows.

4.8. Pathos, *mimēsis,* and theōsis

Photius' performance of emotional assimilation to his subjects presents an opportunity to draw connections between discourses of rhetorically induced sympathy, *mimēsis*, and the Christian doctrine of *theōsis*, or deification. Keeping in mind the dynamic of sympathy and assimilation we saw in Photius and other passages, I would like to return to Gregory of Nazianzus, this time to his first oration on Easter:[44]

χθὲς συνεσταυρούμην Χριστῷ, σήμερον συνδοξάζομαι· χθὲς συνενεκρούμην, συζωο-
ποιοῦμαι σήμερον· χθὲς συνεθαπτόμην, σήμερον συνεγείρομαι ... γενώμεθα ὡς Χριστὸς,
ἐπεὶ καὶ Χριστὸς ὡς ἡμεῖς· γενώμεθα θεοὶ δι' αὐτὸν, ἐπειδὴ κάκεῖνος δι' ἡμᾶς ἄνθρωπος.

Yesterday I was being crucified together with Christ, today I am glorified with Him. Yesterday I was made dead with Him, today I am made alive. Yesterday I was buried with him, today I rise with Him ... Let us become like Christ, since Christ became like us. Let us become gods on his account, since he became human on ours.

---

[44] *Or.* 1.4–5, citing the edition of Bernardi (1978).

4. Lend a Sympathetic Ear

Harrison has shown how the concept of *mimēsis* that is at work in this passage 'permeates' the structures and thought patterns of early Christianity, from baptism to the Eucharist to the emulation of saintly exemplars.[45] Gregory's familiar exhortation to his audience to imitate Christ – to 'become like Christ' – is followed by the more arresting formulation, 'Let us become gods' (γενώμεθα θεοί). Here Gregory is alluding to the doctrine of deification, or *theōsis*, a word which, as Maslov points out, Gregory was the first Christian writer to employ.[46] The doctrine has a rich later history in the Orthodox tradition, and it is an idea central to the thought of Gregory, who for example characteristically states in his oration on the Holy Lights that we 'have been made ... for the *mimēsis* of God, as far as is attainable': πεποιημένους ... εἰς θεοῦ μίμησιν, ὅσον ἐφικτόν (*Or.* 39.7). Gregory's formula – especially the phrase 'as far as is attainable' – puts us in mind of the famous tag from Plato's *Theaetetus* on the philosopher's flight from the world, which eventually became widely known throughout both the Classical and the Christian traditions as one of the definitions of philosophy: it is the 'assimilation to God, as much as possible' (ὁμοίωσις θεῷ κατὰ τὸ δυνατόν, *Tht.* 176a).[47] How then does this 'mimetic assimilation', as Halliwell calls it,[48] play out in the context of a Christian homily? For an idea we can turn again to Gregory's oration on the Nativity. Gregory describes how we are to be drawn to the divine through that part of the divine that we can comprehend:

τῷ δὲ ἀλήπτῳ θαυμάζηται, θαυμαζόμενον δὲ ποθῆται πλέον, ποθούμενον δὲ καθαίρῃ, καθαῖρον δὲ θεοειδεῖς ἀπεργάζηται, τοιούτοις δὲ γενομένοις, ὡς οἰκείοις, ἤδη προσομιλῇ, τολμᾷ τι νεανικὸν ὁ λόγος, Θεὸς θεοῖς ἑνούμενός τε καὶ γνωριζόμενος, καὶ τοσοῦτον ἴσως, ὅσον ἤδη γινώσκει τοὺς γινωσκομένους.[49]

so that it be marvelled at for its incomprehensibility, and being marvelled at that it be desired more, and being desired that it purify, and purifying that it render us God-like, and when we have now become such that He may communicate with us, as with His own (my speech makes a bold utterance), God made one with gods and made known to them, and to such a degree perhaps as He now knows those who are known by Him.

Gregory's audience are to be rendered god-like, to become gods, through a combination of *pothos*, or desire for the divine, of *theōria*, or contemplation of the divine, and of *katharsis*, or purification, which is consistently presented as made possible through fear, or *phobos* of the divine and also as the most important pre-

---

[45] Harrison (2006) 41.

[46] Maslov (2012) 441. For Gregory on *theōsis* see also Tollefsen (2006) and Beeley (2008) 116–22.

[47] For these definitions and their prominence in Late Antique and Byzantine philosophical education, especially the commentators of the Alexandrian school such as David and Elias, see Ševčenko (1956).

[48] See Halliwell (2002) 315 on how for the philosopher, 'an especially active engagement in mimetic "assimilation" ... is to be understood above all as the goal, by this date shared by pagan and Christian thinkers, of fashioning oneself "in the likeness of God"'.

[49] *Or.* 38.7, ed. Moreschini (1990).

138   *Byron MacDougall*

requisite for *theōria*. What, then, do divine *pothos*, *phobos*, *theōria*, and *katharsis* have to do with sympathy, with the sharing of *pathos*? Desire and fear are both examples of *pathē* that lend themselves to being communicated between rhetor and audience via sympathy, but I would also suggest that *katharsis*, or purification, itself is a state that Gregory performs. It is a psychological state – we might even call it a disposition or *diathesis* of the soul – that is conceived of as being shared with the audience through the same dynamics of rhetorically induced sympathy that we have been exploring. Consider again Gregory's account of reading Basil:

ὅταν ἠθικοῖς λόγοις καὶ πρακτικοῖς, καθαίρομαι ψυχὴν καὶ σῶμα, καὶ ναὸς Θεοῦ γίνομαι δεκτικός, καὶ ὄργανον κρουόμενον Πνεύματι καὶ θείας ὑμνῳδὸν δόξης τε καὶ δυνάμεως.[50]

When I read his ethical and ascetic treatises, I am purified in soul and body, and I become a temple that receives God, and an instrument played by the Spirit, singing hymns of divine glory and power.

Reading Basil's works on Christian asceticism induces in Gregory what he calls 'the divine alteration' (τὴν θείαν ἀλλοίωσιν), as he experiences *katharsis* in his soul and body. The reading of Basil produces – sympathetically I would suggest – the feeling of purification in his reading audience, namely Gregory. Gregory and his fellow rhetors would have expected the same dynamic to function between themselves and the audiences of their performances. In particular, I think this applies in Gregory's homily on the Feast of the Holy Lights, the Baptism of Christ, when in the proemium Gregory announces to his audience that

ἡ γὰρ ἁγία τῶν Φώτων ἡμέρα, εἰς ἣν ἀφίγμεθα καὶ ἣν ἑορτάζειν ἠξιώμεθα σήμερον ... ἐνεργεῖ τὴν ἐμὴν κάθαρσιν ...[51]

The Holy Day of Lights, at which we have assembled and which we have deemed fit to celebrate today ... works my own purification ...

Gregory declares to his audience that the present feast is 'working his own purification', and over the course of the oration he performs rhetorically the various stages of that purification, from fear which leads to purification which leads to illumination (*Or.* 39.8). We are to imagine his audience 'following along' and experiencing these stages of purification themselves.[52] In fact, part of this process is made explicit in the passage which I quoted at the beginning of this chapter:

φρίττων καὶ γλῶσσαν καὶ διάνοιαν, ὅταν περὶ Θεοῦ φθέγγωμαι, καὶ ὑμῖν ταὐτὸ τοῦτο συνευχόμενος τὸ ἐπαίνετον πάθος καὶ μακάριον.[53]

---

[50] *Or.* 43.67; see above n. 22.

[51] *Or.* 39.1.

[52] For Gregory's performed *ēthos* and its connection to *theōria* in these and similar passages see Norris (1991) 108–9: 'Moses' ascent up the mount provides the Biblical basis for Nazianzen's description of his own "character", ἦθος, in terms of "contemplation", θεωρία. Gregory mentioned Elijah, Moses and Paul within a similar discussion of ἦθος in 27.9. Ascending involves the level of purification and contemplation already achieved.'

[53] *Or.* 39.11; see above n. 1.

4. Lend a Sympathetic Ear 139

When I speak about God, I experience trembling in both my mind and my tongue, and I pray that you also experience this same praiseworthy and blessed *pathos*.

In these last two passages, Gregory signposts to his audience his own experience of *katharsis* and *phrikē*, the latter a *pathos* of 'fear and trembling' that leads to *katharsis* and on to *theōsis*. He also states explicitly that his goal is for his audience to share in the same 'praiseworthy and blessed *pathos*' that he himself experiences. This is precisely the result that Gregory and his contemporaries would have expected to be brought about through the dynamic of rhetorical sympathy. As Gregory experiences the feeling of *katharsis* in his own soul by reading the ascetic works of Basil, so the members of his Epiphany audience are to experience *phrikē* and *katharsis* when prompted by Gregory's example. They are thus helped along in their goal of approaching *theōsis*, and in Gregory's eyes this progress is made possible by the same power of discourse that enabled him to respond to the experience of reading Basil, or that enabled Dionysius of Halicarnassus to respond emotionally to the experience of reading Isocrates or Demosthenes. We can thus observe how ancient theoretical understandings of rhetorical sympathy were deployed in order to perform active roles in religious life.

Whether this sympathy is effectively communicated depends not only on homilists like Gregory, but also on whether the homilist's audience has been primed by prior experience. This brings us back, in the end, to the relationship between the audience and the subject of discourse. Martin Hinterberger reminds us in this volume that emotions are culturally conditioned, and this goes not only for what we might call the physiological content of emotions.[54] The dynamics of how certain emotional responses are communicated are also culturally determined and learned. One could describe this as the 'prefocussing' of audiences and their emotional responses to narrative, and I have several times now adapted the image of 'priming' that other scholars have introduced.[55] When Gregory writes of his emotional response to reading Basil, he is not only teaching future rhetors like Michael Psellos how to describe rhetorically induced emotional responses; he is also teaching future audiences, as participants in learned discursive culture, about how they are expected to experience sympathy with performed *pathos*. Gregory feels *phrikē* or trembling when he speaks about God, and he prays that his audience will experience the same *pathos* that he feels. We could say that what he is actually praying for is for his audience to have been properly trained in rhetorical culture, and that they have been primed to experience sympathy in response to his own performance of *pathos*.

---

[54] See Hinterberger's chapter in this volume, pp. 303–38.

[55] For 'prefocussing' emotional response to narrative see Carroll (2011) 170. For 'priming' see for example Cairns (forthcoming).

5

Emotions and λόγος ἐνδιάθετος

Πάθη in John Sikeliotes' Commentary on Hermogenes' *On Types of Style**

Aglae Pizzone

Introduction

In ancient Greece the very first systematic theorization of the emotions famously came to be in Aristotle's treatise on rhetoric. The nexus between rhetoric and affective response has been inextricable ever since. It is therefore all the more surprising that, despite both the interest in the history of the emotions in Byzantium[1] and the strong emotional overtones of much of Byzantine rhetoric, no consideration has hitherto been given to the theorizations of the emotions in Byzantine rhetorical treatises. My contribution aims to address this topic, taking its cue from the commentary on Hermogenes' treatise *On Types of Style* authored in the eleventh century by John Sikeliotes.

Sikeliotes' exegetical work seemed a fit starting point for this study, for an array of reasons. Hermogenes' treatise was continuously commented upon in Byzantine classrooms from Late Antiquity onward, from the fifth-century commentary by Syrianos to Planudes' late fourteenth-century exegesis of the whole *Corpus Hermogenianum*. Hermogenes' and pseudo-Hermogenes' treatises were *the* handbook that sustained the rhetorical training of Byzantine elites. On the one hand, looking at the way Byzantine readers interacted with the corpus, negotiating its heritage over time, can tell us much about changing mentalities as well as about cultural-economic patterns shaping the education of the elite in the empire. On the other, Hermogenes was a testing ground of sorts for intellectuals aspiring to be recognized as leading figures in the cultural circles of the capital. To pen an authoritative commentary on the major handbook used in Byzantine classrooms was tantamount to shaping rhetorical teaching at the

---

* I would like to express my deepest gratitude to the Emotions through Time internal reviewers and to Stratis Papaioannou for their observations and notes on the first draft of this contribution: they helped me improve my work tremendously. It goes without saying that the responsibility for any mistake is mine.

[1] See the Introduction to this volume.

142   *Aglae Pizzone*

highest levels. It meant appropriating and subtly transforming Hermogenes'
text by superimposing a new voice on it, one that wanted to be heard. It therefore comes as no surprise that the surviving commentaries are the site of heartfelt polemics not only against previous exegeses, but also against contemporary
competing intellectuals.[2] The eleventh century is known to be a turning point in
Byzantine cultural history, marked by rich and sophisticated literary criticism.[3]
It is therefore crucial, in studying the story of 'Byzantine emotions', to see how
eleventh-century rhetoricians theorized and understood the linguistic expression of emotions as well as their ethical relevance within the framework of a
Christian rhetoric.

   This brings me to my second main point. John Sikeliotes stands as a towering,
though elusive, figure against the background of the lively late tenth- and early
eleventh-century Constantinopolitan cultural landscape.[4] Stratis Papaioannou
has recently been able to trace more precisely the details of his life and oeuvre.[5]
John Sikeliotes was a teacher and a student of philosophy, who most probably
came to Constantinople after witnessing the defeat of the Byzantine army by
the Arabs in Sicily in 964.[6] Active as a court orator, he was the author of several
improvised speeches as well as progymnasmata and was granted the honour of
pronouncing a speech for the emperor Constantine VIII at the Pikridion monastery in the capital.[7] He also most likely authored a highly refined hagiographical
piece, the *Life of Our Holy Father Nikephoros the Monk and Bishop of Miletos*
(*BHG* 1338), which bears striking stylistic and linguistic similarities to the *Commentary* on Hermogenes.[8] From Psellos we learn that he authored commentaries
on Gregory of Nazianzos that are now lost, while his exegesis on Ailios Aristeides is preserved in the form of scholia to the latter's speeches, now freshly
edited.[9] Above all, however, Sikeliotes' importance lies in the fact that, as pointed out by Conley,[10] he was the first to 'Christianize' rhetorical thought by con-

---

   [2] John Tzetzes' twelfth-century commentary, still unedited, is a case in point, as it is ridden
with polemical accents against contemporary fellow literati. The violent outburst of anger
against the rhetor Gregory in the *Historiai* is a direct consequence of Tzetzes' and Gregory's
engagement with Hermogenes' treatise in the Constantinopolitan teaching milieus. See Agapitos
(2017) 22–6 and Pizzone (2022). On the teaching of rhetoric in Byzantium and on the reception
of Hermogenes in particular see Valiavitcharska (2020) and Papaioannou (2021) 78-88. For a
survey of earlier, late antique commentators, see Pepe (2018).
   [3] I will confine myself to mentioning Papaioannou (2013); Bernard (2014).
   [4] On Sikeliotes see Mazzucchi (1990); Conley (2002–3) 145–52; Lauxtermann (2002) 208–9
and n. 32; Papaioannou (2013) 22 n. 61, 34–5; see also n. 5 below; Roilos (2018) 159–66; Betancourt (2018) 135–7.
   [5] Papaioannou (2015) and (2019a).
   [6] Papaioannou (2015) 272–3; (2019a) 665.
   [7] See vi.447.14–448.15 Walz and now Papaioannou (2019a) 663 with a sound critical text and
664–7 for translation and commentary.
   [8] Papaioannou (2015).
   [9] See Roilos (2018) 163 n. 10.
   [10] Conley (2002–3); Papaioannou (2019a) 683–92.

5. *Emotions and* λόγος ἐνδιάθετος 143

sistently using examples from the Holy Scriptures and Gregory of Nazianzos to elucidate Hermogenes' treatise. He thus 'dethroned' Demosthenes, as Conley puts it. More recently Stratis Papaioannou has called attention to the notion of 'political discourse' resurfacing for the first time in Sikeliotes' exegesis and to his attempt to create a high-profile and morally sound rhetoric. As Papaioannou puts it, 'Sikeliotes wishes to promote a rhetoric that in both nature and aims is moral rather than merely aesthetic.'[11] Given the increasing attention to the emotional aspects of communication between the tenth and the eleventh century, looking at the explicit treatment of πάθη in Sikeliotes' exegesis is key to understanding how Byzantine elites handled the moral concerns entailed by a conscious affective manipulation of the audience.

This contribution will therefore investigate the discursive definition of πάθη provided by Sikeliotes. A full understanding of such a definition is crucial, as it represents the cornerstone of subsequent reflections on the nature and function of the emotions in rhetoric. In order to explore the meaning and relevance of πάθη in John's commentary, however, it is necessary to take a step back and look first at some aspects of Sikeliotes' philosophy of language. Πάθη are in fact discussed by John mostly in connection with μέθοδος, or approach, one of the eight components through which speech is created: thought or content, approach, diction, figures of speech, clauses, word order, cadence, and rhythm.[12] Πάθη, qua movements of the soul, are seen as the equivalent of approach specifically when John discusses Hermogenes' λόγος ἐνδιάθετος. That is why we must first dive into the meaning of λόγος ἐνδιάθετος in Sikeliotes' commentary and into the thorny question of the difference between λόγος προφορικός (uttered or outer speech) and λόγος ἐνδιάθετος (internal speech). This discussion will in turn raise further questions on the linguistic – or non-linguistic – nature of the emotions and on their status within Christian discourse. If emotions – experienced and elicited – are seen not just as a powerful tool to manipulate the audience, but, rather, as ontologically connected with innate and truthful speech, their ethical value becomes unquestionable. Emotions, in fact, characterize the most preferable and best possible discursive type from a quintessentially Christian point of view.

5.1. The language of the emotions

The division between λόγος προφορικός and λόγος ἐνδιάθετος, known as a hallmark of Stoicism in Imperial times,[13] is not something new for Hermogenian

---

[11] Papaionannou (2013) 88.

[12] On these elements see Patillon (1988); Kennedy (1994) 216.

[13] A distinction between inner and uttered dialogue is in fact to be found already in Pl. *Tht.* 189e4–90a6. The traditional view ascribed the introduction of the categories λόγος προ-

144 *Aglae Pizzone*

commentaries. In the fourth-century scholia by Sopater a discussion of the two λόγοι serves as an introduction to the whole τέχνη (art),[14] since being τεχνικός (skilled) is precisely the defining trait of the λόγος προφορικός. The latter is the object of two distinct arts, rhetoric and grammar, while λόγος ἐνδιάθετος is assigned to a τέχνη that deals with ἐνθυμήματα and ἐπιχειρήματα (forms of rhetorical syllogisms).[15] In a contribution devoted to Philo of Alexandria, Adam Kamesar (2004) has pointed to similarities between this approach and Stoic-Platonic – Philo's in particular – stances towards rhetoric and philosophy, which are respectively the province of προφορικός and ἐνδιάθετος λόγος. John seems to build on this tradition, but innovates, taking a different approach, one designed to lay the foundations for an ethically sound coexistence of rhetoric and Christianity, thus paving the way for a complete acceptance of 'emotional' discourse.

John's commentary does not address λόγος προφορικός and λόγος ἐνδιάθετος in the prolegomena or in the programmatic prologue to the commentary. The distinction between the two λόγοι is tackled when John elucidates the Hermogenian notion of ἐνδιάθετος style, which, in Hermogenes, has less to do with inner λόγος qua thought or reasoning, and more with a spontaneous and sincere utterance. As Patillon's lucid analysis shows, the distinction in Hermogenes points to a difference between immediate and delayed expression and has to do with both premeditation and metadiscourse. In that it is uttered under the impulse of the moment, without preparation or warning signs for the audience, ἐνδιάθετος discourse expresses both a state, διάθεσις, and the emotions, πάθη, of the soul, which are explicitly mentioned by Hermogenes, from astonishment and fear to pity and sorrow.[16]

This semantic and conceptual area is the springboard that allows John Sikeliotes to bend the traditional antithesis προφορικός/ἐνδιάθετος to his own goals. Λόγος ἐνδιάθετος is mentioned for the first time in the commentary on section 1.11, where Hermogenes illustrates amplification and abundance and has a digression about the mixing of styles, including τὸ πιθανόν, the plausible.[17]

φορικός/λόγος ἐνδιάθετος to the Stoa: cf. Mühl (1962). However, the sources ascribing it to Stoicism are quite late (Sext. Emp. *Math.* 8.275–6 and Porph. *Abst.* 3.2–3). There is now a consensus that the distinction came to the forefront of philosophical discussions within the framework of the debates between Stoics and Academics on the rationality of animals: see Chiesa (1991) and Matelli (1992). Modern scholarship has been particularly interested in whether λόγος ἐνδιάθετος can be taken as composed of pre-linguistic concepts or rather requires a given language of utterance. Panaccio (2017 [1999]) has advocated the former reading at least from Aristotle onwards, arguing that λόγος ἐνδιάθετος, being the source of deliberative processes and intentionality, is situated before human linguistic conventions and any grammatical structure.

[14] On Sopater, see Rabe (1926) 57–70; Hock and O'Neill (2002) 98–112; Cribiore (2009) 58.
[15] This thought ultimately goes back to Arist. *An. Post.* 76b24–6.
[16] 2.7.11–12. Cf. Patillon (1988) 112, 225; (2012) cvii and 170 with notes.
[17] 11.1.6–7 with Patillon (2012) 92 and notes.

5. Emotions and λόγος ἐνδιάθετος

John is thus given the opportunity to explain what πιθανός actually means, thus introducing the notion of ἐνδιάθετος λόγος:[18]

πῶς γίνεται ... τὸ δὲ πιθανὸν καὶ ἀληθὲς, ὃ καὶ ἐνδιάθετον λέγει, ῥηθήσεται· πιθανὸν δὲ κατ' ἐξοχὴν καὶ κατ' ἰσχύν· πάντα μὲν γὰρ πιθανά· ἀλλὰ τῇ τέχνῃ τοῦ ῥήτορος γίνονται πιθανά, καὶ εἰ μὴ τοιαῦτα τῇ φύσει· ... ἀληθὲς δὲ λέγεται διὰ τὸ εἶναι αὐτόπιστον, καὶ κατασκευῶν οὐ δεόμενον, καὶ ὥσπερ ἐξ ἀναμνήσεως εἰσαγόμενον καὶ ἀληθοῦς καὶ βεβαίας κινήσεως τῆς ψυχῆς, καὶ διὰ τὸ μὴ ἀνατραπῆναι δύνασθαι· τοιαῦτα γὰρ τὰ ἀληθῆ· ἐνδιάθετον δέ, ὡς ἐξ ὀρθῆς καὶ ἀδόλου τῆς διαθέσεως προϊὸν ἐκ τοῦ νοηματικοῦ καὶ κατὰ διάθεσιν λόγου· τὸν γὰρ λόγον τῆς ψυχῆς τὸν κρυπτὸν καὶ ἀνεξάκουστον ἀκοαῖς ἐνδιάθετον λέγουσι, καὶ ἐκ διαθέσεως· συνίσταται γοῦν οὗτος μετὰ τῆς ἀκμῆς, ὅταν τινῶν κατηγοροῦντες ἢ κατατρέχοντες καὶ ἐπιτιμῶντες μεταξὺ τραγῳδήσωμεν οἰκτιζόμενοι, εἰρωνευόμενοι, ἤ τι τῶν οἰκείων τῆς ἰδέας ταύτης εἰσάγωμεν, ὡς ταῦτά ἐστι·

I shall say how the plausible and the truthful, which he also calls innate, are achieved: it is persuasive by default and by force; for everything is plausible; however it becomes plausible thanks to the rhetoricians' technique also even if is not such by nature; ... it is said to be truthful because it is credible in itself and does not require confirmation, as if it was introduced from memories or as the result of a truthful and reliable movement of the soul, and because it cannot be refuted. Such are the truthful arguments; and it is [called] innate because it proceeds from the rational and in accordance with the inner disposition, as if from a righteous and honest state; for they define as innate and as coming from inner disposition the discourse of the soul that is hidden and does not reach the ears. This kind is produced with vigour, when we also speak tragically, pitying or using irony, or we introduce anything proper to this type of style, while we accuse or pursue or censure someone, as in the following ...

The following examples show that ἐνδιάθετος λόγος is produced specifically when one wants to convey emotions proceeding directly from the speaker's inner reasoning.[19] The examples used to illustrate sincere λόγος come mainly from Gregory of Nazianzos' oration 39, *On the Holy Lights*.[20] John specifically points to the passage where Gregory launches into a tirade against the rigorism of those who, like Novatus, do not show any pity and empathy towards repentant sinners.[21]

John's choice – Gregory's *Or.* 39 – is far from coincidental. The whole sermon relies on the premise of Gregory ventriloquizing God's voice, through the words uttered by Jesus in John 8:12, 'I am the light of the World.'[22] By saying 'I' Gregory takes up before his congregation the same role as Jesus before the Pharisees in

---

[18] vi.306.18–307.3 Walz.

[19] Exemplified in Hermogenes by metadiscourse: 2.7.27.

[20] Delivered for Epiphany 381. See Daley (2006) 127 and 128–30 for an English translation; Hofer (2013) 166–9. The oration builds on the audience's feelings, and Gregory purposefully wants to communicate his own emotions, having his flock relive them through his words. The oration offers a stark depiction of Gregory himself as a vessel of the divine λόγος.

[21] *Or.* 39.18. Novatus and his followers ruled out the possibility of post-baptism absolution in case of specific sins. See Ferguson (2009) 382–3.

[22] *Or.* 39.2.3–4, ed. Moreschini and Gallay (1990) 150 (= *PG* 36.336B).

146 *Aglae Pizzone*

John's gospel, a passage that resonates with the representation of God as λόγος and of Jesus as carrier of the Father's inner λόγος offered in the evangelic prologue.[23] Right at the beginning of the oration, Gregory plays with the double meaning of λόγος, stating that he expects the congregation to be lifted both by his voice (uttered word) and by the spiritual meaning of his predication (inner word):[24]

ὁρᾶτε τῆς ἡμέρας τὴν χάριν; ὁρᾶτε τοῦ μυστηρίου τὴν δύναμιν; οὐκ ἀπὸ γῆς ἤρθητε; οὐκ ἄνω τέθεισθε σαφῶς ὑψωθέντες ὑπὸ τῆς ἡμετέρας φωνῆς καὶ ἀναγωγῆς; καὶ ἔτι μᾶλλον τεθήσεσθε, ἐπειδὰν εὐοδώσῃ τὸν λόγον ὁ Λόγος.

Do you see the grace of this day? Do you see the power of the mystery? Are you not lifted up from the earth? Are you not clearly placed on high, after having been lifted up by our voice and sublimation? And you will be placed much higher when the Word shall have guided my word.

The sermon moreover stresses time and again the salvific and purifying role of emotions such as fear, compunction, and pity (39.8; 39.11; 39.29). The passage pointed out by John as an example of 'sincere discourse' is devoted precisely to the role played by compassionate weeping in true Christian faith.

Ἐνδιάθετος λόγος is thus presented in Sikeliotes' commentary as a rhetorical mode reproducing the invisible movements of the soul generating emotions in the visible structures of the language. The connection between innate discourse and πάθος is stressed more clearly a little later:[25]

πιθανὸν δέ ἐστι τὸ καὶ ἐνδιάθετον, λόγος τὸ πάθος ἐξαγγέλλων τοῦ λέγοντος, ὅπως διάκειται περὶ τὸ λεγόμενον, ὡς ἐν τοῖς περὶ αὐτοῦ μαθησόμεθα.

Also plausible is what is innate, a discourse showing the emotion of the speaker, what his disposition is regarding what it is said, as we will learn in the passage devoted to it.

John Sikeliotes points here to the lengthy explanation he provides further on in his work, when he comments on innate and truthful style as described in *Id.* 2.7. In that passage Hermogenes talks about 'unaffected and sincere and, as it were, animated discourse'.[26] This definition leads John to look closer into the distinction between προφορικός and ἐνδιάθετος, which he had hitherto not tackled:[27]

ὁ ἐνδιάθετος καὶ ἀληθὴς καὶ οἷον ἔμψυχος λόγος. Λόγου[28] τοῦ ἀπὸ ψυχῆς λογικῆς διττὸν τὸ σημαινόμενον·ὁ μὲν γὰρ ἐν προφορικῇ φωνῇ διὰ στόματος καὶ χειλέων ἐκφερόμενος, καὶ ἔναρθρος καὶ γραφόμενος ὁρᾶται· ὁ δὲ ἐν νοήσει καὶ καθ᾽ ἑαυτὴν τὴν ψυχήν, ὃς καὶ

---

[23] See the commentary on the passage offered by Engberg-Pedersen (2017).
[24] *Or.* 39.2.15–19, ed. Moreschini and Gallay (1990) 152 (= *PG* 36.336C).
[25] vi.308.1–2 Walz.
[26] See Patillon (2012), 170–82.
[27] vi.419.17–420.7 Walz.
[28] The Laur. Plut. 57.5, from the end of the twelfth century, fol. 350ʳ, omits λόγου.

5. Emotions and λόγος ἐνδιάθετος

147

ἐνδιάθετος μὲν ὡς κρυπτὸς καὶ ἐν κινήσει τῆς ψυχῆς ὁρώμενος· τὰς γὰρ ποιὰς κινήσεις τῆς ψυχῆς τουτέστι τὰς μὴ πῆξιν λαβούσας, καὶ εἰς ἕξιν οὐκ ἀποκαθισταμένας τῆς τῶν ἔξω δηλώσεως διαθέσεις καλοῦσι, διὰ τὸ διατίθεσθαι τὴν ψυχὴν πρὸς αὐτὰς κατὰ πάθος ἢ ἀγαθὸν ἢ φαῦλον· ἀληθινὸς δὲ λέγεται, ὅτι πείθει μάλιστα, ὡς ἐξ ἀπλάστου διαθέσεως ἐξερχόμενος, καὶ ἤθους ἀδόλου καὶ ἀπανούργου· ἔμψυχος δὲ ὡς εὐκίνητος καὶ δραστήριος τῶν ἀκουομένων· καὶ τὸ ὅλον εἰπεῖν ὡς ἐνεργός· τοιαῦτα γὰρ τὰ ἔμψυχα.

The innate and truthful and, as it were, animated discourse. Twofold is the meaning of the discourse stemming from the rational soul: the one in uttered voice, produced through the mouth and the lips, is articulated and is to be seen in writing; the other in the mind and in the soul itself, which is also innate, as it is hidden, and to be seen in the movement of the soul. For they call such movements of the soul, i.e. those that have not yet solidified and have not yet turned into states, 'dispositions deriving from pointing out external circumstances', since the soul arranges itself towards them [*sc.* the movements of the soul] according to an emotion, either positive or negative. And it is called truthful because it is most persuasive, as coming from a disposition that is still fluid and an honest and non-malicious character; they call it animated as it is agile and pushes to enact what is heard; and to sum up, active; for these are the characteristics of animated beings.

A close reading of the passage suggests that λόγος becomes visible in two ways. External discourse is perceived through either the ears or the eyes,[29] while inner discourse is hidden but can be perceived through the movements of the soul. Such movements are a series of transitory dispositions that have not yet 'solidified' (τὰς μὴ πῆξιν λαβούσας) into ἕξεις or states/habits and that cause an emotional response in the subject. John builds here on Aristotle's *Categories* 8b27–9a9 and *Metaphysics* 5, 1022b21, where the distinction is drawn between states and dispositions.[30] Emotions are primarily categorized by John through their valence dimension. Πάθη seem to form a code of their own, making perceptible the inner, immediate movements of the soul. Inner discourse, while belonging to the non-articulated (only external λόγος qualifies as ἔναρθρος) and to the pre-linguistic, becomes nonetheless visible (ὁρώμενος) in the πάθη resulting from the movements of the soul towards temporary dispositions. Emotions, therefore, are the means through which inner λόγος makes the movements of the soul perceptible and ἐνδιάθετος λόγος communicable.[31] They are pre-linguis-

---

[29] On ἐνδιάθετος λόγος in Byzantine theories of orality and written discourse see the observations of Messis and Papaioannou (2021).

[30] Brague (1980) 285–307.

[31] A comparable stance is to be found also in Psellos, *Opusculum* 51, 577–82 Duffy, where the distinction between uttered and inner speech is introduced as follows: ἀλλὰ καὶ διττός ἐστιν ὁ λόγος, ὁ μὲν προφορικός, ὁ δὲ ἐνδιάθετος, ἤγουν ὁ ἐν τῇ ψυχῇ θεωρούμενος. περὶ δὲ τοῦ προφορικοῦ ὁ λόγος τῷ Ἀριστοτέλει, περὶ δὲ τοῦ ἐνδιαθέτου οὐδεὶς σκοπὸς διὰ τὸ μηδὲ ποσὸν εἶναι τὸν τοιοῦτον, ἀλλ᾽ εἰ ἄρα ποιότητα ψυχῆς· διάθεσις γάρ τις ἢ ἕξις τὴν σύστασιν ἔχουσα ('However discourse is twofold, the one is uttered, the other is inner, that is to say it is to be seen in the soul. Regarding the uttered discourse, we refer to Aristotle; regarding the inner discourse there is no authority because it is not quantitative by nature, but it is rather a quality of the soul, as it were. For it is a disposition or a state endowed with its own structure'). Inner speech, there-

148   *Aglae Pizzone*

tic, in that they are situated before any given spoken language, and yet they form a perceptible code that can be reproduced in speech. Inner states of mind would hardly be communicable without the bodily symptoms and expressions associated with each emotion. Emotions, in turn, find their language in the relevant performative and discursive practices. This explains the paradox of a rhetorical mode conveying ἐνδιάθετος λόγος, which in theory is pre-linguistic in essence. In fact, John argues, approach (μέθοδος) is the way to go if one wants to communicate how the movements of the soul affect the subject:[32]

μέθοδος, τὸ πῶς δεῖ προφέρειν τὰ νοήματα, κατὰ ποῖον πάθος ψυχῆς, λυπηρὸν, θαυμα-στικὸν, σχετλιαστικὸν, θρηνητικὸν καὶ τὰ ὅμοια. γίνονται μὴν καὶ κατ᾽ ἔννοιαν ἀφελεῖς ἔννοιαι λόγου ἀληθινοῦ· τὰ γὰρ σεμνὰ ἢ τραχέα νοήματα, ὅταν ἀφελῶς μεθοδεύωνται, εἰς τὴν ἰδέαν ταύτην ἐμπίπτουσιν, ὥστε πᾶσαν ἔννοιαν οὕτω μεθοδεύσεις· αὐτίκα γὰρ τὸ τὸν θεὸν ἰδεῖν, καὶ τὰ περὶ αὐτὸν,[33] σεμνὸν ὂν καὶ τὸ πρῶτον τῆς τῆς ἐννοίας σεμνότητος ἀφελῶς καὶ ἐπιεικῶς ἐρρήθη τῷ προφήτῃ καὶ ὄντως ἀληθινῶς, "ὦ τάλας," φησὶν, "ὅτι κα-τανένυγμαι, ὅτι ἄνθρωπος ὢν καὶ ἀκάθαρτα χείλη ἔχων καὶ τὰ ἑξῆς."

Approach, how thoughts have to be uttered, according to which affection of the soul – sad, expressing astonishment, indignant, lamentatory, etc. Simple thoughts of truthful discourse are also achieved according to thought, for solemn and coarse thoughts, when they are approached with simplicity, fall into this style, so that you will be working out a concept as a whole through such approaches; for seeing God and what surrounds him, being solemn in essence and the very apex of the idea of solemnity, has been expressed by the prophet (Isa. 6:5) with simplicity, kindness, and inherent truthfulness: 'Woe is me!', he says, 'For I am stunned; for I am a man of unclean lips; etc.'

This passage is crucial, as John, taking his cue from Hermogenes' apparent internal inconsistencies in defining ἔννοια and μέθοδος[34] (and figures, as we will see), identifies instances in which approach and thought actually overlap, cancelling de facto the gap between inner and uttered discourse. This happens when a given emotion is expressed without *actio* or previous study but as a spontaneous affective outburst: καὶ οὐ μεθ᾽ ὑποκρίσεως καὶ προρρήσεως.[35]

According to John, it is possible to reproduce the core of thought without mediation, just as it is granted to some individuals to see the Lord without veils.[36] The analogy once again resonates with and hints at the multiple Christian/ Johannine meanings of λόγος. When it comes to sincere discourse, this over-

---

fore, also according to Psellos, is hard to pinpoint as it cannot be numerically defined, given the ever-changing nature of psychological dispositions.

[32] vi.420.8–19 Walz.

[33] Walz prints αὐτούς. However, the text hardly makes sense with an accusative masculine plural. Laur. Plut. 57.5, fol. 350ᵛ has αὐτὸν, which makes the sentence much more transparent in its meaning.

[34] Cf. vi.118.11–17 Walz.

[35] vi.425.4–5 Walz.

[36] This viewpoint also speaks to the sensitivity towards sincerity ingrained in Christian discourses about rhetoric: see Messis and Papaioannou (2021) 260–1.

5. Emotions and λόγος ἐνδιάθετος 149

lapping ensures that emotions are communicated without pretence, as a simple reflection of what happens in the soul. The process is explained more clearly a few paragraphs later:[37]

ὅταν γὰρ ὡς ἀληθῶς σχετλιάζῃ τις, διὰ τὸ τὸ πρᾶγμα οἰκτρὸν ἢ παθητικὸν ἢ τοιοῦτον εἶ-ναι, ἔννοια τοῦτο τοῦ ἀληθοῦς, ὡς τὰ τοῦ θεολόγου πάντα· ὅταν δὴ μὴ φύσει τὸ πρᾶγμα, ἢ οἴκτου, ἢ θαυμασμοῦ, ἤ τινος τῶν τοιούτων ἐστί, σχηματίζηται δὲ πρὸς τοῦ λέγοντος εἰς σχετλιασμὸν ἢ εἰς θαῦμα, τότ᾽ ἂν εἴη μέθοδος· μέθοδον γὰρ λέγομεν τὴν διέξοδον τοῦ τρόπου τῆς ἐννοίας, ἃ καὶ σχήματα διανοίας λέγεται· καὶ σαφὴς δήπουθεν ἡ μέθοδος, ὅτι περὶ τὸν τρόπον τῆς ἐννοίας λέγεται καὶ αὐτή ἐστιν ἡ ἔννοια· τὸ γὰρ εὐτελὲς εἶναι τὸ πρᾶγμα τὸν σχετλιασμὸν ἐποίησε κατ᾽ ἔννοιαν, καὶ οὐ κατὰ μέθοδον·

If one is truly indignant, on account of the facts themselves being lamentable or passionate or of such nature, then this is the thought of truthfulness, just like everything in [Gregory] the Theologian. If, then, the facts are not such by nature – I mean either lamentable or to be wondered at or of such a sort – but are shaped by the speaker with a view to complaint or wonder, *then* we have approach. For we call approach the exposition of the manner of the thought, what are also called figures of thought. And without doubt approach is clear, that it is defined with reference to the manner of the thought and it is itself the thought; the fact that the topic was undignified brought about indignation in accordance with thought, and not in accordance with approach.

John's conclusion has momentous consequences.[38] By undoing the absolute dichotomy between λόγος προφορικός and λόγος ἐνδιάθετος, he ultimately expands the relevance of rhetoric. Inner λόγος is not the province of dialectic and logic alone but *can* be rhetorically articulated as well as find a faithful utterance in spoken language. And, most importantly, it becomes the carrier of emotions. John's approach is supported both by his exegesis of Hermogenes and by the exemplary rhetorical practice showcased by Gregory of Nazianzos.

The fact that rhetoric is relevant to both λόγος προφορικός and λόγος ἐνδιά-θετος certainly caught on in eleventh-century Byzantium. John Doxapatres, who in his own commentary on Aphthonios' progymnasmata refers to and makes use of John's material,[39] addresses the definition of rhetoric in relation to λόγος προ-φορικός and λόγος ἐνδιάθετος in the following terms:

ὑπόκειται γοῦν, φασί, τῇ ῥητορικῇ ὁ μὲν λόγος καθάπερ ὕλη ὅ τε προφορικὸς καὶ ὁ ἐν-διάθετος, κοσμεῖ δὲ αὐτὸν ὁ τεχνικός. εἰ γοῦν πᾶσα ὕλη κοσμουμένη λόγῳ κοσμεῖται καὶ διατάττεται, ὁ δὲ λόγος τέχνῃ, καθὸ καὶ τὸν τοῦδε τοῦ παντὸς δημιουργὸν ἀριστοτέχνην φασὶ λόγῳ τὴν ὕλην κοσμήσαντα καὶ τάξαντα καὶ εἰδοποιήσαντα, πῶς οὐχὶ καὶ τὸν δίκην ὕλης τὸν λόγον αὐτὸν κοσμοῦντα λόγον τέχνην εἶναι νομίσομεν;

Discourse – external or innate – is the foundation, as they say, of rhetoric, the stuff of which rhetoric is made, as it were, while the skilled orator is the one who gives discourse an order. If, then, any stuff to which an order is given is ordered and arranged by a rationale [λόγος],

---

[37] vi.422.22–423.26 Walz.
[38] See also Kustas (1973) 121.
[39] Cf. xiv.422.8; 423.2; 424.23 Rabe. The quotation that follows is from xiv.89.26–90.8 Rabe.

but the discourse itself [λόγος] by the [rhetorical] art – just as they say that the creator of everything is the most skilled craftsman, He who arranged and gave order and shape to matter through the λόγος, how can we not consider the rationale [λόγος] that gives an order to discourse, qua the stuff of which it is made, as art?

Playing with the multiple (linguistic, philosophical, and theological) meanings of λόγος, Doxapatres advocates the idea that both silent and uttered discourse underlie rhetoric, thus making explicit the transition implied in Sikeliotes' commentary.[40] Here lies the most significant change as compared to previous Christian stances towards λόγος προφορικός and λόγος ἐνδιάθετος, as the designation of τεχνικός was ascribed exclusively to the former.[41] And this is also the theoretical ground allowing Sikeliotes to reaffirm the pre-eminence of rhetoric over philosophy in the prolegomena to his commentary.[42]

John Sikeliotes' stance towards λόγος ἐνδιάθετος and therefore towards emotions can be traced back to a twofold origin. On the one hand, Byzantine philosophical and theological discourse had moved towards filling the gap between λόγοι since as early as the eighth century. On the other, the doctrine of *schēmata*, as worked out from Hellenistic times onwards,[43] offered the conceptual ground suitable both to address the emotions from the perspective of λόγος ἐνδιάθετος and to bring the latter into the domain of rhetoric.

As far as the first point is concerned, it is John of Damascus to whom we must turn to find a first attempt explicitly to move λόγος ἐνδιάθετος beyond the purely pre-linguistic. In the *Expositio fidei* he complicates the traditional dichotomy between inner and uttered discourse by introducing a third variety of λόγος:[44]

Λόγος ἐστὶν ὁ οὐσιωδῶς τῷ πατρὶ ἀεὶ συμπαρών. λόγος πάλιν ἐστὶ καὶ ἡ φυσικὴ τοῦ νοῦ κίνησις, καθ᾽ ἣν κινεῖται καὶ νοεῖ καὶ λογίζεται οἰονεὶ φῶς αὐτοῦ ὢν καὶ ἀπαύγασμα. λόγος πάλιν ἐστὶν ὁ ἐνδιάθετος ὁ ἐν καρδίᾳ λαλούμενος. καὶ πάλιν λόγος ἐστὶν ἄγγελος νοήματος. ὁ μὲν οὖν θεὸς Λόγος οὐσιώδης τέ ἐστι καὶ ἐνυπόστατος, οἱ δὲ λοιποὶ τρεῖς λόγοι δυνάμεις εἰσὶ τῆς ψυχῆς οὐκ ἐν ἰδίᾳ ὑποστάσει θεωρούμενοι, ὧν ὁ μὲν πρῶτος τοῦ νοῦ φυσικόν ἐστι γέννημα ἐξ αὐτοῦ ἀεὶ φυσικῶς πηγαζόμενον, ὁ δεύτερος δὲ λέγεται ἐνδιάθετος, ὁ δὲ τρίτος προφορικός.

The Λόγος is that which always coexists substantially with the Father. However, in another sense, the λόγος is also the natural movement of the mind in respect of which it is moved

---

[40] That rhetoric takes care of both discourses is made even more explicit by the anonymous *ekthesis* on rhetoric, preserved by a single sixteenth-century manuscript of the Biblioteca Ambrosiana (MS C 257 inf.), where invention is assigned to silent discourse while composition and rhythm are the province of the uttered one (iii.735.6 ff. Walz).

[41] So, for instance, in Basil's homily on John 1:1 (*PG* 31.477A), see Messis and Papaioannou (2021) 260.

[42] See Prolegomena xvi.394.14–28 Rabe with Roilos (2018) 170–1.

[43] For a summary of the Hellenistic theory with further bibliography see Schironi (2018) 171–4.

[44] *Expositio fidei* 13.91–8. Cf. also *Expositio fidei* 35. John of Damascus relies heavily on Nemesius, *De natura hominis* 14.71–2. Cf. Panaccio (2017 [1999]), chapter 2.

5. *Emotions and λόγος ἐνδιάθετος*

and thinks and reasons, as if it were in a sense the light and illumination of the mind. In still another sense, there is the interior λόγος, which is articulated in the heart. And there is also the λόγος which is the messenger of thought. Now, the divine Λόγος is at once substantial and subsistent, while the other three are powers of the soul and cannot be considered in their proper hypostases: the first is a natural product of the mind, continually flowing from it in a natural way; the second we call *endiathetos*; and the third *prophorikos*.

Claude Panaccio has argued against the linguistic character of the ἐνδιάθετος, as described by the Damascene, advocating instead 'the idea of an intellectual and prelinguistic discursivity'. And yet, John of Damascus' text is quite clear in differentiating a primary λόγος, whose activity is described as 'gushing' (πηγα-ζόμενον) from a second typology of inner discourse, whose activity is described as 'talk' (λαλούμενος). The latter, moreover, appears to be located within an embodied dimension (ἐν καρδίᾳ) rather than in a purely cognitive one (τοῦ νοῦ κίνησις). John of Damascus seems to transfer a tripartite ontological scheme – mind, discursive reason, body – to the level of λόγος. If this holds true, then ἐνδιάθετος *is* in fact of linguistic nature.

Be that as it may, the three levels of λόγος described by John of Damascus bear striking similarities with the stance taken by later commentators on Hermogenes. Positing inner discourse as something akin to silent speech and related to affections paves the way for the conceptualization of a Christian, ethically sound rhetoric, one that can reproduce the inner movements of the soul to perfection. Moreover, its ethical value is granted by the fact that those movements, or emotions, are uttered without any help, as we have seen, from performative pretence or studied preparation. Roughly a century before John Sikeliotes, another anonymous commentator on Hermogenes seems to imply the same tripartite scheme:[45]

ἡ ἔννοια ἐνεργοῦσα ποιήσει τὴν μέθοδον· ἡ γὰρ ἔννοια ἀναλογοῦσα τῇ ψυχῇ, ὅταν μὲν ἠρεμῇ καὶ μένῃ καθ' ἑαυτήν, οὐδὲν ἀποτελεῖ· κινουμένη δὲ ποιεῖται, καὶ τοῦτο καλεῖται μέθοδος· ἡ περὶ τὴν ἔννοιαν, καὶ οὐ μόνον ἡ ἔννοια ψυχῆς τάξιν ἐπέχει, καὶ ἡ μέθοδος τῆς κινήσεως, ἀλλ' ἰδίᾳ καὶ ἡ λέξις τοῦ σώματος· ὥσπερ γὰρ οὐ δυνατὸν ἐνεργεῖν τὴν ψυχὴν ἄνευ σώματος, οὕτως καὶ τὴν ἔννοιαν οὐχ οἷόν τε χωρὶς λέξεως· ἀναλογεῖ γὰρ ἡ λέξις τῷ σώματι, καὶ ὥσπερ ἐν τῷ σώματί εἰσιν αἱ μορφαί, οὕτως ἐν τῇ λέξει τὰ σχήματα· καὶ δὴ πάσας τὰς τοῦ σώματος ἰδιότητας εὕροις ἂν ἐπὶ τῆς λέξεως, ὥσπερ καὶ τὰς τῆς ψυχῆς ἐπὶ τῆς ἐννοίας· ἔστι μὲν γὰρ αὐτῇ σχήματα, καθάπερ ἐπὶ τῶν σωμάτων αἱ μορφαί, καὶ μακρὰ καὶ βραχέα κῶλα, τάξιν τοῦ μεγέθους ἐπέχοντα ...

The thought in action will create the approach, for the thought is like the soul when, motionless and on its own, it does not accomplish anything; however, when it is moved, it accomplishes something, and this is called approach: approach concerning thought, and not only does the thought hold the same place as the soul and approach occupy the same place as movement, but diction has the same properties as the body: just as it is impossible for the soul to act without the body, so likewise is it impossible to mobilize thought with-

---

[45] vii.2.883.15–884.7 Walz.

out diction; for diction is analogous to the body, and just as there are forms in the body, so likewise are there figures in diction; and in diction you would find all the properties of the body, just as you find the properties of the soul in thought; it has figures, like the forms of bodies, and short and long *cōla*, occupying the same position as magnitude [for bodies] ...

The anonymous commentator envisages a first stage in which ἔννοια, or thought, is by itself, not moving and without qualification, as it were. At such a stage, thought is not communicable. Communication happens only when thought is mobilized and organized through approach. Approach represents, therefore, the second stage, comparable to λόγος ἐνδιάθετος as conceptualized by John of Damascus. It reproduces the movements of the soul, although it is one step removed from the specificity of diction, which is in turn anchored in the diversity of human languages. Diction represents the third stage, that is to say proper uttered speech. The three closely intertwined stages are further exemplified by the anonymous commentator through the analogy between rhetoric and the psycho-physiological structures of the human being, moving from the invisible to the visible: thought = soul; approach = movements of the soul; diction = body.

John takes exactly the same stance[46] and expands on the comparison between the body of rhetoric and the human body, explaining in greater detail how approach can convey the affections of the soul:[47]

λύσις. εἰκότως· ἐπεὶ γὰρ ὁ λόγος ζῴῳ ἀναλογεῖ, καὶ ἡ μὲν ἔννοια τούτου ἀναλογεῖ τῇ τοῦ ζῴου ψυχῇ, ἡ δὲ μέθοδος τῇ τοιᾷδε κινήσει τῆς ψυχῆς – διάφοροι γὰρ αἱ τῶν ψυχῶν ἐν διαφόροις ζῴοις κινήσεις – ἡ δὲ λέξις τῷ σώματι, καὶ τὸ σχῆμα τῇ τοῦ σώματος μορφῇ, καὶ τὰ κῶλα τοῖς ὀστέοις, καὶ ἡ συνθήκη ταῖς τῶν ὀστῶν ἁρμονίαις, καὶ τοῖς τούτων πέρασιν ἡ ἀνάπαυσις, καὶ ὁ ῥυθμὸς τῇ τοιᾷδε κινήσει τοῦ σώματος, εὐλόγως ἐκεῖ μὲν κατὰ τὴν φυσικὴν ἀκολουθίαν μετὰ τὴν ἔννοιαν τὴν ἐπακολουθοῦσαν ταύτῃ μέθοδον ἔταξεν· ἐνταῦθα δὲ τὴν λέξιν τὴν ἀναλογοῦσαν τῷ σώματι, καὶ τὸ σχῆμα τὸ ἀναλογοῦν τῇ μορφῇ ὡς κατ'αἴσθησιν γνωριμώτερον τῆς μεθόδου τῆς ἀναλογούσης τῇ ψυχικῇ κινήσει προέλαβεν, ὥσπερ δῆτα καὶ ἐπὶ τῶν ἀνθρώπων πρότερον ψυχὴν καὶ σῶμα καταλαμβάνομεν καὶ μορφήν· εἶτα καὶ πρὸς τὴν ψυχικὴν ἐντεῦθεν μεταβαίνομεν κίνησιν.

Solution. It is obvious. For, since the λόγος is similar to a living being, its thought too is similar to the soul of a living being, while the approach is equal to such a movement of the soul – for different living beings possess different movements of the soul – diction is similar to the body and the figure to the form of the body and *cōla* to the bones, and composition to the joints of the bones, and the pause to their ends and the rhythm to such a movement of the body, it makes sense that there [when he compiled his list] he put approach after thought, according to the natural sequence, whereas here he listed diction first, which is analogous to the body, and figures, which are analogous to the bodily form, as they are more discernible through the senses than approach, which is analogous to the movements of the soul, just as we as human beings first grasp soul, body, and form; only later do we transition from there to the psychic movements.

---

[46] Roilos (2018) has emphasized the groundbreaking psycho-physiological approach to rhetoric shown by Sikeliotes.

[47] vi.139.14–140.2 Walz.

5. Emotions and λόγος ἐνδιάθετος 153

Approach, then, represents the code, as it were, or the rhetorical counterpart, of λόγος ἐνδιάθετος. The different dispositions of the soul, or emotions, are among the building blocks of such a code that can be inferred through embodied reactions. This conceptualization is also sustained, as I have anticipated, by the doctrine of *schēmata* that originated in Graeco-Roman times. The issue of figures and their categories is rather thorny.[48] What matters for our purposes, however, is that figures are closely connected to emotions already in Imperial rhetorical theory, as is shown, for instance, by the following passage from Alexander's treatise *On Figures*:[49]

ἔπειτα δὲ κἀκεῖνο λέγοι τις ἄν, ὅτι καὶ ἡ ψυχὴ κατ᾽ἀνάγκην μὲν διηνεκῶς ἐσχημάτισται, ἔστι δ᾽ ὅμως καὶ ψυχῆς κατὰ φύσιν τινὰ κινήματα καὶ παρὰ φύσιν ἐπί τε τῆς καθεστώσης καὶ φρονούσης καὶ ἐπὶ τῆς ἐν πάθεσιν οὔσης, ἀφ᾽ ἧς οἱ παθητικοὶ λόγοι. οὕτω δὴ οὖν καὶ ὁ λόγος ἔστι μὲν [ἢ] κατὰ φύσιν ἢ κατὰ συνήθειαν ἐσχηματισμένος, ὃν οὔπω φαμὲν εἶναι σχῆμα, ἔστι δέ τις καὶ παρὰ ταῦτα ὁ πεπλασμένος, ὃν ἐσχηματίσθαι λέγομεν.

Furthermore, one could also say that the soul assumes by necessity and constantly a certain form, and yet certain movements of the soul are natural while others are unnatural, depending on whether the soul is stable and sensible or immersed in passions, from which we have passionate discourses. In the same way the discourse is formed according to nature or according to habit – and in this case we do not speak of figures yet – but there is also a certain kind of discourse that is shaped against these principles and, in this case, we refer to it as figured.

The text implies the same overlap between the psychological and the linguistic that characterizes John Sikeliotes' commentary, except that figures appear here as the rhetorical counterparts of psychological affections. John himself goes to great lengths to disentangle this problem and pinpoint the difference between figures of thought and figures of speech, as well as their relationship with approach. In fact, at the beginning of his treatise *On Types of Style* Hermogenes stresses that in his view figures of thought and approaches coincide, which is precisely the position advocated by John Sikeliotes. Expanding on this point allows Sikeliotes to clarify the nexus between affections of the soul – the focus is here on the movements of the soul accompanied by reason – figures,[50] thoughts, and approaches:[51]

οὐκοῦν καὶ τὰ τοῦ Λογγίνου κατίδωμεν· εἰ πάθη ψυχῆς τὰ τῆς διανοίας σχήματα καὶ τῶν νοημάτων αὐτῆς ἀλλοιώσεις, μεταβαλλομένης πρὸς τὰ συμπίπτοντα, σχηματισμοὶ ἂν εἴησαν, εἰ δὲ σχηματισμοί, πῶς οὐ σχήματα; ἔχει ἄρα ἡ ἔννοια σχήματα τὰ πάθη τῆς ψυχῆς καὶ τὰς μεταβολάς, ἀλλ᾽ ἐπειδὴ ἐξ ἑκατέρου μέρους ἄνδρες ἔνδοξοι, δεῖ διαιτῆσαι ταῖς δόξαις, ὡς ἑκάτεροι ταῖς ἀντιφάσεσι χρῶνται καλῶς λέγοντες καὶ κακῶς κατ᾽ ἄλλο

---

[48] See Valiavitcharska (2021).

[49] xii.7–14 Spengel. The treatise has survived in an epitomized form: see Kennedy (1994) 228–9.

[50] Cf. Arist. *Int.* 1.1.

[51] vi.120.14–121.13 Walz.

154 Aglae Pizzone

καὶ ἄλλο, ἀλλ' οὐ κατὰ τὸ αὐτό· κακῶς μὲν, ὅτι οἱ μὲν τὰς μεταβολὰς τῆς ψυχῆς πρὸς τοὺς λόγους ψιλὴν ἔννοιαν λέγουσιν, ἀλλ' οὐ σχῆμα, οἱ δὲ τὴν μέθοδον καὶ τὸ πῶς δεῖ ἐξάγειν τὰ νοήματα οὐ σχῆμα, καλῶς δὲ, ὅτι ἑκάτεροι ἐννοίας λέγουσι ταύτας μεθόδους οὔσας, κινήσεις οὔσας τῆς ψυχῆς, τουτέστι τῶν νοημάτων ἐνεργείας, κἂν τῷ τρόπῳ διαφέρωσιν· εἰ δέ εἰσι παρὰ ταύτας ἕτεραι, καὶ οὐκ ὀκτὼ, ἀλλ' ἐννέα ἔσονται τῶν ἰδεῶν τὰ στοιχεῖα, καὶ οὐ τελείαν τὴν διδασκαλίαν ποιεῖται ὁ τεχνικός· τοῦτο δὲ παρ' οὐδενὶ δέδοται· ἔτι δὲ καὶ ὁ τεχνικὸς τὴν μέθοδον διανοίας σχῆμά τί φησι προϊὼν, ὅπου τὴν τάξιν τῶν στοιχείων ἀπαριθμεῖται· ἔστι μὲν γὰρ, φησί, πρῶτον ἡ ἔννοια, μετὰ ταύτην ἡ λέξις, τρίτον τὸ σχῆμα τῆς λέξεως· τὸ δὲ τῆς ἐννοίας, ὅπερ ἦν ἡ μέθοδος, τέταρτον λέγω· ἰδοὺ φανερῶς τὸ τῆς ἐννοίας σχῆμα μέθοδον εἶπε· καὶ πάλιν περὶ τῆς ἐπικρίσεως, ἥτις προδήλως σχῆμά ἐστι, μικρὸν ὕστερόν που ἐρεῖ, εἴτε οὖν σχῆμα ἡ ἐπίκρισις, εἴτε μέθοδος τῶν καλλωπιζόντων ἐστίν· ὥστε τὰ πάθη τῆς ψυχῆς τὰ μετὰ ἐπιστήμης καὶ λόγου γενόμενα σχήματα ὄντα μέθοδοί εἰσι καὶ τρόποι τῆς ἐξαγγελίας τῶν νοημάτων καὶ οὐδὲν ἕτερον, κἄν τινες διαρρήγνυνται φιλονεικοῦντες.

Let us then look also at Longinus' stance:[52] if the figures of the thinking faculty are affections of the soul and modifications of its discursive thinking in response to the events, then they will present configurations, but if they present configurations, how is it possible that they are not figures? So, the thought has as figures the affections and the transformations of the soul; however, as we have distinguished men on both sides, we must vet their opinions, given that they have contrasting points of view: they are both right and wrong on different points, but never on the same one. They are wrong in that some define the changes of the soul expressed by language as simple thoughts, but not as figures, while others do not use the term figure of the approach and the production of thoughts; they are right in that both sides call thoughts the ones that are approaches, which are the movements of the soul, i.e. operations of discursive thinking, even if they are different in their ways; for if there are other thoughts besides these, the elements of each type of style will be nine instead of eight and thus the teaching of the rhetorician is not perfect; but this point of view is not offered by anyone. Moreover, even the rhetorician himself, proceeding in his discourse, refers to the approach of the thinking faculty as figure, in the passage where he enumerates the sequence of the elements. First there is thought, he says, after that diction, third figure of diction; I count as fourth the figure of thought that was approach. Behold: he clearly called the figure of thought approach; and he does it again a little later regarding judgement, which is clearly a figure, [by saying] either judgement is a figure, or an approach [Hermog. *Id.* 1.6] of those who speak with solemnity; so, the affections of the soul that occur with knowledge and language, being figures, are approaches and ways of expressing the thoughts and nothing else, even if some quarrelsome persons argue otherwise.

Crucial for our purposes is that the affections of the soul are seen once again as 'patterns' or configurations, different from 'pure thought' and therefore to be conveyed through language. Approaches are the translation into rhetoric and language of the movements of the soul, be they accompanied by reason or not. In the latter case such movements – that is emotions – appear to be suspended between the pre-linguistic and the linguistic. They might not depend

---

[52] The quotation has been traced by Mazzucchi (1990) 187 to the *Art of Rhetoric* of Cassius Longinus.

5.2. Ethical consequences

on historical, physically uttered languages to be expressed; nonetheless, they are enacted through clearly identifiable – although virtually infinite[53] – patterns that can be categorized and encoded.

5.2. Ethical consequences

Recent criticism on John Sikeliotes' work has emphasized the 'homologies between the constitution of the human body and the composition of rhetorical "ideas". Rhetorical discourse is thus often compared to an animate entity.'[54] Such a homology is clearly at stake also in the equivalence between emotions and approach and is grounded in the very definition of λόγος ἐνδιάθετος. In the case of the emotions, Sikeliotes' theoretical framework has important consequences.

The expression of the emotions is essential to rhetoric just as the movements of the soul are essential to human nature. By building on both Hermogenes' rhetorical interpretation of and the philosophical reflections on ἐνδιάθετος λόγος, Sikeliotes grants emotions a sound ontological status. The rhetorical expression of affective states is not just functional to persuasion and manipulation, but is part of the broader task of rhetoric as conceptualized by Sikeliotes, that is the reproduction and reorganization through language of every aspect of reality. When rhetoric reaches its optimal instantiation, as happens with Gregory of Nazianzos, expressing one's affective states is not an act of pretence or *actio* but just a reflection of the speaker's innermost psychological dispositions, granted by the correspondence between ἐνδιάθετος and προφορικός λόγος. If we look at the *Life of Nikephoros*, whose authorship has recently been ascertained, as we have seen above, it turns out that Sikeliotes' theoretical stance is also reflected in practice by the way he views emotions within the hagiographical tale. In the prologue he expands on the notion of joy, underlining that tales elicit true joy only when words are consequential, inducing Christian fear in the audience.[55]

In a famous essay on the writing of history, published in 1975, Michel de Certeau expanded on the rhetoric of hagiographic discourse, stating that 'the rhetoric of this "monument" is saturated with meaning, but with identical meaning. It is a tautological tomb.'[56] It is the same illusion of perfect referentiality that Sikeliotes tries to ground methodologically in his exegesis by creating a system where Hermogenian theory of discourse and psycho-physiology are tightly connected. Emotions and rhetorical expressions are accepted as a necessary part of this 'epistemology of transparency',[57] which in turn depends very much on the nature

---

[53] *Id.* 2.7.8 and Patillon (2012) 172.
[54] Roilos (2018) 176.
[55] *Life* 1 and Papaioannou (2015) 271.
[56] Certeau (1975) 269.
[57] Certeau (1975) 266.

and worthiness of the topics addressed.[58] Sikeliotes' approach also implies a full acceptance of the whole range of emotions, including the ones with negative valence, as for instance fear, according to Gregory of Nazianzos' model, which we have seen exemplified in *Or.* 39 or at the very beginning of the *Life of Nikephoros*.

This theoretical standpoint also has larger aesthetic consequences. It explains how the use of rhetorically charged affective overtones in contemporary textual production could coexist with a Christian approach to literature. The big enterprise of metaphrastic rewritings, for instance, is characterized by a stark emphasis on pathetic effects.[59] Sikeliotes' take on the emotions and rhetorical approach provided a suitable theoretical justification, showing that this could actually be done without losing the illusion of perfect referentiality that sustained much of Christian literature. The fact that representing the emotions was considered ethically sound when a reflection of ἐνδιάθετος λόγος also points to some distinctive trends in the representation of affective states beyond literature and rhetoric. As has been noted, Byzantine artists were particularly cautious when it came to excessive and violent gestures, just like Sikeliotes, who carefully distinguishes truthfulness from ὑπόκρισις. By contrast, iconographic patterns that conveyed the idea of inner feelings or intimate reflection on one's emotions were largely preferred, especially in the public liturgical space of churches.[60] Such an inner contemplation can ultimately be regarded as the pictorial counterpart of the rhetorical expression of the emotions, qua dispositions of the soul, as theorized and practised by John Sikeliotes in his work. In turn Sikeliotes' stance does not contradict the accepted codes of behavioural conduct, which frowned upon excessive emotional display, as highlighted also by Bernard in his contribution to this volume.[61]

To sum up: the complex theoretical framework advanced by Sikeliotes in his commentary on Hermogenes, building on classical heritage, gives the expression of emotions a consistent ontological and psychological status, one that not only legitimizes them from a Christian moral point of view but is also in dialogue with Byzantine cultural practices well beyond rhetoric.

---

[58] Cf. vi.422.22–423.26 Walz.
[59] Messis and Papaioannou (2013).
[60] Maguire (2017).
[61] See also Maguire (2007b) 288–90 for secular examples (imperial images).

6

Emotional Communities in the Eleventh Century

Bodily Practices and Emotional Scripts

Floris Bernard

Introduction

When we read texts from the past that deal with emotions, we struggle with numerous hermeneutical challenges. There is the problem of language to begin with. Several scholars sympathetic to social constructionism would argue that different languages do not just create different labels for emotions, but also engender different emotional experiences.[1] Emotion terms cannot be readily translated from one language to the other language with the assumption that they cover exactly the same semantic range. Rather, they refer to different emotional scripts as conditioned by different cultures and societal norms and customs.[2]

Moreover, when reading texts from cultures of the past, in contrast to when we have a real-life conversation, we do not fully grasp the unspoken assumptions, the motions of the body, the glances of the eye, the conniving smile. This stems from a lost context of performance, but also from the fact that cultural and social mentalities are so deeply ingrained that they go unspoken, and thus remain elusive to us. From this perspective, emotions are, just like humour, a rather intractable thing to try to understand only from texts.

Finally, texts are a priori a set of verbal statements about emotions, following their own logic, obeying their own laws, and having their own reasons to distort and rehash actual emotional experience. Texts represent emotional strategies rather than psychological records of emotions.[3] For us, probing Byzantine texts, there is nothing left but to describe discursive structures, without claiming that these reflect actual emotional experience.

A way out of this conundrum may be offered by the concept of 'emotional communities', as proposed and elaborated by Barbara Rosenwein.[4] These emotional communities can be defined as groups in which people adhere to the same norms

---

[1] Harré (1986); Lutz (1988), to name only two influential studies.
[2] Wierzbicka (1999).
[3] MacMullen (2003).
[4] Rosenwein (2002), (2006).

of emotional expression and agree on how emotions, and which ones, should be appreciated or repudiated, and in what contexts. Members of an emotional community share a repertory of emotional responses to certain events, within the larger framework of cultural and religious constraints, and, if we are talking about written texts, resources of a literary or rhetorical tradition. They also share a similar emotional vocabulary, and express the same presuppositions about the nature and use of emotions. Instead of trying to reveal actual emotional experience, the displays, the discursive strategies, the textual distortions become meaningful objects of research themselves.

Rosenwein was hugely inspired by the concept of habitus as developed by Pierre Bourdieu.[5] Habitus can be taken to refer to a complex of semi-conscious and unconscious acts and manners by which social agents structure the social world around them, and are in turn structured by them. Importantly, a habitus is acquired through experience and practice, and not consciously learned. Thus, the posture of the body and the expressions on the face are hallmarks of belonging to a social group, even if they are not officially proclaimed entrance requirements of that group. A habitus is not a conscious strategy, and is not reflected upon, but competent social agents have a perfect 'feel' for how to behave in a given social setting.

As a result of all this, we can posit that authors, being social agents, describe, attribute, and prescribe emotions in their texts according to the habitus that regulates the community they live and work in. Whether these utterances are truthful or false in relation to real emotional experiences becomes somehow a moot point. The concept of 'emotional communities' also gives us the opportunity to avoid talking about 'Byzantine anger' or 'Byzantine joy' as monolithic phenomena. Instead, we can split them up into meaningful objects of research, according to the social milieu, group, or class that can be defined as an emotional community. Also, semantic analysis can benefit from this more granular approach. As Rosenwein stresses, emotional communities are bound together not only by the evaluation of emotions, but even by how they talk about emotions and what definitions they attribute to certain terms. The semantic value of words is no longer assumed to be a static notion that can serve as an unquestioned basis to start from. Rather, emotion terms can acquire different meaning and valuations dependent on the social community. Certain charged terms become fault lines and spaces of contest between social groups. Thus texts are indicative of attitudes towards emotions, and tell us something more about the culture-specific biases that create emotional dispositions.[6] Texts follow an emotional script, a term that for this purpose can retain its theatrical connotations.

---

[5] See Bourdieu (1972) for the most fundamental formulation of the concept.
[6] For this last point, see Scherer and Brosch (2009).

6. Emotional Communities in the Eleventh Century

For the analysis of emotional communities, we need to focus on one limited period, its social structures, cultural contestations, solidarities, and antagonisms. The period taken here, roughly from 990 to 1070, is characterized by a kind of polyphony, allowing us to contrast one community with the other. This advantage is offset by an important disadvantage, namely that the communities are chiefly represented by only one person. It would be wrong to see these individuals as the only voice of their community, but on the other hand it cannot be denied that they were important spokespersons and leading figures with such an authority that their writings (or speeches) effectively changed something and helped to cement communities among their disciples and students. Their texts provided behavioural models for communities on how to act and behave. These two persons are Michael Psellos (1018–*ca*. 1080) and Symeon the New Theologian (949–1022). Even if they did not live exactly in the same time period, it can be said that their views and texts greatly influenced social and cultural debates that flared up in the eleventh century and continued in later centuries.

6.1. Michael Psellos: the shaping of the urban gentleman

Let us begin with Michael Psellos, the well-known scholar, orator, and philosopher.[7] The multifarious texts of Michael Psellos have been read in many different ways and with different purposes in mind. I will here follow an approach that situates his intellectual activity in a contemporary context of education and social strife. Psellos thrived in a social milieu that saw education as a stepping stone to power. It is as a teacher that Psellos amassed his influence. Many of his texts need to be seen as accompanying or propping up his 'teaching business'.

Psellos' funeral orations for his students and pupils are a case in point. These texts highlight the embeddedness of Psellos' intellectual activities in a lively contemporary context, and bring out the narrow connection of education with social services and social cohesion. In the highly competitive school context of eleventh-century Constantinople, teacher and pupils together formed a sort of clique, ready to defend each other and rally against other teachers and schools in ritualized competitions. Many letters of Psellos show how his teaching is used to maintain and enhance relationships with the family of pupils, and laid the foundation for important bonds in later life, when former students, as important officials, rendered services to their former teacher.[8]

---

[7] It would not be very fruitful to give an exhaustive bibliography on Michael Psellos. For Psellos in Byzantine intellectual history, see Jenkins (2017). For Psellos in Byzantine literary history, see Papaioannou (2013).

[8] Bernard (2017).

160 *Floris Bernard*

Obviously, funeral orations express sadness and grief. But funeral orations also provide detailed character portraits of the deceased. In doing so, they impart an idealized type of personal behaviour, and, consequently, of emotional expression. It is important to keep in mind that these speeches were pronounced in front of an audience of family and friends, who sought consolation and solidarity in the speech. Thus, the description of a beloved person becomes an ideal type which members of the audience were supposed to identify with and to imitate. Of course, these portraits can be said to be full of *topoi* and not give us faithful descriptions of individualities. But I propose to consider these so-called *topoi* not as immutable laws of the genre, but rather as building blocks of certain ideals that live on in a society or community and in this respect become meaningful objects of research.

First of all, the funeral speeches repeatedly stress the social cohesion among Psellos' students, confirmed by emotional bonds. The group of students is, for example, referred to as a λογικὸς σύνδεσμος, a 'community of letters'.[9] Elsewhere, Psellos uses names of various military units to describe his student body, which underlines the competitiveness and, so to speak, militant nature of these student cliques. In both instances, Psellos states that the community is now threatened in its unity by the death of one of its members. The funeral oration is thus an important ritual moment where a shared display of emotions reaffirms the bonds between teacher and students, and underlines the values of the community.

In the funeral oration for a deceased pupil of his, probably to be identified with Anastasios Lyzix,[10] Psellos emphasizes the importance of emotions and behaviour to the cohesion of his group:[11]

οἷς μὲν γὰρ ὑπόγυια τὰ τῆς φιλίας δεσμά, τούτοις καὶ τὸ ἀποβεβληκέναι, οὓς προσφάτως ἐφίλησαν, οὐ λίαν ὀδυνηρόν, οἷς δὲ ὁ μακρὸς χρόνος εἰς φιλίαν ψυχὰς ἀνεκέρασεν, οἱ τοιοῦτοι πῶς ἂν στέρξαιεν ἀλλήλων στερούμενοι; εἰ δὲ καὶ ὁ τρόπος τῆς συνουσίας καὶ ἡ ταύτης ἀρχὴ οὐ κώμων καὶ πότων ἤρτηται, οὐδὲ τοῦ συγκυβεύειν ἢ συσφαιρίζειν, ἀλλὰ Μουσῶν καὶ λόγων καὶ τῆς ἄλλης χάριτος, πῶς ἂν ἀπαθῶς φέροιεν οἱ τοιοῦτοι διαλυό[μεν]οι;

People whose bonds of friendship are still fresh will not find it too painful if they have to lose those whom they only got to love recently. But those people whose souls are by long time mingled together towards friendship, how could they endure being bereft of each other? And if the character and principle of their companionship do not depend on revelries or drinks, nor on playing dice or ball together, but on Muses and words and other graces, how could such people bear to be separated, without being moved?

Psellos reminds his audience of the bonds of mutual affection, expressed by an expected display of emotions. Friends are said not to bear separation without

---

[9] *Or.* 7.1, ed. Polemis (2014), line 8. For military imagery, see *Or.* 9.5.
[10] Gautier (1978) 89–90.
[11] *Or.* 8.1, ed. Polemis (2014), lines 23–30.

6. Emotional Communities in the Eleventh Century   161

emotion (*apathōs*: a term to keep in mind). To feel and to show emotions at occasions of death is represented as a duty, a ritualized act that keeps the community together. Hence the violent outbursts of grief that we encounter in funeral orations and which sometimes strike us as exaggerated.

At the same time, Psellos' speech defines the relationships between students as emotional bonds of friendship. This bond is rooted in a strong sense of solidarity created by appreciating the same activities from an early age. Education and schooling not only transmit formal knowledge, but also imprint group behaviour, a way of life, on young boys, dictating what to like and what to dislike. The contrast with other groups is deliberately emphasized, thus enhancing its special nature: *their* community is devoted to the Muses, not to trivial games.

Having thus set the stage for the emotional outbursts of grief in his speech, he moves on to the *laudatio* of the deceased Anastasios, giving a detailed description of his inner and outer qualities. Being a self-conscious orator, Psellos announces the key term *ēthē* when character and manners come up in this direct address to the deceased friend:[12]

> ἀλλὰ καὶ τοῖς ἤθεσι καὶ τοῖς σχήμασιν ἐφήρμοστό σοι πάντα καὶ κατάλληλα ἦν πρὸς ἄλ-
> ληλα. ὅ τε γὰρ γέλως σοι αἰδοῖ σύγκρατος καὶ τὴν αἰδῶ ἱλαρὰν ἡ τῆς ψυχῆς χάρις ἐδεί-
> κνυεν, ἀπήνθιστο δέ σοι καὶ τὸ στόμα Μούσαις ἅμα καὶ Χάρισι καὶ οὔθ' αἱ Μοῦσαι τῶν
> Χαρίτων ἄτερ οὔθ' αἱ Χάριτες τῶν Μουσῶν χωρὶς ἐπεδείκνυντο. πρὸς οὐδὲν δέ σοι οὔτε
> ὁ θεατὴς οὔθ' ὁ ἀκροατὴς ἐδυσχέραινεν, [ἀλλ' ὁ μὲν] τῷ ἤθει τερπόμενος καὶ τῷ κάλλει
> τοῦ σώματος, προσθήσω δὲ καὶ τῇ τῆς χειρὸς εὐρυθμίᾳ ἐκ κ[.....] τὸν κάλαμον ἔχοντος
> τοῖς τε ἄλλοις ἀπῄει τερπόμενος.

> But also in your character and outward appearance everything was in proportion and in harmony with each other. Your laughter was restrained by prudence and yet the grace of your soul showed your prudence to be of a cheerful kind. Your mouth blossomed with Muses and Graces alike, and neither did the Muses show themselves without Graces, nor the Graces without the Muses. No one who looked at you or listened to you would be irritated by anything, rather, all were charmed by your character and by the beauty of your body, I would add also by the beautiful rhythm of your hand ... holding the pen, and they would go away delighted.

The personality of Anastasios radiates cheerfulness and gladness, which he transmits to all who meet him. But, importantly, when Psellos speaks about his laughter, he adds that it is 'restrained by prudence (*aidōs*)'. This prudence, in turn, should not be shown in a pure form, but rather qualified by a dose of cheerfulness. Anastasios' cheerfulness is thus refined and restrained rather than ebullient and boundless. *Charis* is a key concept in this: it refers to an innate quality, something that enchants without being overbearing.

Apart from *ēthē*, referring to inner qualities, Psellos also emphasizes Anastasios' *schēma*, which refers to an individual's external appearance. Here, Psellos

---

[12] *Or.* 8.3, ed. Polemis (2014) lines 14–23.

162 *Floris Bernard*

gives the example of Anastasios' beautiful handwriting. Calligraphy was indeed an activity well valued by this public of students and aspiring bureaucrats.

The idea of moderately restrained cheerfulness is best expressed by restrained laughter, and/or the soundless smile. Smiles are ubiquitous in Psellos' praise of individuals. This is, for example, a concise formulation of a graceful personality, to be found in an oration for a certain Radenos, also a deceased pupil of Psellos.[13]

ἡ τῶν ἠθῶν με κρᾶσις ἀνθέλκει, ὁ χαριέστατος τρόπος, ὁ εὐφυέστατος λόγος, τοῦ μειδιά-
ματος τὸ γλυκύ, τοῦ νοήματος τὸ ὀξύ.

The mixture of his personal traits attracted me: his most graceful manners, his naturally gifted speech, the sweetness of his smile, the sharpness of his mind.

Another funeral oration for a pupil, named as Romanos referendarios, contains one of the most detailed discussions of how an emotional script also includes care for the body. Just before this passage, Psellos had praised Romanos' excellence in legal studies.[14]

τοῖς μὲν οὖν ἄλλοις τὰ τοιαῦτα θεωρήματα νέφος ἐπάγει σκεπτομένοις καὶ σκυθρωπό-
τητα, ἐκείνῳ δὲ ἱλαρὰ ἡ ψυχὴ καὶ χαρίεις ἁπανταχοῦ. τοῦτο δὲ πλάτος κατηγορεῖ φύσεως, ὡς, ὅσοι στενοὶ τὴν γνώμην εἰσίν, ἐπὶ πᾶσι χαρίτων ἐστέρηνται καὶ τὴν ἔνδοθεν πλά-
νην ὁ τῶν ὀφρύων δεικνύει δεσμός. ἀλλ' οὐκ ἐκεῖνος τοιοῦτος (πολλοῦ γε καὶ δεῖ). λέγω
δὲ ταῦτα ὁμοῦ τε ἐκείνῳ προτιθεὶς τοὺς ἐπαίνους καὶ τοὺς φαύλους ἐπέχων ζωγράφους,
ὅσοι δὴ κακῶς καὶ τὴν ἀρετὴν καὶ τὰς ἑαυτῶν χρωματουργοῦσι ψυχάς, οὔτ' ἐλευθερίως ζῆν αἱρούμενοι, οὔτε δὴ μεγαλοπρέπειάν τινα τοῖς προσομιλοῦσιν ἐπιδεικνύμενοι,
ἀλλ' ἢν μὴ τὰς τρίχας ἀποτίλωσι καὶ τοὺς ὄνυχας ἀποξεύωσι, μηδ' ἐκπλύνειαν ἑαυτοὺς
ἢ ἀποκαθάρειαν, ἀρκοῦσαν τοῦτο οἰόμενοι ἐπίδειξιν ἀρετῆς. ἔγωγ' οὖν διῳκισμένους
οἶδα τοὺς βίους, καὶ τὸν μὲν πολιτικὸν κατανενόηκα, τὸν δὲ ἀπότομόν τινα καὶ τὴν φύσιν ὑπερφωνήσαντα.

When other people examined these [legal] problems, a cloud of sullenness descended over them, but the soul of this man [i.e. Romanos] was cheerful and graceful under all circumstances. This fact proves the breadth of human nature, because all narrow-minded people are bereft of graces; and the furrowing of their eyebrows is a sign of their inner error. But he was not of that kind, far from it. I am saying this both to express praise for him, and to hold back those miserable painters, who give bad portraits of virtue and of their own souls: they do not choose to live freely, nor do they display any grandeur to their interlocutors. Instead, they consider it as a sufficient sign of their virtue, if they do not cut their hair, nor clip their nails, nor wash or clean themselves. Hence I am aware that lifestyles are far apart, and I consider the one 'urbane' (*politikos*), and the other severe, shouting down nature.

There is a strong idea of distinctness from other groups, based on bodily appearance and emotional display. People like Romanos take delight in intellectual pursuits. Their countenance is marked by cheerfulness and grandeur, qualities that are here, as elsewhere, subsumed by the term *charis*. Not only are these

---

[13] *Or.*3, ed. Gautier (1978), lines 25–7.
[14] *Or.* 9.3, ed. Polemis (2014), lines 16–21.

6. Emotional Communities in the Eleventh Century 163

men full of joy, they also transmit this joy to others. They act more spontaneously, in accordance with human nature (*phusis*). 'Nature' is indeed a key term in Psellos' world view, also playing a role in his views on authorship and discursive resourcefulness, highlighting his authenticity and variability.[15]

The outsiders to this community are clearly contrasted with this. They are characterized by their external appearance, their lack of bodily care, and the facial expression they assume, in this case frowning. And when Psellos observes that they consider this a sign of virtue, there is the implicit assumption that emotional display and facial expressions are consciously used strategies that can be semiotically decoded and have social significance. Without doubt, Psellos has an ascetic kind of monk in view – in a passage in his *Chronographia*, he is more explicit about the extreme display of supposed virtue in certain monks.[16] Here, it is implied that, contrary to those who live 'freely' (if ἐλευθερίως can be translated thus), they abide by unnecessary rules that oppress their nature.

As often, Psellos shows an acute awareness of social distinctions, and is keen to develop his own vocabulary in order to mark these distinctions. Here, he gives his definition of what it means to be *politikos*, a very charged term that he also defines to his own advantage elsewhere.[17] There is an etymological ring referring to the *polis*, the body politic, or even more literally the city, Constantinople, with all its cultural connotations. This is the place (imagined and real) of intense social interactions, where learning and elegant manners are appreciated.[18] The *politikos bios* also more narrowly refers to the meritocratic career path of the civil elite, with which Psellos is so eager to identify himself (and his friends). Spontaneity, innate elegance, and a flexible, cheerful countenance are hallmarks of this emotional script. On the other side, there is the group of monastics or ascetics, defined by the term σκυθρωπότης, that is, sullenness, or a grave countenance.

The same strong idea of distinction is also present in Psellos' funeral oration for Niketas, a former fellow pupil who became his teaching colleague. Psellos describes at length their time together at school as young students. He focuses again on the *ēthē*, the personal traits:[19]

αἱ δὲ τῶν ἠθῶν ὁμοιότητες μιᾶς ἐδόκουν ψυχῆς. οὐ γὰρ τὰ μὲν πρὸς τὴν φύσιν δεξιοί τε καὶ ἴσοι, τὴν δὲ γνώμην ἀλλότριοι, ἀλλὰ χαρίεντές τε ἄμφω καὶ τοῖς καλλίστοις ἐφηδόμενοι καὶ ἤθεσι καὶ παιδεύμασι. τῶν γὰρ ἄλλων σκυθρωπαζόντων καὶ κόμην τρεφόντων, ὥστε ταύτῃ δοκεῖν περιττοί, καὶ τἆλλα ποιούντων οἷς τὸ δοκεῖν θηρᾶται, ἀλλ' οὐ τὸ εἶναι δείκνυται, ἡμεῖς ἐν γλώττῃ ποιούμενοι τὴν ἐπίδειξιν καὶ τὸ περιττὸν ἐν τοῖς παιδεύμασιν ἐνδεικνύμενοι, οὐδὲ τῆς πολιτικῆς ἡμελοῦμεν χάριτος.

---

[15] Papaioannou (2013) 147–52.
[16] Book 6b (*Theodora*) 18, ed. Reinsch (2014).
[17] Book 6b (*Theodora*) 7–8, ed. Reinsch (2014).
[18] See also Cupane (2011).
[19] *Or.* 4.3, ed. Polemis (2014), lines 10–18.

164 *Floris Bernard*

The similarities of our personalities seemed to be those of one soul, since it was not the case that we were talented and equal in our nature, and yet different in opinions. No, we were both agreeable, and we were attracted to the most beautiful lifestyle and subjects of learning. Whereas the others assumed a grave countenance, letting their hair grow to appear special, and doing those other things by which people pursue an external appearance without showing their actual character, we made a display of our eloquence instead, and we showed our distinctiveness in education, without neglecting the urbane elegance.

Psellos creates clear-cut binary oppositions here. On the one hand, there are people like him and Niketas, defined by *politikē charis*, the refinement expected from worldly-wise gentlemen. On the other hand, some people display a sullen countenance (*skuthrōpazein* is again the term used) and neglect their body. Psellos suspects that the other group is even consciously cultivating that image, and he demystifies their appearance. When we consider that in some other texts of Psellos, he defends himself against the accusation of showing off and hypocrisy, we sense that there is a certain struggle going on to lay claim to sincerity. Here is also where 'nature' becomes important in this passage: in Psellos' projected community, this nature shows itself transparently, without efforts to force it to become something else. This passage, like the whole oration, emphasizes the importance of shared education in shaping a certain emotional profile. *Ēthos* and *paideuma* in this fragment are combined social markers, again suggesting that common education at school is as much a training in a desired behaviour as it is an acquaintance with subject matter.

But when we further read the oration for Niketas, it becomes clear that this idealized type of emotional behaviour is by no means uniform or static. It is certainly not so for an author such as Psellos, who values adaptability so much.[20] Thus, when Psellos describes how Niketas became a bishop,[21] his emotional profile changes.[22]

οὐ γὰρ ὥσπερ Φωκίων καὶ Κάτων βαρεῖς καὶ οὐκ ἀνεκτοὶ φανέντες, οὐδὲ κατάλληλοι τοῖς καιροῖς, μετὰ τῶν πραγμάτων καὶ ἑαυτὸν προσαπώλεσεν, οὐδὲ σκυθρωπὴν ἐδείκνυ τὴν ἀρετήν, οὐδὲ μὴ σπουδαίαν τὴν χάριν, ἀλλ᾽ ἕκαστον τῇ τοῦ ἑτέρου σπουδῇ δεικνὺς σπουδαιότερον, ὁμοῦ τε τοῖς ὁμοίοις ὅμοιος ἦν, καὶ τῶν ἐκ μέρους γνωριζομένων καλλί- ων παρὰ πολύ, σκυθρωποῦ τε καὶ χαρίεντος ἐν μέσῳ γενόμενος, ἀμφοτέρους ἂν ἥδυνε, πρὸς μὲν τὸν σκυθρωπάσας συμμέτρως, πρὸς δὲ τὸν ἐμμελῶς χαριεντισάμενος. εἰ γὰρ καὶ γεγηθέναι ἐῴκει τῷ βλέμματι τό τε ἦθος αὐτῷ πρὸς τὸ χαριέστερον ἐτετόρευτο, ἀλλ᾽ ἡ φροντὶς ἔστιν οὗ συνῆγεν τὰς ὀφρῦς καὶ ἐδέσμει τὸν γέλωτα.

He was not like Phokion and Cato, who displayed a grave and unbearable appearance without adapting themselves to the circumstances; he did not lose himself in his occupations, nor did he display a virtue that was sullen, or a grace that was frivolous. Instead, he showed

---

[20] This quality of Psellos' oeuvre is perhaps most adequately discussed by Ljubarskij (1978).
[21] I conclude this from *Or.* 4.7, ed. Polemis (2014), line 5: ἀρχιερωσύνη.
[22] *Or.* 4.7, ed. Polemis (2014), lines 13–24.

6. Emotional Communities in the Eleventh Century 165

that each one of them is more important when used in pursuit of the other. At the same time, he was similar to those who were similar, and he was far more becoming than those who made themselves only partly recognizable. He found the middle between sullen and graceful, and gave sweetness to both: to the one person, he was moderately stern, to the other, he would be lighthearted in a harmonious way. And even if his eyes seemed to rejoice, and his personality leaned towards elegance, still at times worries drew together his eyebrows and held his laughter in check.

Psellos is very keen to point out the moderateness of Niketas' emotions: moving between 'serious' and 'cheerful', he is said to combine both. Psellos attributes much importance to emotional display in his descriptions of social roles, and insists on the key terms *skuthrōpos* and *charieis*. At the end, he again puts forward an image of restraint: the laughter is there, but it is restrained, and Niketas also frowns when this is appropriate. But Psellos remains keen to point out that Niketas rather leaned towards *charis*. So there is not so much a radical change; rather a flexibility dependent on a given role in society. It appears that high office, especially of a clerical kind, brings with it another form of emotional behaviour. In contrast to the schoolboy he once was, Niketas as a bishop cannot laugh out loud and has to show a degree of severity as well.

We need to keep this flexibility in mind. Psellos does not describe persons in terms of fixed types; he is interested in how well they adapt to social roles. With this in mind, we can better understand why in what is perhaps the fullest character portrait in Psellos' oeuvre, that of Constantine IX Monomachos in the *Chronographia*, someone is represented as very cheerful and light-hearted and yet negatively valued.[23] Psellos simply does not find this light-heartedness fitting for an emperor, especially not within the broader argument of the *Chronographia*, whose genre necessitates an emphasis on values such as military valour.

This applies even more to portraits of monks. In his funeral speech for the abbot of the monastery of Horaia Pege, the monastery where Psellos himself had resided, he again puts forward moderateness as a chief virtue:[24]

καίτοι τὰ πολλὰ καὶ χαριεντιζόμενος ἦν, μείλιχα τοῖς προσιοῦσι φθεγγόμενος, ἀλλ᾽ οὐκ ἐν τῷ σκυθρωπῷ τὸ σεβάσμιον, οὐδὲ ἐν τῷ κατηφεῖ τὸ μακάριον, ἀλλ᾽ ἐν τῷ τὴν ἀρετὴν εἰδέναι ἐπιστημόνως μεταχειρίζεσθαι.

And yet, he could also be playful on many occasions, and speak sweetly to people approaching him; he did not look for respectability by being sullen, nor for sanctity by being downcast, but he acquired those by knowing how to handle virtue with expert knowledge.

Psellos emphatically does not deny the abbot all cheerfulness altogether, but cannot of course portray him as a playful character. He censures others who attempted to achieve an impression of sanctity by being excessively sullen. In Psellos'

---

[23] For character portraits in the *Chronographia*, see Lauritzen (2013).
[24] *Or.* 10.26, ed. Polemis (2014), lines 1–4.

166 *Floris Bernard*

world view, monastic people too should be moderate in their emotional profile, and retain a dose of sociability.

The next example is not a funeral speech in the strict sense of the word, but an encomium for Symeon Metaphrastes. As Stratis Papaioannou has keenly observed, this text presents Symeon as an ideal, 'saintly' author.[25] Psellos voices his own ideas about authorship by projecting them on to Symeon. But the text deals not only with authorship as a discursive activity, but also with the *ēthos* of the author and his role in society. Thus, Psellos makes sure to distance Symeon from what he calls 'idle philosophers' (line 89) who did not contribute to society, but rather cared to let their beards grow and to be sullen in their face (line 98: σκυθρωποὶ τοῖς προσώποις γεγόνασιν). Symeon is very different:[26]

καὶ ἐπὶ τούτοις οὐδὲ χαρίτων ἄμοιρος ὁ ἀνήρ, ἀλλὰ κατήρτυτο αὐτῷ πρὸς πᾶσαν σπουδὴν μετ᾽ ἐμμελοῦς παιδιᾶς καὶ ἡ γλῶττα καὶ ἡ διάνοια. μεγαλοπρεπῶς δὲ ἔχων καὶ τῆς στολῆς καὶ τοῦ σχήματος ἅμα δὲ καὶ τοῦ βαδίσματος ἀντήλλαττε τὸ ἦθος πρὸς τὸ φαινόμενον, ἐπίχαρίς τε ὢν καὶ εὐπρόσιτος καὶ αὐτόθεν ἕλκων πάντας τῷ μειδιάματι.

Nor was the man deprived of charm, having trained his tongue and mind to treat any serious matter with the required lightness of touch. Counterbalancing a grand manner, which was apparent in his dress, style, and even the way that he walked, were a character that was full of charm and made him easy to approach, and a smile that immediately drew everyone to him.

Smiles, the way of walking, dressing, and talking, can all be interpreted as indications of someone's social profile. Here, Psellos is again at pains to present a balanced portrait: the charm and accessibility, which situate Symeon in a *politikos* environment, is offset by remarks about the stateliness or grandeur of his manners. Fittingly, the smile is again an ingredient of this portrait.

So far, we have been discussing only positive examples. But it is of course interesting to see how this emotional script contrasts with negative portrayals. I will discuss here just one: in his *Chronographia*, Psellos gives a portrait of someone who is interfering in his own sphere of activities. This figure is Leo Paraspondylos,[27] advisor to emperors, and also for a while a friend of Psellos.[28]

οὗτος γοῦν ὁ ἀνὴρ τὸ ἄχθος τῶν βασιλικῶν διοικήσεων κατωμαδὸν ἀράμενος, φορτικὸς ἔδοξε τοῖς πολλοῖς· τοῦ γὰρ πολιτικοῦ ἤθους, ὡς ἔφην, ἐστέρητο· ὅθεν οὔτε χαριέστατος ὤν, οὔτε τοῖς προσιοῦσι δεξιῶς ὁμιλῶν, ἀλλ᾽ ἀεὶ καὶ πᾶσι τὸ τραχὺ τοῦ ἤθους ἐπιδεικνύμενος, καὶ πᾶσαν ἀποστρεφόμενος ἔντευξιν, καὶ εἰ μή τις εἴποι τὸ ἄρθρον τῆς ὑποθέσεως, ἀλλά τι καὶ προοιμιάσαιτο, βαρυθυμῶν καὶ δεινοπαθῶν ἀπεχθὴς σύμπασιν ὦπτο, καὶ οὐδεὶς προσιέναι ἐβούλετο, ὅτι μὴ πᾶσα ἀνάγκη. ἔγωγ᾽ οὖν τὴν στάθμην τῆς τοιαύτης γνώμης θαυμάζω μὲν, αἰῶσι μὲν ἀλλ᾽ οὐ χρόνοις πρόσφορον ἥγημαι, καὶ βίῳ τῷ μέλλοντι ἀλλ᾽ οὐ τῷ ἐφεστηκότι· τὸ γὰρ ἀπαθὲς πάντη καὶ ἄθελκτον ὑπὲρ πάσας τὰς

---

[25] Papaioannou (2013) 158–62.
[26] *Or. 7*, ed. Fisher (1994), lines 140–6, trans. Papaioannou (2013) 161.
[27] On their relationship, see also De Vries-van der Velden (1999).
[28] Book 6a (*Konstantinos IX*), c. 7, ed. Reinsch (2014). Translation is my own.

6. Emotional Communities in the Eleventh Century   167

σφαίρας τίθεμαι καὶ ἔξω τῆς περιοχῆς τοῦ παντός· ὁ δέ γε μετὰ σώματος βίος, ἅτε πολιτικώτερος, ἁρμοδιώτερος τοῖς παροῦσι καιροῖς, μᾶλλον δὲ τῷ σωματικῷ βίῳ τὸ πάσχον κατάλληλον τῆς ψυχῆς.

This man took over the burden of imperial administration, and in this he appeared to many as an uncouth person, because he lacked, as I have said before, a civilized personality (*politikon ēthos*). As a result, he was not agreeable, nor did he converse skilfully with people who approached him. Instead, he displayed the churlish side of his character to everyone. He was averse to every conversation, and when someone did not bring up the core of a subject immediately, but provided some kind of introduction, he would be indignant and lose his temper, making an odious impression on everyone. Therefore, no one approached him when it was not absolutely necessary. On the one hand, I admire the stability of such a character, but I consider it rather fitting for eternity than for human times, and rather for the future life than the present one. For the quality of always being passionless (*apathēs*) and uncharmed, I would locate it above all spheres and out of our reach. But the bodily life, by virtue of being more civilized (*politikos*), is more apt to our times, and the sensorial part (*to paschon*) of the soul is fitting to the bodily life.

Psellos again considers the use and control of emotions as flexible according to the social context. When having a responsible function, when leading a life in the midst of society, as a *politikos anēr*, the emotional behaviour needs to be in line with this. Leo, by contrast, remained inflexible and passionless (*apathēs*), everything the urbane gentleman is not. The term *apathēs*, if taken generally, seems to elicit some respect from Psellos, before he makes the argument that for a civil function it is not the most appropriate. And elsewhere in this chapter Psellos points out Leo's proneness to anger, or at least impatience with rhetorical frivolities. It is not so much emotionlessness that Psellos finds fault with in Leo, but rather severity, in manners, habits, and also tastes.

Certain key terms again receive an almost explicit definition. In the last sentence of the fragment, the *politikon ēthos* is defined as the lifestyle of the urbanite, imbued with natural *charis*. The notion of 'body' is connected to this; it appears here in a similar role as does 'nature' elsewhere in the Psellian oeuvre. It is a life that does not shun passions, in the sense that there is room for sociability, and for the appreciation of the beautiful and enjoyable things of life.

Also in other genres than the funeral oration, Psellos negotiates the terms and conditions of the emotional community he constructs around him. Letters are a powerful tool to do so.[29] Addressed to acquaintances, and often read aloud in circles of friends, they have the power to confirm, redefine, and demarcate the bonds that hold a community together. And as Margaret Mullett states: 'The Byzantine letter is above all a vehicle for emotion.'[30] Letters frequently discuss and negotiate emotions, either expressing those of the writer, or trying to influence the emotions of the recipient. The latter aspect is perhaps most obvious

---

[29] On Psellos' letters, see now Jeffreys and Lauxtermann (2017).
[30] Mullett (1981) 82.

168 *Floris Bernard*

in consolation letters, which attempt to relieve the grief of the recipient over the death of a family member or friend.[31]

There is no space here to discuss all the nuances and ramifications of epistolary emotions; rather, I would like to bring up two ideas: the emotionality itself of Psellos' emotional community (by which I mean the understanding that its members are allowed, and even encouraged, to give in to, to express emotions), and the emphasis on cheerfulness, charm, and light-heartedness, an emphasis already apparent from the funeral orations discussed above.

The very processes of writing and reading letters are themselves portrayed as acts arousing powerful emotions. An illuminating example is Psellos' letter to his powerful protector in later life, the *caesar* John Doukas. Psellos reassures John about the goodwill of his brother, the emperor Constantine X Doukas. To give evidence of this favourable disposition, Psellos reports how Constantine had appreciated a letter sent by John, and read out aloud by Psellos.[32]

ἔγωγ' οὖν αὐτῷ τὴν σὴν ὑπαναγινώσκων ἐπιστολὴν ἑώρων ὅπως τὰ μὲν ἡδέως προσεμειδία, τὰ δὲ ἱλαρύνετο. ὅτε δὲ ἐπανέγνων αὐτῷ τὸν μοναχὸν καί τὴν ἀθρόαν ἀλλοίωσιν, μικροῦ δεῖν καὶ ἐξεδάκρυσεν.

When I read out your letter to him, I saw how he sweetly smiled at some things, and was gladdened by others. But when I read to him about the monk and the sudden change, he almost burst into tears.

Passages such as this one imply that the performance of letters, in a social setting, gave rise to various emotions, and that these are important indicators of how letters were perceived (and acted upon).

Other letters of Psellos convey the expectation of cheerfulness and avoidance of severity. In a letter to his good friend John Mauropous, Psellos reacts to an apparent reproach of Mauropous that his friend did not take his troubles seriously enough. Psellos reminds him, with playful rhetorical questions, of the cheerful emotional attitude that should govern the exchange of letters.[33]

διατὶ δὲ καὶ τῆς φιλίας τὰς χάριτας οὐκ ἀναιρεῖς, αἱ δὴ τὸ σεμνὸν αὐτῆς μετριάζουσιν, συγκεκραμμένην δεικνύουσιν καὶ τῆς μουσικῆς ἡρμοσμένην; ἀλλὰ τί ἔδει με ποιεῖν, ἐφ' οἷς αὐτὸς αὐτόθεν βαρυθυμεῖς καὶ μὴ φέρεις τὰ δρώμενα, σκυθρωπάζειν ἐν ταῖς ἐπιστολαῖς καὶ ἀμειδὲς φθέγγεσθαι;

Why don't you abandon the graces of friendship altogether, which moderate its seriousness, and show how it [friendship] is mingled with, and adapted to, the art of the Muses? What ought I to have done, in reaction to the events which make you yourself automatically dejected and have problems to endure? Should I in my letters then be sullen and speak without smiles?

---

[31] Littlewood (1999).
[32] Letter 43, ed. Papaioannou (2019), lines 68–72.
[33] Letter 175, ed. Papaioannou (2019), lines 32–7.

6. Emotional Communities in the Eleventh Century 169

There seems to be a set of emotions required to fulfil the laws of the epistolographic genre, which often seem to be as much social codes as they are literary convention. Letters are supposed to bring joy and in adverse situations to console. Thus, being sullen (*skuthrōpazein*) when writing letters, as Psellos here argues, is anathema; a playful smile should always be in the background. This shared understanding of jocularity formed the basis of the many jokes, teasing mockeries and enigmatic *double entendres* in Byzantine epistolography.[34]

The notion of *asteiotēs* subsumes this desire for jocularity and cheerful emotionality, connecting it at the same time with the physical space of our emotional community: the city. *Asteiotēs*, which can be translated as 'urbanity', underlines the elegance of a city-dweller, wilfully contrasting it with the outsider who has coarse manners – also often an outsider in a spatial sense: outside Constantinople.

In a speech against his detractors, Psellos gives his definition of what it means to be *asteios*, implying that it created animosity.[35] The text thus offers an apology for the emotional contours of our community. The discussion centres on the 'graces of character': Psellos stresses how these have come to him naturally. His manners and eloquence are the outcome of nature and talent. They show themselves spontaneously: they are not something that one could just learn as a *technē*. His character is graceful (εὔχαρις), which Psellos explains as adaptability to the circumstances, even giving faithful imitations. This paves the way for a corresponding form of emotional behaviour, again expressed by the restrained laughter, the natural, God-given smile (which Psellos also associates with statues in this text).

There is no other contemporary author who reflects on emotional behaviour with the same intensity and with a similar attention for social roles as Psellos does. Emotional scripts can only be gained indirectly. The poems of Christopher of Mytilene (fl. 1025–50?) about Constantinople and its inhabitants, full of puns, *recherché* jokes, teasing mockeries, may reveal something of the gaiety of contemporary poetry and urban elite culture.[36]

The works of Psellos' teacher and friend John Mauropous (*ca.* 1000–*ca.* 1080) are another matter. Because of their preoccupation with autobiographical apology, Mauropous' poems and letters brim with emotional experience. The epistolary network of himself and his friends is dominated by a distinction between distress and joy (often κατήφεια and χαρά), in which the services offered by him and his friends (and of course the letters themselves) are supposed to turn the negative emotion into the opposite.[37] These oppositional pairs are

---

[34] Bernard (2015).

[35] *Or.* 7, ed. Littlewood (1985), lines 105–20. For a discussion of this passage, see also Papaioannou (2013) 142–4 and Bernard (2013).

[36] De Groote (2012).

[37] Typical examples are Letters 27 and 56, ed. Karpozilos (1990).

170   *Floris Bernard*

connected to facial expressions and bodily postures that are similar to those we find in Psellos. For example, at the apex of his career, when being introduced to the emperors (supposedly with the help of his pupil Psellos), Mauropous wrote a long poem of gratitude in which the following lines appear:[38]

ἄγροικος ἦν χθές, ἀστικὸς δὲ νῦν μάλα·
κάτω νενευκώς, ἀλλὰ νῦν ἄνω βλέπων·
ἄθυμος, ἀλλ᾿ εὔθυμος, ἡδονῆς γέμων·
μικρός, κατηφής, νῦν δὲ λαμπρὸς καὶ μέγας.

I was boorish yesterday, but now I am urbane.
I looked downwards, but now I look upwards;
I was desperate, but now I am happy and full of joy,
I was inconsiderable, dejected, but now brilliant and great.

Mauropous' entry at the court corresponds with a move from outside the city to within, from social insignificance to a high and renowned position, coinciding with his first acquaintance with the imperial family. This social and spatial promotion is coupled with a change in bodily posture, notably downward-looking versus upward-looking, sullenness versus cheerfulness. As the pithy formulation in the first verse of this quotation exemplifies, *agroikos*, the cultural 'boorishness', is associated with a bodily posture, and diametrically opposed to *asteiotēs*, which combines a spatial, physical presence in the city with social status, and a new emotional profile.

6.2. Symeon the New Theologian: the emotional conditioning of the monk

Symeon and Psellos did not live at exactly the same time. But Symeon's impact loomed large over the same period, through the equally formidable figure of Niketas Stethatos, who promoted his cult. Niketas edited Symeon's texts, notably the hymns, and wrote Symeon's *Vita*.[39] It is not far-fetched to say that these texts exercised their influence on people who were contemporaries of Michael Psellos.

Symeon is known as a mystical writer, innovative theologian, and monastic reformer.[40] While his ideas on mystical union have received the most attention from scholars, there can be no doubt that Symeon's texts constitute an effort to prescribe, condition, and regulate the emotions of each individual monk who is a member of Symeon's community, the monastery of St Mammas, which Symeon led from around 990 to 1005. His numerous works, in poetry and prose, whether

---

[38] Poem 54, lines 64–7, ed. Lagarde (1882).

[39] On the relationship between Niketas and Symeon, see Hinterberger (2012).

[40] A selection from the more recent bibliography includes McGuckin (1996); Markopoulos (2008); Turner (1990); and Koder (2011).

6. Emotional Communities in the Eleventh Century

171

catecheses, chapters, or hymns, address the question of how to achieve spiritual perfection. What we would today call emotions play a primordial role in this. Of course, Symeon is directly and indirectly influenced by earlier spiritual writers; his thoughts on emotions are part of a long monastic tradition connecting him with authors such as Theodore Stoudios and John Klimax, ultimately deriving from Evagrios of Pontos and beyond to the first monastic fathers.[41] However, every study of Symeon notices how his teachings are also innovative and idiosyncratic.

Even on the basis of the very superficial sketch I will give here, it will be clear that Symeon's texts are not easy to narrow down to one unified view on emotions. Again, as in Psellos' texts, the evaluation of emotions is context-bound and in the service of a specific argument. The emotional conditioning, or perhaps emotional regime,[42] that Symeon imposed on his community, began at the very moment when the novice had to say goodbye to his family and friends. The following advice comes from a so-called *centurion*, consisting of one hundred brief chapters with exhortations and advice to his monks:[43]

τὴν παρὰ τῶν γονέων καὶ ἀδελφῶν καὶ φίλων σου θλῖψιν ὁρῶν διὰ σὲ γενομένην, γέλα ἐπὶ τῷ ὑποβάλλοντι ταῦτα ποικίλως κατὰ σοῦ γίνεσθαι δαίμονι· καὶ μετὰ φόβου καὶ σπουδῆς πολλῆς ὑποχώρησον.

When you see the sadness that your parents, brothers, and friends feel because of you, laugh at the demon who cleverly devises this attack against you, and retreat, with great fear and haste.

Symeon advises his monks to detach themselves from worldly emotions, of which affectionate sadness within the family is a typical example. Laughter should be used as an antidote to this – a remarkable statement that warns us against supposing a too easy dichotomy between laughter as belonging to the 'secular' world, and tears and avoidance of laughter as typical for the monastic world.

Apatheia (the absence of passions, passionlessness) constitutes an important ideal in Symeon's projected path to spiritual perfection. Symeon talks very frequently about *pathos* and *pathē* (which I will here provisionally translate as 'passions') as something to be eradicated from the soul of his monks. *Apatheia* is put forward as an ideal in many passages in diverse texts. For instance, Symeon summarily states in his *Chapters*: 'He who does not become passionless, or does not know what passionlessness is, such a man will not be able to even have faith, as long as he walks the earth.'[44] Elsewhere, Symeon states that one could fight passions, but will never be able to eradicate them; a pure heart is not bothered

---

[41] See the emphasis on 'heart-work' and cognitive disciplining in a recent study on early monasticism: Dilley (2017).

[42] For the term 'emotional regimes', see Reddy (2001).

[43] *Chapter* 1.17, ed. Darrouzès (1957).

[44] *Chapter* 1.85, ed. Darrouzès (1957): ὁ μὴ γεγονὼς ἀπαθὴς οὐδ᾽ ὃ τί ἐστιν ἀπάθεια οἶδεν, ἀλλ᾽ οὐδὲ πιστεύειν εἶναί τινα τοιοῦτον ἐπὶ τῆς γῆς δύναται.

172 *Floris Bernard*

by any passion. This leads Symeon to define passionlessness as becoming so alien to passions as not to even think of them.[45]

But what are these *pathē* exactly? Can we (as is often done in other contexts) translate *pathē* as 'emotions'? Does Symeon advocate a spiritual state in which his monks are completely free of any emotion? We should consider here that *pathos,* through the meaning of immoral emotions, acquired quite different meanings in Late Antique Christian discourse, and hence Byzantine parlance.[46] The following, rather randomly chosen, short piece of advice is telling:[47]

τὸ πένθος διπλοῦν ταῖς ἐνεργείαις ἐστὶ καὶ ὡς μὲν ὕδωρ, διὰ τῶν δακρύων πᾶσαν σβεννύει τὴν φλόγα τῶν παθῶν καὶ τὴν ψυχὴν ἐκκαθαίρει τοῦ ἐξ αὐτῶν μολυσμοῦ· ὡς δὲ πῦρ, διὰ τῆς παρουσίας τοῦ ἁγίου Πνεύματος ζωοποιεῖ καὶ ἀναφλέγει καὶ ἐκπυροῖ καὶ θερμαίνει τὴν καρδίαν καὶ πρὸς ἔρωτα καὶ πόθον Θεοῦ ἐξάπτει αὐτήν.

Compunction has two forms of effect. As water, it extinguishes the fire of passions (*pathē*) through tears, and cleanses the soul from the defilement of passions. As fire, through the presence of the Holy Spirit it gives life and fire, warms the heart and heats it up, and kindles it towards the love and desire for God.

Perhaps paradoxically to us modern readers, 'passions' are said to be quelled with tears. And the ultimate eradication of passions leads, in our parlance, to other emotions: those of love and desire. Put simply, *pathos* does not mean 'emotion' in our sense, and the ideal monk of Symeon is far from an unemotional being. In fact, the path that Symeon projects for the monk leads to intense emotionality, but of course one that is guided towards devotion to God and the community.

The newly adopted monk is in another chapter urged to do the following:[48]

ὅταν μετὰ πάσης κάθῃ ἐπὶ τραπέζης τῆς ἀδελφότητος καὶ νοερῶς σοι σκιὰ τὰ πάντα τοῖς ὀφθαλμοῖς ὑπογράφωνται καὶ τοῦ ἡδέος τῶν βρωμάτων οὐκ ἐπαισθάνῃ, ἀλλ' ὅλην ἔχεις τὴν ψυχὴν τῷ θαύματι ἔκπληκτον καὶ τοῖς δάκρυσιν ἔμπλεων, τότε γίνωσκε τὴν τοῦ Θεοῦ σοι χάριν οὕτω ταῦτα ὑποδεικνύειν διὰ τὴν ἐκ τοῦ φόβου πολλήν σου ταπείνωσιν, ὅπως ἰδὼν τὰ ποιήματα τοῦ Θεοῦ καὶ διδαχθεὶς τῶν αἰσθητῶν τὴν ἀδράνειαν, εἰς ἀγάπην τῶν νοητῶν μετεγκεντρίσῃς τὸν φόβον σου. καὶ αὕτη ἐστὶν ἡ πνευματικὴ γνῶσις, ἣν καὶ λεγομένην ἀκούεις, ἥτις μέσον τοῦ φόβου καὶ τῆς ἀγάπης εὑρίσκεται καὶ ἀπὸ τούτου εἰς ταύτην διαβιβάζει ἀνεπαισθήτως καὶ ἀκινδύνως τὸν ἄνθρωπον.

When you are seated together with the whole community and all things seem to your eyes shadows in a spiritual sense, and you do not perceive the deliciousness of the food, and your whole soul is shocked with wonder and filled with tears, then recognize that God's grace gives you this sign through the humiliation resulting from fear. Thus, seeing God's creation and learning the weakness of sensible things, stitch your fear on to the love of intelligible things. That is the real spiritual wisdom about which you have heard: it is in between fear and love, transporting man from the former to the latter.

---

[45] *Chapter* 3.31–3, ed. Darrouzès (1957).
[46] See Scrutton (2011) for a thorough discussion.
[47] *Chapter* 3.12, ed. Darrouzès (1957).
[48] *Chapter* 1.32, ed. Darrouzès (1957).

6. Emotional Communities in the Eleventh Century
173

Spiritual wisdom results from the right emotional conditioning of the soul. The monk's insight consists not of thoughts, but of emotions. The soul is made to wonder, filled with tears, and is beset with great fear. The eventual spiritual wisdom is then defined as a state between the two strong emotions of fear and love. The passage also transmits the sense of community: emotions are aroused when all are gathered around the table.

The mystical experience itself, one of the main messages of Symeon's oeuvre, is described as a highly emotional event. In the following passage, the awareness of and union with the divine light is the cause for shouting, falling on the ground, feeling fire within, and shedding many tears, in an act where the rational part of the individual succumbs completely to, as it is said, wonder (ἔκπληξις) and fear (φόβος).[49]

ὁ ἔνδον αὐτοῦ τὸ φῶς τοῦ παναγίου Πνεύματος ἔχων, μὴ φέρων τοῦτο ὁρᾶν, εἰς γῆν πρηνὴς πίπτει, κράζει τε καὶ βοᾷ ἐν ἐκπλήξει καὶ φόβῳ πολλῷ ὡς ὑπὲρ φύσιν, ὑπὲρ λόγον, ὑπὲρ ἔννοιαν πρᾶγμα ἰδὼν καὶ παθών· καὶ γίνεται ὅμοιος ἀνθρώπῳ ποθὲν ἀναφθέντι τὰ σπλάγχνα ὑπὸ πυρός, ὑφ' οὗ φλεγόμενος καὶ τῆς φλογὸς τὸν ἐμπρησμὸν μὴ δυνάμενος φέρειν, ὑπάρχει ὥσπερ ἐξεστηκώς· καὶ μηδὲ ἑαυτοῦ γενέσθαι ὅλως ἰσχύων, τοῖς δάκρυσι δὲ καταντλούμενος ἀενάως καὶ ὑπὸ τούτων καταψυχόμενος, τὸ πῦρ ἐξάπτει τοῦ πόθου σφοδρότερον. ἐντεῦθεν δὲ τὰ δάκρυα προχέει πλειόνως καὶ τῇ τούτων ἐκχύσει πλυνόμενος λαμπρότερον ἀπαστράπτει·

Whoever has inside the light of the most holy Spirit, cannot endure to see it and falls head-on on the ground. He shouts and yells in amazement and fear, seeing and experiencing a thing that is beyond nature, word, or thought. And he becomes similar to someone whose entrails are set on fire. Inflamed by it, not enduring the burning of the flame, he is as if out of himself. Failing to master himself, he sheds tears in abundance, and is refreshed by them, and fans even more the fire of his desire. Hence he sheds more tears, and being washed by their outpouring, he shines forth more brilliantly.

Passages like these abound with images of fire and tears, hotness and coldness, all described as being vividly felt and creating profound bodily changes.

The most important of bodily signs connected with inner experience is tears. Tears have been a recurrent theme in asceticism, and authors such as John Klimax and Theodore the Stoudite often dwell on the significance of tears for the monk, as part of a personal ritual of contrition, and sign of contact with the Holy Spirit, associated with the water of baptism.[50] But in Symeon's writings, tears take this to a much deeper level, as can be gauged by the surprise with which his community received his recommendations on tears.

Many of his sermons dwell on the role of tears as a necessary step in the process of compunction, to purify the soul, and to prepare it for union with God.

---

[49] *Chapter* 3.21, ed. Darrouzès (1957).

[50] For Symeon and tears in the monastic tradition, see Hunt (2004), (2015); the older Hausherr (1944) remains essential. On tears in Byzantine texts in general, see Hinterberger (2006b); and for tears of contrition in poetry, Giannouli (2009).

174 *Floris Bernard*

The following passage is but one example, taken here because it also foregrounds the role of 'nature' and emphasizes how we cannot, and should not, fight against our emotions. It answers to real or imagined objections by monks that for certain people it is impossible to weep.[51]

ὅτι δὲ ἐκ φύσεως τὸ κλαίειν πᾶσιν ἡμῖν πρόσεστιν, αὐτὰ τὰ γεννώμενα βρέφη σε διδαξάτωσαν. ἅμα γὰρ τῷ προελθεῖν τῆς γαστρὸς καὶ πεσεῖν ἐπὶ τῆς γῆς κλαίουσι, καὶ τοῦτο σημεῖον ζωῆς ταῖς μαίαις καὶ ταῖς μητράσιν ἐνδείκνυται. εἰ γὰρ μὴ κλαύσει τὸ βρέφος, οὐδὲ ζῆν λέγεται· κλαῦσαν δὲ δείκνυσιν αὐτόθι ὅτι συνεπόμενον ἡ φύσις ἔχει ἀπὸ γεννήσεως τὸ πένθος ὁμοῦ καὶ τὰ δάκρυα ...

ὡς γὰρ ἡ τροφὴ καὶ ἡ πόσις ἀναγκαία ἐστὶ τῷ σώματι, οὕτω καὶ τὰ δάκρυα τῇ ψυχῇ, ὥστε ὁ μὴ καθ' ἑκάστην κλαίων – ὀκνῶ γὰρ εἰπεῖν καθ' ὥραν, ἵνα μὴ δόξω βαρύς –, λιμῷ τὴν ψυχὴν διαφθείρεται καὶ ἀπόλλυται. εἰ τοίνυν συνεπόμενόν ἐστι τῇ φύσει τὸ κλαίειν ὁμοῦ καὶ τὰ δάκρυα, καθὼς ἀποδέδεικται, μηδεὶς τὸ τῆς φύσεως ἀγαθὸν ἀπαρνήσηται, μηδεὶς ὄκνῳ καὶ ῥαθυμίᾳ τοῦ τοιούτου καλοῦ στερήσειεν ἑαυτόν, μηδεὶς κακίᾳ καὶ πονηρίᾳ καὶ ὑπερηφανίᾳ ψυχῆς ἀλαζὼν γένηται καὶ εἰς ἀντιτυπίαν λίθου παρὰ φύσιν μετενεχθῇ, ἀλλὰ σπουδῇ τῇ καλλίστῃ πρὸς τὰς ἐντολὰς χρησάμενος τοῦ Θεοῦ, φυλαξάτω τὸ μέγα τοῦτο δῶρον,

That weeping is fitting for us all by nature, let newborn babies teach you. From the moment they come out of the womb and fall on earth, they cry, and that is a sign of life for the midwives and mothers. For if the baby does not cry, people say that it does not live. When it cries, it shows on the spot that nature has grief and tears that follow the birth ...

Just as food and drinks are necessary for the body, so are tears for the soul, so that one who does not weep every day (I hesitate to say every hour, lest I should seem too severe) corrupts and loses his soul by starving it. So, if it is a consequence of our nature to weep and to shed tears, as has been shown, let no one deny the good gifts of nature, and let no one, by hesitation and laziness, deprive himself of such a good, or become haughty by evil and meanness and pride of the soul, and be changed, contrary to nature, into the image of a stone, but with all earnest zeal he should pay heed to the commands of God, and guard that great gift.

Tears are not caused by sadness, but by compunction and by being overcome by the all-encompassing power of the Spirit (see the same sermon, lines 199–201). This leads Symeon in this particular passage to argue that tears come to us by nature, and nobody should make his soul so hard as stone as to avoid tears. Tears are a sign of the humble soul which gives in to its natural impulses and does not fight against it. Rather than emotions that one ought to oppose, they are here described as divine gifts against which it would be futile to fight. Symeon stipulates quite precise rules: monks should weep every day, if not every hour. Weeping is a ritual act that is not so much advised as required. It is something active, which monks should seek out and do. It is a spiritual exercise that is in fact an exercise in emotions, with a very physical dimension. At the same time, this pas-

---

[51] *Sermon* 29, ed. Krivochéine (1963–5), lines 218–42.

6. Emotional Communities in the Eleventh Century

175

sage emphasizes the role of nature, and warns against acting against it. Psellos had given exactly the same warning, as we have seen, but with a completely different purpose in mind.

Another sermon of Symeon further dwells on the necessity of compunction and the role of tears, but in an even more specific and ritual dimension.[52] Symeon expects that monks come to communion in tears or having just shed tears (lines 608–50), which again reveals the ritual nature of the tears he has in mind. But several monks admitted to Symeon that they were not able to do so, asking him how they could achieve an emotional state that provoked tears. Without utterly denying this world with everything that is in it, Symeon argues (lines 586–95), without 'walking sullenly all day' (σκυθρωπάζων πορεύεσθαι; see Ps. 37:7), one will never be able to achieve that state where one can 'soak his bed and mattress in tears' (see Ps. 6:7). The biblical quotations point to the wish to have monks suffer all the sufferings present in the Bible. The physicality of tears is not be underestimated: Symeon insists so much on them, portrays them so clearly as an exercise to be performed, speaks about them in such specific terms, that it cannot be taken as just a metaphor for compunction. It is of course easy to see how the Greek verb σκυθρωπάζω acquires a totally different evaluation compared to Psellos' axis of emotional values.

Hence, far from advocating an absence of emotions, one would rather be led to describe Symeon's project of educating and exhorting monks as a project of emotional conditioning or emotional regime. Symeon's moulding of the soul of the monk is not an attempt to eradicate emotions, but rather to embrace them and not resist them. It is an appeal to another kind of emotionality than the one they have been adopting in the normal world.

Symeon's project is not only intent on influencing the inner state of his monks. He is also much concerned with outward display and expression, through bodily movements and facial expressions. In his *Hymn* 4, Symeon couples the renunciation of the world to a set of prescriptions on posture and how to move the body:[53]

> Ἄφες κόσμον ἅπαντα καὶ τοὺς ἐν κόσμῳ·
> μόνον προσλαβοῦ τὸ μακάριον πένθος·
> θρήνησον μόνα τὰ κακῶς σοι πραχθέντα,
> ὅτι ταῦτά σε τοῦ ποιητοῦ τῶν ὅλων
> ἀπεστέρησαν Χριστοῦ καὶ τῶν ἁγίων   [5]
> μηδενὸς ἄλλου φροντίσῃς ἐκτὸς τούτου,
> ἀλλὰ καὶ τὸ σῶμά σου ὡς ξένον ἔχε·
> καὶ κάτω βλέπε ὡς κατακεκριμένος
> καὶ τὴν ἐπὶ θάνατον ὁδὸν βαδίζων
> στέναζε ἀεὶ ἐκ βάθους τῆς καρδίας   [10]

---

[52] *Sermon* 4, ed. Krivochéine (1963–5).
[53] *Hymn* 4, ed. Koder and Paramelle (1969), lines 1–16.

176   *Floris Bernard*

καὶ τὸ πρόσωπον μόνοις δάκρυσι πλῦνε,
τοὺς δὲ πόδας σου τοὺς εἰς κακὰ δραμόντας
μὴ θελήσης ὕδατι νῖψαι μηδόλως·
ναὶ δὴ καὶ τὰς χεῖρας σου συνεσταλμένας ἔχε·
ταύτας ἀναιδῶς πρὸς θεὸν μὴ ἐκτείνης,   [15]
ἃς πολλάκις ἥπλωσας εἰς ἁμαρτίαν·

Leave this world and the people who are in it,
Only attach yourself to blessed compunction.
Bewail only your bad actions,
For these have robbed you of the creator of all,
And of Christ and the saints.   [5]
Do not think of anything else, except this:
To have your body as something alien.
Look down as a condemned one,
And walking the road leading to death
Sigh from the bottom of your heart,   [10]
And do not wash your face but with tears.
Your feet that have walked towards evil,
On no account wash them with water.
And your hands, you should keep them folded,
Do not shamelessly stretch them out to God,   [15]
Since you have often unfolded them for sin.

Symeon's emotional regime contains guidelines about how to express and display emotions, to create the ideal monk, not only in his thoughts, obedience, but in his very behaviour, how he walks, talks, looks, takes care of his body. Hygienic habits are again deemed important: in the monastic ideology of Symeon, washing the face as well as the feet is a sign of attachment to the body, and should thus be shunned.

Conclusions

Obviously, and perhaps self-evidently, many elements in Symeon's emotional community are diametrically opposed to Psellos'. The last example is telling: Psellos abhorred Symeon's ideal unwashed monk. Smiles and tears are not only expressions of inner emotions, but social markers that indicate one's devotion to a given community. The status of the body is very different, and this extends to an entire 'ideology' of bodily care, of which the details were quite precisely watched over. Looking downwards and looking upwards, furrowing eyebrows and relaxing them, form important oppositional pairs. These were all social markers, pinpointing someone's social role. Some key terms such as *charis*, *skuthrōpos*, *pathos*, *apatheia*, *politikos* are charged with emotional meanings and receive very different evaluations and indeed definitions. *Phusis* becomes a point of contention, claimed by both groups, and acquiring very different connotations: for Psellos' community, it is a call for a lifestyle free from oppression by harsh rules, but in the ethics adopted by Symeon, it corresponds to the rightful place of humans and an awareness of sins. Psellos' insistence on giving it a new semantic value, going in a rather different direction, is an important innovation.

Both Psellos and Symeon solicit emotions from the members of their communities, with fixed displays of emotions punctuating important communal gatherings such as eating together or commemorating the dead. They transmit ideal types of emotional behaviour, not least when presenting themselves. By repeatedly insisting on these emotional profiles, they effectively construct emotional regimes. Taking only these two authors into account is avowedly a reductive operation; in the very brief discussion of Mauropous we have seen that inside emotional communities authors employed different strategies, even when sharing the same tenets. Obviously, all this is not invented in the eleventh century; rather, both world views rest upon long traditions of texts describing or prescribing emotional behaviour. The Church Fathers, more specifically, developed a quite detailed and consistent physiognomy of emotional display, encompassing facial expression and bodily posture.[54]

When attempting to understand the broader currents behind Byzantine texts, we should look not only at different theoretical models or ideologies. When studying emotions, an analysis of their theoretical underpinnings should be complemented by practice: how do they describe, ascribe, and redefine emotions, in order to pursue immediate pragmatic goals in a society? How do they read the body: its posture, expressions, and habits? The foregoing should be taken as only a hint of the profits that such an approach could bring.

---

[54] This point definitely needs further research. For laughter, see Halliwell (2008) 471–519. For anger and envy, see Hinterberger (2017a). For a detailed physiognomic description of an angry countenance, see, for instance, Gregory of Nazianzos' *Poem against Anger* (*Poem* 1.2.25); see Oberhaus (1991).

7

'Aren't You Afraid That You Will Suffer the Same?'

Emotive Persuasion in John Chrysostom's Preaching

Jan R. Stenger

Introduction

If we are to believe his massive corpus of homilies, the fourth-century preacher and bishop John Chrysostom in Antioch and Constantinople was constantly fighting a futile battle against unruly behaviour and immorality. Whether it was theatre shows, heavy drinking in the taverns, or visits to brothels, the Christians of both cities were simply not prepared to abide by the moral code that Chrysostom's ascetic ideology wanted to impose on them. One major reason for proneness to debauchery and unrest was that they were enslaved by harmful passions, above all by anger, hatred, and envy. The preoccupation with dissonant or inappropriate feelings is a constant presence in Chrysostom's sermons and writings. In his letter to the monk Stagirius, who was suffering from depression, he sought to cure the addressee of his sorrow (*athumia*) by arguing that he himself was responsible for his affective states.[1] In a letter to another ascetic, named Theodore, Chrysostom did his best to dissuade his friend from unacceptable love for a beautiful woman.[2] And, to add one further example, in the eighteenth Homily on the Statues, delivered in Antioch in AD 387, the preacher upbraided his flock for showing misguided excitement and joy, as they had completed just half of the fasting period.[3] Some of the passages which display an emotional disunity underline that there was something like the right time or measure, a *kairos*, for certain emotions.[4] Chrysostom did not want to ban hilarity from Antioch altogether, but in this particular situation excitement was at odds with the circumstances. Three points emerge from Chrysostom's rebukes and admonitions: first, he pays attention to the situational nature of emotions and, related to that, their cognitive basis, as they involve an assessment of the situation

---

[1] See Wright (2015) 360–2.
[2] *Ad Theod.* 1 (SC 117).
[3] *De stat.* 18.1 (PG 49.179–81).
[4] See, for example, *In Heb. hom.* 11.4 (PG 63.95).

180 *Jan R. Stenger*

at hand; second, his analytic approach indicates an educative impetus, as he, like many ancient philosophers, believed that emotions were educable and could be treated therapeutically; and third, his analytic sharpness notwithstanding, Chrysostom very often in these texts presents himself as a passionate rhetorician, moving his audiences rather than engaging in logical argumentation.

Scholars have elucidated many aspects of the emotions in Chrysostom's preaching and gone to considerable lengths to better understand their centrality in his thinking.[5] The theatricality of grief and joy in his dealing with the Riot of the Statues in Antioch has been shown, as well as their function in the Christian transformation of the city.[6] Recent articles have pointed to the medical and philosophical background of Chrysostom's discussion of human emotions, arguing that, in the manner of a medico-philosophical therapist, he tried to correct pernicious passions as diseases of the soul.[7] In addition, it has been demonstrated using the example of sorrow that Chrysostom was convinced that certain emotions could themselves have a therapeutic effect, for example in deterring people from sinful deeds.[8] This underscores another, fundamental finding, namely that the interconnectedness of sin and passion is central to Chrysostom's Christian anthropology.[9] What has, however, largely escaped the notice of scholars is that Chrysostom, apart from curing passions such as anger and discoursing on the therapeutic nature of emotions, also mobilizes his audience's *pathē* in order to reshape emotional patterns.[10] Foregrounding the preacher's theorization, studies have tended to neglect the rhetorical side of his works and, in particular, his emotional persuasion.

This chapter, therefore, addresses the question of how Chrysostom as a virtuoso orator of the church attempts to tackle the emotional dissonance noted above. How does he utilize the churchgoers' feelings to realign them with what he considers to be appropriate *pathē*? The focus will be on his persuasion techniques, the rhetorical instruments through which he arouses his listeners' emotions in order to redress the balance between proper and inappropriate feelings. For our analysis it will be helpful to think of emotions as narrative scripts, because Chrysostom frequently not only diagnoses an affect, but also depicts how an emotional state translates into action and behaviour. Such an understanding of emotions, as proposed in the field of Classics by Robert Kaster, implies that

---

[5] See, most recently, Papadogiannakis (2018) and (2019), with ample references to scholarship on Chrysostom and individual emotions, and Leyerle (2020).

[6] Stenger (2017).

[7] Mayer (2015); Wright (2015). See also Blowers (2010) on pity.

[8] Leyerle (2015).

[9] See Laird (2012) on Chrysostom's view of how passions affect the human soul and behaviour.

[10] Lanfranchi (2016) on the homilies against the Judaizers is an exception. He also draws attention to the emotional divide between Chrysostom and his audience.

7. 'Aren't You Afraid That You Will Suffer the Same?'

emotional scripts enact the moral values of a culture, represent a configuration of beliefs, desires, and aversions, and are staged in a concrete social setting. According to Kaster, an emotion is 'the whole process and all its constituent elements, the little narrative or dramatic script that is acted out from the evaluative perception at its beginning to the various possible responses at the end'.[11] Drawing on this approach, the following discussion aims (1) to identify the core set of Chrysostom's emotive techniques; (2) to show how emotional persuasion serves the aim of reconfiguring the audience's emotional fabric; and (3) to argue that Chrysostom not only acknowledges the limited therapeutic effect of certain emotions once they have occurred – as in the case of Stagirius' despondency[12] – but translates this insight into his own oratorical practice.

7.1. Chrysostom on the nexus of rhetoric and emotions

Chrysostom himself, it seems, was no stranger to intense feelings. In his tractate *On the Priesthood* he confesses to his own propensity to rage, which made him wonder whether he was suitable for the job of a churchman.[13] Both his self-description and impassioned rhetoric, moreover, corroborated the image of the unrestrained man of God, as the church historian Socrates attributed Chrysostom's downfall in Constantinople in part to his temper, noting that he 'was inclined more to anger than to forbearance'.[14] His own irascibility, however, did not make him blind to the intricate link between human emotions and the power of speech. Time and again he had occasion to comment on, and often censure, the audience's applause and enthusiasm, even frenzy, when he was preaching in the churches of Antioch and Constantinople.[15] Whether or not his indignation at the congregation's frenetic response to his preaching was genuine, his remarks indicate that he was fully aware of the potential of words to manipulate the audience's feelings so that, carried away by their emotions, they were likely to eat out of the orator's hand.

We should not be taken by surprise, then, that Chrysostom discussed the power of certain forms of discourse to have a strong impact on the readers' or listeners' emotions, in particular in teaching settings such as the regular church service. Current scholarship very much emphasizes that Late Antique preaching was firmly embedded in the sophistic culture of that period and that churchmen, normally well-educated leaders, were orators not inferior to secular rhetoricians

---

[11] Kaster (2005), with the quotation on p. 8. See also Papadogiannakis (2019) 312–16 on the use of emotion scripts in Chrysostom's homilies.

[12] See *Ad Stag.* 1.6 (*PG* 47.441).

[13] *De sac.* 3.10.140–90. See also *In Act. apost. hom.* 3.4 (*PG* 60.39). See Leyerle (2001) 192–3.

[14] Socrates, *Hist. eccl.* 6.21 (*PG* 67.725), 6.3 (*PG* 67.669).

[15] *In Matt. hom.* 17.7 (*PG* 57.264); *In Act. apost. hom.* 30.4 (*PG* 60.227); *De stat.* 2.4 (*PG* 49.38).

182 *Jan R. Stenger*

declaiming in the theatres.[16] Fittingly, Chrysostom's job description for the cleric in *On the Priesthood* included, among other essential qualities, a sufficient command of eloquence so that he could reach the faithful, teach, and influence them.[17] He himself had attended a rhetorical school which furnished him with the skills that would enable him to sway the masses and posthumously earned him the name 'Golden Mouth'. Part of the curriculum taught there was persuasion through *pathos*, that is, through putting the audience in a desired emotional state. Aristotle's *Rhetoric*, laying the theoretical foundations, had explained that stirring up the listeners' emotions greatly affected their judgements.[18] Already in the fifth century BC, the sophist Gorgias, likening eloquence to effective drugs, had claimed that speech was 'a powerful lord that can banish fear and remove grief and instil pleasure and enhance pity'.[19]

The Christian preacher possessed also another invaluable resource if he wanted to learn the art of emotive persuasion. It is characteristic of Chrysostom's exegesis of the Holy Scriptures that he draws attention to their masterly rhetoric and explains to his congregation how the biblical books, above all Paul's letters, succeeded in arousing emotions.[20] In the introduction to his homilies on Galatians, for example, Chrysostom discusses at length the Apostle's adaptable eloquence. Apart from instructing his addressees, Paul also displayed in the letter his indignation in order to correct their behaviour.[21] Further, commenting on the Psalms, Chrysostom stresses that it was simply through words that the psalm created anger and fear.[22] Conversely, he sometimes had to acknowledge the limits of emotional persuasion when he noticed with disappointment that the frightening narratives of the Bible fell on deaf ears and proved ineffective.[23] Such comments suggest that mobilizing emotions was a legitimate, and important, instrument in the instruction in faith. The preacher had to speak to the believers' hearts, not to their minds alone. In emblematic fashion, a passage in a homily on Matthew draws an analogy between Chrysostom's attempt to realign his congregation's feelings and teaching pupils in the schools. As the schoolteacher shows the children how to learn to write letters through repeated exercises and inscribe the tablets, so the preacher seeks to erase the harmful passions such as anger and

---

[16] E. g. Maxwell (2006).

[17] *De sac.* 5.

[18] Arist. *Rh.* 1.2, 1356a1–20; 2.1, 1378a19–29; 2.2–11, 1378a30–1388b30 (on individual emotions). However, Aristotle is critical of the rhetoricians' overemphasis on emotional arousal as a means of persuasion (1.2, 1356a14–17). See Konstan (2007) and Dow (2015) *passim*, esp. chapter 7.

[19] Gorg. *Hel.* 8, further 14.

[20] For Chrysostom's image of Paul, especially as a teacher, see Mitchell (2000) and Rylaarsdam (2014) 159–66.

[21] *In Gal. comm.* 1 (*PG* 61.611–12), arguing that in this Paul was following the example of Christ.

[22] *Exp. in ps.* 7.2 (*PG* 55.99).

[23] *In Act. apost. hom.* 19.5 (*PG* 60.156).

envy from his listeners' memory and inscribe instead indelibly good feelings.[24] Intriguingly, the comparison hints at the textual quality of emotions: emotions can be created, and inculcated, by words, and they resemble written letters, as if they were a cultural technique.

The textuality of human emotions is, however, but one side of the matter. Equally important is their performative dimension. Chrysostom has acquired notoriety for his relentless attacks on theatre spectacles. The main reason why he so tirelessly upbraided Christians for their love of the shows is that the mimetic performances on stage had a fatal impact on the spectators' souls. Watching debauchery, lascivious behaviour, and devilish passions on stage threw, he claimed, their souls into turmoil and lured them into immoral behaviour. According to him, it was even possible to read the emotional discomposure in the spectators' faces and demeanour as they returned from the spectacles.[25] Thus, in Chrysostom's eyes passions staged in multimodal performances, including visual and auditory stimuli, had an irresistible emotive effect on the audiences. Unsurprisingly, he was keen to utilize this mechanism, albeit with noble intentions, for the benefit of the Church, turning the gathering of the faithful into an awe-inspiring spiritual theatre.[26] This should remind us that the performative quality was crucial for the texts to realize their persuasive potential. Unfortunately, when examining his preaching we are prevented from recovering the original performance setting of the homilies and can merely speculate on the contribution to the arousal of emotions of the preacher–congregation interaction. Chrysostom's facial expressions, gestures, body movements on the pulpit, and modulations of his voice, as well as the collective responses of his audience, all that must have had a considerable effect on how his preaching was experienced emotionally.

7.2. Choreographing sadness

A unique opportunity for instrumentalizing the congregation's emotional states arose when, in February AD 387, riots erupted in Antioch-on-Orontes, in response to the emperor Theodosius I's tax rises. Public unrest started as the population greeted the ruler's decision with an outcry of rage, then followed insults against the emperor and his family; the enraged citizens marched to the governor's residence to vent their anger and went so far as to overturn the imperial images.[27] After the outburst abated, panic and fear of the emperor's wrath filled

---

[24] *In Matt. hom.* 11.6–7 (*PG* 57.200–1).

[25] *Inan. glor. et ed. lib.* 77–9 (SC 188); *In Lucian.* (*PG* 50.521–2); *In Barlaam* 4 (*PG* 50.682); *Hom. in mart.* (*PG* 50.665–6). Cf. Leyerle (2001) 45–9.

[26] See Jacob (2010).

[27] The riots took place on either 25 or 26 February 387. For the historical events see Van de Paverd (1991) and French (1998).

184 *Jan R. Stenger*

the entire city, with many of the civic elite fleeing to the surrounding mountains in order to save their lives. As a punishment for this insubordination and lese-majesty, Theodosius stripped Antioch of its rank as metropolis and imposed other punitive measures, including the closing of baths and theatres. In the wake of the so-called Riot of the Statues, an official enquiry was held by the imperial magistrates, and some of the leading citizens were executed. Overall, however, Theodosius' reaction turned out to be relatively mild, not least because bishop Flavian had travelled to the court at Constantinople to assuage the ruler's wrath.

Understandably, public sentiment was in turmoil during these days, as collective emotions were running high. Rage, anxiety, and finally, joy of relief were palpable in the public sphere and also left their marks in the speeches of Libanius and John Chrysostom that responded to the eruption of violence.[28] Chrysostom devoted a whole series of homilies to the events, seeing his congregation through the period of crisis and uncertainty.[29] The first of these homilies was preached on 27 February 387, before the beginning of Lent and immediately after the onset of violence and the overturning of the statues.[30] It was based on a passage from 1 Timothy and for the greatest part discussed one of Chrysostom's major concerns, the gap between wealth and poverty.[31] As to the riots, the preacher tried to make sense of the disturbing incidents by arguing that they resulted from the Antiochenes' failure to take action against the blasphemers of God present in the city.[32]

How unsettled the situation in Antioch was in the aftermath of the tumult can be seen right at the beginning of the homily, when Chrysostom exclaims, 'What shall I say or what shall I speak of? The present occasion is one for tears, not for words; for lamentation, not for discourse; for prayer, not for oratory.'[33] With these words, the preacher strikes the tune for the first half of the sermon as he goes on to articulate his grief and terror. Having briefly drawn a parallel to Job's lamentable situation, after he had lost everything, and his friends' wailing, Chrysostom appears to increase the intensity of his feeling of sorrow and despair:[34]

---

[28] See Stenger (2017) on Libanius' and Chrysostom's representation of laughter and tears during the upheaval.

[29] Van de Paverd (1991) gives summaries of these homilies and has established the chronology of the series.

[30] *De stat.* 2 (*PG* 49.33–48). For the date see Van de Paverd (1991) 316–17.

[31] See *De stat.* 2.4 (*PG* 49.39) with 1 Tim. 6:17.

[32] For an analysis of this homily and the role of emotions in Chrysostom's argument, see also Stenger (2019) 177–88.

[33] *De stat.* 2.1 (*PG* 49.33.38–40): τί εἴπω καὶ τί λαλήσω; δακρύων ὁ παρὼν καιρός, οὐχὶ ῥημάτων· θρήνων, οὐχὶ λόγων· εὐχῆς, οὐ δημηγορίας.

[34] *De stat.* 2.1 (*PG* 49.34.38–50): δότε μοι θρηνῆσαι τὰ παρόντα. ἐσιγήσαμεν ἡμέρας ἑπτά, καθάπερ οἱ φίλοι τοῦ Ἰώβ· δότε μοι στόμα διᾶραι σήμερον, καὶ τὴν κοινὴν ταύτην ὀδύρασθαι συμφοράν. τίς ἡμῖν ἐβάσκηνεν, ἀγαπητοί; τίς ἡμῖν ἐφθόνησε; πόθεν ἡ τοσαύτη γέγονε μεταβολή; οὐδὲν τῆς πόλεως τῆς ἡμετέρας σεμνότερον ἦν· οὐδὲν γέγονεν ἐλεεινότερον νῦν. δῆμος

7. 'Aren't You Afraid That You Will Suffer the Same?'

Allow me to mourn over our present state. We have been silent for seven days, just as the friends of Job were. Allow me to open my mouth today and bewail this common disaster. Who, beloved, has bewitched us? Who has envied us? Whence has this enormous change come over us? Nothing was more dignified than our city. Now, never has been anything more pitiable. The people so well ordered and civilized, even like a manageable and tamed horse, always submissive to the hands of its rulers, has now so suddenly become rebellious, as to have perpetrated such evils, as one can hardly dare to mention. I mourn now and lament, not for the greatness of that threat which we expect, but for the excess of the madness which has been manifested.

It is striking how this passage engages the audience and, in particular, appeals to their feelings. The preacher addresses his listeners directly, he poses pressing questions, using an inclusive first-person pronoun so as to establish a community of sufferers. He repeats questions and expressions, employs brief cola and numerous antitheses that throw the dramatic reversal of fate into high relief. The sense of despair and utter sorrow is further intensified by the use of hyperbole, for example when Chrysostom exclaims, 'Before, nothing was more blessed than our city; but now, it has come to pass that nothing is more unpleasing!'[35] To add to the emotional effect of his preaching, he makes use of an array of overt emotional language, of terms such as 'to lament' (*thrēnō*), 'to mourn' (*oduromai*), 'despondency' (*athumia, katēpheia*), and 'fear' (*phobos, deos*). Further, metaphors like 'the heavy mist of sorrow' (τῆς ἀθυμίας τὴν ἀχλύν) and 'the cloud of sadness' (τῆς ἀθυμίας τῷ νέφει) foreground the experiential and embodied qualities of emotions, thereby stimulating the audience's imagination. Some of these figurative expressions had a long pedigree in Greek poetry, going back to Homer's *Iliad*.[36] The metaphor of grief as an enveloping substance also reflected the Greeks' view of the phenomenology of this emotion, as veiling was a spontaneous expression of grief and part of the mourning ritual.[37] All these instruments and techniques employed by Chrysostom evidently serve to not only conjure up an image of the distress debilitating the whole city, but also move the listeners to experience the same feelings as their priest does.

The invitation to join him in mourning becomes even more apparent when we consider the rhetorical presentation of his wailing in greater detail. With the reference to lamentation in the opening of the homily, Chrysostom has

---

εὔτακτος οὕτω καὶ ἥμερος, καὶ καθάπερ ἵππος χειροήθης καὶ τιθασσός, ἀεὶ ταῖς τῶν ἀρχόντων εἴκων χερσίν, ἐξαίφνης τοσοῦτον ἡμῖν ἀπεσκίρτησε νῦν, ὡς τοσαῦτα ἐργάσασθαι κακά, ἃ μηδὲ εἰπεῖν θέμις. ὀδύρομαι καὶ θρηνῶ νῦν, οὐ διὰ τὸ μέγεθος τῆς προσδοκωμένης ἀπειλῆς, ἀλλὰ διὰ τὴν ὑπερβολὴν τῆς γεγενημένης μανίας. The reference is to Job 2:13, the preceding one to Job 2:8, 12. Job was a standard exemplum in Christian consolatory discourse. See Dassmann (1991) 415–17.

[35] *De stat.* 2.1 (*PG* 49.34.57–35.1): οὐδὲν τῆς πόλεως τῆς ἡμετέρας πρότερον μακαριώτερον ἦν, οὐδὲν ἀτερπέστερον γέγονε νῦν.

[36] E.g. Hom. *Il.* 17.591, 20.421.

[37] See Cairns (2016a) 34–6.

186 *Jan R. Stenger*

already suggested to his congregation what they should expect this time from his preaching. Then he asks them to let him bewail the disaster. Later he directs another exhortation to them, using the words of Jeremiah: 'Call for the mourning women, that they may come, and for the cunning women, and let them take up a wailing. Let your eyes run down with water, and your eyelids gush out with tears!'[38] As we can see in the passage quoted above, Chrysostom in a series of questions expresses his inability to pinpoint the cause of Antioch's downfall; he is left wondering who has envied the city so much that he brought it to its knees. Another striking feature of the homily is that it frequently gives a sense of the dimension of the disaster by contrasting the city's former, prosperous state with the current situation of loss and suffocation. Antioch has fallen from dignity to pity; the people, once well ordered like a tame horse, have suddenly become unruly and wrought unspeakable evils. These dramatic reversals, couched in antithesis, intensify the pathos that dominates the first part of the homily. To take the pathos to an even higher level, Chrysostom later in an apostrophe to the mountains and hills calls nature to take up his lament and asks his listeners to call the whole creation into sympathy with their suffering.[39]

We can suppose that all these rhetorical techniques struck a chord with the Christians gathered in the Great Church of Antioch, for what their preacher did in these passages was to adapt a rhetorical form taken from the standard repertoire of epideictic oratory. For occasions of public mourning, rhetorical handbooks, like the treatises of Menander Rhetor from the late third century, recommended the format of the monody, the formal lament in which the speaker was supposed to articulate the community's grief over the loss of a beloved or revered person.[40] Although Menander formulated his guidelines on the monody exclusively with the lament for a deceased person in mind, rhetorical practice had recourse to this form also when cities were struck by disaster, for example by a devastating earthquake.[41] It may be more than coincidence that Chrysostom at one point makes mention of a recent earthquake that shook Antioch, in order to put the scale of the current crisis into context.[42] When we take Menander as representative of the rhetorical stock-in-trade in Late Antiquity, we easily notice that Chrysostom's homily closely follows the long-established pattern and *topoi*

---

[38] *De stat.* 2.2 (*PG* 49.36.42–5): "ἀποστείλατε πρὸς τὰς θρηνούσας, καὶ ἐλθέτωσαν, καὶ πρὸς τὰς σοφὰς, καὶ φθεγξάσθωσαν." ῥεέτωσαν οἱ ὀφθαλμοὶ ὑμῶν ὕδωρ, καὶ τὰ βλέφαρα ὑμῶν καταγέτω δάκρυα. Cf. Jer. 9:17–18. We may note here that Gregory of Nyssa in his funeral oration for bishop Meletius of Antioch (d. AD 381) when mourning his death references the same passage and makes the comparison with Jeremiah lamenting the fall of Jerusalem (Gr. Nyss. *Oratio funebris in Meletium episcopum*, GNO 9.1:451–2).

[39] *De stat.* 2.2 (*PG* 49.36). Chrysostom seems to draw here on the Stoic idea of cosmic sympathy, or the parallel of micro- and macrocosm. See Brouwer (2015) 19–28.

[40] Men. Rhet. *Treatise* 2, pp. 434.10–437.4.

[41] Aristid. *Or.* 18, Smyrna; 22, Eleusis; Lib. *Or.* 60, Daphne; 61, Nicomedia.

[42] *De stat.* 2.2 (*PG* 49.35).

7. 'Aren't You Afraid That You Will Suffer the Same?'

suggested for the formal lament. Menander discusses, among other elements: the complaint against the divine powers and unjust fate; pity induced by reference to visible events and present happenings; references to the happy past; apostrophe; sharing the grief of the bereft relatives; and description of the personal appearance of the deceased. Exactly these elements, albeit adapted to a city, occur in Chrysostom's impassioned speech after the riots. In addition, just as rhetorical monodies of cities and places, like that of the Apollo temple at Daphne by Libanius, make references to mythology in order to come to grips with the loss, Chrysostom draws on the biblical examples of Job and Cain's punishment so that the congregation can make sense of Antioch's ruin.[43] They are invited to identify with Job's relatives and friends who bewailed his fate, and to be horrified by the severity of Cain's chastisement; seeing their own fate in terms of these biblical narratives must have had considerable impact on how the Antiochenes conceptualized their own emotional state in the face of imminent disaster.[44]

By adopting the formal lament Chrysostom activated his audience's feelings; he mobilized their grief and despair, even invited them to respond to his lamentation with collective wailing. We can imagine that his oratorical performance on the pulpit, the multimodal rhetorical *hupokrisis*, would have heightened this effect, turning the preaching into a veritable spectacle of shared sadness. His manipulation of their emotional state was facilitated by the recourse to an engrained pattern or script of emotional behaviour. Late Antique audiences were familiar with the different forms of epideictic oratory, from panegyric to monody, and they knew almost instinctively how to take part in these performances. The script that Chrysostom utilized to great effect was intended, as an emotional choreography, to virtually prescribe how they should feel and experience the situation.

Another means employed for influencing the congregation's emotional experience is narrative, occasionally combined with analogy. To characterize the city's fall into deep melancholy, Chrysostom draws a parallel with bees buzzing around their hive: as smoke has driven away the bees so that the hive has become solitary, fear has driven away the inhabitants of the city. This analogy is then further developed by means of another one comparing desolate Antioch to a garden stripped of leaves and fruits. Immediately after this passage, the homily proceeds with further analogies that, featuring narrative, depict the atmosphere as riddled with anxiety and despair:[45]

---

[43] Lib. *Or.* 60. See Stenger (2018) on Libanius' monody and Chrysostom's deconstruction of it. The references to the biblical Job and to Cain's punishment are in *De stat.* 2.1 (*PG* 49.33–4) and 2.2 (*PG* 49.35).

[44] See Alexiou (1974) on the tradition of the ritual lament, especially 24–35 on the Church Fathers' critique, and appropriation, of traditional practices of lamentation.

[45] *De stat.* 2.1 (*PG* 49.35.17–26): πάντες τὴν ἐνεγκοῦσαν ὥσπερ παγίδα φεύγουσιν, ὥσπερ βάραθρον ἐγκαταλιμπάνουσιν, ὥσπερ πυρᾶς ἀποπηδῶσι· καὶ καθάπερ οἰκίας ἁπτομένης οὐχ

All flee from the place which brought them forth as from a snare; they desert it like a dungeon; they leap out of it as from fire. And just when a house is seized upon by flames, not only those who dwell therein, but all who are near take their flight from it with haste, eager to save their bare bodies, so now, too, when the emperor's wrath is expected to come as a fire from above, everyone presses to escape and save the bare body, before the fire in its progress reaches them.

Other brief narratives evoke the spectres of warfare, captivity, and the siege of a city, to make the congregation feel as if they were vulnerable, like captives. What is striking in these and further comparisons is, for one thing, their plot structure; they do not simply parallel the current state in Antioch with a static tableau, the sight of some object or feature. Rather, they imply a sequence of events and actions, sudden and dramatic reversals, focusing on the experience of those who are exposed to violence and destruction by an almost invisible, anonymous enemy. Further, these miniature tragedies are close-ups of experiences, and of existential ones, at that. The episodes of fire, siege, and battle with their graphic detail zoom in on the heart-breaking suffering, the flight, and fear of the victims. By doing so they reflect, or rather focus, the Antiochenes' emotional experience. Emotions, these episodes suggest, have a narrative structure; they are triggered by events, entail an assessment of the situation, and result in a certain behaviour and actions. Interlaced with covert emotional expressions, that is, phrases that can act as psychological triggers, such as 'siege', 'death', and 'flight', the descriptions evoke in the listeners emotional responses, almost traumatizing them, in order to sustain a level of intense emotionality. Chrysostom is not minded to assuage his audience's fears; quite the reverse: his rhetoric adds fuel to the flames.[46]

Immediately after the eruption of violence in his home town, Chrysostom, rather than allaying his listeners' fear and sadness, decided to step up the intensity of their feelings. He openly encouraged them through emotive persuasion techniques to give free rein to their despair, to fully savour their anxieties and get obsessed with their horror. The arousal of passions, however, was not an end in itself, for once he had prepared the ground, Chrysostom moved on to instruction and constructive exhortation.[47] His ultimate goal was that the congregation shake off their sorrows and return to their former frame of mind or 'habit' (ἔθος, ethos).[48] In a reversal of psychic movements, they were 'to mount on the wings of

---

οἱ τὴν οἰκίαν οἰκοῦντες μόνον, ἀλλὰ καὶ πάντες οἱ πλησίον μετὰ πολλῆς ἀποπηδῶσι τῆς σπουδῆς, γυμνὸν τὸ σῶμα διασῶσαι σπουδάζοντες· οὕτω δὴ καὶ νῦν τῆς βασιλικῆς ὀργῆς καθάπερ πυρᾶς τινος ἄνωθεν ἥξειν προσδοκωμένης, πρὶν ἐπ' αὐτοὺς ὁδῷ βαδίζον ἔλθῃ τὸ πῦρ, ἕκαστος ἐπείγεται προεξελθεῖν, καὶ γυμνὸν διασῶσαι τὸ σῶμα.

[46] Papadogiannakis (2018) 352–3 shows that Chrysostom in the aftermath of the riots emphasized the positive effects of fear. According to the preacher, fear was a catalyst for moral improvement. See also Leyerle (2020) 113–20 on the disciplinary force of fear in his preaching.

[47] For an analysis of the bipartite structure of the homily see Celentano (2016).

[48] See De stat. 2.3 (PG 49.37).

7. 'Aren't You Afraid That You Will Suffer the Same?' 189

hope' to escape the debilitating torpidity.[49] Emotions oriented towards the past and present were to give way to those focused on the future. Thus, his emotive persuasion aimed to intensify negative feelings before replacing them with more helpful ones. One factor that clearly played into Chrysostom's hands was the commonality of grief and fear: everyone could hope that he or she would be part of an emotional community finding their way to renewed confidence.[50]

7.3. Training sympathy

Even a month later Chrysostom sought to capitalize on the fear that had taken possession of the Antiochenes' minds. In the thirteenth homily of the series, preached on Wednesday 24 March 387, he gave an extensive account of the second tribunal that followed the riots, a trial presided over by imperial officials.[51] As a relatively moderate verdict was passed on the city and it was decided that the capital punishment of some of the decurions be suspended, Chrysostom saw an opportunity to point out to his flock the benefits of the fear of hell. Hardly had he climbed the pulpit before he made plain that he was determined to sustain the emotional intensity built up over the preceding weeks. As he had begun in the days before, he now began by exclaiming 'Blessed be God.'[52] In the following lines and paragraphs we then notice further parallels to Homily 2: again, he uses exclamations, a staccato series of questions, pointed antitheses, dramatic reversals, and covert emotional techniques.

One feature, however, stands out. One can hardly think of another homily of his that parades such an extended narrative as this sermon. Meticulously composed and indulging in a plethora of vivid details, the first-person account creates a lively picture of the situation in Antioch and the proceedings of the

---

[49] Metaphors representing hope as a light and insubstantial object or an object that is capable of flying had a long tradition, going back to Archaic and Classical Greek poetry. See Solon 13.36 West; Bacchyl. 3.75; Aesch. fr. 99.22 Radt; Soph. *OT* 487–8. However, it is significant that in the poetic tradition these metaphors emphasize the unreliability and delusional aspects of *elpis*. See Cairns (2016b) 35. Chrysostom uses the metaphor of wings or giving wings also with reference to faith and the spiritual ascent. See, for example, *De paen. hom.* 3.1 (*PG* 49.293.14); *In 1 Cor. hom.* 17.2 (*PG* 61.142.19); 27.4 (*PG* 61.320.63).

[50] I use the term 'emotional community' as defined by Rosenwein (2006) 2: emotional communities are 'groups in which people adhere to the same norms of emotional expression and value – or devalue – the same or related emotions'. Emotional communities are not constituted by one or two emotions but rather by constellations, or sets, of emotions. To analyse these communities, Rosenwein reads related texts, noting all the words, gestures, and cries that signify feelings or the absence of feelings. She is interested in who is feeling what, when, and why (26). See also Papadogiannakis (2018) 348 on Chrysostom's attempts to shape an emotional community.

[51] See Van de Paverd (1991) 64–5 on the historical context.

[52] *De stat.* 13.1 (*PG* 49.135.42–4).

190 *Jan R. Stenger*

tribunal as they were witnessed by the fearful citizens. As rhetorical students exercised to provoke pity with gripping depictions of the sack of cities, so Chrysostom paid remarkable attention to emotions and their expression.[53] Terror, fear, dreadful silence, and distress dominate the scene as Chrysostom relates how he went to the tribunal, joined the crowd in imploring God and shivered before the heavily armed soldiers. What motivated him to insert in his homily such an extraordinary narrative was its effect on the audience. As an introduction to his account, Chrysostom explains that for those who have been delivered from shipwreck it is sweet to remember the dangers on rough sea once they have escaped to the harbour. 'The remembrance of past evils', he adds, 'always makes the present prosperity to appear more strikingly.'[54] He attributes to memory, with emphasis on its narrative quality, a therapeutic effect, if one recollects experienced emotions. With a certain distance both in time and viewpoint, humans are able to assess and understand their own emotional states.

Therefore, the long narrative employs an array of techniques that facilitate the audience's retrieving of the experience they have had the week before. Not only does he make use of overt emotion language, mentioning, for example, terror, fear, and pity, but he also pursues a common strategy recommended by the rhetorical treatises for conveying *pathos*. Especially when he recounts how two women, the mother and sister of one of those under trial, sat down at the vestibule, rolling themselves on the pavement and being terrified by what they heard from inside, Chrysostom slows down his narrative to dwell on the details of this scenario, the movements, the actions, the response of the bystanders, and many other features. The passage certainly conforms to the general recommendations on *ekphrasis*, the technique of conjuring up vivid images through a wealth of graphic information. The *enargeia* created through this instrument was intended to arouse *pathos*, as had been done brilliantly by, among others, the so-called tragic historians of the Hellenistic period.[55] For the congregation to recreate the frightening atmosphere of the day of the trial, Chrysostom, as in Homily 2, foregrounds the experiential quality, the phenomenology of passions, including bodily signs, posture, gesture,

---

[53] Cf. Webb (2009) 73.

[54] *De stat.* 13.1 (*PG* 49.135.48–50): ἡ γὰρ τῶν παρελθόντων κακῶν μνήμη ἀεὶ τὴν ἐνεστῶσαν εὐημερίαν ἀκριβέστερον ὁρᾶσθαι ποιεῖ. This was a commonplace in Antiquity. See e. g. Eur. fr. 133 (*TrGF* 5.1.250): ὡς ἡδύ τοι σωθέντα μεμνῆσθαι πόνων; Verg. *Aen.* 1.203 (*forsan et haec olim meminisse iuuabit*); and Plut. *Mor.* 630e (*Quaest. conv.*). Macrob. *Sat.* 7.2.9–10 has a brief discussion of this psychological mechanism ('at some future time, after misfortune has been endured to the end, the memory of toil is pleasing, when it has subsided').

[55] For the arousal of emotions as the effect of the production of *enargeia* through visualization see Webb (2009) 93–101, 143–4. The imagination involved in *enargeia* is, as Huitink (2019) argues from an enactivist perspective, not an exclusively visual experience but has important physical and embodied aspects. According to Huitink, *enargeia* brings with it an emotional and experiential grasp of what is described. For the 'tragic' qualities of Hellenistic historiography and its aim to arouse empathy see Chaniotis (2013a).

7. 'Aren't You Afraid That You Will Suffer the Same?'

movement, and dress. His depiction even takes on a multimodal quality, as he uses visual and auditory cues, thereby almost giving a tactile quality to his words. This emerges clearly when the narrative is nearing its climax:[56]

> But alone, in shabby clothes, hedged in by so many soldiers, crawling on the ground about the very doors, they suffered more pitiably than those who were on trial within. Hearing the voice of the executioners, the strokes of the whips, the wailing of those who were being whipped, the horrifying threat of the judges, these women endured at every beating sharper pains than those who were beaten.

Here Chrysostom stages a drama of passions before the audience's eyes; he makes them witnesses of this heart-rending scenario so that they cannot resist being profoundly shaken in the same way as the actual onlookers were.[57] More precisely, the narrative with its strong link between *enargeia*, vividness, and the phenomenology of the emotions involved does not turn the listeners merely into witnesses; rather, the description of sensorimotor interaction encourages them to imaginatively place themselves within the narrated world. The narrative skill brought to bear on the entire report goes to great lengths to make the atmosphere of gloom and horror present, at once playing with proximity and distance.[58] Distance, because the act of remembrance is far from the original psychic trauma; but at the same time proximity, as the congregation is impelled to immerse themselves in the narrative and re-experience the emotional turmoil endured by the crowd present at the tribunal.

This intention is also indicated by a short intervening comment made by the narrator immediately following the lachrymose tableau. 'Those men were tortured by the executioners; these women by the despotic force of nature and the sympathy of affections. There was lamentation inside and outside ...'[59] Everyone, even the judges themselves, cannot but share in the universal lament. The mechanism that Chrysostom wants to activate is the natural sympathy (συμπάθεια, *sumpatheia*), the feeling of common humanity, which makes one see oneself in the place of the other.[60] Only if the faithful are overwhelmed by fear

---

[56] *De stat.* 13.1 (*PG* 49.137.43–50): ... μόναι μετὰ εὐτελῶν ἱματίων ἐν μέσῳ τοσούτων ἀπειλημμέναι στρατιωτῶν, χαμαὶ συρόμεναι περὶ τὰς θύρας αὐτάς, τῶν ἔνδον δικαζομένων ἐλεεινότερα ἔπασχον, τῆς τῶν δημίων ἀκούουσαι φωνῆς, τοῦ κτύπου τῶν μαστίγων, τοῦ θρήνου τῶν μαστιζομένων, τῆς φοβερᾶς τῶν δικαζόντων ἀπειλῆς, καὶ καθ' ἕκαστον τῶν παιομένων χαλεπωτέρας ἐκείνων ὑπέμενον ὀδύνας αὗται.

[57] See also his remarks in *In Matt. hom.* 11.2–3 (*PG* 57.194–5), where he states that Matthew with his words sets terror before our eyes and increases the fear.

[58] For similar vivid depictions in Chrysostom's works aiming at making events present see Stenger (2015).

[59] *De stat.* 13.1 (*PG* 49.138.9–12): ἐκείνους μὲν γὰρ οἱ δήμιοι, ταύτας δὲ ἐβασάνιζεν ἡ τῆς φύσεως τυραννὶς καὶ ἡ τῶν σπλάγχνων συμπάθεια· καὶ ἦν ἔνδον θρῆνος, ἔξω θρῆνος.

[60] The term *sumpatheia* had a range of different senses in Plato, the Peripatetics, and the Stoics, from the body-and-soul relationships to a state of general interconnectedness in the natural world. See Brouwer (2015) and Struck (2016) 180–5.

192   *Jan R. Stenger*

and pity, as the gathered crowd was, can the intended effect of the 'tragedy', as Chrysostom calls the episode, occur.

The arousal of strong emotions through vivid storytelling does not merely give the congregation a sense of relief and pleasure once they have escaped the heavy storm. Rather, by going through the tormenting experience once again the faithful are to come to their senses, acknowledge that the disaster has been caused by their misbehaviour and consequently change their conduct. This is the force of the concluding comments to the account:[61]

> Perhaps the tragedy of all that I have told you has greatly softened your hearts, but do not get annoyed. For since I am about to venture upon some more subtle thoughts and beg a gentler state of mind from you, I have done this studiously, so that by the terror of the description your minds shake off all listlessness and withdraw themselves from all worldly cares and with more ease convey the force of the things to be spoken into the depths of your soul.

Thus, Chrysostom exploits the audience's emotional response for his re-education programme. In order to cure their indifference, he first incites their fear and pity because these feelings fulfil an important cognitive function. It is through such emotional experiences that humans become aware of the true nature of things and events. Perhaps more than rational thinking, emotions, as embodied responses to good and evil, have the potential to profoundly reshape the mind.[62] It is certainly no coincidence, then, that Chrysostom considers the cognition of good and evil a 'natural law situated within us' (φυσικὸς ἡμῖν ἔγκειται νόμος τῶν καλῶν καὶ τῶν οὐ τοιούτων).[63]

As the homily proceeds in its remaining part to ethical teaching, it becomes even more apparent that Chrysostom wants to harness the faculty of imagining and recreating feelings for his didactic agenda. Significantly, in this section references to instruction and learning abound. After briefly discussing the shame in the presence of inferiors caused by sinful deeds, he turns to his core lesson, which is predicated on the Golden Rule: 'Do you wish to receive kindness? So be kind to another.'[64] In a series of alternating questions and commands, Chrysostom asks his flock to show mercy and love to their neighbours, instead of

---

[61] *De stat.* 13.2 (*PG* 49.139.38–46): τάχα ἱκανῶς ὑμῶν κατεμάλαξε τὴν καρδίαν ἡ τραγῳδία τῶν εἰρημένων, ἀλλὰ μὴ δυσχεράνητε. καὶ γὰρ ἐπειδὴ μέλλω λεπτοτέρων κατατολμᾶν νοημάτων, καὶ ἀπαλωτέρας δέομαι διανοίας, ἐπίτηδες τοῦτο ἐποίησα, ὥστε τῷ φόβῳ τοῦ διηγήματος τὴν διάνοιαν ὑμῶν πᾶσαν ἀποτιναξαμένην ῥαθυμίαν, καὶ τῶν βιωτικῶν ἀπαναστᾶσαν ἁπάντων, μετὰ πολλῆς τῆς εὐκολίας πρὸς τὸ βάθος τῆς ψυχῆς παραπέμψαι τῶν λεγομένων τὴν δύναμιν.

[62] Cf. Colombetti (2014) on the enactive perspective in cognitive science that cognition and affectivity cannot be separated. She claims '[t]he mind, as embodied, is intrinsically or constitutively affective; you cannot take affectivity away from it and still have a mind' (1).

[63] *De stat.* 13.3 (*PG* 49.139.48–9), referring to his preaching 'of late', probably Homily 12 or also Homily 11.

[64] *De stat.* 13.3 (*PG* 49.140), quoting Matt. 7:12.

7. 'Aren't You Afraid That You Will Suffer the Same?' 193

envying and deceiving one another. The rationale behind his demanding appeal to the imagined interlocutor is that humans possess an innate disposition which enables them to respond properly to vice and virtue.

For we all have a natural disposition to feel indignation along with those who are maltreated (that is why we straightaway become the enemies of those who are insolent, though we ourselves may have suffered nothing) and to sympathize in the pleasure of those who enjoy succour and aid. And we are overwhelmed by the misfortunes of others, as well as by mutual affection. For although critical times may seem to induce a certain dispiritedness, we entertain nevertheless a common love for each other. And at this a certain wise man hinted, saying, 'Every living being loves what is like to it, and man his fellow.'[65]

According to this principle, humans have the natural inclination to identify with others and feel sympathy, even if they only observe others suffering without being affected themselves.[66] It is, thus, characteristic of humans to be bound together, as the members of a body, through a commonality of feelings. In the same way as a disease can affect several parts of the body, the faithful cannot, and must not, solely take care of their own behaviour and conduct, because they are necessarily affected by what their neighbours do or suffer. Since this is a form of embodied knowledge, as Chrysostom's explanation suggests, there is no need for learning; the natural inclination for sympathy is sufficient for steering humans to the right choice between good and evil.[67] As if to give a specimen of his instruction, Chrysostom then directs a series of rebuking questions to his imaginary addressee, thereby impelling everyone in the audience to experience a sense of shame so that they be sobered. Asking them whether they do not feel fear before superiors or shame in the presence of friends, or whether they are not having a bad conscience, he once more points out that they are to learn their lesson even if they only see others being punished.[68] Thus, strong emotions, like fear, shame, envy, aversion, and pity, are instrumental in the process of moral correction.[69] This is the reason why the graphic narrative of fear and grief

---

[65] *De stat.* 13.3 (*PG* 49.141.4–14): καὶ γὰρ τὸ συναγανακτεῖν τοῖς ὑβριζομένοις φυσικὸν ἅπαντες ἔχομεν (εὐθέως οὖν τοῖς ἐπηρεάζουσιν ἐχθροὶ γινόμεθα, κἂν μηδὲν ὦμεν αὐτοὶ πεπονθότες), καὶ τὸ συνήδεσθαι τοῖς ἀντιλήψεως καὶ βοηθείας ἀπολαύουσι, καὶ τὸ κατακλᾶσθαι ἐπὶ ταῖς ἑτέρων συμφοραῖς καὶ τῇ φιλοστοργίᾳ τῇ πρὸς ἀλλήλους. κἂν γὰρ πραγμάτων περιστάσεις δοκῶσι μικροψυχίαν τινὰ εἰσάγειν, ἀλλ' ὅμως ἔχομεν κοινὸν πρὸς ἀλλήλους φίλτρον. καὶ τοῦτό τις σοφὸς αἰνιττόμενος ἔλεγε· "πᾶν ζῷον ἀγαπᾷ τὸ ὅμοιον αὐτῷ, καὶ ἄνθρωπος τὸν πλησίον αὐτοῦ." The quotation is Ecclus. 13:15. For the principle evoked here see Rom. 12:15 and Chrys. *In Rom. hom.* 22.1 (*PG* 60.609–10).

[66] See also Blowers (2010) 13–14 on Chrysostom's use of scenarios of pity for training the congregation to feel mercy. The sympathy or rather contagious effects produced by watching or hearing something happening to others is also discussed in the Pseudo-Aristotelian *Problemata*, Book 7 (esp. 7.7, 887a15–21). See Struck (2016) 182–3.

[67] See *De stat.* 13.3 (*PG* 49.140–1).

[68] *De stat.* 13.4 (*PG* 49.141).

[69] Cf. also *In Matt. hom.* 11.6–7 (*PG* 57.200–1), where Chrysostom discusses his pedagogic

194   *Jan R. Stenger*

encourages the audience to sympathize with their suffering fellows. Such an emotive drama can effectively inculcate in the audience the moral compass that ought to govern the Christian life.

7.4. Shaming the audience

Emotive persuasion was by no means confined to the existential crisis of AD 387. Rather, the techniques discussed so far can be found in one way or another in many homilies of Chrysostom's. If it was his aim in the thirteenth Homily on the Statues to force his listeners into sympathy with the actors of the dramatic scenario, one of his sermons on Matthew took the theatrical element to an even higher level. Preaching on the Beatitudes, he did not rely on logical argumentation alone to elucidate the biblical passage but made use of various emotive techniques in order to impose the moral of Jesus' teaching on his flock. Particularly striking is that the homily very effectively engages the audience by bombarding an imagined interlocutor with a barrage of questions and direct addresses, to the extent that the preacher's monologue is virtually turned into an intense exchange. In one of these passages, Chrysostom purports to recall together with the interlocutor a scene which they have recently witnessed:[70]

> Have you not seen him who owed the ten thousand talents and then, after he was forgiven that debt, choked his fellow servant for one hundred denarii? What great evils he endured, and how he was delivered over to everlasting punishment? Have you not trembled at the example? Aren't you afraid that you will suffer the same?

What his addressee is to learn from this episode is that everyone is likewise the debtor of the Lord and, nonetheless, He endures with forbearance, instead of exacting with brutality of us what we owe. Yet, in fact Chrysostom is not recalling a specific incident in the streets of Antioch, or making up the entire episode, but adapting a well-known parable from the Gospel.[71] However, it is significant that he rewrites the biblical example in such a way that it could have taken place almost anywhere in the late Roman Empire. What he achieves with the creative retelling of the parable is that his audience can relate to the scene more directly than to an event told by Jesus centuries earlier. Chrysostom presents the parable as a quotidian drama, an altercation as it would happen in real life; and he even invites his addressee to watch the violent encounter, as if he were attending some

---

mission and with an analogy suggests that appropriate feelings can be learned in the same way as writing in the schools.

[70] *In Matt. hom.* 15.11 (*PG* 57.238.7–12): οὐκ εἶδες ἐκεῖνον τὸν τὰ μυρία τάλαντα ὀφείλοντα, εἶτα μετὰ τὴν ἐκείνων ἄφεσιν ἀποπνίγοντα τὸν ἑαυτοῦ σύνδουλον ὑπὲρ ἑκατὸν δηναρίων; ὅσα ὑπέστη κακὰ, καὶ πῶς ἀθανάτῳ παρεδόθη κολάσει; οὐ δέδοικας τὸ ὑπόδειγμα; οὐ φοβῇ μὴ καὶ αὐτὸς τὰ αὐτὰ πάθῃς;

[71] See Matt. 18:21–35.

7. 'Aren't You Afraid That You Will Suffer the Same?'

spectacle on the theatrical stage. More importantly, the interlocutor is to identify with the cruel debtor-turned-creditor and expect the same fierce punishment that was inflicted by God on the biblical figure.

If he had explained the moral of the episode in sober terms, the lesson would certainly not have been lost on the congregation. Visualizing immoral behaviour and unacceptable violence in such a theatrical style, however, spoke to the audience with greater immediacy. Every single member of the congregation could immerse himself or herself in the dramatic scenario, adopt the perspective of the inhumane aggressor and thereby realize the evil nature of this behaviour. As if this were not enough, the homily then confronts the listeners with stern questions that, by the implication of threats, are intended to raise the spectre of eternal punishment and instil existential fear. The single episode might, on the face of it, appear too brief to have a sustained effect on the audience's mental state. However, once we place it in the context of the entire homily, it is evident that Chrysostom has carefully arranged a whole sequence of similar emotive scenarios. Not only does he employ an array of overt emotion terms, including 'wrath' (*orgē*, *thumos*), 'shame' (*aischunē*), and 'love', but he also invites his flock to imagine themselves observing a fight in the streets and an angry man in the marketplace.[72]

While the men fighting give themselves over to unbridled aggressiveness, the onlookers – that is, everyone in the church gathering – stand by in indifference or, even worse, feel pleasure at the miseries of others. As we have seen in our analysis of Homily 13 on the Statues, the preacher wants his audience to immerse themselves in the emotional dramas and simulate the feelings that someone would have in the real-life situation.[73] When they imagine themselves taking part in the action, as either agents or bystanders, they become aware of the moral component of their emotions. Affects such as pleasure and pity, so Chrysostom's dramatization suggests, reveal the moral values and attitudes of those who experience them. Inappropriate pleasure at another person's hardship then lays bare the moral depravity of the observer who is moved to *Schadenfreude* and excitement by the offensive sight. In order to drive this point home, Chrysostom also draws attention to the dehumanizing effect of improper emotional responses. First, he reproachfully asks the interlocutor whether he is watching a wild beast fighting or a man, a brother and even member of the same body (*melos*).[74] Then, to increase the shame, he stresses that only shameless persons, slavish natures, take pleasure in brutal acts committed against fellow human beings. And finally, as if every member of his congregation had degraded to such brutishness, he rebukes them, 'Are you inflicting blows, tell me, and kicking and

---

[72] *In Matt. hom.* 15.10 (*PG* 57.236), 11 (237).
[73] See above, pp. 189–91 on the use of narrative in *De stat.* 13.
[74] See Eph. 4:25.

196   *Jan R. Stenger*

biting? Have you become a wild boar or a wild ass? And are you not ashamed, don't you blush at having turned savage and betraying your own nobleness?'[75] These repeated rebukes, which appeal to the fellow feeling everyone ought to have, intend to strip the faithful of their un-Christian emotional dispositions and drag them towards sympathy and love for their neighbours, in particular for the poor and sufferers. Ultimately, the arousal of contradictory emotions, a veritable roller coaster of feelings, is to engender a fundamental change in actions and behaviour. This change, rather unsurprisingly, is itself facilitated by morally charged emotions, as the homily in the concluding part instils hope of the eternal rewards that Jesus holds in store for those who forgive their debtors and offenders.[76]

The questions just quoted warrant a closer look also for another reason. They are, indeed, a key feature of this homily, for the entire long discussion of brutality and harshness is interlaced with passages conveying Chrysostom's moral outrage. Time and again hurling indignant questions at his interlocutor, he expresses his disbelief that members of his flock, of all people, may be thrilled and pleased when they happen to see people beating up each other. 'You see a man behaving himself disgracefully,' he says for example, 'and do not consider yourself disgraceful? Don't you throw yourself between them and scatter the devil's line of battle and put an end to men's miseries?' Relentless in his accusations, Chrysostom some paragraphs later asks indignantly, 'Are you hesitant and do you shirk, hurrying by cruelly and unmercifully? And how do you expect, calling upon God, ever to find Him gracious?'[77] More than once, these enraged questions are followed by stern commands, such as 'Don't look on, but separate them. Don't take delight, but reconcile them. Don't stir up others to the disgraceful sight, but rather scare away and separate those who are assembled.'[78] Here it is worth noting that Chrysostom was well aware that Christ himself and the Apostle Paul, his admired model, had rebuked the disciples and the Galatians, respectively, in such a manner. In the introduction to his commentary on Galatians, he explains in detail Paul's skilful use of the rhetoric of indignation, pointing out that by ex-

---

[75] *In Matt. hom.* 15.11 (*PG* 57.237.44–7): πληγὰς ἐντείνεις, εἰπέ μοι, καὶ λακτίζεις, καὶ δάκνεις; ὗς ἄγριος ἐγένου, καὶ ὄνος ἄγριος; καὶ οὐκ αἰσχύνη, οὐδὲ ἐρυθριᾷς, ἐκθηριούμενος, καὶ τὴν οἰκείαν εὐγένειαν προδιδούς;

[76] *In Matt. hom.* 15.11 (*PG* 57.238). Chrysostom pursues a similar strategy of emotive persuasion in another homily on Matthew in which he pairs terror with encouragement by first conjuring up a frightening prospect of Matthew's warnings and then instilling hope for change (*In Matt. hom.* 11.3, *PG* 57.194–6).

[77] *In Matt. hom.* 15.10 (*PG* 57.236.43–6): ὁρᾷς ἄνθρωπον ἀσχημονοῦντα, καὶ οὐχ ἡγῇ αὐτὸς ἀσχημονεῖν; οὐδὲ εἰσέρχῃ μέσος, καὶ διασκεδάζεις τοῦ διαβόλου τὴν φάλαγγα, καὶ τὰ ἀνθρώπινα διαλύεις κακά; 11 (*PG* 57.237.40–2): ... ὀκνεῖς καὶ ἀναδύῃ, καὶ παρατρέχεις ὠμῶς καὶ ἀνηλεῶς; καὶ πῶς προσδοκᾷς τὸν Θεὸν καλῶν ἵλεών ποτε ἕξειν;

[78] *In Matt. hom.* 15.10 (*PG* 57.236.38–41): μὴ θεώρει, ἀλλὰ διάλυε· μὴ τέρπου, ἀλλὰ διόρθου· μὴ ἑτέρους παρακίνει ἐπὶ τὴν ἀσχημοσύνην, ἀλλὰ καὶ τοὺς συνειλεγμένους ἀποσόβει καὶ διάλυε.

7. 'Aren't You Afraid That You Will Suffer the Same?'   197

hibiting his anger the Apostle intended to correct his addressees' behaviour.[79] Apt adaptor of Paul's pedagogy that he was, Chrysostom in his homily on Matthew pursued the same strategy. Angry questions and open reprimands not only mobilized the audience's emotions, but also conveyed the image of the priest as one who responded to inappropriate comportment with strong feelings.[80] The rhetorical display of his own moral sentiments was a means of sophisticated self-fashioning, the creation of a persona that served the communicative aims of the homily.[81] It was part of Chrysostom's strategic attempt to build his own ethos and 'emotional authority', as the foundation to his claim to the status of an educator of the believers.

The creation of his emotional persona was essential for the effective manipulation of the congregation's feelings, for in order to infuse shame into their souls he had to credibly impersonate the role of the morally superior person who was rightly outraged by their proneness to cruelty. With his performative indignation, Chrysostom cornered the members of his flock so that, in all likelihood, they felt uncomfortable and were filled with remorse, even if they had not committed any of what the homily imputed to them.[82] We do, of course, not know how they in reality responded to Chrysostom's rhetoric of shaming. Some might have blushed in a feeling of guilt, others may have been indignant at the acts of violence and reassured themselves that they were different.[83] What is clear, however, is the aim of reaffirming the Christian code of morality and correcting immoral carelessness.[84] From this pedagogic viewpoint, the display of anger was clearly a sign of the priest's true love for his congregation.[85] His wrath was driven by the wish to rescue their souls from the fire of hell. That was, after all, what Paul had done, who, according to Chrysostom, despite his love 'utters words full of anger – not that he himself felt this way but in order to correct [his ad-

---

[79] *In Gal. comm.* 1 (*PG* 61.612). See Durand (1993) on anger in Chrysostom's works and Rylaarsdam (2014) 184–7 on Paul's mixed method of exhortation.

[80] *De stat.* 16.1 (*PG* 49.161–3), for example, makes a similar display of Chrysostom's anger and harshness.

[81] The importance of the creation of the speaker's representation or performance of his own emotional reaction for persuasion had, of course, been highlighted already by Aristotle. Arist. *Rh.* 1.2, 1356a4–13; 2.1, 1378a6–19. See Dow (2015) 95–100.

[82] The strategy of shaming the audience comes out very clearly also in *De stat.* 16.1 (*PG* 49.161–2), where Chrysostom articulates his own shame and disappointment at his cóngregation's cowardice and foolishness.

[83] *In Eph. hom.* 15.4 (*PG* 62.110) very effectively infuses shame into the congregation: 'Why do all you women blush? I am not addressing all of you' (τί ἠρυθριάσατε πᾶσαι; οὐ πρὸς πάσας ἡμῖν ὁ λόγος·).

[84] See also *In Matt. hom.* 16.7 (*PG* 57.248); *In Eph. hom.* 2.4 (*PG* 62.21). Cf. Durand (1993) 65–6.

[85] Chrysostom explains this principle in the conclusion to *In Act. apost. hom.* 3 (*PG* 60.41–2), with a reference to Prov. 27:6 (ἀξιοπιστότερα γὰρ τραύματα φίλου, ἢ ἑκούσια φιλήματα ἐχθροῦ) and what seems to be an adage (τὰ γὰρ παρὰ φίλων λεγόμενα, κἂν ὕβρις ᾖ, φορητά).

198   Jan R. Stenger

dressees]'.[86] Manipulating the Christians' feelings, even filling them with shame, was a legitimate tactic if it was done for the sake of morality, in order to forge an emotional community founded on Christian virtues. Significantly, at one point, after one of those concatenations of harsh questions, he reminds his interlocutor of the importance of moral emotions, stressing 'you are a Christian': as a member of the community of the faithful, he or she ought to live up to the moral, and emotional, standards that form the church's bedrock.[87]

Conclusion

Our examination of selected examples of Chrysostom's preaching has demonstrated the centrality of emotional persuasion in his ethical instruction. Mobilizing emotions, both positive and negative ones, was a core technique of his moral pedagogy. Steeped in the tradition of classical rhetoric, Chrysostom was cognizant of the great contribution made by *pathos* in the persuasion of large audiences. Unlike philosophers who approached the therapy of passions through rational discourse, he, though drawing on the assumptions and approaches of medico-philosophical therapy, deliberately combined logical argumentation with emotive persuasion. Fully aware of the impact of affectivity on the embodied mind, he sought to capitalize on the experiential dimension of feelings: foregrounding the phenomenology of emotions, their bodily aspects, his rhetoric encouraged the listeners to enact these experiences. This text-induced experience would, so Chrysostom hoped, impel them to re-evaluate their responses to good and evil, in the same way as the real-life emotions would. The passages that we have analysed indicate that the arousal of emotions aimed at a fundamental restructuring of the emotional fabric. In the place of unacceptable rage, foolish fear, and consuming envy, the believers were to cultivate legitimate indignation at sinful acts, sympathy with their fellows, and love for their neighbours. For that reason, emotive persuasion was Chrysostom's instrument of choice in the Christian re-education of entrenched habits. Ethical formation was facilitated by emotional responses to verbally generated stimuli.

For activating the listeners' emotions Chrysostom had a variety of rhetorical techniques at his disposal, from overt emotional terminology to the adaptation of the traditional lament. The most powerful item in his toolkit was breaking down the boundary between discourse and audience, closing the gap between text and real life. For the congregation to be gripped and virtually dragged into the

---

[86] *In 1 Cor. hom.* 14.1 (*PG* 61.115.42–3): ... πάλιν θυμοῦ γέμοντας λόγους ἀφίησιν, οὐκ αὐτὸς ταῦτα πάσχων, ἀλλ' ἐκείνους διορθούμενος. See also *De laud. Paul. hom.* 5 on the Apostle's adaptable rhetoric. Cf. Leyerle (2001) 190.

[87] *In Matt. hom.* 15.11 (*PG* 57.237.49).

7. 'Aren't You Afraid That You Will Suffer the Same?'

scenarios, the homilies employed a range of visualization techniques, including exceptionally detailed depiction and dramatic presentation. The narratives appealed to the audience's senses, putting an almost multisensory scenario before their eyes. The livelier Chrysostom's depictions of weeping women and fighting men were, the more likely were the members of his congregation to be moved by these social dramas, not least because the narratives highlighted the central role of passions in human relationships. Any churchgoer would have responded emotionally to the immediacy of the narratives, immersing themselves in them and, directed by the preacher's emotive rhetoric, simulating the emotions enacted by the imagined characters. Depending on Chrysostom's aims, they were to identify with the pitiable sufferers or the brutish aggressors.

The scenarios were helpful also in another respect, for they visualized the social nature of the emotions that were at the front of Chrysostom's mind. Love, pity, and sympathy, and on the opposite side hate, anger, and envy are feelings inextricably linked with social relationships and interaction. They regulate behaviour between individuals and are indicative of a person's attitudes towards other people. As he aspired to create a truly Christian community, Chrysostom had to uproot divisive feelings and replace them with those that helped establish humane relationships. Therefore, he did his best to instil shame and fear associated with inacceptable emotions, while mobilizing hope and pleasure connected to virtuous conduct. As a result of the preaching situation, the homilies dealt not with the individual's psychic state, but with shared feelings. Love and sympathy were to be felt by every Christian, regardless of existing differences in possession, power, and reputation. In the end, Christians were to be united in an emotional community, so that the dissonance that we noticed at the beginning would disappear.

8

Voicing and Gesturing Emotions

Remarks on Emotive Performance from Antiquity to the Middle Byzantine Period*

Niels Gaul

Introduction

> 'Delivery is to form oneself thoroughly on what is being said – in one's posture, glance/facial expression, and voice – as the best tragic actor might.'[1]

The emotive impact of rhetorical performance was recognized long before the theorization and codification of rhetoric commenced. It can first be traced in the *Iliad* and its characterizations of Menelaos, Nestor, and Odysseus, respectively, who are each said to intone their orations in a specific way and, accordingly, affect their listeners differently; however, this effect is implied rather than explicitly described. Menelaos speaks 'loud and clear' (μάλα λιγέως) and can thus be followed easily. Nestor's style is 'sweeter than honey' (μέλιτος γλυκίων). Odysseus' 'powerful voice', by contrast, proclaims 'deep from within his chest words like a winter storm' (ὄπα ... ἐκ στήθεος μεγάλην / ἔπεα νιφάδεσσιν ἐοικότα χειμερίῃσιν).[2]

---

* This article was completed with generous funding support from the European Research Council (ERC) under the European Union's Horizon 2020 research and innovation programme (grant agreement no. 726371, PAIXUE). I am grateful to the Emotions through Time network members, and Douglas Cairns and Martin Hinterberger in particular, for their helpful comments and observations; all remaining shortcomings are entirely my own. Like any piece straddling chronological and disciplinary boundaries, this chapter cannot achieve uniformity in referring to past figures: while Classicists retain the time-honoured, anglicized and latinized versions of ancient Greek names, Byzantinists have in recent years, and for good reason, moved towards strict transliteration. This necessitates an arbitrary break somewhere; in this chapter, I have by and large anglicized those ancient writers where the established version makes an audible difference (e. g. Thucydides, Plato, Aristotle, Plutarch), and transliterated everyone else.

[1] *Introduction to the Art of Rhetoric*, ed. Walz (1832–6) 6.35.16–19: ἡ δὲ ὑπόκρισίς ἐστιν ἵνα καὶ τῷ σχήματι καὶ τῷ βλέμματι καὶ τῇ φωνῇ, ὡς ἂν τραγῳδὸς ἄριστος καλῶς τοῖς λεγομένοις συσχηματίζηται.

[2] *Il.* 3.212–15; 1.249; 3.216–24. Later rhetoricians came to equate these styles with different

The first more systematic treatment of such matters survives in Aristotle's *Rhetoric*.[3] Alongside the rhetor's character and proofs, Aristotle introduces the art of affecting an audience's emotional disposition (ἐν τῷ τὸν ἀκροατὴν διαθεῖναι πως, 1.2, 1356a3) as one of the three means of persuading the listener. This is followed, in Book 2, by a survey of key emotions and their impact.[4] In Book 3, finally, under the heading of 'delivery' (ὑπόκρισις; the same term denotes 'acting' in the theatre), Aristotle turns to the significance of emotive performances and, following Plato,[5] declares that 'it is not sufficient to know what one ought to say, but one must also know how one ought to say it' (οὐ γὰρ ἀπόχρη τὸ ἔχειν ἃ δεῖ λέγειν, ἀλλ' ἀνάγκη καὶ ταῦτα ὡς δεῖ εἰπεῖν, 3.1, 1403b15–17); in fact, he lays claim to being the first to treat this subject systematically.[6]

Since initially poets had performed their own compositions, acting, Aristotle says, emerged comparatively late in the context of tragedy and rhapsody;[7] as its primary means he identifies the voice:

This [= performance/delivery] is situated in the voice, as to how it ought to be used for [representing/expressing] each particular emotion; when it [the voice] should be loud, as it were, when soft, when intermediate; and how the pitch, that is, shrill, deep, and intermediate, should be used; and what rhythms for each subject. For there are three factors that they [= orators] consider: volume, harmony, rhythm.[8]

In an ideal world, no such theatrics would have been required. In that ideal world, facts and content would have been the decisive factors in determining the success of any rhetorical performance – a point Aristotle emphasizes (one notes the repetition of δίκαιον): 'for it is right that one should aim at nothing more in a speech than how to avoid exciting pain or pleasure. For the right thing is to fight the case with the very facts, so that everything else that is be-

---

rhetoricians and thus different levels of style (*genus subtile, genus medium*, and *genus grande*), as attested in Dionysios of Halikarnassos or Quintilian: see Schulz (2013) 84.

[3] The *Rh. Al.*, now ascribed to Anaximenes of Lampsakos, does not say much about either emotions or their performance, but discusses 'lively' performance techniques, such as interrogating one's opponent in court: Chiron (2007).

[4] Arist. *Rh.* 2.2–11; this catalogue has received ample attention; cf. Konstan (2007) 413–19 with further literature and Vogiatzi (2019) 175–216 for the Byzantine commentators' response to it.

[5] *Resp.* 3, 392c7–8: ἅ τε λεκτέον καὶ ὡς λεκτέον.

[6] Arist. *Rh.* 3.1, 1403b35–1404a1, ed. Kassel (1976): οὔπω δὲ σύγκειται τέχνη περὶ αὐτῶν, ἐπεὶ καὶ τὸ περὶ τὴν λέξιν ὀψὲ προῆλθεν· καὶ δοκεῖ φορτικὸν εἶναι, καλῶς ὑπολαμβανόμενον; trans. Freese and Striker (2020) 349: 'But no treatise has yet been composed on matters of delivery, since the matter of style itself has only lately come to notice; it is thought to be vulgar, and rightly so.'

[7] On the vocal abilities of actors see e.g. Pickard-Cambridge (1968) 167–71; Cooper (2004) 145–6.

[8] Trans. Freese and Striker (2020) 349 (modified); Arist. *Rh.* 3.1, 1403b27–32: ἔστι δὲ αὐτὴ [= ὑπόκρισις] μὲν ἐν τῇ φωνῇ, πῶς αὐτῇ δεῖ χρῆσθαι πρὸς ἕκαστον πάθος, οἷον πότε μεγάλῃ καὶ πότε μικρᾷ καὶ μέσῃ, καὶ πῶς τοῖς τόνοις, οἷον ὀξείᾳ καὶ βαρείᾳ καὶ μέσῃ, καὶ ῥυθμοῖς τίσι πρὸς ἕκαστα. τρία γάρ ἐστιν περὶ ἃ σκοποῦσιν· ταῦτα δ' ἐστὶ μέγεθος ἁρμονία ῥυθμός.

8. Voicing and Gesturing Emotions   203

side demonstration becomes superfluous' (ἐπεὶ τό γε δίκαιόν ἐστι μηδὲν πλέον ζητεῖν περὶ τὸν λόγον ἢ ὥστε μήτε λυπεῖν μήτ᾽ εὐφραίνειν· δίκαιον γὰρ αὐτοῖς ἀγωνίζεσθαι τοῖς πράγμασιν, ὥστε τἆλλα ἔξω τοῦ ἀποδεῖξαι περίεργα ἐστίν, 3.1, 1404a4–7) and which, in fact, recalls his opening statement.[9] In the real world, however, emotional manipulation often prevails. Therefore, those carried the day, Aristotle continues, who best exploited their voice's volume, harmony, and rhythm, in poetic competitions as well as political contests (καὶ κατὰ τοὺς πολιτικοὺς ἀγῶνας), 'owing to the corruptness of our constitutions' (διὰ τὴν μοχθηρίαν τῶν πολιτειῶν, 1403b34–5): a point he re-emphasizes towards the end of the paragraph.[10] Aristotle therefore concedes that 'since the whole business of rhetoric is to influence opinion, we must pay attention to it' – the matter of emotive performance, that is – 'not as being right, but necessary' in a specific situation (ἀλλ᾽ ὅλης οὔσης πρὸς δόξαν τῆς πραγματείας τῆς περὶ τὴν ῥητορικήν, οὐχ ὡς ὀρθῶς ἔχοντος ἀλλ᾽ ὡς ἀναγκαίου τὴν ἐπιμέλειαν ποιητέον, 1404a1–3).[11]

***

This chapter examines one specific aspect of the ways in which ancient Greek and Byzantine practitioners of oratory – often disregarding Aristotle's and other philosophers' concerns – sought to express emotions and, in turn, arouse and manipulate those of their audiences.[12] Ideas of how emotions are transmitted from author/rhetor to actor[13]/orator (often separate roles in Greek Antiquity but coinciding in the same individual in Byzantium) to audience have changed considerably over time: while Antiquity privileged identification as in Plato's metaphor of magnetizing rings in the *Ion*,[14] recent advances in cognitive and neuro-science have foregrounded concepts such as narrative empathy, motor resonance, or embodied narratology, which seek to capture the emotional transactions and immersions that occur within and between author, actor, and audience in the processes of writing/composing, reading/performing, and listening.[15] Devised for a framework that seems compatible with ancient and Byzantine performative realities – not least as it can be applied to both silent reading and public per-

---

[9] Arist. *Rh.* 1.1, 1354a24–5: οὐ γὰρ δεῖ τὸν δικαστὴν διαστρέφειν εἰς ὀργὴν προάγοντας ἢ φθόνον ἢ ἔλεον ('it is not right to pervert the judge by moving him to anger or envy or pity').

[10] Arist. *Rh.* 3.1, 1404a7–8: ἀλλ᾽ ὅμως μέγα δύναται, καθάπερ εἴρηται, διὰ τὴν τοῦ ἀκροατοῦ μοχθηρίαν ('nevertheless, as we have just said, it is of great influence owing to the depravity of the listener', trans. Freese and Striker (2020) 349). See Lossau (1971).

[11] But note that Vogiatzi (2019) 189 argues that 'there is no reference that indicates that Aristotle considers emotions as having a negative influence on the judgment, namely as confusing or altering the judgment in a way opposing to reason'.

[12] For a recent 'wholesome' approach cf. Serafim (2017).

[13] I follow the terminology of social performance introduced by Alexander (2006): 'actor' here refers to whoever performs a rhetorical composition, rather than a theatrical actor, from whom ancient orators sought to be carefully distinguished; cf. Gaul (2018).

[14] See Andrea Capra's chapter in this volume.

[15] See e.g. Keen (2013); Wojciehowski and Gallese (2011); Cave (2016).

204 *Niels Gaul*

formance – Noël Carroll's concept of criterial prefocusing, for example, offers a plausible alternative to the long-standing idea that audiences ought to identify with the emotions of the text they listen to:[16]

> The first step in the elicitation of an emotional response from the audience is a criterially prefocused text – a text structured in such a way that the description or depiction of the object of our attention is such that it will activate our subsumption of the event under the categories that are criterially relevant to certain emotional states.[17]

Such prefocusing becomes possible when, as in the examples here examined, authors/actors 'share a background (an ethos, a moral and emotive repertoire, a cognitive stock, and so on) with audiences'.[18] This approach helps not least explain the emotional asymmetries which are often at play since, as Carroll argues, the emotions projected by an actor and felt by the audience are rarely identical but rather vectorially converging (e.g. sympathy for lovers rather than actual love; pity for a tragic figure rather than actual grief; etc.).[19]

While the rhetorical/narrative strategies of the text performed are perhaps the most important tools in stirring the audience's emotions, this chapter focuses on the two instruments without which no orator could transmit and amplify these emotion(s); both are key to making 'salient the features of situations that are criterially relevant to the arousal of pertinent emotions':[20] voice and gestures. The former was defined by volume, harmony/pitch, and rhythm; the latter includes both posture – the static way of carrying oneself – and gesticulation, posture's dynamic counterpart. While modern theory recognizes voice and gestures as interdependent parts of any language system,[21] the status of the latter has not always been universally accepted. Aristotle himself situated the performance of character and emotions in the voice; his disciple Theophrastos may have been the first to differentiate between 'the movement of the body' (τὴν κίνησιν τοῦ σώματος) and 'the tension of the voice' (τὸν τόνον τῆς φωνῆς).[22] The only ancient account of delivery that pays detailed attention to both voice and gestures survives in Marcus Fabius Quintilianus' *Institutio oratorica* (11.3), composed in the late first century AD.[23]

---

[16] Closely related to the question of whether a rhetor ought to feel the emotion s/he seeks to transmit that was first raised by Theophrastos *in anonymi proleg. RG* 6.35–6. See below p. 209 for Demosthenes' accusation that the absence of tears showed that Aischines' emotions were feigned; in one instance, Herodes Attikos had tears in his eyes (Philostr. *VS* 574).

[17] Carroll (2001) 228.

[18] Carroll (2001) 230.

[19] Carroll (2015) 320–5.

[20] Carroll (2015) 322.

[21] E.g. Goldin-Meadow (2003).

[22] *Rhetores graeci*, ed. Rabe (1896) 14.177.3–8 follows a correction in the manuscript; but see Matelli (2016) 96–7, who argues for the original reading, τὸν τόνον τῆς ψυχῆς.

[23] Cf. e.g. Graf (1991) and J. Hall (2004).

8. Voicing and Gesturing Emotions

This chapter, then, examines through time which voice/gesture constellation ancient Greek and Byzantine theoreticians and practitioners of rhetorical performance considered ideal in order to transmit and arouse emotions. Such an 'emotive transfer' from actor to audience, if successful – that is, if the actor is judged as authentic by the audience – creates a feeling of performative flow.[24] Crucially, for a performance to persuade the audience, the emotions that were voiced or gestured had to be perceived as in line with the orator's character:[25] not his 'real' character, however defined, but a rhetorically construed literary persona to suit the circumstances, and as attested in the progymnasmatic exercise of *ēthopoiïa*.[26] An unsuccessful performance, by contrast, would fail to convey to the audience the emotions the rhetor sought to arouse.[27]

While this chapter focuses on rhetorical performances, theatre is never far off. Until fairly recently, ancient theatre has been studied largely in separation from ancient law-courts and assemblies with their judicial and deliberative rhetoric; this has changed with the realization that both theatrical and oratorical performances lend themselves to being analysed as instances of social performance; this is not to say, however, that ancient practitioners were not acutely aware of the different requirements for a performance to succeed, and audiences did not approach both types of performance with very different expectations.[28] In fact, there seems a progressive development from ancient Athenian oratory with its uneasy relationship to theatre and acting (especially embodied in the figure of Aischines as an actor-turned-rhetor) via the rhetorical performances of the Second Sophistic physically occupying theatrical spaces, to the Byzantine *theatron* that, for all we know, was no longer tied to a theatre setting proper but bestowed its name on any occasion at which a rhetor stepped 'into the middle' in order to perform epideictic rhetoric.[29] A competitive, agonistic component certainly ran through both ancient oratory and theatre, be this the ten judges in the theatre or the vast number of judges – from 200 up to 1,500 – in the law-courts, visually separated from the mass of the audience by being seated on their *prohedriai* or by being placed behind the *dryphaktoi*.[30] This competitive component continued in the Byzantine Middle Ages. By contrast, the judge in a

---

[24] For a recent summary of performance studies approaches to Attic oratory see Serafim (2017) 3–5.

[25] Swearingen (1994).

[26] Gaul (2014) 259–69, with further literature. For the earliest Middle Byzantine treatment of *ēthopoiïa* see Ioannes Sardianos' commentary on Aphthonios' *progymnasmata*, ch. 9, ed. Rabe (1896) 194–214.

[27] Keen (2013) points out that equally, 'extreme personal distress in response to narrative usually intrerrupts and sometimes terminates the narrative transaction'.

[28] Harris (2017).

[29] Mullett (1984); Gaul (2011) 17–53 and (2020) 354–9, with further literature; and see below, pp. 217–18.

[30] Serafim (2017) 27 with further literature.

Byzantine *theatron* was set apart socially rather than physically, usually by virtue of being the highest-ranking member of the audience or the performer's patron/patroness, though one cannot exclude that he, or more rarely she, may occasionally have been placed on a dais, throne, or the like, especially if oratory was performed in the emperor's presence.[31]

It is also worthwhile remembering at the outset that the emotional relation between actor and audience was – and is – in fact reciprocal;[32] its delicate balance could easily be disturbed by either of the two parties.[33] Unexpected audience reactions could easily set an orator off track. Examples are attested in the cases of Demosthenes and the sophist Herakleides. As the youngest member of the embassy, Demosthenes – according to his opponent, Aischines – froze in the fierce presence of Philip of Macedon in 346 and could not continue his delivery even when encouraged by the king to take heart.[34] When Herakleides performed at Septimius Severus' court and the emperor's entourage behaved very differently from the audiences he was accustomed to, less willing to applaud than Herakleides' own students and the urbane audiences he usually addressed, and when he perceived vibes of *phthonos* from his fellow sophist Ailios Antipatros – Severus' private secretary and tutor to the emperor's sons – Herakleides panicked and froze mid-sentence.[35]

This chapter takes a *longue durée* perspective, from the ten Attic orators to the eleventh century (and occasionally beyond) and proceeds in chronological order: I first look at some ancient material before glancing at the Second Sophistic and, finally, arriving in the Middle Byzantine period. For limits of space, I will not attempt to highlight any specific emotion[36] or any specific strategy of pre-focusing a text, e.g. by offering vivid *ekphraseis* to the audience.[37] I will also not discuss other aspects of voice, such as its role in constructing masculinity, or the role of the body as the carrier of voice.[38]

8.1. Ancient rhetoric

Aristotle's treatment of the emotive aspects of rhetoric may have been the first systematic one, but not the first altogether. Brief mentions of emotive practice

---

[31] Gaul (2018) 229–31.

[32] See Pais (2016) for insightful comments from a modern perspective.

[33] Hall (1995) 43–4; Korenjak (2000); Worthington (2017).

[34] Aeschin. 2.20–39; cf. also Philostr. *VS* 508 and, e.g., Roisman (2007) 395; Worthington (2017) 16 and 24–5.

[35] Philostr. *VS* 614, ed. Stefec (2016) 121 (2.75).

[36] Especially *ekplēxis* would merit a more detailed treatment (Gaul (forthcoming).

[37] Cf. Byron MacDougall, Mircea Grațian Duluş and Jan R. Stenger's chapters in this volume.

[38] Gleason (1995) 82–158; Gunderson (2000); Duncan (2006); Roisman (2007); Lachenaud (2013).

8. Voicing and Gesturing Emotions

preceded it, such as Sokrates' description of the sophist Thrasymachos of Chalkedon, as part of the survey of rhetorical practices in Plato's *Phaedrus*:

> To me it seems that the strength of the Chalkedonian [= Thrasymachos] prevails by means of art among the tearful orations, which are drawn from old age and poverty, and *he is also strong*, as he said, *at rousing many people to anger, and then again to charm them by soothing those who are angry*, and most powerful in constructing and abolishing calumnies on whatever grounds.[39]

By contrast, the ideal, factual rhetor is represented by the figure of Perikles, who was singled out in Aristotle's *Athenian Constitution* and whose moderation (σω-φροσύνη) and 'calm voice modulation' (πλάσμα φωνῆς ἀθόρυβον) were praised by Plutarch.[40] Often contrasted with the latter is Kleon, who, Aristotle claims, in the vein of Thrasymachos seemed to corrupt the citizens with his emotional assaults and was the first to shout and slander from the bema: unlike the other rhetors, he was not speaking 'with decency' (ἐν κόσμῳ).[41] This is again mirrored by Plutarch, who maintained that Kleon was 'the first to shout when speaking publicly' (πρῶτος ἐν τῷ δημηγορεῖν ἀνακραγών, *Nik.* 8). Aristophanes made fun of Kleon's voice as resembling that of a scorched pig (ἔχουσα φωνὴν ἐμπεπρη-μένης ὑός, *Vesp.* 36). Importantly, such differences also translate into the realm of gestures. Perikles always kept one hand under his garment (τὴν χεῖρα συνέ-χειν ἐντὸς τῆς περιβολῆς), so as to stop himself from gesticulating.[42] This corresponds with Paul Zanker's reading of the Vatican statue of Sophokles, whom he interprets as a model citizen:

> The mantle carefully draped about his body enfolds both arms tightly ... The drapery allows even the legs little room for movement. Yet at the same time ... the position of the advanced leg and the one arm propped up conveys a sense of energy and a commanding presence. Thus this particular pose, with very limited mobility and both arms completely immobilized, along with the self-conscious sense of 'making an appearance', would be particularly appropriate for an orator.[43]

This gesture further corresponds with the depiction of a rhetor on an Attic amphora in the Louvre dating to *ca.* 480 BC and, indeed, a statue of Aischines him-

---

[39] Pl. *Phdr.* 267c7–d3 (emphasis added): τῶν γε μὴν οἰκτρογόων ἐπὶ γῆρας καὶ πενίαν ἑλ-κομένων λόγων κεκρατηκέναι τέχνῃ μοι φαίνεται τὸ τοῦ Χαλκηδονίου σθένος, ὀργίσαι τε αὖ πολλοὺς ἅμα δεινὸς ἀνὴρ γέγονεν, καὶ πάλιν ὠργισμένοις ἐπάδων κηλεῖν, ὡς ἔφη· διαβάλ-λειν τε καὶ ἀπολύσασθαι διαβολὰς ὁθενδὴ κράτιστος.

[40] Arist. *Ath. Pol.* 27–8.1 (ἕως μὲν οὖν Περικλῆς προειστήκει τοῦ δήμου, βελτίω τὰ κατὰ τὴν πολιτείαν ἦν, τελευτήσαντος δὲ Περικλέους πολὺ χείρω); Plut. *Per.* 5. Cf. also Plut. *Per.* 8.6: περὶ τὸν λόγον εὐλαβής.

[41] *Ath. Pol.* 28.3: ὃς δοκεῖ μάλιστα διαφθεῖραι τὸν δῆμον ταῖς ὁρμαῖς, καὶ πρῶτος ἐπὶ τοῦ βήματος ἀνέκραγε καὶ ἐλοιδορήσατο, καὶ περιζωσάμενος ἐδημηγόρησε, τῶν ἄλλων ἐν κόσμῳ λεγόντων; Schulz (2013) 86–7.

[42] Plut. *Mor.* 800c (*Praec. Ger. Reip.*).

[43] Zanker (1995) 43–50 with fig. 25; the following quotation on pp. 44–5.

208 *Niels Gaul*

self, nowadays in the Museo Nazionale at Naples.[44] The latter in turn claimed that Solon's statue in the agora of Salamis, which must have been very similar in appearance 'with his arm hidden inside [his mantle]' (ἐντὸς τὴν χεῖρα ἔχων), represented the latter appearing before the Athenian assembly:[45] a claim immediately ridiculed by Demosthenes.[46] Kleon, by contrast, wore a belt around his garment (περιζωσάμενος), presumably in order to have his hands free for gesticulation.[47]

Further evidence for the importance of the voice comes from Isokrates in the context of the contemporary controversy of the orality vs literariness of rhetoric.[48] Isokrates emphasizes that orations performed orally (λόγοι λεγόμε-νοι) positively differ from orations that are being read (λόγοι ἀναγιγνωσκό-μενοι):[49] 'how much discourses that are performed orally, with regard to their persuasive power, differ from those which are being read' (ὅσον διαφέρου-σιν τῶν λόγων εἰς τὸ πείθειν οἱ λεγόμενοι τῶν ἀναγιγνωσκομένων). Isokrates continues:

> And they [the members of the audience] have concluded this with good reason: for when a discourse is robbed of the reputation of the speaker, of his voice and the variations which are made in rhetorical delivery; besides, if it is robbed of urgency and keen interest in the subject matter; when it has not a single accessory to support its contentions and enforce its plea, but is deserted and stripped of all the aids which I have mentioned; and when someone reads it aloud without persuasiveness and without impressing his character onto it, but as if taking an inventory of something – in these circumstances it naturally, I think, seems to be insufficient to its hearers.[50]

Isokrates thus equally identified the orator's voice and its modulation as the key tool of delivery. He ties this firmly into a plausible display of character (*ēthos*), that becomes the *conditio sine qua non* of arousing emotions, thus demonstrating the

---

[44] Zanker (1995) figs 27 and 26. Quint. *Inst.* 138 refers to this as a Greek custom but assumes that some gestures were employed nonetheless: 'Accordingly [as their arms were kept within their clothes] they must have used different gestures from ours in the prooemium' (*itaque estiam gestu necesse est usos esse in principiis eos alio quorum bracchium veste continebatur*), trans. Russell (2002) 157.

[45] Aeschin. 1.25.11–13, ed. Martin and Budé (1927): τοῦτ' ἔστιν, ὦ ἄνδρες Ἀθηναῖοι, ὑπόμνημα καὶ μίμημα τοῦ Σόλωνος σχήματος, ὃν τρόπον ἔχων αὐτὸς διελέγετο τῷ δήμῳ τῶν Ἀθηναίων; cf. Zanker (1995) 45–7 and Boegehold (1999) 79.

[46] Dem. 19.251.

[47] Plut. *Mor.* 800c (*Praec. Ger. Reip.*).

[48] Ritoók (1991); Mariß (2002); Edwards (2007).

[49] Isoc. *Phil.* 25–7.

[50] Trans. Norlin (1928) 261 (modified); Isoc. *Phil.* 26: καὶ ταῦτ' οὐκ ἀλόγως ἐγνώκασιν· ἐπει-δὰν γὰρ ὁ λόγος ἀποστερηθῇ τῆς τε δόξης τῆς τοῦ λέγοντος καὶ τῆς φωνῆς καὶ τῶν μεταβολῶν τῶν ἐν ταῖς ῥητορείαις γιγνομένων, ἔτι δὲ τῶν καιρῶν καὶ τῆς σπουδῆς τῆς περὶ τὴν πρᾶξιν, καὶ μηδὲν ᾖ τὸ συναγωνιζόμενον καὶ συμπεῖθον, ἀλλὰ τῶν μὲν προειρημένων ἁπάντων ἔρημος γέ-νηται καὶ γυμνός, ἀναγιγνώσκῃ δέ τις αὐτὸν ἀπιθάνως καὶ μηδὲν ἦθος ἐνσημαινόμενος ἀλλ' ὥσπερ ἀπαριθμῶν, εἰκότως, οἶμαι, φαῦλος εἶναι δοκεῖ τοῖς ἀκούουσιν.

8. Voicing and Gesturing Emotions

209

inextricable connection between Aristotle's categories of character and delivery. Futher corroboration for this comes from Demosthenes, who made authenticity of voice, and thus character, an essential criterion of the display of emotions. The citizens of Athens, he wrote/performed in his successful attempt to slander his opponent, Aischines, 'thought it befitting that the one who would speak over the bodies of the slain and magnify their virtue ... should not lament their fate feigning with his voice, but express the mourning of his very soul'.[51] Demosthenes continues to claim that his own sincerity was widely recognized, whereas Aischines' – the actor by training – was not;[52] the discrepancy between text and performance in the latter's case showed that his purported emotions were not genuine, but an act of *hupokrisis*. Demosthenes continues to accuse Aischines of failing to display the emotions expected from 'an honest and loyal citizen': 'He shed no tears; he did not suffer any such pain in his soul; he vociferated, he exulted, he strained his throat' (οὐδ' ἐδάκρυσεν, οὐδ' ἔπαθεν τοιοῦτον οὐδὲν τῇ ψυχῇ, ἀλλ' ἐπάρας τὴν φωνὴν καὶ γεγηθὼς καὶ λαρυγγίζων, 18.291). One notes that 'true emotion' would, in this instance, have required the facial expression of weeping.[53] In Demosthenes' twist, for this lack of sincerity, Aischines' strategy failed: rather than succeeding in offering proof against Demosthenes, he undid himself by demonstrating that 'in all those distressing events he had had no feeling in common with the other citizens': 'Yet a man who claims to care, as this one here now does, for our laws and constitution, should have this if nothing else, namely the ability to grieve and feel joy over the same things as the many.'[54] Demosthenes' description suggests, in terms of performance theory, an acute failure on Aischines' part to come across as authentic.[55]

In conclusion to this first part, there can be no doubt that voice modulation was considered the primary tool of conveying emotions (and a corresponding character). The ideal ancient orator made prudent use of his voice and limited his gestures to the bare minimum.[56] Yet while rhetorical theory seems to have frowned

---

[51] Dem. 18.287: εἶτα καὶ προσήκειν ὑπολαμβάνοντες τὸν ἐροῦντ' ἐπὶ τοῖς τετελευτηκόσι καὶ τὴν ἐκείνων ἀρετὴν κοσμήσοντα ... μηδὲ τῇ φωνῇ δακρύειν ὑποκρινόμενον τὴν ἐκείνων τύχην, ἀλλὰ τῇ ψυχῇ συναλγεῖν. Easterling (1999); Duncan (2006) 58–89; Schulz (2013) 87–9; and Serafim (2017) all draw mainly on Aeschin. 2 and 3 and Dem. 18 and 19.

[52] Dem. 18.287: τοῦτο δ' ἑώρων παρ' ἑαυτοῖς καὶ παρ' ἐμοί, παρὰ δ' ὑμῖν οὔ. See especially Duncan (2006) 58–89 for Demosthenes' skilful exploitation of Aischines' social background and early career and the latter's lasting success in branding Aischines as a 'third-rate actor'; see also Duncan (2006) 65–6 and *passim* and Serafim (2017) 18.

[53] Something a theatrical actor would not have learnt to do, given that performance was masked.

[54] Dem. 18.291: καίτοι τὸν τῶν νόμων καὶ τῆς πολιτείας φάσκοντα φροντίζειν, ὥσπερ οὗτος νυνί, καὶ εἰ μηδὲν ἄλλο, τοῦτό γ' ἔχειν δεῖ, ταὐτὰ λυπεῖσθαι καὶ ταὐτὰ χαίρειν τοῖς πολλοῖς. Cf. also Duncan (2006) 80.

[55] Alexander (2006) 54–7.

[56] Boegehold (1999) 6 and 79 concedes that the ideal rhetor did not gesticulate but assumes this rule had become obsolete by the fourth century BC and proceeds to postulate frequent gestures; equally, Serafim (2017) 31.

210   *Niels Gaul*

upon the use of gestures, it is equally clear that they were widely used by the fourth century BC at the latest:[57] it is again Demosthenes who observed that Aischines imitated his words and gesticulation (ῥήματα καὶ σχήματα μιμούμενος, 18.232). On this occasion, Aischines seems to have visualized Demosthenes' (sexually) ambiguous gesture of standing up and scratching his head;[58] on a different occasion, he called Demosthenes out for dramatically whirling about on the spot.[59]

8.2. The Second Sophistic

Aischines offers a convenient connection from ancient to Deuterosophistic rhetoric: already for Philostratos, he was the key figure linking the so-called 'Ancient' (ἀρχαία) with the 'Second' (δευτέρα) Sophistic.[60] According to Philostratos, after leaving Athens in voluntary exile Aischines perfected the type of extempore performance that was to become the hallmark of the Second Sophistic period and its Late Antique and, subsequently, Medieval/Byzantine heirs:[61]

Setting forth extempore orations fluently and in an inspired manner, he first carried this praise. For up to his time speaking in the inspired manner had not yet become the custom in the efforts of the sophists, but it originates from Aischines, who improvised as though he were carried away by a divine impulse, like those who exhale the oracles.[62]

'Speaking in an inspired manner' seems to imply a state of emotional 'unhingedness' on the part of the performer, that may well have transmitted itself on to the audience; again there is emphasis on voice rather than gestures.

Yet the Augustan literary critic, Dionysios of Halikarnassos, clearly did not share any of the Classical reservations against gesture when describing Demosthenes' delivery:

One topic remains for me to discuss, namely about delivery: how the man adorned his discourse – for this is a necessary virtue with regard to orations and especially regarding political orations ... Realizing that the nature of delivery is twofold, he [Demosthenes] worked hard on both parts. For both the emotions of his voice and the gestures of his body he achieved with great effort, as he wanted to have the best, although his nature was not well suited towards these ends.[63]

---

[57] See e.g. Graf (1991) and J. Hall (2004).

[58] See e.g. Plut. *Pomp.* 48.7, Luc. *Rhet. Did.* 11; Duncan (2006) 78 on κίναδος/κίναιδος.

[59] Aeschin. 3.167; cf. Worthington (2017) 23.

[60] For Philostratos' famous terminology, cf. *VS* 481, ed. Stefec (2016) 2–3 (1.3.1–2).

[61] Philostr. *VS* 482, ed. Stefec (2016) 3–5 (1.4.2, 1.5). Cf. Van Hook (1919) on Alkidamas' neglected treatise.

[62] Philostr. *VS* 509, ed. Stefec (2016) 26 (1.43.1): τὸν δὲ αὐτοσχέδιον λόγον ξὺν εὐροίᾳ καὶ θείως διατιθέμενος τὸν ἔπαινον τοῦτον πρώτως ἠνέγκατο. τὸ γὰρ θείως λέγειν οὔπω μὲν ἐπεχωρίασε σοφιστῶν σπουδαῖς, ἀπ' Αἰσχίνου δ' ἤρξατο θεοφορήτῳ ὁρμῇ ἀποσχεδιάζοντος, ὥσπερ οἱ τοὺς χρησμοὺς ἀναπνέοντες.

[63] Dion. Hal. *Dem.* 53: εἰς ἔτι μοι καταλείπεται λόγος ὁ περὶ τῆς ὑποκρίσεως, ὡς κεκόσμηκε

8. Voicing and Gesturing Emotions 211

Dionysios thus assumed that Demosthenes used frequent gestures, albeit without offering any detail; further down, he offers a close reading of several passages and seeks to reconstruct their ideal delivery. On Demosthenes' *Third Philippic* oration (§ 26) he comments thus:

Surely this demands an overwhelmingly angry and tragic manner of delivery? What, then, are the tones and accents of voice, the facial expressions and manual gestures that portray anger and grief? Those which men actually experiencing these emotions employ; for it would be silly to reject real life, and look for another school to teach us delivery.[64]

Dionysios' answer to his own rhetorical question does not disclose what gestures precisely an angry man would make; but it clearly assumes and endorses the use of gestures alongside voice modulation. Ultimately, however, Dionysios' approach to Classical oratory was one based on *reading* (ἀναγνούς), rather than performance, and delivery is not one of his main concerns.[65] Yet his overall stance ties in well with Quintilian's obervation that performance had become more lively in his time than it had been in Cicero's days: 'But today a rather more agitated form of delivery has come into fashion, and is expected',[66] and Dionysios may well have drawn on contemporary practices when reconstructing Demosthenes' performances.

This more agitated approach certainly seems to hold true for Deuterosophistc performances; with rhetoric turning into epideictic entertainment that literally happened in theatrical spaces, the state of emotional arousal of both rhetors and audiences increased.[67] It suffices here to point to Ailios Aristeides' climactic tricolon θόρυβος, εὔνοια, ἐνθουσιασμός that neatly summarizes the boiling atmosphere around his performances,[68] even if with a fair bit of exaggeration: one member of the audience could not be told from the next as they were standing shoulder to shoulder. With Aristeides' very first word, 'the whole audience rose

---

τὴν λέξιν ἀνήρ, ἀναγκαίας ἀρετῆς οὔσης περὶ λόγους καὶ μάλιστα τοὺς πολιτικούς ... διττὴν δὲ τὴν φύσιν αὐτῆς οὖσαν ὁρῶν, περὶ ἄμφω τὰ μέρη σφόδρα ἐσπούδασε. καὶ γὰρ τὰ πάθη τὰ τῆς φωνῆς καὶ τὰ σχήματα τοῦ σώματος, ὡς κράτιστα ἕξειν ἔμελλεν, οὐ μικρῷ πόνῳ κατειργάσατο, καίτοι φύσει πρὸς ταῦτα οὐ πάνυ εὐτυχεῖ χρησάμενος.

[64] Trans. Usher (1974) 443; Dion. Hal. *Dem.* 54: οὐ δι' ὀργῆς τ' οὖν ταῦτα ὑπερβαλλούσης καὶ οἴκτου λέγεσθαι προσήκει; τίνες οὖν εἰσιν ὀργῆς καὶ ὀλοφυρμοῦ τόνοι καὶ ἐγκλίσεις καὶ σχηματισμοὶ προσώπου καὶ φοραὶ χειρῶν; ἃς οἱ κατ' ἀλήθειαν ταῦτα πεπονθότες ἐπιτελοῦσι. πάνυ γὰρ εὔηθες ἄλλο τι ζητεῖν ὑποκρίσεως διδασκαλεῖον, ἀφέντας τὴν ἀλήθειαν.

[65] Dion. Hal. *Isoc.* 5 and 13; on Dionysios of Halikarnassos, cf. e.g. Wiater (2011).

[66] Trans. J. Hall (2004) 157; Quint. *Inst.* 11.3.184: *sed iam recepta est actio paulo agitatior et exigitur et quibusdam partibus convenit.* See also Athanasios, *Prol. Syll.*, ed. Rabe (1896) 177.8, and *Rhetorica ad Herennium*; cf. Hall (2007) and Schulz (2013) 107–62.

[67] On Deuterosophistic performances see Schouler (1987); Schmitz (1997) 197–231; Korenjak (2000); Connolly (2001); Whitmarsh (2005) 23–40; Cavallo (2007); Capano (2013); Schmitz (2017); Thomas (2017).

[68] *Hieros logos* 5: τό γε τοῦ θορύβου τε καὶ τῆς εὐνοίας, μᾶλλον δέ, εἰ χρὴ τἀληθὲς εἰπεῖν, ἐνθουσιασμοῦ, τοσοῦτον παρὰ πάντων συνέβη ὥστε οὐδεὶς ὤφθη καθήμενος οὔτ' ἐπὶ τοῦ προαγῶνος οὔθ' ἡνίκα ἀναστὰς ἠγωνιζόμην.

212 *Niels Gaul*

to their feet and lived through pain, joy, and fascination[69] and emphatically nodded along with what was being said – and by inventing shouts of praise not ever heard, everybody sought to increase his own cultural capital by judging Aristeides to be the greatest sophist.

Philostratos' *Lives of the Sophists*, while generally not overly interested in aspects of performance, nevertheless offers a few pertinent examples. One encounters demonstrative theatricality e.g. in Polemo's performance technique (reported by Philostratos from Herodes Attikos' letter to Barbarus), whose trick was, whilst arriving in a litter because of his gout,

that he used to rise to such a pitch of excitement that he would jump up from his chair when he came to the most striking conclusions in his argument, and whenever he rounded off a period he would utter the final clause with a smile, as though to show clearly that he could deliver it without effort, and at certain places in the argument he would stamp the ground just like the horse in Homer.[70]

Given that most sophists performed standing, Polemo's gesture was certainly bespoke. Even more theatrical was Dio Chrysostom, who – while in exile – styled himself as Odysseus and performed with the help of props (his own clothing):

He often came to the camps in the rags he customarily wore, and when after Domitian had been assassinated he saw the soldiers verging towards rebellion, he could not contain himself at the sight of the disorder that had broken out, but naked he leaped on to an high altar and began his harangue thus:
'Then Odysseus of many counsels was stripped of his rags'
and having said this and revealed himself, that he was no pauper, nor whom they believed him to be, but the wise Dio, he breathed a spirited accusation of the tyrant; and he convinced the soldiers to better consider in their actions what seemed good to the Romans. And indeed the persuasion of the man was capable of enchanting also those not versed in Greek.[71]

---

[69] Asyndetic tricolon: ὤδινον, ἐγάνυντο, ἐξεπλήττοντο.

[70] Trans. Wright (1921) 121; Philostr. *VS* 537, ed. Stefec (2016) 52–3 (1.74.7): φησὶ δὲ αὐτὸν ὁ Ἡρώδης καὶ ἀναπηδᾶν τοῦ θρόνου περὶ τὰς ἀκμὰς τῶν ὑποθέσεων, τοσοῦτον αὐτῷ περιεῖναι ὁρμῆς, καὶ ὅτε ἀποτορνεύοι περίοδον, τὸ ἐπὶ πᾶσιν αὐτῆς κῶλον σὺν μειδιάματι φέρειν, ἐνδεικνύμενον πολὺ τὸ ἀλύπως φράζειν, καὶ κροαίνειν ἐν τοῖς τῶν ὑποθέσεων χωρίοις οὐδὲν μεῖον τοῦ Ὁμηρικοῦ ἵππου. According to the *Rhetorica ad Herennium* 3.27, the occasional stamping of the foot (*pedis dexteri rara supplaudio*), alongside pacing and rapid movements of the right arm, was suitable 'to express forcefulness in debate' (Hall (2007) 225).

[71] Philostr. *VS* 488, ed. Stefec (2016) 8–9 (1.14.4–5): θαμίζων δὲ ἐς τὰ στρατόπεδα ἐν οἷσπερ εἰώθει τρύχεσι, καὶ τοὺς στρατιώτας ὁρῶν ἐς νεώτερα ὁρμῶντας ἐπὶ Δομετιανῷ ἀπεσφαγμένῳ, οὐκ ἐφείσατο ἀταξίαν ἰδὼν ἐκραγεῖσαν, ἀλλὰ γυμνὸς ἀναπηδήσας ἐπὶ βωμὸν ὑψηλὸν ἤρξατο τοῦ λόγου ὧδε·
'αὐτὰρ ὁ γυμνώθη ῥακέων πολύμητις Ὀδυσσεύς' [*Od.* 22.1],
καὶ εἰπὼν ταῦτα καὶ δηλώσας ἑαυτόν, ὅτι μὴ πτωχὸς μηδ' ὃν ᾤοντο, Δίων δὲ εἴη ὁ σοφός, ἐπὶ μὲν τὴν κατηγορίαν τοῦ τυράννου πολὺς ἔπνευσε, τοὺς δὲ στρατιώτας ἐδίδαξεν ἄμεινον φρονεῖν τὰ δοκοῦντα Ῥωμαίοις πράττοντας. καὶ γὰρ ἡ πειθὼ τοῦ ἀνδρὸς οἵα καταθέλξαι καὶ τοὺς μὴ τὰ Ἑλλήνων ἀκριβοῦντας; trans. Wright (1921) 21.

8. Voicing and Gesturing Emotions

This episode also has interesting implications for the sophistication and expectation of audiences, given that on this occasion, Dio's audience seems to have been made up of soldiers whose command of Greek proved insufficient to follow the details of the argument.

However, there was also the danger of overdoing gesticulation and spoiling the effect:

[Skopelianos] had an extremely melodious voice, and he would often smite his thigh in order to arouse both himself and his hearers.[72] He excelled also in the use of covert allusion and ambiguous language, but he was even more admirable in his treatment of the more vigorous and grandiloquent themes. It is said that at these times [when treating grandiloquent themes relating to the Persians] he would sway to and fro more than usual, as though in a Bacchic frenzy,[73] and when one of Polemo's entourage said of him that he beat a loud drum, Skopelianos took to himself the sneering jest and retorted: 'Yes, I do beat a drum, but it is the shield of Ajax.'[74]

Such witticisms are typical of Philostratos' sophists; whatever reservations against the use of gestures there may have been in Antiquity, by the Second Sophistic period, such inhibitions were no longer in place. However, not all gestures achieved the desired effect. In one of his customary anecdotes, though not pertaining to a performance of oratory, Philostratos commented on Polemo's witty reaction to an actor's performance:

Again, when a tragic actor at the Olympic games in Smyrna pointed to the ground as he uttered the words, 'O Zeus!' then raised his hands to heaven at the words, 'and Earth!', Polemo, who was presiding at the Olympic games, expelled him from the contest, saying: 'This fellow has committed a solecism with his hand.'[75]

While these passages foreground gestures, elsewhere Philostratos makes clear that emotions kept being transmitted through prefocused texts and voice modulation; his most explicit statement in this respect pertains to Antiochos of

---

[72] The *Rhetorica ad Herennium* 3.27 classifies *feminis plangor* as suitable for lament (*conquestio*) when aiming at a heightened tone (*amplificatio*); cf. J. Hall (2004) 146 and (2007) 225.

[73] Cicero, too, approved of this gesture (*Brut.* 278). The *Rhetorica ad Herennium* 3.26 recommends gentle movement of the body – *paululum corpus a cervicibus demittemus* – as suitable for demonstrative passages.

[74] Trans. Wright (1921) 83–5; Philostr. *VS* 519–20, ed. Stefec (2016) 36 (1.55.8–10): περιῆν δὲ αὐτῷ καὶ εὐφωνίας, καὶ τὸ φθέγμα ἡδονὴν εἶχε τόν τε μηρὸν θαμὰ ἔπληττεν ἑαυτόν τε ὑπεγείρων καὶ τοὺς ἀκροωμένους. ἄριστος μὲν οὖν καὶ σχηματίσαι λόγον καὶ ἐπαμφοτέρως εἰπεῖν, θαυμασιώτερος δὲ περὶ τὰς ἀκμαιοτέρας τῶν ὑποθέσεων … ἐλέγετο καὶ σείεσθαι μᾶλλον ἐν ταύταις, ὥσπερ βακχεύων, καί τινος τῶν ἀμφὶ τὸν Πολέμονα τυμπανίζειν αὐτὸν φήσαντος λαβόμενος ὁ Σκοπελιανὸς τοῦ σκώμματος "τυμπανίζω μέν", εἶπεν, "ἀλλὰ τῇ τοῦ Αἴαντος ἀσπίδι".

[75] Trans. Wright (1921) 131; Philostr. *VS* 542–3, ed. Stefec (2016) 56–7 (1.77.8): ἀγωνιστοῦ δὲ τραγῳδίας ἐν τοῖς κατὰ τὴν Σμύρναν Ὀλυμπίοις τὸ 'ὦ Ζεῦ' ἐς τὴν γῆν δείξαντος, τὸ δὲ 'καὶ γᾶ' ἐς τὸν οὐρανὸν ἀνασχόντος, προκαθήμενος τῶν Ὀλυμπίων ὁ Πολέμων ἐξέωσεν αὐτὸν τῶν ἄθλων εἰπὼν 'οὗτος τῇ χειρὶ ἐσολοίκισεν'.

214 *Niels Gaul*

Aigai, who shrewdly exploited *ēthopoiïa* continuing a long tradition of law-court oratory.[76] Antiochos

> handled the emotions more skilfully than any other sophist, for he did not spin out long monodies or abject lamentations, but expressed them in a few words and adorned them with ideas better than I can describe, as is evident in other cases that he pleaded, but especially in the following.[77]

Philostratos proceeds to give two examples of *ēthopoiïai*, in which Antiochos excelled, and thus takes us back to the issue of successful, i.e. authentic representation of character. The first example deals with a girl that gave birth after rape; in his *meletē* Antiochos assumed the figure of the paternal grandfather and exclaimed: 'Give up the child, give it up already before it can taste its mother's milk!',[78] with anaphora and temporal adverb ἤδη creating a sense of urgency. In the second example, a castrated man – again impersonated by Antiochos – cleverly exploited a gap in the agreement of a tyrant, who abdicated on the condition of immunity for himself, in the latter's contract with the people; the eunuch slew the former tyrant. Antiochos 'threw in an ingenious argument while he set forth the eunuch's personal grievance: "With whom, pray", cried he, "did he make this agreement? With children, women, boys, old men, and men: but I have no name in that contract."'[79]

8.3. The (Middle) Byzantine period

From Deuterosophistic theatrics, the Byzantines inherited the term *theatron* to denote rhetorical performances.[80] But did they subscribe to the same ideals of performance? With the decline of secular oratory towards the end of Late Antiquity, emotive performance moved into the church.[81] While much can be inferred about performative contexts from the surviving corpora of homilies, it seems to remain an open question whether and to what degree Late Antique preachers employed gesture; no description of an actual performance seems to have survived. Nor are portraits in Byzantine manuscripts particularly helpful,

---

[76] Cf. Serafim (2017) 91–111.

[77] Trans. Wright (1921) 187–9; Philostr. *VS* 569, ed. Stefec (2016) 81–2 (2.23.3–5): καὶ τὰ πάθη ἄριστα σοφιστῶν μετεχειρίσατο· οὐ γὰρ μονῳδίας ἀπεμήκυνεν οὐδὲ θρήνους ὑποκειμένους, ἀλλ᾽ ἐβραχυλόγει αὐτὰ ξὺν διανοίαις λόγου κρείττοσιν, ὡς ἔκ τε τῶν ἄλλων ὑποθέσεων δηλοῦται καὶ μάλιστα ἐκ τῶνδε.

[78] Philostr. *VS* 569, ed. Stefec (2016) 81 (2.23.4): 'ἄποδος', ἔφη, 'τὸ παιδίον, ἄποδος ἤδη, πρὶν γεύσηται μητρῴου γάλακτος.'

[79] Philostr. *VS* 569, ed. Stefec (2016) 82 (2.23.5): 'τίσι γάρ', ἔφη, 'ταῦτα ὡμολόγησε; παισὶ γυναίοις μειρακίοις πρεσβύταις ἀνδράσιν· ἐγὼ δὲ ὄνομα ἐν ταῖς συνθήκαις οὐκ ἔχω.'

[80] On this practice and the terminological shift, see Gaul (2020) 354–9.

[81] Cf. e.g. Jan Stenger's chapter in this volume.

8. Voicing and Gesturing Emotions 215

as these tend to depict their object in the act of writing rather than preaching. However, one passage in Psellos' well-known essay on Gregory Nazianzen's style might imply the use of gesture.[82] When discussing Gregory's approach to the three genres of rhetoric, Psellos wrote:

> He [Gregory] advises by weaving censure with admonitions and by smoothing it with different methods of presentation. He practises judicial discourse in mellifluous and piercing voice; for his *movement* has pulses and hissings and the intensity of his breath makes frequently excited leaps. When he advises, he resembles a stream of oil that flows silently and enters into the soul calmly. When he fights against his opponents, he resembles brimstone and storms and the fiery bursts of clouds.[83]

Given that Psellos seems to focus on Gregory's voice in this paragraph and his metaphors of movement ('the pitch jumps'), Papaioannou's suggestion to take κίνησις as an allusion to the Hermogenian form of vivacity (γοργότης) seems perhaps more plausible than to assume a physical gesture. Given the emotive nature of preaching, it is in any case not surprising that whatever contemporary reference is made in the twelfth-century commentaries on Aristotle's *Rhetoric* concerns reading in church, rather than the performance of oratory in court or 'theatrical' contexts. The anonymous twelfth-century commentary on Aristotle's *Rhetoric* explains:

> and initially the poets themselves performed the tragedies] for example Sophokles: when he introduced slaves as speakers, he imitated them and spoke in barbaric tongue; when he introduced women in speaking roles, he spoke like a woman; *just as nowadays those who [publicly] read the passions of martyrs do.*[84]

The Anonymus also expanded on Aristotle's statement about the use of the voice quoted above, and offered considerable detail:[85]

> This method of delivery is considered as part of the voice, that is to say, of the reading performance: how one must utilise the act of reading towards the emotions. For if the persona, about whom the oration, is angry, one must use a loud and harsh voice;[86] if grieving and wailing one must use a sharp voice; if ill, a middle voice. And how must one use the

---

[82] See Papaioannou (2017b) 140 n. 89.

[83] Trans. Papaioannou (2017b) 140; Psellos, *On Gregory's Style,* 308–14, ed. Levy (1912) (emphasis added): συμβουλεύει τε γὰρ τὸ τῆς ἐπιτιμήσεως εἶδος συμπλέκων ταῖς παραινέσεσι καὶ ταῖς μεθόδοις καταλεαίνων· καὶ δικάζεται εὔηχόν τι φθεγγόμενος καὶ τορόν· σφυγμούς τε γὰρ αὐτῷ καὶ σιγμοὺς ἡ **κίνησις** ἔχει καὶ πηδᾷ θαμὰ διεγειρόμενος αὐτῷ ὁ τόνος τοῦ πνεύματος. καὶ συμβουλεύων μὲν ἔοικεν ἐλαίου ῥεύματι ἀψοφητὶ ῥέοντι καὶ εἰσδύνοντι εἰς τὴν ψυχὴν ὁμαλῶς, πρὸς δὲ τοὺς ἀντιθέτους ἀγωνιζόμενος θείῳ καὶ καταιγίδι καὶ τοῖς ἐκ τῶν νεφῶν ἐκπυρινισμοῖς.

[84] Anon. *Comm. in Arist. Rh.* 3.1, 1403b21, ed. Rabe (1896) 159.5–8 (emphasis added): καὶ γὰρ αὐτοὶ οἱ ποιηταὶ ὑπεκρίνοντο τὰς τραγῳδίας, οἷον ὁ Σοφοκλῆς, ὅταν παρεισῆγε δούλους λέγοντας, ἐμιμεῖτο αὐτοὺς καὶ ἔλεγε φωνὰς βαρβαρικάς, ὅταν δὲ παρεισῆγε γυναῖκας λεγούσας, ἔλεγεν ὡς γυνή, **καθάπερ καὶ νῦν οἱ ἀναγινώσκοντες τὰ μαρτυρογράφια ποιοῦσιν.**

[85] See *Rh.* 3.1, 1404b27–32 on p. 202 above.

[86] The famous anecdote about Demosthenes and his client comes to mind, whom Demosthenes needed to provoke to sound like a man angry and wronged (Plut. *Dem.* 11.2–3).

216　　　　　　　　　　　　　　　　　　*Niels Gaul*

pitches of the voice? For we want either to employ a sharp voice (if the persona grieves, about whom the oration) or a grave voice, if the person is heroic and angry. The rhythm is composed [accordingly] and appears plainly from such composition: for the rhythm will be different if we speak first in anapaests and then in dactylics; and another would be effected, either indeed humble or middle, if we spoke in dactylics first, and only then in anapaests: for with regard to [different] emotions the rhythm needs to be adjusted as well.[87]

Just like the Anonymus, his contemporary Stephanos equally made reference to homiletic practice and the reading of the Gospels:

Delivery is of utmost importance in poetry and prose orations: just as [John] Chrysostom, when he studied Abraam's affairs, imitated him exceedingly well, and Sarah and Isaac and the slaves and the Ismailites.[88] This is also clear from those around Aischines and Demosthenes: Aischines declaimed in tragic style when he went to Philip, performed well, won, and was crowned; Demosthenes, who was not very skilled with regard to performance, suffered defeat, and thence their rivalry began. Performance means to express things appropriate to every emotion with like voice: if someone imitates a tyrant or Polymestor, it is necessary to use a loud voice; if a woman, such as Hekabe or Polyxene, a low voice and as if interrupted from emotion (*pathos*). But one must also use the pitches in a fitting manner: for this reason also, those who learn to read the holy Gospels are first introduced to the pitches of the words, being taught the acute, long drawn-out, grave, and soft voice.[89]

This passage leaves no doubt as to the importance of voice and pitch (τόνος) in arousing emotions. Further down, Stephanos commented on the onomatopoetic qualities of voice, intriguingly evoking the example of a Latin church bell: 'The tongue is most imitative when imitating music, a trumpet, a Latin bell, swallows or frogs, as nowadays with us the singers [in church] and then the comic poet:

---

[87] Anon. *Comm. in Arist. Rh.* 3.1, 1403b27–9, ed. Rabe (1896) 159.14–25: ἔστι δὲ αὕτη ἡ τῆς ὑποκρίσεως μέθοδος θεωρουμένη ἐν τῇ φωνῇ ἤτοι ἐν τῇ ἀναγνώσει, πῶς δεῖ χρᾶσθαι τῇ ἀναγνώσει πρὸς τὰ πάθη· εἰ γὰρ ὀργιζόμενόν ἐστι τὸ πρόσωπον, περὶ οὗ ὁ λόγος, δεῖ χρᾶσθαι μεγάλῃ φωνῇ καὶ τραχείᾳ, εἰ δὲ λυπούμενον καὶ θρηνοῦν, δεῖ χρᾶσθαι ὀξείᾳ φωνῇ, εἰ δὲ νοσαζόμενον, μέσῃ. καὶ πῶς τοῖς τόνοις τῆς φωνῆς χρηστέον· ἢ γὰρ ὀξεῖαν φωνὴν ἀφιέναι μέλλομεν· εἰ θρηνεῖ τὸ πρόσωπον, περὶ οὗ ὁ λόγος, ἢ βαρεῖαν, εἰ ἡρωικόν ἐστι τὸ πρόσωπον καὶ ὀργιζόμενον. ὁ ῥυθμὸς σύγκειται καὶ ἀναφαίνεται ἐκ τῆς τοιᾶσδε συνθήκης· ἄλλος γὰρ ῥυθμὸς γίνεται, εἰ πρῶτον ἀναπαίστους εἴπωμεν, εἶτα δακτύλους, καὶ ἄλλος ἂν ἀποτελεσθῇ, ἢ ταπεινὸς δηλονότι ἢ μέσος, εἰ τοὺς δακτύλους πρῶτον εἴπωμεν, εἶτα τοὺς ἀναπαίστους· καὶ γὰρ πρὸς τὰ πάθη ὀφείλει καὶ ὁ ῥυθμὸς ἐξαλλάττεσθαι.

[88] A reference to Chrysostom's commentary on Genesis.

[89] Stephanos, *Comm. in Arist. Rh.* 3.1, 1403b22–7, ed. Rabe (1896) 309.12–25: ἡ ὑπόκρισις μέγιστόν ἐστιν ἔν τε ποιήσει καὶ ἐν πεζοῖς λόγοις· ὡς ὁ Χρυσόστομος τὰ κατὰ τὸν Ἀβραὰμ μελετήσας ἐμιμήσατό τε τοῦτον ἄριστα καὶ τὴν Σάρραν καὶ Ἰσαὰκ καὶ τοὺς δούλους καὶ τοὺς Ἰσμαηλίτας· ὡς καὶ ἐκ τῶν περὶ Αἰσχίνην καὶ Δημοσθένην δεδήλωται· ἐτραγῴδησε μὲν γὰρ παρὰ Φίλιππον ἰὼν Αἰσχίνης καὶ καλῶς ὑπεκρίθη καὶ νενίκηκε καὶ ἐστεφάνωται, ὁ δὲ Δημοσθένης μὴ ἔχων εἰς τὴν ὑπόκρισιν ἡττήθη κἀντεῦθεν αὐτοῖς ἡ διαμάχη ξυνέπεσεν. ἔστιν οὖν ὑπόκρισις τὸ ἑκάστῳ πάθει κατάλληλον τὴν ἐξαγγελίαν διὰ τῆς ποιᾶς φωνῆς ποιεῖσθαι· εἰ μὲν γὰρ τύραννον ἢ Πολυμήστορα μιμοῖτο, δεῖ μεγάλῃ χρῆσθαι φωνῇ, εἰ δὲ γυναῖκα οἷον Ἑκάβην ἢ Πολυξένην, μικρᾷ καὶ οἷον ὑπὸ τοῦ πάθους διακοπτομένῃ. ἀλλὰ καὶ τοῖς τόνοις χρηστέον ἁρμοζόντως. διὰ τοῦτο καὶ οἱ τὰ ἅγια εὐαγγέλια ἀναγινώσκειν μανθάνοντες μυοῦνται πρῶτον τοὺς τόνους, ὀξεῖαν καὶ συρματικὴν καὶ βαρεῖαν καὶ λείαν ἐκπαιδευόμενοι.

8. Voicing and Gesturing Emotions

"brekekekex", "koax koax", "tio tio", "threttanelo", "ui ui", and myriads other such instances.[90] While their effects are not detailed, it is safe to assume that such voice modulations served an affective purpose with the listener in both representing and, in turn, eliciting emotions. Once again the emphasis on voice over gestures in these passages suggests that the former was considered the more important affective instrument.

This also holds true for rhetoric performed at the imperial court. In a well-known passage, Psellos commented on the qualities of his own voice, that helped him gain access to Emperor Konstantinos IX Monomachos. Psellos emphasized that this was a gift of nature and that his tongue (γλῶττα) was considered particularly graceful.[91] He added more detailed comments on what makes a model rhetor in the funeral oration for his one-time friend, the law-professor-turned-patriarch Ioannes Xiphilinos. In the passage describing Xiphilinos', and Psellos' own, rise at the imperial court, the latter depicted Xiphilinos as an ideal rhetor:

His tongue was overflowing and as if from a fountain, the words welled out of it, and his apprehension of a given subject was not based on the consultation of books, but memory kept everything inside his soul[92] ... He did not acquire a clear (loud) voice through exercise, but was fortunate to be granted such a voice in an almost supernatural way. When he enacted the emperor's utterances, or any other subject that had been assigned to him, his speech resembled thunder in the sky (βροντάς). He was standing in the middle, or rather was surrounded by the crowd; he resembled a solid and fixed column, neither disturbed nor losing his head by what was said by those around him; rather, he kept his composure and showed the firmness of his character.[93] As soon as he began speaking, using a prolific but honey-sweetened tongue, he made a proper division of the chapters of his subject: he went up to its most important point, making it the starting point of his speech. At the beginning and middle of his oration he was thoughtful and pensive, but at the end of his discourse he became pleasant and beautiful.[94] Through his harmonious, flowery style he made clear that his speech had come to its conclusion smoothly.[95]

---

[90] Stephanos, *Comm. in Arist. Rh.* 3.1, 1404a19, ed. Rabe (1896) 310.35–311.4: μιμητικωτάτη γὰρ ἡ γλῶττα μιμουμένη καὶ μουσικὴν καὶ σάλπιγγα καὶ κώδωνα Λατινικὸν καὶ ἀηδόνας καὶ βατράχους, ὡς σήμερον παρ᾽ ἡμῖν οἱ ψάλται καὶ τότε ὁ κωμῳδὸς 'βρεκεκεκέξ' καὶ τὸ 'κοὰξ κοάξ' [Ar. *Ran.* 209–10, 215, 220, etc.] καὶ τὸ 'τίο τίο' [Ar. *Av.* 237] καὶ τὸ 'θρεττανελό' [Ar. *Plut.* 290, 296] καὶ τὸ 'ὒ ὒ' [Ar. *Plut.* 895] καὶ ἄλλα μυρία τοιάδε.

[91] Psellos, *Chronographia*, 6.44–5, ed. Reinsch, 124–5. Psellos' emphasis on his natural capacities, as opposed to family pedigree, represents the approach of the second-tier literati coming to the fore in the tenth and eleventh centuries; cf. Gaul (2014) 243–58. Social dynamics of such kind had already been at work in the controversy between Demosthenes and his *homo novus* opponent, Aischines – cf. Duncan (2006) 82–4.

[92] Xiphilinos' memory certainly aided with extempore speaking.

[93] I.e. his authenticity.

[94] Cf. Philostr. *VS* 612: καὶ γὰρ ἐπίχαρις καὶ ἀγαλματίας.

[95] Trans. Polemis (2015) 189–90 (modified); Psellos, *Or. fun.* 3 (for Ioannes Xiphilinos) 9.5–15, ed. Polemis, 126–7: ἐκάχλαζε γὰρ αὐτῷ ἡ γλῶττα ... καὶ αὐτόθεν τὰ πηγαῖα ἐχεῖτο νάματα καὶ ἡ ἐπιστροφὴ τούτῳ τῶν ἐπιβολῶν οὐκ εἰς βιβλία τὰ πλείω, ἀλλ᾽ ἡ μνήμη πάντα συνήθροιζε τῇ ψυχῇ ... λαμπροφωνίαν δὲ ἤσκησε μὲν οὐδαμῶς, εὐμοίρησε δὲ ταύτης ὑπερφυῶς, καὶ εἴτε βασιλείους φωνὰς ὑποκρίνοιτο, ἄνωθεν ταύτας ἡφίει ὥσπερ βροντάς, εἴτε τι ἄλλο λέγειν ἐπε-

218 *Niels Gaul*

Psellos leaves no doubt that Xiphilinos, other than reflecting his determination in his posture, achieved his affective impact primarily, if not entirely, through voice modulation: like the ideal rhetor of old, he stands in the middle of the *theatron* resembling 'a solid and fixed column' (στήλη ἀσφαλὴς καὶ ἀκίνητος), that is, with little or no gesturing; his soon thundering, soon honey-sweet tongue evokes the image of the Homeric orators that opened this chapter – in fact combines several of their qualities into the sole figure of Xiphilinos – while his posture is reminiscent of Odysseus' in the well-known passage in the third book of the *Iliad*.[96]

The situation is somewhat more ambiguous in the case of another brilliant performer that Psellos introduces, the *chartoularios* Ioannes Kroustoulas, who – as suggested by the anonymous commentator on Aristotle – seems to have performed *martyrologia* and other hagiographical pieces in the church of the Chalkoprateia in downtown Constantinople:

> Everyone who was present there and had listened to the man suffered immediate change in respect to his soul and came to feel contentment, even if he were a stone, or rock, or iron, or an uncontrollable beast greedy of blood. For such charm trickled from his lips and so harmonious was his voice and in such a manner did he subdue the listeners by enchantments and charm those with good cheer, that even if someone (for permit me to boast briefly about this man!) had to receive the miseries of Odysseus, these would immediately fill his entire soul with gladness.[97]

τέτακτο. ὁ δὲ ἐν μέσοις ἐγκείμενος, μᾶλλον δὲ τῶν πέριξ ἑστηκὼς μέσος, ἥδραστο μὲν ὥσπερ τις στήλη ἀσφαλὴς καὶ ἀκίνητος, οὐ τοῖς ἑκατέρωθεν λόγοις θορυβούμενος ἢ κλονούμενος, ἀλλ' ἐφ' ἑαυτοῦ μένων καὶ τὴν τοῦ ἤθους πῆξιν ἐπιδεικνύμενος. ἀρξάμενος δὲ λέγειν πλατείᾳ ὁμοῦ τῇ γλώττῃ καὶ μελιχρᾷ, διῄρει μὲν ὥσπερ εἰκὸς τὴν ὑπόθεσιν, ἀναβαίνων δὲ εἰς τὴν τοῦ ὑποκειμένου ἀκρόπολιν, ἐκεῖθεν ἠφίει τοὺς λόγους, σύννους μὲν καὶ περιεσκεμμένος ἄνω τε καὶ περὶ τὰ μέσα γιγνόμενος, πρὸς δὲ τῷ τέλει τῆς ὑποθέσεως χαρίεις τε καὶ ἀγαλματίας φαινόμενος, καὶ ὅτι συνέκλεισεν ὁμαλῶς τὴν ὅλην περίοδον καὶ τὴν τομὴν τοῦ λόγου συνεπεράνατο, ἐμμελῶς ταῖς ἐξανθούσαις ἐπιδεικνύμενος χάρισι.

[96] *Il.* 3.217–22: ἀλλ' ὅτε δὴ πολύμητις ἀναΐξειεν Ὀδυσσεὺς / στάσκεν, ὑπαὶ δὲ ἴδεσκε κατὰ χθονὸς ὄμματα πήξας, / σκῆπτρον δ' οὔτ' ὀπίσω οὔτε προπρηνὲς ἐνώμα, / ἀλλ' ἀστεμφὲς ἔχεσκεν ἀΐδρεϊ φωτὶ ἐοικώς· / φαίης κε ζάκοτόν τέ τιν' ἔμμεναι ἄφρονά τ' αὔτως. / ἀλλ' ὅτε δὴ ὅπα τε μεγάλην ἐκ στήθεος εἴη / καὶ ἔπεα νιφάδεσσιν ἐοικότα χειμερίῃσιν (Odysseus 'rose quickly / but just stood there, his eyes fixed on the ground. / He did not move his staff forward or backward / But held it steady. You would have thought him / A dull, surly lout without any wit. But when he / Opened his mouth and projected his voice |/ The words fell down like snowflakes in a blizzard'; trans. Lombardo (1997)). Cf. n. 2 above.

[97] Psellos, *Or. min.* 37.157–64, ed. Littlewood (1985) 142: οὐκ ἔστιν οὖν ὅστις ἐκεῖσε παραγενόμενος καὶ τοῦ ἀνδρὸς ἀκούσας οὐκ εὐθὺς τὴν ψυχὴν ἠλλάγη καὶ πρὸς εὐθυμίαν μετεληλύθει, κἂν λίθος ἦν, κἂν πέτρα, κἂν σίδηρος, κἂν θὴρ αἱμοβόρος καὶ ἀκατάσχετος. τοσαύτη γὰρ χάρις τῶν τούτου χειλέων ἀπέσταζε καὶ τοιοῦτος ὑπῆρχε τὴν φωνὴν ἐναρμόνιος καὶ οὕτως κατέθελγε τοὺς ἀκούοντας καὶ κατεκήλει τοὺς εὔφρονας, ὥστε, κἂν εἴ ποτέ τις (δότε γάρ μοι καὶ βραχύ τι καυχήσασθαι περὶ τοῦ ἀνδρός) τὰς τοῦ Ὀδυσσέως εἶχε κακότητας ἀπολαβεῖν, αὐτὰς αὐτίκα καὶ θυμηδίας ἐμπλῆσαι τὴν ψυχὴν ἅπασαν. This text is now available in an excellent translation-cum-commentary by Papaioannou (2017a), who also promises a more thorough analysis of the text (forthcoming).

8. Voicing and Gesturing Emotions

While the passage again emphasizes the importance of voice, there was certainly a dramatic gesture involved *before* Ioannes started his performance when, on the basis of a small sign, Psellos claimed to be able to figure out Ioannes 'from a small sign':

for when he entered the spot of his reading he was not one who retained his solemn posture and his restrained manner towards everything, but as if transforming himself into the noble spirit of a wild beast, he moved aside with his hand the monastic piece of clothing that we usually call *periauchenion*;[98] he took the candle and showed himself calm and firm in his will[99] – all but speaking with his posture and offering a model for how a reader ought to perform.[100]

This again suggests that, like Xiphilinos, Kroustoulas asumed a fairly immobile posture – holding a candle would have made gesturing all but impossible – in order to visualize the strength of his character and convey it to the audience. While these gestures immediately preceded the actual delivery, it is less clear whether Kroustoulas moved anything but his voice while he was performing his reading.[101] Whether one assumes that Kroustoulas made use of gestures during his actual performance depends on one passage of Psellos' intriguing encomium in particular: ἑώρων γοῦν αὐτὸν ἀτενῶς καὶ πάντοθεν λεπτολογούμενος ἀνηρεύνων εἰς τὰς ἐκτάσεις, εἰς τὰς ἀφέσεις, τὰς ὑποκρίσεις, τὰς μεταβάσεις, τὰς ἐκτοπίσεις, καὶ πάντοθέν μοι διέσῳζε τὸ ἀκέραιον.[102] The beginning reads fairly straightforwardly: 'I observed him intently and examined him from every aspect, studying for myself every detail'. Papaioannou renders the following *termini technici* as 'how he stretched out his hands, how he would start off, how he would perform, how he would shift his body, how he would change his spot',[103] arriving at the image of an animated performance. With good reason: in Psellos, ἔκτασις is more often than not specified as 'extending one's hands' (ἔκτασις χειρῶν) and μετάβασις frequently assumes a spatial connotation,[104] while ἐκτόπισις is a hapax

---

[98] Was this in order to free his arm(s) for gesturing?

[99] Compare above n. 97, about Xiphilinos: ἀλλ᾽ ἐφ᾽ ἑαυτοῦ μένων καὶ τὴν τοῦ ἤθους πῆξιν ἐπιδεικνύμενος.

[100] Trans. Papaioannou (2017a) 226 (modified); Psellos, *Or. min.* 37.61–9, ed. Littlewood (1985) 139: εὐθὺς γὰρ τὸν ἄνδρα καὶ παραυτίκα διέγνωκα καὶ τὸ βραχὺ σημεῖον τὴν ὅλην μοι μαρτυρίαν παρέσχηκεν· οὐδὲ γὰρ τοιοῦτος ἦν ὁποῖος εἰσέδυ τὸν τόπον πατήσας τῆς ἀναγνώσεως, οὐδὲ μετὰ τοῦ σεμνοῦ παρέμενε σχήματος καὶ τοῦ συνεσταλμένου πρὸς πάντα φρονήματος, ἀλλὰ θηρὸς ὥσπερ μεταμφιασάμενος γενναιότητα τό τε ῥάκος τῆς χειρὸς ἐπανέστρεψεν, ὃ δὴ συνήθως περιαυχένιον ὀνομάζομεν, καὶ τὸν κηρὸν λαβὼν σταθηρὸς τὴν γνώμην ἐδέδεικτο, μονονουχὶ διὰ τοῦ σχήματος προσφθεγγόμενος καὶ τυπῶν ὁποῖον δεῖ πάντως τὸν ἀναγινώσκειν ὀφείλοντα γίγνεσθαι. Compare Quint. *Inst.* 11.3.137 for arrangements of dress; cf. Graf (1991) 44–5.

[101] Psellos offers a definition of an accomplished reader at *Or. min.* 37.97–112.

[102] Psellos, *Or. min.* 37.147–9 (emphasis added).

[103] Papaioannou (2017a) 230.

[104] Ἔκτασις χειρῶν: Psellos, *Orr. pan.* 2.785, 14.53; *Or. hag.* 3a.36 and 694; μετάβασις: *Chron.* 5.1.6, ed. Reinsch (2014) 80.

in his surviving (vast) *oeuvre*, and is rarely attested anywhere else. Papaioannou's gestural reading is thus very likely. However, in the present context it may
be worthwhile indicating that ἔκτασις and μετάβασις can both assume a slightly
different technical meaning: the lengthening of a syllable and the transition from
one topic to another, respectively; the first is attested as such in Psellos' favourite
critic, Dionysios of Halikarnassos, while the second goes back to the *Odyssey*.[105]
With the meaning of ἐκτόπισις somewhat unclear – 'the removal of something (a
passage?) (to another spot)' – one might perhaps countenance an interpretation
of these terms as referring to voice modulation and content arrangement, rather
than physical movements: 'with regard to his lengthenings, departures, interpretations,[106] transitions, displacements(?)'.

The paragraph continues:

And from all this, for me he maintained his purity. *For* soon he appeared as if smooth [a
smooth air], soon he was considered some fresh breeze: *for* he gave breath to the oration,
made the right stresses, often employed a rough voice, frequently furnished it with wings
[= gave it an air of excitement], and thoroughly regaled those present with his well-
sounding rhythms: some passages he pronounced by somehow weaving various styles
together; others with single-sidedness,[107] others without conjunctions; the cases/cadences
of the words, which the philosophers call the ends of words and syllables by analogy, he
offered in fitting expressions.[108]

It seems as if Psellos was using the rest of the paragraph to give examples for his
initial assessment ('*For* soon … soon …; *for* he gave …' – a causality seems implied throughout): given that the remainder of this paragraph deals exclusively
with Kroustoulas' voice and reading technique, one cannot fully exclude the possibility that Psellos was here referring to the latter's voice modulation throughout,
rather than any physical movements. If so, then Psellos' ideal eleventh-century
rhetor evoked emotions by voice rather than gesture. Either way, the emotional
impact of Kroustoulas' delivery was such that

over and above these he made some cry and shed wondrous tears from the eyes, what
everybody very reasonably calls indications of one's soul; others [he made] laugh and

---

[105] Dion. Hal. *De comp. verb.* 25: τί δ᾽ ἐστὶ τοῦτο; τὰ γράμματα ὅταν παιδευώμεθα, πρῶτον μὲν τὰ ὀνόματα αὐτῶν ἐκμανθάνομεν, ἔπειτα τοὺς τύπους καὶ τὰς δυνάμεις, εἶθ᾽ οὕτω τὰς
συλλαβὰς καὶ τὰ ἐν ταύταις πάθη, καὶ μετὰ τοῦτο ἤδη τὰς λέξεις καὶ τὰ συμβεβηκότα αὐταῖς,
ἐκτάσεις τε λέγω καὶ συστολὰς καὶ προσῳδίας καὶ τὰ παραπλήσια τούτοις. For μετάβασις see
Luc. *Hist. conscr.* 55; as a rhetorical figure: Quint. *Inst.* 9.3.25. Cf. *Od.* 8.492.

[106] 'Deliveries' in the plural does not seem to make much sense in this context.

[107] Another rare technical term, as observed by Papaioannou (2017a) 230 n. 26.

[108] Psellos, *Or. min.* 37.149–56, ed. Littlewood (1985) 142: νῦν μὲν γὰρ λεῖος ὥσπερ ἐφαίνετο,
νῦν δέ τις αὔρα νενόμιστο· πνεῦμά τε γὰρ παρεῖχε τῷ λόγῳ, καὶ ἐποίει τόνους ἐτραχύνετό τε
πολλάκις καὶ τὴν φωνὴν ἐπτέρου καὶ τοῖς εὐήχοις ῥυθμοῖς τοὺς παρόντας κατέτερπε· καὶ τὰ
μὲν κατὰ συμπλοκήν πως προῆγε, τὰ δὲ κατὰ μονομέρειαν, τὰ δ᾽ ἄλλα συμβολῆς ἄτερ, τὰς δὲ
πτώσεις πάντων τῶν λόγων, ἄσπερ δὴ πέρατα λέξεων ἢ συλλαβῶν ἀναλόγως ὀνομάζουσιν οἱ
φιλόσοφοι, κατὰ τοὺς εἰκότας λόγους παρείχετο.

8. Voicing and Gesturing Emotions 221

give themselves over to pleasures; yet others he rendered to weeping and wailing. One of these, as the words touched his soul, took off his garment and gave it to the beggar [there] (for the church is not short of these) and preferred to be naked on Christ's behalf and the reward [to be received] from there, which offers manifold blessings in return and provides the ever-lasting life.[109]

Certainly for the Late Byzantine period, as for all periods under consideration, exaggerated gesticulation during performance was a risky enterprise that could easily backfire, as the well-known example of Nikephoros Choumnos shows:

> You convoke *theatra* for your own sake, calling together men of presently great reputation, who listen to your ever so great wisdom and your [intellectual] prowess and over-boldness against Plato and those other men of old with great names. And you yourself sit amidst those men [amidst your own *theatron*], and while your texts are being read, you celebrate mystic rites and you applaud [your own texts] with manifold unpleasant gestures, soon jumping up from your stool, soon collapsing and contracting [on it, performing] all [possible] gestures and bendings of your head and neck, and manifold twistings and turnings of your body, going mad and offering [many] occasions of laughter and much to talk about to the listeners and spectators, when they would later leave your *theatron*.[110]

This is to be taken *cum grano salis*, as Choumnos does not perform himself on this occasion; nevertheless, for Theodoros Metochites' vitriolic criticism to work, it must have been based on assumptions of how a literatus should act.

Conclusion

While the Second Sophistic bestowed the concept of *theatron* and extempore rhetoric on Byzantine literati, it is somewhat less certain that it transmitted its more enlivened fashion of performance to the Byzantine Middle Ages. From the limited evidence here discussed, a statue-like rhetor was perceived as an ideal orator, whereas abundant gesturing was prone to criticism and ridicule:

---

[109] Psellos, *Or. min.* 37.274–81, ed. Littlewood (1985) 146: τοὺς μὲν γὰρ ἐπὶ τούτοις ἐποίει θρη-νεῖν καὶ δεινὰ τῶν ὀφθαλμῶν καταρρέειν τὰ δάκρυα, ἃ ψυχῆς μηνύματα λέγουσι καὶ λίαν εἰκό-τως ἅπαντες, τοὺς δὲ γελᾶν καὶ ἐκκεχύσθαι ταῖς ἡδοναῖς, τοὺς δὲ παντάπασιν ἐδίδου κλαυθ-μῷ. εἷς δέ τις τούτων, ἁψαμένων αὐτοῦ τῆς ψυχῆς τῶν ῥημάτων, τὸν χιτῶνα ἀποδυσάμενος τῷ πένητι δέδωκεν (οὐδὲ τούτων γὰρ ὁ νεὼς ἠμοίρει) καὶ γυμνιτεύειν προείλετο διὰ Χριστὸν καὶ τὴν ἐκεῖθεν ἀντίδοσιν, ἣ δὴ πολλαπλασίους ἀντιπαρέχει τὰς χάριτας καὶ ζωὴν πρυτανεύει τὴν ἀεὶ διαμένουσαν.

[110] Theodore Metochites, *Or.* 14.27.1–11, ed. Ševčenko (1962a) 253: καὶ θέατρα συγκαλεῖς ἑαυ-τῷ καὶ τοὺς νῦν ἐλλογίμους, ἀκροασαμένους τῆς σῆς μεγίστης σοφίας καὶ κράτους καὶ τόλμης κατὰ Πλάτωνος καὶ τῶν παλαιῶν ἐκείνων μεγαλωνύμων ἀνδρῶν· καὶ μέσος προκαθήμενος, ἀναγινωσκομένων τῶν σῶν, ὀργιάζεις καὶ ἐπικροτεῖς παντοίοις ἀηδίας σχήμασι, νῦν μὲν ἀνα-πηδῶν τοῦ σκίμποδος, νῦν δὲ συμπίπτων καὶ συνιζάνων καὶ χειρονομίαις πάσαις καὶ κεφαλῆς κλίσεσι καὶ αὐχένος, καὶ στροφαῖς καὶ ἀντιστροφαῖς παντοίαις τοῦ σώματος, ἐξοιστρούμενος καὶ γέλωτος ἀφορμὰς καὶ πλείστην διατριβὴν τοῖς λόγοις ἔπειθ᾽ ὕστερον ἐξιοῦσιν ἀπὸ σοῦ τοῖς ἀκροαταῖς τε καὶ θεαταῖς παρέχων.

222 *Niels Gaul*

emotions were thus to be conveyed through voice, rather than gesturing. It is not entirely clear whether Psellos endorsed a motionless style of performance throughout; the passages discussed above seem ambiguous in this respect: in context, it is perhaps more likely that the various technical terms allude to voice modulation rather than physical movement. On the other hand, there can be no doubt that Psellos endorsed facial expressions (βλέμμα) such as tears.[111] At the very beginning of this chapter we saw the anonymous commentator on Hermogenes equally include posture (σχῆμα) alongside glance and voice.[112] If there was a change from the Deuterosophistic to the Middle Byzantine period, the reason is likely to be found in the mitigating influence of Christianity. Though one could easily imagine John Chrysostom and his Late Antique contemporaries gesticulating wildly, there is seemingly no explicit evidence for this; the predominance of the homiletic genre throughout the Middle Byzantine period and well into the tenth century, with the concomitant habitus of humbleness and self-effacement, may well have prevented strong gesturing to develop. But then again, just as in Antiquity, theory and practice may well have differed.

The revival of classicizing rhetoric in ninth-century Byzantium, growing out of the homiletic tradition, is likely to have emphasized, at least initially, a more restrained performance technique. Michael Psellos, in the famous essay on reading Gregory Nazianzen, explicitly pitches Gregory against the 'more coarse' of the sophists:

As for myself, whenever I read him – and I do this often, initially for the sake of philosophy but soon after for entertainment – I am filled with indescribable beauty and charm. On numerous occasions, I even abandon what I have been studying and, leaving behind the intended meaning of his theology and spirited away in my senses, I enjoy spring in the rose-gardens of his words. Realising that I have been carried away, I adore my ravisher and cover him with kisses.[113]

---

[111] Such as in his treatise *On Gregory's Style*, 372–7, ed. Levy (1912): ὁποῖον δ᾽ ἂν ἐμπέσοι τῷ λόγῳ πρόσωπον, εὐθὺς τοιοῦτός ἐστιν ὁ τοσοῦτος· μετατίθεται γὰρ πρὸς τὸ πάθος τοῦ λέγοντος, καὶ νῦν μὲν ἐπιτέγγει δακρύοις τοὺς ὀφθαλμούς, νῦν δὲ εὐθυμεῖ ... νῦν δὲ σχετλιάζει καὶ ποτνιᾶται καὶ κατακλᾶται τοῖς ὀδυρμοῖς; trans. Papaioannou (2017b) 144: 'Whatever persona happens to be introduced in his speech, Gregory, a man of such majesty, immediately assumes. He changes himself and adopts the emotion of the one who is speaking: at times he wets his eyes with tears; at times he is full of cheer ... and at times he complains, implores, breaks down with lamentations.'

[112] However, he did so without specifying what an ideal posture consisted of.

[113] Trans. Papaioannou (2017b) 127; Psellos, *On Gregory's Style*, 46–51: ἔγωγ᾽ οὖν ὁσάκις αὐτῷ ἐντυγχάνω, προσομιλῶ δὲ θαμά, προηγουμένως μὲν φιλοσοφίας ἕνεκα, παρεπομένως δὲ καὶ ψυχαγωγίας, ὥρας ἀμυθήτου πληροῦμαι καὶ χάριτος· καὶ καταλιμπάνω πολλάκις περὶ ὃ ἐσπούδακα καὶ τὸν νοῦν τῆς θεολογίας ἀφεὶς τῇ ῥοδωνιᾷ ἐνεαρίζω τῶν λέξεων καὶ κλέπτομαι ταῖς αἰσθήσεσι· καὶ γνοὺς ὅτι κέκλεμμαι, εἶτα δὴ ἀγαπῶ καὶ καταφιλῶ τὸν συλήσαντα. Incidentally, this latter phrase might have to be understood more literally than hitherto assumed; recent research on Latin Medieval manuscripts suggests that they were touched and kissed in significant places.

8. Voicing and Gesturing Emotions 223

Psellos continues:

If I am forced to return from the phrasing to the meaning, I feel pain because I am enraptured no longer, and lament the addition as though it were a privation. The beauty of his speech is not like the one practised by the more coarse among the sophists. Theirs is a matter of display and theatre, which might charm someone once, but make him grow edgy on a second encounter, for without having smoothed the edges of their lips, they ventured upon their writings with audacity rather than art. Gregory's beauty, however, is not like that (far from it!). His is like the harmonious beauty of music.[114]

As one reads on, it becomes clear that Psellos is more concerned with style and composition than actual performance technique – he likens Gregory to Lysias, Isokrates, Demosthenes, Aischines, and Plato, and concludes that he was less like Thucydides, Niketes of Smyrna, or Skopelianos (displaying intimate knowledge of Philostratos' *Lives of the Sophists*).[115]

With more work required to reach any definite conclusions,[116] our argument may have come full circle: while Byzantine ideals of style and composition remained firmly embedded in the Deuterosophistic rhetorical tradition, Byzantine ideals of delivery, under the mitigating influence of the Christian ideals of humility and moderation, may have come to realign themselves with the Platonic/Aristotelic emphasis on rhetoric brought to life by the skilled and prudent use of an orator's voice, that shunned an abundance of gestures.

---

[114] Trans. Papaioannou (2017b) 127–8; Psellos, *On Gregory's Style*, 51–9: κἂν ἀναχωρῆσαι τῆς φράσεως ἐπὶ τὸν νοῦν βιασθῶ, ἀλγῶ ὅτι μὴ καὶ αὖθις συλῶμαι καὶ ὡς στέρησιν τὴν προσθήκην ὀδύρομαι. ἔστι γὰρ τὸ κάλλος αὐτῷ τοῦ λόγου οὐχ οἷον οἱ παχύτεροι τῶν σοφιστευσάντων ἠσκήσαντο, ἐπιδεικτικόν τε καὶ θεατρικόν, ᾧ τις ἅπαξ θελχθεὶς ἔπειτα δὶς προσομιλήσας προσοχθίσειε – τοὺς γὰρ ὄχθους τῶν χειλέων μὴ ἀπολεάναντες οἱ ῥήτορες οὗτοι ἐθάρσησαν τὰ συγγράμματα τόλμῃ πρὸς τοὺς λόγους ἢ τέχνῃ χρήσαμενοι – ἀλλ᾽ οὐ τοσοῦτον αὐτῷ τὸ κάλλος (πολλοῦ γε καὶ δεῖ), ἀλλ᾽ οἷον τὸ ἐκ μουσικῆς ἐναρμόνιον.

[115] Psellos, *On Gregory's Style*, 94–7.

[116] And importantly, to include Byzantine visual material. My current impression is that the Church Fathers were depicted in the act of writing rather than preaching, thus allowing no conclusions on their gesturing. In the Bzyantine-inspired, Norman Capella Palatina and the cathedral of Monreale, St Paul is shown stepping forward with his right leg and with his right hand raised and finger pointing, while preaching to the Jews.

Part III: Literature

9

Mental Conflict from Homer to Eustathius*

Douglas Cairns

Introduction

My subject in this chapter is mental conflict, i. e. the situation that arises when a person is subject to conflicting motives or impulses to act.[1] This focus on motivation entails a focus on affectivity – because (as a matter of fact) without affect we have no motive for doing anything.[2] In keeping with our theme in this volume, the context in which I want to explore that topic is Homeric psychology – how the Homeric poems represent the process, how that representation has been understood by scholars, how it should be understood, and how it was understood by Eustathius in his Homeric Commentaries.

9.1. Homer

One very common (though not the only) way of representing mental conflict in Homer is in terms of the relation between a person and his or her 'psychic organs'. There are many of these: *thumos, phrenes, kradiē, ētor*, and more. For an older tradition of scholarship, the existence of these 'psychic organs' illustrates the primitiveness of Homeric concepts of self and agency. For Bruno Snell, the explanation of mental process in terms of the promptings of *thumos*, other organs, and the gods makes Homeric man 'a battleground of arbitrary forces and uncanny powers'; 'Homeric man has not yet awakened to the fact that he possesses in his own soul the source of his powers'.[3] Snell's is an approach that Ar-

---

* I am grateful to Martin Hinterberger, Aglae Pizzone, Filippomaria Pontani, and Matteo Zaccarini for assistance with and comments on this chapter, and to the Leverhulme Trust for making possible the volume and the project that lies behind it. I draw also on research funded by the Arts and Humanities Research Council (A History of Distributed Cognition) and the European Research Council (Advanced Grant 741084, Honour in Classical Greece).

[1] For orientation, see Price (1995).

[2] The idea is at least as old as Hume. In modern affect theory it is especially associated with (in the first wave) Silvan Tomkins (e. g. (1984) 163–4) and (more recently) Antonio Damasio (1994), but the general principle is much more widely accepted: see e. g. Boddice (2018) 95–7.

[3] Snell (1953) 19–22 (quotations pp. 21–2).

228   *Douglas Cairns*

thur Adkins summarizes succinctly when he endorses the claim that 'Homeric Man ... has a psychology and a physiology in which the parts are more evident than the whole.'[4]

But more recent scholarship has made this approach untenable. First, it has been shown that in a large number of occurrences, above all when used adverbially (i. e. with prepositions or in the dative), the use of the words denoting the so-called 'psychic organs' can be less a matter of semantic specificity than of metrical convenience, so that these terms exhibit substantial degrees of overlap and redundancy (as in the recurrent pleonasm κατὰ φρένα καὶ κατὰ θυμόν).[5] We need to treat the 'psychic organs' as a family rather than as independent variables. But by far the most prominent member of that family is *thumos*. *Thumos* occurs over 750 times in the poems, roughly twice as often as (the next most common term) *phrēn/phrenes*. *Thumos*, cognate with Indo-European words meaning 'smoke' (including Latin *fumus*),[6] is one of a number of terms in Greek which associate psychological activity with air and breath.[7] The link between *thumos* and breath is immediately clear in the Homeric poems when (for example) dying warriors breathe out their *thumos* on the Iliadic battlefield,[8] or the *thumos* (with the *psuchē*) is breathed out in a swoon,[9] only to be breathed in again when the person revives.[10]

But the functions of *thumos* in Homer extend far beyond living and breathing. By metonymy (in which aspects of the physical body felt to play a role in mental functioning come to serve as ways of referring to those functions) and in various forms of metaphor (chiefly reification and personification), Homeric *thumos* is implicated in a wide range of mental functions. Common to just about all of these, however, is an implication of motivational force.[11] Both because of its range, frequency, and salience, and because of its specific association with motivation, *thumos* is the term we shall concentrate on here.

---

[4] Adkins (1970) 15–27 (quotation p. 26). Similar views are encouraged by the 'laundry list' approach to Homeric psychology, in which (in themselves useful) lists of different functions are merely set side by side: see especially Caswell (1990); Sullivan (1995).

[5] See Jahn (1987), esp. 182–211; the table on 186–92 shows at a glance that most of the functions of *thumos* we shall consider below are not functions of *thumos* alone. For κατὰ φρένα καὶ κατὰ θυμόν as pleonastic, see p. 210.

[6] See Beekes (2009) 564.

[7] See Onians (1954) 44–6, 49–56, 67–79; Bremmer (1983) 56; Clarke (1999) 130–3.

[8] *Il.* 4.522–4, 13.653–4; similarly, the *thumos* of the dying horse, Pedasus, is breathed out and flies off at *Il.* 16.468–9, and at 3.293–4 sacrificial animals lie gasping on the ground, short of *thumos*, after the sacrificial knife has removed their *menos*, or vital force.

[9] As when Sarpedon's *psuchē* leaves him and he gasps out his *thumos*, but is revived by a blast of wind, *Il.* 5.696–8.

[10] *Il.* 22.466–75, *Od.* 24.345–50. For 'gathering one's *thumos*' (etc.) as getting one's breath back, cf. *Il.* 21.417, *Od.* 5.458. A straightforward identification of *thumos* with breath is complicated by its assimilation to the heart as something that can 'beat' in the chest (*Il.* 7.216, 23.370–1).

[11] See Cairns (2019c).

9. Mental Conflict from Homer to Eustathius 229

This association with motivation means that, even when *thumos* is at its most 'cognitive', it is also never without an element of affectivity. We see this clearly in a passage in *Od.* 9 (294–306):

> ἡμεῖς δὲ κλαίοντες ἀνεσχέθομεν Διὶ χεῖρας,
> σχέτλια ἔργ᾽ ὁρόωντες· ἀμηχανίη δ᾽ ἔχε θυμόν.   295
> αὐτὰρ ἐπεὶ Κύκλωψ μεγάλην ἐμπλήσατο νηδὺν
> ἀνδρόμεα κρέ᾽ ἔδων καὶ ἐπ᾽ ἄκρητον γάλα πίνων,
> κεῖτ᾽ ἔντοσθ᾽ ἄντροιο τανυσσάμενος διὰ μήλων.
> τὸν μὲν ἐγὼ βούλευσα κατὰ μεγαλήτορα θυμὸν
> ἄσσον ἰών, ξίφος ὀξὺ ἐρυσσάμενος παρὰ μηροῦ,   300
> οὐτάμεναι πρὸς στῆθος, ὅθι φρένες ἧπαρ ἔχουσι,
> χείρ᾽ ἐπιμασσάμενος· ἕτερος δέ με θυμὸς ἔρυκεν.
> αὐτοῦ γάρ κε καὶ ἄμμες ἀπωλόμεθ᾽ αἰπὺν ὄλεθρον·
> οὐ γάρ κεν δυνάμεσθα θυράων ὑψηλάων
> χερσὶν ἀπώσασθαι λίθον ὄβριμον, ὃν προσέθηκεν.   305
> ὣς τότε μὲν στενάχοντες ἐμείναμεν Ἠῶ δῖαν.

We held our hands up to Zeus and wailed to see his terrible deeds; helplessness took hold of our *thumos* (ἀμηχανίη δ᾽ ἔχε θυμόν). But when the Cyclops had filled his great belly, eating human meat washed down with unmixed milk, he stretched out among the sheep and lay inside the cave. I planned in my great-hearted *thumos* (βούλευσα κατὰ μεγαλήτορα θυμόν) to go close to him, draw my sharp sword from beside my thigh, and stab him in the chest, where the *phrenes* hold the liver, feeling for it with my hand. But a second thought restrained me (ἕτερος δέ με θυμὸς ἔρυκεν): for, where we were, we too would perish in sheer destruction, since we would not be able to push away with our hands from the lofty door the huge stone he'd put there. And so, lamenting, we awaited the holy Dawn.

When Polyphemus kills and eats two of his companions, Odysseus has at first no immediate plan of action: helplessness grips his *thumos*, and that of the others (295). But once the monster has finished his meal, Odysseus' first thought is of violent revenge: he plans in his proud *thumos* to approach the Cyclops and kill him (9.299–302).[12] But another *thumos* restrains him (ἕτερος δέ με θυμὸς ἔρυκεν, 302): if he kills Polyphemus, they have no way of getting out of the cave. In the phrase ἕτερος θυμός, *thumos* means something like 'thought' or 'impulse', but the ἕτερος θυμός is also personified as the subject of ἔρυκεν. One impulse is more impulsive than the other: the impulse to take revenge and the better judgement that restrains that impulse are equally 'a *thumos*'. But each *thumos* also has indissoluble cognitive and affective aspects. Each evaluates a situation, imagines a possible future, and provides a basis for action. The ἕτερος θυμός inhibits a hot-headed, passionate course of action, but as well as prudent, longer-term plan-

---

[12] Note the synecdoche and enallage in κατὰ μεγαλήτορα θυμόν: the 'organ' is qualified by an adjective that properly qualifies the agent, so that, on a superficial/literal interpretation, its qualities appear to depend on a further 'organ' of its own. It would be entirely wrong to see this as presenting the individual as a Russian doll of nested homunculi.

230 *Douglas Cairns*

ning, it also involves a projection of future states of affairs that encompasses a strong desire to survive, and it motivates Odysseus to change his mind.

The *thumos* is implicated in various other ways in the phenomenon of 'being in two minds'. Deliberation is something that the *thumos* itself can do,[13] but more often it is something that a person does, with or without explicit reference to the *thumos*.[14] At *Il.* 13.455–9 it is Deiphobus himself who 'ponders in two ways', whether to do *x* or *y*, before deciding to pursue an instance of *x*:

> Δηΐφοβος δὲ διάνδιχα μερμήριξεν   455
> ἤ τινά που Τρώων ἑταρίσσαιτο μεγαθύμων
> ἂψ ἀναχωρήσας, ἢ πειρήσαιτο καὶ οἶος.
> ὧδε δέ οἱ φρονέοντι δοάσσατο κέρδιον εἶναι
> βῆναι ἐπ᾽ Αἰνείαν ...

Deiphobus pondered in two ways, whether he should withdraw and team up with one of the great-hearted Trojans, or make an attempt on his own. As he was considering the matter in this way it seemed better to him to go after Aeneas ...

Here there is no explicit reference to *thumos*, *phrenes*, or the like. This does not mean that one can deliberate without using one's *thumos* (etc.); just that deliberation is ordinarily an activity carried out by an agent him- or herself, and that, when the mode of doing so is specified, this adds little or nothing to the meaning – the adverbial reference to a 'psychic organ' simply specifies that deliberation is a process that takes place within the mental apparatus of the person.[15] The agent owns the process; the reasons for each alternative are the agent's

---

[13] As (e. g.) when Telemachus describes the very dilemma that Penelope will go on to present in terms of the 'arousal' of her *thumos* (*Od.* 19.524) as something that 'her *thumos* ponders in two ways' (μητρὶ δ᾽ ἐμῇ δίχα θυμὸς ἐνὶ φρεσὶ μερμηρίζει, *Od.* 16.73); cf. 20.38 (discussed below), where Odysseus' *thumos* ponders how to defeat the Suitors.

[14] With the *thumos*: see e.g. the variations on the formula μερμήριξε δ᾽ ἔπειτα κατὰ φρένα καὶ κατὰ θυμὸν (*Il.* 5.671, 8.169; *Od.* 4.117, 10.151, 20.10, 24.235); other expressions with μερμηρίζω (*Od.* 10.50, 16.237); variations on the formula ἧος ὃ ταῦθ᾽ ὥρμαινε κατὰ φρένα καὶ κατὰ θυμόν (*Il.* 1.193, 11.411, 17.106, 18.15; *Od.* 4.120, 5.365, 424, 6.118); other expressions with ὁρμαίνω (*Il.* 14.20, 21.137, 24.680; *Od.* 2.156); cf. Caswell (1990) 45–7, 73. For passages in which the person simply 'ponders' (μερμηρίζει, ὁρμαίνει, etc.), without mention of the *thumos* (or another 'psychic organ'), see *Il.* 10.28, 12.199, 13.455–9, 20.17; *Od.* 2.325, 3.169, 4.146, 533, 789–94, 843, 6.141–6, 9.554–5, 15.300, 16.256, 261, 18.90–4, 19.52. In *Il.* 14.159–61 and *Od.* 20.93 the person does not initially deliberate κατὰ θυμόν, but subsequent reference to the *thumos* suggests (what we might in any case suppose) that the involvement of the *thumos* or another 'organ' can often be assumed; deliberation also makes use of the *phrenes* alone (*Il.* 2.3, 10.4, 503–7, 16.435, *Od.* 1.427, 2.93, 3.151, 4.843, 10.438, 11.204, 18.435, 22.333–7, 24.128), and occasionally also of other 'psychic organs' (*ētor*, *Il.* 1.188–9; *kēr*, *Od.* 7.82–3, 18.344–5, 23.85–6). See Jahn (1987) 273–85, 291–3.

[15] For this as a fundamental function of locutions involving *thumos*, see Jahn (1987) 7–8, 107–8, 210–15, 225–32. States of mind that are not expressed in behaviour can be said to be 'hidden in the *thumos*' (*Od.* 18.406–7); just so, Odysseus commands Eurycleia not to cry out in celebration of the Suitors' deaths, but to 'rejoice in [her] *thumos*' (*Od.* 22.411), and he himself pities Penelope in his *thumos*, with no visible tears or audible sobs (*Od.* 19.209–11). (Jahn (1987) 104, 106–10, after Ameis-Hentze-Cauer *ad loc.*, rightly sees that this is also the function of the atypical locution

9. Mental Conflict from Homer to Eustathius 231

reasons. What reference to the *thumos* can sometimes add is a sense of the phenomenology of deliberation as a subjective experience.

In a subcategory of deliberation scenes, the agent's deliberation is followed by direct speech that is described in the narrator's speech-introduction formula as an address to the *thumos*. These speeches are attributed either to humans, using the formula 'vexed, he said to his great-hearted *thumos*',[16] or to gods, with 'shaking his head he said to his *thumos*'.[17] For Shirley Darcus Sullivan, it is addresses to the *thumos* above all that 'emphasize the distinctness of person and *thumos*';[18] but, as Hayden Pelliccia has demonstrated, this is not the case.[19] All these speeches either have no audience or addressee at all, or else they have no audience and an addressee who is not meant to hear. Functionally, the *thumos* is just a sounding board for the agent's thoughts, expressed as direct speech; two cases in *Odyssey* 5, where the supposed address to the *thumos* is recapitulated in a regular deliberation formula, with the person as subject ('while he was pondering these things in his *phrēn* and in his *thumos*'), make this especially clear:[20] the agent's address to the *thumos* and the agent's deliberation, in, with, or in respect of the *thumos*, are the same process.

In a smaller subset of these speeches, the speech that the narrator introduces as an address to the *thumos* contains the line 'But why has my dear *thumos* said this to me in conversation?'[21] The *thumos* is addressed, and then in some sense credited with speech. But we should note that the question goes unanswered; it serves only as the conclusion of the ruminations that were introduced by the narrator as an address to the *thumos*. And it is also significant that these speeches are not addressed to the *thumos* by their speakers: in fact, they all begin 'Ah me' (ὤ μοι ἐγώ(ν)). Just as the *thumos* is not actually addressed, so no actual speech is ever attributed to it (in any Homeric passage): the *thumos* simply performs two conventional functions, first as sounding board for the speaker's deliberations, then as a convenient scapegoat as source of the rejected alternative.[22] The functions of these two locutions emerge clearly in the one passage in which the phrase 'But why has my dear *thumos* said this to me in conversation?' occurs in a speech that is *not* introduced by 'vexed, he said to his great-hearted *thumos*'.

χαῖρε νόῳ at *Od.* 8.78.) Such interiority can also be conveyed by referring to the body language of the personified *thumos* (e.g. its smile, *Od.* 20.300–2; its shiver, 23.215–16).

[16] ὀχθήσας δ᾽ ἄρα εἶπε πρὸς ὃν μεγαλήτορα θυμόν – *Il.* 11.403, 17.90, 18.5, 20.343, 21.53, 552, 22.98, *Od.* 5.298, 355, 407, 464.

[17] κινήσας δὲ κάρη προτὶ ὃν μυθήσατο θυμόν – *Il.* 17.200, 442; *Od.* 5.285, 376.

[18] Sullivan (1995) 58, 69.

[19] See Pelliccia (1995) 121–3, 136–46, 200–3, 212–13, and *passim*.

[20] εἷος ὁ ταῦθ᾽ ὥρμαινε κατὰ φρένα καὶ κατὰ θυμόν, *Od.* 5.365 (picking up the address to the *thumos* at 355) and 424 (picking up the address to the *thumos* at 407).

[21] ἀλλὰ τίη μοι ταῦτα φίλος διελέξατο θυμός; *Il.* 11.407, 17.97, 21.562, 22.122.

[22] See Pelliccia (1995) 203–11, 267. On the 'self-distancing' that this represents, cf. Gill (1996) 187–8.

At *Il.* 22.376–88 Achilles is not out of contact – he's addressing a real audience. And so the narrator does not make him address his *thumos*. But his speech is like the other *thumos*-speeches in that Achilles attributes to his *thumos* a proposal that he himself has just made – because he is rejecting it (ἀλλὰ τίη μοι ταῦτα φίλος διελέξατο θυμός; 385).

The longest of these so-called *thumos*-dialogues is Hector's monologue in *Il.* 22.98–130:

> ὀχθήσας δ' ἄρα εἶπε πρὸς ὃν μεγαλήτορα θυμόν·
> "ὤ μοι ἐγών, εἰ μέν κε πύλας καὶ τείχεα δύω,
> Πουλυδάμας μοι πρῶτος ἐλεγχείην ἀναθήσει,   100
> ὅς μ' ἐκέλευε Τρωσὶ ποτὶ πτόλιν ἡγήσασθαι
> νύχθ' ὕπο τήνδ' ὀλοὴν ὅτε τ' ὤρετο δῖος Ἀχιλλεύς.
> ἀλλ' ἐγὼ οὐ πιθόμην· ἦ τ' ἂν πολὺ κέρδιον ἦεν.
> νῦν δ' ἐπεὶ ὤλεσα λαὸν ἀτασθαλίῃσιν ἐμῇσιν,
> αἰδέομαι Τρῶας καὶ Τρῳάδας ἑλκεσιπέπλους,   105
> μή ποτέ τις εἴπῃσι κακώτερος ἄλλος ἐμεῖο·
> Ἕκτωρ ἧφι βίηφι πιθήσας ὤλεσε λαόν.
> ὣς ἐρέουσιν· ἐμοὶ δὲ τότ' ἂν πολὺ κέρδιον εἴη
> ἄντην ἢ Ἀχιλῆα κατακτείναντα νέεσθαι,
> ἠέ κεν αὐτῷ ὀλέσθαι ἐϋκλειῶς πρὸ πόληος.   110
> εἰ δέ κεν ἀσπίδα μὲν καταθείομαι ὀμφαλόεσσαν
> καὶ κόρυθα βριαρήν, δόρυ δὲ πρὸς τεῖχος ἐρείσας
> αὐτὸς ἰὼν Ἀχιλῆος ἀμύμονος ἀντίος ἔλθω
> καί οἱ ὑπόσχωμαι Ἑλένην καὶ κτήμαθ' ἅμ' αὐτῇ,
> πάντα μάλ' ὅσσά τ' Ἀλέξανδρος κοίλης ἐνὶ νηυσὶν   115
> ἠγάγετο Τροίηνδ', ἥ τ' ἔπλετο νείκεος ἀρχή,
> δωσέμεν Ἀτρεΐδῃσιν ἄγειν, ἅμα δ' ἀμφὶς Ἀχαιοῖς
> ἄλλ' ἀποδάσσεσθαι ὅσα τε πτόλις ἥδε κέκευθε·
> Τρωσὶν δ' αὖ μετόπισθε γερούσιον ὅρκον ἕλωμαι
> μή τι κατακρύψειν, ἀλλ' ἄνδιχα πάντα δάσασθαι   120
> κτῆσιν ὅσην πτολίεθρον ἐπήρατον ἐντὸς ἐέργει·
> ἀλλὰ τίη μοι ταῦτα φίλος διελέξατο θυμός;
> μή μιν ἐγὼ μὲν ἵκωμαι ἰών, ὃ δέ μ' οὐκ ἐλεήσει
> οὐδέ τί μ' αἰδέσεται, κτενέει δέ με γυμνὸν ἐόντα
> αὔτως ὥς τε γυναῖκα, ἐπεί κ' ἀπὸ τεύχεα δύω.   125
> οὐ μέν πως νῦν ἔστιν ἀπὸ δρυὸς οὐδ' ἀπὸ πέτρης
> τῷ ὀαριζέμεναι, ἅ τε παρθένος ἠΐθεός τε
> παρθένος ἠΐθεός τ' ὀαρίζετον ἀλλήλοιιν.
> βέλτερον αὖτ' ἔριδι ξυνελαυνέμεν ὅττι τάχιστα·
> εἴδομεν ὁπποτέρῳ κεν Ὀλύμπιος εὖχος ὀρέξῃ."   130

Vexed, he said to his great-hearted *thumos*: 'Ah me! If I go now inside the gates and the walls, Polydamas will be first to set up a reproach against me, for he bade me lead the Trojans back to the city on that accursed night when brilliant Achilles rose up. But I would not obey him. Aye, it would have been much better if I had. Now, since I have ruined my people by my own recklessness, I feel shame before the Trojans and the Trojan women with trailing robes, lest someone inferior to me will say: "Hector trusted in his own might

9. Mental Conflict from Homer to Eustathius   233

and ruined his people." That is what they will say. Then, for me, it would be much better to go against Achilles, and kill him, and come back, or else perish gloriously at his hands in front of the city. But what if I put down my bossed shield and my mighty helmet, and prop my spear up against the wall and go on my own initiative to face blameless Achilles and promise him that I will give Helen back to the Achaeans, to take away, and all the possessions that Alexandros brought to Troy in the hollow ships, which was the beginning of the quarrel, and also that the Achaeans should divide up all that is hidden within the city. I could also take an oath for the Trojans in council not to hide anything away, but distribute everything, all the property that the lovely citadel confines within … But why has my dear *thumos* said this to me in conversation? I *could* go up to him, but he will show me no pity nor will he respect me, but rather kill me, naked as I am, just like a woman, once I have taken off my armour. There is no way now to whisper sweet nothings from a tree or a rock, such as a young man and a young maiden whisper to each other. Better join in conflict as soon as possible. Let us see to which the Olympian grants the glory.'

Here, it is clear that the apparent 'dialogue' with the *thumos* represents Hector's emotional turmoil (ὀχθήσας, 98) as he reflects on the situation he finds himself in: he has ignored Polydamas' advice to retire within the walls (99–103, a reference to Book 18) and so has ruined his people through his own recklessness (104) – a self-condemnation that is reflected also in the charges that he expects others to level against him (105–7). Hector is fully aware that *he* will have to answer in future for *his* previous decisions, decisions that *he himself* condemns. He then considers his options in the present, contemplating an attempt to reach an accommodation with Achilles (111–21). But this, he realizes, is a futile fantasy (122 ff.) – 'But why has my dear *thumos* said this to me in conversation? If I approach him … he'll kill me … Better to join battle as soon as possible: let's see to which of us the Olympian grants the boast of victory.'

So Hector (a) addresses himself; (b) blames himself for his previous decisions; (c) weighs his options; and (d) comes eventually to a decision that, given his past mistakes and his present circumstances, he regards as 'better' for him. The fact that he is said by the narrator to speak all these words to his *thumos*, and then rejects a course of action that he himself entertained by describing it as a proposal of his *thumos*, in no way detracts from his own sense of agency and responsibility.

Many of the points I have been making emerge clearly in a highly individual passage of *Odyssey* 20. Odysseus lies sleepless in the antechamber of his own house, plotting harm for the Suitors in his *thumos* (μνηστῆρσι κακὰ φρονέων ἐνὶ θυμῷ, 5), when the laughter of his female servants, who sleep with the Suitors, stirs up the *thumos* in his chest (τοῦ δ' ὠρίνετο θυμὸς ἐνὶ στήθεσσι φίλοισι, 9). Internal, silent, but still emotionally charged deliberation continues, as Odysseus ponders in his *phrēn* and in his *thumos* (πολλὰ δὲ μερμήριζε κατὰ φρένα καὶ κατὰ θυμόν, 10) whether to kill the women on the spot or let them sleep with the Suitors one last time (10–13). Then 'his heart within him barks' (κραδίη δέ οἱ ἔνδον ὑλάκτει, 13): the doings of a physical organ stand in metonymy for

234 *Douglas Cairns*

the emotional experience with which the organ is associated. The organ in this case is the heart, even though it was the *thumos* that was aroused only four lines earlier. This is not an experience independent of the arousal of the *thumos*, but another way of referring to that experience, or to its intensification. The heart's reaction also involves metaphor – it barks. That this is understood as metaphor, i.e. as a mapping from one domain (animal behaviour) to another (psychological experience), is made crystal clear by the simile that follows – the heart barks like a dog defending her pups (14–16):[23]

> ὡς δὲ κύων ἀμαλῆσι περὶ σκυλάκεσσι βεβῶσα
> ἄνδρ' ἀγνοιήσασ' ὑλάει μέμονέν τε μάχεσθαι,   15
> ὥς ῥα τοῦ ἔνδον ὑλάκτει ἀγαιομένου κακὰ ἔργα.

As a dog standing over her tender pups barks at a man she doesn't recognize and is eager to fight, so it barked within him in his resentment at their wrongdoing.

It is clear that these experiences remain those of Odysseus as agent, and the thoughts remain his thoughts – the heart barks, but it is Odysseus who resents the women's offences (ὥς ῥα **τοῦ** ἔνδον ὑλάκτει **ἀγαιομένου** κακὰ ἔργα, 16).

In a (unique) variation on the speech-introduction formula in which a character is said to address his *thumos*, Odysseus is then described as beating his breast and addressing his *kradiē* (στῆθος δὲ πλήξας κραδίην ἠνίπαπε μύθῳ, 17). In an even more striking variation, the 'psychic organ' is then – here and here alone – actually addressed and spoken to, using second-person verbs (18–21):

> "τέτλαθι δή, κραδίη· καὶ κύντερον ἄλλο ποτ' ἔτλης,
> ἤματι τῷ, ὅτε μοι μένος ἄσχετος ἤσθιε Κύκλωψ
> ἰφθίμους ἑτάρους· σὺ δ' ἐτόλμας, ὄφρα σε μῆτις   20
> ἐξάγαγ' ἐξ ἄντροιο ὀϊόμενον θανέεσθαι."

'Endure, heart: you've endured worse in the past, on that day when the irresistible force, the Cyclops, ate my strong companions. But you endured, until *mētis* led you out of the cave, thinking that death was imminent.'

This takes personification of the *kradiē* further than personification of the *thumos* is ever taken.[24] But still, though the heart is addressed, it does not speak. And

---

[23] The way that the simile in 14–15 illustrates the 'barking' metaphor in 13 and 16 refutes those who argue that there can be no concept of metaphor before the coining of the term *metaphora* or that Homer has no such concept; see Leidl (2003) 38 (with reference to Porphyry, *Homeric Questions* 6). A conscious and knowing approach to the use of such imagery is also suggested by the pun, κύντερον ('more dog-like', i.e. worse), in 18. We see the same phenomenon at *Od.* 19.204–7, where Penelope's skin or cheeks (in a common metaphor for grief, love, etc.) 'melt' (τήκετο, 204, 208) in a way that is compared to melting snow on a mountain (205–7). In this case, the metaphor is a familiar, conventional one, while in the case of the barking heart it is a novel one (albeit based in conventional metonymies and personifications); in both cases, the amplification by means of a simile indicates deliberate, artistic use of metaphorical concepts that in other contexts might be used in a purely conventional way.

[24] See Pellicccia (1995) 175–6, 178; Gill (1996) 184.

9. Mental Conflict from Homer to Eustathius

235

yet, after Odysseus has 'restrained the dear heart (ētor) in his chest' (ὡς ἔφατ᾽, ἐν στήθεσσι καθαπτόμενος φίλον ἦτορ, 22), the kradiē does obey and endure (τῷ δὲ μάλ᾽ ἐν πείσῃ κραδίη μένε τετληυῖα / νωλεμέως, 23–4). There appear to be two interlocutors, even if one of them merely listens and obeys. But the lines in which Odysseus reminds the kradiē of its past (18–21) show that this is so only by means of a poetic conceit. This is clear not only because the experiences of the heart are transparently those of Odysseus himself, and not only because the personified mētis in line 20 is itself also, like the heart, an avatar of Odysseus, a reference to the way he outwitted the Cyclops by calling himself Outis and the pun by which this becomes μή τις (~ mētis) at 9.410. The persistence of Odysseus as operative agent, despite the personification of kradiē and mētis, is also clearly demonstrated by ὀϊόμενον in 21, which betrays the fact that all this is Odysseus' way of addressing himself. The participle agrees in sense with σε, the heart, in 20: 'you', the heart, endured, and μῆτις led 'you' out of the cave, but the thought of imminent death is in effect attributed to the only agent on the scene who is capable of being qualified by a masculine participle, Odysseus himself.[25] The use of the masculine participle betrays a reluctance to attribute to the heart the thought that it, the heart, as opposed to Odysseus, the person, was in danger of death. The striking personification of the barking heart emphasizes the phenomenology of Odysseus' experience in this tense, dramatic context, and conveys it vividly and effectively to the audience. It heightens the tension of the situation in which Odysseus is, for a moment, tempted to jeopardize his long-term plan by giving way to a powerful impulse for revenge. But though its metaphors of self-division dramatize vividly the process of deliberation and impulse control, they also leave Odysseus, the real agent, in control throughout.

Even though it focuses on the kradiē, the passage is also informative about the functions of the thumos. There is a unity that underpins the shifts – in the passage and in its immediate context – between Odysseus, his thumos, and his kradiē. The reflections of Odysseus himself in 5 and 9–13 involve thumos in its regular adverbial function (ἐνὶ θυμῷ, 5; κατὰ φρένα καὶ κατὰ θυμόν, 10), amplifying, more or less tautologously, the interiority of mental events. The thumos is then itself aroused in 9, before this is represented as the indignation of the kradiē in 13–21. These are stages of a single mental process. Just as there is no functional difference between thumos in 9 and kradiē in 13–21, so the address to the kradiē in 18–21 is immediately summarized as a rebuke to the ētor in 22.[26] The heart, once again called kradiē, obeys in the next line, but Odysseus himself tosses and turns, deliberating how to obtain his revenge (μερμηρίζων, / ὅππως

---

[25] Cf. Halliwell (1990) 40 n. 9; Pelliccia (1995) 223 n. 203.

[26] Cf. Pelliccia (1995) 177 n. 123, with Jahn (1987) 201–9, on Austauschbarkeit. Similarly, κατὰ φρένα καὶ κατὰ θυμόν forms a single adverbial expression, pleonastically modifying μερμήριζε in 10.

236 *Douglas Cairns*

δὴ μνηστῆρσιν ἀναιδέσι χεῖρας ἐφήσει, / μοῦνος ἐὼν πολέσι, 28–30).[27] But after Athena appears in the guise of a mortal woman and reminds him how close to his goals he is (30–5), the very same process of deliberation is attributed to the *thumos* in 37–40:

> "ναὶ δὴ ταῦτά γε πάντα, θεά, κατὰ μοῖραν ἔειπες·
> ἀλλά τί μοι τόδε θυμὸς ἐνὶ φρεσὶ μερμηρίζει,
> ὅππως δὴ μνηστῆρσιν ἀναιδέσι χεῖρας ἐφήσω,
> μοῦνος ἐών· οἱ δ' αἰὲν ἀολλέες ἔνδον ἔασι."   40

'Yes, all you have said, goddess, is in order; but the *thumos* in my *phrenes* ponders this one thing, how I can get my hands on the shameless Suitors, alone as I am; they are always together indoors.'

But immediately, the ponderings of the *thumos* become, once more, those of Odysseus himself (41–3):[28]

> "πρὸς δ' ἔτι καὶ τόδε μεῖζον ἐνὶ φρεσὶ μερμηρίζω·
> εἴ περ γὰρ κτείναιμι Διός τε σέθεν τε ἔκητι,
> πῇ κεν ὑπεκπροφύγοιμι; τά σε φράζεσθαι ἄνωγα."

'Besides, there is this even greater thing I ponder in my *phrenes*: if I were to kill them, by Zeus's grace and yours, where could I escape to? I bid you think on that.'

Throughout, the reflections and motivations that this passage represents, whether attributed to Odysseus, his *thumos*, his *kradiē*, or his *ētor*, are those of Odysseus himself. As a metonymy and a metaphor, the *thumos* is credited with a variety of cognitive and affective functions and occasionally used to dramatize situations of deliberation, self-division, and self-control; but these remain ways of representing the personal agency of Homeric characters.

9.2. The barking heart as paradigm of motivational conflict

The remarkable passage in *Odyssey* 20 is bound to stick in the mind; and in fact it becomes emblematic of the phenomenon of motivational conflict. In the body–soul dualism of Plato's *Phaedo* 94c–e it is the body that is the source of affective phenomena such as *epithumiai*, *orgai*, and *phoboi* (called τὰ τοῦ σώματος παθήματα at 94d) and Odysseus' address to his *kradiē* becomes an image for the soul's control of the affections of the body.[29] In the *Republic*, however,

---

[27] Thus, the passage combines two conventional objects of deliberation, whether to do *x* or *y* and how to do what one has decided to do; see Pelliccia (1995) 220–3; Gill (1996) 184.

[28] See Pelliccia (1995) 222.

[29] Τί οὖν; νῦν οὐ πᾶν τοὐναντίον ἡμῖν φαίνεται ἐργαζομένη, ἡγεμονεύουσά τε ἐκείνων πάντων ἐξ ὧν φησί τις αὐτὴν εἶναι, καὶ ἐναντιουμένη ὀλίγου πάντα διὰ παντὸς τοῦ βίου καὶ δεσπόζουσα πάντας τρόπους, τὰ μὲν χαλεπώτερον κολάζουσα καὶ μετ' ἀλγηδόνων, τά τε κατὰ τὴν γυμναστικὴν καὶ τὴν ἰατρικήν, τὰ δὲ πραότερον, καὶ τὰ μὲν ἀπειλοῦσα, τὰ δὲ νουθετοῦσα,

9. Mental Conflict from Homer to Eustathius

motivational conflict occurs not between soul and body, but between parts of the soul. The existence of one of these, the *thumoeides*, is then established not by the so-called 'Principle of Opposites' (that, if the same thing appears to do or undergo opposites in the same respect and with regard to the same object, then we are dealing not with one thing but with more than one, 436b–c), but rather by intuitions about the phenomenology of the motivations involved. It is in that context that Odysseus' barking heart is used as an indication that angry emotions can oppose reason, just as the example of Leontius showed that they can oppose desire (441b–c):

ναὶ μὰ Δί', ἦν δ' ἐγώ, καλῶς γε εἶπες. ἔτι δὲ ἐν τοῖς θηρίοις ἄν τις ἴδοι ὃ λέγεις, ὅτι οὕτως ἔχει. πρὸς δὲ τούτοις καὶ ὃ ἄνω που [ἐκεῖ] εἴπομεν, τὸ τοῦ Ὁμήρου μαρτυρήσει, τὸ –
στῆθος δὲ πλήξας κραδίην ἠνίπαπε μύθῳ·
ἐνταῦθα γὰρ δὴ σαφῶς ὡς ἕτερον ἑτέρῳ ἐπιπλῆττον πεποίηκεν Ὅμηρος τὸ ἀναλογισά-μενον περὶ τοῦ βελτίονός τε καὶ χείρονος τῷ ἀλογίστως θυμουμένῳ.

'Yes, by Zeus, you're right,' I said; 'and besides, one could see the thing you're talking about in animals. In addition to these examples, what we said above, Homer's 'He struck his chest and addressed his heart', will also bear witness. For there Homer has clearly represented as one thing rebuking another that element that has reflected about the better and the worse and that which rages without so reflecting.'

Plato uses Homer for his own purposes in both *Phaedo* and *Republic*; these dialogues differ both from Homer and from each other in the ways in which they explain the phenomenon in question. But neither supports an interpretation of the Homeric passage that detracts in any way from Odysseus' agency (regardless of his conflict with his *kradiē*). The passage at *Republic* 4, 441b–c, in particular,

---

ταῖς ἐπιθυμίαις καὶ ὀργαῖς καὶ φόβοις ὡς ἄλλη οὖσα ἄλλῳ πράγματι διαλεγομένη; οἷόν που καὶ Ὅμηρος ἐν Ὀδυσσείᾳ πεποίηκεν, οὗ λέγει τὸν Ὀδυσσέα·
στῆθος δὲ πλήξας κραδίην ἠνίπαπε μύθῳ·
τέτλαθι δή, κραδίη· καὶ κύντερον ἄλλο ποτ' ἔτλης.
ἆρ' οἴει αὐτὸν ταῦτα ποιῆσαι διανοούμενον ὡς ἁρμονίας αὐτῆς οὔσης καὶ οἵας ἄγεσθαι ὑπὸ τῶν τοῦ σώματος παθημάτων, ἀλλ' οὐχ οἵας ἄγειν τε ταῦτα καὶ δεσπόζειν, καὶ οὔσης αὐτῆς πολὺ θειοτέρου τινὸς πράγματος ἢ καθ' ἁρμονίαν;
Well then, do we not now find that the soul acts in exactly the opposite way, leading those elements of which it is said to consist and opposing them in almost everything through all our life, and exercising despotic control over them in every way, sometimes inflicting harsh and painful punishments (as in gymnastics and medicine), and sometimes milder ones, sometimes threatening and sometimes admonishing, speaking to the desires and passions and fears as if it were distinct from them and they from it, as Homer has shown in the *Odyssey* when he says of Odysseus:
He struck his chest and addressed his heart:
'Endure, heart, you have borne worse than this.'
Do you suppose that, when he wrote those words, he thought of the soul as a harmony which would be led by the affections of the body, and not rather as something fitted to lead and master them, and itself a far more divine thing than a harmony?

238   *Douglas Cairns*

shows that for Plato, as for Homer, the behaviour of the *kradiē* is evidence for a source of motivation that might just as well be associated with the *thumos*.

The iconicity of the barking heart passage[30] clearly extends more widely in ancient discussions of mental conflict: having become emblematic of the Platonic approach, it then becomes an issue in debate between Platonists and Stoics on the nature of the soul and the relation between reason and emotion. We see this debate in action in Galen's attack on Chrysippus' work, *On the Emotions*, at *PHP* 3.3.21–2:[31]

ἔστιν ὅτε δὲ οὐδέτερον εἰς τοσοῦτον ἰσχυρότερόν ἐστιν ὡς ἐφέλκεσθαι παραχρῆμα θάτερον, ἀλλ' ἐναντιοῦταί τε πρὸς ἄλληλα καὶ διαμάχεται καὶ νικᾷ τῷ χρόνῳ θάτερον, ἐπ'
Ὀδυσσέως μὲν ὁ λογισμός, ἐπὶ Μηδείας δ' ὁ θυμός, ὡς δύο ὄντα αὐτὰ μόρια τῆς ψυχῆς ἢ
εἰ μὴ μόρια, πάντως γε δυνάμεις τινές. ὁ δὲ Χρύσιππος οὔτε μόρια ψυχῆς ταῦτ' εἶναι νο-
μίζων οὔτε δυνάμεις ἀλόγους ἑτέρας τῆς λογικῆς ὅμως οὐκ ὀκνεῖ τῶν Ὀδυσσέως τε καὶ
Μηδείας ἐπῶν μνημονεύειν ἐναργῶς καταβαλλόντων τὴν δόξαν αὐτοῦ.

Sometimes neither element is strong enough immediately to subdue the other, but they oppose each other and fight it out, and in time one of them wins – reasoning, in Odysseus' case, *thumos* in Medea's, on the basis that they are two parts of the soul, or, if not parts, then at least some sort of power. But Chrysippus, though he thinks neither that they are parts of the soul nor that there exist non-rational powers distinct from the rational, still does not shrink from mentioning the words of Odysseus and Medea that clearly refute his own doctrine.

Here and elsewhere, Galen defends Platonic tripartition, but in (what he takes to be) a literalist sense, derived no doubt from the *Timaeus*.[32] Even from his account, it emerges that Chrysippus used the example of Odysseus (like that of Medea) to deny not only the fragmentation of the personality but also the partition of the soul. One would dearly like to know exactly what Chrysippus wrote: but it seems likely that he used Medea's monologue (on her *thumos*) and Odysseus' address to his *kradiē* to illustrate a Stoic model of the emotions as judgements in which an initial impression requires the agent's assent, so that mental conflict is explained in terms of vacillation between a succession of such judgements.[33] Again, this is a different model from Homer's; but it is still not one

---

[30] Cited also at *Resp.* 3, 390d. For the passage as a commonplace, cf. (e.g.) Petr. *Sat.* 132: 'Non et Vlixes cum corde litigat suo, et quidam tragici oculos suos tanquam audientes castigant?' Over a millennium later, it is cited by Anna Comnena, *Alexiad* 14.3.6, a sign (as Pontani observes, (2005) 160) of her culture and Homeric learning.

[31] On Galen and Chrysippus, see Tieleman (1996) and (2003); Staden (2000); Gill (2007) and (2010a); Schiefsky (2012). Cf. the anti-Stoic, Platonist arguments for reason–passion conflict in Plutarch, *Mor.* 441b–454c (*De virt. mor.*) (with frequent citations of Homer and other literary sources, as well as of Chrysippus).

[32] For the spatial separation of the elements of the tripartite soul, see *Tim.* 69c–71d; and for the importance of this passage for Galen's literalist conception, see Graver (2007) 74–5. Even so, however, in insisting that *logismos* and *thumos* are parts or powers, Galen still cannot help resorting extensively to metaphor in order to talk about them.

[33] See e.g. Plut. *Mor.* 441c–d, 446f–447a (*De virt. mor.*), with Graver (2007) 71, 73. For the

9. Mental Conflict from Homer to Eustathius

that posits centres of agency that somehow detract from or supplant the agency of the person.

To put all of this in context, it is worth remembering that the correct conclusion here – that the only real agents in these scenarios are the individuals themselves – is one that is both available and explicitly drawn throughout Antiquity. We saw that Homer clearly represented Odysseus' *kradiē*, both in its barking and in its past experiences in the cave of the Cyclops, as a metaphor. At the conclusion of *Republic* 9, too, Plato explicitly presents the tripartite model as 'an image of the soul in words' (588c–d).[34] Aristotle, for his part, points out not only that it is properly the person, not the soul, that thinks and feels (*De an.* 1.4, 408b13–15), but also that talk of phenomena such as justice in the soul is a metaphor that involves treating aspects of the personality as if they were agents (*EN* 5.11, 1138b5–13). Talk of parts of the soul, for him, is context-specific – different forms of enquiry use different models, and the parts may be distinct only in account, like convex and concave in the circumference of a circle (*EN* 1.13, 1102a26–32).

9.3. Eustathius

Which brings us to Eustathius, whom I discuss especially because the much-criticized amplitude of his notes in fact affords the best access we have to a learned Byzantine's understanding of Homeric psychology, but also because, as will emerge below, his observations on the relevant passages still have much to teach us. In the *Iliad* commentary, in particular, Eustathius in general exhibits a detailed and well-informed understanding of the so-called 'psychic organs' in Homer. He regularly distinguishes between *phrenes* as body part and as function.[35] In one passage, he identifies *thumos* with the thymus gland.[36] As psychological functions, he regularly regards *thumos* and other members of the family as interchangeable:[37] at 4.391.28 Van der Valk (on *Il.* 20.195) he notes that 'casting [*ballein*] x in one's *thumos* is the same as placing [*tithenai*] it in one's *phrenes* (τὸ δὲ ἐν θυμῷ βαλεῖν εἴη ἂν ἴσον τῷ ἐν φρεσὶ θήσειν)'.[38] Though later Greek usage leads him to emphasize those Iliadic passages in which *thumos* may

---

view that motivational conflict is a possibility in Stoic theory at all stages of its development, see Cooper (1998); Gill (1998); Graver (2007) 69, 75–81; Gill (2010b) 152.

[34] See Cairns (2017d).

[35] See Keizer's index II to Van der Valk, *s.v.*

[36] See 4.426.24 Van der Valk (on *Il.* 20.402–6).

[37] He also considers *phrenes* and *prapides* to be identical as bodily organs, at 3.257.12–14 (on *Il.* 11.579) and 4.23.6–7 (on 17.111).

[38] Cf. e.g. 2.793.5–7 (on *Il.* 9.537); also 2.361.9–11 (on 6.444), where he equates *thumos* and *kradiē*, and 4.554.14 (on *Il.* 21.563), *thumos* and *ētor*. In the *Odyssey* commentary, cf. 1.73.11–13 Stallbaum = 1.322.17–19 Cullhed (on *Od.* 1. 427), *phrenes* and *ētor*.

240 *Douglas Cairns*

be thought of as a source of anger or even (mis)understood as an anger term,[39] he is also aware that in Homer *thumos* performs functions that are attributed in later Greek to *psuchē* or *nous*.[40] On occasion, he discusses whether 'anger' or *psuchē/nous* best captures the sense.[41]

Eustathius' explicit understanding of the presentation of mental conflict in Homer emerges in his commentaries on three of the four Iliadic *thumos*-dialogues,[42] on Achilles' speech at *Iliad* 22 (which has the 'but why ...' formula, but not the 'he said to his *thumos*' formula), and on the passage involving Odysseus' 'barking heart' in the *Odyssey*. What is immediately striking is that Eustathius interprets all these scenes functionally, in terms of what they contribute to the characterization of the speaker. This is integral to his approach as a teacher of rhetoric, reflecting an interest in the means by which speeches affect their audiences,[43] but it also reflects his assumption that the Homeric poems themselves constitute indirect ways of expressing meanings that can be formulated more straightforwardly and prosaically.[44] He is alert to the use of figurative language and he interprets that language, too, in functional terms – the relevant locutions represent ways of talking about personal agency. Eustathius is absolutely clear that the only genuine agent in any of these scenes is the person, the character himself.

At 3.222.9–15, on Odysseus' monologue at 11.401–10, Eustathius writes:

ἐφ' οἷς ἐπάγει κατὰ σχῆμα λόγου, οἷον καὶ ἐν Ὀδυσσείᾳ κεῖται, ὅπου Ὀδυσσεὺς κινδύνῳ θαλασσίῳ ἐναπείληπτο, ὅτι "ὀχθήσας δ' ἄρα εἶπε πρὸς ὃν μεγαλήτορα θυμόν· ὤμοι, ἐγὼ τί πάθω; μέγα μὲν κακὸν αἴ κε φέβωμαι πληθὺν ταρβήσας, τὸ δὲ ρίγιον, αἴ κεν ἁλώω μόνος", καὶ τὰ ἑξῆς. εἶτα ἐπιρρωνύων ἑαυτὸν καὶ πείσας μένειν, ἐπάγει γνωμικῶς "ἀλλὰ τιή [*sic* Van der Valk] μοι ταῦτα φίλος διελέξατο θυμός;"

To which he adds in figurative language, such as is also found in the *Odyssey* [5.298], where Odysseus had been trapped by danger at sea: 'Deeply troubled he spoke to his own great-

---

[39] 1.13.13–22 (on *Il.* 1.1), 2.824.7–12 (on 9.637), 825.1–3 (on 9.639). Cf. and contrast 2.751.8–11 (on 9.436). In the *Odyssey* commentary, cf. 1.99.38–100.4 Stallbaum = 1.436.3–18 Cullhed (on *Od.* 2.315), 2.96.41 Stallbaum (on *Od.* 15.212).

[40] *Psuchē*: 1.26.20, 2.133.2, 2.137.13–15, 2.307.19, 2.323.2, 2.383.9, 2.441.13–14, 2.835.11, 3.132.3, 3.153.27–8, 3.206.21–2, 3.696.7–16, 3.837.25–9, 4.424.16, 4.425.6, 4.572.21, 4.790.7–9; *nous*: 3.108.18–19, 3.766.13–14, 3.788.5–6. In the *Odyssey* commentary, cf. 1.62.14 Stallbaum = 1.276.26–7 Cullhed on *Od.* 1.322–3 (*psuchē*). Also 1.30.21 Stallbaum = 1.136.8–9 Cullhed on *Od.* 1.114 (*ētor* as *psychē*).

[41] At 2.383.8–12 (on *Il.* 6.523) he hedges his bets between 'anger' and 'mind'; 3.118.20–1 (on 10.495) between *psuchē* and *orgē*. At 3.696.7–16 (on *Il.* 16.24) he goes for *psuchē*, not *cholos*.

[42] I did not find anything relevant in his notes on Menelaus' monologue in *Il.* 17.

[43] On Eustathius' aims and audience, see Cullhed (2016) 2*–4*, 9*–33* (esp. 17*–25* on Eustathius and Byzantine rhetorical education); cf. Pontani (2005) 171–2; Nünlist (2012); Pizzone (2016); Van den Berg (2018). (Cullhed has three systems of pagination: Roman numerals for prelims; asterisked Arabic for introduction; and Arabic for text and translation.)

[44] For Eustathius' view that the Homeric poems themselves are *paraphraseis*, see Signes Codoñer (2014) 80–1.

9. Mental Conflict from Homer to Eustathius 241

hearted *thumos*, "Ah me, what will become of me? It will be a great evil if I run, fearing their multitude, yet more chilling if I am caught alone ..."' Then, to encourage himself and persuade himself to remain, he adds, didactically: 'But why has my dear *thumos* said this to me in conversation?'

The narrator's statement that Odysseus addressed his *thumos* is said to be 'figurative language' (κατὰ σχῆμα λόγου), appropriate to a situation (as in *Odyssey* 5) where a character is isolated and in danger – Eustathius has noticed that this formula is confined to situations in which the speaker is out of contact with any actual addressee.[45] The function of the question ἀλλὰ τίη μοι ταῦτα φίλος διελέξατο θυμός; is then explained wholly in terms of the character and motivation of the agent, as a way of encouraging oneself and strengthening one's resolve.[46] In a further comment on the same passage (223.6–9 on 404), Eustathius notes that the beginning of the speech (in which words that the narrator presented as an address to the *thumos* actually become an address to the self) represents 'being in two minds', whereas the break-off formula ἀλλὰ τίη μοι ... resolves that division into one:

ἰστέον δὲ ὅτι τὸ "ὤμοι ἐγώ" καὶ ἑξῆς, μεταποιηθὲν οἷον "μέγα μὲν κακόν, αἴ κε τόδε γένηται, ῥίγιον δέ, ἐὰν τόδε", εἴποι ἂν ὁ ἐν κινδύνῳ διχογνωμονῶν. εἰ δὲ στήσει τὴν διχόνοιαν εἰς ἕν, ἐρεῖ ἂν προσφυῶς τό· ἀλλὰ τί μοι ταῦτα φίλος διελέξατο θυμός;[47]

'Ah me etc.', reformulated as 'a great evil, if *x* happens, but worse, if *y* does', is the kind of thing you'd say if you were in danger and in two minds.[48] If you resolve the dilemma, then as a natural development you might say: 'But why has my dear *thumos* said this to me in conversation?'

In other cases, too (on 21.562, 22.122–5, and 22.385) ἀλλὰ τίη μοι ... is explained functionally, as a way of repudiating an ill-judged proposal:

καὶ μέχρι τούτων ἐλθὼν καὶ συνεὶς ὅτι οὐ καλῶς ἐνταῦθα νοεῖ, ἐγκόπτει τὸν ἐφεξῆς εἰρμὸν τοῦ λόγου, καὶ ἀφεὶς ἀναπόδοτον κατὰ σχῆμα ἐλλείψεως ἐπισημαίνεται τὸ κακόβουλον, εἰπὼν "ἀλλὰ τί μοι ταῦτα φίλος διελέξατο θυμός;"

Coming to that point and realizing that he is now not thinking right, he checks the sequence of his argument and leaving it without *apodosis* in the form of an ellipse[49] he marks the misjudgement, saying, 'But why has my dear *thumos* said this to me in conversation?' (*Comm. Il.* 4.553.9–12 on 21.562)

---

[45] See above n. 19 and context.

[46] Σ bT *Il.* 11.403–10 describes the passage as the representation of thought in terms of speech.

[47] Eustathius occasionally (and naturally, but without regard for the metre) writes τί for τίη.

[48] The locution εἴποι ἂν recurs in these passages: see the comments cited below on 21.562, 22.122, with Nünlist (2012) 495–6, 499–503 on this and similar phrases as a typical marker of rhetorical instruction in *ēthopoïïa*.

[49] On Eustathius' interpretation of text and punctuation here, see Erbse 5.254 on Σ bT *Il.* 21.556–61.

242   *Douglas Cairns*

καὶ ὅτι ὁ μεταβουλευσάμενος καὶ οἷον εἰπὼν ἐν ἑαυτῷ, ὡς ἕτερός με θυμὸς ἀνῆκεν, εἴποι
ἂν καὶ τό "ἀλλὰ τί μοι ταῦτα φίλος διελέξατο θυμός;"

Note that one who has changed his mind and who, as it were, says inwardly to himself,
another *thumos* sent me forth,[50] might also say 'But why has my dear *thumos* said this to
me in conversation?' (*Comm. Il.* 4.553.23–554.2 on 21.562)

καὶ μέχρι τούτου ἀπρόσκοπτος καὶ νῦν ἐλθὼν ὁ Ἕκτωρ τῇ φράσει, τὸ ἐντεῦθεν οἷον χω-
λεύσας καὶ ἀναπόδοτον ἐάσας τὸ νόημα διὰ τὸ ἀσύμφορον τοῦ βουλεύματος, λέγει, ὡς
καὶ πρὸ τούτου ὁ Ἀγήνωρ, ἑαυτὸν ἐφ' οἷς εἶπε μεμφόμενος, τὸ "ἀλλὰ τίη μοι ταῦτα φίλος
διελέξατο θυμός; ..."

Though Hector has not slipped up in his expression so far, now limping, as it were, and
leaving the thought unfinished (without *apodosis*) on account of the inconvenience of the
conclusion to his deliberation,[51] he says (as did Agenor earlier), reproaching himself for
what he said, 'But why has my dear *thumos* said this to me in conversation?' (*Comm. Il.*
4.585.3–7 on 22.122–5)

ὅτι σύνηθες τῷ ποιητῇ, ὡς προέγνωσται, ἀνωφελέσιν ἐννοίαις ἐπιλέγειν τὸ "ἀλλὰ τίη
μοι ταῦτα φίλος διελέξατο θυμός"; οὕτως ὁ Ἀγήνωρ ἔφη, οὕτως ὁ Ἕκτωρ. οὕτω καὶ νῦν
Ἀχιλλεύς, ὃς εἰπὼν ὡς πολέμαρχος "εἰ δ' ἄγετ' ἀμφὶ πόλιν σὺν τεύχεσι πειρηθῶμεν, ὄφρα
ἔτι γνῶμεν Τρώων νόον ὅν τινα ἔχουσιν, ἢ καταλείψουσι πόλιν ἄκρην τοῦδε πεσόντος, ἢ
μενοῦσιν Ἕκτορος οὐκέτ' ἐόντος", μεταμέλεται εἰπὼν τὸ "ἀλλὰ τίη μοι ταῦτα" καὶ ἑξῆς.

As we noted before, it is in the poet's manner to follow unhelpful considerations with the
phrase: 'But why has my dear *thumos* said this to me in conversation?' Agenor used it; so
did Hector. And now Achilles: speaking like a general, he says 'Come, let us go in armour
about the city to see if we can find out what purpose is in the Trojans, whether they will
abandon their high city, now that this man has fallen, or are minded to stay, though Hector
lives no longer.' Then he changes his mind and says 'But why ...?' (*Comm. Il.* 4.634.23–
635.4 on 22.385, 381–4)

The comment on 22.122, however, goes further in pointing out that the whole
speech amounts to a dialogue that Hector conducts with himself:[52]

ἐν δὲ τῷ "ἀλλὰ τί μοι ταῦτα φίλος διελέξατο θυμός" ὅπερ πᾶς εἴποι ἂν μεταμελόμενος
ἐφ' οἷς βεβούλευται, τὸ "διελέξατο" πρωτότυπόν ἐστι ῥῆμα τοῦ τῆς διαλέξεως ὀνόμα-
τος, πραγματικῶς οὕτω λεχθέν. τρόπον γάρ τινα τοιαῦτα ἑαυτῷ διελέξατο Ἕκτωρ· εἰσε-
λεύσομαι τὸ τεῖχος; ἀλλ' αἰδοῦμαι διὰ τάδε. ἀλλ' ἱκετεύσω; καὶ μὴν σκληρὸς ὁ Ἀχιλλεύς.
ἀντιστήσομαι ἄρα.

In 'But why has my dear *thumos* said this to me in conversation' – which anyone might
say when regretting what s/he has resolved to do – 'said in conversation' is the original
verb from which the noun 'conversation' is coined, used here with reference to the subject

---

[50] Eustathius' own formulation. For ἕτερος θυμός cf. *Od.* 9.302 (discussed above) and for θυμὸς ἀνῆκεν cf. *Il.* 7.25, 21.395.
[51] For the explanation in terms of sentence structure/ellipse, cf. Σ AbT on 22.111–22 (with
Erbse's note, 5.291).
[52] Though Eust. on 99–110 picks up Σ bT on 99–130 (5.290 Erbse), this point is his own.

9. Mental Conflict from Homer to Eustathius 243

matter. For, in a way, Hector was conversing with himself when he said things like: shall I go inside the wall? But I'm ashamed, because ... So shall I supplicate? But Achilles is harsh. Then I'll face him. (*Comm. Il.* 4.588.16–20)

Eustathius does not take literally either the address to the *thumos* or the rejection of the *thumos*'s supposed proposal. Instead, he proposes to interpret πραγματι- κῶς, taking the successive options that Hector rehearses as *tantamount* to dialogue (or even perhaps to dialectic) in a way that justifies the use of the verb διελέξατο.[53] He is clear that the real agent here is Hector. He is absolutely right.

Eustathius' concentration on individual agency and motivation also allows him to see what many modern commentators have overlooked or denied, namely that Hector's *aidōs* in *Il.* 22.99–110 is strongly self-directed, representing Hector's judgement of his own failure. Eustathius explicitly points out that Hector's own self-criticism is identical to the verdict that he attributes to the hypothetical critic (τὸ δὲ "ἀτασθαλίαις ὤλεσα λαόν" ταὐτόν ἐστι τῷ "ἧφι βίηφι πιθήσας ὤλεσε λαόν", 'I ruined the people by my recklessness' is the same thing as 'He trusted in his might and ruined the people', 4.584.6–7 on 104), and observes that the hypothetical critic himself is an effective way of intensifying Hector's pain (4.583.6–13 on 99–110):

καὶ ὅρα ὅτι τε εὐγενῶς ὁ Ἕκτωρ ἐπονειδίστου σωτηρίας θάνατον εὐκλεῆ ἀνθαιρεῖται, καὶ ὡς ὁμολογῶν αὐτὸς ὑπὸ ἀτασθαλίας ὀλέσαι λαόν, ὅμως ὑπό τινος ἑτέρου κακωτέρου, ὅ ἐστι δυσγενοῦς ἢ δειλοῦ, ἀκοῦσαι οὐκ ἀνέχεται ὅπερ αὐτὸς ὁμολογεῖ. δι᾽ οὗ δείκνυται, ὡς πολλὰ φαῦλα συνειδότες πολλοὶ σφίσιν αὐτοῖς οὐκ ἀνέχονται ὑφ᾽ ἑτέρων αὐτὰ ὀνει- δίζεσθαι, οὕτω τις καὶ ἑαυτὸν τύπτων ἢ τὰ οἰκεῖα κατασωτευόμενος ἢ τοὺς ἑαυτοῦ κα- ταβλάπτων οὐκ ἂν ὑπὸ ἄλλων αἱροῖτο ὥσπερ οὐ πάσχειν, οὕτως οὐδ᾽ ἀκούειν τοιαῦτα.[54]

Note that Hector nobly chooses death with renown instead of deliverance with disgrace, and that, though he himself agrees that he recklessly ruined his people, still he cannot bear to hear from some other, worse – i. e. low-born or cowardly – person a charge that he himself accepts. Thus it becomes clear that, just as many people who have many bad things on their conscience cannot stand to be reproached for them by another, so too someone who harms himself or squanders his resources or damages his family would not choose even to hear such things from others, much less undergo them at others' hands.

Talking about other people, and what they might say, can be a way of talking about oneself, of representing one's state of mind and mental processes.[55] Talking about one's *thumos* or one's *kradiē*, and imagining them as interlocutors in a dialogue with oneself, performs a similar function.[56]

---

[53] See Van der Valk 4.588 *ad loc.*: 'Eust. ipse; de re cf. Eust. 1192, 45 (cum annot.), ubi Eust. egit de philosophis vel viris doctis, quos vocat διαλεκτικούς – de voce διάλεξις cf. etiam ad Eust. 1155, 3 – Monet etiam artem dialecticam nunc reipsa (πραγματικῶς, cf. Vol. II, p. LXVIII) nostro loco illustrari.'

[54] On the moral aspects, cf. and contrast Σ bT on 22.99–130.

[55] See further Cairns (2020b).

[56] Christopher Gill (1996) has (acutely) seen internalization of interpersonal dialogue as characteristic of ancient Greek models of the personality. George Herbert Mead, by contrast,

244   *Douglas Cairns*

It is notable that Eustathius clearly sees these passages as variants on a theme: he draws links between them and employs the same kind of functional, etho-poetic, and stylistic explanation in each case. Not surprisingly, then, he takes the same approach to the 'barking heart' in *Od.* 20 (*Comm. Od.* 2.223–4 Stallbaum):

κραδίη δέ οἱ ἔνδον ὑλάκτει. ἐπεὶ δὲ σκληρὸν δοκεῖ ἐπὶ καρδίας τὸ ὑλακτεῖν, ἐπάγει συνή-θως ἐπὶ θεραπείᾳ τῆς λέξεως, ὁποῖα καὶ ἐν ἄλλοις παρεσημάνθη, παραβολὴν ταύτην. ὡς δὲ κύων ἀμαλῇσι περὶ σκυλάκεσσι βεβῶσα ἄνδρα ἀγνοιήσασα ὑλάει μέμονέν τε μάχε-σθαι, ὥς ῥα τοῦ ἔνδον ὑλάκτει, καρδία δηλαδή, ἀγαιομένου κακὰ ἔργα. καὶ οὕτω θερα-πεύσας τὸ τὴν καρδίαν ὑλακτεῖν τῇ κατὰ τὴν κύνα περὶ τοῦ ὑλακτεῖν παραβολῇ ἐπάγει …

'His heart within him barked.' Since it seems harsh to predicate 'barking' of the heart, as usual he adds to give a suitable context to [lit. 'to heal'] the word (as was noted elsewhere) this simile: 'As a dog standing over her tender pups barks at a man she doesn't recognize and is eager to fight, so it – *sc.* the heart – barked within him in his resentment at their wrongdoing.' And in this way, having healed the expression 'barking heart' by means of the simile of the dog barking, he adds … (2.223 on 20.6 ff.)

τὸ δὲ, τέτλαθι κραδίη, ἀπὸ μέρους ἀντὶ τοῦ, σὺ, ὦ Ὀδυσσεῦ. διὸ καὶ ὑποκαταβὰς ἔφη· ὀϊ-όμενον θανέεσθαι, σὲ δηλονότι τὸν Ὀδυσσέα.

'Endure, my heart' is synecdoche for 'You, Odysseus …' That's why, a bit later, he says 'when you thought you were going to die', where 'you' is clearly Odysseus. (2.223–4 on 20.18)

ὅτι καὶ ἐνταῦθα καθάπτεσθαι τὸ λογικῶς ἀποτείνεσθαι, οἷον, ἐν στήθεσσι καθαπτόμενος φίλον ἦτορ, τουτέστιν ὡς πρὸς τὴν καρδίαν ἀποτεινόμενος. διὸ καὶ ἐπάγει· τῷ δὲ μάλα ἐν πείσῃ κραδίη μένε, ἤγουν τὸ ῥηθὲν ἦτορ, τετλυῖα.

Here, *kathaptesthai* means 'to upbraid rationally', i. e. 'assailing his dear heart in his chest' means 'inveighing against the heart'. That's why he adds 'And indeed his *kradiē* – *sc.* the aforementioned *ētor* – endured and remained obedient.' (2.224 on 20.22–3)

Eustathius notes the departure from standard usage in 'his heart within him barked' and points out that the harshness is softened by the way that the phrase is amplified by the simile (ἐπεὶ δὲ σκληρὸν δοκεῖ ἐπὶ καρδίας τὸ ὑλακτεῖν, ἐπά-γει συνήθως ἐπὶ θεραπείᾳ τῆς λέξεως …). He sees the equivalence of *kradiē* and *ētor*,[57] and notes that καθαπτόμενος φίλον ἦτορ is used here in a non-physical sense. Perhaps most strikingly of all, he states quite plainly that Odysseus' ad-dress to his heart involves synecdoche and so amounts to nothing more than a form of self-address (τὸ δὲ, τέτλαθι κραδίη, ἀπὸ μέρους ἀντὶ τοῦ, σὺ, ὦ Ὀδυσ-σεῦ),[58] correctly adducing the gender of the participle, ὀϊόμενον, as conclusive proof of the contention that the *kradiē* (and, he might have added, the *mētis* as

---

saw it as a feature of personality development in general (e.g. Mead (1964) 141). For internal dialogue as a fundamental aspect of the phenomenology of human thinking, see Ferneyhough (2016). Cf. (e.g.) thought (διάνοια) as internal dialogue at Pl. *Soph.* 263e.

[57] Cf. n. 38 above.

[58] Cf. his note on *Od.* 2.39 (1.80.31–2 Stallbaum = 1.354.27–356.1 Cullhed), where, adducing

9. Mental Conflict from Homer to Eustathius 245

well) are transparent figures for aspects of Odysseus' personality (ὀϊόμενον θανέεσθαι, σὲ δηλονότι τὸν Ὀδυσσέα). Consistently, Eustathius locates agency
at exactly the right level – that of the human agent. This reflects an approach
that is characteristic of Eustathius: in a few of his remarks, there are precedents
in the scholia,[59] but the concentration on agency and character (or at least
on motivation and situational appropriateness), together with the focus on the
function of utterances in depicting agency, motive, and character, are features
that reflect Eustathius' own agenda, aims, and methods.

On the issues that have concerned us in this chapter, Eustathius gets things
right.[60] We might say that this is largely because, on the matter of agency and
mental conflict, he takes a pre-theoretical, intuitive approach. That would be
an oversimplification: Eustathius' own methods and interests very much reflect
his specific twelfth-century Byzantine cultural context and the literary and
rhetorical theories of his day.[61] But even if we do regard his approach to agency
and mental conflict as broadly intuitive and common-sense in nature, there
is still a lesson in this that is worth learning. To treat other human beings as
agents is a fundamental element of our cognitive make-up.[62] The strong predis-
position that we have to do so is essential if we are going to be able successfully
to negotiate the natural and social environments in which we live. Whatever
model of the personality – of the 'psychic organs', of the *psuchē*, or of the parts
of the *psuchē* – our ancient sources, from Homer to Eustathius, may prefer, none
of them dispenses with the category of the agent or denies that effective agency
is a feature of persons. Even if some of them do believe in sub-personal levels of

---

Od. 20.22 (ἐν στήθεσσι καθαπτόμενος φίλον ἦτορ) as a parallel, he observes οὕτω καὶ τὸ καθαπτόμενος φίλον ἦτορ, ἀντὶ τοῦ ἑαυτῷ λαλῶν.

[59] I find nothing similar to any of Eustathius' acute observations on the 'barking heart' passage in the *Odyssey* scholia, though (as Pontani notes, (2005) 172) these are fewer in number
for the *Od.*, especially for the later books. On Eustathius' sources, see Pontani (2005) 173–8;
Pagani (2017).

[60] The generally negative view of Eustathius as a reader of Homer (as in Wilson (1996) 196–
200) has given way in recent years to much more nuanced assessments. Pontani (2005) 172 gives
a balanced and ultimately positive view of the value of Eustathius' commentaries ('nella lettura
e nella riflessione sul testo omerico, egli si rivela rispetto a Tzetze un compagno infinitamente
più preciso, costante, affidabile; per noi, poi, una fonte di inestimabile valore'). A similar appreciation guides Cullhed (2016), as well as various authors (esp. Hunter, Nünlist, Pizzone, and
Van den Berg) in Pontani, Katsaros, and Sarris (2017).

[61] A renewed interest in character and characterization in twelfth-century culture can be
traced, for example, in the approach of Isaac Porphyrogenitus and John Tzetzes to the (by then)
traditional, physiognomically inspired pen portraits of Homeric heroes called *eikonismoi* (see
Pralon (2015) on Isaac; Lovato (2017) on Tzetzes). Isaac (son of Alexios I and brother of Anna
Comnena) is also the author of notes on the *Iliad* preserved in MS Par. gr. 2682 which in some
respects reflect approaches that we can trace more fully in Eustathius: see Pontani (2006), esp.
576 on Isaac's remarks on personification (in *Il.* 8.183, 18.501), 580 on physiognomics, and 582–3
on the passions. For a complementary interest in individual characterization in contemporary
Comnenian art, see Linardou (2016), esp. 176, 179–82.

[62] See now Gallagher (2020).

agency (or in external, superhuman agents that influence human beings), nonetheless human agency remains fundamental both in their explanations of human behaviour and as the source domain for the metaphors by which they construct models of sub-personal or supra-personal agency. We who study the history of ideas, of mentalities, and of emotions typically focus on diachronic change and cultural difference, and the world is all the better for that. But there are limits to the range of historical and cross-cultural variation that we can expect to find. And sometimes we need to emphasize that too.

10

Ekphrasis and Emotional Intensity
in the *Homilies* of Philagathos of Cerami*

Mircea Grațian Duluș

> 'When all is said and done, there is only one
> means and only one method of treatment avail-
> able, and that is teaching by word of mouth. That
> is the best instrument, the best diet, and the best
> climate. It takes the place of medicine and cautery
> and surgery. When we need to cauterize or cut,
> we must use this. Without it all else is useless.'
> John Chrysostom, *On the Priesthood* 4.3 (trans.
> Neville, 115)

Introduction

The effectiveness of words to impress themselves upon the hearer and their ability to mold the soul, for virtue or sin, is frequently emphasized by the Fathers.
As John Chrysostom observes, words are the preferred ground of the Devil, who
'tries to hurt us in every way, but especially through our tongues and mouths.
He finds no instrument so suitable for deceiving and destroying us as an undis-
ciplined tongue and a mouth that is never closed.'[1] Speech is that which must
be reclaimed back from the diabolical ensnarement and put at the service of
salvation. In Christian terms it must convey the sacramental *economy* of Christ's
incarnation and the redemption of the flesh. Holy eloquence implies a strategy
of seduction because '[t]o arouse emotionally, to seduce, is to force a path not in

---

* This chapter is based on my PhD dissertation, 'Rhetoric, Exegesis, and Florilegic Structure
in Philagathos of Cerami: An Investigation of the Homilies and of the Allegorical Exegesis of
Heliodorus' *Aethiopika*' (Central European University Budapest, 2018). I would like to express
my heartfelt gratitude to Prof. Douglas Cairns and Prof. Niels Gaul for having invited me to
participate in this project. The completion of this chapter was supported by the Ministry of
Education and Research, CNCS/CCCDI – UEFISCDI, project number PN-III-P3-3.6-H2020-
2020-0154/contract no. 52/2021. I thank the Ministry for their support and Prof. Andrei Timotin
for setting up the project.

[1] Chrys. *Catech. bapt.* 4.30, ed. Wenger (1970).

the spirit but in the entire body of the listener or spectator, and in occupying it, to become the master of what it digests and rejects'.[2] Its aim is the redirection and transformation of emotion or passion (πάθος) into the service of virtue.

This chapter aims to explore the strategies of emotional arousal in the homilies of Philagathos of Cerami.[3] Philagathos was an influential preacher in the Norman Kingdom of Sicily during the reigns of Roger II (1130–54) and William I (1154–66).[4] He displays a fine ability to stir the emotions of his audience by drawing on a wide repertoire of rhetorical devices, such as *synkrisis, antithesis, diēgesis, ekphrasis, ēthopoiïa* and *thrēnos*.[5] Similarly, the usage of sensory imagery for describing illness, stench, decomposition, or desire was meant to elicit emotion in his listeners. The same end is achieved by the structure of the homilies, which convey a strong sense of rhythmical flow produced by the usage of clausular stress regulation and various tropes such as chiastic structures, the conspicuous usage of *homoioteleuton*, anaphora, alliteration, or symmetrical clauses like antithesis and parallelism.[6] However, the distinctive mark of Philagathos' homiletic corpus is their ecphrastic mode.[7] The South Italian preacher lingers on descriptions of mourning, lamentation, madness, dancing, images of despair or arousal of desire, falling into temptation, astonishment, as well as visual illustrations of pleasure and pride. Philagathos' ecphrastic technique draws on a wide array of sources. The most frequently cited patristic authority is Gregory of Nyssa. Although they are most often unacknowledged, Philagathos used Gregory's works for rhetorical effect, encyclopaedic lore and spiritual interpretation. The next most frequently cited Christian sources are Maximus Confessor, Cyril of Alexandria, Michael Psellos, Makarios Magnes, and Gregory the Theologian. However, what singles out Philagathos' homiletic writing is the usage of authors belonging to the Second Sophistic, such as Procopius of Gaza, Aeneas of Gaza, Lucian of Samosata, Alciphron, Synesius, and the ancient novelists Achilles Tatius and Heliodorus.[8] In fact, the compositional technique of Philagathos'

---

[2] Mondzain (2005) 59.

[3] Philagathos' homiletic corpus is only partially critically edited; most notably Rossi-Taibbi (1969) edited thirty-five sermons; then, Caruso (1974) 109–32 edited another three homilies; next, Zaccagni (2011) 149–63 edited another homily; finally, Torre (2012) 105–51 has published two other homilies and Bianchi (2009) 307–31 a fragment from a homily addressed to the Virgin; a significant number of homilies is still only available in Scorsus' edition (Paris 1644) reprinted in *PG* 132, coll. 135–1078.

[4] Rossi-Taibbi (1969) liv–lv; Duluș (2011) 56–8; (2018) 32–6.

[5] For Philagathos' handling of rhetorical techniques see Duluș (2018) 93–195.

[6] For Philagathos' usage of clausular endings see Perria (1982).

[7] For the aspects involved in assessing innovation and originality in Byzantine sermons see Cunningham (1995) 67–80.

[8] Philagathos' usage of rhetorical models has been the subject of numerous investigations; see for this Zaccagni (1998); Bianchi (2005); Torre (2008); Corcella (2009), (2010), (2011a), (2011b); Bianchi (2011a), (2011b); Duluș (2011); Torre (2011); Zaccagni (2011); Amato (2012); Duluș (2020), (2021); for a comprehensive analysis of Philagathos of Cerami's *oeuvre* see Duluș (2018).

10. Ekphrasis and Emotional Intensity in the Homilies of Philagathos of Cerami 249

sermons reflects the entrenched Byzantine florilegic habit centred on the quotation (most often unacknowledged) and adaptation of sanctioned authorities. By highlighting the incorporation of various rhetorical models into the story of salvation, this chapter will address Philagathos' ecphrastic technique devoted to creating scenes of extreme emotional intensity with a threefold emphasis on the representation of wantonness, bereavement, and the depiction of mixed and conflicting emotions in the homilies.

This chapter embraces Henry Maguire's observation that the rhetoricity of Byzantine homilies represents and shapes a historically specific form of religious experience.[9] Analysing the interaction between Latin liturgical drama and the Byzantine rhetorical imagination in Southern Italy, Maguire explained that 'rhetoric became for the Byzantines another kind of visual drama, one that maintained the fixed forms and good order of icons'.[10] As Maguire puts it, 'the techniques of rhetoric [i.e. *ekphrasis, diēgesis, synkrisis, antithesis*] enabled the Byzantines to create a drama of images, in which the icons themselves spoke to each other and to their audience, without losing any of their fixity and good order. Through rhetoric, the Byzantines created a true "drama" of images, rather than a counterfeit performance of actors'.[11] The characterization of the Byzantine homily as a rhetorical form concentrated on the display of emotions, or as 'an internal drama' according to Maguire's terminology, offers a broader perspective for approaching Byzantine rhetoricized homilies. Indeed, the 'dramatic' sermon may be perceived as the counterpart of the doctrine of the icon, the other medium that represents to sight the deeds of Scripture. However, it should be clarified that Byzantine literary sensitivity restricted the semantic field of drama to depicting scenes of extreme emotional intensity without the provision of staged dramatic representations (play-acting). The single Byzantine tragedy, the Euripidean cento *Christos Paschon*, as Panagiotis Agapitos cogently commented, was 'not a testimony for the staging of passion plays in Byzantium. Rather, it is a witness to the rediscovery of drama as a vehicle for the rhetorical display of πάθη, πένθη, θρῆνοι, and οἰμωγαί.'[12] For the Byzantines did not perceive ancient tragedy as a performed theatrical spectacle but as a recited rhetorical representation.

Furthermore, as Andrew Walker White recently argued, the rhetorical dimension embedded in the various genres of Byzantine sacred literature, sermons included, is informed by the anti-theatrical ritual aesthetic that lies at the heart of Orthodoxy.[13] In opposition to the 'spectacles and the madness of stadiums',

---

[9] Maguire (1977), (2003), (2007b).

[10] Maguire (2003) 219.

[11] Maguire (2003) 219.

[12] Agapitos (1998) 142–3; see also Puchner (2017) 62–8; on the *Christos Paschon*, see Mullett's chapter in this volume.

[13] White (2015) 51–73.

250   *Mircea Grațian Duluș*

the Christian message was asserted through rhetorical performance that enacted a 'spiritual theatre of the mind', as Patricia Cox Miller put it.[14] The difference between the two kinds of spectacles, pagan and Christian, revolves around *mimēsis*. The ancient mimetic paradigm going back to Plato casts the audience into the roles of the poetic characters to the extent that 'the world of the poem *becomes* the world of the mind imaginatively (re)enacting it'.[15] Eric Havelock explained Plato's fundamental hostility to poetry, and to Homer in particular, in terms of the cultural condition of an oral society that experienced literature and poetic representations as radical performativity, which could profoundly alter human behaviour through its subversive emotional effects.[16] In a Christian context this performativity was problematic since the aesthetic pleasure produced by literature and particularly by tragedy implied an aesthetic distance disconnected from those who are suffering when figured by fictional and staged events, as stated by Augustine:[17]

> What is it that a man desires to be made sad, beholding sorrowful and tragic things, which he himself would not like to suffer? And yet he desires as a spectator to feel pain, this very pain is his pleasure. What is this but miserable madness? ... This is usually called misery when someone suffers a misfortune himself and commiseration when he suffers with others. But, after all, of what sort is this pity when it comes to fictional and staged events? For the audience member is not compelled to help anyone but he is invited only to feel pain and the more he feels pain the more he likes the author of those imagined stories.[18]

The irresistible appeal of the culture of spectacles derived from the effort made for aesthetic ends to suffuse the imaginary 'with a power that would make it one with reality in the minds of the spectators'.[19] In terms of *mimēsis*, the goal of the Christian recollection of the sacred history was altogether different in that it was not intended to elicit aesthetic gratification but rather to incorporate scriptural events inwardly by simultaneously looking at the redeemed yet sinful self and by positing a salvation still in the future.[20]

But this pairing of the Byzantine rhetoricized homily which animated a 'drama of images' with the Western liturgical drama invites the question: why was the quest for vividness in representing the story of salvation not accompanied in the East by the development of liturgical drama or religious theatre? The answer to this question lies in the nature of Byzantine religious art and the ac-

---

[14] On the notion of 'spiritual theatre of the mind' or 'mental theatre', denoting the rhetorical mode of the Christian discourse in Late Antiquity (i. e., with reference to the martyr narratives) see the excellent contribution of Miller (2005) 25–52.

[15] Halliwell (2002) 53.

[16] Havelock (1963).

[17] The intricate interplay between aesthetic emotions and the emotions experienced in real life is analysed by Munteanu (2009) 117–47.

[18] August. *Conf.* 3.2; trans. Munteanu (2009) 122.

[19] Auguet (1972) 103; see also Castelli (2005) 124.

[20] Krueger (2014) 84; White (2015) 52.

10. Ekphrasis and Emotional Intensity in the Homilies of Philagathos of Cerami 251

cess to the holy it aims to provide.[21] Iconophile thought insisted that the icon is merely the manifestation of absence, as it abandons consubstantiality with its model. Mondzain insightfully comments: 'the icon attempts to present the grace of an absence within a system of graphic inscription. Christ is not in the icon; the icon is toward Christ, who never stops withdrawing. And in his withdrawal, he confounds the gaze by making himself both eye and gaze.'[22] The icon precisely seeks to avoid the 'materialistic' and 'realistic' aspects implied in theatrical representations which figure the prototypes through human beings and thereby draw them into the order of reference. As it does not possess an objective reality, the icon cannot be reduced to realism or theatrical spectacle.[23] In other words, 'to say that the icon wanted to be a picture and not an idol or representation is to say that it institutes a gaze and not an object'.[24] The dynamic relationship with its prototype was asserted by the written name that always accompanies the person portrayed in the icon and by the ascription of specific physiognomic traits for each major saint. As Henry Maguire puts it, 'holy persons could be portrayed in paintings according to their approved portrait types, but they could not be portrayed in plays by any individual acting in a costume'.[25]

The theology of the icon impacted on every form of Byzantine religious representation. The first liturgical commentary written after Iconoclasm, the *Protheoria*, and the Liturgical Poem based on it written by Nicholas and Theodore of Andida in the late eleventh century, likens the divine liturgy to the representation of Christ in an icon.[26] The same iconic function is ascribed to sermons, which are intended to lead the audience to perceive divine realities.[27] In this connection it is significant to note that among the patristic texts invoked for legitimizing the cult of icons at the second Council of Nicaea in 787 were ecphrastic sermons that scrutinized and shaped the effect of images upon their viewers. One such testimony is Asterius of Amasea's (*ca.* 330–420) description of the martyrdom of Saint Euphemia as it was represented in a painting near the tomb of the saint. As he reaches the description of tortures, the homilist records the emotional effect of the images: 'From this point, I weep and the suffering cut short my discourse. For the painter had smeared drops of blood so manifestly that it seemed to pour truly from the lips and you would depart singing a dirge.'[28]

---

[21] This subject has received extensive scholarly attention; see e.g. Nelson (1989); Belting (1994); Nelson (2000), (2005); Barber (2007); for a recent re-evaluation see Betancourt (2016).

[22] Mondzain (2005) 88.

[23] Mondzain (2005) 91.

[24] Mondzain (2005) 70; Puchner (2017) 87.

[25] Maguire (2003) 217.

[26] Betancourt (2015).

[27] See on this James (2003) 232; (2004) 528–9.

[28] Trans. Castelli (2000) 467; Ast. Am. *Hom.* 11.4.2–4, ed. Datema (1970) 155: δακρύω δὲ τὸ ἐντεῦθεν καί μοι τὸ πάθος ἐπικόπτει τὸν λόγον· τὰς γὰρ τοῦ αἵματος σταγόνας οὕτως ἐναργῶς ἐπέχρωσεν ὁ γραφεὺς ὥστε εἴποις ἂν προχεῖσθαι τῶν χειλέων ἀληθῶς καὶ θρηνήσας ἀπέλθοις.

252   *Mircea Graţian Duluş*

In other words, *ekphrasis* offered a tool for decoding and relating the painted representations with the desired emotional response.

Apart from its instrumental relation with iconic doctrine, the ecphrastic sermon draws on the Classical rhetorical tradition. It may suffice here to note that the arousal of emotions is intrinsic to the function of *ekphrasis*.[29] The ability of language to emotionally affect the audience is conveyed by the term *enargeia*, 'vividness' (ἐναργεία), which represents the appeal to the audience's imagination in order to achieve seeing through hearing.[30] As Ruth Webb explains, *enargeia* is constitutive to *ekphrasis*, which is thought to express a similar function with visual art: 'it is a vivid visual passage describing the subject so clearly that anyone hearing the words would seem to see it'.[31]

In what follows, I will first present ecphrastic accounts of violence and suffering in relation to the massacre of the Holy Innocents (*Hom.* 24 Rossi-Taibbi) and the resurrection of the Son of the Widow of Nain (*Hom.* 6 Rossi-Taibbi). Then, I will explore Philagathos' substantial treatment of impudence and desire in relation to the story of Tamar (*Hom.* 22 Rossi-Taibbi) and Salome's lascivious dancing (*Hom.* 35 Rossi-Taibbi). Finally, I will consider Philagathos' proneness for describing mixed and at times contradictory feelings for conveying extreme emotional turmoil, such as those elicited by the Transfiguration (*Hom.* 31 Rossi-Taibbi) and the Resurrection of the Lord (*Hom.* 27, *PG* 132; *Hom.* 34, *PG* 132).

10.1. *Ekphraseis* of bloodshed and mourning

With sheer intensity, Philagathos explored the emotions of bereavement and grief in two exegetic contexts: in relation to the massacre of the Holy Innocents (*Hom.* 24 Rossi-Taibbi) and the resurrection of the Son of the Widow of Nain (*Hom.* 6 Rossi-Taibbi). For a Christian preacher seasoned in rhetoric, the potential for ecphrastic development of these Gospel stories was manifest.[32]

In what regards the massacre of the Holy Innocents, Philagathos introduced the account after citing and refuting anti-Christian reprimands that chastised Christ for not preventing Herod's massacre and derided his flight to Egypt. Philagathos forcefully begins:

ἦν μὲν καὶ ἄλλας αἰτίας προσθεῖναι τῆς τῶν νηπίων σφαγῆς, ἀλλ᾽ ἐνηχεῖ μου τὰς τοῦ νοὸς ἀκοὰς ὁ τότε γενόμενος θόρυβος, καὶ τὸ κατὰ τῶν παίδων ἀπηνέστατον πρόσταγμα, καὶ

---

[29] See e.g. Webb (1997a).

[30] For the concept of *enargeia* see Webb (2009) 87–106; for the Byzantine understanding of the term see Papaioannou (2011); for *enargeia* and iconicity see the excellent account in Tsakaridou (2013) 49–71.

[31] James and Webb (1991) 5–6.

[32] For the application of this technique in the exegetic tradition of interpreting the massacre of the Holy Innocents see e.g. Barkhuizen (2007) 29–50.

10. Ekphrasis and Emotional Intensity in the Homilies of Philagathos of Cerami 253

ἡ ἀκουσθεῖσα φωνὴ ἐν Ῥαμᾷ, καὶ τὸ Οὐαί, καὶ ὁ θρῆνος ὁ τῆς Ῥαχὴλ ἐκεῖ τὸν λόγον ὑφέλ-
κεται. ἀλλὰ ποῖος ἐφίκοιτο λόγος, εἰς τοσούτου πάθους ἀφήγησιν; τίς ἀξίως ἐκτραγῳδή-
σειε τῆς συμφορᾶς ἐκείνης τὸ μέγεθος; ὦ θέας ἀπευκτῆς, ὦ γνόφου δεινοῦ, κατασχόντος
τότε τὴν Βηθλεέμ. ὦ γυναικῶν ὀλολυγῆς, οἰμωγῆς τε παίδων ἁρπαζομένων εἰς ὄλεθρον.
(*Hom.* 24.6, ed. Rossi-Taibbi (1969) 158)

Indeed, other reasons for the massacre of children could be added, but the uproar that then
arose resounds in the ears of my mind, as well as the atrocious command given against the
children, and the voice heard in Ramah, and the woe, and Rachel's lamentation, which in
that place was weighing upon her speech [Matt. 2:17–18]. But what word could be seemly
for recounting a suffering as great as this? Whoever could describe appropriately with
woeful words the magnitude of that misfortune? Oh horrendous spectacle! Oh terrible
darkness, which at that time spread over Bethlehem! Oh loud cry of women, and children's
weeping when snatched away towards destruction!

The opening questions expressing anxiety and hesitation over the rhetor's ability to find words adequate to the misfortune are a well-established convention in
laments. Gregory of Nyssa formulated similar questions in relation to the same
New Testament episode in his *Homily on the Nativity*, which seems to have inspired Philagathos' formulations.[33] Philagathos recreates the scene of the massacre by dwelling first on what is heard: the atrocious command and the shrieks
of women and children. By arousing the sounds of the (imagined) original scene,
the homilist invites the audience to recreate the events in their own mind. In the
ancient ecphrastic tradition, speech and sound had an intrinsic ability to arouse
pathos, and in particular pity (ἔλεος).[34]

Philagathos' description closely follows the rhetorical tradition which prescribes for *ekphraseis* of war to 'describe the wounds and the deaths and the grief,
and in addition the capture and enslavement of some and the victory and tro-
phies of the others'.[35] First, the homilist presents the massacre unfolding in time:

ἐθρήνουν πατέρες, προσέπιπτον τοῖς στρατιώταις, ἱκέτευον, **καὶ μήτηρ περιεκέχυτο
παῖδα**, πατὴρ δὲ ἀνεκαλεῖτο γονήν. ὥρμα γυνὴ πρὸς φυγήν, φόρτον τοῖς ὤμοις τὸ παιδίον ἐπάγουσα· ἀλλ' ἦν τῶν ὑπηρετῶν ὁ δρόμος ὀξύτερος. ἀλλήλοις δὲ συνεκρούοντο,
καὶ φωναὶ συμμιγεῖς ἀνηγείροντο· ἠπείλουν οἱ στρατιῶται **δεινόν τι καὶ δρακοντῶδες,
ἠγριωμένοις δεδορκότες τοῖς ὄμμασιν.** ὠλόλυζον μητέρες αἵμασι πεφυρμέναι καὶ δά-
κρυσιν· ὠλοφύροντο νήπια ἐλεεινῶς συγκοπτόμενα. τὰ γὰρ ξίφη, ὡς ἔτυχεν, ἐπ' αὐτὰ
φερόμενα ἀθλίως ἠκρωτηρίαζε· καὶ τὸ μὲν χειρῶν ἀπεστέρητο, τὸ δὲ τὼ πόδε συντριβὲν
ἐξ ἡμισείας ἀπώλετο· **ἄλλο κατεάγη τὴν κεφαλήν, τοῦ σώματος τὰ καίρια παρασπώμε-
νον**, τὸ δὲ ὅλον ἐτέμνετο, ὡς ὁ θυμὸς ἐδίδου αὐτοματίζων ἑκάστῳ τὸν θάνατον. ὦ πόσοι
παῖδες, μέσον τμηθέντες, ἡμίθνητοι μεμενήκασι, μηδὲ τελευτὴν ὀξυτέραν κερδαίνον-
τες, ἀλλὰ κατὰ βραχὺ δαπανώμενοι. παῖς παρέθεε τῇ μητρὶ καὶ ψελλιζούσῃ φωνῇ τὴν

---

[33] Gr. Nyss. *Nativ.* (*PG* 46.1145): τίς ἂν ὑπογράψειε τῷ λόγῳ τὰς συμφοράς; 'Who could describe by word these terrible misfortunes?'
[34] Webb (1997a) 115.
[35] Aelius Theon, *Exercises*, *Ekphrasis*, ed. Patillon (1997) 119.14–21; trans Kennedy (2003) 46.
See also Hermog. 10.13–20 Rabe.

254   *Mircea Graţian Duluş*

τεκοῦσαν ἀνεκαλεῖτο. Ἀλλὰ στρατιώτης ἐξάπινα εἰσδραμών, ἀφηρεῖτο τῷ ξίφει τὴν κε-
φαλήν· **φθεγγομένου δ' ἄρα τοῦδε, ἡ κάρα κατεμίχθη τῇ κόνει.** ἐξάγει γάρ με ὁ λόγος
τὰ τῆς ποιήσεως φθέγξασθαι· (*Hom.* 24.6–8, ed. Rossi-Taibbi (1969) 158–9)

The fathers wailed, they fell down before the soldiers kneeling, beseeching them; *a mother
embraced her child* and a father called his offspring. A woman rushed out fleeing, carrying
the child as a burden upon her shoulders, but the henchmen's running was faster. [7.] They
collided with each other and mingled voices arose. The soldiers *uttered terrible and snake-
like threats, flashing forth with savage eyes.* The mothers wept bitterly, drenched by blood
and tears; the babes sobbed when pitiably cleaved asunder. For the swords, randomly
raining down upon them, inflicted horrendous mutilations. One was deprived of hands,
while one died with feet cut in half. *Another had his head cut off, the body's most important
part severed*; another one was entirely cut, since wrath acting spontaneously brought death
to every single one. *Oh, how many children cut in half lay half-dead, not even having the
benefit of a swifter death*, but expired only slowly. *A child ran to his mother, and called her
with faltering voice.* But a soldier rushing towards him with the sword immediately severed
his head; and '*while he was yet speaking his head was mingled with the dust*' (for the speech
leads me to utter poetical words).

The description amasses aural and visual imagery most prominently derived from
Gregory of Nyssa's *Homily on the Nativity*[36] and Procopius of Gaza's *Monody for
Antioch*, of which only a few fragments survive.[37] The *Monody*, written in relation
to the devastating earthquake of 526 that flattened Antioch, furnishes Philagathos
with the gruesome details of the massacre. However, Philagathos' accumulation
of cruel details conforms to a well-established Christian rhetorical pattern for describing this episode inherited from descriptions of war and calamities.[38] Concluding the first section of the *ekphrasis*, Philagathos recalls an Iliadic episode
featuring Diomedes beheading Dolon: 'Diomedes sprang upon him with his
sword and smote him full upon the neck, and shore off both the sinews, and even
while he was yet speaking his head was mingled with the dust' (φθεγγομένου δ'
ἄρα τοῦ γε κάρη κονίῃσιν ἐμίχθη).[39] The narrative context in the *Iliad* refers to
Dolon, who despite being a fast runner was hopelessly hunted down by Diomedes
and Odysseus in a swift pursuit with help from the goddess Athena. Vividly, this
poetical appropriation dovetails with the context of the sermon, as it connotes the
hopelessness of the children's flight and their unavoidable death.

---

   [36] Gr. Nyss. *Nativ.* (*PG* 46.1145): ἀλλ' ἀκροᾶται τοῦ ἄλλου ἤδη φθεγγομένου καὶ **ψελλι-
ζομένη τῇ φωνῇ τὴν μητέρα** μετὰ δακρύων **ἀνακαλοῦντος.** τί πάθῃ; τίς γένηται; τῇ τίνος
ἀντιβοήσει φωνῇ; τῇ τίνος οἰμωγῇ ἀντοδύρηται; 'And she was listening as the other was ere
now speaking and calling in tears her mother with a faltering voice. Oh, what is to befall her?
Who could take this? By whose voice could her cry be answered? By whose weeping could her
lamentation be surpassed?'
   [37] For the allusions to Procopius of Gaza's *Monody* in Philagathos' sermons see Corcella
(2010) 31–4 and Duluş (2020) 472–97; for monody as rhetorical genre see Men. Rhet., *On
Epideictic* 2.16 (ed. and trans. Russell and Wilson (1981) 200–7).
   [38] See for this Maguire (1981) 24–7; Barkhuizen (2007) 31–3.
   [39] Hom. *Il.* 10.455–7 (trans. Murray (1924) 469).

10. Ekphrasis and Emotional Intensity in the Homilies of Philagathos of Cerami   255

The next section describes the aftermath of the calamity, reflecting the chronological progression of the event as demanded by this type of *ekphrasis*. The emphasis is placed on the emotions that seized the inhabitants of Bethlehem:

πᾶσαν ἡλικίαν τὸ πάθος τότε συνείληφε, καὶ τραγῳδίας Ἐρινὺς τῇ Βηθλεὲμ ἐπεκώμαζε, τοῖς οἴκοθεν αὐτὴν πολέμοις μαστίζουσα. καὶ πρεσβύτης μὲν ἐδυσχέραινε τὸν μακρὸν χρόνον καταιτιώμενος, ὡς πάθεσιν αὐτὸν τοῖς παροῦσι τετηρηκότα, καὶ τὸν θάνατον ὡς βραδύνοντα κατεμέμφετο· ἡ δὲ μήτηρ ὅτι καὶ γέγονε μήτηρ ὠδύρετο· ἐμακαρίζοντο δὲ παρθένοι καὶ στεῖραι, καὶ θηλυτόκοι καὶ ἄγονοι. τάχα δὲ καὶ ταῖς τοιαύταις κοινὸν ἦν τὸ τῆς συμφορᾶς ἐξ ἑταιρείας ἢ αἵματος ἢ τρόπου ἀνακοινούμενον. (*Hom.* 24.8, ed. Rossi-Taibbi (1969) 159)

Calamity struck every generation at that time and a tragic Erinys assaulted Bethlehem, scourging it with internecine fights. And the old man wailed, cursing his many years, for having kept him alive only to bring him the present misfortunes, and he blamed death for being slow to arrive; whereas the mother lamented that she had become a mother; happy instead were the virgins and the barren women, and those who had begotten girls, or the childless lot. Yet perhaps even these women participated in the misfortune because of friendship, kinship, or natural affection.

This imagined grief aimed to incite emotion in the audience. Yet Philagathos' account does not stop here. For, augmenting the vividness of his literary description, Philagathos inserts the *ekphrasis* of a painting of the massacre, which he professed to have seen with his own eyes:

εἶδον ἐγὼ τοῦτο τὸ πάθος χρώμασι γεγραμμένον ἐν πίνακι, καὶ πρὸς οἶκτον ἐκινήθην καὶ δάκρυα. ἐγέγραπτο γὰρ ὁ μὲν τύραννος ἐκεῖνος Ἡρώδης ἐφ᾽ ὑψηλοῦ τινος θρόνου σοβαρῶς ἐφεζόμενος, δριμύ τι καὶ θηριῶδες ὁρῶν κεχηνότι τῷ βλέμματι. ὀρθὸν δὲ στήσας ἐν κολεῷ τὸ ξίφος, τὴν λαιὰν ἐπ᾽ αὐτῷ διανέπαυε, τὴν <δὲ> δεξιὰν προτείνων ἐπιτάττειν ἐῴκει τοῖς στρατιώταις ἀνηλεῶς θερίσαι τῶν νηπίων τὴν ἄρουραν. οἱ δὲ θηριοπρεπῶς ἐπιθρώσκοντες, ἀφειδῶς τὰ δείλαια κατεμέλιζον. (*Hom.* 24.9, ed. Rossi-Taibbi (1969) 159)

I saw this [scene of] suffering painted with hues on a panel, and I was moved to pity and tears. For that tyrant Herod was depicted sitting on a high throne haughtily, looking with wide open eyes, fierce and savage. While he rested his left hand upon the upraised and sheathed sword, he stretched forth his right hand [and] seemed to be ordering the soldiers to cut off the mothers without pity. And lurching like beasts they slaughtered mercilessly the wretched [children].

The emotional response evoked by Philagathos' statement of being 'moved to pity and tears', besides disclosing the conventional emotional reaction that a work of art sought to arouse, alludes to the function of the image in Christian religious worship.[40] For it was precisely the emotional impact of religious art that asserted its effectiveness. The transfiguration of the gaze turned upon the icon was a seminal justification for its use. Gregory of Nyssa expresses a similar emotion aroused by painting of the Sacrifice of Isaac: 'I often saw the

---

[40] James and Webb (1991) 9–11.

256 *Mircea Graţian Duluş*

representation of this suffering in painting, and I could not pass by this spectacle without [shedding] tears, so vividly the art brought the story before my eyes.[41] In a different context, Philagathos cites the iconophile principle that the image is anagogical, as it mediates the manifestation of the divine:

ἡ γὰρ τιμὴ τῆς εἰκόνος, ὡς ὁ μέγας εἶπε Βασίλειος, ἐπὶ τὸ πρωτότυπον ἀναφέρεται.[42] καὶ οὕτω διὰ τῆς αἰσθήσεως πρὸς εὐσέβειαν μειζόνως χειραγωγούμεθα. ὁρῶμεν γὰρ ἐν τοῖς ἱεροῖς ἐκτυπώμασι τὸν Δεσπότην ἡμῶν καὶ Θεὸν ἐκ Παρθένου παραδόξως τικτό-μενον, ὑπὸ μάγων δωροφορούμενον, πρεσβυτικαῖς ὠλέναις τοῦ Συμεὼν βασταζόμενον, γυμνὸν ἐν τοῖς ποταμίοις ῥεύμασι προφητικῇ δεξιᾷ χειραπτούμενον, ἐνεργοῦντα τὰ πα-ράδοξα θαύματα **ῥήματι μόνῳ καὶ ὁρμῇ τοῦ θελήματος, τὴν τῶν τεθνηκότων ἐπὶ τὸν βίον** αὖθις **ἀνάλυσιν, τὸν κατὰ τῶν δαιμόνων φόβον, τὴν διὰ θαλάσσης πορείαν ὑπο-χερσουμένου τῇ βάσει τοῦ ὕδατος, τὰς ἐν ἐρήμῳ δαψιλεῖς ἑστιάσεις,**[43] τοῦ προδότου τὴν τόλμαν, τὸ ἀσεβὲς ἐκεῖνο κριτήριον, τὴν στρῶσιν, τὴν ταφήν, τὴν ἀνάστασιν, τὴν εἰς οὐρανοὺς ἀναφοίτησιν· καὶ ταῦτα ὁρῶντες ἐντετυπωμένα τοῖς χρώμασιν, ἐναργῶς αὐτὰ βλέπειν οἰόμεθα· οἶδε γὰρ γραφὴ παριστᾶν ὡς ἐν ὄψει τὰ πράγματα. (*Hom.* 51.7, ed. Zaccagni (2011) 154–5)

In fact the honour paid to the icon, as great Basil said, *passes to the archetype*. And in this manner through the perception of the senses we are greatly led to piety. For we behold in the holy representations our Lord and God miraculously born from the Virgin, endowed with gifts by the wise men from the East, lifted up by the aged arms of Simeon, touched by the right prophetic hand when naked among the streams of the river, [then] effecting ex-traordinary miracles *by the mere utterance of a word and exercise of His will, the restoration of the dead to life* anew, *the fear with which He inspired devils, His walking through the sea by the surface of the water turned into solid ground [for His feet], His abundant banquets in the wilderness*, the daring of the traitor, that wicked judgement, the spreading [on the Cross], the burial, the Resurrection, the ascent into Heaven. And beholding these things impressed with colours we believe to see them as manifestly present. For painting has the capacity to represent the events as if they were [unfolding] before the eyes.

Icon and *ekphrasis* have a similar function in that both seek to make present through sense perception the incarnational ministry of Christ. But by em-phasizing the emotional response, *ekphrasis* served 'as a paradigm of what the viewer in the church should be experiencing in front of an image'.[44]

---

[41] Gr. Nyss. *Deit. fil.* (*PG* 46.572c): εἶδον πολλάκις ἐπὶ γραφῆς εἰκόνα τοῦ πάθους, καὶ οὐκ ἀδακρυτὶ τὴν θέαν παρῆλθον, ἐναργῶς τῆς τέχνης ὑπ᾽ ὄψιν ἀγούσης τὴν ἱστορίαν.

[42] Bas. *Spir.* (*PG* 32.149c).

[43] Philagathos' enumeration is inspired by Gr. Nyss. *Or. catech.* 23.18–28, ed. Mühlenberg (1917): **ἐν ῥήματι μόνῳ καὶ ὁρμῇ τοῦ θελήματος** παρ᾽ αὐτοῦ γινομένην, **τήν τε τῶν τεθνηκό-των ἐπὶ τὸν βίον ἀνάλυσιν,** καὶ **τὸν** [κατὰ] **τῶν δαιμόνων φόβον,** καὶ τῶν κατὰ τὸν ἀέρα πα-θῶν τὴν ἐξουσίαν, **καὶ τὴν διὰ θαλάσσης πορείαν,** οὐ διαχωροῦντος ἐφ᾽ ἑκάτερα τοῦ πελάγους καὶ τὸν πυθμένα γυμνοῦντος τοῖς παροδεύουσι κατὰ τὴν ἐπὶ Μωϋσέως θαυματουργίαν, ἀλλ᾽ ἄνω τῆς ἐπιφανείας **τοῦ ὕδατος ὑποχερσουμένης τῇ βάσει** καὶ διά τινος ἀσφαλοῦς ἀντιτυπί-ας ὑπερειδούσης τὸ ἴχνος, τήν τε τῆς τροφῆς ὑπεροψίαν ἐφ᾽ ὅσον βούλοιτο καὶ **τὰς ἐν ἐρημίᾳ δαψιλεῖς ἑστιάσεις** τῶν ἐν πολλαῖς χιλιάσιν εὐωχουμένων …

[44] James and Webb (1991) 12.

10. Ekphrasis and Emotional Intensity in the Homilies of Philagathos of Cerami   257

As the technique of *ekphrasis* demands, Philagathos' language aims to reflect the events he describes.[45] To achieve this stylistic quality, the homilist appropriated snippets referring to savagery from Cyril of Alexandria's *Commentary on the Twelve Prophets*. First, the characterization of the soldiers, who are 'springing like beasts' – οἱ δὲ θηριοπρεπῶς ἐπιθρώσκοντες – is indebted to Cyril's exegesis of Mic. 2:10–11: 'He distilled into their mind and heart an intoxication through error in which they rightly perish in a frenzy befitting wild animals (θηριοπρεπῶς ἐπιθρώσκοντες) employing utter audacity and abuse.[46] Second, Philagathos' statement that the soldiers 'chopped unmercifully the wretched [lads]' (ἀφειδῶς τὰ δείλαια κατεμέλιζον) goes back to Cyril's exegesis of Mic. 3:1–4: '[Y]ou made savage and heartless attacks on my sheep ... skinning the sheep, tearing their flesh, chopping it unmercifully (καταμελίζοντας ἀφειδῶς) and, as it were, cooking it in a pot.'[47] In addition, the homilist seems to have modelled his exposition after Procopius of Gaza's *Description of the Image* ("Εκφρασις εἰκόνος).[48]

Philagathos recounts the scene as if it were unfolding in time, with Herod seeming to order the slaughter of the children, followed by the soldiers' onslaught and the mothers' gathering the scattered limbs and bewailing the deaths of their children. By this temporal progression, Philagathos follows the recommendation to chronologically divide the actions in his *ekphrasis* into stages: preparation, action, and aftermath. The final stage of the description representing the aftermath of the slaughter is a catalogue of excessive gestures of bereavement that confounds the senses of sight and sound:

ἔγραψεν ὁ ζωγράφος καὶ τὰς ἀθλίας μητέρας οἰκτρὸν συνιστώσας θρῆνον καὶ τοῖς αἵμασι κιρνώσας τὰ δάκρυα. καὶ ἡ μὲν ἔτιλλε τὰς κόμας, ἡ δὲ τοῖς ὄνυξι τὰς παρειὰς περιέδρυφεν· ἄλλη διέρρησσε τὸν πέπλον, καὶ τὰ στέρνα παραγυμνοῦσα τὸν μαστὸν ὑπεδείκνυ καταλειφθέντα τοῦ θηλάζοντος ἔρημον· ἑτέρα δὲ τοῦ κατακοπέντος παιδίου τὰ διεσπαρμένα μέλη συνέλεγε· καὶ ἄλλη νεοσφαγὲς ἐν τοῖς γόνασι κρατοῦσα τὸ νήπιον, πικρῶς ὠλοφύρετο. (*Hom.* 24.9, ed. Rossi-Taibbi (1969) 159)

The painter also represented the miserable mothers, lamenting piteously as they mixed their tears with blood. And one tore her hair, another scraped the skin of her cheeks with her nails, another tore her robe, and laying bare her chest, showed her breast, now without the feeding baby. Another gathered the scattered limbs of the slaughtered child. And another holding on her knees her newly murdered child wept bitterly.

Next, Philagathos enhances the vividness of the visual representation by attributing a lament to the depicted feminine figures. This practice of assigning speech to the depicted characters is buttressed by iconic theology which encouraged the viewers to imagine the words of the sacred characters when beholding the icon:[49]

---

[45] Webb (2009) 57.

[46] Trans. Hill (2008) 209; Cyr. *Os.-Mal.* 1.640.8–11 Pusey.

[47] Trans. Hill (2008) 213; Cyr. *Os.-Mal.* 1.645.14–19 Pusey.

[48] See on this Duluş (2020) 490–2.

[49] James and Webb (1991) 10–11; Maguire (1974) 129–30; this principle was expressly stated

258   *Mircea Graţian Duluş*

καὶ ἐπειδὴ μὴ εἶχεν ὁ τεχνίτης φωνὴν ἐνθεῖναι τοῖς χρώμασιν, ἐσήμανε τοὺς θρήνους τοῖς γράμμασιν. ἐδόκει γὰρ ἐπιτραγῳδεῖν ὧδέ πη τὸ γύναιον· "ὢ παιδίον δυστυχὲς ἀθλιωτέρας μητρός, ἐλάνθανες ἄρα ξίφει καὶ θανάτῳ ἀώρῳ τικτόμενον. ὢ μάτην γονίμου γαστρός, ὢ ζηλωτῆς εὐτεκνίας, ἐπ' ὀλίγον μὲν εὐφρανάσης, ἐπὶ πλέον δὲ ἀνιώσης τὴν δειλαίαν ἐμέ. ὢ μελῶν ἁπαλῶν, καὶ γλώττης ψελλιζούσης ἡδύ, νῦν δὲ φεῦ σιγησάσης ἐσχάτην σιγήν. ὢ δεξιᾶς ἀδίκου ξιφήρους, ὅτι μὴ πρὸ σοῦ, παιδίον, τὴν τεκοῦσαν ἀπέκτεινεν. ἔγρεο, σπλάγχνον ἐμόν, ἀποτίναξον τὸν βαρὺν τοῦτον ὕπνον, ὅν σοι ὁ ἀπηνὴς στρατιώτης ἐνέθηκεν, ὑφαπλώθητι ταῖς ἀγκάλαις τῆς σῆς ἀθλίας μητρός, ἐπιλαβοῦ τοῦ πρίν σοι ποθουμένου μαζοῦ, ἐπίδειξον τὸ γλυκὺ καὶ σύνηθες ἐκεῖνο μειδίαμα." ἀλλ' οὐκ ἀφῆκε τὸ ἀπηνὲς τοῦ τυράννου ἐπίταγμα. τοιαῦτα λέγειν ἐῴκει, καὶ συνεῖρεν ἴσως τὰ τῆς Νιόβης καὶ τῆς Ἀλκήστεως· "μάτην ἄρα σε, τέκνον, ἐξεθρεψάμην, / μάτην ἐμόχθουν καὶ κατεξάνθην πόνοις. / ζηλῶ δ' ἀγάμους καὶ γυναῖκας ἀτέκνους· / βέλτιον γὰρ μὴ τεκεῖν ἢ τίκτειν εἰς δάκρυα." (*Hom.* 24.10–11, ed. Rossi-Taibbi (1969) 159–60)

And since the artist could not provide a voice to the hues, he imprinted the lamentations in letters. For it seemed that the woman lamented in this manner: 'Oh, hapless child of a miserable mother, unaware of the sword, and engendered for an untimely death! Oh womb, fertile in vain! Oh, fruitfulness admired, though it gladdened me a little, yet wretchedness wholly returned to me! Oh, tender limbs and sweetly bumbling tongue, yet now, alas, keeping everlasting silence! Oh, unrighteous right hand, armed with a sword, that it did not slay the mother before you, child! Awake, my child, shake off this heavy sleep, which the cruel soldier has imposed on you! Compose [yourself] upon the elbows of your miserable mother! Grasp your once beloved breast! Show forth that sweet and constant smile!' But the tyrant's cruel command did not permit it. [11.] It appeared seemly to say such words and perhaps to utter the words of Niobe and Alcestis with them:

> 'In vain, oh child, I nourished you,
> In vain, I laboured and was worn out by toils;
> I envy the unmarried lot and the childless women;
> For it is better not to have given birth than giving birth to tears.'

The *ekphrasis* ends with a cento of four verses from Euripides, which recall the atrocious suffering of Niobe and Alcestis.[50] Philagathos' selection is again well considered, for he amassed images loaded with emotions that dovetail with the theme of the sermon. The first two verses give voice to Andromache's lament from Euripides' *Troiades* (*Trojan Women*).[51] Andromache uttered these words at the moment she heard that her baby son, Astyanax, was condemned to die. The third verse alludes to the story of Niobe.[52] According to the myth, Niobe

---

at the second Council of Nicaea in 787: 'When we see on an icon the angel bringing the good news to the Virgin, we must certainly bring to mind the story of the angel – that the angel Gabriel was sent from God to the Virgin; and he came to her and said: 'Hail, O favoured one, the Lord is with you, blessed are you among women' (trans. Sahas (1986) 98).

[50] For the Byzantine appropriation of Euripides see Mullett in this volume.

[51] Eur. *Tro.* 758–60: διὰ κενῆς ἄρα / ἐν σπαργάνοις σε μαστὸς ἐξέθρεψ' ὅδε, / μάτην δ' ἐμόχθουν καὶ κατεξάνθην πόνοις. 'In vain and all in vain, / This breast in swaddling-bands hath nurtured thee' (trans. Way (1959) 417).

[52] The verse is often cited in the rhetorical tradition; see e.g. Apth. *Prog.* 10.35–6 Rabe (1926): ὡς ἔδει τὴν ἀρχὴν μὴ τεκεῖν ἢ τίκτειν εἰς δάκρυα. τῶν οὐ τεκόντων οἱ στερηθέντες εἰσὶν ἀτυ-

10. Ekphrasis and Emotional Intensity in the Homilies of Philagathos of Cerami   259

lost all of her twelve children (even more according to some versions), slain by Apollo and Artemis. The last verse is reminiscent of Euripides' *Alcestis*. It is part of Admetus' lamentation over the loss of Alcestis, who consented to die in his stead.[53] It should be noted that this imitation of emotional patterns from Classical texts constituted the bedrock of rhetorical training.[54] In all likelihood, Philagathos derived the verses from a rhetorical compilation that grouped them according to the theme of bereavement. By interweaving in his account of the massacre pictorial and auditory imagery, the homilist effects a sense of vivid sensory perception. The intensity of the scene is conveyed by 'seeing' in the painting the quasi-temporal unfolding of the massacre, while at the same time 'hearing' through an *ēthopoiïa* the comfortless mothers' lamentation.

Overall, Philagathos' account of the massacre stands apart from other Late Antique and Byzantine representations of this New Testament episode by its extension. For he gave a twofold account of the slaughter. After a detailed initial account, the homilist restated the story in his *ekphrasis* of the painting. At this point one may ask the following question: what meaning should be given to Philagathos' propensity for depicting suffering and loss? Why did the homilist insist on visualizing scenes of extreme cruelty, disfigurement, and suffering?[55] One possible answer is that he perceived the account to have a salvific effect on the audience. This is in tune with the Christian ascetic mindset, for which suffering and illness are avenues of salvation.[56] But by cherishing vivid imagery Philagathos upholds a traditional mode of articulating Christian identity performed through visuality. For *ekphrasis* played a vital role in preserving the memory of Christian suffering.[57] Its *logoi* subverted the pagan spectacular culture by creating 'an anti-theatre able to compete in evocative effectiveness with the profane performance, but under an opposing banner: a kind of spiritual theatre consisting only of words'.[58]

The second extensive treatment of loss and bereavement surfaces in the sermon 'On the Raising of the Son of the Widow of Nain'. The sermon is the peak of Philagathos' propensity for emotional evocation. It encloses descriptions

---

χέστεροι· 'As a result, I ought not to have given birth to start with, rather than giving birth to tears. Those deprived are more unfortunate than those not having given birth' (trans. Kennedy (2003) 116).

[53] Eur. *Alc*. 880–2.

[54] The rhetorical school exercises trained students to compose character sketches by imitating Classical figures; see e.g. Kennedy (2003) 116–17.

[55] Such gruesome details of the massacre are often recorded in Christian exegesis; for Romanos Melodos see Barkhuizen (2007).

[56] See on this Crislip (2013).

[57] See also Castelli (2005), who convincingly argued that the Christian accounts of martyrdom reframed the logic of Roman spectale by performing 'a sort of Christian counter-spectacle' in which the problem of the gaze remained central.

[58] Lugaresi (2017) 126.

260   *Mircea Graţian Duluş*

of a wide range of emotions, from excessive displays of sorrow to astonishment and great happiness.[59] The sermon was performed at the Monastery of Christ Saviour (San Salvatore) in Messina shortly after the death of its first cantor.[60] As he begins his sermon in front of the monastic congregation of the monastery, the homilist describes his pain while looking at the empty seat of his departed friend:

ἄλλην ὑπόθεσιν ὡρμημένος προοίμιον τοῦ λόγου ποιήσασθαι, ἐξετράπην πρὸς ἄλλο τὸν νοῦν, ὦ θεοσύλλεκτε θίασε. ἐπιβαλὼν γὰρ τὸν ὀφθαλμὸν πρὸς τὸν εὐώνυμον τῆς ἐκ-κλησίας χορὸν καὶ κενὸν ἑωρακὼς τὸν τόπον τοῦ ἀδελφοῦ ἡμῶν, ὃν πρὸ μικροῦ τὸ τοῦ θανάτου δρέπανον ἐξεθέρισε, ἰλιγγίασα δακρύων ὑποπλησθείς. εἰμὶ γὰρ οὐκ ἀνδρεῖος ἀνταγωνίσασθαι πρὸς τὴν διὰ θανάτου τῶν φίλων διάζευξιν, ἀλλ᾽ ἀτεχνῶς ἀφιλόσοφος. καὶ ἐλέγχει με αὐτίκα καταρρέον τὸ δάκρυον, καὶ ἀναστρέφεται τὰ σπλάγχνα τῇ μνή-μῃ καὶ ἡ καρδία σπαράσσεται, λογιζομένου τῆς ζωῆς ἡμῶν τὸ ὠκύμορον. (*Hom.* 6.1 ed. Rossi-Taibbi (1969) 37)

Although I had been eager to make another argument as introduction to my speech, my mind is turned to another thing, O company gathered by God. For when I cast my eye to the left choir of the church and I saw empty the place of our brother, whom the sickle of death cut out a little time before, I lost my mind, having been filled with tears. For I am not strong to struggle against the pain at the parting of friends taken away by death, but truly uninstructed (ἀτεχνῶς ἀφιλόσοφος). And now the streaming of tears betrays me, and my inward parts are shaken by the memory [of the person] and my heart is torn apart when I think about the shortness of our life.

The sermon exhibits an ecphrastic perspective on the events leading to the resurrection of the widow's son. Philagathos' acknowledgement that he was un-able to maintain his composure in the face of the horror of death corresponds to an ecphrastic stategy that aims to lead the audience to share the speaker's state of mind.[61] In this sense, Quintilian, the first-century teacher of rhetoric, notes that 'the main thing as regards arousing the emotions ... lies in being moved by them oneself'.[62]

Clearly, the Gospel account (Luke 7:11–15) presenting Christ approaching the city, then the sight of the dead man, the large crowd, and the short address, con-tains the kernel for a powerful evocation, which was seized by Philagathos. In this sermon, the preacher's ability to conjure the absent sight reaches virtuoso levels. The same emphasis on depicting emotions observed in the sermon on the massacre of the Holy Innocents in the twofold account of the slaughter is illus-trated again here in the compositional structure of the homily. For, in its first

---

[59] For an introduction to Byzantine funerary literature see Agapitos (2003) 5–22.

[60] This is indicated in the Italo-Greek branch of the manuscript (Ἐλέχθη ἐν τῇ μεγάλη μονῇ τοῦ Σωτῆρος Ἀκρωτηρίου ἀποθανόντος τοῦ πρωτοψάλτου – 'Pronounced at the Great Monastery of the Saviour of the Promontory <in Messina> after the death of the protopsalt'). See Rossi-Taibbi (1969) lv.

[61] For this function of *ekphrasis* see Webb (2009) 149.

[62] Quint. *Inst. Orat.* 6.2.26: 'Summa enim ... circa mouendos adfectus in hoc posita est, ut moueamur ipsi.'

10. Ekphrasis and Emotional Intensity in the Homilies of Philagathos of Cerami 261

part, it encloses a lengthy citation from Gregory of Nyssa's *De opificio hominis*,[63] which incorporates almost all of Nyssen's account of the episode of Christ raising Lazarus, while in the second part Philagathos introduces his own description, so that he is able to present the episode twice over. First, the preacher acknowledges his reliance on Nyssen's words by saying: 'for I would be mad if I were to change the words of Nyssen in this place' (μαινοίμην γὰρ εἰ τὰς ἐν τούτῳ φωνὰς τοῦ Νυσσαέως ἀμείψαιμι).[64] Philagathos' testimony alludes to the Byzantine practice of authorship centred on *mimēsis*. In this tradition, to speak with authority and persuasion meant to speak through the voice of sanctioned models.[65]

The guidelines on how to write a monody were outlined by Menander of Laodicea (late third century) and remained highly influential in Byzantine culture. The rhetor was advised to address the appearance of the fallen young and to refer to the three periods of time, the visible events, the manner of death, the gathering attending the funeral, the grief of the mother and father, the beautiful past and the bright hopes aroused by him.[66] All these elements pre-eminently feature in Gregory of Nyssa's account on the Widow of Nain, which Philagathos quoted *in extenso*. Besides this appropriation, Philagathos puts forward his own account in which he incorporates all the rhetorical tropes recommended in laments. What stands out in Philagathos' report is the florilegic perspective which is meant to emphasize the emotions felt by the characters of the sacred event. Thus, the homilist absorbed evocative imagery from Basil of Caesarea's *Homily on Psalm 44*, Gregory of Nyssa's *Sermons on the Beatitudes* and *Life of Saint Macrina*, Gregory of Nazianzos' *In Praise of the Maccabees* (Oration 15), then the *Life and Miracles of St Nicholas of Myra*, Heliodorus' *Aethiopica*, Nylus of Ancyra's *Epistle 6* and perhaps Pseudo-Nilus of Ancyra's *Narrations*.[67]

Particularly evocative is Philagathos' descriptions of the youth's slowly withering away, as Menander advised:

πῶς παραστήσω τῷ λόγῳ, ὅπως ὁ μὲν νέος τῷ σφοδρῷ πυρετῷ κατὰ βραχὺ ἐμαραίνετο, ἡ δὲ μήτηρ παρίστατο περιδεὴς καὶ ὑπότρομος, ἀπηνθρακωμένη τὰ σπλάγχνα, πεφρυγμένη τὰ χείλη, κεκαρμένη τὴν κόμην, γυμνὴ τὰ στέρνα, ἀπαρακάλυπτος τὴν κεφαλήν, ἐλπίδι καὶ φόβῳ μεριζομένη, ἐνατενίζουσα τῷ παιδὶ ἀσκαρδαμύκτῳ καὶ κεχηνότι τῷ βλέμματι, καὶ ὥσπερ αὐτῷ συνεκπνέουσα, ἕως κατὰ βραχύ, **ὑπορρεούσης αὐτῷ τῆς τοῦ σώματος ἕξεως καὶ τῶν φυσικῶν τόνων ἐλαττουμένων** καὶ δαπανωμένου τοῦ πνεύματος, ὁ παῖς ἐναπέψυξε. πῶς εἶδε; πῶς ὑπέμεινε; πῶς οὐ συναπῆλθε τῷ τελευτήσαντι; ἐμὲ γοῦν τοσοῦτον ἀνεπτέρωσεν ἡ ἀνάμνησις, ὡς δοκεῖν παρεῖναι τῷ τόπῳ καὶ ὁρᾶν τὰ τοῦ δράματος. (*Hom.* 6.8, ed. Rossi-Taibbi (1969) 40)

---

[63] *Hom.* 6.5–6, ed. Rossi-Taibbi (1969) 38–40 = Gr. Nyss. *Hom. opif.* (*PG* 44.217d–220b).

[64] *Hom.* 6.5, ed. Rossi-Taibbi (1969) 38–9.

[65] For this cultural attitude of absolute deference to authorities see Odorico (1990); on the same subject see Odorico (2011).

[66] Cf. Men. Rhet. *On Epideictic* 2.16.435.1–436.21 (ed. Russell and Wilson (1981) 202–7).

[67] For a detailed mapping of sources in this sermon see Duluş (2018) 93–107.

262 *Mircea Graţian Duluş*

How can I put into words, that as the youth withered away in a short time because of a violent fever, the mother stood fearfully by, quivering, burning up her entrails, withering her lips, tearing her hair, baring her chest, unveiling her head, *divided between hope and fear, gazing steadfastly at the unblinking child, with eyes open wide*, and almost breathing out her life along with him, *while the condition of his body gradually decayed and the strength of his body diminished*, and when the soul was spent, the child expired. How can one look upon this? How might one endure it? How would one not depart from this life together with the deceased?

The emphasis on violent gestures of bereavement, the rhetorical questions, and the vibrancy of the images portraying the suffering of the widow conjures strong emotional responses. Of course, these displays of grief reflect a literary convention in laments.[68] Philagathos' characterization of the young person lying on the bier with 'eyes open wide, unblinking' is particularly striking. In the funeral ritual the eyes and the mouth were closed immediately after death ensued.[69] This image seems to be appropriated from Pseudo-Nilus of Ancyra's *Narrations* (a Late Antique monastic tale of martyrdom), which presents a salient lexical and contextual parallelism with the homily. In Pseudo-Nilus' *Narrations* a mother is described lamenting for her dead boy while gazing 'with eyes open wide, without blinking' – ἀσκαρδαμυκτῶν κεχηνότι τῷ βλέμματι.[70] Furthermore, Philagathos, as Menander advised, describes how the youth slowly withered away. For this the homilist turned to Basil of Caesarea's interpretation of *Psalm* 44, which vividly depicted the dissolution of humankind's perishable nature.[71]

Philagathos assumes an ecphrastic perspective, as if he was present at the events themselves, for he states: 'The remembrance therefore provoked me to such a [discourse], so that I seemed to be present at the site and behold the tragic events' (ἐμὲ γοῦν τοσοῦτον ἀνεπτέρωσεν ἡ ἀνάμνησις, ὡς δοκεῖν παρεῖναι τῷ τόπῳ καὶ ὁρᾶν τὰ τοῦ δράματος).[72] As we have noted, this statement is a *topos* recalling the definition of *ekphrasis* as a 'speech placing the thing shown before the eyes' and thus turning the speaker or the audience into spectators. As Ruth Webb explained, *ekphrasis* 'is a form of language which achieves the linguistically impossible, appealing to the sense of sight, and bringing the referent into the presence of the audience'.[73] Indeed, by acknowledging his own affection Philagathos draws the congregation along to feel a consonant emotional experience.

---

[68] See on this Maguire (1977) 126–7.

[69] Cf. Alexiou (2002) 5.

[70] Ps.-Nil. *Narr.* 6.1.11–12, ed. Conca (1983).

[71] Bas. *Hom. in Ps.* (*PG* 29.388): εἰς ἀκμὴν δὲ ἐλθὼν, καὶ τὸ στάσιμον τῆς ἡλικίας ἀπολαβὼν, πάλιν ἄρχεται κατὰ μικρὸν ὑφαιρεῖν πρὸς τὸ ἔλαττον, **ὑπορρεούσης αὐτῷ λεληθότως τῆς τοῦ σώματος ἕξεως, καὶ τῶν σωματικῶν τόνων ἐλαττουμένων**, ἕως ἂν, ὑπὸ γήρως κατακαμφθεὶς, τὴν εἰς ἔσχατον δυνάμεως ὑφαίρεσιν ὑπομείνῃ.

[72] *Hom.* 6.8, ed. Rossi-Taibbi (1969) 40.

[73] Webb (2009) 52.

10. Ekphrasis and Emotional Intensity in the Homilies of Philagathos of Cerami   263

Next, the preacher emphasizes the turmoil which seized the entire city, which was clearly thought to produce emotion in his listeners:

ἡ μὲν γὰρ πόλις Ναὶν πᾶσα συνέρρει ἐπὶ τῇ ἐκκομιδῇ τοῦ νεκροῦ, καὶ θροῦς ἐγεγόνει πολὺς **καὶ θρῆνος ἦν συμμιγής, ἀνδρῶν** οἰμωγή, **γυναικῶν ὀλολυγή,** παρθένων **κω-κυτός,** παίδων κλαυθμυρισμός, **πάντα δακρύων ἀνάμεστα.** (*Hom.* 6.9, ed. Rossi-Taibbi (1969) 40)

For the entire city of Nain came together for the burial of the deceased, and a great noise arose and *the lament was confused, a wailing* of men, *the shrill shouts* of women, *a screeching* of maidens, the crying of children, *an utter welter of tears.*

Here, the template for expressing the poignancy of grief is derived from Achilles Tatius' novel. Philagathos readjusted to the context of the sermon the *ekphrasis* of the storm from Book 3. The homilist picked up the lurid representation of despair, which seized the passengers when the ship wallowed helplessly through the waves, and the whistling wind: 'It was a pandemonium of noise: roaring waves, blustering wind, the shrill shouts of women, the hoarser cries of men, the sharp commands of sailors, an utter welter of various wailings.'[74]

In the next scene Philagathos explicity connects the ecphrastic evocation with the emotional effect it sets out to arouse. The dismal spectacle draws forth the beholder's tears:

ὁ δὲ νέος ἔκειτο ἐκταθεὶς ἐπὶ τοῦ σκίμποδος ὕπτιος, οἷα πεύκη τις ὑψίκομος ἢ κυπάρισσος, ἣν ἀνέμων διέσεισε προσβολὴ καὶ αὐταῖς ῥίζαις ἐξήπλωσεν, ἐλεεινὸν θέαμα καὶ δακρύων ὑπόθεσις, ἄρτι μὲν τὸν τῆς παρειᾶς ῥόδον μεταβαλὼν εἰς ὠχρότητα, δεικνὺς δὲ καὶ οὕτω τοῦ κάλλους τὰ λείψανα. ἡ δὲ ἀθλία μήτηρ, οἷς ἐποίει καὶ οἷς ἐφθέγγετο, πλέον τῶν εἰς αὐτὴν βλεπόντων ἐπεσπᾶτο τὰ δάκρυα, **ὥσπερ τις ὄρνις πορθουμένους ὁρῶσα τοὺς νεοσσούς, ὄφεως προσερπύσαντος,** περιποτᾶται τὴν καλιὰ περιτρύζουσα καὶ ἀμύνειν οὐκ ἔχουσα. καὶ τάχα τὰ τοῦ Μιχαίου ἐν αὐτῇ ἐπεπλήρωτο· "κόψεται καὶ θρηνήσει, περιπατήσει ἀνυπόδητος καὶ γυμνή· ποιήσεται κοπετὸν ὡς δρακόντων, καὶ πένθος ὡς θυγατέρων Σειρήνων." (*Hom.* 6.9, ed. Rossi-Taibbi (1969) 40)

The youth lay stretched out on his back upon the bier, like a towering pine or a cypress tree, which the onslaught of winds has violently shaken and torn out by its roots,[75] a pitiable spectacle and occasion for tears; even though the rose of his cheek has become pale, it still reveals the remnants of a great beauty. The wretched mother, by the things she did and by the words she uttered, drew out with greater force the tears of those gazing at her, *just as a bird watching her young being devoured, when a snake creeps in to attack, twitters around her nest chirping shrilly all over* and yet *without being able to defend them.* And perhaps the words of Micah are being fulfilled in her: 'Therefore I will wail and howl, I will go stripped and naked: I will make a wailing like the dragons, and mourning as the owls' [Mic. 1:8].

---

[74] Trans. Winkler (1989) 209; Ach. Tat. 3.2.8: συμμιγὴς δὲ πάντων ἐγίνετο βοή· ἐρρόχθει τὸ κῦμα, ἐπάφλαζε τὸ πνεῦμα, **ὀλολυγμὸς γυναικῶν, ἀλαλαγμὸς ἀνδρῶν,** κελευσμὸς ναυτῶν, **πάντα θρήνων καὶ κωκυτῶν ἀνάμεστα..**

[75] For the association of death with the cypress tree see Alexiou (2002) 202.

264 *Mircea Grațian Duluș*

It is again worth noting that Philagathos picks up emotionally intense imagery from the literary tradition. The parallel with the famous bird omen in the second book of the *Iliad* (2.311–320) is immediately apparent. Recounted by Odysseus, the omen presents a snake crawling up a tree to the highest branch in order to devour eight sparrow chicks (νεοσσοί, 311) and their mother (2.310–16). As she flies around wailing for her children (ὀδυρομένη, 315), the snake grapples her wing and enfolds her in his deadly coils. According to John Heath, 'no image in Homer describes the horrible loss of animal young combined with the destruction of the parent in such graphic and sympathetic fashion'.[76] Although Philagathos may have been acquainted with this Iliadic episode, his rendition is demonstrably filtered through Heliodorus' reworking.[77] In the novel the episode is embedded in Kalasiris' lament over the loss of Charikleia and Theagenes:

"καὶ τίς ἦν ἡ πλάνη, ὦ πάτερ, ἣν λέγεις;" "παίδων" ἔφη "πρὸς λῃστῶν ἀφαιρεθεὶς καὶ τοὺς μὲν ἀδικοῦντας γινώσκων **ἐπαμῦναι δὲ οὐκ ἔχων** εἰλοῦμαι περὶ τὸν τόπον καὶ θρήνοις παραπέμπω τὸ πάθος, **ὥσπερ** οἶμαί **τις ὄρνις ὄφεως αὐτῇ τὴν καλιὰν πορθοῦντος ἐν ὀφθαλμοῖς** τε τὴν γονὴν θοινωμένου προσελθεῖν μὲν ὀκνεῖ φεύγειν δὲ οὐ φέρει, πόθος γὰρ ἐν αὐτῇ καὶ πάθος ἀνταγωνίζεται, τετριγυῖα δὲ **περιποτᾶται** τὴν πολιορκίαν εἰς ὦτα ἀνήμερα καὶ οἷς ἔλεον οὐκ ἐγνώρισεν ἡ φύσις ἀνήνυτον ἱκετηρίαν τὸν μητρῷον προσάγουσα θρῆνον."

'What do you mean when you say you were lost, Father?' 'Robbers have taken my children. I know who they are who do me wrong, but there is nothing I can do in retaliation. So I hover around this place trying to assuage my sorrow with tears. I suppose I am rather like a bird whose nest is plundered and chicks devoured by a snake before her very eyes; she dare not go near but cannot bear to fly away; her heart is torn between desire and despair, and she twitters and flutters around the sack of her home, but her pleas and the grief she feels for her young are wasted on cruel ears that nature has left unacquainted with compassion.' (Trans. Morgan (1989) 395; Heliod. *Aeth.* 2.22.4)

Now, the woeful helplessness of the young birds and the emphasis on the grief of the mother, who is defenceless to protect her children, is surely a felicitous simile for conveying the misery of the widow in the sermon.

As recommended in the rhetorical treatises, the arousal of the audience's feeling of pity is accomplished by the detailed description of the sight of the drama.[78] In this sense, Philagathos lingers on evoking the doleful procession outside the gates of the city. The climactic scene features the widow embracing the corpse of her son upon seeing the grave diggers:

ὡς δὲ τῆς πύλης τῆς πόλεως ἔξω ἐγένοντο, τοῦ πλήθους ἐφεπομένου τῇ ἐκφορᾷ, μακρόθεν ἰδοῦσα τοὺς τὸν τάφον ὀρύττοντας, **ἐμμανὴς ἐπὶ** τὸν κράβαττον **ἵεται·** καὶ περιχυθεῖσα τῷ πτώματι καὶ μέλεσι μέλη τοῖς τοῦ παιδὸς τὰ ἑαυτῆς συναρμόσασα, **ἀπρὶξ εἴχετο**

---

[76] Heath (1999) 401.

[77] On this Iliadic allusion within Heliodorus' overall engagement with the Homeric epics see Elmer 2008 (414–15).

[78] Webb (1997a) 121.

10. Ekphrasis and Emotional Intensity in the Homilies of Philagathos of Cerami   265

καὶ γοεροῖς κατησπάζετο θρήνοις· "τέκνον, λέγουσα, τοιοῦτός σοι θάλαμος ἑτοιμάζεται; τοιαύτη σοι παστὰς καλλωπίζεται;" (*Hom.* 6.12, ed. Rossi-Taibbi (1969) 41)

When they proceeded outside the gates of the city, the multitude flocked to the burial, [and] when she saw from afar those digging the grave, *maddened she threw herself upon the bier; and she embraced the corpse and bound her own limbs to the limbs of the child, and hung on him in a clinging embrace, tearfully sobbing out her mournful lamentations.* 'O my child,' she said, 'what kind of wedding is prepared for you? How is this bridal chamber adorned for you?'

This dramatic imagery owes much to Heliodorus' novel. Philagathos weaves into his *ekphrasis* the scene recounting the reaction of Charikleia as she caught sight of Theagenes after a long separation: 'as if the sight of him had stung her to a frenzy, she threw herself upon him, flung her arms around his neck, and hung in a clinging embrace, tearfully sobbing out her greeting' (ὥσπερ οἰστρηθεῖσα ὑπὸ ὄψεως ἐμμανὴς ἐπ' αὐτὸν ἵεται καὶ περιφῦσα τοῦ αὐχένος ἀπρὶξ εἴχετο καὶ ἐξήρτητο καὶ γοεροῖς τισι κατησπάζετο θρήνοις).[79]

Then, Philagathos through an *ēthopoiïa* enhances the intensity of the widow's lamentation.[80] As is known, the rhetorical exercise of *ēthopoiïa* or the imitation of the character of a person aimed at describing internal psychological states, expressed through direct speech:

"τέκνον, λέγουσα, τοιοῦτός σοι θάλαμος ἑτοιμάζεται; τοιαύτη σοι παστὰς καλλωπίζεται; ἔγρεο, φίλτατε, καὶ γηραιᾷ μητρὶ θρηνούσῃ ἐπάκουσον. ἀποτίναξον τὸν βαρὺν τοῦτον ὕπνον τὸν ἀώρως χυθέντα σοι· οἴκτειρον μητρὸς πολιὰν καὶ σπλάγχνα φρυγόμενα. οἴμοι, σιωπᾷς καὶ τὸ γλυκὺ στόμα κατέσχε σιγὴ καὶ ζόφος[81] περικέχυται ταῖς λαμπάσι τῶν ὀφθαλμῶν. καὶ σὺ μὲν ὑπὸ λίθον οἰκήσεις τραχὺν καὶ σκότος βαθύ, ἐγὼ δὲ βλέψω τὸν ἥλιον; οὐ μὲν οὖν, οὐκ ἔστιν εἰκός. πρὸς τῷ σῷ τάφῳ πήξομαι τὴν καλύβην, καὶ τάχα μοι φανήσῃ καὶ λαλοῦντος ἀκούσομαι,[82] μᾶλλον δὲ συνταφήσομαί σοι, ποθούμενε, καὶ τοῖς σοῖς νεαροῖς ὀστέοις σάρκες γηραιαὶ συντακήσονται." οὕτως ἐπετραγῴδει, μὴ ἐπισπεῦσαι συγχωροῦσα τοῦ νεκροῦ τὴν κηδείαν, ἀλλ' ἐμφορεῖσθαι τοῦ πάθους ζητοῦσα, ἐπὶ πλεῖστον αὐτῷ τοὺς ὀδυρμοὺς παρατείνουσα.[83] (*Hom.* 6.12, ed Rossi-Taibbi (1969) 41–2)

'O my child,' she said, 'what kind of wedding is prepared for you? How is this bridal chamber adorned for you? Awake, my darling, and listen your old mother lamenting. Shake off this heavy sleep, which rushed upon you in such an untimely manner! Have pity on your mother's hoary age and hear. *Alas! You are silent and that sweet mouth withheld by silence and darkness* spread upon the lamps of your eyes. You dwell beneath a rough

---

[79] Heliod. *Aeth.* 7.7.5 (trans. Morgan (1989) 494).

[80] For this rhetorical technique in Byzantine homiletics see e. g. Cunningham (2003).

[81] Heliod. *Aeth.* 2.4.3: οἴμοι, σιωπᾷς καὶ τὸ μαντικὸν ἐκεῖνο καὶ θεηγόρον στόμα σιγὴ κατέχει καὶ ζόφος τὴν πυρφόρον καὶ χάος τὴν ἐκ τῶν ἀνακτόρων κατείληφεν·

[82] Proc. Gaz. *Monodia per Antiochia* 1.16–21, ed. Amato (2014) 463: πρὸς τῷ σῷ τάφῳ πήξομαι τὴν παστάδα, καὶ τάχα μοι φανήσῃ καὶ λαλοῦντος ἀκούσομαι.

[83] Gr. Nyss. *Hom. opif.* (*PG* 44.220.23–5): τί τοίνυν πάσχειν εἰκὸς ἦν ἐπ' αὐτῇ τὴν μητέρα; οἱονεὶ πυρὶ τοῖς σπλάγχνοις ἐγκαταφλέγεσθαι, ὡς πικρῶς ἐπ' αὐτῷ παρατείνειν τὸν θρῆνον, περιπλεκομένην προκειμένῳ τῷ πτώματι, ὡς μὴ ἂν ἐπισπεῦσαι τῷ νεκρῷ τὴν κηδείαν, ἀλλ' ἐμφορεῖσθαι τοῦ πάθους, ἐπιπλεῖστον αὐτῷ τοὺς ὀδυρμοὺς παρατείνουσαν·

266 *Mircea Grațian Duluș*

stone and deep darkness, and shall I see the sun? But no, this is not just. *On your grave I shall fix a hut, and perhaps you would come forth to me, and I shall hear you talking,* or rather I shall bury myself with you, my darling, and aged flesh will be consumed along with your youthful bones.' In this manner she bitterly lamented, not *hastening to accede to the funeral of the deceased, but seeking to have her fill of suffering, the wailing was stretched out by her to the greatest extent.*

As can be observed, the insertion of literary snippets and passages filled with pathos and emotion is a constant Philagathean practice. For the widow's speech, Philagathos draws on Heliodorus' novel, precisely on Theagenes' bewailing the death of Charikleia, and on Procopius of Gaza's lost *Monody for Antioch*. The citation from Gregory of Nyssa deserves to be highlighted, for it offered Philagathos a model and a justification for his exploration of grief.[84] Through the voice of Gregory, Philagathos acknowledges the tremendous power of grief and offers his congregation a paradigm for relinquishing their anguish.

Overall, the biblical story offered a typological model through which the community confronted its loss.[85] Philagathos' ecphrastic evocation was effective, for he immediately adds: 'But now since I behold your eyes imbued with tears out of compassion and since the intensity of my voice faded out in the remembrance of the events, after having banished away the eyes' tears let us move towards the most graceful meaning of the story' (ἀλλ' ἐπείπερ ὁρῶ τοὺς ὑμῶν ὀφθαλμοὺς ἐκ συμπαθείας διανοίας τεγγομένους τοῖς δάκρυσι, κἀμοὶ δὲ τῇ μνήμῃ τῆς φωνῆς ὁ τόνος ἐκκόπτεται, φέρε τὰ δάκρυα τῶν ὀφθαλμῶν ἀπομάξαντες ἐπὶ τὸ τῆς ἱστορίας μετέλθωμεν χαριέστατον).[86] The statement serves as a point of transition that marks the end of his ecphrastic intensification of sorrow and the beginning of his attempt to bring solace and genuine hope to his mournful congregation. This division of the sermon bespeaks the imprint of the Christian lamentation tradition, particularly of Gregory of Nyssa's funeral orations. Hans Boersma eloquently described this pattern emerging from Gregory of Nyssa's orations as a twofold process. First, Gregory acknowledges the overwhelming power of grief and even encourages his congregation to grieve, assuming 'that once their mourning has exhausted itself, they will be open to the hope that the gospel offers. Gregory wants the passions to be depleted so that the message of hope can then be properly heard by the reasoning faculty.'[87]

As a parallel, Philagathos presents a similar emotional trajectory. For, in the second part of the sermon, the homilist affectionately portrays how Christ alleviated the widow's grief and led her mind to the comforts of faith:

---

[84] For Gregory of Nyssa's engagement with grief and loss see e.g. Warren Smith (2001) and Boersma (2014).

[85] For the early Byzantine representation of grief articulated through biblical portraits see Ashbrook Harvey (2017b).

[86] *Hom.* 6.13, ed. Rossi-Taibbi (1969) 42.

[87] Boersma (2014) 57.

10. Ekphrasis and Emotional Intensity in the Homilies of Philagathos of Cerami   267

καὶ ἰδὼν τὴν χήραν οὕτως ἡμίγυμνον, αἵματι φυρωμένην καὶ δάκρυσιν, εὐσπλαγχνίσθη ὁ φύσει φιλάνθρωπος ἐκ τῆς ἐνούσης αὐτῷ περὶ τὸν ἄνθρωπον ἀγαθότητος, καὶ φωνὴν ἀφίησι τῇ γυναικὶ ὄντως θείας χάριτος ἔμπλεων· "μὴ κλαῖε". ὦ θεία φωνὴ τοσοῦτον ἄχθος λύπης κουφίσασα. εἰ γάρ τις ἕτερος μὴ κλαίειν αὐτῇ ἐπετέλλετο, ἆρα οὐκ ἂν ἀπέπτυσε τὴν νουθέτησιν καὶ ὡς ἐχθρὸν τὸν νουθετοῦντα παρηγκωνίσατο; ἀκμάζουσα γὰρ λύπη παραμυθητικῶν λόγων ἐστὶν ἀνεπίδεκτος, ὥσπερ τὰ τῶν ῥευματικῶν νοσημάτων κακοηθέστερα ἐπιξαίνεται μᾶλλον πρὶν πεπανθῆναι θεραπευόμενα. εἶπε γὰρ ἴσως δριμύ τι ἀπιδοῦσα καὶ βλοσυρόν· "ὦ τῆς ἀκαιρίας ἄνθρωπε, ὁρᾷς οἷον κάλλος ὁ θάνατος πρὸ ὥρας ἐμάρανε καὶ ὅτι ἄπειμι τῇ γῇ κατακρύψουσα τὸ ἐμὸν φῶς, τῆς ζωῆς μου τὴν ἄγκυραν. καὶ ὡς ἐπὶ μετρίῳ τινὶ πάθει φιλοσοφεῖν ἐπιτάττεις καὶ **μὴ κλαῖε** λαλεῖς· ὡς ἔοικεν, **ἐξ ἀδάμαντος ἢ σιδήρου τὰ σπλάγχνα κεχάλκευσαι**." ἀλλ᾽ οὐδὲν τοιοῦτον ἐφθέγξατο ἡ γυνή· ὁμοῦ δὲ ἤκουσε καὶ σεσίγηκε. διατί; ὅτι τοι σὺν τῷ δεσποτικῷ λόγῳ καὶ γλυκεῖά τις παραψυχὴ ἐνέσταξεν ἐν τῇ ταύτης ψυχῇ, πρὸς ἀγαθὴν ἐλπίδα τὸν νοῦν διεγείρουσα. ἔστη οὖν πρὸς τὸ μέλλον μετέωρος. ἀλλὰ τί μὴ θᾶττον ἐπάγω τὸ γλυκὺ τοῦ διηγήματος καὶ παράδοξον; (*Hom.* 6.13–15, ed. Rossi-Taibbi (1969) 42)

And seeing the widow in this manner half naked, drenched by blood and tears, He was shaken [Luke 7:13], being by nature compassionate as He unites [human nature] in Him out of His goodness towards man, and He addressed the woman with a voice full of divine grace: 'Do not weep' [Luke 7:13]. O divine voice, that you relieve such a huge burden of grief! For if another had ordained her not to cry, would she not have spurned the admonition and cast off the admonisher as if an enemy? Truly, when grief is in full bloom it does not accept words of consolation, just as when swellings when scratched before they soften and suppurate break open afresh in a more virulent manner. [14.] Perhaps looking at Him, she might have said something stern and grim: 'O senseless man, behold what beauty untimely death has withered and that I go to bury my light in the earth, the anchor of my life. And for the sake of moderate suffering you command me to remain indifferent and tell me, "Do not cry?" It seems *your heart is forged from adamant or steel*.'[88] [15.] But the woman felt nothing of the kind. As soon as she heard, 'Do not cry', she fell silent. For what reason? Because with the word of God, He instilled a sweet consolation in this soul, lifting up her mind towards good hope. For she stood exalted regarding the future. But why do I delay to add what is the sweetness of the story and what admirable [in it]?

Just like Gregory of Nyssa, Philagathos recognizes that the power of grief is often indomitable in the face of death. But after the frothing of sorrow the homilist describes the astonishing joy of restoration. Philagathos conjures the visual details of the scene and pays greatest attention to the upheavel of emotions.

The astonishement and wonder triggered by the miracle is marked by first spotlighting the gravediggers who threw their shovels down as their tears were changed into joy (εἰς χαρὰν). Then, to infuse liveliness into his exposition, Philagathos supplies the scene with internal spectators who are confounded by the miracle to the point of disbelief: 'Fear and consternation seized those gathered there, and some of them, I think among those who were more simpleminded, wiped their eyes, as if believing that they beheld these things in a dream (τοὺς συνελθόντας ᾕρει δέος καὶ ἔκπληξις, καί τινες, οἶμαι, τῶν ἁπλουστέρων

---

[88] Pindar, fr. 123.4–5.

τοὺς ὀφθαλμοὺς ἀπέματτον, ὡς ἐν ὀνείρῳ ταῦτα βλέπειν οἰόμενοι).[89] Finally, the sermon outlines the trajectory of the widow's emotional experience from sorrow and grieving (πένθος) to great happiness (ἀγαλλίασιν).

10.2. Exploring the art of seduction: Philagathos on Herodias, Salome, and Tamar

The centrality of *ekphrasis* for depicting emotions is exposed in Philagathos' sermon 'On the Beheading of St John the Baptist' (*Hom.* 35 Rossi-Taibbi). In this sermon Philagathos offered an elaborate ecphrastic account of the events leading up to St John's death. It integrates an *ekphrasis* of St. John the Baptist, of Herodias' arts of seduction, of Salome's alluring appearance, as well as a vivid portrayal of the emotions that divided Herod's soul when the prophet chastised him. Besides, the sermon includes an *ekphrasis* of Herodias' daughter's (whom Flavius Josephus identifies as Salome) lascivious dance, which has few parallels in Byzantine homiletic writing:

ἤδη δὲ τοῦ πότου ἀκμάζοντος, ὁ δειπνοκλήτωρ γενόμενος πάροινος ἄλλην παρασκευά-ζει τοῦ δείπνου τρυφήν. θυγάτριον ἦν τῇ Ἡρωδιάδι ἐκ τῶν τοῦ Φιλίππου νομίμων κη-δευμάτων τεχθέν, **ἀστεῖον μὲν καὶ τὴν ὄψιν οὐκ ἄωρον, ἄλλως δὲ ἰταμὸν** καὶ προπετὲς καὶ ἀναίσχυντον, καὶ ὡς ἀληθῶς τῆς ἀσπίδος μητρὸς ἀπεικόνισμα. ταύτην **κοσμήσασα** ἡ μοιχαλὶς μήτηρ **ἁβρότερον** καὶ νυμφικῶς περιστείλασα, πρὸς τοὺς εὐωχουμένους ὀρ-χησομένην ἐξέπεμψεν. ἡ δέ, ὡς ἐν μέσῳ γένοιτο τῶν δαιτυμόνων, **πρὸς τῷ μὴ αἰσχυνθῆ-ναι κορικῶς ἀποξύσασα τῶν προσώπων πᾶσαν αἰδῶ**, ὥσπερ κορυβαντιῶσα ἐβάκχευε, σοβοῦσα τὴν κόμην, ἀσέμνως λυγιζομένη, ἀνατείνουσα τὴν ὠλένην, παραγυμνοῦσα τὰ στέρνα, θάτερον τοῖν ποδοῖν ἀναστέλλουσα, τῇ ταχείᾳ τοῦ σώματος συστροφῇ παρα-γυμνουμένη, καὶ τάχα τι καὶ τῶν ἀπορρήτων ὑποδεικνύουσα, ἀναιδεῖ τε προσώπῳ τοὺς τῶν ὁρώντων ὀφθαλμοὺς εἰς ἑαυτὴν ἐπιστρέφουσα, καὶ σχήμασι παντοδαποῖς ἔμπληκτα ποιοῦσα τῶν θεατῶν τὰ φρονήματα. (*Hom.* 35.8, ed. Rossi-Taibbi (1969) 242)

Then, when the drinking was in full swing, the inebriated host procures another delicacy for the feast. Herodias had a little daughter born from her legitimate marriage with Philip, *charming and not unappealing in appearance but far too forward*, reckless and shameless, truly the representation of her viperish mother. The adulterous mother *embellishing her daughter rather gracefully* and dressing her up in wedding clothes sent her out dancing in front of those *sumptuously feasting*. And she stepped out among the guests *instead of being ashamed as a girl should be, and wiping off all modesty from her countenance* danced as if filled with Corybantic frenzy, wildly moving her hair, twisting herself indecently, lifting up her elbows, disclosing her breast, raising up one of her two feet, laying herself bare by the swift bending of her body, and perhaps revealing something of those parts which are unfit to be mentioned; with unabashed expression she turned the eyes of the beholders towards herself, and by gestures of every kind she stupefied the spectators' minds.

---

[89] *Hom.* 6.16, ed. Rossi-Taibbi (1969) 43.

10. Ekphrasis and Emotional Intensity in the Homilies of Philagathos of Cerami   269

In the Gospels, Salome is merely reported as having 'pleased' Herod.[90] Yet Philagathos gives an amplified description of Salome's performance, which, the homilist explained, stupified the spectators' minds (ἔμπληκτα τὰ φρονήματα) and provoked Herod's ominous oath. First, we should note that the description of Herodias' daughter incorporates vignettes on impudence plucked from Alciphron's letters, Procopius of Gaza's *Description of the Image* and Heliodorus' *Aethiopica*.[91] Since the allusions to the latter play a more prominent role, an overview of them is here needed. Thus, the characterization of Herodias' daughter as ἀστεῖον μὲν καὶ τὴν ὄψιν οὐκ ἄωρον, ἄλλως δὲ ἰταμὸν ('charming and not unappealing in appearance but far too forward') seems to recall three contexts from Heliodorus' novel. First, it imitates Arsake's portrayal of Theagenes and Charikleia in Heliod. *Aeth.* 7.10.4 as γύναιόν τι ξενικὸν οὐκ ἄωρον μὲν ἄλλως δὲ ἰταμὸν. Second, the description of Herodias' daughter as 'not unappealing in appearance' (τὴν ὄψιν οὐκ ἄωρον) mirrors the caracterization of the slavegirl, Thisbe.[92] Just like Demainete, Thisbe illustrates in the novel the negative image of *erōs*, lustful desire and seduction.[93] Third, the adjective ἀστεῖον recalls the characterization of Demainete in Heliodorus' novel as γύναιον ἀστεῖον μὲν ἀλλ' ἀρχέκακον (Heliod. *Aeth.* 1.9.1). It may thus be concluded that the homilist simultaneously recalled several literary contexts about impudence for depicting Herodias' daughter.

A close analogy to Philagathos' *ekphrasis* of Herodias' daughter's dance in terms of vividness is Basil of Seleucia's sermon *In Herodiadem*.[94] In Basil's sermon, Salome's performance is pictured as 'a true image of her mother's wantonness with her shameless glance, her twisting body, pouring out her soul (ῥεούσῃ ψυχῇ), raising her hands in the air, lifting up her feet she celebrated her own unseemliness with her semi-naked gestures'.[95] From an ethical point of view, these descriptions reiterate the unanimous condemnation of 'lascivious dancing' in patristic literature.[96] But they also bear witness to the fundamental correlation between vision and desire in Christian religious experience. According to the Gospels, vision is capable of arousing lust by a mere look.[97] In addition,

---

[90] Matt. 14:6 and Mark 6:22.

[91] The preacher borrows from Charope's reply to her daughter Glaucippe in Alciphr. *Ep.* 1.12.1: δέον αἰσχύνεσθαι κορικῶς, ἀπέξυσαι τὴν αἰδῶ τοῦ προσώπου. For the imprint of Procopius' *ekphrasis* on Philagathos' sermon see Duluş (2020) 485–6; for an overview on Philagathos' overall engagement with the ancient novel see Duluş (2021).

[92] Heliod. *Aeth.* 1.11.3: Θίσβη παιδισκάριον ἦν αὐτῇ ψάλλειν τε πρὸς κιθάραν ἐπιστάμενον καὶ τὴν ὄψιν οὐκ ἄωρον. 'She had a slave girl by the name of Thisbe, who could sing to the harp and not unappealing looking' (trans. Morgan (1989) 361).

[93] See for this Morgan (1989) 108–9; Dowden (1996) 267–85.

[94] Bas. Sel. *Oratio XVIII in Herodiadem* (*PG* 85.226D–236C).

[95] Trans. Webb (1997b) 136 (slightly modified).

[96] See for this Puchner (2017) 68–74.

[97] Matt. 5:27–8: 'You have heard that it was said to those of old, "You shall not commit

270 *Mircea Grațian Duluș*

the Church Fathers continually emphasized that even the sensuous images once represented by means of words are able to inflame the imagination and to foment wantoness just like sight itself.[98] For instance, in a homily on John's Gospel, John Chrysostom describes the emotional effects triggered by the mere enunciation of the name of the dancer:

> For as soon as the tongue has uttered the name of the dancer, immediately the soul has figured to itself his looks, his hair, his delicate clothing, and the man himself who is more effeminate than all ... Were you not somewhat affected when I gave this description? But do not be ashamed, nor blush, for the very necessity of nature requires this, and so disposes the soul in the state in which it is placed by the power of the reported things. But, if I speak about them myself, you feel a certain degree of emotion at the hearing (ἐπάθετέ τι πρὸς τὴν ἀκρόασιν), while standing in the church, and at a distance from these things, consider what most likely they feel, who actually sit in the theatre itself, enjoying great licence, being outside this venerable and frightful assembly, who both see and hear those things with much shamelessness.[99]

Thus, this authoritative voice openly recognizes that theatrical imagery is able to stir the imagination and to unleash potentially sinful reactions. But, the appeal to provocative imagery and its significance is closely related, as Lugaresi pointed out, to the spatial dimension within which such evocations take place.[100] From Chrysostom and presumably Philagathos' point of view, the uncontaminated vantage point of the liturgical chronotope is able to turn such sensuous imagery into an antidote to sin. The vividness of such evocations would enable the audience to stare at their own unseemliness and to reflect on the reasons for their moral corruption. It may be instructive to note that Philagathos employs similar theatrical imagery for depicting the demonic snares and the workings of desire in the homily 'On the Prodigal Son':

τῷ μὲν γὰρ σωφρονοῦντι, καὶ λογισμῷ γενναίῳ τῶν παθῶν κατευμεγεθοῦντι, ῥαγδαῖον ἐπιφέρουσι πόλεμον, πανταχόθεν περιιστῶντες τὰ θέλγητρα, μέλιτι τὸ δηλητήριον παραρτύοντες, καὶ χρυσαῖς φιάλαις κιρνῶντες τὸν θάνατον. ἐπειδὰν δὲ εἴσω παγίδος συσχῶσι τὸ θήραμα, καὶ τὴν ψυχὴν ἐν ἕξει τοῦ κακοῦ δουλαγωγήσωσι, τότε δὴ τότε δυσχερῆ ποιοῦσι τῶν κακῶν, τὴν ἀπόλαυσιν, ὡς ἂν διακαῶς ἔχοιεν πρὸς αὐτὰς, τῷ τῆς ἐπιθυμίας οἴστρῳ νυττόμενοι· κατὰ τὰς δεινὰς τῶν ἑταιρίδων, αἳ μέχρι τότε τοὺς νέους ἀγρεύουσι νεύμασι, καὶ λυγίσμασι καὶ καγχάσμασι, καὶ συνθήμασιν, ἕως ἂν ἅψωσι τῆς

---

adultery." But I say to you that whoever looks at a woman to lust for her has already committed adultery with her in his heart.'

[98] See for this Webb (1997b) 131–4.

[99] Chrys. *Hom. in Jn.* 18.4 (*PG* 59.119–20).

[100] In relation to Chrysostom, Lugaresi (2017) 144 explained that the appeal to sensuous imagery is meant 'to make spectacles an object of the word, i.e., to rhetoricize them, in a manner of speaking, and to conduct this operation under conditions of relative safety, i.e., no longer in a chronotope of theatricality, on the contrary in an antithetical one, which is the church'. For the importance of liturgy in assessing the language of desire employed by Christian homilists see Ashbrook Harvey (2009).

10. Ekphrasis and Emotional Intensity in the Homilies of Philagathos of Cerami   271

ἐπιθυμίας τὸ πῦρ. εἶτα μεταβάλλουσαι ἀκκίζονται, τοὺς ἐραστὰς ὑποκνίζουσαι. (*Hom.* 17, *PG* 132.384D–385A)

Against the chaste, the noble-minded, and the one prevailing over the passions they [i.e. the demons] wage a raging war, placing all around allurements, seasoning the poison with honey and pouring death in golden bowls. After they have captured the prey in the snare and have made even the soul enslaved to the habit of evil, then, only then, they render arduous the gratification procured from evils, for when men searingly strive for pleasures they are pierced by the madness of desire not unlike those dreadful enticements of courtesans, which only hunt after the young with gestures, with sinuous movements of the body, with laughter and compliances till they ignite the fire of desire; and then changing themselves, they affect indifference, exciting the lovers.

In a way that parallels his account of Salome's 'lascivious dancing', Philagathos' rather theoretical exposition of pleasure and desire is confined to visuality. By incorporating several novelistic allusions, the homilist turns his listeners into spectators of a courtesan who enacts in front of them the process of seduction itself.[101]

Philagathos addressed the same subject in his homily on the story of Tamar (Gen. 38). In the Book of Genesis Tamar pretended to be a prostitute to trick her father-in-law, Judah, into fathering a child with her. After his first two sons died, Judah was reluctant to give her his last and youngest son Shelah as the law of 'levirate marriage' prescribed. When Tamar realized this, she contrived a scheme in order to bear Judah a child and thus to continue the messianic line. Philagathos' interest in this story is undoubtedly prompted by the inclusion of Tamar in the genealogy of Christ recorded in the Gospel of Matthew (Matt. 1:1–17). The Greek exegetic tradition considered her inclusion as a token for Christ's assumption of sinful human nature and the adoption of Gentiles into God's salvific design.[102] Within this tradition that condemns Tamar for sexual depravity, Philagathos' account distinguishes itself by the emphasis on the theatrical and visual dimension of her arts of seduction:

ἐτεθνήκει Σαυὰ ἡ τοῦ Ἰούδα γυνή. καιρὸς ἦν τῆς τῶν προβάτων κουρᾶς, ἔδει δὲ τὸν Ἰού-δαν δι' ἐκείνης τῆς κώμης διελθεῖν ἐς τὰ ποίμνια. τοῦτο ἡ Θάμαρ ὡς ᾔσθετο, ἀπεδύσατο τὰ πενθικά, ἐνεδύσατο τὰ νυμφικά, ἐπλάσατο ἤθη ἑταιρικά, μετήμειψεν ἑαυτὴν εἰς τὰ πορνικά, προσέθηκε κάλλη κομμωτικὰ καί, περί τι χαμαιτυπεῖον ἀγχοῦ τῆς λεωφόρου καθίσασα καὶ ὁδοιδοκοῦσα, ἐκαραδόκει τοῦ πενθεροῦ τὴν διέλευσιν. ἤδη δὲ κλινούσης ἡμέρας, ἵετο Ἰούδας καὶ μετ' αὐτοῦ οἰκέτης ποιμήν (Εἴρας ὁ ποιμὴν ἐκαλεῖτο). ὡς οὖν ἡ Θάμαρ εἶδεν αὐτοὺς πλησιάσαντας, τοῦ δράματος ἄρχεται, τοσαῦτα πλαττομένη, ὅσα αἱ δι' ἀκολασίας ὑπερβολὴν **ἀποξύσασαι τῶν προσώπων** πᾶσαν αἰδώ, νεύμασι καὶ καγ-χάσμασι καὶ λυγίσμασι τὸν κηδεστὴν εἰς πόθον ὑφάπτουσα· ἀνακαλύπτουσα μὲν ἐπ'

---

[101] For the novelistic allusions implied in this passage see Duluş (2021) 128–9.

[102] This interpretation was not universal; the Syriac exegetic tradition, as Ashbrook Harvey (2009) 33 pointed out, considered Tamar's behaviour 'admirable and even glorious since it led to the reality of Christ's incarnation through Mary'.

272   Mircea Graţian Duluş

ὀλίγον τὸ θέριστρον, ὅσον τὸ κάλλος ἐνδείξασθαι, εἶτα κρύπτουσα τὴν μορφήν· ὁμοῦ τε
λανθάνουσα τίς εἴη, καὶ ὑποκνίζουσα τῶν ὁρώντων τὸν ἔρωτα. (*Hom.* 22.8–9, ed. Rossi-
Taibbi (1969) 144)

Sava the wife of Judah died [Gen. 38:12]; it was the time of shearing the sheep, and it was
fated that Judah had to pass through her village [i. e. Tamar's] to reach the flocks. As Tamar
apprehended this, she stripped off her mournful clothing, dressed in bridal attire, put on
her trappings, then reclining before a brothel near the road and lying there in wait she
watched eagerly her father-in-law passing by. Well, when the day was already declining
Judah came accompanied by his shepherd servant (the shepherd was called Eiras). Therefore, as Tamar saw them drawing near, she begins her play, contriving such things as could
wipe off through the excess of wantonness all shame from their faces, inflaming her father-
in-law towards desire, by gestures, by laughter, by sinuous movements; uncovering for a
moment her veil, just so much as to reveal her beauty, and yet keeping hidden her bodily
shape, both at once hiding who she was and yet arousing the lust of the beholders.

Philagathos amplifies a story rich in dramatic detail by recalling literary contexts
of love, desire, and seduction. Thus, to depict Tamar's feigned wantonness (ἀποξύσασαι τῶν προσώπων πᾶσαν αἰδῶ) Philagathos draws on Alciphron's fictional
character, Glaucippe (*Ep.* 1.12.1: δέον αἰσχύνεσθαι κορικῶς, ἀπέξυσαι τὴν αἰδῶ
τοῦ προσώπου). As we noted above, by this snippet Philagathos also depicted
Salome's licentious dance.[103] Then, the reference to Tamar's means of inflaming
Judah's desire seems modelled on the Heliodorean episode of Thisbe seducing
Knemon 'with looks, gestures, and various other tokens' (βλέμμασι νεύμασι συνθήμασιν).[104] Along these lines, Philagathos continues:

ἁλίσκεται οὖν τῷ κάλλει ὁ βέλτιστος Ἰούδας καί, νομίσας χαμαιτυπεῖον εἶναι καὶ μίαν
τῶν τὰς ἡδονὰς πωλουσῶν, χρῆται τῷ οἰκέτῃ προαγωγῷ, καὶ μηνύει ὑποδέξασθαι τοῦτον ἐν τῇ νυκτί, ἐπαγγειλάμενος αὐτῇ πέμψειν ἔριφον· ἡ δὲ ἁρπάζει τὸ ῥῆμα περιχαρῶς,
ἀκκισαμένη μηδέν. ἐπεὶ δὲ νὺξ αὐτοὺς ἐκοινώσατο, καὶ εἴσω δικτύων ἡ Θάμαρ εἶχε τὸ
θήραμα, κολακείαις αὐτὸν ὑποχαυνώσασα καὶ αὖθις **τοῖς ἀκκισμοῖς ἀναφλέξασα**, ἐνέ-
χυρα ζητεῖ τῆς τοῦ ἐρίφου ἀποστολῆς τὴν ῥάβδον καὶ τὸν ὁρμίσκον καὶ τὸν δακτύλιον. ὁ
δὲ τοῖς ἱμέροις αὐτῆς γεγονὼς ὅλως ἐξίτηλος, ἀποζώννυται τὴν ζώνην εὐθύς, τὴν ῥάβδον
γοργῶς, δίδωσι πρὸς τούτοις καὶ τὸν δακτύλιον. (*Hom.* 22.9, ed. Rossi-Taibbi (1969) 144)

Thereupon the illustrious Judah is seized by her beauty and, thinking that she was one
of those who offer pleasures for sale, he uses his servant as a pander, and makes known
through him that he would welcome her at night, promising that he would send her a
young goat. She grasps his offer with alacrity, while affecting no indifference. When the
night brought them together and Tamar had the prey in the net, while she made him puff
up with conceit through her flatteries and then again inflamed him through her prudish
indifference, she requested as pledge for sending her the promised goat, the staff, the cord,
and the signet [Gen. 38:18]. Judah, having become entirely ravished by the yearning after
her, forthwith takes off the cord, quickly throws off the staff, gives even the signet for these
[allurements].

---

[103] *Hom.* 35.8, ed. Rossi-Taibbi (1969) 242.
[104] Heliod. *Aeth.* 1.11.3.

10. Ekphrasis and Emotional Intensity in the Homilies of Philagathos of Cerami   273

Furthermore, the reference to the simulated indifference of the courtesans to inflame their lovers has a thematic parallel in Heliodorus' novel. It is reminiscent of Isias from Chemnis' arts of seduction enacted by feigning indifference to her husband's attentions (cf. Heliod. *Aeth.* 6.4.1: ἀκκισμοὺς ἀναπλάσαι κατ' ἐμοῦ). By such imagery Philagathos led his listeners to witness the biblical story as if through sight. But since Tamar is included in the messianic line, the exposition is subservient to a theological meaning that makes vivid the abyss of sin and the reason for which Christ descended into the world, to take upon himself the guilt and shame of sin (2 Cor. 5:21). Furthermore, as Susan Ashbrook Harvey pointed out, by being enacted during the liturgy such dramatic narratives opened up a social space wherein emotions could be explored and confronted 'while yet being relegated to a "safe distance" – the mythic realm of the biblical past'.[105]

10.3. Describing conflicting and interacting emotional states

The prominence of emotions in Philagathos' *Homilies* is perhaps most apparent in his fondness for depicting conflicting emotional states. Although present in manifold ways in Greek literature, notably in tragedy and the lyric poetry of Sappho and Anacreon, the conflict of emotions takes on an increased prominence with the Greek novel, as Massimo Fusillo convincingly argued.[106] In fact, Philagathos' leaning towards describing emotional shifts and conflicting emotions simultaneously experienced by the characters of the sacred story precisely relies on the ancient novel.

A good example for this is the description of Herod's emotions in *Hom.* 35. Philagathos reports that Herod's soul was divided by 'shame, love, and anger' when St John rebuked him over his unlawful liaison with her brother's wife, Herodias:

Hom. 35.5, ed. Rossi-Taibbi (1969) 240–1	Ach. Tat. 5.24.3
ὁρῶν γὰρ Ἡρώδης ῥαγδαίως τὸν προφήτην τοῖς ἐλέγχοις τοῦτον μαστίζοντα, ἀνυποστόλῳ τε θάρσει τὸ δυσῶδες τῆς φαύλης πράξεως ἐκπομπεύοντα, **πολλοῖς ἐμερίζετο τὴν ψυχήν, αἰσχύνῃ, ἔρωτι καὶ θυμῷ· ᾐσχύνετο** τοῦ κήρυκος τὸ ἀξίωμα, **ὠργίζετο** ἐλεγχόμενος, ὁ **ἔρως τὴν ὀργὴν** ἐπὶ πλέον ἀνέφλεγε, καὶ τέλος ἡ φιληδονία νικᾷ τὸ ἀνδράποδον.	ὡς δὲ προϊοῦσα καὶ τοῖς λοιποῖς τῶν γεγραμμένων ἐνέτυχε, πᾶσαν μαθοῦσα τὴν ἀλήθειαν ἐμεμέριστο πολλοῖς ἅμα τὴν ψυχήν, αἰδοῖ καὶ ὀργῇ καὶ ἔρωτι καὶ ζηλοτυπίᾳ. ᾐσχύνετο τὸν ἄνδρα, ὠργίζετο τοῖς γράμμασιν, ὁ ἔρως ἐμάραινε τὴν ὀργήν, ἐξῆπτε τὸν ἔρωτα ἡ ζηλοτυπία, καὶ τέλος ἐκράτησεν ὁ ἔρως.

---

[105] Ashbrook Harvey (2017b) 202.
[106] Fusillo (1999); on this theme see also Montiglio (2010); Cummings (2017); Smith (2021); for the philosophical, and particularly Platonic underpinnings of psychological conflict in the ancient novel see Repath (2007); this theme is often exploited in *ekphraseis* of works of art; see on this Maguire (1974) 132–4; (1977) 166–71.

274   *Mircea Grațian Duluș*

Hom. 35.5, ed. Rossi-Taibbi (1969) 240–1	Ach. Tat. 5.24.3
For Herod seeing the prophet violently flogging him with rebukes and parading the filthiness of his foul deeds openly and fearlessly, *had his soul torn apart by many conflicting emotions – shame, love, and anger; he was ashamed* before the herald's standing, *enraged* when chastised; *for love greatly inflamed the anger* and the lust for pleasure prevails at last over the one who has been taken captive.	But when she read on, the rest of the letter told her the whole story, and she felt her soul torn apart by conflicting emotions: shame, anger, love, and jealousy – she was ashamed to face her husband; the letter made her angry, but her anger withered away before her love, which was in turn inflamed by her jealousy. In the end her love prevailed. (Trans. Morgan (1989) 246)

Philagathos' depiction was manifestly inspired by Achilles Tatius' novel.[107] The preacher accommodates into the sermon the description of emotions which seized Melite when she read Kleitophon's letter to the formerly supposed-dead Leukippe, shortly after the unforeseen return of her husband Thersander. Philagathos, therefore, avails himself of this moment when Melite discovers the truth that both Thersander and Leukippe are alive for grasping the psychological complexity beneath Herod's turmoil.

Philagathos applies a similar imaginative re-enactment of emotions surounding the episode of the Transfiguration of the Lord. The event narrated in Luke (9:27–36) is part of a larger section devoted to the identity of Jesus. Immediately after the Lord was recognized by Peter as 'the Christ, the Son of the Living God' (Matt. 16:16; cf. Luke 9:20), he announced to them the approaching Passion and death. Then the Lord took Peter, James, and John 'up to a high mountain' – by tradition Mount Tabor – and was 'transfigured before them' (Luke 9:28). Overwhelmed by that miraculous experience, Peter said 'Master, it is good for us to be here' (Luke 9:33). Philagathos goes on recreate these condensed emotional shifts for his listeners, saying:

καὶ ἀκούων ταῦτα, **πολλοῖς ἐμερίζετο τὴν ψυχήν· λύπῃ, θυμῷ, ἀπορίᾳ** ἐπυρπολεῖτο τὰ σπλάγχνα, τοῦ Διδασκάλου μέλλων χωρίζεσθαι, ἔζεε τῷ θυμῷ, ἐννοῶν τῶν Ἰουδαίων τὸ τόλμημα, ἰλιγγία περὶ αὐτοῦ διαπορῶν· "πότερον ἀπολίπω μόνον παθεῖν τὸν καθηγητήν, ἢ καὶ αὐτὸς χωρήσω μετ' αὐτοῦ πρὸς τὸν θάνατον;" **τούτοις τοῖς πάθεσι μεριζόμενος**, ἀπαρακαλύπτως μὲν ἐπισχεῖν τὸν Κύριον καὶ κωλῦσαι τῆς ὁρμῆς οὐκ ἐτόλμησεν (ἅπαξ γὰρ τοῦτο τολμήσας, εἰλήφει τῆς προπετείας τὰ ἐπιτίμια ἀκούσας. "ὕπαγε ὀπίσω μου, Σατανᾶ")· τὴν δὲ τοῦ ὄρους ἡσυχίαν ἰδὼν καὶ τοὺς προφήτας δορυφοροῦντας καὶ τὴν νεφέλην ἐπισκιάσασαν, ἐνενόησεν ὡς, εἰ ἐνταῦθα μένοιμεν, τὰς ἐπιβουλὰς τῶν Ἰουδαίων ἐκκλίναιμεν. (*Hom.* 31.30–1, ed. Rossi-Taibbi (1969) 217)

Upon hearing these things, Peter had his soul torn apart by many conflicting emotions; he was inwardly consumed by grief, by anger, by perplexity, that he was going to be separated from the Teacher; he was boiling with anger when considering the daring of the Jews, astonished about Him and pondering what to do: 'Shall I leave the teacher to suffer

---

[107] On this novelistic passage see Cummings (2017) 323–4; Repath (2007) 75–6.

10. Ekphrasis and Emotional Intensity in the Homilies of Philagathos of Cerami   275

alone or shall I go with Him to death?' Divided by such conflicting emotions, he did not dare openly to obstruct the Lord and restrain his desire (for he attempted this just once, as he had received the penalties for his rashness when he heard 'Get thee behind me, Satan' [Matt. 16:23]; for as he beheld the stillness of the mount and the prophets attending by and the cloud overshadowing them, he thought that if we stay here, we will avoid the snares of the Jews.

Thus, the vivid description of Peter's feelings who had his soul 'torn apart by many conflicting emotions' and the explanation given to each emotion, grief at the separation from the Teacher, anger at the Jews, perplexity at Christ's announcement of his Passion is structurally modelled on the same episode from *Leukippe et Kleitophon*, which Philagathos used for portraying Herod's emotions.

We can also trace the theme of emotional conflict in the sermon for the Fifth Eothinon (Luke 24:13–35) which portrays the emotions which seized the Apostles as they were walking to the village of Emmaus:[108]

'Abide with us, for it is towards evening, and the day is far spent' [Luke 24:29]. He wittingly accepted, intending to lead them up to a purer knowledge. In that place the table and the unleavened bread was set before; for it was the third day after the leaven was lifted on the Feast of the Passover. Then, as he knew, he revealed himself in the breaking of bread, and having been seen anew he concealed [himself] and a new emotion seized the disciples, divided between joy and tears. Whom they sought, they had, and whom they had they did not recognize, and whom they found they lost. For having seen him, they rejoiced, for having been bereft of him they wailed, they grieved for not having known him, they repented for what they had carelessly said. In all likelihood they blamed their own sluggishness, because the grace of his teaching had not led them to the knowledge [of him]. 'Did not our heart burn within us while He talked with us on the road, and while He opened the Scriptures to us?' [Luke 24:32].

This is one of the passages from Philagathos' *Homilies* which prompted Henry Maguire to note the opposite approaches to the dramatization of the Gospel story in the Greek rhetorical tradition versus the Latin liturgical plays.[109] Maguire noted that the emphasis on the emotional shifts experienced by the two disciples conveyed in the sermon is 'at far greater depth than the Latin plays'.[110] Indeed, the most arresting aspect in Philagathos' artful description are the anti-

---

[108] *Hom.* 27 (PG 132.656B–C): "μεῖνον μεθ' ἡμῶν, ὅτι πρὸς ἑσπέραν ἐστὶν καὶ κέκλικεν ἤδη ἡ ἡμέρα." ὁ δὲ τὴν ἧτταν ἑκὼν ἀπεδέχετο, μέλλων ἐμβιβάζειν αὐτοὺς εἰς ἀκραιφνεστέραν ἐπίγνωσιν. ἐκεῖ τράπεζα παρατίθεται, καὶ ἄρτος ἄζυμος· τρίτη γὰρ ἦν τῆς ἐν τῷ Πάσχα τῆς ζύμης ἄρσεως. καὶ τότε, ὡς ἔγνω ἐν τῇ κλάσει τοῦ ἄρτου φανεροῖ ἑαυτὸν, καὶ φανεὶς αὖθις ἀπεκρύπτετο, καὶ πάθος τοὺς μαθητὰς κατειλήφει καινὸν, χαρᾷ καὶ δάκρυσι μεριζόμενον. ὃν γὰρ ἐζήτουν, εἶχον, καὶ ὃν εἶχον ἠγνόουν, καὶ ὃν εὗρον ἀπώλεσαν· ἔχαιρον ἰδόντες, ἔκλαιον στερηθέντες, ἠνιῶντο μὴ γνωρίσαντες, μεταμελοῦντο ἐφ' οἷς προπετῶς διελέγοντο. τὴν σφῶν νωθείαν ὡς εἰκὸς κατεμέμφοντο, ὅτι μηδὲ τῆς διδασκαλίας ἡ χάρις πρὸς ἐπίγνωσιν αὐτοὺς ἐπηγάγετο. "οὐχὶ ἡ καρδία ἡμῶν καιομένη ἦν [ἐν ἡμῖν] ὡς ἐλάλει ἡμῖν ἐν τῇ ὁδῷ, ὡς διήνοιγεν ἡμῖν τὰς γραφάς;"

[109] Maguire (2007b) 229–30.

[110] Maguire (2007b) 229.

276   *Mircea Graţian Duluş*

thetical assertions: 'Whom they sought, they had, and whom they had they did not recognize, and whom they found they lost.' What has escaped previous commentators is that the template for these formulations, although not literally cited by the homilist, is the final sequence of Heliodorus' novel, which features Charikleia, and Theagenes about to be offered as a human sacrifice. At that moment, Sisimithres and Persinna reveal the truth of Charikleia's royal descent, which brings a complete reversal of fortunes:

> By these events [the divine intervention] brought into the most perfect harmony the greatest opposites, joy and sorrow blended together; tears mingled with laughter; the most hideous horror transformed into celebration, those who wept at once laughed; those who grieved at once rejoiced; *they found those whom they had not sought and lost those whom they thought to have found*; and finally the expected human slaughter was transformed into a sacrifice free of all stain.[111]

We must underline here Philagathos' competence in conveying astonishment and bewilderment by relying on the novel. For this was the poetic aim of the *topos* of conflicting emotions according to Fusillo.[112]

The same theme is explored in the homily 'For the Eighth Resurrection Gospel Reading', our final example. The assigned Gospel lection is John 20:11–18, which describes the day of the Lord's Resurrection, when Mary Magdalene went to the tomb.[113] The pericope presents Mary Magdalene standing outside the tomb weeping, her dialogue with the angels, and finally her conversation with Christ, whom she did not recognize at first. Philagathos relied on the novel for describing the emotional shifts undergone by Mary Magdalene as her desolation was changed into joy as she recognized Jesus. In short, this is a context apt to recall the novel. In the words of Philagathos:

> So Mary, astounded by the shape of the angels and struck down with amazement, was standing quivering in front of that incredible sight. The angels in fact, so as to deliver her from her agony, as though seeking curiously to know the cause of her tears, led her by their appearance and voice to believe that the Lord was stolen. 'Woman, why are you weeping? [John 20:15] Why do you suppose that someone carried out a theft, while he was guarded by such sentinels? You see the angels sitting one at the head and the other at the feet [John 20:12] and do you still consider the treasure to have been plundered? Moreover, who [could be] this reckless corpse-robber or unashamed grave-burglar that would steal the king while he was guarded by angelical array?' But the Magdalene was so much without sense that nothing from the present happenings was she able to figure out. Be-

---

[111] Trans. Morgan (1989) 586, slightly modified; Heliod. *Aeth*. 10.38.4: ὑφ᾽ ἧς καὶ τὰ ἐναντιώτατα πρὸς συμφωνίαν ἡρμόζετο, χαρᾶς καὶ λύπης συμπεπλεγμένων, γέλωτι **δακρύων κεραννυμένων**, τῶν στυγνοτάτων εἰς ἑορτὴν μεταβαλλομένων, γελώντων ἅμα τῶν κλαιόντων καὶ χαιρόντων τῶν θρηνούντων, **εὑρισκόντων οὓς μὴ ἐζήτουν καὶ ἀπολλύντων οὓς εὑρηκέναι ἐδόκουν**, καὶ τέλος τῶν προσδοκηθέντων **φόνων εἰς εὐαγεῖς θυσίας μεταβαλλομένων**. Furthermore, the wording from this passage (i. e. δακρύων κεραννυμένων) has a close parallel in Philagathos' *Hom*. 35.7, ed. Rossi-Taibbi (1969) 24: δάκρυσι κεραννύμενοι.

[112] Fusillo (1999) 65.

[113] For the Byzantine cycle of the Eothina Gospel pericopes see Janeras (1986) 55–69.

10. Ekphrasis and Emotional Intensity in the Homilies of Philagathos of Cerami   277

sides, she held fast to her conceit and said: 'They have taken away my Lord, and I do not know where they have laid Him' [John 20:13]. What she said to Peter and to John before, she now spoke to the angels. But, oh admirable perseverance! Oh praiseworthy curiosity! [For] her beloved did not overlook her; the one searched after did not let her be plunged into disbelief, but beholding the fervent desire all at once he was standing there. 'For having turned around she saw Jesus standing there, and did not know that it was Jesus' [John 20:14]. But what was that which persuaded her to abandon the conversation with the angels and to turn back? From the countenance and the posture of the angels, she felt that someone shadowed her back. For when the Lord appeared, the angels leapt up forthwith from their sitting, indicating by their shifting of sight the one standing by. So then, Mary when she saw this turned her gaze. She did not recognize who was the one who asked her: 'Woman, why are you weeping? Whom are you seeking?' [John 20:15].[114]

It is spectacular to observe that the description of Mary Magdalene's bewilderment at the tomb is modelled after Heliodorus' novel. For the homiletic scene is reminiscent of the astonishment which seized the Ethiopian queen Persinna when Charikleia produced the crucial recognition token of her true royal identity. Charikleia disclosed the band (ταινία) on which her mother Persinna wrote 'in royal Ethiopian script'[115] to explain the motives which led her to expose Charikleia. The novelistic episode to which we turn is illustrative of Philagathos' reading of the novel:

καὶ ἅμα λέγουσα τὴν συνεκτεθεῖσαν ἑαυτῇ ταινίαν ὑπὸ τῇ γαστρὶ φέρουσα προὔφερέ τε καὶ ἀνειλήσασα τῇ Περσίννῃ προσεκόμιζεν. ἡ δὲ ἐπειδὴ τὸ πρῶτον εἶδεν ἀχανής τε καὶ **αὖος ἐγεγόνει** καὶ χρόνον ἐπὶ πλεῖστον τὰ ἐγγεγραμμένα τῇ ταινίᾳ καὶ τὴν κόρην αὖθις ἐν μέρει περιεσκόπει· **τρόμῳ** τε καὶ παλμῷ συνείχετο καὶ ἱδρῶτι διερρεῖτο, χαίρουσα μὲν ἐφ᾽ οἷς εὕρισκεν ἀμηχανοῦσα δὲ πρὸς τὸ τῶν παρ᾽ ἐλπίδας ἄπιστον, δεδοικυῖα δὲ τὴν ἐξ Ὑδάσπου τῶν φανερουμένων ὑποψίαν τε καὶ ἀπιστίαν ἢ καὶ ὀργήν, ἂν οὕτω τύχῃ, καὶ τιμωρίαν. ὥστε καὶ τὸν Ὑδάσπην ἐνορῶντα εἰς τὸ **θάμβος** καὶ τὴν συνέχουσαν **ἀγωνίαν** "ὦ γύναι" εἰπεῖν "τί ταῦτα; ἢ τί **πέπονθας** πρὸς τὴν δεικνυμένην γραφήν;" ἡ δὲ "ὦ βασι-

---
[114] *Hom.* 34 (PG 132.673C–676B): ἡ μὲν οὖν Μαρία, ἐκπλαγεῖσα τῇ μορφῇ τῶν ἀγγέλων **καὶ αὖος γεγονυῖα**, τῷ παραδόξῳ θεάματι **ὑπότρομος** ἵστατο· οἱ δὲ ἄγγελοι, λύοντες αὐτὴν **τῆς ἀγωνίας**, φιλοπευστοῦσι δῆθεν τὴν τῶν δακρύων αἰτίαν μαθεῖν, διὰ τῆς ἐμφανείας καὶ τῆς φωνῆς ἀπάγοντες αὐτὴν τοῦ οἴεσθαι κλαπῆναι τὸν Κύριον. "γύναι, τί κλαίεις;" τί νομίζεις κλοπὴν ὑποστῆναι τὸν ὑπὸ τοιούτων φυλάκων φρουρούμενον; ὁρᾷς ἀγγέλους ἐφεζομένους, ἕνα πρὸς τῇ κεφαλῇ, καὶ ἕνα πρὸς τοῖς ποσὶ, καὶ συληθῆναι νομίζεις τὸν θησαυρόν; καὶ τίς οὗτος νεκροσύλης ἀναιδὴς, ἢ τυμβωρύχος θρασὺς, ὡς βασιλέα κλέψαι παρατάξει ἀγγελικῇ φυλαττόμενον; ἀλλ᾽ ἦν ἄρα ἡ Μαγδαληνὴ τοσοῦτον ἠλίθιος, ὡς μηδέν τι τῶν ὄντων ἐκ τούτου καταστοχάσασθαι· ἔτι γὰρ τῆς αὐτῆς ὑπολήψεως εἴχετο, καὶ φησι· "ἦραν τὸν κύριόν μου, καὶ οὐκ οἶδα ποῦ ἔθηκαν αὐτόν." ὁ πρότερον εἶπε Πέτρῳ καὶ Ἰωάννῃ, τοῦτο καὶ τοῖς ἀγγέλοις λαλεῖ. ἀλλ᾽, ὦ τῆς καλῆς καρτερίας! ὦ τῆς ἐπαινετῆς πολυπραγμοσύνης! οὐ παρεῖδεν αὐτὴν ὁ ποθούμενος· οὐκ ἀφῆκε τῇ ἀπιστίᾳ βυθίζεσθαι ὁ ζητούμενος· ἀλλὰ τὸν ζέοντα πόθον ἰδὼν, αὐτομάτως ἐφίσταται. "στραφεῖσα γὰρ ὀπίσω καὶ θεωρεῖ τὸν Ἰησοῦν ἑστῶτα καὶ οὐκ ᾔδει ὅτι Ἰησοῦς ἐστιν." τί δὲ τὸ πεῖσαν αὐτὴν καταλεῖψαι τὴν μετ᾽ ἀγγέλων διάλεξιν, καὶ ὑποστρέψαι εἰς τὰ ὀπίσω; ἐκ τῆς τῶν ἀγγέλων ὄψεως καὶ τοῦ σχήματος ᾔσθετό τινος ἐπισκιάσαντος αὐτῇ τὸ μετάφρενον. ἐπιστάντος γὰρ τοῦ Κυρίου, οἱ ἄγγελοι εὐθὺς **τῆς καθέδρας ἀνέθορον**, τῇ μεταβολῇ τῆς ὄψεως τὸν ἐπιστάντα δηλώσαντες. ὃ δὴ Μαρία θεασαμένη τὴν ὄψιν ὑπέστρεψεν· οὐ μὴν ἐπέγνω, τίς ἦν ὁ πυθόμενος· "γύναι, τί κλαίεις; τίνα ζητεῖς;"
[115] Heliod. *Aeth.* 4.8.1.

λεῦ" εἶπε "καὶ δέσποτα καὶ ἄνερ, ἄλλο μὲν οὐδὲν ἂν εἴποιμι πλέον, λαβὼν δὲ ἀναγίνωσκε· διδάσκαλός σοι πάντων ἡ ταινία γενήσεται."

And with these words she brought forth the band that her mother had laid out beside her and that she wore around her waist, unfolded it, and presented it to Persinna. The instant she saw it, the queen was struck down with amazement, and some time passed while she scrutinized first the writing on the band and then the girl; she was seized with a fit of palpitations, perspiration streamed from every pore, as joy at the return of what had been lost combined with perplexity at this incredible and unlooked-for turn of events, and with fear that Hydaspes might be suspicious and incredulous at these revelations, possibly even angry and vengeful; so that even Hydaspes became aware of his wife's anguished astonishment and said: 'What is this woman? Why are you so affected by the appearance of this document?' 'Sire,' she answered, 'lord, husband. I have nothing more to say. Take the band and read it. It will tell you all there is to tell.' (Trans. Morgan (1989) 567; Heliod. *Aeth.* 10.13.1–3)

This epiphanic moment of great emotional intensity when Persinna recognized the band she embroidered is alluded to in the sermon. Philagathos' appropriation is certified by the lexical choices and the contextual parallelism with the novel. Mary Magdalene 'struck down with amazement (αὖος γεγονυῖα) was standing quivering (ὑπότρομος) in front of that incredible sight' literally corresponds to Persinna's reaction (αὖος ἐγεγόνει καὶ … τρόμῳ τε καὶ παλμῷ συνείχετο) at the sight of the band. But the parallelism does not stop here. The question Jesus asked, 'Woman, why are you weeping?' ("γύναι, τί κλαίεις;") comes close to the question Hydaspes asked, 'What is this woman?' ("ὦ γύναι" εἰπεῖν "τί ταῦτα;"). Undoubtedly, Philagathos perceived a similarity between the two scenes and triggered his association. Besides, the band in the novel is the teacher (διδάσκαλος) through which the identity and the fullness of Charikleia's divinely ordained destiny are comprehended (cf. Heliod. *Aeth.* 4.9.1). This aspect equally invited a correspondence with the 'band' of Scripture which disclosed the identity of Jesus Christ as the Son of God and eternal divine wisdom. It is also tempting to see in the formulation 'the angels leapt up forthwith from their sitting' (οἱ ἄγγελοι εὐθὺς τῆς καθέδρας ἀνέθορον) another parallel with the opening scene of the novel, which presents the bandits 'thunderstruck with wonder and terror' when Charikleia, whom they thought to be a goddess, leapt up from the rock (Heliod. *Aeth.* 1.2.5: καὶ ἅμα λέγουσα ἡ μὲν τῆς πέτρας ἀνέθορεν). The thematic parallelism with Christ's apparition is worth noting, for the appearance of Charikleia is assimilated to the epiphany of a deity.[116]

The intense realism and liveliness conjured by the novelistic *topos* of conflicting emotions offered Philagathos a powerful instrument to present the dramatic tension embedded in the Gospels.

---

[116] See on this Edsall (2002) 121–3; the possible Heliodorean allusion acquires further credit when considering that the same novelistic episode is involved in *Hom.* 6.12, ed. Rossi-Taibbi (1969) 41–2.

Conclusion

The management of emotions figures prominently in Philagathos' understanding of Christ's redemptive activity. The focus of this analysis was placed on the exercise of *ekphrasis* and the associated concept of *enargeia*. This is Philagathos' chief rhetorical strategy throughout the sermons for promoting the emotional involvement of the faithful in the biblical event reactualized through vivid discourse. By exciting a similar zeal in the listener's mind, biblical occurrences become 'history' in the proper (Christian) sense in so far as they actualize the redemptive movement of creation towards eschatological fulfilment. Pre-eminently, Philagathos' ecphrastic elaborations bring to light the refinement and the extent of his learning. The array of rhetorical models which inform these compositions is dazzling, precluding a clear distinction between Classical and Christian terminology of emotions. The distinct Christian perspective is embedded in the interplay between *ekphrasis*, iconic doctrine, and Christian anthropology which takes the emotions as prerequisite for deification.

11

Tragic Emotions?

The *Christos Paschon*

Margaret Mullett

Introduction

In 1983 W. B. Stanford was very coy about explaining why there was no study of the emotions in Greek tragedy: 'perhaps because emotions are so subjective and so hard to define or perhaps because scholars prefer to discuss what goes on in the mind rather than what involves the heart. Or perhaps because the spectre of the affective fallacy warns them off.'[1] Today we are in a different position. We can agree on the issue of definition: 'everyone knows perfectly well what emotion is but no one can define it'.[2] We can deal with the affective fallacy,[3] and forty years later the neuroscience looks very different, so that everyone wants to know what goes on in the brain, whatever about mind and heart.[4] And it is clear that 'tragedy essentially arouses powerful emotions'.[5]

In this chapter I want to look at emotions in the only surviving Byzantine tragedy, or, more accurately, trilogy of tragedies, the *Christos Paschon*. Strangely enough, I have not found a previous attempt at analysis – strangely for two reasons: first because studies of emotions in Greek tragedy[6] predate the recent interest in Classical[7] or Byzantine[8] emotions (and might perhaps have discour-

---

[1] Stanford (1983) 1.

[2] Fehr and Russell (1984); cf. Cairns (2017a): '"Emotion" is a contested term with no agreed definition and a particular history of its own.'

[3] Indeed by the time of Stanford's publication both reader-response approaches and *Rezeptionstheorie* had responded to Wimsatt and Beardsley's affective fallacy: Fish (1970) and Iser (1976). See also narratological developments with Phelan (1996) and Rabinowitz (1998).

[4] Again the birth of cognitive neuroscience can be traced to the late 1970s, before Stanford's book, see Passingham (2016) 2–3, though positron emission tomography (PET) was an innovation of the 1980s and functional magnetic brain imaging (fMRI) in the 1990s. For the connection to emotion see Colombetti (2014).

[5] Taplin and Billings (2010).

[6] As well as Stanford see Konstan (1991); Belfiore (1992); Lada (1993), (1996).

[7] A full list would now be a long one. High points are Cairns (1993), followed by a series of individual works, collaborative projects, and edited volumes: Braund and Gill (1997), which includes Webb (1997a); Konstan (2006b) as the peak of a series of studies of individual emotions

282   *Margaret Mullett*

aged any recent rush of work on tragic emotions).[9] Second because it was well known in the Byzantine eleventh and twelfth centuries that the master of emotion in poetry was Euripides[10] – and the *Paschon* is an Euripidean cento, 'a dramatic hypothesis in the manner of Euripides' (Titulus; Hypothesis line 3, ed. Tuilier (1969) 125). Euripides was probably more popular in Byzantium than at any time before the past fifty years. For Anna Komnene, he was *the* tragedian as Homer was *the* poet, and it is Euripides that Michael Psellos chooses to compare (oddly to us) with George of Pisidia.[11] His plays, or at least those of 'the selection',[12] were key to the school syllabus.[13]

11.1. The text

The *Christos Paschon* comprises 30 + 2602 (+ possibly 8) iambic lines in twenty-five manuscripts from the middle of the thirteenth century on.[14] It is regarded as anonymous, though the manuscript tradition ascribes it to Gregory of Nazianzos.[15] Herbert Hunger and Wolfram Hörandner convincingly resited it in the twelfth century,[16] and authorship has been variously ascribed to Con-

---

(pity (in 2001), anger, envy/spite/jealousy, shame, *praotēs* (all 2003), *storgē* and *chara* (in 2010)) as well as many general studies, and Chaniotis (2012d) followed by further outcomes of projects in Oxford and Princeton.

[8] Maguire (1977) was first into the field. The first study of a single emotion, *phthonos*, was Hinterberger (2013a) and the first overview Hinterberger (2010). The first collected view is again by Hinterberger (2006a), now followed by Constantinou and Meyer (2019) and Mullett and Ashbrook Harvey (forthcoming). Drpić (2016) 296–331 pursued *pothos* (desire, yearning) in inscriptions on objects, responding to Mullett (1999) on letters, Binning (2018) examines wrath and fear in Pantokrator images and inscriptions, and Gerstel (2019) has looked at awe in monumental inscriptions in the painted churches of late Byzantine villages. See also Burrus (2008) on shame.

[9] But see Konstan (1991), Ruffell (2008), Munteanu (2012), and Cairns (2021).

[10] See the rather puzzling *sunkrisis* of Psellos, *On Euripides and George of Pisidia*, ed. Dyck (1986), and comment in Agapitos (1998a) 138. See now on this and on the popularity issue Marciniak (2022).

[11] The popularity of Euripides had increased over the Roman period; see Cribiore (2001a) 244: 'Euripides was by far the most popular of the tragedians in the Greco-Roman world.' As for the present day, see (in the context of a revival of interest in Greek tragedy since the 1970s) Hall (2004) 5: 'In the first half of 1995 more Euripides was performed in London than any other playwright, including Shakespeare.'

[12] On 'the selection' of ten plays as distinct from the nine 'alphabetical' plays, the 'triad', or indeed the theatrical repertory of around thirty plays proposed by Pertusi, see Dodds (1944) xlvii–lii; Turyn (1957); Zuntz (1965).

[13] Zuntz (1965) 255. With Cribiore (2001b) we begin to understand how this might have worked in the schoolroom rather than on the manuscript page.

[14] Edited by Brambs (1885); Tuilier (1969).

[15] All twenty-five manuscripts attribute the work to Gregory: Tuilier (1969) 75–116.

[16] Since Hunger (1968a), the text has been redated to the twelfth century. Tuilier in his edition (1969) opted for the authorship of Gregory of Nazianzos, and in 1984 the twelfth-century dating was queried on palaeographical grounds by Alfonso Garzya, but rigorous work enabled

11. *Tragic Emotions?*

stantine Manasses, John Tzetzes, and Theodore Prodromos.[17] It is a tissue of lines and half-lines from four plays of Euripides: *Medea, Hippolytus, Rhesus,* and *Bacchae,* plus rather fewer from *Hecuba, Orestes, Phoenissae,* and *Troades;* there are some quotations from other plays, mainly *Prometheus Bound* and *Agamemnon.*[18] But the vast majority of the quoted text (1,078 of 1,304 lines) is drawn from the four plays, and almost a majority of the whole text (1,293 of 2,531 lines, omitting hypothesis and prayers) is spoken by the Theotokos, its protagonist. Another characteristic of the text is that like other twelfth-century pieces it is generically complex. As well as its dramatic form and its texture of cento it is also an extended Virgin's lament, or at least contains eleven different laments and two described laments: the proportion of lament is about one-third of the whole.[19] As well as further generic issues (is it a tragedy? a cento? a Virgin's lament?), there is also the possibility that it is not unitary. The French editor Tuilier has suggested that the text is a trilogy, one play for each day of the weekend, to comprise first the Crucifixion, second the Burial, and third the Resurrection, and I adopt this view here.[20]

It has been studied by Byzantinists trying to prove the existence or otherwise of a Byzantine drama,[21] by Margaret Alexiou on the Virgin's lament,[22] recently by Elizabeth Bolman on the Galaktotrophousa,[23] and technical aspects of its nature as lament or cento have been considered,[24] but wider issues of reception,[25] iden-

---

Wolfram Hörandner to respond in 1988 using lexical arguments; these were contested by Garzya in 1989, but supported by Follieri in 1991/2. Though the contextual argument for the twelfth century may seem overwhelmingly persuasive, revisiting the issue is probably a desideratum.

[17] Respectively Horna (1929); Dübner (1846) iv–v; Hilberg (1886).

[18] Identified with varying levels of persuasiveness in both Brambs (1885) and Tuilier (1969); also quoted are *Alcestis, Andromache, Helen, Iphigenia at Aulis* and *Iphigenia among the Taurians, Phoenissae,* and Lycophron's *Alexandra,* as well as biblical and apocryphal texts. It is by no means a complete cento. The choice of texts is interesting in that it is not based on the Byzantine triad – though this neither proves nor disproves a Late Byzantine date for the triad. For a different selection of Euripidean plays, *Troades* and *Alcestis,* in another twelfth-century text see Duluş in this volume.

[19] Commentators have suggested that the work is suffused with lament, e.g. Brown (2012) 153. See Mullett (forthcoming a).

[20] Support for this suggestion comes from the fact that the first (Crucifixion) section ends at lines 1130–3 with the end of the *Medea,* a marker of closure, and also that the three main characters change in each part: in the first the Theotokos, Christ, and John the Theologian; in the second the Theotokos, John the Theologian, and Joseph of Arimathea; in the third, the Theotokos, Mary Magdalen, and Christ.

[21] For a judicious treatment see Marciniak (2004) 89–95; See also Kazhdan and Epstein (1985) 140–1.

[22] Alexiou (1975) 122–4.

[23] Elizabeth Bolman quoted it at the Theotokos conference, Oxford, August, 2006, in a paper which will form part of a book on the Middle and Late Byzantine Galaktotrophousa.

[24] For lament see Bernier-Farella (2015) and Mullett (forthcoming a); for cento Bryant Davies (2017) and Mullett (forthcoming b).

[25] Mullett (2021).

284 *Margaret Mullett*

tity,[26] performance,[27] and purpose[28] have not, or only very recently, been considered.[29] Classicists have been more concerned to use the text to understand the manuscript tradition of *Bacchae* than to see it as a work in its own right, but that also looks to have changed recently.[30]

In this chapter I want to look at emotions (represented in the text and designed to be evoked by the text) both in terms of emotional trajectory and also in terms of the emotion words used. Finally I want to ask what is added to the mix by the underlying cento, and what is added by the potential of performance, so looking at emotions over time: in fifth-century Athens as well as twelfth-century Byzantium.

If we look for the structure of the text, the hypothesis which sets out the action is unhelpful. It describes at the heart of the piece a mourning, groaning Theotokos and a Christ who suffers ἀδίκως. The playwright's *prosōpa* are the mother, the disciple John the Theologian, and the *korai*, the women of Galilee, who form the chorus. Already we see that the familiar title is misleading (the Theotokos is in each play the protagonist), and we shall soon see that the hypothesis is a very inadequate description of the text.[31] Each of the three plays (if we accept Tuilier's suggestion of a trilogy) has its own three actors plus messengers and chorus; each has its own emotional atmosphere and trajectory. First to emotions in the text.

11.2 Emotional trajectories

11.2.1. The Crucifixion

The first play, the Crucifixion play from lines 1 to 1133, deals with the Passion proper, from the Last Supper to the death on the cross. Its structure takes us from an introduction by the Theotokos and chorus, setting the scene through an account of the Fall, through three messenger speeches and three responsive laments to (at 727) the sudden address by Christ to the Theotokos, and their conversation, to his death, framed by two more laments, and finally other reactions by John the Theologian (including a lament) and the chorus, ending with yet another lament. The Virgin stands strongly, impassively, throughout, receiving blow after blow, and the emotions fly around her. The tension throughout is between her fear of the crowd and the enemies of Christ, and her desire to be as close as possible to her son in his suffering. She curses, wails, rejoices,

---

[26] Mullett (2021).
[27] Mullett (forthcoming c).
[28] Pollmann (1997).
[29] An exception is Dostálová (1982).
[30] Alexopoulou (2013); Bryant Davies (2017).
[31] Brambs (1885) 25–7; Tuilier (1969) 124–6.

11. Tragic Emotions?

stands strong in her confidence, shows *storgē*,[32] caring affection,[33] towards her son, anger towards Judas and other tormentors of her son, and hope for the future. The texture is shot through with lament: seven of the eleven laments of the trilogy are in this play, but even elsewhere the emotional mix is powerful, and the Theotokos' overall *apatheia* (emotionlessness) means that the chorus takes much of the emotional burden.[34]

The play opens with a long (ninety lines) speech by the Theotokos, giving the context for the events which unfold. She discusses the daring and lust of Eve for the fruit and offers a counterfactual reading: if the serpent had not appeared in Paradise, seduced Eve, and she had not persuaded Adam to eat, there would have been no Fall and so no Incarnation, no Passion. The Theotokos would not have been a mother forever virgin, would not have heard her son called to justice, would not have seen him covered with injuries, or felt the cruel flame which consumed her, stirred her spirit, pierced her heart as Symeon predicted at the Presentation. But in the words (*Med.* 168) of the Nurse in *Medea*, all now is enmity, closest ties are diseased (1.37). Eve did precipitate the Fall and weeps accordingly, feels disgust for the world, and takes no joy in it. At 1.61 Mary turns to herself, in the words of Hecuba (*Hec.* 736), and lays out the story of the Annunciation, where she voices Andromache on Astyanax (1.77, *Tro.* 747 ff.); she felt such joy, an *erōs* (passionate love)[35] which could not be contained, despite the threat of the sword in her innards. She announces that she wanted to set out in the night to see the passion of her son, but that the women had persuaded her to wait for day.

At 1.91, after this powerful speech, the exchanges between chorus and Theotokos (1.91–128) are matter-of-fact, as they establish action in the city, a night crowd following a force armed with swords and torches, and the approach of the first messenger (1.129–266). The Theotokos is not sure what the threat is, the women try to prepare her, though she does not establish the extent of their fear, and the messenger is unwilling to reveal the worst, which is that Jesus has been betrayed by a friend: fearing and daring and friendship are spelt out as the

---

[32] Greek emotion terms will be discussed below in the section on emotional discourse.

[33] See Lewis (1960) 39–68, who translates it as 'affection', and Tsironi (forthcoming).

[34] To begin with, the chorus ramps up fear and tension, seeming always to know more than the Theotokos at 91–2, 95–7, speaking the first αἲ αἲ αἲ αἲ of the play at 100, insisting that her son is dying, that she will not see him again in life, twisting the knife in the wound and inciting the Virgin's curse by telling her about Judas. By the second lament the chorus takes part, urging the Theotokos to advance to a point of vantage, emphasizing fear, trembling, and tears. At 560–7 and 598–604 they acclaim the Virgin, recalling the Annunciation, and at 611–38 the two half-choruses insist she is mourning, weeping non-stop; even the third messenger has a fallen face and eyes full of tears; Peter at 809–11 howls, groans, moans. They support the Theotokos, observing but not remarking, as she, at 837–53, realizes that Christ is dead, and then the two half-choruses insist that she is different from other women and can bear the grief, as she launches into lament 6. They insist on the horror of the scene but promise that God will have his revenge.

[35] Lewis (1960) 111–40 does not translate, though he regards it as sexual love, 'being in love'.

286 *Margaret Mullett*

messenger tells of the Last Supper, the Garden, the Betrayal, and the flight of the disciples in a speech heavy with foreboding and fear. From 1.267 the Theotokos responds with the Virgin's curse (1.267–357, the first lament of the trilogy) towards Judas, a standard part of the lament of the Virgin in Christian tradition. She shows anger, disgust at his shamelessness, and daring, and relapses into tears as the chorus join her (1.358–61), to be challenged by her for weeping too soon.

At 1.361–2 they announce the next messenger, who baldly reports the condemnation to death of Jesus by scribes and elders (1.376–418). He confesses admiration for Jesus, and reports close observation of his manner (silent, sad), and the failure of Pilate to prevent his death in the face of the crowd. He ends with Orestes, 'He will die today' (1.418, *Or.* 948). At 1.419 the Virgin launches into the second lament (1.419–77), which is really a second curse in both anger and grief against the *phthonos* (envy)[36] of the Jews, recognizing the long-dreaded prophecy and reacting emotionally. The chorus (1.437–8) offers a mild rebuke (a feature of the Virgin's lament tradition) that she is talking so much when her son is dying; she ripostes (1.439–40) with anger and shock that they would fail to show confidence in the saviour of the world. They tell her (this time, 1.441–3) to step forward and see if he is living or dead. She weeps and laments (1.444–77), and they decide to follow at a distance as fear rises palpably among them but she is determined to follow Christ to the tomb, and beyond, for in the midst of fear she expresses hope in the Resurrection with the joy to come. The chorus (1.560–7, 1.598–604) offers *chairetismoi* as she recalls the Annunciation, and anxiety in the tempest speech of Hecuba in the *Troades* (1.558–9, *Tro.* 475–7). As she sees a third messenger, he begins (at 1.639) in similar stately mode, begging her not to turn from him in disgust.

The messenger claims to be a disciple, to be as affected as she is, and takes at least sixteen lines to get to the point, which is the story (1.657–81) of what happened once the crowd and Christ had left the city: the crucifixion, the beating, the vinegar and hyssop. Her response is a third lament (1.682–726) as she begs the women to come with her, denying fear to join him. And though the chorus demurs, ramping up the sense of a hostile crowd, it is clear that from 1.690 to 1.727 they move to the foot of the cross, voicing lament as they go. Fear and grief are in counterpoint here.

At 1.727 the first play reaches its climax as Christ speaks, and the third actor, John the Theologian, is revealed, and is persuaded to behold his mother as she him, her son. Christ asks why she weeps, as she launches into her fourth lament (1.738–808), addressed to Christ, a very watery one, with the *Medea* line 'women are born for tears' (*Med.* 928) used for the third time at 1.748. Christ promises

---

[36] Fundamentally Hinterberger (2013a); Konstan (2006d) 111–28 connects it with indignation and distinguishes it from jealousy, *zēlotupia*, 219–43, and Kaster (2005) makes the connections with shame, disgust, and regret. See Sanders (2014) 33–57 on vocabulary.

11. Tragic Emotions? 287

rewards and urges confidence, and Mary claims faith and confidence, but confesses that grief wipes out confidence. She demands punishment for the crowd and forgiveness for Peter, who is announced by the chorus (1.809–11), lamenting offstage, horribly, remorsefully. Christ promises both to her, and begs her to avoid hate (revulsion), even of those who unjustly crucified him. She notes his lack of hate and anger and wonders at the scale of that rage; at 1.834–7 Christ waves her away and tells us he is leaving her.

From 1.838 the fifth lament allows us to see the Theotokos grasping, first intellectually then emotionally, the fact that he is dead, calling on her son to console her, talk to her, return to look after her in old age and bring incomparable joy to the human race. John the Theologian offers comfort at 1.932–82 (and laments himself briefly, 1.998–1007), voicing confidence and hope in the bright light of the third day. The chorus point out that she is unlike other women; how can she bear the sight of her dead son? The Theotokos takes this as a slight (smears are a part of the lament tradition) and prepares herself to weep and to wait for vengeance on the murderers. As the chorus soothe her, at 1.1071–94 she sees a soldier pierce Christ's side with a lance, and the chorus reinforce the horrific sight – φρικτόν, twice (1.1101, 1105), and creation joins in: the earth trembles, stones are ripped up, tombs open, and the soldier falls shaking to earth.

At 1.1110 the Theotokos addresses Christ in a final, seventh lament (1.1110–33), in which the *phthonos* of the deicides is recalled as she cries out in confusion: what is she to do, how will she bury him? How will she get him down from the cross? The end resolves with faith in that all will come out well as God's will against all expectation.[37]

So in this play a dense atmosphere of different emotions surrounds a Theotokos struggling not to yield herself to the grief of the seven laments which form such a high proportion of the text. At the climax with Christ on the cross, though, she weeps and mourns; she also steps into her role as intercessor, achieving punishment for the deicides and forgiveness for Peter. The play moves from the remembered joy of Annunciation and Incarnation through mounting fear, anger, and grief to a temporary confidence.

What is the audience expected to feel in this most tragedic of the three plays? Is it fear and pity for the suffering Christ, who did not, as the prologue tells us, deserve his fate? Or is it rather for the protagonist, a woman who expects to lose her son, watches him die and faces the future, mourning as Byzantines mourned for their sons every day? I tend to the latter view.

---

[37] Lines 1.1130–3 echo *Med.* 1415–18, the last lines of each play, but while *Med.* looks backwards at the action, τοιόνδ᾽ ἀπέβη τόδε πρᾶγμα ('such is the outcome of this story', 1419), *Christos Paschon* 1 looks forward to God's solution in 3, the Resurrection, imbuing ἀέλπτως, 1.1131, with a sense of hope.

288   *Margaret Mullett*

11.2.2. The Burial

This play, lines 1134 to 1905, changes the *dramatis personae*. The Theotokos carries out two important ritual acts, accompanied by John the Theologian and Joseph of Arimathea (Nikodemos is also present but is silent except in 2.1466–9). The subject matter is highly unusual, unique in Medieval drama, touched on only briefly at the end of the Crucifixion play of the Cyprus Passion cycle,[38] and could perhaps only have been written in the twelfth century, when the cycle of scenes of Passion and Resurrection were being expanded, as part of the development which Henry Maguire saw as giving a greater weight to emotion in the eleventh to thirteenth centuries.[39]

The play proceeds calmly through the aftermath of the Crucifixion, in the latter part of Friday. A conversation between John the Theologian and Joseph (2.1134–1246) sets the scene before the Theotokos enters at 2.1163 or preferably[40] 2.1247; the Deposition follows (at 2.1275–1308), the Threnos (2.1309–1444), the Entombment (2.1445–94), and the Teleutaios Aspasmos (2.1495–1601). The men depart, Joseph for exile (by 2.1810), and then the women to John's house, where they will await the day of resurrection (2.1903–5),[41] and the Theotokos delivers lament 10 (2.1818–31) at the house. A messenger arrives at 2.1863 to announce that a guard has been set on the tomb.

Unlike the non-stop action and progression of the Theotokos and chorus to the foot of the cross, and even more speedy action in the third play, this play appears more static, with minimal action at Golgotha and the tomb, a kind of television bottle episode, with the conspirators working in friendship against a background of fear. The chorus has very little to do until the Theotokos holds court again at the house.[42] The magnificent set piece Threnos and Teleutaios Aspasmos make up for any lack of action, though the only conflict is how great a part the Theotokos will take in proceedings, and the major tension comes from fear of interruption by the authorities or the mob.

At 2.1134 John the Theologian hails Joseph arriving with the answer to the Theotokos' worries at the end of the previous play. He has a tomb and permis-

---

[38] *Cyprus Passion Cycle*, ed. Mahr (1947) 199.20–206.5.

[39] Maguire (1977).

[40] This would entail Joseph at 2.1163–71 addressing an absent Theotokos, free of fear unlike the other disciples; this allows John 1223–39 to recall a mourning Theotokos and Joseph to mention her at 1241–2 as if absent; she can then enter at 1247 and greet the newcomers.

[41] When do they leave for the house? If at 2.1811, there is little time to get there before the tenth lament at 1818–31, but John the Theologian points it out to the women as they go at 1814 and tells them to stay there. So the women sleep during lament 8 and are roused 1832–62 to receive the fourth messenger at 1863.

[42] They chime in at 2.1433 after Joseph's account of Judas' hanging (but the line could be given to Joseph), are addressed towards the end of the Teleutaios Aspasmos, and again by the Theologian at 2.1810. At the house one half-chorus contrasts its sleep with the Theotokos' vigil and mourning; the other claims not to be able to sleep because of it; they are roused at 1855 and announce the fourth messenger at 1860–2. They end the play, 1903–5, with *Phoenissae* 727.

11. Tragic Emotions?

sion from Pilate, but he also wonders how to manage the deposition. There is a sense of the proprieties of mourning – Joseph weeps as much as is proper from someone not part of the family. At 2.1169 fear of the authorities and the crowd is mentioned and John counters with a long disquisition on the third day, when sadness will turn to joy and the virtuous anger of the Father will punish the murderers. He also (2.1223–39) gives an extraordinary account of a very different Theotokos from the stoic and majestic queen of the Crucifixion play, indulging in *thrēnoi* and *gooi*, throwing herself at the cross, trying to wake the corpse, and we have direct speech too (at 2.1227–30 and 2.1235–8). John's Theotokos ends with a word of confidence, asking John why he was so despairing: this speech in general plays off faith, hope, and despair. Joseph appreciates the account but advises John to keep her away from the savage and terrifying crowd, at which the Theotokos enters, praising her brave friends in the words of Medea on Aegeus (*Med.* 765). She presses them to get on with the deposition, to hurry so that she can hold her son (2.1252–7).

From 2.1258 to 1309 is the Deposition, in which the main issue is whether the Virgin will receive the body or not; the men refuse to let her, telling her to hide lest the murderers get her, that there is nothing she can do but weep and moan, but she again says, unanswerably, that she will be cowardly if she fails to weep over her dead son, wash him, embrace him, and bury him. And they comply, telling her and the chorus to hold out their arms to receive the body.

From 2.1309–1426 is the formal Threnos (lament 8), in which she speaks to the dead son, embracing him, asking how she can express her grief. She details his features and asks why he abandoned her; how will she survive? A second section ranges through the past (the Fall), the present (the Incarnation), and the future (cursing Judas and Pilate again), and returns in the third section to an address to Jesus, whom she now holds with a shroud, whom she once held in nappies. She ends with the *phthonos* of Judas and his punishment, fulfilling the shape of Greek ritual laments and the subject matter of the Virgin's lament.

As she ends at 2.1426 Joseph informs her that Judas has been found hanged, and after she expresses her gratitude, she tells Joseph and Nikodemos to take the body to the tomb, and they shuffle along with her instructions to 1488. At 2.1492 the Theotokos tells the women that Christ is buried and urges them to come and see the body. She flinches and says she cannot bear to see, they begin to move off, then she stops them and demands to say goodbye to her dead.

This (2.1505–1609), the Teleutaios Aspasmos, is the ninth lament and deals with new material: the descent into Hades, slanders against her, and then she addresses Christ again with a confident view of conquests of the future and at 1585 the expulsion of the Jews. How to groan over you? How to bewail your murder? God's *orgē* (anger),[43] the hope for a glorious future, play off her mourning and

---

[43] See Konstan (2006b) 41–76 on the relationship of *mēnis*, *cholos*, and *orgē*.

290   *Margaret Mullett*

groaning; this moment is pivotal, where grief and hope are more equal than before. She closes the section with a word to the women telling them they cannot speak the traditional chants but should glorify him with gentle laments, naming him the living King. She then urges the women to withdraw to the house of John, whom Christ gave her as a son.

A long section, 2.1620–1817, engineers the protagonists' exit from the stage, drawn between fear and friendship. The Theotokos says positively the final, very touching, word to Christ: 'I'm leaving you alone now, going to the house of the son you gave me' (2.1630–3). John the Theologian is sure that there will be eternal punishments for Judas in hell, and Joseph at 2.1700–11 echoes Cadmus in *Bacchae* (1352–6 and 1364–9) when he wonders whether he will be exiled, and John looks forward to the Resurrection. He promises Joseph a reward and assures him of Christ's triumph over death. The Theotokos urges him to go and tell men about this triumph over death, and John urges them to rejoice and not to fear, and finally joy breaks through and defeats fear. At 2.1810 John, once they have finally left, scoops up the women of Galilee and takes them to his house, where the Virgin sings a short lament, no. 10 (2.1818–31). She and the chorus alternate talk of sleeping with weeping; she determines to weep as she waits to see Christ alive again.

At 2.1860 a messenger, one of the disciples, is spotted, offering anxious news, which brings back the cloud of fear: a guard has been set on the tomb, which has been sealed. The Theotokos scorns these measures and notes that it only means that the guard will be witnesses to the Resurrection. With the chorus's intention to rest quietly in the house, waiting for the darkness of the night, the second play ends.

So this play is set within a framework of fear, that the respectful duty to the dead will be interrupted by violence, but shows male friendship and the Virgin's great set pieces of grief triumphant. The trajectory is here from fear and sadness to confidence and joy but the progression is far from even.

How is the audience expected to respond in this case? To mourn with the Theotokos, to feel release and relief when the work of the burial party is done? To recall through this non-liturgical experience their own ritual participations in the Holy Week liturgy, though services at this point were not developed into a full-blown *epitaphios thrēnos*?[44] To share the growing confidence of the actors that Christ will rise on the third day and to begin to set grief aside? All these, I would suggest.

---

[44] For the dating and development of the *epitaphios thrēnos*, by the fourteenth century celebrated on Good Friday evening, but preceded from the tenth or eleventh century by a Good Friday compline service with kanon of the lamenting Virgin plus a Holy Saturday orthros service, see Ševčenko (2011), in which she complicates and finesses the previously received view of a 'new' Komnenian Good Friday compline service.

11.2.3. The Resurrection

This play, 1906–2531, has many more comparanda than either of the others, and they range from Romanos' Easter hymn[45] to the Benediktbeuern plays,[46] and images of the Myrrhophores in Byzantine art.[47] The three actors play the Theotokos, Mary Magdalen, and a succession of supernatural apparitions. After an introduction (3.1906–2042) in which the women find their way to the tomb in the half dark, a first section offers three different experiences of the Resurrection (3.2043–93, 2094–115, 2116–72), then a comic subplot of Pilate, the priests, and the guard (3.2194–377) while Mary Magdalen travels to inform the disciples, then a recapitulation section (3.2421–79) in which many more accounts of the Resurrection are included (the problem with this play is dealing with gospel harmony so that it can be played credibly). A final section (3.2480–531) brings Christ to appear to the Ten and send out the Apostles. A note of confidence, despite denunciation of the *thumos*, *thrasutēs*, and *tolmēria* (anger,[48] rashness, and daring) of the murderers, gives way through shudders and shivers and astonishment at the supernatural apparitions to the great joy (*chara*, *gēthosunē*) of Easter.

At 3.1906 the Theotokos hails the dawn and wonders who might go and check out the tomb, lest the women might stumble on the *thumos* of the murderers. Mary Magdalen offers to go as scout, while needling the Virgin; she wants the privilege of first seeing the risen Christ. She is still sleepy, and the chorus are sleepier, all owing a lot to *Rhesus* at this point. Apart from the joy of the women the section is atmospheric but not overly emotional. They go, and the Virgin sings her last lament, no. 11 (3.2019–30), on the last possible occasion as they reach the tomb.

They then at 3.2031–3 see that the guards have deserted the tomb, still worrying about the crowd, described as *thrasus*, but the Theotokos urges them to keep going – but who, she wonders, will roll away the stone? Mary Magdalen, in surprise, sees the stone rolled away and resolves to go and tell the disciples. The Theotokos shudders and sees an angel, together with the guards scattered below as if dead. The angel urges them not to fear – as do all the apparitions – and tells them that Christ is risen and has gone to Galilee. Again Mary Magdalen offers to go to the disciples. At 3.2094–6 Magdalen sees someone she recognizes and the Theotokos steps in to respond to the *Chairete*, as they are seized by joy and fear. Christ tells them not to fear and tell his brothers to go to Galilee. The Theotokos sings a hymn to joy and light (3.2108–15) and at 3.2116 the Magdalen announces

---

[45] Romanos, *I Resurrection*, ed. Grosdidier de Matons (1967) 380–420; on *chara* in this text see Krueger (forthcoming).

[46] *Verses pascales de tres Maries*, ed. Dronke (1994) 92–100.

[47] Ousterhout (2013).

[48] On the wide semantic range of *thumos* (soul, life, spirit, courage) see Kanavou (2013) 173–4.

292 *Margaret Mullett*

the arrival of the chorus – they decide to go to the tomb with them. A young man greets them, and they react with *phobos* and *thambos* and *tromos* (fear, astonishment, and trembling). Magdalen again offers to go to Peter, and the chorus shows an extreme level of fear.

At 3.2174 a messenger, a friend, arrives and announces the ascent from Hades, and then details a subplot (to line 2377) in which the guard go to the priests and are bribed into telling Pilate that the disciples stole the body. The guard laments for its lost professional credibility at 2295, and the emotions are much cruder than in the rest of the play: lots of fear, anger, shame, vexation, terror, and symptom-metonymies such as *tromos* and *phrikē*.[49] The cover-up works, though the messenger thinks the guard will start to tell the story. He ran to the Theotokos with *gēthosunē*. The Theotokos writes the priests off as showing the insolence of *phthonos* but hails friends to visit the tomb again without fear.

At 3.2421 a recapitulation section reminds us of episodes which did and didn't happen in the story so far, the Theotokos is described as *charma tou genous* ('the joy of the [human] race'), and amazement, trembling, fear, and joy are reiterated. At the end the story of Emmaus is told, and the chorus then at 2480–503 recounts the appearance of Christ to the Ten, asking why they were afraid and offering proof of the Resurrection.

So this play takes us from the hope of the end of the second play to full belief in the *deus ex machina* appearance at the very end. Atmospheric fearful sleepiness and a sense of competition between the two women Myrrhophores (the Theotokos and the Magdalen), plus a final display of grief, lead us to the experiences of Easter Sunday. We see three episodes in detail, and in each one joy fights with shock and fear as we observe different emotional reactions to the different supernatural figures: the Theotokos' calm acceptance of her place, the Magdalen's ambition and willingness, the chorus's terror and unwillingness to accept what has happened. In the subplot we see more mundane emotions played out: fear of exposure, annoyance, and full-blown hate and terror can be seen, but the messenger's message is that Christ has risen, and he greets it with *gēthosunē*, a signal for what follows. In the recapitulation the women tremble, are amazed, and rejoice anew.

There is little doubt that in this play, where the plot takes us from a bad place to a happier one, we are also expected to react with joy and fear (3.2447–8, καὶ τούσδ' ἀπαστράπτοντας ἰδοῦσ' ἐνθέως / ἔστην καταπλαγεῖσα χαρᾷ καὶ φόβῳ), awe at the extraordinary events of the weekend and overwhelming joy at the central truth of Christianity. We join at 3.2532 a prayer to the Pantanax and at 2572 another to the Parthenos, prayers for mercy and protection.

---

[49] See Cairns (2013a) for shuddering and shivering.

11.3. Emotional discourse

So far we have made no distinction between the ways in which these emotional maps are set out. In fact they are marked by a mixture of emotion words, stage directions, and deduced emotions. A closer look at the explicit emotional terminology shows words of love (ἀγάπη, ἔρως, πόθος, στοργή, φιλία) most often used (sixty-nine times), followed by words of fear (φόβος, δέος, θάμβος, τάρβος, θροέω) fifty-one times, sadness (λύπη, πένθος, ἀνία, ἄλγος, ὀδύνη) forty-two times, and joy (χαρά, χάρμα, τέρψις, γῆθος, γηθοσύνη) forty-one times. Next comes hope (ἐλπίς) with thirty-three. Words of care and anxiety (μέριμνα, φροντίς, μέλω) figure sixteen times, then anger words (ὀργή, θυμός, χόλος) appear sixteen times, and envy (φθόνος, ζῆλος) fifteen times. Revulsion (στυγός) with ten, disturbance/surprise (ἔκπληξις, καταπλαγεῖσα(ι), τάραγμα) with nine, pity (οἶκτος) with seven, and shame (αἰσχύνη, αἰδώς) with six come last. There is no νέμεσις, ἐπιχαιρεκακία, or ἐνθουσιασμός, all of which are in Stanford's list, or the Byzantine emotions of ἀκηδία, κατάνυξις, and χαρμολύπη. It is worth looking at the four emotions at the top of the list, since a closer look alters the order, with sadness and fear at the top. Love is complicated by πόθος (with thirteen occurrences) and especially φιλία with forty-nine, even excluding the noun φίλος (thirty-eight examples). The strong showing of joy excludes any use of the χαιρ- root in greeting. Grief is interesting: if we include only λύπη and ἀνία, sadness is at a level with anger and care; adding the twenty-four instances of the more physical ἄλγος and ὀδύνη more than doubles the tally. Πένθος, which the adds the dimension of ritual response, adds only two, but θρῆνος twenty-four and γόος eight more. In this part of the range, grief is grieving: something you do rather than something you feel. And it shows that emotion words are only part of the picture: grief is signalled in lament by its resident *topoi* and by the inarticulate words and ululations. Embedded stage directions which refer to affects, tears, groaning, shaking, quivering, and so on, are another means where emotions, notably fear and grief, have easily recognizable physical manifestations: shivering, shuddering, and quaking add forty, groaning, howling, and weeping sixty-three. And much of the time we deduce emotion from a combination of indicators; in mimesis, as in life, we do not always need to be told.

This becomes clear when we compare equivalent passages in rhetorical works of the twelfth century. So, in Nikephoros Basilakes' *ēthopoiia*, *What the Theotokos Would Say When She Embraces Her Son When Being Prepared for Burial*,[50] we find some lament *topoi* (swaddling clothes/winding sheet; who will fittingly lament you?), though not a high proportion of those collected by Margaret

---

[50] Ed. Beneker and Gibson (2016) 206–22. On Nikephoros Basilakes see Pizzone (2014).

Alexiou.[51] Tears drip, they are warm, disciples mourn (or are not there to do so), she grieves, *thrēnoi* are mentioned. She is *philoteknos* (child-loving)[52] and addresses Christ as σπλάγχνον ἐμόν; the only emotion to be named is *chara*. In contrast to this mimetic work Nicholas Mesarites' *ekphrasis* of the mosaics in the church of the Holy Apostles[53] immediately bristles with emotion and emotion words. Mildness, gentleness, anger, terror, and cruelty in section 14, the Pantokrator image, anger, and joy in the Luke and Simon panel, joy three times in the Annunciation. The raising of Lazaros (26) offers sorrow as well as tears, gladness, compassion, and fear. With the Betrayal (27), we reach the same narrative span as our text, and find *phthonos*, hatred, joy, and sorrow. The Crucifixion (17) is devoid of emotion terms but when we reach 28, the women, we are directed to a turning point in the emotional spectrum of the piece: joy, we are told, gives way to sorrow. And in an explosion of emotion we meet affection, depression, gloom, grief, and, as the women approach the tomb, fear, amazement, horror. Their blood drains away, their complexions are yellow, their pulses slow, but they regain their courage and find strength. The guards are thunderstruck, even in sleep seized by fear, and sluggish, listless as though hung-over. The *Chairete* at 29 brings tears of joy and feet smothered in kisses, and Thomas at 34 is overcome by fear, just as the disciples at Tiberias in 35 show joy despite the angry waves. When you cannot show you must tell – in order to arouse the impression of showing.[54]

The handling of emotion terms in the *Christos Paschon* falls between these extremes, more than in the *ēthopoiïa*, fewer than in the *ekphrasis*. The emotional trajectories of Mesarites and our text are very similar. The remembered joy of the Annunciation, the envy and hatred and sorrow of the Betrayal are matched in the *Paschon* by the shift from joy and love through fear and anger to grief and confidence. The second play has no equivalent in Mesarites and takes us from fear through *philia* (friendly affection)[55] and grief to hope. And the overblown emotional tempest of Mesarites 28 does, like the Resurrection play of the *Paschon*, take us from fear and hope to amazement and joy. There are three emotional trajectories in our text, not one, and none of these is the same as the expected trajectories of fifth-century drama.

---

[51] Alexiou (1974).

[52] Similar compounds, e.g. *philomētor, philopator*, were popular at the top of the Komnenian family, especially in the generation after Alexios I.

[53] Ed. and trans. Downey (1957). On Nicholas Mesarites see Angold (2016); Macrides (2020).

[54] On *ekphrasis*'s goal of bringing the subject vividly before the eyes of the reader see Webb (2009).

[55] Konstan (2006b) 169–84 calls it the 'most general widely used term for love' in Classical Greek usage; Lewis (1960) 69–109 translates 'friendship'. It is the standard Byzantine Greek term for friendship, whether instrumental, erotic, or affective, symmetrical or asymmetrical.

11.4. What does the cento add?

But there is another way in which emotions are mobilized in the trilogy. We need to appreciate the part played by the cento texture in all three plays, and I shall take each in turn, looking at the use of the four major source texts.[56] We have noted in passing the way that the Theotokos, in the first play in particular, voices the strong women of the source texts: Medea and Agave, helping to establish the centrality and majesty of the protagonist. The use of the *Medea* in the first (Friday) play is thoughtful and considered. The quotations are not random or mechanical: they are not pulled from anywhere at any time, nor do they steal large tracts of text consistently for any actor. They do not smack of parody. Nor is this a school exercise, concerned to show off skills, self-conscious and boasting; the author has thought carefully about his source plays, identified speeches with the greatest emotional impact, and reminded his audience of them and their relevance to the ultimate drama of the Passion. Occasionally there is a self-referential word for the audience: the use at 1.1014–15 of *Med.* 1224–30, the sting in the tail for 'crafters of polished speeches' of the description of the death of Creon and his daughter, quoted at greater length than usual, could be a wry remark intended for the *theatron*.[57]

The quotations can be whole lines, half-lines, very occasionally a short chunk of five or six lines, and sometimes bow to the sense of a speech rather than specific words. Sometimes a series of individual words or syntactical patternings suggests a continuing reference which could be picked up by the audience. An example is the use made of the Nurse's opening speech on might-have-beens echoed in the Theotokos' speech on the Fall. It is important who voices lines. The Theotokos voices Medea (and the use increases towards the end as the horror deepens) but also Jason, and the horror of Medea's crime is used to underline her implacable opposition to Judas and to the threatening crowd, though not to the children of the crowd (an unusually non-anti-Semitic sentiment for a Byzantine). At the climax of the first play (1.731–837) the dialogue between Christ and the Virgin is an affecting exploration of the nature of 'good' news, thick with reminiscences of the Paedagogus puzzled when Medea reacts to his 'good news' with

---

[56] Scholarship has been slow to put the text in the context of Late Antique cento, which we now understand a great deal better after the work of Mark Usher (1998), Scott McGill (2005), and Sigrid Cullhed (2015). Bryant Davies (2017) highlights the oddity of the text as cento and isolates longer passages (chunks) to demonstrate how the text both offers and takes away typological characters for the Theotokos, comparing and contrasting, making tragedy possible but ultimately subverting the exercise. In Mullett (2021) I look at cento as spolia; here I concentrate on how already emotion-heavy passages in the source texts are used to paint emotion on to the biblical plot.

[57] For *theatra* as performance foci in the intellectual and literary society of Komnenian and later Constantinople, see Mullett (1984); Marciniak (2007); Gaul (2018), (forthcoming).

296   *Margaret Mullett*

tears (*Med.* 1012; 1.731), and of Jason's obtuseness when he announces their new fortune to the children (*Med.* 922, 924, 925, 929; 1.730, 733, 738, 737).

Much of the source play goes unused: our author goes for moments of high emotion or horror or dramatic tension – Medea's farewell to the children, the death of Jason's bride, Medea weeping once the die is cast and she cannot go back on her actions – and uses them to heighten the emotional content of his text. It is highly likely that the author knew what he was doing: Psellos on Euripides points us in this direction.[58] Some lines are used three or four times, sometimes two sides of a question (for example Jason and Medea on parenting) are combined to add texture. Parts of the Women of Corinth speech are used, not to hammer home a feminist message, but to signal how Mary is different from other women: her maternity did not involve the pain of childbirth.

In *Hippolytus* the exchange between Phaedra and the chorus as they overhear Hippolytus berating the Nurse inside (*Hipp.* 565–600), that excruciating cocktail of horror and shame and fear and desire, is used in all three plays but most often in the first one, and most speeches in this exchange are used. They are used by the Theotokos in her realization speech (1.848–9), awaiting the news of the third messenger (1.605–9, 610–12), in her reply to the first messenger and his to her (1.133–4) and in the Virgin's curse (1.284). Sometimes there are simpler equivalences of emotion. At 1.142 the Theotokos' horror at the messenger's news recalls the horror of Theseus reading the suicide note (*Hipp.* 874); at 1.423–5 the Theotokos on the Jews recalls Theseus' (unjust) revulsion at Hippolytus; the Theotokos in her last two speeches to the living Christ (at 1.802 and 828) echoes the sadness of Hippolytus saying goodbye to Theseus (*Hipp.* 1454), and the shock of realization that Christ is dead (at 1.853) mirrors Hippolytus seeing Phaedra dead (*Hipp.* 906). Eleven of the fourteen lines of this speech, from 902 to 915, are used, mostly in the first play but in various less parallel circumstances, in Virgin's lament and chorus; any heightened emotion is useful to support any emotion. Aspects of lament, for example in the fifth lament after the death of Christ (1.847–931), enlist elements from the death of Hippolytus (*Hipp.* 1215–17: the earth mourns), Hippolytus finding Phaedra (*Hipp.* 905–7: it was not long ago), Theseus and Hippolytus as Hippolytus dies (*Hipp.* 1408–10: would I could die), and Theseus' lament for Phaedra (*Hipp.* 839: I am more destroyed than

---

[58] Panagiotis Agapitos (1998a) 138 explains: Psellos in his *sunkrisis* of Euripides and George of Pisidia, ed. Dyck (1986) 44, 'concentrates specifically on *pathos* as the essence of drama'. This is much more to the point than the Byzantine commentary tradition, which does not emphasize emotion or 'the tragic'; though we should note that we do not have any clearly dated Middle Byzantine scholia to precede those of Triklinios, Thomas Magister, and Moschopoulos. In their absence the Psellos *sunkrisis* takes on more weight. If the little treatise in MS Barocci 131 is by Psellos as Browning (1963) suggests, its emphasis on πάθη τε καὶ πράξεις in sections 1 and 2 is supportive.

11. Tragic Emotions? 297

you); in this case rather than the mythical situation mirroring the biblical one, a heightened specific emotion, here of grief, accentuates the Virgin's own grief.

With *Bacchae* an undertow of horror pulls the emotions of Theotokos and chorus: reactions to messengers' news as in *Bacch.* 1030 and 1.438; Agave's moment of *anagnōrisis* at *Bacch.* 1280 informs the Theotokos' at 1.444; the Theotokos at 1.1046–62 after the death of Christ, between laments 6 and 7, makes use of Cadmus and Agave reassembling the bits of Pentheus (*Bacch.* 1244–7 and 1259–62), and 1.1075 on the bloody wounds of Christ takes further colour from the account of maenads on the mountain at *Bacch.* 742. In *Rhesus* blame (the driver of Hector, *Rhes.* 835; the Theotokos of Judas, 1.275;), the promise of punishment (Odysseus in *Rhes.* 894, Judas in 1.277) match their associated emotions, and the grief and horror of the driver's description of the damage to Rhesus' body in *Rhes.* 790, 794 ramps up the description of the piercing of Christ's side in 1.1080–5.

In the second, the Burial, play, the major set pieces are enhanced by rich use of highly emotion-laden passages from the four source texts. The deposition section sees the Theotokos at her entrance voicing Medea triumphant after the interview with Aegeus and about to reveal her plans to the chorus (*Med.* 765, 2.1250), and again in the debate over whether she will herself hold Christ echoing the again triumphant Medea receiving the news of the death of Creon and his daughter (*Med.* 1127–8, 2.1298–9); she orders the men to get Christ down in the words of Artemis telling Theseus to take Hippolytus in his arms (*Hipp.* 1431–2, 2.1301–2), interlaced at the moment of deposition with Medea to the messenger (*Med.* 1127–8, 2.1298–9), Agave on Dionysus (*Bacch.* 1147, 2.1300), and Hector being woken in *Rhesus* (*Rhes.* 7, 2.1304); while Joseph's technical business with hammer and nails (2.1263–5 after her entrance at 1247) reflects Agave preparing to nail up her trophy (*Bacch.* 1213–15). The Threnos uses Hippolytus' farewell to Troezen (*Hipp.* 1097, 2.1316), Cadmus' lament over Pentheus (*Bacch.* 1314–15, 2.1342–3), the Muse's first speech and Hector's reply (*Rhes.* 917–18, 959; 2.1341, 1378), and the farewells to the children by Jason and Medea (*Med.* 1069–71, 1413–14; 2.1314–21, 1317–18), plus the bride's cry of pain (*Med.* 1183, 2.1332). The announcement of the hanging of Judas from 2.1429 and the Entombment at 2.1453–6 are particularly complex and are analysed below. The Teleutaios Aspasmos is less densely inhabited, beginning with Hippolytus' farewell (*Hipp.* 1358–61, 1098–1101, 2.1489–91, 1495–8), and Medea's call to the children to go into the house (*Med.* 1076, 2.1499), and a doom-laden use of *Medea* 1223–4 spread over twenty lines, settling soon into heavy borrowing from *Bacchae* which contrasts the arrival of Dionysus in Thebes (*Bacch.* 1–56, 2.1535–1603) and the beginning of his cult with this key point in the creation of a cult of Christ, closing, however (at 1609–10), with a repetition of *Med.* 1076: Medea to the children.

Let us look now at the third, the Resurrection, play. In general it is heavily dependent on *Rhesus*, which suits both the blundering about in the dark and the misplaced and disavowed sleeping of the chorus; it carries also an element of danger. The introduction from 1906 to 2030, the dawn sequence with the setting out of the women, and the selection of a scout, is particularly indebted; Agave's waking up of the Bacchants (*Bacch.* 692) at 1994 is well integrated. Sinister undertones caused by the use of the family conflict of *Medea* are defused by the *Rhesus*-like exhortations not to bump into the guards in the night (*Rhes.* 570, 3.1980). The subplot of guards, priests, and Pilate from 2207 to 2377 makes use of the sense of an army by night in *Rhesus* with two scenes of Hector berating the chorus (*Rhes.* 52–75 and 808–19) which intercut throughout this section, offering a general sense of danger, which is increased when at 2227–9 Pentheus' threat to attack the Bacchants (*Bacch.* 778–80) suggests an equivalent threat to the Myrrhophores. The series of shocks that make up the narrative are well conveyed by the Magdalen's echoing at 2122–3 Hippolytus discovering the corpse of Phaedra (*Hipp.* 912–13) and the messenger describing to Hector (*Rhes.* 265–300) the shock of the arrival of the Thracian army at Troy.

More specifically, Christ is prefigured by Rhesus as an arriving saviour (at the first appearance of the angel, 3.2058, *Rhes.* 618), by the dying Hippolytus' chastity as appreciated by Artemis (*Hipp.* 1419, 3.2179), and by Dionysus instructing the Bacchants on what to do next (*Bacch.* 60), as Christ instructs the Apostles (3.2519): singing triumphal chants, preaching in the palace. The Theotokos is often Hector, the strong commander waiting for an expected saviour,[59] and Mary Magdalen is Dolon the volunteer.[60] More consistently the Myrrhophores, wandering over the landscape in search of Jesus, are evoked in terms of the maenads in the two messenger speeches of *Bacchae*.[61] But while this character-sketching is helpful, the main contribution of the cento to this play is atmospheric, its poetic sleepiness and half-light setting the scene for an event with no precedent, no referent in earlier literature.

It may help to look at two examples in a little more detail. The announcement of the hanging of Judas from 2.1427 to 1432, with the Virgin's reaction from 1434 to 1446, uses three viewpoints (the chorus, Theseus, and Hippolytus) on Phaedra's and Hippolytus' tragedies, all heavy with blame:

---

[59] The Theotokos voices Hector (for example 1.88 and 498) when debating whether to get nearer to see what is happening to Jesus (*Rhes.* 63), while deciding to send a volunteer to the tomb (*Rhes.* 141, 161, 181; 3.1917, 1933–5, 1969, 1972), when enquiring whether Christ has left Hades/Rhesus has arrived (*Rhes.* 280; 3.2186), in the Virgin's curse (1.274, echoing Hector's fears that Odysseus has run into Dolon and killed him, *Rhes.* 861), while readying for the Entombment/burial of Rhesus (*Rhes.* 959; 2.1378), and looking forward to the day of deliverance (3.2010, *Rhes.* 991, the end of Hector's last speech).

[60] In 3.1941–51, 1964–75 the Magdalen volunteers as in *Rhes.* 124, 126, 154, 156–60, 223, and asks for a reward as in *Rhes.* 161–5, 181–90.

[61] 3.1994 and 2018 on waking up the Myrrhophores use *Bacch.* 692–3, the first messenger on waking up the maenads. 3.2013, 2014, 2015, the Myrrhophores setting off for the tomb, use *Bacch.* 1086, 1089–91, the women leaping after Agave.

11. Tragic Emotions?   299

ἤδη κέκριται παντάδικος ἐνδίκως
μύστης ὁ παγκάκιστος ἐκδοὺς Δεσπότην·
ὦπτο κρεμαστοῖς ἐν βρόχοις ἠρτημένος·
βρόχων δὲ θᾶσσον ὑψόθεν χαμαιριφὴς
πίπτει πρὸς οὖδας μυρίοις οἰμώγμασι·
κακοῦ γὰρ ἐγγὺς ὢν ὁ τάλας οὐκ ἔγνω. (2.1427–32)

The formal Threnos has ended at 1426 with the Theotokos addressing Judas in a second Virgin's curse, condemning his *phthonos*. Joseph chips in with the news that Judas has been found hanged. His first two lines are original, then he uses at 2.1429 κρεμαστοῖς ἐν βρόχοις ἠρτημένη, *Hipp.* 779, the chorus's response to the Nurse's heavily charged discovery of the hanged Phaedra. The chorus has foreshadowed the discovery in 764–75, emphasizing the queen's shame, revulsion, pain, and passion, and then the Nurse and chorus exchange exclamations, ἰοὺ ἰού, φεῦ φεῦ, οὐ σπεύσετ' around the bare announcement. It is not the first time the poet of the *Paschon* has used the line: it has appeared in the first messenger's recounted (or imagined?) overhearing of someone in the garden accusing Judas and looking forward to his fate. But here it now takes on the immediacy and the emotional context of its use in *Hipp.*, and it is reinforced in 1430–2 by the use of *Bacch.* 1111–13 with the horror of the second messenger's account of Pentheus' fall from the tree, his cries and realization that his end is close.

The chorus responds with an original line, and then the Virgin responds at 2.1434, voicing Theseus' judgemental response, *Hipp.* 1169–72, to the news of Hippolytus' accident:

ὦ θεοί, Πόσειδόν θ'· ὡς ἄρ' ἦσθ' ἐμὸς πατὴρ
ὀρθῶς, ἀκούσας τῶν ἐμῶν κατευγμάτων
πῶς καὶ διώλετ'; εἰπέ, τῷ τρόπῳ Δίκης
ἔπαισεν αὐτὸν ῥόπτρον αἰσχύναντά με;

Our poet uses about half of 1169 in 2.1434: ὦ τέκνον, ὡς ἄρ' ἐστὶ σὸς Πατὴρ μέγας, and then the first half of 1172 in 2.1436: ἔπαισεν αὐτὸν ῥόπτρον, ὡς προδόντα σε, and proceeds through *Bacch.* 995, and a medley of *Rhesus*, to her conclusion at 2.1445: she uses *Hipp.* 614, Hippolytus' condemnation of Phaedra after her death: ἀπέπτυσ' οὐδεὶς ἄδικος ἐστὶ μοι φίλος. Here the substitution of ἀσεβὴς Θεῷ absorbs the ἄδικος ἐστὶ μοι of Euripides while adding an extra dimension. The shock, emotion, and disapproval of the Hippolytan passages enriches reactions to the hanging of Judas.

In a second example, the Entombment at 2.1453–6 has another knot of borrowed emotion, leading into a short lament passage at 2.1461–5:

κρύψατε γοῦν πρόσωπον ὡς τάχος πέπλοις·
ψαύσατε χερσί, θαψατ' ἐν τάχει νέκυν,
τὸν κατθανόντ' Ἄνακτ' Ἰουδαίων ὕπο·
αἴρειν φοράδην τὸν νεόδμητον χρεών. (2.1453–6)

This time it is drawn from four different plays, each taking up a different line. The moment of Hippolytus' death at *Hipp*. 1458 and his instruction to his father to cover his face, κρύψον δέ μου πρόσωπον ὡς τάχος πέπλοις, used at 2.1453, is followed at 2.1454 by another line close to the end of a play; Jason's inability to bury the children underlines the importance of pressing on with the Entombment: ψαῦσαί τε χεροῖν θάψαι (*Med.* 1412). Line 2.1455 uses Cadmus' account at *Bacch*. 1226 of how he 'went to the mountain and brought back the son the maenads killed': τὸν κατθανόντα παῖδα μαινάδων ὕπο. The bare account concludes the description of the 'endless labour of searching' to find scattered body parts. Finally, the φοράδειν early in the line at 2.1456 recalls *Rhes*. 888, in which the chorus sees the Muse arriving by *mēchanē* with the body of Rhesus in her arms, before she launches into her lament at *Rhes*. 890. Fear as well as grief are evoked. So here the ritual actions of collecting, veiling, carrying, and burying are expressed in terms of what are arguably the most emotion-laden lines of each of the four source plays.

It is worth noting that the emotion lies in character and plot, not in vocabulary. There are cases of clusters of emotion words which do duplicate emotion words in the source texts. For example, the section of the Virgin's curse 1.292–357 picks up at 292 θάρσους from *Med.* 469 and at 295 ἀναίδει' from *Med.* 472, both in Medea's speech to Jason, at 355 στένουσα and πεπληγμένη, both from *Hipp*. 38 in Aphrodite's opening speech on Phaedra, and at 357 δακρύοις from *Med.* 928, Medea to Jason, weeping over the children. And in the Virgin's fifth lament, after she realizes at 853 that Christ is dead, a similar sequence of varied emotions are drawn from passages of high emotion in the source texts. At 864 ποθοῦσα is taken from *Hipp*. 912, where Hippolytus sees the corpse of Phaedra, at 915 and 918, ἐλπίδας and ζηλωτόν come from *Med.* 1032 and 1036, Medea speaking to the children before she kills them. φιλτάτη at 918 is from *Med.* 1071, her final farewell to the children. So passages of high emotion in the *Paschon* lean on passages of high emotion in the source texts, word by word. But these examples are exceptions: more often emotion words in our text are original, and clusters of emotion words do not depend on emotions in the source texts. Even in the examples we have looked at there are as many original emotion words as words gleaned from the source texts. But we have already seen that in the announcement of Judas' hanging and in the Entombment a rich overlay of emotional episodes in the various texts works without specific borrowings of emotion terms. It would seem that emotion words are not necessary where emotional contexts can be evoked.

So the cento texture shows off learning, sets up parallels for consideration, offers Byzantine readings of ancient plays, creates atmosphere, builds character, and injects the drama with already emotion-laden text. It does this sometimes by mirroring situations (or reversing them, child on parent for parent on child), sometimes by matching specific emotions rather than situations, sometimes by

11. Tragic Emotions?

301

using any heightened emotion in the source text, or preferably source texts, as a loaded palette knife for the depiction of the *Paschon*'s emotion.

11.5. Performance

Finally, we might ask what performance, whether staged, rhetorical, or noetic,[62] adds to representation or indeed to narrative. What is the power of *mimēsis* over *diēgēsis*? Shared emotion, whether empathy or sympathy,[63] must play a large part,[64] as an audience relives its own losses and mourning and advances with the actors from fear and grief and indignation through *tharsos*, confidence, to awe and joy. This was surely also how Byzantines were able to read the not always transparent emotions of painted representations, through shared personal and liturgical experience. Emotions in the theatre are vicarious, felt not about real life, but the life of the person observed by the person feeling them, and generous, in that we care about the feelings of others.[65] And they are contained, in a special time and space, to bring greater focus. But there is more. Tragedy appeals to judgement, and other cognitive functions.[66] Learned receivers, 'full-knowing readers' like Joe Pucci's,[67] appreciate the fragments of other passions, other tragedies, but also see beyond, to an undeserving *pathos*, to ironies of *peripeteia* as the much maligned villains, as in the Resurrection subplot, enable, unknown to themselves, the salvation of mankind and the happy ending, and to literal *anagnōriseis* as flawed male disciples fail, through terror and despair, to see for themselves the miracle of salvation. Mimesis, and I would suggest

---

[62] The debate over the performability of the *Christos Paschon* continues; see most recently Puchner (2017) and Mullett (forthcoming c).

[63] On the difference between feeling with and feeling for see Halliwell (2002) 78; Cairns (2017b) 72–3; and, exhaustively, Feagin (1996) 83–142. See, however, Colombetti (2014) 186: 'the distinction between empathy and sympathy is not as clear as some may think'; for her, sympathy depends on what she calls basic empathy. In our case it is the sharedness which matters; see Pfister (1988) 37 on audience: 'the collective aspect increases the intensity of the reception'. On 'empathy' see also Cairns, pp. 24–7 above.

[64] It has been argued that theatre is a 'feeling-machine', designed to stimulate feelings through such triggers as lighting, sound, movement, *mise en scène*, pacing, structure, characterization, human proximity. See Hurley (2010) 36–57, and for Greek drama Meineck (2018).

[65] Taplin (1978) 168.

[66] The interrelationship between cognition and emotion has been at issue since Aristotle: Taplin (1986) 173; Heath (1987) 71. Lada (1993) argues for the intertwining of affective and cognitive processes in tragedy, and Ruffell (2008) for different configurations of affect and cognition for tragedy and comedy. Konstan (2006b) 20 notes that scholarship has increasingly recognized that emotions 'typically and perhaps necessarily' involve a substantial cognitive component; Colombetti (2014) confirms that cognition is necessarily affective (xvi), that evaluation is essential to emotional episodes (111), and that appraisal is embodied (83). The cognitive/affective antithesis appears to be no longer as current as it once was.

[67] Pucci (1998).

the cento texture also, offers that sense of distance which allows reflection on emotion, faith, and human frailty, but it also allows flawed and recognizable human emotions to play out the drama, the greatest drama, of the Byzantine era.

It is not immediately comprehensible why a twelfth-century author should have chosen to represent the Easter story in tragic form.[68] As we have seen, the plot is not very conducive to tragedy, and so the trajectory of emotions is like no fifth-century tragedy. But I would suggest that it was the potential of tragedy to focus emotion that appealed to the author, and the possibility of a Euripidean cento that gave it added depth. Using emotions reused through time and envisaged as performed, these plays show us Byzantine emotions in action, in conflict, and in resolution.

---

[68] For literary contexts which may have encouraged the choice see Mullett (2020). These include the prominence of rhetoric in the twelfth century, the revival of ancient genres, including forms of cento and dialogue, an increased awareness of tragedy and appearance of stichomythia, and an increased use of direct speech.

12

Alazoneia and *Aidōs/Aischunē* in Anna Komnene's and Niketas Choniates' Histories*

Martin Hinterberger

Introduction

The present chapter is motivated by a special interest in emotional concepts and terminology. I shall try to analyse the typical elements of *alazoneia* ('arrogance') and *aidōs/aischunē* ('shame') episodes in Byzantine historiographical texts, particularly from the twelfth and thirteenth centuries. What are the triggering circumstances? Are there recurrent patterns? What are the bodily symptoms and the metaphors linked to them? It will quickly become clear that the texts I am working with emphasize the behavioural aspect of emotions; to a high degree their internal experience, 'the feeling aspect', i. e. their phenomenology, remains in the dark.

These emotional episodes are couched in the traditional language of Byzantine learned literature, strongly influenced by ancient Greek literary models, while the same applies also to the imagery connected with emotions and the metaphors used. I am very much intrigued by the question of how these ancient terms (and concepts) relate to the author's twelfth/thirteenth-century present. In approaching this question, the juxtaposition of original classicizing texts and simplifying *metaphraseis* can prove helpful.

Why *aidōs/aischunē* (shame) and *alazoneia* (arrogance)? Both emotions are key driving forces for the plot of Niketas Choniates' *History* and, to a lesser degree, Anna Komnene's *Alexiad*. Moreover, both are 'self-conscious emotions' related to respect for social norms, and they are sometimes viewed as two diametrically opposing poles[1] – already in Plato's chariot allegory the noble horse

---

* This chapter has greatly profited from the judicious comments made by the two anonymous reviewers. I am also indebted to John Davis and Chris Schabel for emending my English.

[1] On shame and arrogance/pride as opposite self-conscious emotions see Lewis (2000) 623, particularly: 'Pride occurs when one makes a comparison or evaluates one's behavior vis-à-vis some standard, rule or goal (SRG) and finds that one has succeeded. Shame or guilt, on the other hand, occurs when such an evaluation leads to the conclusion that one has failed'; see also Konstan (2006b) 100 with further bibliography as well as e. g. Lelord and André (2001) 203.

304 *Martin Hinterberger*

is characterized by *aidōs*, and the unruly one by *alazoneia*.[2] Furthermore, both emotions are linked to characteristic behavioural patterns with clear bodily symptoms. And finally, both are terminologically intriguing.

Emotions are a complex phenomenon of human life, consisting of various constituent parts.[3] Emotions involve judgements and evaluations, and they also display physical aspects in the form of their typical neurophysiological and visceral changes, their subjective symptomatology, and their embodied expression (for instance, the facial expression accompanying emotion).[4] One fundamental assumption of my investigation is that emotions, because they involve judgments and evaluations to a significant degree, are culturally conditioned and that they undergo historical change, as do social norms and cultural values.[5] Accordingly, Byzantine emotions are approached here as being in principle different to modern, as well as ancient, emotions. This is particularly true for emotions such as *aidōs*/*aischunē* and *alazoneia* that are more than others connected to standards and rules created by a certain culture.[6]

I should also mention that my point of departure is the evidence of the ancient and Byzantine texts which I compare, not modern concepts. This means that I try to understand what Byzantine *alazoneia*, *aidōs*, and *aischunē* mean and to trace the development of these concepts from ancient Greek times, even though in explaining these emotions I have to use the modern terms arrogance and shame (in as precise a way as possible). It is not my primary aim, however, to investigate which Byzantine concepts correspond to our modern understanding of arrogance or shame. Since Byzantine emotions have barely been investigated and there is almost no research on the topic of the present chapter,[7] all results will have a strongly provisional character.

This chapter is about emotions in historiography, with a special focus on historiographical texts of the twelfth and thirteenth centuries. Byzantine historiography is especially rich in emotional episodes, particularly when compared to modern historiography (excepting, of course, the special case of biography), where emotions are virtually absent, since they do not represent 'hard facts'.

---

[2] Pl. *Phdr.* 246a–256e.

[3] In my opinion, component models such as the one developed by Scherer (1984) are more apt to explain historical change in emotions. Various researchers, such as e. g. Colombetti (2014), would, however, deny that components can be distinguished.

[4] See Cairns (2003) 12–13.

[5] See for more details Stearns (2002); Plamper (2012); Matt and Stearns (2014) 1–13; Schnell (2015).

[6] Cf. Lewis (2000) 624 and 626–7 ('All of us have beliefs about what is acceptable for others and for ourselves in regard to standards having to do with actions, thoughts and feelings. This set of beliefs, or SRGs, constitutes the information one acquires through culturalization in a particular society').

[7] See generally Hinterberger (2010a). On Byzantine arrogance and pride see Magdalino (1984), (1989).

12. Alazoneia and Aidōs/Aischunē 305

Yet, in Byzantine historiography emotions are significant causes of historical events.[8] However, historiographical texts do not always and necessarily include emotional episodes. It makes an important difference whether or not emotions are presented as a determinant factor in history (or historiography).[9] See for example the following two accounts of Emperor Aemilian's death (AD 253):

Αἰμιλιανὸς ἐβασίλευσεν ἔτος ἕν, καὶ ἐσφάγη ἐν τῷ παλατίῳ ὑπὸ τῶν στρατιωτῶν. (Georg. Cedr. *Chron.* 281, ed. Tartaglia (2016) 458, eleventh/twelfth century)

Aemilian reigned one year, and was then slaughtered in the palace by his soldiers.

ὁ βασιλεὺς Αἰμιλιανὸς ... ἦν μὲν ἀνὴρ ἀγαθὸς τὰ πολέμια καὶ κρείττων τῶν ἐναντίων, ἥττων δὲ τῶν εὐτυχημάτων. ἐπῆρτο γὰρ αὐτῷ τὸ φρόνημα ἐπὶ τοῖς κατορθώμασι καὶ τῶν ὑπὸ χεῖρα δεινῶς κατωφρύωτο. ἔνθεν τοι καὶ ἀπηχθάνοντο αὐτῷ τὸ στρατιωτικὸν φῦλον καὶ ἐμίσουν σφοδρῶς. καὶ ὃν πολεμοῦντα ἐθαύμαζον, τοῦτον εὐτυχοῦντα διὰ τὴν ἀλαζονείαν ἀπεβδελύττοντο· ἀνῃρήκασι γοῦν ἐξαπιναίως αὐτῷ ἐπιθέμενοι μῆνας τέσσαρας βασιλεύσαντα. (Mich. Psel. *Hist. synt.* 46, ed. Aerts (1990) 30.14–23, eleventh century)

The emperor Aemilian ... was a clever man in warfare and better than his adversaries, but he was not equal to his successes. He became haughty due to his achievements and he behaved very superciliously towards his subjects. Hence the soldiery disliked him and intensely hated him. Thus, the one whom they admired at war, the same did they abhor because of his arrogance after success. Suddenly they rushed upon him and killed him. He ruled four months. (Trans. Aerts (1990) 31, slightly adapted)

If we compare these two passages we readily recognize the fundamental difference between the two versions of the same event. In the first case, the fact of Aemilian's murder is simply stated: Aemilian was killed. In the second case it is explained *why* the events took the specific turn: Aemilian had become arrogant (ἐπῆρτο, διὰ τὴν ἀλαζονείαν), a fact which in turn generated the hatred of his entourage, which subsequently led to his assassination.

Why is historiography, i.e contemporary history, richer in emotions than other Byzantine literary genres, particularly in comparison with chronicles, the other important genre which gives an account of past events? Historiography has a stronger narrative character than chronography, which often simply states events. Historiography instead presents also causes, motives for human behaviour.[10] Historiography does much more to explain why the events narrated took place in the way they did. This seems to be a characteristic element of the narrative mode.

---

[8] See Hinterberger (2003). On emotions in ancient historiography see Damon (2017) and the stimulating questions raised by Sanders (2012) 159–65.

[9] Cf. Ljubarskij (1992) 83.

[10] Cf. Hinterberger (2013a) 370–425.

306 *Martin Hinterberger*

12.1. *Alazoneia* – arrogance

I have rendered *alazoneia* – the Greek key term used in the above episode from Psellos' *Short History* – with 'arrogance'. What do we mean by 'arrogance'? According to the definition given by the *Oxford English Dictionary* (= *OED*), 'arrogance' means 'the assertion of unwarrantable claims in respect of one's importance; undue assumption of dignity, authority, or knowledge'. Synonyms of 'arrogant' are (e. g.) 'haughty, conceited, self-important, egotistic, full of oneself, superior'. 'Modest' appears as the opposite of 'arrogant' – and modesty, as we shall see further below, corresponds with *aidōs*. Etymologically, arrogant is linked to Latin *arrogare*, 'to claim something for oneself'. One could also say that arrogance is the condemnable version of pride, which according to the *OED* is 'a high or overweening opinion of one's own qualities, attainments or estate, which gives rise to a feeling and attitude of superiority over and contempt for others'. Pride as 'the exhibition of this quality in attitude, bearing, conduct or treatment of others' is a synonym of arrogance and haughtiness.[11] As antonyms of pride, shame and humility are recorded. Vanity is another closely related term. It is defined as 'high opinion of oneself; self-conceit and desire for admiration'. Its antonym is again 'modesty'. The last term to be mentioned is conceit, 'an overweening opinion of oneself; overestimation of one's own qualities, personal vanity or pride' (*ODE*). The word ultimately derives from Latin *concipere* (English 'conceive'), which means it has to do with the 'concept' one has about oneself, how one conceives of oneself. In sociological or psychological studies, arrogance usually appears as an excessive and therefore negative form of pride, but is not treated as an emotional category in itself. In order to differentiate the latter from appropriate and therefore positive pride, Lewis (2000) uses the term 'hubris'.[12]

---

[11] English 'pride', like e. g. German *Stolz*, has both a positive and a negative meaning, whereas French has two different words, namely *fierté* for positive and *orgueil* for negative pride. Konstan (2006b) 90 and 100 briefly discusses possible reasons why ancient Greek had no word for positive pride (in contrast to negative pride/arrogance, namely *hubris*). Cairns (2022), however, makes a strong case for the existence of the phenomenon 'positive pride' in ancient Greek texts despite the lack of a single label. Also during the Byzantine period, Greek continues to lack a term for positive pride. In modern Greek the term *huperēphania/perēphania/periphaneia* has both negative and positive connotations; the semantic development of ancient/Byzantine negative *huperēphania* to ambivalent modern *perēphania* might have been influenced by the ancient/Byzantine positive term *periphaneia*, 'good reputation, glory', that became synonymous with *huperēphania* during the Byzantine centuries. The history of these terms would certainly deserve an in-depth investigation. On modern Greek *perēphania* and its semantic relation to other pride terms see the concise overview in Babiniotis (2002) 1836.

[12] Lewis (2000) 629–30 ('Hubris is defined as exaggerated pride or self-confidence ... It is an example of pridefulness, something dislikeable and to be avoided') and 634–5. When speaking of negative pride, Dyson (2006) occasionally uses the terms 'arrogance' and 'hubris'; see e. g. 5–6, 10, 14.

Besides *alazoneia*, the basic arrogance-related terms in Byzantine Greek are *huperēphania* ('pride'), *kenodoxia* ('vanity'), *eparsis* ('haughtiness'), *oiēsis* ('conceit'), *huperopsia* ('arrogant contempt'), and *tuphos* ('conceit, vanity, pride'); all of them share the idea of 'having a high opinion of oneself', μέγα φρονεῖν. Other closely related terms such as *kauchēma*, *kompos*, or *megalēgoria* are originally connected to the concept of boasting or bragging.[13] With the exception of *kenodoxia*, all these emotional terms were already used in Classical Greek.[14]

The terms *alazoneia* and *alazōn* appear relatively late in ancient Greek literature,[15] and it seems that other terms, such as *hubris*, were used to refer to the concept of 'arrogance' earlier (see below). *Alazoneia* and *alazōn* first appear in texts that ridicule or condemn character flaws such as arrogance.[16] Judging from the prominent place the *alazōn* has as a stock character in Aristophanes' comedies, the *alazōn* ('arrogant boaster') seems to have been a conspicuous phenomenon in Classical Athens.[17] Xenophon, on the other hand, defines the *alazōn* specifically as someone who for the sake of profit wishes to appear what he is not (e. g. rich or brave) or who promises to do what he cannot.[18] Yet, despite their apparent significance in everyday Athenian life, 'arrogance' and 'pride' do not belong to the emotions prominently treated in philosophy. When referring to human beings, and not a horse as in the already mentioned passage in *Phaedrus*, Plato contrasts the *alazōn* with the truth-loving person: the *alazōn* is a liar.[19] Also Aristotle only briefly comments on *alazoneia*, construing it as 'boastfulness', which together with *alētheia* and *eirōneia* constitutes one of his many theoretical conceptual triads. *Alētheia* is the virtuous mean, whereas *alazoneia* is

---

[13] The translations to English are of course mere approximations. In particular, it is difficult to render the term *tuphos* differently than as a mixture of English terms. On its usage in Christian texts see the entry in Lampe (1961) 1420–1. The combination of *tuphos* and *alazoneia* appears e. g. in Plut. *Artax.* 20.2.1.

[14] Ribbeck (1882), particularly 51–4. Julius Pollux, *Onomasticon* 146, lists the following roughly synonymous terms: αὔχημα, ἀλαζονεία, κόμπος, σεμνολογία, μεγαληγορία, μεγαλορρημοσύνη, ὑπερφρόνησις, ὑπεροψία, τερατεία, and ὑπερηφανία. On this second-century writer and his lexicon organized by topic see Dickey (2007) 96. Polybios (second century BC) seems to have been the first author to use *kenodoxia*, *kenodoxos*, and *kenodoxeō* systematically (see *TLG*). On the use of *kenodoxia* by Christian writers see the detailed entry in Lampe (1961) 741–2.

[15] The words *alazōn* and *alazoneia* or their derivatives do not appear in Homer, Hesiod, Herodotus, or the three Classical tragedians; see *TLG*.

[16] Next to Aristophanes' comedies, these are the Aesopian fables, which are, however, difficult to date with precision. See in particular fables 33, 156, and 234, ed. Hausrath and Hunger (1959–70), where boastful characters are depicted.

[17] Ribbeck (1882); Cornford (1934) 132–256; Whitman (1964) 26–7.

[18] Xen. *Cyr.* 2.2.12: ὁ μὲν γὰρ ἀλαζὼν ἔμοιγε δοκεῖ ὄνομα κεῖσθαι ἐπὶ τοῖς προσποιουμένοις καὶ πλουσιωτέροις εἶναι ἢ εἰσὶ καὶ ἀνδρειοτέροις καὶ ποιήσειν ἃ μὴ ἱκανοί εἰσιν ὑπισχνουμένοις, καὶ ταῦτα φανεροῖς γιγνομένοις ὅτι τοῦ λαβεῖν τι ἕνεκα καὶ κερδᾶναι ποιοῦσιν.

[19] E. g. Pl. *Resp.* 8, 560c (ψευδεῖς δὴ καὶ ἀλαζόνες). For more attestations see Ribbeck (1882) 4.

308 *Martin Hinterberger*

a pretence towards the greater and *eirōneia* a pretence to the lesser.[20] *Alazoneia* is more conspicuous in the work of Aristotle's followers. Thus, it is the topic of one of Theophrastus' character portraits (character 23). Not surprisingly, Theophrastus' understanding of *alazoneia* corresponds with Aristotle's: *alazoneia* is the pretence of non-existing goods, achievements, or virtues, boastful talk about made-up achievements.[21] *Alazoneia* here seems to be not so much an emotion, but an attitude. In the following character sketch 24 *huperēphania* is treated. Here, the proud man is primarily described as a snob, who behaves in a condescending way towards others.[22] The Aristotelian philosopher Ariston too devoted a treatise to *huperēphania*, in which he gave advice on how to counter one's own arrogance. Interestingly, Ariston seems to construe *megalopsuchia* as the positive counterpart of *huperēphania*. Whereas in this treatise the term *alazoneia* is not mentioned at all, in the following one on *authadeia* ('wilfulness, presumptuousness'), though again not prominent, *alazoneia/alazōn* appears as a component of the main subject. Ariston defines *authadeia* as a mixture of *oiēsis* ('conceit'), *huperēphania* ('pride/arrogance'), *huperopsia* ('arrogant contempt'), and also *alazoneia*.[23] Apparently the other philosophical schools were not much interested in pride-related emotions. Much later, though not focusing on *alazoneia* itself, Plutarch (first to second century) mentions arrogance in his treatise on self-praise, since self-praise is one of the characteristics of the *alazōn*.[24]

As already mentioned, *hubris* is another term that might have covered at least partly the concept of 'arrogance' before the term *alazoneia* gradually replaced *hubris* in this function.[25] While *hubris* frequently denotes insolent and arrogant behaviour, usually a slight, it may also be used for the expression of the underlying dispositional emotion, i. e. arrogance.[26] Despite their close semantic connection,

---

[20] Arist. *Eth. Nic.* 2, 1108a20–3: ἡ μεσότης ἀλήθεια λεγέσθω, ἡ δὲ προσποίησις, ἡ μὲν ἐπὶ τὸ μεῖζον ἀλαζονεία καὶ ὁ ἔχων ταύτην ἀλαζών, ἡ δ' ἐπὶ τὸ ἔλαττον εἰρωνεία καὶ εἴρων ὁ ἔχων αὐτήν.

[21] Theophr. *Char.* 23.1: ἀμέλει δὲ ἡ ἀλαζονεία δόξει εἶναι προσποίησίς τις ἀγαθῶν οὐκ ὄντων.

[22] Theophr. *Char.* 24.1: ἔστι δὲ ἡ ὑπερηφανία καταφρόνησίς τις πλὴν αὐτοῦ τῶν ἄλλων. See also Sorabji (2000) 221.

[23] Ariston, fr. 13.6 Wehrli: καὶ διαιρεῖν μεγαλοψυχίαν ὑπερηφανίας, ἀλλὰ μὴ συμφύρειν ὡς ἓν καὶ ταὐτόν· διαφέρει γὰρ ὅσον καὶ ἐπὶ τοῦ σώματος οἰδήσεως εὐεξία. On the combination of various emotions see fr. 14.1: ὁ δ' αὐθάδης λεγόμενος ἔοικε μὲν εἶναι μεικτὸς ἐξ οἰήσεως καὶ ὑπερηφανίας καὶ ὑπεροψίας, and 14.4.2–3: τῷ μὲν οὖν αὐθάδει τά τ' ἐκ τῆς οἰήσεως καὶ τῆς ὑπερηφανίας καὶ ὑπεροψίας εἰ μὴ καὶ τῆς ἀλαζονείας δυσχερῆ παρακολουθεῖ. See also Sorabji (2000) 221–2 on Ariston's treatment of pride, and 25–6 on the fragmentary tradition of his work.

[24] E. g. Plut. *Mor.* 540c9 (*De laude ipsius*).

[25] This development of the relation between *hubris* and *alazoneia* seems to have been similar to the development of the relation between *nemesis* and *phthonos* covering the concept 'envy', where the use of *nemesis* is restricted to a relationship between the divine and the human; cf. Milobenski (1964) 8.

[26] Cairns (1996a); Konstan (2006) 100.

12. Alazoneia and Aidōs/Aischunē

the terms *alazoneia* and *hubris* are only rarely combined.[27] In post-Classical and Byzantine Greek, however, *hubris* tends to express exclusively a specifically insolent behaviour,[28] while *alazoneia* seems to have taken over entirely the meaning of 'arrogance'. This becomes particularly clear if we cast a brief glance at an early Byzantine text. In Agathias Scholasticus' *History* (sixth century), which continues Procopius' *Wars*, *alazoneia* is presented as a key concept for the understanding of the course of historical events. *Alazoneia* ('arrogance'), says Agathias, equals injustice and directly leads to disaster. Before turning to contemporary attestations for this underlying principle, Agathias refers to examples from the past, particularly to Xerxes' presumptuous attack against the Greeks, who had not wronged him. Not only in this passage does Agathias rely on Herodotus, but instead of retaining the term *hubris* of Herodotus' text, the Byzantine historian uses *alazoneia* for the characterization of Xerxes' behaviour.[29] Moreover, Agathias couples *alazoneia* with the term *atasthalos* ('wanton'), exactly as Herodotus (and other Classical authors) links it to *hubris*.[30] A different kind of arrogance in Agathias' text is the attitude of certain persons who in Agathias' time presumed to explain natural disasters with the laws of physics, rather than God's inexplicable will – another instance of what the ancients would clearly have called *hubris*.

In the Early Christian period, pride-related concepts gradually change significance. Thus, *huperēphania* ('pride'), *kenodoxia* ('vanity'), and *alazoneia* ('arrogance') are all explicitly condemned in the New Testament.[31] John Chrysostom depicts *kenodoxia*, the display of riches and splendour or 'vanity', as a wild

---

[27] To the best of my knowledge, the only attestation in Classical literature is Pl. *Phdr.* 253e, where both nouns characterize the unruly horse.

[28] See the entry 'hybris' in Kazhdan (1991b) 959 (particularly the definition 'injury to another person through word or deed').

[29] Agathias, *Hist.* 2.10.4, ed. Keydell (1967), 53.33–54.2: Ξέρξης δὲ ἐκεῖνος ὁ πάνυ καὶ τὰ τοῦ Ξέρξου θαύματα τῷ ἄρα γε τρόπῳ ὑπὸ τῶν Ἑλλήνων νενίκηται ἢ ὅτι ὁ μὲν ἀλαζών τε ἦν καὶ ἀτάσθαλος καὶ καταδουλωσόμενος ᾔει τοὺς οὐδὲν ἠδικηκότας μόνῳ δὲ τῷ πλήθει πίσυνος καὶ τῇ τῶν ὅπλων παρασκευῇ εὐβουλίᾳ οὐ μάλα ἐχρῆτο, οἱ δὲ ὅσιά γε δρῶντες ὑπὲρ τῆς σφετέρας ἐλευθερίας ἠμύνοντο ...; cf. Hdt. 7.8–10 and 8.109.3. On Herodotus' influence on Agathias in general see Karpozilos (1997) 439. Xerxes remained a paragon of arrogance throughout the Byzantine centuries; see e. g. Nic. Chon. *Or.* 16.171.18–20, ed. Van Dieten (1972): τοῦ παρασπόνδου καὶ κομπάζοντος τὰ ὑπέραυχα, καὶ οὐδ' ὅσα Ξέρξης ἠλαζονεύετο καθ' Ἑλλήνων θάλασσαν ἀπογαιῶν καὶ ἤπειρον θαλαττῶν (referring to the sultan of Ikonion), or *Or.* 4.31.4–5.

[30] For the connection between *atasthalos* and *hubris* see also Cairns (1996a) 15.

[31] Jas. 4:6 and 1 Pet. 5:5, both quoting Prov. 3:34: κύριος ὑπερηφάνοις ἀντιτάσσεται, ταπεινοῖς δὲ δίδωσιν χάριν. Phil. 2:3: μηδὲν κατ' ἐριθείαν μηδὲ κατὰ κενοδοξίαν, ἀλλὰ τῇ ταπεινοφροσύνῃ ἀλλήλους ἡγούμενοι ὑπερέχοντας ἑαυτῶν. Gal. 5:26: μὴ γινώμεθα κενόδοξοι. 1 John 2:16: πᾶν τὸ ἐν τῷ κόσμῳ, ἡ ἐπιθυμία τῆς σαρκὸς καὶ ἡ ἐπιθυμία τῶν ὀφθαλμῶν καὶ ἡ ἀλαζονεία τοῦ βίου, οὐκ ἔστιν ἐκ τοῦ πατρός. Under the heading *huperēphania*, Prov. 3:34 was incorporated in various florilegia or lexica (e. g. Jo. Damas. *Sacra parallela*, PG 96.104.37; *Suda* Y290, ed. Adler (1928–38, 4.654–5)) and frequently quoted by famous authors, e. g. Euseb. *Praep. evang.* 11.13.8.3–4, ed. Mras (1954–6); Greg. Naz. *Or. funebris in laud. Bas.* 57.6, ed. Bernardi (1992) 248.30–1.

310 *Martin Hinterberger*

beast and demon threatening the relationship between God and the Christian.[32] Particularly in monastic environments, *huperēphania* ('pride') and *kenodoxia* ('vanity') came to be considered two of the major vices (consequently both were incorporated into the group of seven deadly or cardinal sins in the West), and were of course utterly condemned.[33] Characteristically, according to Christian mythology, it was pride and arrogance that was at the origin of the fall of Satan – who raised himself above God.[34] It is for this reason that *huperēphania* is occasionally regarded as the 'mother of all evils'.[35] Euagrios Pontikos (fourth century) observes that *kenodoxia* consists in the desire to be seen (πρὸς τὸ θεαθῆναι, cf. Matt. 6:1) and that it is connected to a certain type of dreams about great achievements.[36] He also warns that *kenodoxia* is a most dangerous vice, since every success against it at the same time increases and invigorates it.[37] According to John Klimakos (seventh century), *kenodoxia* and *huperēphania* belong to the highest steps the monk or nun has to face on the ladder he or she climbs up to perfection (steps 22 and 23 of the *Heavenly Ladder*).[38] Accordingly, 'pride' and 'vanity' were much discussed, and efforts were made to give definitions; see e.g. Basil of Caesarea (fourth century):[39]

κενόδοξός ἐστιν ὁ ψιλῆς ἕνεκεν τῆς ἐν κόσμῳ δόξης ποιῶν τι ἢ λέγων.

Vain is he who does or says something for the sake of a little glory in the world.

In contrast to *huperēphania*, *kenodoxia* almost always has to do with the desire for the admiration of others or with the display of superiority (through, for example, one's dress, or a certain kind of behaviour). *Huperēphania*, on the other hand, does not: it is described as a conviction of superiority, as a turning away from God, which may even lead to rivalry with God (cf. Satan) and, in the end, to madness.[40] Although usually *kenodoxia* is presented as a first step in the direction

---

[32] Chrys. *De vana gloria*, ed. Malingrey (1972).

[33] See Knuuttila (2004) 141–2.

[34] See e.g. Mich. Glyc. *Carm. de carcere*, ed. Tsolakes (1959) 504–5: ἄλλος εἰς χοῦν κατήγετο τοῦ Ἅιδου καὶ πυθμένα, / ὡς ἀλαζὼν καὶ σοβαρός, ὡς ἄλλος Ἑωσφόρος; cf. also Hinterberger (2013a) 199–200. According to another version, however, it was envy that caused Satan's fall. See also Kelly (2006) 197–8 and Sorabji (2000) 335–7.

[35] See e.g. *Apophthegmata patrum* 8.6.6–7, ed. Guy (1993–2005): ὑπερηφανία ἡ μήτηρ πάντων τῶν κακῶν.

[36] Euagr. Pont. *Peri logismōn* 3.14–23 and 28.1–15 (see also 15.1–15 and 21.1–32), ed. Géhin, Guillaumont, and Guillaumont (1998).

[37] Euagr. Pont. *Praktikos* 30.1–3, ed. Guillaumont and Guillaumont (1971). See also 13.1–13 and 14.1–7 on vanity and pride.

[38] *PG* 88. There are numerous stories about conceited monks and their final fall into sin, when they thought they were already sure of victory over the demon of 'arrogance'; see Kulhánková (2014), esp. 142 and 146.

[39] Bas. Caes. *Regulae brevius tractatae*, Inter. 52, *PG* 31.1117B.

[40] Euagr. Pont. *Praktikos* 14.6–7, ed. Guillaumont and Guillaumont (1971); *Peri logismōn* 21.25–6, ed. Géhin, Guillaumont, and Guillaumont (1998), and see also 13.1–13 and 14.1–7 on

12. Alazoneia and Aidōs/Aischunē 311

of *huperēphania*, Dorotheos of Gaza (sixth century) treats both emotions without distinguishing them terminologically from each other. Using exclusively the term *huperēphania* he differentiates two types of 'pride', one in relation to the monk's brothers (in other texts usually called *kenodoxia*), the other in relation to God (*huperēphania* proper). Furthermore, he distinguishes secular *huperēphania* (based on garments or riches, or, on the other hand, on natural gifts – the latter being superior, i. e. less reprehensible) from its monastic variant (based on monastic achievements).[41]

In contrast to *kenodoxia* and *huperēphania*, *alazoneia* is less neatly conceptualized in Christian texts. The reason for this neglect may be that *alazoneia* had not achieved the full status of a sin, but was rather seen as a vice accompanying vanity and pride. In theoretical texts it appears only on the margin of the discussion of the more significant concepts of *kenodoxia* and *huperēphania*. See e. g. Maximus the Confessor (seventh century):[42]

ἡ κενοδοξία ποτὲ μὲν ἀναιρουμένη, ποτὲ δὲ μένουσα, τίκτει τὴν ὑπερηφανίαν· καὶ ἀναιρουμένη μὲν οἴησιν ἐμποιεῖ· μένουσα δὲ ἀλαζονείαν.

Vanity, whether it is eradicated or whether it remains, begets pride. When it is eradicated, it generates self-conceit; when it remains it produces arrogance.

Here *alazoneia* appears as a kind of pride generated by vanity.

The discussion of emotions by the above-mentioned authors gained a sort of canonical status for the following centuries. Excerpts like the ones quoted above were incorporated into florilegia under headings such as Περὶ κενοδοξίας or Περὶ ὑπερηφανίας καὶ ταπεινοφροσύνης.[43] These collections of various passages on a specific *pathos* constitute an invaluable source for the study of emotions.

Is there any real distinction between *alazoneia* ('arrogance') on the one hand, and *huperēphania* ('pride') and *kenodoxia* ('vanity') on the other? We shall attempt to answer this question on the basis of a close reading of historiographical texts, starting with two passages which give us particularly focused descriptions of *alazoneia*.

According to Michael Psellos' account of Emperor Aemilian's death (see above), arrogance is generated by success or good fortune and achievements (εὐτυχήματα, κατορθώματα), which overwhelm the arrogant person so that

---

vanity and pride. The connection between pride and madness can be found already in ancient Greek philosophy (the example being Xerxes); Sorabji (2000) 222.

[41] Doroth. Gaz. *Didaskaliai* 2.31–2, ed. Regnault and De Préville (2001); see also 16.168.19–21, where he interprets ἀλαζονεία τοῦ βίου as κενοδοξία.

[42] Max. Conf. *De caritate*, cent. 3.61, *PG* 90.1036B. Cf. the translation in Palmer, Sherrard, and Ware (1981) 93.

[43] See e. g. *Florilegium Patmense* chs 22 and 45, ed. Sargologos (1990). On florilegia and emotions see generally Hinterberger (2013a) 89–94. *Tapeinotēs* (or *tapeinophrosunē*) is regularly regarded as the opposite or antidote of pride; cf. already above, note 31 (Prov. 3:34 or Phil. 2:3).

312   *Martin Hinterberger*

'his attitude becomes haughty' (ἦν ἀνὴρ ... ἥττων τῶν εὐτυχημάτων. ἐπῆρτο γὰρ αὐτῷ τὸ φρόνημα ἐπὶ τοῖς κατορθώμασι καὶ τῶν ὑπὸ χεῖρα δεινῶς κατω-φρύωτο). *Epairomai* literally means 'to rise up'. Aemilian lifts himself above his former comrades, now subjects, and treats them haughtily; he looks down on them, and he behaves in a superior manner towards them; he believes himself to be above others. *Katophruoomai* is a derivative of *ophrus*, 'eyebrow', meaning 'to raise the eyebrows against someone' and used here in the metaphorical sense of treating someone arrogantly (cf. English 'supercilious' – we shall come back to this metaphorical use below). This haughty behaviour stirs the soldiers' hostility, hatred, and disgust (ἀπηχθάνοντο, ἐμίσουν, ἀπεβδελύττοντο). They had admired Aemilian when they were fighting together, but now they despise and detest him because of his arrogance (διὰ τὴν ἀλαζονείαν). Arrogance appears as haughty and superior behaviour, behaviour regarded as inappropriate.

Soldiers and generals seem to have been particularly prone to arrogance, as the next passage we are going to analyse suggests.[44] In this case, however, the protagonist is a positive hero, the father of the ruling emperor Nikephoros Botaneiates (1078–81), to whom Michael Attaleiates' *History* (eleventh century) is dedicated.[45] Michael Botaneiates did not act as might have been expected as 'normal', namely in an arrogant way. He was not overwhelmed by 'arrogance', although circumstances favoured the appearance of this emotion. For the triggering situation is the same as before: he is a successful and famous soldier, admired and praised for his accomplishments. As in the previous passage, the verb θαυμάζω ('to admire') is used also here, as well as εὐπραγία ('achievement'), a synonym of εὐτύχημα. Others in his place would have had a 'raised or superior attitude' (μέγα φρονῶν) because of their achievements (κατορθώματα) and would have become haughty because of arrogance (ἀλαζονείᾳ κατεπαιρόμενος), and they would have ceased behaving in a friendly manner towards others and keeping company with them.[46] Rather they would raise themselves (ἐμαυτὸν ὑπεραίρων) above the others and, out of their pride, imagine themselves to be superior.

In addition to the features already mentioned by Psellos, two new characteristics appear here: the arrogant man does not keep company with others, he is a snob, and he boasts of his superiority. The latter two traits, says Attaleiates, are also to be found in those who are ensnared by the 'vice of vanity' (τῷ πάθει τῆς

---

[44] Plautus' *Miles gloriosus* comes to our mind.

[45] Mich. Attal. *Hist.* 171.17–23, ed. Pérez Martín (2002): τί δέ; οὕτως ἔχων εὐκλείας καὶ εὐ-πραγίας ὁ ἀνὴρ καὶ παρὰ πάντων θαυμαζόμενός τε καὶ δοξαζόμενος καὶ τοῖς ἐξ ἔργων μεγα-λουργήμασι σεμνυνόμενος, μέγα φρονῶν ἦν ἐπὶ τοῖς ἑαυτοῦ κατορθώμασι καὶ ἀλαζονείᾳ κα-τεπαιρόμενος τῶν πολλῶν καὶ τοῖς ἀστικοῖς ὡς ἀγοραίοις τισὶ καὶ ἀόπλοις μὴ εὐθύμως καὶ προσηνῶς ὁμιλῶν καὶ συναυλιζόμενος ἀλλ᾿, ὥσπερ τινὲς τῶν κεκρατημένων τῷ πάθει τῆς κε-νοδοξίας, ἑαυτὸν ὑπεραίρων καὶ τῷ κόμπῳ τερατευόμενος τὸ ἀνόμοιον, οἷα φιλεῖ τοὺς πολλοὺς ποιεῖν τῶν στρατιωτῶν; οὐμενοῦν.

[46] Cf. also the snob in Theophrastus' character 24 on *huperēphania*.

κενοδοξίας). I am not certain whether Attaleiates wants to say that *kenodoxia* is a related emotion, overlapping with *alazoneia* in certain aspects, or that *kenodoxia* is the term used for (more or less) the same emotion, though in another – i.e. generally religious or monastic – context, or perceived from such a point of view (although the secular and the religious sphere are of course not neatly separated). I tend to believe the latter, and therefore translate *pathos* as 'vice'.

Before we proceed, I shall summarize the basic elements of Byzantine 'arrogance' so far, its script: (allegedly) special achievements trigger a high opinion about oneself which is expressed through certain actions such as disdainful and generally unkind behaviour, bragging, or the rejection of other human beings. Apart from the central terms *alazoneia*, *huperēphania*, and *kenodoxia* – which are not clearly distinguished from each other – *eparsis*/*epērmenos* and *heauton huperairō* ('haughtiness'/'haughty'), *oiēsis* ('conceit'), μέγα φρονῶν ('thinking big'), and *kompos* ('bragging') are other significant terms and locutions used for the arrogant person's description. Thus, the general concept of *alazoneia* does not differ significantly from ancient Greek standards, nor do the terms used.

The following remarks will focus on two twelfth/thirteenth-century texts, Anna Komnene's *Alexiad* and Niketas Choniates' *History*.[47] From the passages examined below, the constituents of typical arrogant behaviour in Niketas Choniates' and Anna Komnene's Histories can be extracted. Both texts are quite rich in episodes that feature arrogance, and they were transposed to a stylistically lower level, so-called *metaphraseis*, in the mid-fourteenth century.[48] When cited, the original passages will be accompanied by their simplified fourteenth-century versions. It is easily observable that in the simplified *metaphraseis* the terminological plethora of the classicizing texts is reduced to a restricted set of terms and that the key term in the *metaphraseis* appears to be *alazoneia* and, to a lesser degree, *eparsis*. Interestingly, the term *kenodoxia* is absent from either text as well as from their *metaphraseis*.

In the two eleventh-century historiographical texts by Michael Psellos and Michael Attaleiates respectively examined above, arrogance is presented as a negative character trait which afflicts soldiers in particular. In Choniates, we

---

[47] Ed. by Reinsch and Kambylis (2001) and Van Dieten (1975) respectively. In both sections (*alazoneia*, *aidōs/aischunē*), I shall present, against chronological order, first passages from Choniates and then from the *Alexiad*, because Choniates' text is richer in emotional episodes and the *metaphrasis* of his text has come down to us almost entirely whereas from the *metaphrasis* of the *Alexiad* only a small part has been preserved.

[48] Ed. by Hunger (1981) and Davis and Hinterberger (forthcoming) respectively. In the latter edition Byzantine spelling habits concerning diacritics and the *iota subscriptum* are respected. On *metaphraseis* and the metaphrastic process see generally Hinterberger (2014a). The database of corresponding classicizing and koine terms, constructed in the framework of the research project The Vocabulary of Byzantine Classicizing and Literary Koine Texts: a Database of Correspondences, funded by the A. G. Leventis Foundation and conducted at the University of Cyprus, was a useful tool for the present study; see generally Hinterberger (2017c).

314 *Martin Hinterberger*

have examples of the same phenomenon. During a military campaign against the Turks, it is Emperor John's nephew, John Komnenos, who manifests such a high conceit of himself that he refuses to follow imperial orders that would humiliate him.[49] The entire episode is presented as a Byzantine failure caused by irrational arrogance (*tuphos*) and anger (*thumos*).[50] Apart from being arrogant (*phronēmatias, gauros*), John's behaviour is characterized as impudent (*anaidēs*). When he is finally forced to obey, he decides to defect to the Turks. In the *metaphrasis* the emotion terms corresponding with *phronēmatias, gauros*, and *anaidēs* are *epērmenos, alazōn*, and *adiantropos*.

In another episode, Emperor Isaak Angelos' young cousin Konstantinos became haughty (ἐπαρθείς) after a few (insignificant, as Choniates says) military successes. He is so proud of himself and convinced of his own value (i.e. conceited) that he rebels against the emperor and commits the extreme act of insubordination.[51] The *metaphrasis* retains the word ἐπαρθείς, explaining that the reason for Konstantinos' haughtiness was *alazoneia*.[52]

---

[49] Nic. Chon. *Hist.* 35.42–36.49: μάχης γὰρ ἐνισταμένης μετὰ Περσῶν, ἱππότην ἐπίσημον ἐξ Ἰταλίας ὁρμώμενον ἄνιππον θεασάμενος ἐκέλευσε παρεστῶτι τῷ ἀνεψιῷ ἀποβῆναι τοῦ Ἀραβίου ἵππου, ᾧ ἦν ἔποχος, καὶ δοῦναι τοῦτον τῷ Ἰταλῷ, μὴ χατίζοντα ἵππων τὸν ἀνεψιὸν ἐπιστάμενος. ὁ δὲ φρονηματίας ὢν καὶ γαῦρος πλέον τοῦ δέοντος τῷ τοῦ βασιλέως ἀντέστη κελεύσματι, ἐμβριθεστέραν, ἵνα μὴ λέγοιμι ἀναιδεστέραν, τὴν ἀντίρρησιν ποιησάμενος· καὶ τὸν Λατῖνον ἐξουθενῶν προυκαλεῖτο εἰς ἀντιμάχησιν ὡς τὸν ἵππον, εἰ περιγένοιτο, δικαίως ἀποληψόμενον. Cf. *Metaphrasis Chon.* 1.13.5: μάχης γὰρ ἐνισταμένης μετὰ Περσῶν, Φράγγον ἐπίσημον ἀνδρεῖον ὁ βασιλεὺς χωρὶς ἀλόγου βλέψας, παρισταμένου τοῦ ἀνεψιοῦ αὐτοῦ μεθ' ἵππου Ἀραβικοῦ, ὥρισεν αὐτὸν πεζεῦσαι ἀπὸ τοῦ ἀλόγου αὐτοῦ καὶ δοῦναι αὐτὸ τῷ Ἰταλῷ ὡς γινώσκων ἔχειν καὶ ἕτερον ἵππον τὸν ἀνεψιὸν αὐτοῦ. ὁ δὲ ἐπηρμένος ὢν καὶ ἀλαζὼν καὶ πλέον τοῦ πρέποντος, ἀντέστη τῷ ὁρισμῷ τῷ βασιλικῷ ἀγριώτερον, ἵνα μὴ εἴπω ἀδιαντροπώτερον, τὴν ἀπόκρισιν ποιησάμενος, τὸν Λατῖνον ὑβρίζων καὶ κράζων πρὸς ἀντιμάχησιν καὶ "εἰ καταβάλει με οὗτος, δικαίως καὶ τὸν ἐμὸν ἵππον λάβη."

[50] Nic. Chon. *Hist.* 35.39–41: ἴσως δ' ἂν καὶ τῆς Νεοκαισαρέων ἐκράτησε βασιλεύς, εἰ μὴ κατὰ συγκυρίαν ἀπρόοπτον αὐτῷ προσέστη τῦφος ἄλογος αὐτοθελής καὶ θυμὸς παντάπασιν ἀκυβέρνητος τοῦ ἀδελφιδοῦ Ἰωάννου. Cf. *Metaphrasis Chon.* 1.13.5: ἴσως δὲ καὶ τὴν Νεοκαισάρειαν ἐκράτησεν ὁ βασιλεύς, εἰ μὴ συνέβαινε παραλόγως θυμωθῆναι τὸν βασιλέα ἐπὶ τῷ ἀνεψιῷ αὐτοῦ Ἰωάννη. Here the anonymous metaphrast misunderstood Choniates' text. It was the emperor's nephew who became arrogant and angry, not the emperor.

[51] Nic. Chon. *Hist.* 435.53–61: ἀλλὰ δέον τὰ λυσιτελῆ ταῦτα τῇ πατρίδι καὶ ταῖς ἐκεῖσε πόλεσιν αἱρεῖσθαι τὸν Κωνσταντῖνον, ὁ δὲ τὴν ἐναντίαν ἐτράπετο. ἐπαρθεὶς γὰρ τοῖς μικροῖς ἀγωνίσμασι τούτοις ὡς τὰς φρένας ἀστατῶν τῇ νεότητι ἤρξατο ὑποποιεῖσθαι τοὺς συνόντας αὐτῷ ἀρχηγοὺς κἂκ τῶν ἐγχωρίων στρατιωτῶν ὁπόσους τὸ γένος αἰδεσίμους ἐγίνωσκε καὶ περιδεξίους εἰς ἔργα πολέμια. οὐκοῦν καὶ βραχεῖαν ἐκ τούτων ῥοπὴν ἐσχηκὼς πρὸς τὴν τῶν κατ' ἔφεσιν ἐκπεράτωσιν τῆς στρατηγίδος ἀνθαιρεῖται στολῆς τὴν βασίλειον καὶ τοὺς πόδας εἰς ἑτοιμασίαν τῆς τυραννίδος φοινικοβαφὲς ἀμφιέννυσι πέδιλον. Cf. Magoulias (1984) 239.

[52] Cf. *Metaphrasis Chon.* 14.5.5: ἔπρεπε τοίνυν καὶ τὸν Κωνσταντῖνον, ἐπεὶ τοιοῦτος ἐν τοῖς βαρβάροις ἐγένετο δόκιμος, βοηθῆσαι καὶ τῇ πατρίδι αὐτοῦ, καὶ τὰ πρὸς ὠφέλειαν τῆς βασιλείας ποιεῖν, αὐτὸς δὲ τὸ ἐναντίον εἰργάσατο. ἐπαρθεὶς γὰρ ἀπὸ νεότητος, καὶ τῆς ἧς εἶχεν ἀλαζονείας, ἐπιπλέον δὲ καὶ διὰ τὰς νίκας ἃς κατὰ τῶν ἐχθρῶν ἐνεδείξατο, ἤρξατο μεταχειρίζεσθαι τοὺς μετ' αὐτὸν ὄντας στρατηγοὺς καὶ τοὺς ἑτέρους ὅσοι ἐκ γένους ἦσαν λαμπροῦ καὶ περιδέξιοι πρὸς ἔργα πολεμικά, οἵτινες καὶ ὑπήκουσαν αὐτῷ καὶ πληρῶσαι τὰ πάντα πρὸς τὸν σκοπὸν αὐτοῦ ὑπεσχέθησαν· ἀντὶ γοῦν τοῦ στρατηγὸς εἶναι, ἀναγορεύεται βασιλεὺς καὶ κόκ-

12. Alazoneia and Aidōs/Aischunē 315

Yet civil dignitaries are also prone to arrogance, such as Konstantinos Mesopotamites, who as 'chancellor' of Alexios III Angelos had mediated during a serious conflict of the imperial couple in the course of which Empress Euphrosyne had been banned from the palace (see on this more below). When Euphrosyne finally returned to the palace, Mesopotamites too 'raised his eyebrow' (ἀνέσπα τὴν ὀφρύν) and walked around 'mincingly' (βλακῶδες), believing that he could achieve everything with the emperor.[53] Here, as in other cases, the simplified version is more specific, rendering Choniates' somewhat unclear βλακῶδες with μετὰ ἀλαζονείας, 'arrogantly'.[54] Also when patriarch Basil Kamateros met the usurper and anti-hero of the *History* Andronikos I Komnenos (AD 1183–5) for the first time, he noticed the latter's 'arrogant way of walking' (ἀγέρωχον βάδισμα) as well as an 'eyebrow-raising pride' (ὀφρὺν ἐπιλλώπτουσαν ὑπεροψίαν).[55] The *metaphrasis* renders *agerōchos* as *alazonikos*. Interestingly, in both cases *alazoneia* expresses itself through the way in which the arrogant person walks.

In Choniates' *History*, arrogance is not a solely male privilege. Theodora, Emperor Manuel's niece and lover, who already had illegitimately 'arrogated' more or less all imperial rights, refused to walk on the palace floor if it had not been cleaned beforehand. She demands too much, and steps beyond the accepted limits.

αὐτίκα τοίνυν καὶ ἡ ἀνιψιὰ Θεοδώρα, ἣ καὶ ὡς ἔφημεν ἐπλησίαζε, βασιλικωτάτης μετεῖχε δορυφορίας καὶ μόνον οὐ διαδουμένη καὶ τῶν ἀρχείων σαρουμένων παριέναι ἤθελε, καὶ κατὰ φυσικὴν μὲν ἰδιότητα σοβαρὰν ἕλκουσα τὴν ὀφρὺν καὶ ἄνω τὸ ὄμμα τείνουσα, τὸ δὲ πλέον ἀγέρωχον βλέπουσα. (Nic. Chon. *Hist.* 204.91–5)

κινα ὑποδύεται. In the sequel, Konstantinos' behaviour is characterized as ἀκαταστασία ('lack of order') and ἀπιστία ('illoyalty, rebellion').

[53] Nic. Chon. *Hist.* 489.47–51: ὁ δὲ Μεσοποταμίτης Κωνσταντῖνος ... ἀνέσπα τὴν ὀφρὺν καὶ βλακῶδες ἔβαινε διὰ τὴν τῆς δεσποίνης ἐπάνοδον. καθ' ὅν, οἶμαι, λόγον μηδ' ἐξαρκεῖν αὐτῷ ἐς τιμὴν τὸ παρὰ βασιλεῖ δύνασθαι τὰ πάντα οἰόμενος. Cf. Magoulias (1984) 269.

[54] *Metaphrasis Chon.* 15.14.1: ὁ δὲ Μεσοποταμίτης Κωνσταντῖνος ... εἰσερχόμενος εἰς τὰ βασίλεια καὶ τὰ ὀφρύδια ἐπάνω κρατῶν, καὶ μετὰ ἀλαζονείας περιπατῶν, καθότι πάλιν ἐξ οἰκονομίας ἐκείνου εἰσῆλθεν ἡ δέσποινα εἰς τὰ βασίλεια, οὐδὲ τὴν ἣν εἶχεν ἐκ βασιλέως τιμὴν ἀρκετὴν εἶναι πρὸς αὐτὸν ὑπελάμβανε. On the adjective βλακώδης expressing an arrogant attitude see *Suda* B317, ed. Adler (1928–38, 1.474) explaining βλακεία as ὑπεροψία, μωρία. The combination of βλακεία and ἀλαζονεία appears e. g. in Plut. *Mor.* 47e (*De recta ratione audiendi* 1–2).

[55] Nic. Chon. *Hist.* 252.81–253.85: ὁ δὲ τότε πρώτως Ἀνδρόνικον θεασάμενος, ἐπεὶ κατηθρήκει περιεργότερον βλέμμα γοργόν, ὑποκαθήμενον φρόνημα, σοφιστικὸν καὶ περίεργον ἦθος, ἡλικίας ἀναδρομὴν ἐς πόδα δέκατον μικροῦ ἀνατείνουσαν, ἀγέρωχον βάδισμα, ὀφρὺν ἐπιλλώπτουσαν ὑπεροψίαν, φροντιστικόν τε καὶ ἐπὶ συννοίας ἀεὶ ἄνθρωπον. Cf. *Metaphrasis Chon.* 9.8.1: ὁ δὲ πατριάρχης τότε πρῶτον τὸν Ἀνδρόνικον θεασάμενος, ἐπεὶ κατεσκόπευσε καὶ εἶδεν αὐτὸν ἀκριβῶς ἔχοντα βλέμμα γοργόν, φρόνημα καὶ ἦθος περίεργον καὶ σοφιστικόν, ἡλικίαν μακρὰν μέχρι καὶ δέκα ἴχνη ποδῶν ἀναβαίνουσαν, περιπάτημα ἀλαζονικόν, ἐπάνω ἔχοντα τὰς ὀφρῦς, φροντιστικὸν καὶ σύννουν. See also Mich. Psel. *Or. min.* 14.165–6, ed. Littlewood (1985) 57: τὰς ὀφρῦς ἀνατείνουσι καὶ μετὰ σοβαροῦ προΐασι τοῦ βαδίσματος.

316   *Martin Hinterberger*

His niece Theodora with whom, as we have related, he had sexual intercourse, was a member of the imperial retinue except that she did not wear a crown; supercilious by nature, she would enter the palace only when it was swept clean, as she arched her eyebrow in conceited disdain. (Trans. Magoulias (1984) 116)

Theodora's *alazoneia* manifests itself again through the raised eyebrow, the eye looking upward, and the arrogant gaze. As before, the *metaphrasis* translates the bodily signs of arrogance into the emotion itself:[56]

ἦν γὰρ καὶ κατὰ φύσιν ἀλαζονικὴ, ἄνω τὰ ὄμματα ἐπηρμένα βλέπουσα.

For she was arrogant by nature, with her eyes looking up in a conceited way.

According to Choniates, Empress Euphrosyne, the wife of Alexios III Angelos, was a capable woman in administrative and political matters, and she would have deserved admiration 'if she had known her limits' (μέτρα and ὅροι).[57] Because of her successes, however, she became so conceited and arrogant (τυφομανής, a term which is attested only in Choniates)[58] that she committed outrageous acts (ἀθέμιτα, ἀτόπημα), such as dabbling in magic or demolishing ancient statues that stood in the Forum of Constantinople.[59] Choniates regards these actions as 'arrogant' (*huperēphanōs*), but also as 'impudent' (*anaidōs*). The corresponding arrogance terms in the *metaphrasis* are *alazoneia* and *eparsis*, whereas the shameless act is characterized as *adiantropōs*.[60]

---

[56] *Metaphrasis Chon.* 8.2.2: αὐτίκα τοίνυν ἡ ἀνεψιὰ αὐτοῦ Θεοδώρα, ἣν εἴπομεν ὅτι συνεμίγετο, βασιλικὴν εἶχε ἔξοδον τὲ καὶ λαμπρότητα, μόνον μὴ μετέχουσα εὐφημίας καὶ στέμματος· ὅτε γὰρ ἔμελλε διὰ τοῦ παλατίου ἐλθεῖν, εἰ μὴ φιλοκαλημένα ἦσαν τὰ μάρμαρα, ἐπάνω περιπατῆσαι μὴ ἤθελε· ἦν γὰρ καὶ κατὰ φύσιν ἀλαζονικὴ, ἄνω τὰ ὄμματα ἐπηρμένα βλέπουσα.

[57] Nic. Chon. *Hist.* 519.39–520.57: ἦν δ᾿ ἂν οὐκ ἀποσπούδαστα ταῦτα, οὐδὲ τοῦ ἄγασθαι πόρρωθεν, ὡς ὑπὸ γυναικὸς κατορθούμενα, εἴπερ ᾔδεσαν μέτρα καὶ ὅροις ὑπήγοντο· νῦν δὲ τὸ ἄγαν τυφομανὲς καὶ πολυσπερχὲς τῆς δεσποίνης καὶ τὸ δοκοῦν ἴσως δεόντως ἀκριβωθῆναι ἠχρείου τε καὶ διέφθειρεν ὡς νέφεσιν ἥλιος τοῖς ἐπιγινομένοις ἀπευκταίοις ἀφαυρούμενα. τραπομένη γὰρ ἐς προγνώσεις τῶν ἐσομένων ἀρρητουργίαις καὶ μαντείαις προσέκειτο καὶ πολλὰ τῶν ἀθεμίτων εἰργάζετο, ὥστε καὶ τοῦ Καλυδωνίου συὸς τὸ ῥύγχος ἀπέτεμεν … καὶ τὸν καλλίνικον Ἡρακλῆν, τῶν Λυσιμάχου ἔργων τὸ κάλλιστον ὄντα, χειρὶ βαλόντα τὴν κεφαλὴν τῆς λεοντῆς ὑπεστρωμένης κοφίνῳ καὶ τὰς ἰδίας τύχας ὀλοφυρόμενον, πολλαῖς κατὰ νώτου ξᾶναι διενοεῖτο. Ἡράκλεις τοῦ ἀτοπήματος καὶ παπαὶ τῶν ἐπὶ σοὶ τολμωμένων, ἥρως ἄλκιμε, μεγαλόθυμε. τίς σοι Εὐρυσθεὺς τοιοῦτον πώποτε προύθηκεν ἄεθλον; ἢ τίς Ὀμφάλη, ἐπίτριμμα ἐρώτων καὶ κακότεχνον γύναιον, οὕτως ὑπερηφάνως σοι προσενήνεκται; οὐ ταῦτα δὲ μόνον ἀναιδῶς διεπράττετο, ἀλλὰ καὶ ἄλλων ἀνδρεικέλων ἀφῄρει μόρια καὶ σφυρῶν καταφοραῖς ἐκαρατόμει ἕτερα. Cf. Magoulias (1984) 285.

[58] The adjective τυφομανής seems to have been coined by Choniates (attested here, *Hist.* 519.41, and 595.11). Cf. Trapp (1994–2017) 1831, where it is rendered as 'von rasender Arroganz'. The adjective, πολυσπερχής, too, is a quite recherché term which apart from Choniates is also used by Eustathios of Thessalonike; see Trapp (1994–2017) 1345 ('sehr emsig').

[59] On Choniates' negative characterization of Euphrosyne see Garland (1997) 286–93 and Hill (1997) 92–3.

[60] *Metaphrasis Chon.* 16.7.1–3: τὰ γοῦν παρ᾿ αὐτῆς γινόμενα ἵνα ἐθαυμάζοντο καὶ ἐπαινοῦντο, εἰ μέτρα καὶ ὅρους ἐγίνωσκε καταστάσεως, ἡ ἀλαζονεία δὲ ταύτης καὶ ἡ ἔπαρσις καὶ τὸ ὑπολαμβάνειν ὅτι τὰ πάντα παρ᾿ αὐτῆς κατὰ ἀκρίβειαν καὶ πρὸς τὸ συμφέρον οἰκονομοῦνται

12. Alazoneia and Aidōs/Aischunē 317

Arrogance, then, is a serious character flaw for Byzantines – a strong feeling of superiority, based on false assumptions[61] about one's value, which usually manifests itself in the breach of appropriate behaviour, particularly in disobedience towards the emperor. But it appears to be much more significant and serious in the case of foreigners who behave arrogantly towards the Byzantines.

One such is the Hungarian general Dionysios, who out of arrogance boasted about his upcoming victory:

[οἱ Παίονες] … φρονηματισθέντες οὕτω μετὰ κόμπου ἐπῄεσαν. οὗτος δὲ ὁ Διονύσιος, ὅτε πρώτως ἠκηκόει τὸν Ἴστρον διαβῆναι Ῥωμαϊκὴν στρατιάν, γεγαυρωμένος ὢν ἐπὶ ταῖς προτέραις νίκαις, ἃς ἤρατο κατὰ Ῥωμαίων, μεγαλορρημονῶν ἔλεγεν ὡς εἰς κολωνὸν αὖθις ἐσεῖται ἀγηοχὼς τὰ τῶν ἐν πολέμῳ πεσόντων Ῥωμαίων ὀστᾶ, καὶ οἷα τροπαίῳ τούτοις ὡς καὶ ἄλλοτέ ποτε χρήσαιτο. (Nic. Chon. Hist. 153.26–32)

And thus [the Hungarians] … became arrogant and attacked the Byzantines with boisterousness. When this Dionysios, who prided himself in his previous victories over the Byzantines, first heard that the Byzantine army had crossed the Danube, he boastfully said that he would erect a column out of the bones of the Byzantines fallen in battle and he would use them [i.e. the bones] as a symbol of victory as already once before. (Cf. Magoulias (1984) 87)

In the *metaphrasis*, Choniates' arrogance-related terms φρονηματισθέντες μετὰ κόμπου are rendered as μετὰ ἐπηρμένου φρονήματος καὶ ἀλαζονείας, while γεγαυρωμένος and μεγαλορρημονῶν are summarized as ἔπαρσις.[62]

Other such arrogant foreigners were the German kings Conrad III and Henry VI, the latter's envoy Henry of Kalden, and the Sicilian Aldouinos. In their arrogance the German kings disobey orders of the Byzantine emperor, or they make inappropriate demands; therefore, they are also characterized as impudent.[63]

Aldouinos (i.e. Baldwin), on the other side, a high-ranking dignitary of the Norman king William II of Sicily,[64] because of the good fortune he had experi-

---

ἠχρείωσε καὶ διέφθειρεν ὥσπερ καὶ τὰ νέφη τὸν ἥλιον· ἐξετάζουσα γὰρ μαθεῖν τὰ μέλλοντα ἔμπροσθεν γεγενῆσθαι, εἰς γοητείας καὶ μαντείας ἐνέσκηψε, καὶ πολλὰ τῶν ἀτόπων εἰργάζετο … οὐ ταῦτα δὲ μόνον ἀδιαντρόπως διέπραξεν, ἀλλὰ καὶ ἄλλων στηλῶν ἱσταμένων τῶν μὲν τοὺς ὄρχεις αὐτῶν ἀπέκοπτεν, ἄλλα δὲ μετὰ βαρέων κατὰ κεφαλῆς κρούων συνέτριβε.

[61] See οἴομαι in Nic. Chon. Hist. 489.51; cf. above, note 53. In the *metaphrasis*, repeatedly the verb ὑπολαμβάνω is explicitly used in order to clarify that a 'false belief' is meant; see e.g. *Metaphrasis Chon.* 10.6.8, 15.14.1, and 16.7.1–2 (cf. notes 54, 60, and 74).

[62] *Metaphrasis Chon.* 6.1.8: μετὰ ἐπηρμένου φρονήματος καὶ ἀλαζονείας κατὰ τῶν Ῥωμαίων ἤρχοντο. ὅτε καὶ λέγεται τὸν Διονύσιον εἰπεῖν ἀκούσαντα περάσαι τὴν τῶν Ῥωμαίων στρατιὰν τὸν Δάνουβιν μετὰ ἐπάρσεως, ὅτι πεσοῦνται τὰ ὀστᾶ αὐτῶν ὡσεὶ βουνὸς ἐν τῷ τόπῳ τούτῳ.

[63] On Conrad III see Nic. Chon. Hist. 65.95–1 (ὑπερεφρόνει, βλακευόμενος; cf. *Metaphrasis Chon.* 2.7.12: ἀλαζονευόμενος); on Henry VI, *Metaphrasis Chon.* 15.10.2 (ἀλαζονικὸς and ἀδιαντρόπως; cf. Nic. Chon. Hist. 475.37–8, but less explicit); on Henry of Kalden, Nic. Chon. Hist. 476.61–2 (βαρὺς τὴν ὀφρύν; cf. *Metaphrasis Chon.* 15.10.3: ἐπηρμένος). The Germans' claims are characterized as ἀλαζονεῖαι and κόμποι (Nic. Chon. Hist. 476.63–4; cf. *Metaphrasis Chon.* 15.10.3: καυχήματα).

[64] See also Schmidt (1997) 171.

318   *Martin Hinterberger*

enced, became 'swollen (ἐξοιδούμενος/πεφυσιωμένος) like a wineskin' – another quite usual metaphor used for the arrogant man, already in ancient Greek[65] – and wrote an insolent letter to Emperor Isaak, ridiculing him:

ὁ δ' Ἀλδουῖνος ἀγέρωχος ὢν καὶ ἄλλως ὡς ἔδειξε, τότε δὲ καὶ ταῖς ἐνεστώσαις τύχαις ὡς ἀσκὸς ἐξοιδούμενος, οὐκ ἐνεγκὼν τὰ ἐπεσταλμένα ἀμείβεται τὸν βασιλέα λόγοις κομψευτικοῖς. τό τε γὰρ ξίφος αὐτοῦ ἐκωμῴδησεν … (Nic. Chon. *Hist.* 365.65–8)[66]

Aldouinos, generally being an arrogant man as became clear, was at that time swollen like a wineskin because of his successes, and therefore he could not tolerate the [emperor's] letters and replied to the emperor with mocking words. For he ridiculed his [the emperor's] sword … (Cf. Magoulias (1984) 202)

Also, in Anna Komnene's *Alexiad*, Bohemund of Sicily, who became conceited and arrogant after he cunningly escaped from the Byzantines' hands, sends a scornful message to Emperor Alexios:

ὁ δὲ τῶν μὲν ἄλλων ὑπερεώρα πάντων, ἀνεζήτει δὲ τὸν δοῦκα τῆς πόλεως. ἦν δὲ ἄρα οὗτος Ἀλέξιός τις θέματος Ἀρμενιακοῦ γενόμενος. ὃν θεασάμενος, μετὰ σοβαροῦ τοῦ βλέμματός τε καὶ σχήματος καὶ σοβαρᾷ τῇ φωνῇ χρώμενος καὶ ὅλως βαρβαρικῇ, ἀπαγγεῖλαι προσέταττεν Ἀλεξίῳ τῷ αὐτοκράτορι ὅτι "σοὶ ἐγὼ Βαϊμοῦντος ἐκεῖνος ὁ τοῦ Ῥομπέρτου, ὃν ὁ ἀνέκαθεν χρόνος καὶ σὲ καὶ τὴν ὑπὸ σὲ βασιλείαν ἐδίδαξεν, ὁπόσος τίς εἰμι τὴν ἀνδρείαν καὶ τὴν ἔνστασιν … εἰ γὰρ τὴν ἀντιπέραν ἤπειρον καταλάβοιμι καὶ Λογγιβάρδους καὶ πάντας Λατίνους καὶ Γερμανοὺς καὶ τοὺς καθ' ἡμᾶς Φράγγους ὀψαίμην, ἄνδρας Ἄρεως μνήμονας, πολλῶν φόνων καὶ πολλῶν αἱμάτων τὰς σὰς ἐμπλήσω καὶ πόλεις καὶ χώρας, ἕως ἂν ἐπ' αὐτοῦ Βυζαντίου τὸ δόρυ πηξαίμην." εἰς τοσοῦτον ἄρα ὁ βάρβαρος ἀλαζονείας ἐπῆρτο. (Anna Comn. *Alex.* 11.12.5–6)

However, he treated them all with contempt and asked for the *doux* of the town. The *doux* happened to be a certain Alexios of the Armenian theme. When Bohemund saw him he looked at him haughtily and with haughty bearing and speaking haughtily in his barbarian language ordered him to give Alexios the Emperor the following message. 'This message I send to thee, I, that Bohemund the son of Robert, who has in these past years taught thee and thy Empire how strong I am in courage and perseverance … For as soon as I reach the continent opposite and see the men of Lombardy, and all the Latins and Germans and the Franks, our subjects and most warlike men, I shall fill thy towns and countries with many murders and much bloodshed until I plant my spear on Byzantium itself.' To such a pitch of arrogance was the barbarian carried. (Trans. Dawes (1928) 299, slightly adapted)

---

[65] See e.g. φύσημα and other derivatives of φυσάω in LSJ. Cf. also Euagr. Pont. *Praktikos* 14.4, ed. Guillaumont and Guillaumont (1971): φυσιοῦσθαι, or Agathias, *Hist.* 2.30.5, ed. Keydell (1967) 80.25: τοὺς … ἀλαζόνας … καὶ πέρα τοῦ δέοντος ἐξωγκωμένους, or Nic. Chon. *Hist.* 438.52: μετὰ φυσήματος; cf. *Metaphrasis Chon.* 14.6.2: ἀπὸ τῆς τοιαύτης ὑπεροψίας καὶ σοβαρότητος. Also Lewis (2000) 630 regards being 'puffed up' as a major characteristic of *hubris*.

[66] Cf. *Metaphrasis Chon.* 12.3.4: ὁ δὲ Ἀλδουῖνος ἀλαζονικὸς ὤν, τότε δὲ καὶ πλέον τοῦ πρέποντος ὑπὸ τῆς νίκης ὡς ἀσκὸς πεφυσιωμένος πρησθείς, μὴ ἐνεγκὼν τὰ παρὰ τοῦ βασιλέως γεγραμμένα ἀντέγραψε καὶ αὐτὸς γελῶν καὶ ἐξουδενῶν τὴν τοῦ βασιλέως σπάθην.

12. Alazoneia and Aidōs/Aischunē 319

The metaphrast renders the classical adjective *sobaros* with *epērmenos* and *alazonikos*.[67]

In *Alex*. 10.10.6 Anna recounts the outrageous lack of respect of one French nobleman who dared to sit on the emperor's throne. Alexios ignored him, 'knowing the Latins' arrogant nature'.[68] Interestingly, another French nobleman, count Baldouinos (i. e. Baudouin of Boulogne), appears thereafter on the scene, lifting his countryman from the throne and explaining to him that the Byzantine emperor does not sit with his subjects and that one must respect the customs of the land (τὰ ἔθη τῆς χώρας τηρεῖν).

The common feature in all these passages is the lack of respect for Byzantine authority or the emperor on the Westerner's part. Apart from a few individual cases of arrogant behaviour mentioned above (German kings, Henry of Kalden, Baldwin), rather frequently Choniates declares 'arrogance' to be a contemptible character trait of Westerners in general.[69] Thus, he writes, the Venetians had become rich among the Byzantines and for this reason they became also arrogant and impudent (αὐθάδειάν τε καὶ ἀναίδειαν μετεδίωκαν). They demonstrated animosity toward the Byzantines and disregard for the emperor's orders.[70]

---

[67] *Metaphrasis Alex*. 112–15: ὁ δὲ τοὺς μὲν ἄλλους πάντας παρέβλεπεν, ἐγύρευε δὲ τὸν δοῦκα. ἦν δὲ ἐκεῖσε Ἀλέξιός τις ἀπὸ τοῦ θέματος τοῦ Ἀρμενιακοῦ· ὃν ἰδὼν μετὰ ἐπηρμένου βλέμματος καὶ σχήματος καὶ ἀλαζονικῇ φωνῇ χρησάμενος εἶπε τῷ Ἀλεξίῳ· εἶπε τῷ βασιλεῖ, ὅτι ἐγώ εἰμι ὁ Βαϊμοῦντος ἐκεῖνος ὁ τοῦ Ῥομπέρτου υἱός· ὃν ὁ χρόνος ἐδίδαξέ σε τὸ τίς εἰμι καὶ πόσος εἰς ἀνδρείαν καὶ τὴν φρόνησιν ... ἐνταῦθα γὰρ ἐλθὼν πᾶσαν τὴν Λογγιβαρδίαν καὶ τοὺς Νορμάνους καὶ τοὺς Φράγγους καὶ Ἀλαμάνους κατὰ σοῦ καὶ τῶν σῶν χωρῶν κινήσω, ἕως ἂν τὸ κοντάριν μου εἰς τὴν Πόλιν πήξω· εἰς τοσαύτην ἀλαζονείαν ἐπήρθη ὁ βάρβαρος. In the *Suda*, Σ756/7, ed. Adler (1928–38, 4.394), σοβαρός is explained as ὑπερήφανος, ἐπαιρόμενος. αὐθάδης, ἔξω τοῦ δέοντος φερόμενος. See also σοβαρότης ('arrogance', a new term) in Lampe (1961) 1244 as well as the compound adjectives σοβαροπρόσωπος, σοβαρότροπος, σοβαρόφρων in Trapp (1994–2017) 1582.

[68] Anna Comn. *Alex*. 10.10.6: τολμήσας τίς ἀπὸ πάντων τῶν κομήτων εὐγενὴς εἰς τὸν σκίμποδα τοῦ βασιλέως ἐκάθισεν. ὁ δὲ βασιλεὺς ἠνείχετο τούτου μηδέν τι φθεγξάμενος, πάλαι τὴν ἀγέρωχον τῶν Λατίνων φύσιν εἰδώς. παρελθὼν δὲ ὁ κόμης Βαλδουῖνος καὶ ἁψάμενος αὐτοῦ τῆς χειρὸς ἤγειρεν ἐκεῖθεν καὶ πολλὰ καταμεμψάμενος ἔφη· "... οὐδὲ γὰρ ἔθιμον τοῖς βασιλεῦσι Ῥωμαίων συνέδρους ἔχειν τοὺς ὑπ᾿ αὐτούς. δούλους δὲ ὁμότας τῆς αὐτοῦ βασιλείας γεγονότας χρὴ καὶ τὰ ἔθη τῆς χώρας τηρεῖν." See also Reinsch (1996) 354. The corresponding passage of the *metaphrasis* is not extant.

[69] E. g. Westerners in general: Nic. Chon. *Hist*. 199.53–4: ὑψαυχεῖν τε γὰρ τοὺς ἄνδρας καὶ τὸ φρονεῖν εἶναι ἀκαταπλήκτους τε καὶ ἀταπεινώτους (cf. *Metaphrasis Chon*. 8.1.2: τοὺς κατὰ τὴν δύσιν Λατίνους ... ἀλαζονικοὺς ὄντας καὶ ἐπηρμένους) or more specifically the Sicilian Normans: Nic. Chon. *Hist*. 357.60: τοὺς ὑψαύχενας (cf. *Metaphrasis Chon*. 12.2.5: τοὺς ὑψαύχενας τούτους καὶ ἀλαζόνας Φράγγους) and 358.90–1: ὑψαύχενες καὶ γαῦροι καὶ ... κομπάζοντες (cf. *Metaphrasis Chon*. 12.2.7: καυχωμένους, ἀλαζόνας καὶ ἐπηρμένους). The same can be observed in Anna's *Alexiad*, although there the motive is less conspicuous. See e.g. Anna Comn. *Alex*. 10.6.6: ὁποῖα Λατῖνος ὑψαύχην, and 10.10.6: τὴν ἀγέρωχον τῶν Λατίνων φύσιν.

[70] Nic. Chon. *Hist*. 171.52–5: οὐκοῦν καὶ περιβαλόμενοι πλοῦτον πολὺν αὐθάδειάν τε καὶ ἀναίδειαν μετεδίωκαν, ὡς μὴ μόνον ἀναρσίως ἔχειν Ῥωμαίοις, ἀλλὰ καὶ τῶν βασιλικῶν ἀνεπιστρόφως ἀπειλῶν τε καὶ ἐντολῶν. Cf. *Metaphrasis Chon*. 6.5.1: εἰς ἀλαζονείαν καὶ ἀδιαντροπίαν ἐνέπεσον.

320   *Martin Hinterberger*

Choniates' combination *authadeia* and *anaideia* is rendered as *alazoneia* and *adiantropia* in the *metaphrasis*, the latter term being the low-style word generally corresponding with high-style *anaideia* or *anaischuntia*.[71] And it is the Westerners' arrogance which is presented as the motivating force behind their devastating assaults on the Byzantine Empire. In a long digression occasioned by the Norman sack of Thessalonike in 1185 and the arrogant way Westerners treat their defeated enemies, Choniates declares the following: Westerners are like the envious and satanic serpent wishing to destroy the paradise on earth, the Byzantine Empire.[72] There is an unbridgeable gulf separating the two 'nations' – the opposition is forcefully expressed by αὐτοὶ μέν – ἡμεῖς δέ. Latins are arrogant (ὑψαυχενοῦντες, ἐξ ὑπερηφανίας, τὸ ὑπέροφρυ καὶ τὸ κομπηρὸν, κόρυζα[73]), whereas the Byzantines' major characteristics are τὸ λεῖον τοῦ ἤθους and τὸ ὑποκαταβαῖνον χαμαὶ διὰ τὸ τοῦ φρονήματος μέτριον, i.e. moderation, modesty, and humility – the Westerners' arrogance is thus developed into the very reason for the disaster that befell Byzantium.

οὕτω μέσον ἡμῶν καὶ αὐτῶν χάσμα διαφορᾶς ἐστήρικται μέγιστον καὶ ταῖς γνώμαις ἀσυναφεῖς ἐσμεν καὶ κατὰ διάμετρον ἀφεστήκαμεν, εἰ καὶ σώμασι συναπτόμεθα καὶ τὴν αὐτὴν πολλάκις κληρούμεθα οἴκησιν. ὅθεν καὶ αὐτοὶ μὲν ὑψαυχενοῦντες ὡς τὰ πολλὰ καὶ τὸ τοῦ σχήματος ἐξ ὑπερηφανίας ὑποκρινόμενοι ὄρθιον ὡς πτέρναν φιλοῦσι τηρεῖν καὶ περιεργάζεσθαι τὸ λεῖον τοῦ ἤθους ἡμῶν καὶ ὑποκαταβαῖνον χαμαὶ διὰ τὸ τοῦ φρονήματος μέτριον, ἡμεῖς δὲ τὸ ἐκείνων ὑπέροφρυ καὶ τὸ κομπηρὸν καὶ σεμνὸν καὶ τὴν κόρυζαν οἷά τινα κεφαλὴν ἄνω ὑποβλεπόμενοι τείνουσαν ἐπ' αὐτῆς τὴν πορείαν τιθέμεθα φλῶντες ἐς δεῦρο τῇ δυνάμει Χριστοῦ τοῦ πατεῖν ἐπάνω ὄφεως καὶ σκορπίων ἐξουσίαν βραβεύοντος καὶ τὸ μηδὲν ἐντεῦθεν παθεῖν ἢ καὶ ἠδικῆσθαι παρέχοντος. (Nic. Chon. *Hist*. 301.27–302.37)[74]

---

[71] On *adiantropia* see Trapp (1994–2017) and Kriaras (1967–) *s. v.* as well as below, pp. 327 and 336

[72] Nic. Chon. *Hist*. 301.17–27: τί δ' ἂν κακὸν εἴη παρεικὼς ἀτέλεστον ἀνὴρ μισορρώμαιος καὶ τοσαύτην ἀποθησαυρίσας ἐν ἑαυτῷ καθ᾽῾Ελληνος ἀνδρὸς τὴν ἀπέχθειαν, ὁποίαν οὐδ᾽ ὄφις αὐτὸς ὁ ἀρχαῖος τοῦ ἀνθρωπίνου γένους ἐπίβουλος συνειληφὼς πάλαι ἀπέτεκεν, ἐπεὶ καὶ παραδείσῳ μὲν ἄντικρυς παρὰ τοῖς καταρατοτάτοις Λατίνοις εἰκάζεται ἣν ἡμεῖς ἐλάχομεν οἰκεῖν καὶ ἀποκαρπεύεσθαι, καὶ δυσέρωτες ὄντες τῶν παρ᾽ ἡμῖν ἀγαθῶν κακογνωμονοῦσιν ἀεὶ περὶ τὸ ἡμέτερον γένος καὶ κακῶν εἰσι τέκτονες διὰ παντός. κἂν φιλεῖν πλάττωνται, τὸν καιρὸν ὑποδυόμενοι, μισοῦσιν ὡς ἔχθιστον· κἂν ὁ λόγος αὐτοῖς εὐπροσήγορος καὶ ὑπὲρ ἔλαιον ῥέων ἀψοφητὶ ἀπαλύνηται, ἀλλὰ βολίδες εἰσὶ καὶ οὕτως αὐτοὶ καὶ μαχαίρας ἀμφιστόμου τομώτεροι. This passage and the comparison with the serpent-devil suggest that the Latins were driven by *phthonos*, 'envy', against the Byzantines, who enjoyed their paradise as Adam and Eve had done; cf. Hinterberger (2013a) 189–208 and 288–9.

[73] The term *koruza* literally means 'snot' and is metonymically used for arrogance in Choniates and other Byzantine classicizing authors (while in ancient Greek it is generally used in the metaphorical sense of 'stupidity', cf. LSJ *s. v.*). The *metaphrasis* renders *koruza* regularly as *alazoneia*.

[74] Cf. *Metaphrasis Chon*. 10.6.8: καὶ μέσον ἡμῶν καὶ αὐτῶν μέγα χάσμα διαφορᾶς ἐστὶ, καὶ κατὰ τὰς γνώμας πολὺ κατὰ διάμετρον ἀφεστήκαμεν, κἂν καὶ ἐν τοῖς σώμασι συναγώμεθα καὶ τὴν αὐτὴν γῆν πολλάκις κατοίκησιν ἔχωμεν. ὅθεν καὶ αὐτοὶ μὲν ὀρθὰς καὶ ὑψηλὰς κρατοῦντες τὰς κεφαλάς, καὶ τὸ ὀρθὸν ὑποκρίνοντες ἐκ τῆς ἀλαζονείας αὐτῶν, ἡμᾶς δὲ περιεργάζονται καὶ ὑπολαμβάνουσιν εἰς τὰς πτέρνας κεῖσθαι αὐτῶν, διὰ τὸ τοῦ φρονήματος μέτριον καὶ τοῦ ἤθους

12. Alazoneia and Aidōs/Aischunē 321

Between us and them the greatest gulf of disagreement has been fixed, and we are separated in purpose and diametrically opposed, even though we are closely associated and frequently share the same dwelling. Overweening in their arrogant display of straightforwardness, the Latins would stare up and down at us and behold with curiosity the gentleness and lowliness of our demeanour; and we, looking grimly upon their superciliousness, boastfulness, and pompousness, with the drivel from their nose held in the air, are committed to this course and grit our teeth, secure in the power of Christ, who gives the faithful the power to tread on serpents and scorpions and grants them protection from all harm and hurt. (Cf. Magoulias (1984) 167)

Again, when narrating the conquest of Constantinople in 1204, Choniates enumerates the Latins' outstanding character traits: besides their total lack of compassion for their defeated enemies, these are ὁ χαλκοῦς αὐχήν, ἡ ἀλαζὼν φρήν, ἡ ὀρθὴ ὀφρύς, ὁ μετέωρος ὀφθαλμός, 'the bronze [i. e. stiff] neck, the arrogant spirit, the high brow, the eye looking upwards' – all signs of arrogance.

τοιαῦθ', ὡς ἐκ πολλῶν βραχέα δοῦναι τῇ ἱστορίᾳ, οἱ ἐξ ἑσπέρας στρατοὶ κατὰ τῆς Χριστοῦ κληρονομίας παρηνομήκασιν, ἐπ' οὐδενὶ τῶν ὅλων τὸ φιλάνθρωπον ἐνδειξάμενοι, ἀλλὰ πάντας ἀποξενώσαντες χρημάτων καὶ κτημάτων, οἰκημάτων τε καὶ ἐσθημάτων, καὶ μηδενὸς τῶν πάντων μεταδόντες τοῖς ἔχουσι. ταῦτα ὁ χαλκοῦς αὐχήν, ἡ ἀλαζὼν φρήν, ἡ ὀρθὴ ὀφρύς, ἡ ἀεὶ ξυριῶσα καὶ νεανισκευομένη παρειά, ἡ φιλαίματος δεξιά, ἡ ἀκροχολῶσα ῥίν, ὁ μετέωρος ὀφθαλμός, ἡ ἄπληστος γνάθος, ἡ ἄστοργος γνώμη ... (Nic. Chon. *Hist.* 575.59–66)[75]

Such then, to make a long story short, were the outrageous crimes committed by the Western armies against the inheritance of Christ. Without showing any feelings of humanity whatsoever, they exacted from all their money and chattel, dwellings and clothing, leaving to them nothing of all their goods. Thus behaved the bronze neck, the haughty spirit, the high brow, the ever-shaved and youthful cheek, the bloodthirsty right hand, the wrathful nostril, the eye looking upward, the insatiable jaw, the loveless attitude ... (Cf. Magoulias (1984) 316)

In the *metaphrasis*, these bodily symptoms of *alazoneia* are rendered as ὁ χαλκὸς τράχηλος, ἡ ἀλαζονικὴ φρόνησις, ἡ ὀρθὴ καὶ ἐπηρμένη ὀφρύς, ὁ ὑψηλὰ βλέπων ὀφθαλμός. When the conquerors distributed their booty, the Byzantine lands, they displayed again blind arrogance (τυφομανής, rendered as ἐπηρμένος καὶ ἀλαζονικός in the *metaphrasis*) and madness.[76]

τὸ ταπεινόν, ἡμεῖς δὲ τὴν ἐκείνων ἀλαζονείαν καὶ τὴν ὑπέροφρυν καὶ ὑψηλὴν κεφαλὴν τὴν ἐπάνω βλέπουσαν τῇ δυνάμει Χριστοῦ καταπατοῦμεν, τοῦ ἐπάνω ὄφεων καὶ σκορπίων ἐξουσίαν δωρησαμένου ἡμῖν πατεῖν καὶ τὸ μηδὲν ἐξ αὐτῶν παθεῖν φοβεῖσθαι ἢ μόνον τὸ ἀδικεῖσθαι.

[75] Cf. *Metaphrasis Chon.* 20.6.1: ταῦτα ὡς ἐκ πολλῶν ὀλίγα τῇ ἱστορίᾳ ἐγράψαμεν, ἀφ' ὧν οἱ δυσικοὶ Λατῖνοι κατὰ τῆς τοῦ Χριστοῦ κληρονομίας παρηνόμησαν, μηδένα τῶν ἁπάντων φιλανθρωπευσάμενοι, ἀλλὰ πάντας καὶ χρημάτων καὶ κτημάτων ἀποξενώσαντες καὶ ὁσπητίων καὶ ῥούχων, καὶ μηδένα τῶν ἁπάντων μεταδόντες τι ἀφ' ὧν εἶχον. ταῦτα ὁ χαλκὸς τράχηλος, ἡ ἀλαζονικὴ φρόνησις, ἡ ὀρθὴ καὶ ἐπηρμένη ὀφρύς, τὸ ἀείποτε ξυριζόμενον καὶ νέον φαινόμενον μάγουλον, ἡ δεξιὰ χεὶρ ἡ ἀείποτε τὰ αἵματα χέουσα, ἡ ὀργῆς γέμουσα μίτυς, ὁ ὑψηλὰ βλέπων ὀφθαλμός, ἡ ἄπληστος καὶ ἀχόρταστος κοιλία, ἡ ἄστοργος γνώμη ...

[76] Nic. Chon. *Hist.* 595.10–21: ὡς δὲ καὶ κλήρους πόλεων καὶ χωρῶν ἤρξαντο βάλλειν, ἣν ἰδέ-

322 *Martin Hinterberger*

In the passages analysed above, Niketas Choniates as well as Anna Komnene use a broad variety of terms to express the concept of 'arrogance'. Apart from the common terms *alazoneia*, *eparsis*, and *huperēphania* – *kenodoxia* is conspicuously absent – we find *phronēmatias/phronēmatizomai* ('having a high opinion of oneself'), *koruza* (literally 'snot', metaphorically 'stupidity, foolishness'), and *tuphos* ('arrogance, madness' and its derivative *tuphomanēs*), the adjectives *agerōchos*, *authadēs*, and *sobaros*, as well as the verbs *brenthuomai* and *semnunomai*.[77] Other terms such as *huperopsia* ('contempt', literally 'to-look-beyond') denote bodily signs or symptoms of arrogance and are used metonymically instead of *alazoneia*: the arrogant person's eye looks upward (ὑψηλὰ βλέπειν, μετέωρος ὀφθαλμός) or beyond other people (ὑπερορᾶν). This 'overlooking', ignoring, and disdainful character seems to be the essential quality of the arrogant gaze (σοβαρὸν βλέμμα), whereas it is less clear how the arrogant voice (σοβαρὰ φωνή) sounded or what the arrogant way of walking (ἀγέρωχον βάδισμα) looked like. In the *metaphrasis*, this broad terminological variety is almost entirely reduced to the three basic terms *alazoneia*, *eparsis*, and *huperēphania* (the latter is, however, rare).[78] Another mental image is that of a swollen body elicited by the comparison of the arrogant person with a swollen wineskin (ὡς ἀσκὸς ἐξοιδούμενος). Two other bodily signs which are conspicuous in Choniates are the raised eyebrow (*ophrus*) and the high neck (*hupsauchēn*) – in the *metaphrasis* usually rendered with the same basic terms mentioned above. A few more words on these corporeal expressions of arrogance are appropriate.

As we have seen, Choniates frequently uses the noun *ophrus* 'eyebrow' metonymically in the sense of 'arrogance' (cf. English 'to be supercilious').[79] This meaning appears already in ancient Greek (and is explained in Byzantine lexica such as the *Suda* as *alazoneia* and rendered as such in the *metaphrasis*). Accordingly, locutions such as ἀνασπάω τὴν ὀφρύν or ἕλκω σοβαρὰν τὴν ὀφρύν, 'to raise an arrogant eyebrow', are used in the sense of 'to become arrogant', even

---

σθαι καὶ θέσθαι διὰ πλείστου ὅτι τοῦ θαύματος ἀνδρῶν τυφομανῶν μὴ ξυμβλητὴν ἀπόνοιαν, εἴτ' οὖν παράνοιαν εἰπεῖν οἰκειότερον. Cf. *Metaphrasis Chon.* 21.5.1: ὡς δὲ καὶ κλήρους πόλεων καὶ χωρῶν ἤρξαντο βάλλειν, τότε ἵνα εἶδε τίς καὶ ἐθαύμασεν ἀνδρῶν ἐπηρμένων καὶ ἀλαζονικῶν τοσαύτην ἀπόνοιαν ἢ μᾶλλον μωρίαν εἰπεῖν ἀληθέστερον.

[77] See LSJ on these terms and their use in ancient Greek as synonyms of *alazōn*. See also Ribbeck (1882) 53–4. The *Suda*, A202, explains *agerōchia* as *huperēphania* and *agerōchos* as *alazōn* (ed. Adler 1928–38, 1.23). For βρενθύεται, Hesychius (*Lex.* B1100) gives the explanations μεγαλοφρονεῖ, ὑπερηφανεύεται, ἐπαίρεται. On *sobaros* see above, note 67.

[78] Based on the results of the research project mentioned above (note 48), a detailed list of lexical correspondences between Choniates' *History* and the *metaphrasis* of this text is available in the form of searchable PDF files from the website of the Interdepartmental Postgraduate Program in Byzantine Studies and the Latin East of the University of Cyprus: see www.ucy.ac.cy/byz/el/news-and-announcements (accessed 3 August 2021).

[79] On eyebrows expressing emotions other than arrogance (in particular anger, fear, and contempt) see Ekman (2003) 139, 168, and 185.

12. Alazoneia and Aidōs/Aischunē 323

when there is no actual body language or a reference to body language is not the point – so the physical expression has become a name for the emotion itself.[80] In an interesting passage of his *Chronographia*, Michael Psellos explains the symbolic meaning of different forms of eyebrows when presenting Basil II as an ideal ruler also in his appearance.

τὸ μὲν οὖν ἦθος αὐτῷ τοιοῦτον, τὸ δὲ εἶδος εὐγένειαν κατηγόρει φύσεως· τό τε γὰρ ὄμμα χαροπὸν καὶ λαμπρὸν, καὶ ἡ ὀφρὺς οὐκ ἐπικειμένη καὶ σκυθρωπάζουσα, οὔτε θηλυπρεπῶς κατ' εὐθεῖαν ἐκτεταμένη γραμμὴν, ἀλλ' ὑπερκειμένη καὶ τὸ ἀγέρωχον τοῦ ἀνδρὸς ὑπεμφαίνουσα· (Mich. Psel. *Chron.* 1.35.4, ed. Reinsch (2014))

So much for his character. As for his appearance, it betrayed the nobility of his nature. For his eyes were light-blue and bright, the eyebrows not overhanging nor sullen, nor yet extended in one straight line as is becoming for women, but they were high above his eyes and indicative of his pride. (Trans. Sewter (1969) 48, slightly adapted)

Raised eyebrows here, too, are indicative of arrogance or pride.[81] Choniates also uses the adjective *huperophrus*, 'with high eyebrows', a classicizing word, yet not attested in Classical literature. It is sporadically used by Gregory of Nazianzos, is frequent in Cyril of Alexandria, and appears in lexica where it is explained as *alazōn* or *huperēphanos*.[82] Its broader use is attested only from the twelfth century on, when like other classicizing literary terms, it was 'unearthed' by the intellectuals of the Komnenian era, and further developed.[83] The compound verb ὑπεροφρυάζομαι ('be arrogant') which derives from this adjective is only attested in Niketas Choniates and his brother Michael.[84]

Repeatedly, Choniates calls arrogant persons *hupsauchēn*, 'with a high neck' (cf. English 'stiff-necked'); the Western enemies of Byzantium in particular are characterized with this adjective.[85] In Classical Greek literature, the adjective

---

[80] On the meaning and use of these locutions in Ancient Greek see LSJ *s.v.* ὀφρύς.

[81] Since Psellos' general portrait of Basil II as well as the above description of his appearance is rather positive, τὸ ἀγέρωχον probably designates positive pride, a rather rare phenomenon in Byzantine as well as ancient literature. Reinsch's translation of this passage, too, suggests such an interpretation; see Reinsch (2015) 102.

[82] E.g. Ps.-Zonar. *Lexicon* 1768.20 (ἀλαζών, ἐπηρμένος, ed. Tittmann (1808)). *Suda* Y344 (ὑπερήφανος, ed. Adler (1928–38, 4.659)). Phot. *Lexicon* 623.11 (ὑπερήφανος, ed. Theodoridis (1982–2013)). On its usage in patristic texts see Lampe (1961) 1441. As a rare variant of ὑπέροφρυς, ὕψοφρυς is used in a thirteenth-century poem, again characterizing a Westerner (Ἰταλός); cf. Trapp (1994–2017) 1909.

[83] Apart from Choniates, the term *huperophrus* is used more than once by Constantine Manasses, Euthymios Malakes, Theodore Prodromos, and Eustathios of Thessalonike as well as by the thirteenth-century author George Pachymeres. The *TLG* was of great help for this investigation. On other Classical/classicizing terms that were resuscitated and partly reinterpreted during this period see Hinterberger (2014b).

[84] See Trapp (1994–2017) 1866 ('überaus hochmütig sein').

[85] See also Schmidt (1997) 169 n. 35. ὑψαύχην characterizes Westerners also in other contemporary texts, such as Anna Comn. *Alex.* 10.6.6: ὁποῖα Λατῖνος ὑψαύχην; Georg. Acropol. *Epitaph. Io. Ducae* 7, ed. Heisenberg and Wirth (1978), 17.2–4: καὶ ὁ ὑψαύχην κατέπιπτε καὶ ὁ

324   *Martin Hinterberger*

hupsauchēn is attested in Plato's *Phaedrus* (253d), where in combination with *alazoneia* it is used as an attribute of the arrogant horse, one of the two horses symbolizing two parts of the tripartite soul.[86] This very passage is frequently quoted in treatises on horses (*hippiatrika*). *Hupsauchēn* appears often together with *gauros*.[87] Both terms seem to be initially restricted to the characterization of a horse. Thus, its figurative meaning is related to the image of a horse's neck which is 'high' and 'straight', and it is particularly associated with an unruly, 'arrogant' horse. In lexica and scholia the term *hupsauchēn* is regularly explained as *alazōn* or *hupsēlophrōn* ('thinking high').[88] Choniates uses also the derivative verb *hupsaucheneō*, 'have a straight neck, i.e. be arrogant'. In other texts this verb seems to have been occasionally confused with *hupsaucheō*, a derivative of *aucheō*, 'to boast', since both concepts, the 'high neck' and boastful behaviour, were associated with arrogance.[89]

On the other hand, an inclined, lowered neck is a sign of humility and subjection. To lower one's neck means to recognize the other's authority. Choniates describes a peculiar ritual which expresses the act of submission and shows utter humility:[90] a man lies down and invites others to step on his neck. Thus, for instance, patriarch Michael Oxeites, who had been forced to abdicate, invites his fellow monks to step on his neck after returning from the patriarchal throne to his monastery (AD 1140).[91]

τὰς ὀφρῦς ἐπαίρων ὑπεχαλᾶτο τοῦ κεναυχήματος καὶ τὸ φύσημα κατεβέβλητο. In the same meaning the word ὑψηλοτράχηλος (in combination with ἀγέρωχος) is used by Theodore Prodromos (an older contemporary of Choniates). Characteristically, Prodromos describes the island of Corfu, at that time under Norman occupation, and its inhabitants with these adjectives. Equally characteristically, he praises Emperor Manuel for his human treatment of the enemies; Theo. Prod. *Poem. hist.* 30, ed. Hörandner (1974) 99–101: καὶ τὴν ὑψηλοτράχηλον ᾐχμαλωτίσω πόλιν / καὶ τὸν ἀγέρωχον λαὸν τὸν ἐν αὐτῇ καθεῖλες / κἂν μετὰ τὴν καθαίρεσιν ἐχρήσω φιλανθρώπως. For ὑψηλοτράχηλος see also Trapp (1994–2017) 1907, 'mit hohem Nacken, stolz'.

[86] See on this simile Sorabji (2000) 95 and Knuuttila (2004) 13. On the horse metaphor concerning *alazoneia* see already Ribbeck (1882) 2 (and 52). Greg. Naz. *In novam Dominicam* 620.27, *PG* 36) too speaks about a ὑψαύχην ἵππος καὶ ἀγέρωχος. Also in the Aesopian fable *On Horse, Ox, Dog and Man*, *hupsauchēn* appears as a quality common to horse and arrogant man (Fable 107.16–17, ed. Hausrath and Hunger (1959–70), 1.133).

[87] E.g. Them. Βασανιστὴς ἢ φιλόσοφος 248b11. On *gauros* see LSJ *s.v.*

[88] See e.g. Ps.-Zonar. *Lexicon* 1790.29, ed. Tittmann (1808), or *Etym. Gudianum* 546.42, ed. Sturz (1818).

[89] See LSJ *s.v.*

[90] E.g. Nic. Chon. *Hist.* 234.80: καὶ τὸν αὐχένα παντὶ τῷ βουλομένῳ παρέχει πατεῖν. This ritual looks very much like the Roman *calcatio colli* ('trampling the neck'), a ritual frequently performed during a triumph, with the winner putting his foot on the vanquished enemy's neck. This ritual was well known in Byzantium and the West, but appears to have been restricted to a military context. The scenes from Choniates discussed here obviously allude to the military ritual. On the *calcatio colli* in Byzantium see McCormick (1986) 310 and 315 as well as Signes Codoñer (2014a) 193 with further bibliography.

[91] Nic. Chon. *Hist.* 79.80–7: μετὰ τὸν Ὀξείτην Μιχαὴλ … ὑπεκστάντα τῆς ὑπερτάτης τῷ βουλομένῳ καθέδρας καὶ πρὸς τὴν νῆσον τὴν Ὀξεῖαν ἀποφοιτήσαντα, καθ' ἣν τὸν ἄσκευον

12. *Alazoneia and Aidōs/Aischunē* 325

The bodily signs associated with *alazoneia*, particularly the 'overlooking glance', may also express disdain or contempt, emotions often connected to pride and arrogance. But in several instances, as we have seen, *alazoneia* is also accompanied by a lack of shame, *anaideia*.

12.2. *Aischunē/aidōs* – shame

The second emotion we deal with in this chapter is shame. The *OED* gives a detailed definition of the word's principal meanings in English: (a) 'The painful emotion arising from the consciousness of something dishonouring, ridiculous, or indecorous in one's own conduct or circumstances (or in those of others whose honour or disgrace one regards as one's own), or of being in a situation which offends one's sense of modesty or decency.' Other meanings of the term are (b) 'fear of offence against propriety or decency, operating as a restraint on behaviour; modesty, shamefastness' and (c) 'disgrace, ignominy, loss of esteem or reputation'. Modern emotion studies largely agree that shame is a self-conscious emotion that involves a negative perception of the self with reference to culturally determined standards and rules. When experiencing shame, one sees oneself as deficient through the eyes of others and one feels weak, inferior, and submissive. Shame is a painful and negatively valenced experience.[92]

Besides the stylistically neutral or even low-style term *entropē* (discussed in more detail below), classicizing Byzantine authors use two major shame-related terms, which they had inherited from ancient Greek, *aidōs* and *aischunē* (as well as the derivative verbs *aideomai* and *aischunomai*). In ancient Greek, both terms roughly correspond to English 'shame', but they do not totally overlap. Their differentiation, if they are distinguished at all, seems to vary from author to author and certainly changes diachronically. Generally, one could perhaps say that *aidōs* also means 'respect' (in post-Classical Greek this becomes the principal meaning) and a 'sense of shame', whereas *aischunē*, along with 'shame', also expresses 'guilt' (as a state of mind) and 'disgrace' (as a state of affairs).[93] Despite a

---

βίον καὶ ἀπέριττον ἐκ παιδὸς ἐπανήρητο· ἔνθα καὶ τὸν οἰκεῖον ἀποδοχμώσας αὐχένα πρὸς τῇ εἰσόδῳ τοῦ προνάου πατεῖν παρεῖχε τῷ εἰσιόντι παντὶ μοναχῷ, λέγων ἀξυμφόρως ἑαυτῷ τὴν ἡλικιώτιδα καὶ φίλην ἡσυχίαν παρώσασθαι καὶ ἐπ᾽ οὐδενὶ ξυνοίσοντι τὸν θρόνον ἀναβῆναι τὸν ὑπερύψηλον. Cf. Magoulias (1984) 47.

[92] Fontaine (2009). See also Lewis (2000) 628–9: 'Shame is the product of a complex set of cognitive activities: individuals' evaluation of their actions in regard to their SRGs and their global evaluation of the self.' Lelord and André (2001) 187–228 provide a good overview of contemporary shame (and its connection to embarrassment and guilt).

[93] On ancient shame see Cairns (1993) and Konstan (2006b) 91–110. Cairns (1993) 2 gives the following definition of ancient *aidōs*: '*aidōs* is an inhibitory emotion based on a sensitivity to and protectiveness of one's self-image'. LSJ defines *aidōs* as 'reverence', 'awe', 'respect', 'sense of honour'.

326 *Martin Hinterberger*

high degree of semantic overlap and interchangeability between the two terms during the Classical period,[94] the Stoics distinguished positive and proactive *aidōs* from negative and reactive *aischunē*,[95] a distinction that might not have been valid broadly, but influenced theoretical discussion in Late Antique and Byzantine times. Thus, Nemesius of Emesa (fourth/fifth century) declares in his influential treatise on human nature that the ancients frequently used the terms *aidōs* and *aischunē* without difference, but that they are 'now distinguished' along the following lines: *aidōs* is a fear due to expected reproach, while *aischunē* is a fear due to one's having done a disgraceful deed.[96] Note, however, that again this distinction or even the use of the very terms might have been restricted to learned discourse, since low-register texts of the same period do not use the term *aidōs* much, let alone distinguish it from *aischunē* along the lines suggested by Nemesius.[97] The definition given by Nemesius was almost verbatim taken over by the prominent theologian John of Damascus (eighth century).[98] Moreover, the differentiation (closely following the original Stoic text) can be found in various Byzantine lexica.[99]

It seems that over the centuries, first the noun *aidōs* as well as the verb *aideomai* (the latter, however, to a lesser degree), but later also *aischunē* and *aischunomai*, gradually disappeared from the spoken language, while at a later stage their place was taken over by *entropē* and *entrepomai* (literally 'turning towards').[100] It is difficult to determine with precision the various stages of this

---

[94] On the synonymy of the terms *aidōs* and *aischunē* see Cairns (1993) 415 and Williams (1993) 194 n. 9.

[95] See e. g. Chrysippus, fr. 416, line 17–20 (preserved in Nemesius). A similar distinction has been observed already for Herodotus: see Williams (1993) 194 n. 9. On Stoic philosophy and emotions see Graver (2007); on Stoic views concerning shame see Graver (2007) 208–9.

[96] Nemes. Emes. *De nat. hom.* 21, ed. Morani (1987) 81.19–82.3: αἰδὼς δὲ φόβος ἐπὶ προσδο-κίᾳ ψόγου (κάλλιστον δὲ τοῦτο τὸ πάθος), αἰσχύνη δὲ φόβος ἐπ' αἰσχρῷ πεπραγμένῳ (οὐδὲ τοῦτο δὲ ἀνέλπιστον εἰς σωτηρίαν). ταύτῃ δὲ διαφέρει αἰδὼς αἰσχύνης, ὅτι ὁ μὲν αἰσχυνόμε-νος ἐφ' οἷς ἔπραξε καταδύεται, ὁ δὲ αἰδούμενος φοβεῖται περιπεσεῖν ἀδοξίᾳ τινί. καλοῦσι δὲ οἱ παλαιοὶ πολλάκις καὶ τὴν αἰδὼ αἰσχύνην καὶ τὴν αἰσχύνην αἰδώ, καταχρώμενοι τοῖς ὀνόμασι. On the treatment of shame by Nemesius see also Knuuttila (2004) 109.

[97] For instance, the word αἰδώς does not appear in the *Apophthegmata patrum* (fifth century; see Guy (1993–2005), vol. 3, 257–8), and it is extremely rare in other low-style texts such as the *Life of Symeon the Younger Stylite*, the *Life of Theodoros Sykeotes*, or John Moschos' *Pratum spirituale* (all beginning of seventh century) as well as Theophanes' *Chronicle* (beginning of ninth century), whereas αἰσχύνη is quite frequent in these texts. When it is used in these texts, *aidōs* means 'reverence' and is often related to the religious sphere. But *entropē* too is absent (with one exception in John Moschos). In a lexicon to Gregory of Nazianzos' poems (probably ninth century) αἰδέομαι is explained with αἰσχύνομαι; Kalamakis (1992) 147. In the *Septuagint* the term *entropē* is used almost always in combination with *aischunē* (six out of seven attestations). In this (collection of) text(s) *aischunē*/*aischunomai* is the dominant shame term.

[98] Jo. Damas. *Expositio fidei* 29.4–6, ed. Kotter (1973) 81.

[99] E. g. Ps.-Zonar. *Lexicon* 1816.6–8, ed. Tittmann (1808).

[100] Already Ammonius (or rather Herennius Philo, second century) interprets *aidōs* and *aischunē* as two forms of *entropē*; Ammon. *Diff.* 17: αἰδὼς καὶ αἰσχύνη διαφέρει, ὅτι ἡ μὲν αἰδώς

12. Alazoneia and Aidōs/Aischunē   327

intriguing terminological development, but by the twelfth/thirteenth century at the latest *entropē/entrepomai* has basically replaced *aidōs/aideomai* and *aischunē/aischunomai* in the simple written and probably also the spoken language. Characteristically, our two Byzantine classicizing historiographical texts use both classical terms, avoiding *entropē*, with only one exception: when Choniates laments the fall of Constantinople, quoting the Old Testament prophet Isaiah.[101] But if we look in the *metaphraseis*, which are composed in simple written koine, we observe that *aidōs* is always replaced by *entropē*, the low-register equivalent, whereas *aischunē* is sometimes retained but otherwise also replaced by *entropē*.[102] Interestingly, *aischunē* is only retained when the term *aischunē* designates an objective state of affairs, disgrace (in German, *Schande*, meaning (c) of the word 'shame' above), not a subjective state of mind; in this sense *aischunē* occasionally also replaces the noun *oneidos* ('reproach, disgrace') of Choniates' original. In any case, the spoken and simple written language got along quite well with only one term (*entropē*) for the emotion shame.

Since the living language, it seems, did not support two different concepts and ancient Greek texts were not consistent in their use of the two old terms, I ask myself: along what dividing lines did Byzantine authors apply the terms *aidōs* and *aischunē*? Are they used interchangeably, or did they adopt a distinction, perhaps along the Stoic lines? The investigation of a few shame episodes in Niketas Choniates and Anna Komnene will shed some light on this question.

12.2.1. Aischunē

On a pretext, Patriarch Theodosius (AD 1179–83) was condemned by the synod, ousted from his residence and confined to the Pantepoptes monastery in Constantinople. When he triumphantly returned to the Hagia Sophia, crowds of people hailed the patriarch, whereas the metropolitans who had voted against him hid in their houses because they feared for their lives, were utterly ashamed (*aischunē*), and felt guilty. They also were ridiculed by the people:

οὕτω δὲ ἡ προπομπὴ μυριάνθρωπος ἦν, ὡς μόλις περὶ βαθεῖαν ἑσπέραν ἐπαναζεῦξαι τὸν προπεμπόμενον ἐς τὸν μέγαν τῆς ἁγίας Σοφίας νεών ... τοσαύτη δ' αἰσχύνη τὰ τῶν θεμένων αὐτὸν ὑπόδικον ἀρχιερέων ἐκάλυψε πρόσωπα, ὡς μὴ μόνον τὰς δημοσίους παρό-

---

ἐστιν ἐντροπὴ πρὸς ἕκαστον ὧν σεβασμίως τις ἔχει, αἰσχύνη δ' ἐφ' οἷς ἕκαστος ἁμαρτὼν αἰσχύνεται ὡς μὴ δέον τι πράξας. καὶ αἰδεῖται μέν τις τὸν πατέρα, αἰσχύνεται δὲ ὃς μεθύσκεται. See on this text Dickey (2007) 94–6. On early Christian attestations of *entropē/entrepomai* in the sense of 'shame/be ashamed' see Lampe (1961) 483–4. On the use of *aidōs, aischunē*, and *entropē* as synonyms see also below, n. 127.

[101] Nic. Chon. *Hist.* 578.35–6 (= Isa. 54:4): μὴ φοβοῦ, ὅτι κατῃσχύνθης, μηδὲ ἐντραπῇς, ὅτι ὠνειδίσθης.

[102] Moreover, *anaideia* is rendered as *adiantropia*, *anaidēs* as *adiantropos*. On *adiantropia* see Trapp (1994–2017) and Kriaras (1967–) *s. v.* On the correspondence of shame terms in Choniates' *History* and its *metaphrasis* see again the list of corresponding terms mentioned above (note 78).

328

Martin Hinterberger

δους ἐκτρέπεσθαι διὰ τὸ εἰς τὸν ἀρχιθύτην ἀμπλάκημα καὶ τὸ ἐκείνων ἐντεῦθεν παγκαταγέλαστον, ἀλλὰ καὶ τὸ θανεῖν ὑποβλέπεσθαι. (Nic. Chon. *Hist.* 243.24–31)[103]

So huge was the number of people who joined in the procession that ... he returned to the Great Church of the Holy Wisdom of God only late in the evening. So great was the shame that covered the faces of the bishops for condoning his trial that they avoided the public ways not only because of their sin against the patriarch and the universal derision heaped on them as a result but also because they were afraid that they might be killed. (Trans. Magoulias (1984) 135)

In another episode, the Serbian leader Stephen Nemanja (Desa), who had repeatedly rebelled against Emperor Manuel Komnenos (and for this reason is also called arrogant, Nic. Chon. *Hist.* 159.94, cf. ὀφρύος), was forced to demonstrate his submission to the ruler by paying his respects (AD 1172).[104] But after having done so, he regretted this humiliating action and felt shame (ἠσχύνετο) and anger (ὠργίζετο) for having submitted himself.

ἐξιὼν γὰρ ἀπὸ προσώπου τοῦ βασιλέως πολλοῖς ἅμα τὴν ψυχὴν ἐμερίζετο πάθεσιν. ἠσχύνετο ἐφ᾽ οἷς τῷ βασιλεῖ προσελήλυθεν, ὠργίζετο ὧν ἕνεκα πέπονθεν, ἐπαθαίνετο οἷς τῆς γνώμης παρεκτροπὰς θριγγίοις ὅρκων ἑαυτῷ ἀπετείχισε. (Nic. Chon. *Hist.* 136.58–61)[105]

When he left the emperor, his soul was torn by many passions. He was ashamed for submitting to the emperor; he was angry about what had happened to him, and he was agitated by the fact that the oaths he had sworn did not permit him to change his mind. (Cf. Magoulias (1984) 78)

In both the case of the metropolitans, although they are also concerned about what people are saying about them now and in the future, and the case of Stephen Nemanja, the shame in play is basically retrospective and has to do with humiliation, the 'loss of face', and disgrace. In the first episode we also observe guilt (note the word *amplakēma*, a high-style synonym of *hamartia*, 'sin').

---

[103] Cf. *Metaphrasis Chon.* 9.4.2: οὕτω δὲ ἡ προπομπὴ μυριάνθρωπος ἦν, ὡς μόλις πρὸς βαθεῖαν νύκτα εἰς τὸν μέγαν ναὸν τῆς τοῦ θεοῦ ἁγίας Σοφίας φθάσαι ... τοσαύτη δὲ ἐντροπὴ τὰ τῶν ὑποδίκων ἀρχιερέων ἐκάλυψε πρόσωπα, ὡς μὴ μόνον ἔξω ἔρχεσθαι ἤθελον διὰ τὸ πάντας καταγελᾶν αὐτούς, ἀλλὰ καὶ οἴκοις καθήμενοι τὸν θάνατον αὐτῶν προέκρινον.

[104] In the *metaphrasis*, Nemanja's behaviour is explicitly characterized as 'arrogant', particularly because he dared to attack the Byzantine troops without declaring war, instead of waiting for their attack, whereas Choniates uses circumlocutions: *Metaphrasis Chon.* 6.2.2: ὁ δὲ Νεεμὰν τοσοῦτον ἀλαζὼν ἦν, ὡς μηδὲ προσμεῖναι τὸν Πεδιάτην, ἀλλὰ κατ᾽ αὐτοῦ ἐξελθεῖν ... κατολίγον δὲ τὴν ἀλαζονείαν ἀφεὶς καὶ τὴν ὀφρὺν ἀποθέμενος, τέλος τὴν αὐτοῦ κεφαλὴν τοῖς τοῦ βασιλέως ποσὶν ὑποτίθησι. Cf. Nic. Chon. *Hist.* 159.94.4: Νεεμὰν οὕτως ἀναρσίου μετῆν φρονήματος, ὡς εὐθὺς ἐξενεγκεῖν ἀκήρυκτον πόλεμον ... ἀεὶ δέ τι περικόπτων τῆς προλαβούσης ὀφρύος καὶ ὑφαιρῶν τέλος τοῖς ἐκείνου ποσὶ τὴν οἰκείαν ὑποτέθεικε κεφαλήν. On the historical background see Magdalino (1993) 79.

[105] Cf. *Metaphrasis Chon.* 5.4: ἐξελθὼν γὰρ ἀπὸ προσώπου τοῦ βασιλέως μετεμέλετο ἐφ᾽ οἷς ἔπραξεν, ἐντρέπετο διότι προσῆλθε καὶ προσέπεσε τῶ βασιλεῖ, καὶ ἐπαθαίνετο ἐν τοῖς ὅρκοις οἷς ὤμοσε, καὶ ὠργίζετο ὧν ἕνεκα ἔπραξε.

12. Alazoneia and Aidōs/Aischunē 329

According to Choniates, Andronikos Komnenos (ruled AD 1183–5), having finally attained the imperial throne, was not ashamed (οὐκ ᾐσχύνετο) when sleeping with his predecessor's young fiancée. Not only was the former emperor his nephew whom he had had killed, but the girl was only 10 years old. The latter fact not only breached social norms, but also formal canonical law (note ἀθεμί-τως in line 4).

τῆς δὲ μυσαρᾶς πράξεως ταύτης οὕτω τετελεσμένης ἁρμόζεται Ἀνδρονίκῳ πρὸς συμβί-ωσιν Ἄννα ἡ τοῦ βασιλέως Ἀλεξίου μνηστή, θυγάτηρ οὖσα τοῦ τὴν ἀρχὴν τῶν Φράγγων διέποντος. καὶ οὐκ ᾐσχύνετο Κρονίων ἀπόζων ἀνεψιοῦ γυναικὶ μιλτοπαρήῳ καὶ τρυφε-ρᾷ καὶ μήπω τὸ ἑνδέκατον ἔτος ἐξηνυκυίᾳ μέλλων ἀθεμίτως συγκατακλίνεσθαι καὶ πα-ραγκαλίζεσθαι ὁ πέπων τὴν ὀμφακίζουσαν, ὁ ὑπέρωρος τὴν ἡλικίαν, τὴν ὀρθοτίτθιον νεάνιδα, ὁ ῥικνὸς καὶ χαλαρὸς τὴν ῥοδοδάκτυλον καὶ δρόσον ἔρωτος στάζουσαν. (Nic. Chon. Hist. 275.12–276.19)[106]

When this loathsome deed had been accomplished, Andronikos married Anna, Emperor Alexios' wife, daughter of the king of the Franks. And he, an old man, was not ashamed to sleep unlawfully with his nephew's red-cheeked and tender spouse who had not yet com-pleted her eleventh year, the overripe suitor the unripe maiden, the dotard the damsel with pointed breasts, the shrivelled and languid old man the rosy-fingered girl dripping with the dew of love. (Trans. Magoulias (1984) 153, slightly adapted)

This is not proactive shame, since Andronikos is not inhibited to sleep with the young lady. With the negated verb *aischunomai* Choniates expresses not so much that Andronikos lacked the sense of shame that would have prevented him from committing this impropriety, but that he did not experience shame or guilt when he should have done so, not only retrospectively after the deed, but already when committing it.

12.2.2. Aidōs

Niketas Choniates draws a rather negative portrait of Empress Euphrosyne, the wife of Alexios III. In the previous section, we have already discussed Euphrosyn-e's arrogance.[107] In Book 15 Choniates narrates an episode that was shameful for both the empress and her husband. The author concedes that Euphrosyne was energetic and eloquent as well as a cunning politician. Yet, the fact that she had acquired more power than her weak husband and that she used this power self-consciously and in ways she independently thought fit constituted, in Choniates' eyes, a transgression of tradition and the established order. By assuming such

---

[106] Cf. *Metaphrasis Chon.* 10.1.2: τῆς δὲ μισαρᾶς ταύτης πράξεως ἐλεεινῶς πληρωθείσης, λαμβάνει εἰς γυναῖκα ὁ Ἀνδρόνικος τὴν τοῦ Ἀλεξίου τοῦ βασιλέως μεμνηστευμένην, θυγατέ-ραν οὖσαν τοῦ ῥηγὸς τῶν Φράγγων. καὶ οὐκ ἐντρέπετο ὁ βρωμόγερος τοῦ ἀνεψιοῦ αὐτοῦ τὴν γυναῖκα νέαν οὖσαν καὶ τρυφεράν, τὸν ἑνδέκατον χρόνον τότε πληρώσασαν, παρανόμως συμ-μίγεσθαι καὶ περιπλέκεσθαι, ὁ γηραιὸς καὶ τὴν ἡλικίαν ὑψηλός, τὴν νεάνιδα καὶ τρυφεράν, ὁ τὰ μάγουλα ζαρωμένος, τὴν τριακονταφυλλοκόκκινον καὶ ἐρωτικήν.

[107] See above, p. 316.

330   *Martin Hinterberger*

great power and acting like an emperor, the empress 'dishonoured the veil of *aidōs*'[108] – the expression 'dishonour the veil of *aidōs*' in all probability harks back to Gregory of Nazianzos' funeral oration for his sister Gorgonia, presented in this text as the ideal of womanhood, in contrast to women 'dishonouring the veil of modesty'.[109] Quite fittingly, in the *metaphrasis*, the corresponding term specifically is not just *entropē*, but *gunaikeia entropē*, 'female modesty/sense of shame'. For this shameless transgression of social boundaries, Euphrosyne was publicly censured ('booed and whistled at'), and her behaviour caused her husband *aischunē*, 'disgrace'. Apart from her outweighing her husband in political capability and power, it was a specific affair that illustrates Euphrosyne's 'shamelessness' and the emperor's disgrace resulting therefrom.[110] Having taken the government into her hands, the empress sought to stop corruption at the court and appointed Konstantinos Mesopotamites chief minister. For this reason, her relatives, who had profited from the lack of control, turned against her and falsely accused her of 'shamelessly sleeping' with her lover and, more seriously, of plotting against the emperor's life.[111] Consequently, her alleged lover was killed and Euphrosyne was in danger of being condemned as an adulteress and even of incurring the death sentence. Since the hard evidence for her guilt was shaky, the emperor's counsellors pleaded for a more cautious handling of the affair. According to their reasoning, the emperor would greatly disgrace himself if, after condemning his wife as an adulteress, he later had to accept her back in the palace as innocent.[112] Thus, it was decided that the empress merely had to leave the palace secretly, a fact that again disgraced the emperor. But in the face of this unforeseen and unintended development, the empress's slanderous relatives regretted the shame they had brought to their family, particularly because they were blamed by and subjected to the insults of the Constantinople's inhabitants, but also suffered from bad conscience (cf. the metropolitans' disgrace and feeling guilty above).[113] After six months of banishment, Euphrosyne was allowed to

---

[108] Nic. Chon. *Hist.* 460.86–7: τὸ κάλυμμα τῆς αἰδοῦς ἀτιμάσασα ἐκλώζετο καὶ διεσυρίττετο καὶ εἰς ὄνειδος ἦν τῷ ταύτην ἁρμοσαμένῳ. Cf. *Metaphrasis Chon.* 15.4.3: τὴν γυναικείαν ἐντροπὴν ἀπορρίψασα, διὰ τοῦ γουργούρου αὐτῆς κλώζους καὶ ἐρευγμοὺς ἐποίει, καὶ σφυριγμοὺς μεγάλους ἐξέφερεν ἀπὸ τοῦ στόματος αὐτῆς, ἅπερ ἦσαν εἰς αἰσχύνην καὶ ὄνειδος τοῦ ταύτης ἀνδρός. Again the Metaphrast partly misunderstood Choniates' text ('being booed' became 'produced noises').

[109] Greg. Naz. *Or.* 8.9.21–2, ed. Calvet-Sebasti (1995) 264: ἀκούετε τῶν γυναικῶν ὅσαι λίαν ἐπιδεικτικαὶ καὶ ῥᾴθυμοι, καὶ τὸ κάλυμμα τῆς αἰδοῦς ἀτιμάζουσαι.

[110] Nic. Chon. *Hist.* 483.36: τάραχος ὃς τὰ κατὰ τὸν βασιλέα ᾔσχυνε. Cf. *Metaphrasis Chon.* 15.13.1: εἰς ἐντροπὴν μεγάλην ἐνέβαλε.

[111] Nic. Chon. *Hist.* 486.32: ἀναίδην συγκατακλινομένη. Cf. *Metaphrasis Chon.* 15.13.10: ἀδιαντρόπως.

[112] Nic. Chon. *Hist.* 488.90: τὴν αὐτὸς αὐτοῦ αἰσχύνην διατεχνώμενος ἐσεῖται. Cf. *Metaphrasis Chon.* 15.13.15: ἔνι καὶ ἐντροπὴ μεγάλη.

[113] Nic. Chon. *Hist.* 489.28–30: ἐφ' οἷς τὸ γένος ᾔσχυναν ἤχθοντο, εἰ καὶ μὴ εἰς ὅσον ἔδει καὶ δυσφορεῖν, καὶ οἱ ὀνειδισμοὶ δὲ τοῦ λεὼ καὶ αἱ κερτομίαι τούτοις ἐμπίπτουσαι κατεπίεζον.

12. Alazoneia and Aidōs/Aischunē

return to the imperial palace, thanks to the intervention of Mesopotamites, who, as we have already seen, became arrogant because of this important achievement.

In this presentation of the events, *aidōs* and *aischunē* appear as clearly distinguished ('a sense of shame' vs 'the objective state of shame'), but closely related to one another. According to Choniates, *aidōs* is what a woman, especially an empress, should experience, but Euphrosyne does not. *Aidōs* should prevent a woman from transgressing social norms. Moreover, Euphrosyne's (alleged) lack of *aidōs* reflects badly on her husband as well as on her family and causes *aischunē* 'shame/disgrace' to both.

There is another case of female *aidōs* is Choniates' *History*. The Vlach leader Chrysos, who had rebelled against the emperor Alexios Angelos, was bribed into agreeing to peace with a marriage arrangement (AD 1199). The emperor 'gave' him one of his kinswomen, the daughter of the protostrator Manuel Kamytzes, who was, however, already married and had first to divorce her husband. During the wedding banquet Chrysos drank and ate to excess, while the bride restrained herself and ate and drank modestly. She did so out of respect (αἰδουμένη) for the law of the newlyweds. Her cautious behaviour, however, enraged Chrysos and made him speak arrogantly (μεθ' ὑπεροψίας – μετὰ ἀλαζονείας in the *metaphrasis*) to her.

> τελεσθέντων δὲ τῶν νυμφευμάτων καὶ τῆς γαμηλίου δαιτὸς παρατεθείσης, ὁ μὲν Χρύσος ἐζωροπότει καὶ ἤσθιε τενθευόμενος, ἡ δὲ γυνὴ τὸν τῶν νεονύμφων αἰδουμένη νόμον ἐγκρατῶς εἶχε τῶν παρακειμένων. ἐπιταχθεῖσα δὲ πρὸς τοῦ νυμφίου συμμετέχειν ἐκείνῳ βρώσεως καὶ μὴ οὕτως αὐτίκα δράσασα εἰς ὀργὴν ἐκμαίνει τὸν ἄνδρα. ἀμέλει καὶ πλεῖστα καθ' ἑαυτὸν ὑποβαρβαρίσας καὶ θυμομαχήσας ἐφ' ἱκανὸν μεθ' ὑπεροψίας ἔφησεν ὕστερον "μὴ φάγῃς, μηδὲ πίῃς" Ἑλληνίδι φωνῇ. (Nic. Chon. *Hist.* 507.60–508.66)[114]

> When after the wedding ceremony the banquet had been served, Chrysos was drinking and eating heavily, while his wife, respecting the law of the newlyweds, was eating and drinking only cautiously of the dishes set before her. When he ordered her to participate in the feasting and she did not obey him immediately, he got furious. For some time he muttered to himself bitterly in his barbaric language, and later said to her full of arrogance in Greek: 'Do not eat nor drink.' (Cf. Magoulias (1984) 280)

Note that the *metaphrasis* more explicitly states that Chrysos' wife 'was embarrassed to eat' (φαγεῖν ἠνεντρέπετο). In this revealing episode, Choniates stages the clash of Byzantine cultural conventions with barbarian ones. Respect

---

Cf. *Metaphrasis Chon.* 15.13.17: ἠνεντρέποντο ἐφ' οἷς εἶπον, εἰ καὶ μὴ τοσοῦτον ὅσον ἔπρεπεν. οἱ ὀνειδισμοὶ δὲ καὶ ὕβρεις αἱ εἰς αὐτοὺς παρὰ τοῦ πλήθους τοῦ λαοῦ γινόμεναι πικρῶς ἐδάμαζον τὴν αὐτῶν συνείδησιν.

[114] Cf. *Metaphrasis Chon.* 16.1.11: γενομένου δὲ τοῦ γάμου καὶ τῆς τραπέζης τεθείσης, ὁ μὲν Χρύσος ἔτρωγεν ἀπλήστως καὶ ἔπινεν· ἡ γυνὴ δὲ τὸν νόμον τῶν νεονύμφων κρατοῦσα φαγεῖν ἠνεντρέπετο. ὁρισθεῖσα δὲ παρὰ τοῦ γαμβροῦ μετ' ἐκεῖνον φαγεῖν, καὶ μὴ ἐκ τοῦ παρ' αὐτίκα τοῦτο ποιήσασα, ἐμάνη, καὶ πολλὰ βαρβαρίσας καὶ θυμωθεὶς, μετὰ ἀλαζονείας ὕστερον εἶπε "μὴ φάγῃς, μηδὲ πίῃς."

332   *Martin Hinterberger*

for Byzantine norms of good behaviour presupposes modesty and a sense of shame, whereas disregard for these social rules is perceived as shamelessness and arrogance. The Byzantine noblewoman who was married off to a barbarian feels respect for social conventions, whereas the barbarian bridegroom arrogantly (i. e. without respect, ignoring) violates these rules.

Anna Komnene presents her mother Eirene Doukaina, Alexios Komnenos' wife, as a very modest person who only reluctantly appeared in public. When she was forced to do so, she was utterly ashamed (*aidōs*). Her shame manifested itself through blushing (*eruthēma*). Her (sense of) shame (*aidōs*) inhibited her even from speaking publicly. But this strong sense of shame was overcome by her love for her husband Alexios, who wanted to have her with him during his campaigns.

ὁ γὰρ τρόπος ἐκείνης τοιοῦτος τίς ἦν· οὐ πάνυ τι δημοσιεύεσθαι ἤθελεν, ἀλλὰ τὰ πολλὰ μὲν οἰκουροῦσα ἦν ... ἐπειδὰν δὲ μέλλοι δημοσιεύσειν ἑαυτὴν κατά τινα χρείαν ἀναγκαιοτάτην ὡς βασιλίδα, αἰδοῦς τὲ ὑπεπίμπλατο καὶ ἐρύθημα εὐθὺς ἐξηνθήκει ταῖς παρειαῖς. καὶ ἡ μὲν φιλόσοφος Θεανὼ τοῦ πήχεος αὐτῆς γυμνωθέντος, ἐπειδή τις παίζων εἰρήκει πρὸς ταύτην "καλὸς ὁ πήχυς", "ἀλλ' οὐ δημόσιος" εἶπεν ἐκείνη. ἡ δὲ βασιλὶς καὶ μήτηρ ἐμή, τὸ τῆς σεμνότητος ἄγαλμα, τὸ τῆς ἁγιότητος καταγώγιον, μὴ ὅτι γε πήχυν ἢ βλέμμα δημοσιεύειν ἠγάπα, ἀλλ' οὐδὲ φωνὴν ἐκείνης ἤθελεν εἰς ἀσυνήθεις παραπέμπεσθαι ἀκοάς· τοσοῦτον ἦν ἐκείνη χρῆμα θαυμάσιον εἰς αἰδῶ. ἐπεὶ δὲ ἀνάγκη οὐδὲ θεοί, φησί, μάχονται, ἀναγκάζεται πρὸς τὰς συχνὰς τοῦ αὐτοκράτορος ἐκστρατεύσεις αὐτῷ παρακολουθεῖν. κατεῖχε μὲν αὐτὴν ἡ σύμφυτος αἰδὼς ἔνδον τῶν βασιλείων, τὸ δὲ πρὸς τὸν αὐτοκράτορα φίλτρον καὶ ἡ διάπυρος πρὸς ἐκεῖνον ἀγάπη ἐξῆγεν αὐτὴν καὶ μὴ βουλομένην τῶν ἀνακτόρων διὰ ταυτασὶ τὰς αἰτίας· ... (Anna Comn. *Alex.* 12.3.2–4)[115]

For her way was like that: she did not wish to show herself in public, but most of the time stayed at home ... Whenever she had to appear in public at some important ceremony, she was overcome with shame and a blush at once suffused her cheeks. The woman philosopher Theano once bared her elbow and someone playfully remarked, 'What a lovely elbow!', 'But not for public show', she replied. Well, the empress, my mother, the image of propriety, the dwelling-place of saintliness, so far from being pleased to reveal to the common gaze an elbow or her eyes, was unwilling that even her voice should be heard by strangers. Her sense of shame was really extraordinary. But since not even gods, as the poet says, fight against necessity, she was forced to accompany the emperor on his frequent expeditions. Her innate sense of shame kept her inside the palace; on the other hand, her affection and burning love for him compelled her, however unwillingly, to leave her home. There were two cogent reasons ... (Sewter (1969) 374–5, slightly adapted)

Although *aidōs* appears here in two slightly different forms, namely (a) 'proactive shame', the emotion anticipating the transgression/violation of moral rules (ἐπειδὰν δὲ μέλλοι δημοσιεύσειν ἑαυτὴν ..., αἰδοῦς τὲ ὑπεπίμπλατο), and

---

[115] Cf. *Metaphrasis Alex.* 155–9: ἐκείνη δὲ οὐκ ἠγάπα παρρησιάζεσθαι, ἀλλ' ἤθελεν ἐντὸς τοῦ οἴκου αὐτῆς εὑρίσκεσθαι ... εἰ δὲ καὶ διὰ τὴν τῆς βασιλείας χρῆσιν ἀνάγκη ἦν παρρησιασθῆναι, τότε ἀπὸ τῆς ἐντροπῆς τὰ μάγουλα αὐτῆς ἐκοκκίνιζον ... τοσαύτην εἶχεν ἐκείνη τὴν ἐντροπήν. ἐπεὶ δὲ ἠναγκάζετο παρὰ τοῦ βασιλέως κατηκολούθει αὐτῷ καὶ εἶχε μὲν τὴν ἐντροπὴν ἔνδοθεν, ἡ τοῦ βασιλέως δὲ ἀγάπη καὶ μὴ θέλουσαν ἀπὸ τῶν παλατίων ταύτην ἐξέβαλεν ...

12. Alazoneia and Aidōs/Aischunē   333

(b) a 'sense of shame' inhibiting the infringement of moral/social rules (οὐδὲ φωνὴν ἐκείνης ἤθελεν εἰς ἀσυνήθεις παραπέμπεσθαι ἀκοάς· τοσοῦτον ἦν ἐκείνη χρῆμα θαυμάσιον εἰς αἰδῶ), it basically is inhibitory shame.[116] In the *metaphrasis* both occurences are rendered as *entropē*. Moreover, we observe parallels with the *alazoneia* episode about Empress Euphrosyne presented above: there the empress, apparently without inhibition, did not restrict her activities to the household (*oikouria*), which in itself, though, is not condemned by Choniates.[117] Anna Komnene, however, stresses that Eirene Doukaina wished to stay inside the palace, but was nevertheless forced to leave it occasionally. The aim of this emphasis may have been to fend off criticism against Eirene Doukaina for accompanying Alexios on his campaigns and thus violating the rules of appropriate female behaviour.[118]

In Byzantine historiography we basically come across emotions ascribed to other persons.[119] This attribution is based on the observation of a specific behavioural pattern. Quite frequently this attribution is based on very little hard evidence, and instead built on the hypothesis that in a given situation a person would experience a certain kind of emotion or a set of emotions. A lot of emotions in these texts are inferred emotions, emotions that were expected or supposed to be elicited by specific circumstances. Autobiographical declarations about emotions, confessions by the emotional subject, on the other hand, are very rare.[120] But there are a few in Anna's *History*.[121]

---

[116] For a Byzantine woman, public appearances (i. e. showing themselves to men that were not members of the household) were generally regarded as an infringement of female *aidōs*, as is e. g. stated in Emperor Leo VI's novel 48, lines 16–18, ed. Troianos (2007) 174–6. See also Greg. Naz. *Or.* 8 (*Funeral Oration for Gorgonia*) 9.1–2, ed. Calvet-Sebasti (1995) 262: ὁ μὲν δὴ θεῖος Σολομὼν ... ἐπαινεῖ καὶ οἰκουρίαν γυναικός. On the fundamental association between *aidōs* and the visual as well as *aidos* as a self-protective emotion in Antiquity see Cairns (1996b).

[117] Nic. Chon. *Hist.* 519.36–8: εὑρίσκει δὲ καὶ τὴν σύνευνον Εὐφροσύνην μὴ πάντη τὴν οἰκουρίαν ἀσπασαμένην, ἀλλὰ κατὰ στασιωτῶν καὶ δημοκόπων κἀκείνην ἀνδρισαμένην. See also above, p. 316.

[118] Hill (1997) 92.

[119] Damon (2017) distinguishes three 'types' of emotions in ancient historiography: (a) in the story, as a matter of historiography, (b) the emotional effects on the audience, i. e. emotions provoked by historiography, and (c) emotions in the author. In Byzantine historiography type (a) is the most conspicuous one, whereas type (c), which we are going to discuss here, is rather rare.

[120] Interestingly, in the *metaphrasis* of Choniates' *History* there are two occasions where the author declares that shame prevents him from giving more details, whereas in the corresponding passages of Choniates' original version other authorial expressions are used (simply 'I cannot' or 'the law of History does not allow me'; *Metaphrasis Chon.* 15.2.3: τὰ ὀνόματα εἰπεῖν αἰσχύνομαι, cf. Nic. Chon. *Hist.* 456.78–9: τὰ δὲ ὀνόματα προφέρειν οὐ δύναμαι, and *Metaphrasis Chon.* 16.11.1: φεῦ τῆς μιαροτάτης γνώμης καὶ ῥυπαρᾶς. αἰσχύνομαι γὰρ περὶ τούτων πλέον εἰπεῖν, cf. Nic. Chon. *Hist.* 525.88–9: φεῦ τῆς ῥυπαροτάτης γνώμης. οὐ γάρ τι πλέον ὁ τῆς ἱστορίας νόμος εἰπεῖν ἐπιτρέπει μοι.

[121] On Anna's appearance as emotional author in the *Alexiad*, see Neville (2019) and Hinterberger (1999) 301–2. I wonder whether there is a fundamental difference between such autobiographical emotional scenarios and other scenarios ascribed to a third person (Damon's types

334 *Martin Hinterberger*

In chapter 13 of the first book of the *Alexiad*, Anna Komnene refers to events far away in the West, namely the outbreak of the Investiture Controversy between the German emperor Henry IV and Pope Gregory VII. In particular she mentions the brutal treatment of the imperial ambassadors by the pope:[122]

τούτων οὖν ἀκούσας ὁ πάπας τῶν λόγων κατὰ τῶν πρέσβεων εὐθὺς ἐμεμήνει καὶ αἰκισά-
μενος πρότερον ἀπανθρώπως, εἶτα καὶ κείρας τὰς κεφαλὰς καὶ ἐπικείρας τοὺς πώγωνας,
τὰς μὲν ψαλίσι, ξυρῷ δὲ τοὺς πώγωνας, καὶ ἄλλό τι προσεξεργασάμενος ἀτοπώτατον καὶ
βαρβαρικὴν ὕβριν ὑπερελαύνων ἀφῆκεν. εἶπον ἂν καὶ τὴν ὕβριν, εἰ μή με καὶ γυναικεία
καὶ βασιλικὴ ἐπεῖχεν αἰδώς· ἐκεῖνο γὰρ οὐχ᾽ ὅπως ἀνάξιον ἀρχιερέως τὸ παρ᾽ ἐκείνου
πραχθέν, ἀλλ᾽ οὐδ᾽ ὅλως ἀνθρώπου χριστιανικὸν ἐπιφερομένου καὶ τοὔνομα. ἐβδελυξάμην καὶ τὸ ἐνθύμημα τοῦ βαρβάρου, μήτοιγε τοὔργον, ἐπεὶ καὶ τὸν γραφέα κάλαμον καὶ
τὸν χάρτην ἐμόλυνα ἄν, εἰ τὸ πραχθὲν κατὰ μέρος διεξήειν ... καὶ ταῦτα ἀρχιερέως ... καὶ
ταῦτα προκαθημένου τῆς οἰκουμένης ἁπάσης γενομένου, ὥσπερ οὖν οἱ Λατίνοι λέγου-
σί τε καὶ οἴονται· ἔστι γὰρ καὶ τοῦτο τῆς ἀλαζονείας αὐτῶν. (Anna Comn. *Alex.* 1.13.3–4)

When the pope heard these words, he immediately took his anger out on the envoys sent by Henry. To begin with, he maltreated them savagely, then cut their hair and beards, the one with scissors, the other with a razor, and finally he did something else to them which was quite improper, going beyond the insolent behaviour one expects from barbarians, and then sent them away. I would have given a name to the outrage, but as a woman and a princess, a sense of shame forbade me. What was done on his orders was not only un-worthy of a high priest, but of any man at all who bears the name of Christian. Even the barbarian's intention, let alone the act itself, filled me with disgust; if I had described it in detail, reedpen and paper would have been defiled ... And this was the work of a high priest. More it was the doing of the Supreme high priest, of him who presided over the whole inhabited world (according to the claims and the belief of the Latins – another ex-ample of their arrogance). (Trans. Sewter (1969) 62)

Anna explicitly says that the ambassadors' hair and beards were cut, and that something else, something totally outrageous (ἀτοπώτατον) was done to them which her female and royal sense of shame (γυναικεία καὶ βασιλικὴ αἰδώς) forbids her (ἐπέχει) to name.[123] The thought of it alone fills her with disgust (ἐβδελυξάμην),[124] to write it down would defile her writing instruments. The most shocking aspect of this story was that the outrage was committed by the supreme leader of the Church, the supreme priest of the entire world 'as they erroneously think' – οἴονται here already suggests 'conceit' and 'arrogance'. For this, Anna says, is *also* part of their arrogance (ἔστι γὰρ καὶ τοῦτο τῆς ἀλαζο-νείας αὐτῶν). If I interpret this passage correctly, the entire episode, not just the

---

(a) and (c)), an essential difference beyond that of a different point of view. For instance, certain emotions such as envy or arrogance are almost exclusively ascribed to a third person.

[122] The alleged maltreatment of the imperial ambassadors during the synod in Rome in AD 1076 relies on an antipapal rumour; cf. Reinsch (1996) 58.

[123] We do not know what exactly Anna had on her mind – perhaps something pertaining to the sexual sphere; cf. Nic. Chon. *Hist.* 520.52, where the term ἀτόπημα is mentioned con-cerning the mutilation of the sexual organs (in this case, however, of statues – see above, p. 316).

[124] Cf. arrogance provoking disgust in Mich. Psel. *Hist. synt.* 46; see above, p. 312.

12. Alazoneia and Aidōs/Aischunē 335

end concerning the Latins' false claim of world leadership, expresses their utter arrogance, meaning their non-conformity with Byzantine standards of good and correct behaviour.

In a similar passage Anna refers to the abominable Bogomil heresy, whose leader, Basil, allegedly performed a miracle:

τὰ μὲν οὖν τοῦ τέρατος τούτου ταύτη ἐχέτω. ἠβουλόμην δὲ καὶ πᾶσαν τὴν τῶν Βογομί-λων διηγήσασθαι αἵρεσιν, ἀλλά με κωλύει καὶ αἰδώς, ὥς πού φησιν ἡ καλὴ Σαπφώ, ὅτι συγγραφεὺς ἔγωγε γυνὴ καὶ τῆς πορφύρας τὸ τιμιώτατον καὶ τῶν Ἀλεξίου πρώτιστον βλάστημα, τά τε εἰς ἀκοὴν πολλῶν ἐρχόμενα σιγῆς ἄξια βούλομαι μὲν γράφειν, ἵνα τὸ πλῆρες τῆς τῶν Βογομίλων παραστήσω αἱρέσεως, ἀλλ' ἵνα μὴ τὴν γλῶτταν μολύνω τὴν ἐμαυτῆς, παρίημι ταῦτα. (Anna Comn. *Alex.* 15.9.1)

I will say no more about this miracle. It was my intention to expound the whole Bogomilian heresy, but 'shame' as the lovely Sappho somewhere remarks, 'forbids me'. For I am woman-writer born in the Porphyra, most-honoured and first born of Alexios' children. What was common hearsay, had better be passed over in silence. Despite my desire to give a full account, I cannot – for if I did my tongue would be sullied. (Sewter (1969) 499–500, slightly modified)

Again the author shies away from telling the whole story, because her sense of shame forbids her from doing so (ἀλλά με κωλύει καὶ αἰδώς). This sense of shame is appropriate for her because she is a woman and she is Emperor Alexios' first-born child (ἔγωγε γυνὴ καὶ τῆς πορφύρας τὸ τιμιώτατον καὶ τῶν Ἀλεξίου πρώτιστον βλάστημα).[125] Here, as in the previous passage, Anna presents *aidōs* as a primarily female and also princely emotion.[126] She underlines this fact by quoting Sappho (fr. 137 L–P), the most famous woman author of Antiquity, also familiar to the learned Byzantine intellectuals of her time.

Anna, a woman, is writing particularly about women (her mother and her-self) and referring to ancient female exempla. What is the full meaning of these exempla? In the first case, Anna compares her mother's (sense of) shame to the emotion of the ancient philosopher Theano, whom her mother of course surpasses. In the second instance, by quoting Sappho, Anna identifies herself with the ancient woman author and her sense of appropriateness.[127]

---

[125] Anna presents herself in similar terms in the prologue to the *Alexiad* (Pro. 1.2).

[126] *Aidōs* as a princely and female emotion is a common topic in ancient literature; see for instance Nausikaa or Penelope in Homer; cf. Cairns (1993) 120–4, for a discussion of the relevant passages.

[127] The story about Theano was not particularly widespread (see the attestations collected by Broderson (2010), but it had been incorporated into John Stobaeus' anthology (4.23.49a2), from where it could easily reach a broader public. In Antiquity Theano was regarded as a general paragon of modesty; see Cairns (1996b), 81–2. Sappho's line, on the other hand, was cited in Aristotle's *Rhetoric* (1, 1367a11), and from there it found its way into numerous commentaries on this work. Particularly interesting is Stephen the Grammarian's commentary (twelfth century?), which gives three synonyms for the verb 'to be ashamed', namely ἐντρέπομαι, αἰδοῦμαι, αἰσχύ-νομαι (280.30–5, ed. Rabe (1896)): εἴτε ὁ Ἀλκαῖος ὁ ποιητὴς ἤρα κόρης τινὸς ἢ ἄλλος τις ἤρα,

336   *Martin Hinterberger*

In juxtaposing these two groups of shame passages, the following can be observed: the two terms *aidōs* and *aischunē* seem indeed to express two differentiated concepts, quite similar to the Stoic differentiation mentioned above. There is a tendency to apply *aischunē* as retrospective shame/disgrace and guilt, or shame experienced not only after committing a shameful or disgraceful act, but also while committing it, whereas *aidōs* is more inhibitory and proactive (the woman blushes already before showing herself publicly, or is inhibited by shame to eat) – yet this differentiation is not absolute. Another distinction between the two terms may run along lines of gender: *aischunē* is experienced by men, *aidōs* by women. At least, this is the case in our two texts. In one contemporary text, however, an encomiastic poem dedicated to Manuel Komnenos, *aidōs* and concomitant blushing is presented as a positive trait of the emperor's character.[128]

The comparison of shame terms in our two texts and their respective *metaphraseis* leads to results similar to those in the previous arrogance section. A relatively rich variety of shame terms in Choniates and Anna Komnene corresponds with one single central term in the *metaphraseis*, namely *entropē*. This means that whatever semantic differentiation between *aidōs* and *aischunē* may have been intended in the two classicizing texts has disappeared in their *metaphraseis*. The same is true for the derivative stems formed with *alpha privativum*, *anaid-* and *anaischunt-*, which correspond with *adiantrop-*. Interestingly, the ancient adverb *anedēn* (originally not connected to shame circumstances or etymologically related to *aidōs*) is almost always used as a shame term and therefore frequently spelled with αι (instead of traditional ε) in the manuscripts of Choniates' *History*. In the *metaphrasis* it always corresponds with *adiantropōs*, regardless of its meaning in Choniates' original (which means *anedēn* is occasionally misunderstood). Metaphorical terms such as *aneruthriastōs* ('without blushing') in the sense of 'shamelessly' always correspond with *adiantropōs*.

Conclusion

We have shed some light on the conceptualization of arrogance- and shame-related emotions in twelfth/thirteenth-century Byzantine historiography. Whereas in Classical Greek *alazoneia* primarily meant 'boastfulness', in twelfth/thirteenth-century texts (and probably in a broader chronological range of texts as well)

παράγει οὖν ὅμως ἡ Σαπφὼ διάλογον· καὶ λέγει ὁ ἐρῶν πρὸς τὴν ἐρωμένην "θέλω τι εἰπεῖν πρὸς σέ, ἀλλὰ ἐντρέπομαι, αἰδοῦμαι, αἰσχύνομαι", εἶτ᾽ αὖθις ἀμοιβαδὶς ἡ κόρη λέγει πρὸς ἐκεῖνον "ἀλλ᾽ ἐὰν ᾖς ἀγαθὸς καὶ ὃ ἔμελλες πρὸς μὲ εἰπεῖν ἦν ἀγαθόν, οὐκ ἂν ᾐδοῦ καὶ ᾐσχύνου οὕτως, ἀλλὰ μετὰ παρρησίας ἔλεγες ἂν βλέπων πρὸς μὲ ἀνερυθριάστως." In this passage, it is also interesting to note that in the original context the words are uttered by a male figure.

[128] Prodr. Mangan. *Carm.* 9.60–71, ed. Jeffreys and Jeffreys (2015). In this case *aidōs* is motivated by public praise.

alazoneia means a sense of superiority and exaggerated self-esteem which manifests itself in disregard and disrespect for established social rules, in particular Byzantine social rules in contrast to foreign, non-Byzantine rules. Boasting may still accompany *alazoneia*, but it is no longer essential to its concept. Whereas *kenodoxia* and, to a lesser extent, *huperēphania* have strong religious connotations, 'arrogance' is an emotion which is generated in the 'world'.[129] Frequently a 'high neck' and a 'raised eyebrow' are used metonymically instead of *alazoneia*. In the two texts we focused on, we observe the tendency that the terms *aidōs* and *aischunē* express two forms of shame, the one proactive, the other retroactive – which means very much in accordance with the Stoic theory – and they appear gender-related.

Juxtaposing Anna Komnene's and Niketas Choniates' original Histories with their fourteenth-century *metaphraseis*, we observe a general trend towards de-metaphoricization and a concomitant reduction of emotional terms. Whereas in the Histories a plethora of ancient and classicizing Byzantine Greek terms are used, in the Byzantine koine of the *metaphraseis* basically one single term (*entropē*) is used for 'shame', and two terms (*alazoneia* and *eparsis*) for arrogance. This is in tune with the general simplifying character of these *metaphraseis*.

When I decided to engage with *alazoneia* and *aidōs/aischunē* I did so primarily not because they were conceptually linked (although they clearly are), but because they were conspicuous in two texts, Choniates' *History* and Anna Komnena's *Alexiad*. So, why are they important? And how are they linked? *Alazoneia* is prominent in Choniates' narrative because besides the moral decadence of the Byzantine ruling class (their own arrogance included), it is the Westerners' arrogance that is presented as the essential cause for the disaster that befell Byzantium, the driving force behind the Latin attack on Thessalonike and even more the attack on Constantinople. *Aidōs*, on the other hand, is significant in Anna's *History* because it appears as a major constituent of female virtue, in a text written by a woman, giving more place than usual to (imperial) women. Both *aidōs/aischunē* and *alazoneia* are strongly related to the concept of *taxis* or *katastasis*, 'order',[130] and to the transgression of social norms, while *alazoneia* as well as the absence of *aidōs/aischunē* has to do with a lack of respect. In the case of arrogance, the impudent behaviour is triggered by an exaggerated self-esteem.

---

[129] The *Life of Kyrillos Phileotes* composed by Nicholas Kataskepenos is a hagiographical text contemporary with Anna Komnene's *Alexiad*. Not surprisingly, out of the range of pride and arrogance emotions Nicholas focuses on the vices of *kenodoxia* and *huperēphania*. Most interestingly, however, in the rare cases where he uses the word *alazoneia*, the author refers to matters of the 'world', usually to arrogance as a character trait of Westerners; Nicol. Catascep. *Vita Cyril. Phil.*, ed. Sargologos (1964) 36.1.3: τὸν ὑπερνεφῆ καὶ ἀλαζόνα Βαϊμοῦνδον ἐκεῖνον; 47.11.8–9: Ῥωσέλην τὸν Φράγγον, ὃς τῇ οἰκείᾳ ἀλαζονείᾳ θαρρῶν ἐπήρθη κατὰ τοῦ βασιλέως.

[130] On the importance of this concept for the Byzantine society see Magdalino (1989) 197–8. See the key terms *akatastasia/katastasis* in *Metaphrasis Chon.* 14.5.5 and 16.7.1–2 (cf. above, nn. 52 and 60).

For this reason, *alazoneia* and *anaideia* occur together in some of the passages we have analysed,[131] and in a certain sense Byzantine *alazoneia* and *aidōs/aischunē*, as today arrogance and shame, constitute two opposite ends on a scale of 'appropriateness'.

---

[131] See particularly Choniates' presentation of Empress Euphrosyne (above, pp. 316 and 329), or the Venitians (above, pp. 319–20). Morevover, the arrogance of the Bulgarian leader Asan (*thrasus/alazonikos*) is characterized as impudence (*anaideia*); see Nic. Chon. *Hist.* 369.67–9 and *Metaphrasis Chon.* 12.6.3.

13

Angry Warriors in the Byzantine *War of Troy**

Stavroula Constantinou

13.1. Emotions and anger

Like its French prototype, Benoît de Saint-Maure's twelfth-century *Roman de Troie*,[1] the Byzantine Greek *War of Troy* (Ὁ Πόλεμος τῆς Τρωάδος), an anonymous vernacular work of the thirteenth century consisting of about 14,400 fifteen-syllable verses,[2] is replete with references to emotions and affective expressions that influence the poem's meaning and structure.[3] In general, emotions in the two works take a double form. On the one hand, they are conditions

---

** Some of the ideas that inform this chapter's arguments were developed within the framework of the project Network for Medieval Arts and Rituals (NetMAR), which received funding from the European Union's Horizon 2020 research and innovation programme under grant agreement No. 951875. The opinions expressed in this document reflect only the author's view and in no way reflect the European Commission's opinions. The European Commission is not responsible for any use that may be made of the information it contains.

[1] Benoît de Sainte-Maure was a cleric in the circle of King Henry II and Eleanor of Aquitaine. His *Roman de Troie (ca.* 1165) is one of the three so-called 'Romances of Antiquity' – the other two are the anonymous *Roman de Thèbes* and *Roman d'Enéas* (1150–65) – that were composed in the form of octosyllabic rhymed couplets and were presented as Romance 'translations' of important Latin texts (Huchet (1989); Burgess and Kelly (2017) 3–4). Concerning the *Roman de Troie*, as Benoît informs us, it is based on two Medieval accounts of the Trojan War: Dares Phrygius, *De excidio Troiae historia* and Dictys Cretensis, *Ephemeris de bello Troiano*. The *Roman de Troie*, which is the largest of the romances of Antiquity, consists of 30,316 verses, and it was extremely popular in the Middle Ages, as attested by the relatively large number of manuscripts transmitting the poem and by its numerous influences (Burgess and Kelly (2017) 1–3).

[2] Elizabeth Jeffreys argues that *The War of Troy* was written between 1267 and 1281 (Jeffreys (2016), (2019)). It is also suggested, not quite persuasively, that it was composed in Frankish Greece, in the Morea (Jeffreys (1993)). Even though *The War of Troy* is much shorter than its French counterpart (less than half), it is by far the largest Byzantine vernacular text. Most scholars, Jeffreys included, have seen *The War of Troy* as a 'more or less close translation from its Western original' (Beaton (1996) 135–6; see also Shawcross (2003) 140; Lentari (2014) 8. For a discussion of Byzantinists' treatment of Late Byzantine fiction that is based on Western models, see Constantinou (2013) 227–9). This conclusion does not represent the reality. *The War of Troy* is as much a rewriting of the *Roman de Troie* as the latter constitutes a rewriting of Dares and Dictys. For a detailed discussion of *The War of Troy* as a rewriting, see Constantinou (2021).

[3] In contrast to the *Roman de Troie*, *The War of Troy* has not attracted much scholarly attention. The few studies focusing on the Greek poem include the following: Papathomopoulos

340   *Stavroula Constantinou*

characterizing the heroes or heroines. On the other hand, they are reactions to incitements leading to actions that in turn provoke further actions through which the narrative unfolds.

The centrality of emotions in both epic poems becomes obvious at the outset. Their narrative is set in motion through King Peleus' (Πήλεος, ancient Greek Pelias) extremely strong fear that his nephew, Jason, who is famous for his exceptional bravery, will push him off his throne and snatch his crown (**φόβον εἶ-χεν ἀπόρρητον** μήπως ἐξαναστάντος / ἐπάρῃ τὸ βασίλειον καὶ τοῦτον ἐξηβάλῃ, *The War of Troy* 15–16; emphasis added). Fear leads Peleus to create a deadly trap for Jason. Taking advantage of his nephew's thirst for honour, Peleus asks him to undertake a quest that no man could achieve: to get the Golden Fleece. Upon Jason's agreement, the king's fear is converted into great happiness (καὶ ταῦτα εὐθὺς ὡς ἤκουσεν ὁ βασιλεὺς Πηλέος, / **ὅλος χαρὰ** ἐγένετο, **ὅλος ἦν θυμηδία**, *The War of Troy* 98–9; emphasis added). Overcome with joy, Peleus sends for the skilful artisan, Argus, who is commanded to build the most suitable ship for Jason's trip to Colchis. Peleus' joy is later substituted by anger when, beyond his expectations, Jason manages with Medea's help to succeed in his quest. However, he does not show his anger. He rather appears happy and full of love for his nephew, whom he now honours (ὁ Πήλεος ἐτίμησε τὸν Ἰασοῦν μεγάλως· / οὐκ ἔδειξέ τον πρόσωπον τάχατε **χολιασμένον** / … ἀλλὰ **χαρὰν** τοῦ ἔδειχνε καὶ **ἀγά-πην πληρεστάτην**, *The War of Troy* 734–7; emphasis added).

At this point, the story involving Peleus and Jason reaches its happy ending: it begins with fear and ends with happiness, while, in between, these and other characters' emotions play an essential part. In what follows, the omniscient narrators of the *Roman de Troie* and the *War of Troy* undertake to narrate another, much longer, story, which dominates the rest of the two works. This is the story of Troy, regarding the city's first and second sacks by the Greeks. The two works also present the fate of the women of Priam's family and those of the most important Greeks (Diomedes, Agamemnon, Menelaus, Odysseus, and Pyrrhus) and the surviving Trojans (Aeneas and Anthenor) who help the Greeks conquer Troy. In all cases, as the following analysis will also demonstrate, emotions are prominent. Whereas the poems start with Peleus' fear, they end with a different feeling. The narrative of the *Roman de Troie* closes with Circe's joy upon welcoming back the son she has with Odysseus, Telegonus, whom she considered dead. In her happiness, Circe does not fail to mourn for Odysseus, who is no longer alive. The Greek poet, on the other hand, ends his own narrative with the grief that the assassination of Achilles' son, Pyrrhus, causes to the Greeks.[4]

---

and Jeffreys (1996) xiii–cxxv; Jeffreys (2007), (2013); Lentari (2014); Soltic (2014); Goldwyn (2018) 155–77; Markopoulos (2019); Constantinou (2019b), (2020).

[4] The episode with Circe and Telegonus appears earlier in *The War of Troy* (14080–7). In

13. Angry Warriors in the Byzantine War of Troy   341

As is the case with the first Troy tale that has come down to us, Homer's *Iliad*, anger is one of the two Medieval poems' most important feelings.[5] In fact, as has been pointed out, 'anger and epic seem to go hand in hand. If different genres are particularly associated with different emotions, then epic surely lays claim to anger.'[6] In short, the centrality of anger in the Medieval epic works in question is the result of a generic convention that goes back to Homer. It has to be added, however, that epic anger is gender-specific, since it is chiefly displayed by male characters and it constitutes the emotion which defines the warrior.[7] For instance, when the Greeks decide to attack Troy for a second time, the omniscient narrator provides short portraits of their most significant warriors, beginning with Agamemnon, their leader. In most cases, the narrator starts from the warriors' appearance, and then moves to their virtues. Anger is presented as one of these virtues, thus appearing as an extremely positive and necessary characteristic of the warrior:

> ὁ Ἀχιλλεὺς ὁ θαυμαστὸς ἔλαμπεν ὑπὲρ πάντας·
> κάλλος εἶχεν ἀπόρρητον, ἀνδρείαν ἐξηρημένην·
> μακρύς, πλατὺς στὸ στῆθος του, λιγνὸς ὡς πρὸς τὴν μέσην·
> χοντρὰ τὰ μέλη, φοβερά, τὰς χεῖρας καὶ τοὺς πόδας·
> εὔμορφα ὀμμάτια, ἀπόκοτα, ἄγρια καὶ θυμωμένα·
> μαλλία σγουρά, ξανθόχροια, πρέποντα πρὸς τὰ κάλλη·
> πρόσωπον χαρωπότατον πρὸς φίλους, ἐγνωρίμους,
> πολλὰ χολιαστικώτατον πρὸς ἐχθρούς, ἀντιδίκους.
> (*The War of Troy* 2086–93)

---

the Greek poem, however, Circe's joy is soon transformed into sorrow for the loss of Odysseus. In this case, Circe's happiness does not last, and she does not experience any mixed feelings.

[5] Neither Benoît nor the anonymous poet seems to have had a direct knowledge of the Homeric work. However, there are a number of parallels between Homer's epics and the two Medieval poems. After all, the works upon which the *Roman de Troie* is based constitute rewritings of the *Iliad* and the *Odyssey*. Some of the similarities and differences between *The War of Troy* and the *Iliad* will be revealed through the following analysis. For Homer and the uses of the Troy matter in Byzantium, see Browning (1975); Nilsson (2004); Goldwyn (2015).

[6] Braund and Most (2003b) 3. For Homeric anger see, for example, Muellner (1996); Koziak (1999); Harris (2001) 131–56; Cairns (2003); Most (2003); Walsh (2005); Konstan (2010a); Kalimtzis (2012) 5–21.

[7] In Homer, female anger is mostly expressed by goddesses (Koziak (1999) 1074–7). In *The War of Troy*, where the Olympian gods and goddesses play a much lesser role, goddesses' anger is almost non-existent. The only exception is Minerva's anger towards the Greeks for stealing the Palladium from her temple (*The War of Troy* 11926), and for abusing Cassandra after the second sack of Troy while she was taking shelter in the temple of the goddess (*The War of Troy* 12879). Mortal women displaying anger in *The War of Troy* are the Amazons, who do so as warriors (10996–11000). The only exception of a woman who is not a warrior showing anger in *The War of Troy* is the queen Hecuba after she witnesses the murder of her daughter Polyxena at the Greeks' hands (12483–8). Hecuba's rage could be described as 'female', as it is incited by her motherly grief and not by an act of dishonour, as is mostly the case with male anger. For the correlation between maternal sorrow and anger in Greek antiquity, see Loraux (1998 [1990]).

342 Stavroula Constantinou

> Achilles, the magnificent, was shining above all.
> He had ineffable beauty, awe-inspiring bravery.
> He was tall, broad-breasted, with a thin waist
> and with thick, fearful [bodily] parts, hands and feet;
> [he had] beautiful, bold, wild and angry eyes;
> curly, blond hair, shaped according to the laws of beauty;
> [he had] the most cheerful face to friends and acquaintances,
> but [it became] extremely angry against enemies, opponents.[8]

Achilles' constant anger is first detected in his eyes, which are both beautiful and wild, bold and wrathful. The dual character of his eyes reflects his double face, which becomes extremely joyful before friends and acquaintances, while it appears exceptionally angry against enemies and rivalries.[9] Achilles' facial expression of extreme antithetical feelings exposes both his relationships with other men, who are either friends or enemies, and his unrestrained character. In fact, this first presentation of the hero warrior's contradictory emotionality is in full accordance with his later behaviour towards his best friend Patroclus, on the one hand, and his worst enemy Hector, on the other.

To a large extent, as is mostly the case with the Homeric works, anger in the *Roman de Troie* and *The War of Troy* has an Aristotelian sense.[10] In his *Rhetoric*, Aristotle defines anger as follows:

> ἔστω δὴ ὀργὴ ὄρεξις μετὰ λύπης τιμωρίας [φαινομένης] διὰ φαινομένην ὀλιγωρίαν εἰς αὑτὸν ἢ <τι> τῶν αὑτοῦ, τοῦ ὀλιγωρεῖν μὴ προσήκοντος ... καὶ πάσῃ ὀργῇ ἕπεσθαί τινα ἡδονήν, τὴν ἀπὸ τῆς ἐλπίδος τοῦ τιμωρήσασθαι. (*Rh.* 2.2, 1378a30–2, 1378b1–2)

> Let us take anger, then, to be the impulse, accompanied by pain, for visible retaliation in response to visible disparagement by a man who has no business disparaging one or people dear to one ... It also follows that every instance of anger is accompanied by a certain feeling of pleasure based on the expectation of achieving retaliation.[11]

For Aristotle, anger is a man's personal concern created by an external factor. It is the desire to restore a man's honour and status that have been affected by another man's wrongdoing. As an immediate, yet legitimate, reaction to misconduct, anger springs from pain. At the same time, anger generates desire for revenge through which the initial victim is transformed into a perpetrator. Thus, while anger is born of distress, it ends in delight.

---

[8] Unless otherwise indicated, translations are my own.

[9] For anger's association with the face and the eyes, see also below, § 13.4.

[10] Douglas Cairns has shown in a seminal article that anger in Homer is chiefly as Aristotle would have it: a response to an insult. There are, however, instances in which anger is provoked by events or situations where no offender is involved: Cairns (2003). This is valid also for the *Roman de Troie* and *The War of Troy*, as the aforementioned example of Peleus' anger towards Jason for the latter's achievements demonstrates.

[11] Trans. Waterfield (2018) 61. For anger in Aristotle see, for instance, Harris (2001) 93–8; Konstan (2003); Kalimtzis (2012) 73–126.

13. Angry Warriors in the Byzantine War of Troy

Such an approach to anger is expressed through the words and deeds of a number of heroes in *The War of Troy*. One of them is King Priam, who is enraged due to Troy's sack by the Greeks, the murder of his parents, and the abduction of his sister Hesione, who, instead of being treated according to her status as a princess, becomes the concubine of a mere soldier (Telamon). Priam confesses: ποτὲ καρδίαν χαιράμενην οὐ μὴ ἔχω εἰς τὸν κόσμον, / ἕως οὗ τὴν ἐκδίκησιν ἐπάρω τῆς Τρωάδος ('I shall never find happiness in the world, / unless I take revenge for Troy', *The War of Troy* 1182–3). Priam's pain is transformed into pleasure as soon as his honour is restored by dishonouring the Greeks through the seizure of Helen, who replaces Hesione. This act causes in turn the Greeks' anger, so that they seek to re-establish their own honour by destroying Troy for a second time.[12]

Aristotelian anger, which is accompanied by both pain and pleasure, is unavoidably associated with a number of other feelings: sorrow, shame, hope, desire, and joy. Often, as Priam's example mentioned above indicates, this is also the case with the angry heroes of the two Medieval poems. A case in point from the Greek camp, which also involves the kidnapping of a woman, concerns the cuckold husband, Menelaus, who is angry towards Paris for dishonouring him, while at the same time he is ashamed of and feels sorrow at being deprived of his wife, Helen. Upon seeing Menelaus in such a bad emotional state, his brother Agamemnon reminds him of the pleasures of revenge, which all Greeks are prepared to take on his behalf (*The War of Troy* 1976–2013).

As one of the most prominent feelings of the massive *Roman de Troie* and *The War of Troy*, male anger takes various forms, is expressed and experienced in many ways, and has different uses and functions. These are mostly determined by the ways in which enraged heroes, who undertake different roles, such as those of the king (e. g. Peleus and Laomedon), the husband (e. g. Menelaus and Priam), and the warrior (all participants in the Trojan wars), interact with both each other and other characters of the narrative, male and female. On the literary level, anger also serves as a rhetorical device supporting the works' poetic form, as a technique of characterization, and as a means of advancing and sustaining the plot.[13]

---

[12] The first destruction of Troy was also incited by the Greeks' anger at not being allowed to stay in Trojan land on their way to Colchis. Jason and his comrades were gravely offended by the way Laomedon, the Trojan king, had treated them: Ταῦτα εὐθὺς ὡς ἤκουσεν, ὁ Ἰασοῦς ἐθλίβη / καὶ ἠλλοιώθη ἡ ὄψις του ἀπὸ θυμοῦ μεγάλου. / τοὺς ἄρχοντας ἐσύντυχε μετὰ χολῆς μεγάλης: / "μὰ τὸν θεόν, ὦ ἄρχοντες, εὐγενικοὶ στρατιῶται, / ἄτιμον πράγμαν ἔποικεν οὗτος ὁ βασιλέας, / ὅτι μὲ τέτοιαν χολὴν νὰ μᾶς ἀπιλογιάσῃ, / νὰ ἐβγοῦμε ἀπὸ τὴν χώραν του μετὰ πολλῆς αἰσχύνης" ('Upon hearing these words, Jason was immediately saddened. / His face was transformed by great anger. / He spoke to the lords with great anger: / "By God, lords, noble soldiers, / this king has done a dishonourable thing: / to send us away in such an angry manner, / to have to abandon his county with a lot of shame"', *The War of Troy* 174–80).

[13] For the aesthetic uses of emotions in Byzantine literature, see Constantinou (2019b).

344   *Stavroula Constantinou*

13.2. The warrior as an angry man

The confines of this chapter do not allow an examination of all forms, expressions, experiences, and operations of male anger in the two Medieval epics. Thus, the following analysis focuses on *The War of Troy* and investigates some important aspects of the poem's most prominent type of anger, that of the warrior. More specifically, it deals with the vocabulary, the physiology, the signs, and the effects of the warrior's anger, as well as with its involvement in the characterization of the protagonist warriors of the two opposing camps, Achilles and Hector, who in the work under discussion are depicted as equals in battle; it is not always clear who will eventually survive and who will be killed first.[14] In the end, each hero's death is achieved through treachery. Achilles manages to kill Hector while the latter is attacking another Greek warrior. As for Achilles, he is murdered while he is in the temple of Minerva to meet Polyxena, with whom he is in love.

Being the bravest and most competent warriors, the two heroes are also the angriest ones. They get enraged more often than anyone else, and they display their wrath both in and beyond the battlefield. Their anger is directed at various targets: the whole army of their enemies, individual warriors with whom they get involved in single combat (including their fight against each other), and members of their own camps (e.g. Achilles' anger against the Greeks for not following his advice to abandon the war, an outcome that would enable the hero to marry Polyxena; Hector's rage against Andromache and Priam for not allowing him to go to battle on a particular day). The two heroes' fury lies at the centre of a number of episodes, while at the same time it considerably determines the course of the war and their own fate. As formulated by Matilda Tomaryn Bruckner, 'both Achilles and Hector are propelled to their encounter with death by the fury of their anger, exploded when they see the comrades they abandoned on the verge of defeat without their aid'.[15] Inevitably, most references to anger in *The War of Troy* concern Achilles and Hector.

In sum, the analysis undertaken in the rest of this essay concerns, on the one hand, the warrior's anger as an emotion that has a cultural history (how it was understood, described, expressed, and experienced in past cultures) and, on the other, anger as a rhetorical and narrative device which fashions poetic diction and creates characters whose words and actions shape the plot. The two aspects are inseparable, and the one cannot be understood without the other for two reasons. First, they become available to us through the literary text: the voice of its narrator and the words and behaviour of its heroes. Second, the narrator's and the heroes' understanding of anger must reflect social conventions about

---

[14] This constitutes a deviation from their Homeric counterparts. In the *Iliad*, Achilles is superior to Hector. See Schein (1984) 89–167.

[15] Tomaryn Bruckner (2010) 137.

13. Angry Warriors in the Byzantine War of Troy

345

this very emotion: its characteristics and the situations where its experience and performance are expected.[16] 'Narrative literature', according to Jeff Rider, 'shares the structure of an emotion, reflects, purveys, and plays with the ambient emotionology of time and place in which it was created.'[17] Thus, approaching the warrior's anger in *The War of Troy* as a rhetorical and narrative means goes hand in hand with approaching its cultural specifics as mirrored in the same poem.

As far as the cultural specifics of anger and the warrior's characterization are concerned, three elements of the Aristotelian anger are relevant here – and possibly to other Medieval or later works featuring angry male characters.[18] First, Aristotle understands anger as reaction to actions whose consequences affect a man's status and honour. Second, anger for Aristotle is a special kind of judgement, mostly justified, about a man's self and place in a certain society or about those of his friends. Third, in contrast to modern practice, Aristotle does not see anger as a bad feeling, but treats it as an emotion with both a negative and positive sense.

In the *War of Troy* – and, of course, in the *Roman de Troie* – the warrior's anger that could be described as Aristotelian is simultaneously a collective emotion, since it defines the members of two armies. As a collective emotion, anger is here understood through Barbara Rosenwein's concept of 'emotional community'. According to Rosenwein, 'emotional communities are groups ... that have their own particular values, modes of feeling, and ways to express those feelings'.[19] A certain emotional community might be detected in different contemporary societies, such as the Greek and Trojan ones that populate *The War of Troy*.

Both the Greek and Trojan warriors, despite their different origins, have shared values and 'adhere to the same norms of emotional expression and value – or devalue – the same or related emotions'.[20] Concerning anger in particular, the aristocratic warriors of the *War of Troy*, either Greek or Trojan, get angry for the same reasons and display their rage in similar ways. Similar also is the rhetoric employed by our anonymous poet to express in words and in poetic ways why and how these very warriors become enraged.

---

[16] White (1998) 137.

[17] Rider (2011) 6.

[18] It needs to be noted that the Aristotelian theory of anger has proved extremely influential, since it has informed, either consciously or unconsciously, the work of many authors from Antiquity to Modernity. See Konstan (2010a) 9–18 (ancient Greek and Latin authors); Stewart (2000) 67 and Hinterberger (2017a) 328 (Church Fathers); Hinterberger (2010a) 132–3 (Byzantine authors); Spencer (2017) 501 (Medieval Western authors); and Frevert (2011) 40–70, 89–95 (Early Modern and later authors). Regarding later literary works with angry male characters, Inna Kupreeva has reminded me of D'Artagnan's and the Musketeers' anger in Alexandre Dumas's novel *Les trois Mousquetaires* (March–July 1844), which has also an Aristotelian sense and thus has many parallels with the warrior's anger in the *Roman de Troie* (and *The War of Troy*).

[19] Rosenwein (2006) 3.

[20] Rosenwein (2006) 2.

The discussion that follows is divided into two interconnected parts. The first and larger part (§ 13.3) concerns the verbal expressivity of the warrior's anger. It examines how the anonymous poet communicates the warrior's anger to his audiences: the terminology and the tropes he uses, which, as will be shown, often reflect contemporary medical approaches to anger. In the second part (§ 13.4), the analysis moves from verbal to bodily expressions of anger, discussing its physiology and facial manifestations that also appear to be based on relevant medical discourses. Within the framework of the two parts, the relationship between anger and characterization is further revealed, since the poet employs the rhetoric of anger and refers to its physiology in an attempt to both portray the temperament of individual warriors and explain the reasons behind their actions. Unavoidably, the discussion focuses on the two most exemplary warriors: Achilles and Hector, whose expressions of anger, as already stated, lie at the heart of the war narrative, and thus prove decisive for the unfolding of the plot.

13.3. The vocabulary and rhetoric of anger

As many scholars have noted, Homer's most common term for anger is *cholos*.[21] Interestingly, the most frequent word for anger in *The War of Troy* is a word with the same root: *cholē* (χολή). In general, Byzantine authors use the two terms as synonyms. As John of Damascus (*ca.* 675–749) writes in his short discussion on anger, 'anger (*thumos*) … is called both "*cholē*" and "*cholos*"' (θυμὸς … καὶ χολὴ λέγεται καὶ χόλος; *Exposition of the Orthodox Faith*, 30.2–3).[22]

The word *cholē*, which literally means 'bile', points to an understanding of the bodily basis of anger that was also acknowledged by Late Antique and Byzantine authors. For example, Nemesius, the Bishop of Emesa (late fourth century), drawing also on Aristotle's account of anger in the *De anima*, makes the following etymological remark, which is later adopted by John of Damascus: θυμὸς δέ ἐστι ζέσις τοῦ περὶ καρδίαν αἵματος ἐξ ἀναθυμιάσεως τῆς χολῆς ἢ ἀναθολώσεως γινομένη· διὸ καὶ χολὴ λέγεται καὶ χόλος ('Anger is the boiling of the blood about the heart which is produced by the exhalation of the bile or turbidity. It is for this reason that it is called both *cholē* and *cholos*'; *On the Nature of Man*, 20.81.2–3).[23]

Nemesius' definition of anger, along with the physiological explanation of anger terminology, reveals the influence of the Hippocratic theory of humours, which was popularized by Galen and his followers and largely adopted in Byzantine medicine.[24] In Galenic and post-Galenic humoral theory, according to

---

[21] See, for example, Harris (2001) 341; Cairns (2003) 25; Kalimtzis (2012) 5.
[22] Ed. Kotter (1973).
[23] Ed. Morani (1987). See Arist. *De an.* 403a31.
[24] For the humoral theory in the Hippocratic and Galenic corpus see, for example, Hankinson (2008) 217–24; Vogt (2008) 308–12; Jouanna (2012) 335–60; King (2013). As for Galen's

13. Angry Warriors in the Byzantine War of Troy

which the human body contains four liquids (humours) – blood, yellow bile, black bile, and phlegm – anger is related to an overproduction of yellow bile in the liver or stomach through which the four humours' balance in the blood is disrupted: καὶ θυμοὶ ... πλείονα τὸν τῆς ξανθῆς χολῆς ἀθροίζουσι χυμόν ('Angry emotions ... collect a larger quantity of the yellow bile'; Pseudo-Galen, *On Humours* 19.488.11–13).[25]

As a synonym of *cholē*, anger is also linked to the sense of taste – it is equated with a bitter bodily fluid involved in the digestion of food[26] – revealing a conception of anger similar to that of Aristotle: anger as (initially) unpleasant and painful. The anonymous Byzantine poet does not refrain from making clear *cholē*'s (i. e. anger's) equivalence with bitterness, as demonstrated, for instance, in these two verses: νὰ χολιάσῃς τοὺς Ἕλληνας, νὰ τοὺς παραπικράνῃς and μετὰ μεγάλης τῆς χολῆς, μετὰ πολλῆς πικρίας ('To *irritate* the Greeks, to highly *embitter* them'; 'with a *great anger*, with *a lot of bitterness*' (*The War of Troy* 12387 and 13055; emphasis added).[27]

Our poet also uses extensively the verb *choliazō* (χολιάζω) – a vernacular version of the verb *cholaō* – and its derivatives *choliakos, choliastikos, choliasmenos* (χολιακός, χολιαστικός, χολιασμένος).[28] These words are employed for all types of angry men depicted in *The War of Troy*. To refer to a greater or the greatest degree of anger performed by his heroes, the Byzantine poet utilizes a superlative adjective (e. g. χολιαστικώτατος) or phrases such as πολλά χολιασμένος ('very angry'), πάμπολλα χολιασμένος ('extremely angry'), ἐκ τὴν χολὴν τὴν φοβερὰν ('due to his great anger'), and χολιακὸς εἰς ἄκρον ('an angry man to the highest limit'). As a rule, when anger is presented as excessive, either in these or other terms, the angry man is a Troy warrior.

In addition to *cholos*, Homer uses various words to describe different kinds of anger: *kotos, mēnis, nemesis, thumos, achos, menos*.[29] The Byzantine poet, in contrast, employs the aforementioned *cholē* interchangeably with *thumos* (θυμός) and *orgē* (ὀργή) for all types of anger.[30] Nevertheless, he has the tendency

---

legacy in Byzantium and the Medieval West, see Nutton (2007), (2008); Jouanna (2012) 341–59; Bouras-Vallianatos (2015).

[25] Ed. Kühn (1821–33). For the medical understanding of anger, see also below.

[26] πικρὸν δὲ τὴν ξανθήν [χολήν] ('Yellow bile is bitter', Galen, *On Hippocrates' 'Nature of Man'* 15.80.7, ed. Mewaldt (1914)).

[27] Cf. the following statement from an anonymous post-Galenic medical treatise, *On the Constitution of the Universe and of Man* 2.3, ed. Ideler (1841): ὅσοι δὲ ἀπὸ ξανθῆς χολῆς τυγχάνουσιν, οὗτοί εἰσιν ὀργίλοι καὶ πικροὶ καὶ εὔτολμοι καὶ σώματά εἰσιν ὕπωχροι καὶ ξανθόχροοι ('Those who are composed of yellow bile are quick-tempered, bitter, daring; regarding their bodies, they are greenish and have yellow skin', trans. Jouanna (2012) 342).

[28] These *cholē* terms are also found in other Byzantine vernacular texts, both earlier and later (e. g. *Digenis Akritas, Spaneas, Livistros and Rodamne*, the Byzantine *Achilleid*, and *Chronicle of Morea*).

[29] Harris (2001) 50–70; Cairns (2003) 21–37; Kalimtzis (2012) 11–12.

[30] Already in the fifth century BC, *mēnis* had generally been substituted by *thumos* and *orgē*:

348   *Stavroula Constantinou*

to associate *cholē* and *orgē* with the body, whereas he mostly links *thumos* with the mind: ἐκ τὸν θυμὸν ὑπάγαινε νὰ ἔβγῃ ἐκ τὸν νοῦν του ('He was about to lose his mind out of his anger', *The War of Troy* 10962).

After *cholē*, the most frequent term for anger in *The War of Troy* is *thumos,* along with the words deriving from it: *thumoumai, thumomenos, thumodēs* (θυμοῦμαι, θυμωμένος, θυμώδης). However, the *thumos* terms involved in the articulation of different degrees of anger are much more varied than those of the *cholē* words given above: μέγας θυμός ('great anger'), ὅλος θυμοῦ ('wholly angered'), ἐθυμώθη φοβερά ('he was greatly angered'), θυμώδης λίαν ('very bad-tempered'), πολλὰ θυμωμένος ('very angry'), μετὰ θυμοῦ θυμωμένοι ('they were enraged with anger'), μὲ τέτοιαν ἴραν τοῦ θυμοῦ ('with such an enraged anger').

It should be noted that in the last two examples the immensity of anger is highlighted through the repetition of anger terms within the same verse. The last example (μὲ τέτοιαν ἴραν τοῦ θυμοῦ; 'de tel aïr' in the *Roman de Troie*, 9921) is interesting also from a linguistic point of view. Here, the Greek poet transliterates the French word *aïr* ('anger') as ἴραν.[31] *Orgē* and its derivatives *orgizomai, orgistikos,* or *orgisthikos* (ὀργίζομαι, ὀργιστικός, or ὀργισθικός) appear much less frequently in the Greek poem. Some other and much less-used words expressing anger include the verbs *aganaktō* (ἀγανακτῶ) and *mainomai* (μαίνομαι), as well as the latter's derivative, *mania* (μανία) through which anger, as is also the case in Homer,[32] is associated with madness.

In addition to repetition and hyperbole,[33] the Greek poet also employs other tropes to point to the warrior's anger and its intensity. These include irony, metaphor, and simile. In general, ironic statements referring to a hero's anger are made in the voice of the narrator, who at times chooses to describe the anger's degree not within the course of the narrative, but through an authorial intrusion. For example, after presenting the reason for a hero's anger and before going on to narrate its effects, the narrator turns to his audience. His ironic intrusion is

---

Harris (2001) 52. From the first century AD onwards and up to the Byzantine era *cholos, thumos,* and *orgē* are used interchangeably: Harris (2001) 54; Hinterberger (2010a) 133; (2017a) 336–7.

[31] Papathomopoulos and Jeffreys translate the word ἴρα as 'violent blow,' a translation that does not take into consideration the word's relationship with the emotion of anger: Papathomopoulos and Jeffreys (1996) 748.

[32] Clarke (1995) 151; Hershkowitz (1998) 136–44; Clarke (2004) 81.

[33] Some other characteristic examples include the following: (1) repetition: μετὰ θυμοῦ, μετὰ χολῆς πρῶτος εἰς αὔτους κρούει, γεμάτος ἦτον τὴν χολὴν καὶ τὸν θυμὸν ὡσαύτως, κακόγλωσσος καὶ χολιακὸς εὑρίσκετον, θυμώδης ('with anger, with irritation he strikes them first', 'he is full of anger and similarly full of rage', 'he was ill-tongued and bad-tempered, characterized by anger', *The War of Troy* 3541, 4383, and 11235); (2) hyperbole: ἐκ τὸν θυμὸν τὸν μέγαν/ὑπάει νὰ θνήξῃ ζωντανός, ἐὰν μὴ τὸν ἐκδικήσῃ, τόσα ἄγριος εἰς τὸ πρόσωπον ἔνι καὶ χολιασμένος,/ὅτι τινὰς οὐδὲν τολμᾷ νὰ τὸν ἀνατηρήσῃ, ἐκ τὸν θυμὸν ὑπάγαινε νὰ ἔβγῃ ἐκ τὸν νοῦν του ('out of his great anger/he is about to die alive, unless he avenges him', 'he has such a wild face and he is so angry/that nobody dares to look at him', 'he was about to lose his mind out of his anger', *The War of Troy* 995–6, 6740–1, 10962).

13. Angry Warriors in the Byzantine War of Troy   349

normally no longer than a verse that takes the form of a conditional sentence: ἐὰν ἐθυμώθη τίποτε, κανεὶς μηδὲν ἠρώτα ('If he was in any way angry let no one ever ask'). By asking in such a way for the evaluation of the hero's emotionality, the narrator encourages the audience's involvement in the poem's world while at the same time he serves poetic purposes concerning the work's metrical form and rhetoric.

In other instances, the narrator enters the hero's mind and communicates his thoughts and intentions as these are determined by his angry feelings:

> ὁ"Εκτωρ ὁ θαυμάσιος ἐξῆλθεν ἐκ τὴν πόρταν·
> καλὰ ἐφαίνετον ἄνθρωπος νὰ ἔναι χολιασμένος.
> σπουδάζει εἰς τοὺς"Ελληνας νὰ ῥίψῃ τὴν χολήν του·
> δείξει τους θέλει σήμερον τὸ πόσον τοὺς ἀγάπα.
> (*The War of Troy* 3280–3; emphasis added)

> Hector the magnificent came out of the gate.
> It is quite obvious that the man is angry.
> He is eager to *vent his cholē* upon the Greeks.
> He wants to show them how much he *loves* them today.

The ironic words of the last hemistich allow the narrator to highlight and present more powerfully the ferocity of Hector's anger as he is about to enter the battlefield. Through this irony, the hero's anger is linked to another feeling, the opposite of love.[34] The coexistence of anger and hatred in the warrior's emotional life drive him to perform more violent, and thus more heroic, deeds on the battlefield. Hector, who finds himself in such an emotional state, causes considerable damage to the Greek army on that very day.

In addition to irony, this short passage also entails one of the poem's metaphors for expressing anger: ῥίπτει τὴν χολήν του (*The War of Troy* 3282), which literally means 'he throws his bile', and thus creates the image of a warrior taking revenge on his enemies by pouring an unpleasant liquid upon them.[35] Another relevant metaphor found in *The War of Troy* reads as follows: 'he sells his *cholē*' or 'he sells his *thumos*' (πουλεῖ τὴν χολήν του, θυμὸν πουλεῖ), implying that, by acting out his anger through attacking his enemies, the warrior receives a payment that represents the Aristotelian pleasure achieved through retaliation.[36] These

---

[34] For a reading of the Aristotelian approach to the relationship between anger and hatred, see Kalimtzis (2012) 125–33.

[35] For the use of metaphors in the expression of emotions, see Kövecses (2003).

[36] Other variations of the metaphor of transaction involving enemies include the verbs 'pay', 'get paid', and 'buy': οὐ μὴ νὰ ζήσῃς πλεώτερον, ἐδὰ θέλεις **πληρώσει**/τὴν χωρισίαν ἣν ἔποικες ἐμὲν καὶ τοῦ ἀδελφοῦ μου./ἐδὰ δι' αὐτὴν νὰ **πληρωθῶ**, ἐκδίκησιν νὰ πάρω ('you are not going to live any longer, you are going to *pay* here/the separation you created between me and my brother./I am going to *be paid* for it here, to take revenge' (*The War of Troy* 5128–30; emphasis added); ὁ"Εκτωρ ἐθυμώθηκε, μέγαν κακὸν τοῦ ἐφάνη·/λέγει: "ἐδὰ ἐντροπιάσθηκα, ἂν μὴ τὸ **ἐξαγοράσῃς**." /καλὴν σπαθέαν τὸν ἔδωκε, κόπτει του τὸν βραχιόνα ('Hector got angry, it seemed to him a great evil; /he says: "I have been ashamed in this, you will have to *buy* it

350   *Stavroula Constantinou*

metaphors graphically express the social dimension of anger as exemplified by Aristotle: the soldier's anger acquires meaning when it is transformed into violence directed against the adversarial community of warriors.

However, neither of these two anger metaphors exists in Homer or the *Roman de Troie*. Furthermore, they do not seem to have been used by any other Byzantine author. A *TLG* search has produced no results other than the examples found in *The War of Troy*. It should be mentioned, however, that some Byzantine authors employ the verb 'throw' (ῥίπτω) to create a metaphor for other emotions, such as arrogance, sorrow, and fear. A case in point is the anonymous poet of the romance *Livistros and Rodamne* (possibly thirteenth century), with which *The War of Troy* shares a number of linguistic similarities.[37]

In *Livistros and Rodamne*, the protagonists are, for instance, advised by other characters to ῥίψε το τὸ κενόδοξον, ἄφες τὸ ἠπηρμένον.[38] καὶ τοὺς ὀπίσω πι-κρασμοὺς ῥίψε, ξενώθησέ τους, καὶ ῥίψε, ῥίψε τὸ λοιπὸν ἀποτουνῦν τὸν φόβον ('Throw vanity, leave pride behind'; 'and throw, abandon the previous sorrows'; 'and throw, throw fear from now on', *Livistros and Rodamne* 1421, 2485, 3144).[39] In these examples, to throw an emotion means to get rid of it in a process during which the hero or heroine is first invited to come to terms with his or her own emotionality and then to try to control it, an achievement that leads to emotional maturity. In *The War of Troy*, in contrast, when the warriors throw their anger they do not get rid of it, but they vent it on their enemies, and the angrier they get the better.

Other common metaphors for anger included in *The War of Troy* belong to the category of container metaphors: χολὴν βαστάζουσι μεγάλην, ὅλος θυμοῦ γεμᾶτος, or ὅλος θυμοῦ ἐπλήσθη ('they hold great *cholē*' and 'he was completely filled with *thumos*'), which, unlike the previous set of anger metaphors, can be found both in Homer and other Byzantine literature from different periods.[40] In the first example, the metaphor produces the image of warriors holding vessels

---

[your slight] *off*.' / He gave him a good cutting, he cut his arm', *The War of Troy* 5138–40; emphasis added).

[37] Jeffreys (2019). Most earlier texts having such a metaphor are epistles (e.g. ἔξω ῥίπτων τὸν φόβον ἀπὸ τοῦ δεῦρο, 'throwing anger out from now on', Theodorus Studites, *Epistulae* 552.18, ed. Fatouros (1992).

[38] There are other Byzantine texts, however, in which the verb ἀφίημι ('to abandon') is used for anger. See, for example, 'and you, abandon the *cholē*' (καὶ σὺ τὴν χολὴν ἄφες, John Stobaeus, *Anthology* 3.14.7.40, ed. Hense and Wachsmuth (1894)); ἄφες τὸ μακρὸν βρύγμα, τὸν μέγαν χόλον ('abandon your huge bellowing, your great anger', trans. Jeffreys (2012) 83 with a minor modification of my own), Theodoros Prodromos (twelfth century), *Rhodanthe and Dosikles* 5.56, ed. Marcovich (1992).

[39] Ed. Agapitos (2006).

[40] For container metaphors for anger in Homer, see Padel (1992) 2–26; Cairns (2003) 18, 22, 25, and 31. For examples of the use of similar metaphors in Byzantine literature see, for instance, *Life of Thekla* 1.5.14 (ed. Dagron (1978) 168–283); *Passion of Romanos* § 4.78 (ed. Halkin (1989) 33–54); Anna Komnene, *Alexiad* 4.8.2.9–10 (ed. Kambylis and Reinsch (2001)); Theodoros Prodromos, *Rodanthe and Dosicles* 2.293–4 (ed. Marcovich (1992)).

13. Angry Warriors in the Byzantine War of Troy 351

filled with bile, while in the second it is the warrior's own body that is transformed into a vessel full of anger. The metaphor of the body as vessel in particular suggests the accumulation of a power within a highly pressurized holder that is about to burst upon the warrior's enemies.

In fact, the container metaphors represent an earlier phase in the development of the warrior's anger than the one expressed in the first set of metaphors presented above ('to sell/pay for/get paid for/buy his *cholē*' and 'to throw his *cholē*'). The container metaphors refer to the anger's arousal and to its subsequent, and often instantaneous, growth which keeps increasing until it reaches its highest degree. The transaction and other relevant metaphors, on the other hand, concern the point at which a hero is about to soothe his anger by selling or throwing it to the enemy who is forced to pay dearly for it.[41]

The last figure to be discussed in this part, simile, takes two forms when it refers to the warrior's anger: animal and fire similes, which are also employed in the *Iliad*.[42] Unlike many of their Homeric counterparts, the animal and fire similes of *The War of Troy*, apart from one exception (9488–92), are in Richard Buxton's words 'short', for they 'do not contain a verb',[43] and also because they normally do not exceed the limits of a single verse line. Furthermore, the Byzantine poet's similes do not point to a 'parallel world' presenting 'alternatives, a set of possibilities on which to gaze if the traumas of the battlefield become overwhelming'.[44] They are, in contrast, rhetorical devices that, like the other tropes examined above, present in a striking way the warrior's anger and its intensity.

The Byzantine poet employs animal similes more frequently than fire similes. The animals to which the angry warrior is likened are wild beasts including lions, leopards, tigers, wolves, and rabid dogs that are used with the same sense: all beasts stand for extreme anger which supersedes human limits. Sometimes two different beasts are mentioned in a single simile to further emphasize anger's excessiveness and the hero's beastly aggression: λέοντας, τίγρις ἄγριος οὐ μὴ νὰ ἐδιαφεντεύθη ('A lion, a wild tiger, he [Hector] would not be subdued', *The War of Troy* 4790). At other times the hero's ferocity is so vast that it even surpasses that of beasts: πλεώτερον ἦτον ἄγριος λέοντος ἢ παρδάλου ('He [Hector] was more wild than a lion or a leopard', *The War of Troy* 6712).

---

[41] In other Byzantine texts, the target's perspective is also presented through the use of transaction metaphors. For instance, we read in Theodoros Prodromos' novel *Rhodanthe and Dosikles* 2.293–4 (ed. Marcovich (1992), emphasis added): πλήσοι δὲ θυμοῦ καὶ πρὸς ὀργὴν ὀτρύνοι, / καὶ κερδανῶ μὲν τοῦ τεκόντος τὸν χόλον ('[he] would be full of rage and stirred to anger, / and I would *gain* my father's fury', trans. Jeffreys (2012) 45).

[42] Compared to Homer, the anonymous Byzantine poet uses similes to a much lesser degree. The bibliography on Homeric similes is vast. For animal and fire similes in Homer in particular see, for example, Whitman (1958) 128–53; Clarke (1995); Alden (2005); Heath (2005) 39–51, 119–67; Ready (2011) 42–8, 61–9.

[43] Buxton (2006) 146.

[44] Buxton (2006) 153.

As long as Achilles and Hector are alive and participate in battle, all the animal similes appearing in the poem are employed to describe the immense ferocity through which their equal exemplarity as warriors is highlighted. Their victims, on the other hand, are likened to peaceful domestic animals: ἐμπρός του οἱ Τρῶες ἔφευγαν ὡς ἄρνες ἀπὸ λύκον ('At his [Achilles'] presence, the Trojans fled as sheep [escape] a wolf', *The War of Troy* 4422). When Hector is fatally stabbed in the back by Achilles in the course of the tenth battle, an animal simile is used for the first time to refer to the Trojans' collective anger, as their immense desire to avenge the death of their leader brings them together: ὅλοι ὡς λυσσιάροι νὰ ἔμπωσι, τὸν Ἕκτωρ νὰ ἐκδικήσουν ('All are about to enter [battle] like rabid dogs to take revenge for Hector', *The War of Troy* 7465).

When Achilles is killed by Paris in the execution of Hecuba's plot, animal similes that were previously employed to describe the Greek hero's anger are from this point onwards utilized for his son, Pyrrhus. Presented as his father's double, Pyrrhus arrives at Troy to both avenge his killing and take his place as the leader of the Myrmidons: ἔμπροσθεν πάντων ὥδευεν ὡς λέων χολιασμένος ('He was marching in front of all of them like an angry lion', *The War of Troy* 10889). In this example, the simile is directed to both the warrior and the beast. Pyrrhus rushes to battle like a lion, whereas the beast, which is described as 'angry', behaves like him. The angry lion that has the same emotional state as the warrior is humanized, while Pyrrhus, who acts like a lion, is animalized.

Fire similes liken anger to the characteristics and products of fire (flame colour, light, heat, burning, energy, and ashes). The angry feelings they describe are not as extreme as those highlighted by the bestial similes. Accordingly, they are not reserved for the two exceptional warriors (Achilles and Hector), but they are used to refer to the anger of more individual heroes. Another important difference between the fire and animal similes concerns the situations in which they are used. Unlike animal similes, the fire ones are not employed during fighting, but in verbal confrontations between opponents. Whereas animal similes concern an anger that leads to violent and murderous acts, fire similes are associated with verbal duels in which threats of violence are expressed.

In most cases, fire similes are employed to illustrate how a hero's anger is excited by words that he finds offensive. When, for example, the Trojan Anthenor asks Telamon to return Hesione, the prize he acquires for his bravery during the first sack of Troy, he ἄναψεν ὡς ἡ λάβρα ('lights up like a fire', *The War of Troy* 1400). Nestor's angry reaction to Anthenor's words is also presented by means of a fire simile. In this case, the simile is part of a comment made by the omniscient narrator: ἐκ τὸν θυμόν του ἐγίνετον ἡ ὄψις του, ὡς εἰκάζω, / ὡς τέφρα, κόνις γέγονεν ... ('as a result of his anger, his face became, as I assume, / like ash, it became powder ...', *The War of Troy* 1458–9).

The association of anger with fire in these similes, like the metonymical *cholē* terms, also has a medical background. According to Galen, εἴ γε δὴ καὶ τοῖς θυ-

13. *Angry Warriors in the Byzantine War of Troy* 353

μωθεῖσι ... αὔξησις τῆς ἐμφύτου γίνεται θερμότητος. ὁ μέν γε θυμὸς οὐδ' ἁπλῶς αὔξησις, ἀλλ' οἷον ζέσις τίς ἐστι τοῦ κατὰ τὴν καρδίαν θερμοῦ ('an increase in innate hotness arises ... in those experiencing anger ... Anger is not simply an increase, but as it were a kind of boiling of the hot in the heart').[45] Moreover, the humour that is responsible for anger, yellow bile, as Galen notes elsewhere, has the properties of fire: θερμὴ μὲν καὶ ξηρὰ τὴν δύναμίν ἐστιν ἡ ξανθὴ χολή, καθάπερ τὸ πῦρ ('the yellow bile is hot and dry in power, just as the fire').[46] Here Galen, like our poet, uses a figurative language to give a physiological explanation of anger.

In sum, the rhetoric of anger in *The War of Troy*, as is the case with a number of Greek literary texts from Antiquity to Byzantium,[47] seems to be influenced by contemporary medical discourses, and thus it reflects a cultural understanding of the embodiment of anger. Physicians, on the other hand, employ literary discourses to illuminate their own approaches to anger. Such an example is Galen, who, apart from using rhetorical tropes in his medical treatises, extensively quotes Chrysippus' quotations from Homer and ancient Greek tragedy, in his attempt to refute the Stoic's explanations of anger according to which, like all emotions, it is a kind of judgement.[48] Yet, in so doing, Galen produces a medical work including a mosaic of canonical ancient Greek literature. But it is about time to move from the vocabulary and rhetoric of anger to the Byzantine poet's approach to the physiology of anger. Even though the poem's references to the embodiment of anger are much fewer than the emotion's rhetorical expressions, they serve the same purpose: to stress anger's immensity as a force which disturbs both body and mind.

13.4. The embodiment of anger

To a large extent, the embodiment of anger in *The War of Troy*, as will be further demonstrated, echoes current medical theory about the emotion's physiology.

---

[45] Trans. Singer (2017) 170; *On the Preservation of Health* 6.138.6–8, ed. Kühn (1821–33).

[46] Trans. De Lacy (2005) 503 with modification; *On the Doctrines of Hippocrates and Plato* 8.4.21.23–4, ed. De Lacy (2005).

[47] For ancient Greek literature, see Jouanna (2012) 69. Other Byzantine literary texts which are in dialogue with contemporary medical treatises include hagiography, historiography, and poetry (Reinsch (2000) 96–7; Dennis (2001); Constantinou (2010); Bouras-Vallianatos (2016)). Cf. also the following verses from Theodoros Prodromos' *Catomyomachia*: [θυμὸς] ἐστιν ... / ... ζέσις τις αἵματος πρὸς καρδίαν ('Anger is some boiling of the blood around the heart', 297–8, ed. Hunger (1968b)).

[48] De Lacy (1966); Tieleman (1996) 219–48; Cullyer (2008). A Byzantine counterpart of Galen is Meletius the Monk, whose medical treatise *On the Constitution of Man* (possibly ninth century; ed. Cramer (1836)), which is to a large extent based on Galen's work (Oberhelman (2015) 10), has many quotations from literary texts (e. g. the Homeric epics (at least twenty-five references) and the work of Hesiod (at least three references)).

354   *Stavroula Constantinou*

The Byzantine poet thus understands the warrior's anger as both a bodily and mental state. In so doing, he reflects the Aristotelian theory which makes a distinction between a physical and philosophical understanding of anger while at the same time arguing that a genuinely scientific theory requires the combination of both:

διαφερόντως δ᾽ ἂν ὁρίσαιντο ὁ φυσικὸς [τε] καὶ ὁ διαλεκτικὸς ἕκαστον αὐτῶν, οἷον ὀργὴ τί ἐστιν· ὁ μὲν γὰρ ὄρεξιν ἀντιλυπήσεως ἤ τι τοιοῦτον, ὁ δὲ ζέσιν τοῦ περὶ καρδίαν αἵματος καὶ θερμοῦ. τούτων δὲ ὁ μὲν τὴν ὕλην ἀποδίδωσιν, ὁ δὲ τὸ εἶδος καὶ τὸν λόγον. ὁ μὲν γὰρ λόγος ὅδε τοῦ πράγματος, ἀνάγκη δ᾽ εἶναι τοῦτον ἐν ὕλῃ τοιᾳδί, εἰ ἔσται. (*De an.* 1.1, 403a29–403b3).

But a natural scientist and a dialectician would define each of these differently – for example, what anger is. For a dialectician it is a desire for retaliation or something like that, whereas for a natural scientist it is a boiling of the blood and hot stuff around the heart. Of these, the natural scientist gives the matter, whereas the dialectician gives the form and the account. For this is the account of the thing, although it must be in matter of such-and-such a sort if it is to exist. (Trans. Reeve (2017) 4)

According to a physician like Galen, as suggested earlier, the heart is the seat of the arterial system that is associated with anger: ὁ δέ γε θυμὸς οἷον ζέσις τις καὶ κίνησις σφοδρὰ τῆς θυμοειδοῦς δυνάμεως ἐν τῷ σώματι τῆς καρδίας αὐτῷ καθιδρυμένης ('And rage is as it were a boiling and vigorous motion of the spirited capacity which is seated in the actual body of the heart').[49] The idea that the bodily reaction, which is related to anger, takes place in the heart or involves the heart is found already in Homer (e.g. μοι οἰδάνεται κραδίη χόλῳ, 'my heart is swelling with anger', *Il.* 9.646),[50] and is repeated by later authors.[51]

    The poet of *The War of Troy*, too, sees the swelling of the heart as a bodily manifestation of anger. In the whole poem, however, there are only two references to the angry warrior's swelling heart. The first concerns Hector, while the second is about Achilles. Both references are made when the two heroes find themselves in a similar situation, which is another instance of their parallel treatment by the poet. This occurs when the heroes' armies are almost destroyed by the enemy as a result of their absence from the battlefield.

---

[49] Trans. Reeve (2017) 4; *On the Differences of Fevers* 8.283.7–9.

[50] For the bodily swelling incited by anger in Homer see, for example, Clarke (1999) 61–126; Harris (2001) 142; Cairns (2003) 25; Ready (2011) 34–5.

[51] Cf. Nemesius' definition, quoted above (p. 346), and see also Basil of Caesarea's definition of anger in his *Commentary on the Prophet Isaiah*, which uses similar language to that of Nemesius and John of Damascus quoted above: ἔστι δὲ θυμὸς ζέσις περὶ καρδίαν αἵματος, παρὰ τὸ οἱονεὶ ἐξ ἀναθυμιάσεως τῶν χυμῶν, συνιστάμενον οἴδημα περὶ τὴν καρδίαν ('Anger is a boiling of the blood about the heart, which is produced by the exhalation of the humours, creating a swelling about the heart', 5.181.13–15, ed. Trevisan (1939)) and that of John Chrysostom in his fifty-third Homily: Ὅταν γὰρ τὸ πάθος ἔνδοθεν διεγείρηται, καὶ ἡ καρδία οἰδαίνῃ ... ('When the passion [anger] is developed inside, and the heart swells ...', in *PG* 54.470.60–1.

13. Angry Warriors in the Byzantine War of Troy 355

In the first case, Hector is forced by his family to avoid fighting on the first day of the tenth battle due to a dream of his wife, Andromache, that foretells his death on that very day. Since a soldier's avoidance of battle is treated as a dishonourable act, Hector gets angry for having to undergo such a humiliation. His anger follows a climactic development, and it reaches its peak when Hector realizes the severe consequences of his inactivity:

> ὁ Ἕκτωρ ἀκρομάζετον, ἤκουσε τὴν ὀδύνην
> καὶ τὸν χαμὸν τὸν ἔπαθαν ἐκείνην τὴν ἡμέραν
> καὶ πῶς τοὺς ἐτροπεύσασιν, ἐμπάσαν τους στὴν πόλιν.
> ἡ χολή του ἀνέβαινεν ἐπάνω εἰς τὸ κεφάλιν·
> ἐπρήσθη ἡ καρδία του ἐκ τὴν πολλὴν πικρίαν.
> τινὰς οὐδὲν ἀποτολμᾷ νὰ τὸν ἀνατηρήσῃ.
> (*The War of Troy* 6947–53)

> Hector was listening, he heard about the suffering
> and the bereavements they had on that day
> and how they [Greeks] defeated them, made them to return to the city.
> His *cholē* was rising to the head.
> His heart swelled because of the great bitterness.
> Nobody dared to face him.

In this passage, Hector's bodily behaviour during anger includes both a swelling of the heart and a rising of the yellow bile to the head. According to Galen, when there is an extreme production of humours, these reach the head:

> οἷον εἰ πλῆθος εἴη περιεχόμενον ἀτμῶν ἢ χυμῶν, ἐπισκοπεῖσθαι, πότερον διὰ μέγεθος πυ-
> ρετῶν οἱ χυμοὶ χυθέντες τε καὶ οἱονεὶ ζέσαντες ἐπὶ τὴν κεφαλὴν ὥρμησαν, ἢ διὰ τὴν τοῦ
> μέρους ἀρρωστίαν ἢ διὰ τὴν ἐν παντὶ τῷ σώματι πλησμονήν. (*Ad Glauconem de medendi
> methodo* 11.62.7–11)

> If an excess of vapours or humours happens to be contained there, see whether due to the intensity of the fever the humours have been liquefied, and boiling, so to speak, have attacked the head, thanks either to the weakness of that part or else to an excess throughout the body. (Trans. Van der Eijk (2008) 294.)

In his commentary *On the Hippocratic Epidemics*, Galen mentions that during anger the head gets particularly hot. This internal bodily reaction is externalized on the face of the angry person, who has gleaming eyes and a red countenance.[52] Possibly this medical explanation is also the subtext of an anger metaphor used

---

[52] *In Hippocratis librum VI epidemiarum*, 17B, 259.14–15, 260.1–4: φαίνεται οὖν ἐναργῶς ἐν ταῖς ὀξυθυμίαις μείζονά τε καὶ σφοδρότερον ἡ καρδία ποιουμένη τὸν σφυγμὸν ἅμα ταῖς καθ' ὅλον τὸ ζῷον ἀρτηρίαις ... τοῦ δὲ πρὸς τὴν κεφαλὴν ἀναφέρεσθαι τό τε ὑγρὸν καὶ τὴν θερμασίαν πλείονα σημεῖόν ἐστι τὸ κατὰ τοὺς ὀφθαλμούς τε καὶ τὸ πρόσωπον ὅλον ἔρευθος ('It is thus quite obvious that during anger the heart makes greater and intensifies simultaneously the pulse in all the arteries of a living being ... As for the liquid and the heat in the head, they are mostly shown in the flashing eyes and the redness of the whole face').

356   *Stavroula Constantinou*

by the poet of *The War of Troy*: τὸ πῦρ ἀπὸ τὸ πρόσωπον ἔπνεε τοῦ θυμοῦ του ('The fire of his anger was blowing from the face', 13976).

As suggested by the above-quoted verse, 'Nobody dared to face him', the excessive production of yellow bile in Hector's body as a symptom of his anger that finds its way up to the head is quite discernible in his face. The Trojans realize the immensity of Hector's rage through the appearance of his face, and, being afraid of becoming the victims of his anger, they do not look him straight in the eyes. In fact, the transformation of Hector's face due to his anger is explicitly described earlier:

> ... ἀπὸ τὴν πικρίαν ἵδρωνε καὶ ἐθυμοῦτο.
> πολλὰ τὸν ἐχολιάσασιν, ὅταν τὸν ἐκρατοῦσαν·
> ἀπὸ κάτω εἰς τὸ ἔλμον του <τοῦ> ἀλλάσσετον ἡ ὄψις.
> τὰ ὀμμάτια του ἐπρήσθησαν, ὡς φλόγα κοκκινίζουν·
> (*The War of Troy* 6708–11)

> He was sweating out of bitterness and he was angry.
> They angered him greatly by keeping him [away from battle].
> His face was transformed under the armour.
> His eyes swelled, they became red like a flame.[53]

Here another bodily symptom of Hector's bitter anger is included, that is sweat. Sweat could be explained as the result of the great heat that, according to Galen, is produced within the body during anger. Furthermore, the hero's eyes do not just turn red, but they are also swollen. This is another bodily reaction that has a medical explanation. In the Hippocratic corpus, the swollen eyes constitute a sign of mental disorder.[54] Hector's swollen eyes in this case suggest that his anger is escalating, reaching its highest degree.

Indeed, Hector is about to kill his wife for keeping him away from war. Anything that would disturb his established status as an exemplary warrior is considered by him a madness; that is why he attacks his wife with a great ferocity, which equals the aggressiveness he displays against the Greeks during combat. On the face of it, Hector's anger seems justified. However, the knowledge provided by the narrator that Andromache is right to insist that the hero should not leave the walls of Troy on that very day renders Hector's wrath problematic. The hero's maddening anger, which prevents him from seeing the message of Andromache's prophetic dream that is clear to all the other Trojans, his father included, becomes the reason for his death. The loss of Hector is, of course, much worse than his short absence from battle, as it marks the beginning of Troy's downfall. Hector's rage in this episode is the only case in which it acquires a negative sense. This is probably the reason why the poet presents its embodiment in such detail.

---

[53] The expression of anger in the eyes is found also in Homer (see Cairns (2003) 42).
[54] Thumiger (2017) 92–4.

13. Angry Warriors in the Byzantine War of Troy

357

Hector is disturbed in both body and mind. It is impossible for him to see the disastrous consequences of returning to battle.

As far as Achilles is concerned, the physiology of his anger is described, yet not in the same detail as that of his Trojan counterpart. Achilles' anger has two phases. First, he gets angry with the Greeks. This happens when he makes a pact with the Trojans to convince his camp to abandon the war and to be offered Polyxena as wife in exchange. To this end, Achilles summons the Greeks to argue that the war against the Trojans confers dishonour rather than honour on them, for, as he goes on to say, they have lost more than thirty thousand illustrious warriors for the sake of Menelaus' wife. Achilles' words provoke the angry reaction of the other Greeks, who claim the exact opposite: it is for their honour that they participate in this war, and if they give it up now they will be dishonoured. Feeling insulted by the Greeks' disrespectful behaviour towards him, the angry Achilles decides to abandon the war so that they might realize his military value and the truth of his words.

Anger isolates Achilles and his soldiers from the rest of the Greek camp. For over six months, they stay away from battle. Without their help, the Greeks are about to lose the war. In their attempt to regain Achilles' friendship and assistance, the Greeks show their respect to the hero and acknowledge his bravery. As a result, Achilles' anger is softened, and he sends his soldiers to the Greeks' aid, but he does not return to the battle, to keep the oath he has given to the Trojans, as he is madly in love with Polyxena. His army is soon devasted. At this point, the second phase of his anger starts. Now he is infuriated with the Trojans:

> πολλὰ βαρὺ τὸν φαίνεται εἴ τι ἀκούῃ καὶ βλέπῃ·
> πολλὰ ἐστενέφθη, ἐθλίβηκεν, ἐνθύμησιν ἐχάσε.
> πολλὰ γοργόν, ἐγλήγορα, φοραίνει τὸ λουρίκιν,
> ἡ καρδία του ἐπρήσθηκεν ἀπὸ θυμοῦ μεγάλου.
> τὸ ἔλμον τοῦ ἐφόρεσαν, πηδᾷ, καβαλλικεύει·
> ἐπῆρε τὸ σκουτάριν του καὶ ἕνα χοντρὸν κοντάριν.
>
> ...
>
> τίποτε οὐκ ἔχει ἐνθύμησιν ἀγάπης ἢ φιλίας.
> ἐδὰ καὶ ἃς φυλάγωνται, ἂν θέλουν, Τρωανῖτες.
> (*The War of Troy* 9477–82, 9484–5)

> Whatever he hears and sees seems very bad to him.
> He is very gloomy, saddened, he forgets his promise.
> Swiftly and very quick he puts on his armour.
> His heart swells from the great anger.
> He puts on his helmet, he jumps, he mounts his horse.
> He takes his buckler and a thick spear.
>
> ...
>
> He has no memory of either love or friendship.
> Here and now, the Trojans should spare themselves, if they want.

358   *Stavroula Constantinou*

As the last verse implies, when Achilles returns to battle, like Hector previously, he resorts to extreme violence, slaying more than a thousand Trojans like a 'hungry wolf' eating the victims and drinking their blood without restraint (*The War of Troy* 9488–503). That is how he avenges the loss of his soldiers. Yet, in contrast to Hector's anger against his wife, that of Achilles against the Greeks does not acquire a negative sense, since he eventually returns to battle. His return is welcomed by all the Greeks, whose victory over the Trojans is now secured.

Conclusion

Through the use of Aristotle's anger theory and Rosenwein's concept of 'emotional community', the preceding discussion has attempted to bring to the fore the cultural specifics and literariness of the warrior's anger, while at the same time it has revealed certain similarities and differences between Homeric anger and that in *The War of Troy*, thus allowing an illumination of the former through the latter and vice versa. Yet the comparison with Homer has been indispensable for yet another reason. As Kostas Kalimtzis rightly argues, 'the long road that led to an understanding of anger begins with Homer':[55] 'His descriptions of the passions became part of the human intellectual inheritance that could be shared across all cultural boundaries ... Homeric descriptions of the hero's *thumos* or *cholos* are the first steps to understanding human anger.'[56]

In fact, the warrior's anger is not only an ancient or Medieval phenomenon, but also exists in later and contemporary cultures. The clinical psychiatrist, Jonathan Shay, who has examined the moral wounds of contemporary war, has clearly exposed the universality of Homeric anger: 'Homer's starting point is ... *menis*, indignant wrath. I believe it is also the first and possibly the primary trauma that converted subsequent terror, horror, grief, and guilt into lifelong disability for Vietnam veterans.'[57] Consequently, the 'Emotions through Time' project, which apart from anger explores a variety of emotions from Antiquity to Byzantium, may not only prove illuminating for the cultural historian, but also provide answers to contemporary issues. For instance, Homeric works and – I would add – their later adaptations, as Shay has demonstrated, make us aware of military and social practices that are more effective than our own in restoring the soldiers' emotional health.[58]

---

[55] Kalimtzis (2012) 5.
[56] Kalimtzis (2012) 3.
[57] Shay (2003 [1994]) 21.
[58] Shay has used also the *Odyssey* in his attempt to deal with combat trauma (Shay (2002)). His books have been welcome in military circles and seem to have transformed the lives of many soldiers (Shay (2003) i–xxiii).

Part IV
Art and Ritual

14

Visualizing and Enacting Emotions*

The Affective Capacities of the *Litē*

Vicky Manolopoulou

Introduction

The Byzantines referred to annual religious processions with the term *litē*, which means supplication. The term and other cognate words have inherited the meaning of supplication from Antiquity. For example, the term *litaneuō* is used in Homer to refer to acts of supplication between equals, men and men and gods and gods, whilst the vocabulary for prayer is different and only used for men and gods.[1] In Byzantium, however, the meaning of *litē* is reserved to describe collective supplication addressed to God. Although there are other types of procession with religious elements, the term is used for the collective, public, outdoor, liturgical ecclesiastical procession with supplicatory character, led only by the bishop or his representative.[2] *Litai* were meant to be performed by the faithful, namely the entire body of the Church (the *ekklēsia*), including – at times – the emperor and the patriarch. They took place in both cities and villages at critical moments: these included natural phenomena such as droughts, volcanic eruptions, and earthquakes, distressful events such as enemy attacks, but also joyful events such as the translation of relics, welcoming of holy figures, and dedication of churches. They were also performed at annual commemorations of such events and other feasts. These processions belong to what is commonly referred to as the stational liturgy in so far as they involve the use of more than one site for the celebration of the day. By the tenth century, almost one-fifth of Constantinopol-

---

* First and foremost, I would like to thank the editors of this volume for their meticulous work and constructive comments. I am especially grateful to the two reviewers for their comments and all Emotions through Time contributors for the interesting discussions, particularly Margaret Mullett, for her invaluable support. Thanks are also due to Panos Theodoropoulos and Maroula Perisanidi for their suggestions and Joe Skinner for his unceasing encouragement. All errors and oversights are entirely my own.

[1] Pedrick (1982) 128. For a discussion of emotions in relation to supplication, see Crotty (1994).

[2] Baldovin (1987) 206–9. See also Manolopoulou (2016) 25–30.

362   *Vicky Manolopoulou*

itan churches were used during the year for this type of activity (Fig. 14.1). The
Typikon of the Great Church[3] prescribed what was to be celebrated in the city of
Constantinople throughout the liturgical year: people were to gather at a church
where, at some point after readings and hymns, a procession would exit and then,
led by the patriarch or his representative, move towards one of several stations.[4]

During these processions people forged emotional communities[5] where specific emotions were to be evoked and understood and collective emotion was
experienced.[6] Whilst the role of emotions in ritual has attracted the attention
of scholars working on periods from Antiquity to Byzantium, there has been
little work to date on emotion and Late Antique and Byzantine liturgical processions.[7] Emotion and ritual are inextricably interwoven not only because of the
affective relationship networks[8] created between performers and spectators but
also because of those existing and created between people and the divine.[9] Rather
than focusing on emotions of the individual, the main aim of this chapter is to
show how the performance of processions aimed to create an 'atmosphere'[10] that
enabled the participants to attune to an emotional community and its understanding of the relationship between human and divine emotion.[11]

---

[3] For a discussion of the available textual, visual, and material sources for the study of *litai* in
Constantinople, see Manolopoulou (2016) 12–17 and in Brubaker and Wickham (2021).

[4] For a detailed description of how the liturgical rite was performed, see a comprehensive
summary from Marinis (2014) 21–3. For the history and evolution of the Byzantine rite see Taft
(1992). Specifically, for the way the stational ritual was performed, see Taft (2006) 44–7, discussing the eleventh-century Byzantine service book Paris Coislin. 213, fols 79ᵛ–83ᵛ. For a comparison of the stational liturgies of Rome, Jerusalem, and Constantinople see Baldovin (1987).
For a spatiotemporal analysis and a phenomenological approach to these processions, see
Manolopoulou (2016), (2019).

[5] 'Groups in which people adhere to the same norms of emotional expression and value – or
devalue – the same or related emotions', Rosenwein (2006) 2.

[6] By collective emotion I mean here emotions that emerge when people come together or
form crowds either during ritual, or other events. For a theoretical discussion on collective
emotions see von Scheve and Ismer (2013).

[7] Manolopoulou (2013), (2016). The theme of processions from Antiquity to Byzantium
was explored in the workshop Moving through Time: Processions from the Classical Past to
Byzantium, Institute of Classical Studies, London (June 2018), organized by V. Manolopoulou,
H. Cornwell, and I. Papadogiannakis. For cult communities and emotional communities, see
Chaniotis (2013c) 172.

[8] The affective fields: this term was first introduced by Harris and Sørensen (2010).

[9] Manolopoulou (2013), (2016). See also, for example, in an earlier context, Chaniotis (2013c)
170: 'the emotions range from gratitude and hope to the fear of god, the joy at the extra-ordinary
character of the festive day, and the pride for a community's achievements. In such communal
celebrations, certain emotions are prescribed or expected; others are banned. Festivals invite the
community to participate in public excitement, prescribing a certain mood for the occasion, and
striving for a higher purpose.' For a discussion of processions, their staging, and their meaning
in Hellenistic cities see Chaniotis (2013b).

[10] 'the emotional experience engendered by being in a particular place and situation', Harris
and Sørensen (2010) 153.

[11] For a similar approach to Greek ritual see Chaniotis (2011).

14. Visualizing and Enacting Emotions

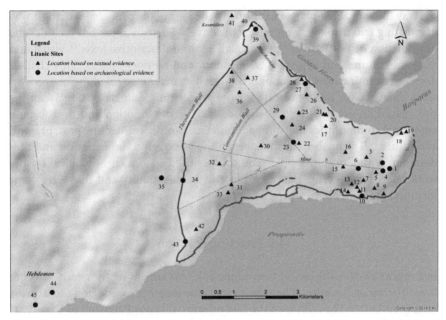

Figure 14.1. Sites used in religious processions according to the tenth-century *Typikon* of the Great Church. 1. Great Church (Hagia Sophia); 2. Theotokos Chalkoprateia; 3. Prodromos at Sphorakiou; 4. Million; 5. St John at Dihippion; 6. Forum of Constantine; 7. SS Cosmas and Damian at Dareiou; 8. SS Peter and Paul at Triconch; 9. Nea Ekklesia; 10. SS Sergios and Bacchos; 11. Michael at Addas; 12. St Thekla; 13. St Panteleimon at Narsou; 14. St Thomas at Amantiou; 15. Forty Martyrs at the Bronze Tetrapylon; 16. St Anastasia; 17. St Prokopios at Chelonio; 18. St Menas; 19. St Paul at the Orphanage; 20. St Metrophanes; 21. St Stephen at Zeugma; 22. St Stephen at Constantinianae; 23. St Polyeuktos; 24. All Saints; 25. SS Constantine and Helen; 26. St Laurentios; 27. St Euphemia; 28. St Elijah; 29. Holy Apostles; 30. Prodromos at Eremias; 31. Old Golden Gate; 32. St Mokios; 33. Heleninianae (St Thyrsos and Theotokos); 34. Pege Gate; 35. Theotokos Pege; 36. St George at Deuteron; 37. Theotokos at Petra; 38. St George at Sykes; 39. Theotokos Blachernae; 40. Pteron Gate; 41. SS Cosmas and Damian at Kosmidion; 42. Theotokos Jerusalem; 43. Golden Gate; 44. Tribunal; 45. Saint John and Prodromos at Hebdomon; a. Acropolis; b. Forum Tauri; c. Forum Bovis; d. Forum of Arkadios; e. column of Marcian; f. Mokios cistern. (From Manolopoulou (2019).)

The first part of the chapter examines processions as a way of enacting emotion collectively and argues that they contributed to shaping and communicating ideas about divine and human emotion.[12] The second part focuses on the performative dimension of procession, the affective properties of its various components, and

---

[12] This chapter recognizes emotion to be natural, embodied but also socially constructed. Durkheim (2001 [1912]); Hochschild (1979); Gordon (1981); Hochschild (1983). For a critical overview of the work of sociologists on emotion see Bericat (2016).

364   *Vicky Manolopoulou*

the way these enabled people to attune to the idea of the procession being a way of enacting and displaying emotion collectively. Such an approach includes the examination of normative,[13] performative,[14] and descriptive texts,[15] visual and material culture, and experiences of indoor and outdoor spaces. This chapter does not examine how emotional communities that are created during processions change over time, but rather how processions, as part of the Byzantine rite, played an essential role in shaping ideas about emotion and thus forging emotional communities that aimed to traverse time by connecting past, present, and future.[16] The analysis is anchored in the Middle Byzantine period and predominantly in Constantinople. The sources used span a chronological framework referring to events that took place in Late Antiquity and that were commemorated in later periods.

14.1. Enacting emotion

In the year AD 806, the city of Constantinople was lamenting the death of its beloved patriarch, Tarasios. The whole city came together as one body to express grief (*penthos*).[17] The author of the Life of Saint Tarasios Patriarch of Constantinople, Ignatios, describes it as follows (the *vita* was written sometime in AD 843–7): 'Then all the city did not stop mourning with inconsolable grief and tears over him, who was her guardian and protector.'[18] According to Ignatios, Tarasios' funerary rite brought together the emperor, people from all backgrounds (πᾶσα τύχη καὶ ἡλικία),[19] the Church, the monks, in short, the entire community. The whole city (πᾶσα ... ἡ πόλις) was as one body – as Ignatios describes – weeping in lament for the significant loss. Collective expression of emotion, in this case, does not necessarily reflect the emotions of the individuals that formed the body of the city (although it is not impossible that grief was felt at an individual level),

---

[13] I.e. texts prescribing how processions should be celebrated, such as the *Typikon* of the Great Church.

[14] I.e. texts that were performed, such as hymns or homilies.

[15] I.e. texts that provide direct or indirect descriptions of processions, such as histories. For similar methodology in discussing the aesthetics of Hellenistic processions see Chaniotis (2013c).

[16] This was achieved during the liturgy. See Louth (2013a) 122–40.

[17] For a discussion of *penthos* and *lupē* (grief) see Chryssavgis (1989) 127; Hunt (2004) 3–16; Hinterberger (2010a) 129–30. Communities can perform emotion collectively during ritual, and this forges group identity: for emotion and communal activity, see also Durkheim (2001 [1912]) 289–304.

[18] Ignatios, *Life of Tarasios* 62.1–2, ed. and trans. Efthymiadis (1998) 156, 202: πᾶσα δὲ τοῦτον ἡ πόλις ἀπαρακλήτῳ πένθει καὶ δάκρυσιν ὡς αὐτῆς ὀδυρομένη κηδεμόνα καὶ προστάτην οὐκ ἔληγεν.

[19] Ignatios, *Life of Tarasios* 64.9–10, ed. and trans. Efthymiadis (1998) 159, 203.

but rather relates to the way the group identified emotions appropriate to the situation.[20]

The words chosen to describe the strength of the emotion of grief link Tarasios' death to the loss of a paternal figure and guardian (κηδεμόνα καὶ προστάτην). Ignatios calls Tarasios the 'New Moses' who saved the Church from heresy, and he links Tarasios with the prophets who 'appeared as harbours of salvation sent by God'. The Church in agony and fear was 'tossed up and down as if she were a ship at sea and was risking the loss of its cargo'. The saint as a 'skilful sea-fighter' brought the Church 'to harbour'.[21] Ignatios' colourful imagery refers to the role that Tarasios played during the Iconoclastic controversy – a historical event that was central implicitly or explicitly in many commemorations during the liturgical year – and to his philanthropic work. The saint was buried three days after his death on 25 February at the monastery of All Saints in Constantinople. The funerary procession was accompanied by monks 'showing their sorrow and weaving hymns with tears'.[22] The procession was joined by a big crowd desiring to see the body of the saint, to the point that the emperor had to send the military to control the crowd.[23] Tarasios' commemoration must have passed into the liturgical calendar sometime after the Triumph of Orthodoxy in AD 843. By the tenth century, his *synaxis* was celebrated at the Great Church,[24] also highlighting his Constantinopolitan origins.[25]

Tarasios' funerary procession and later commemoration was a way to shape ideas about emotion or, in other words, a way to forge an emotional community. Ritualized mourning and enactment of collective emotion involving processions also took place in the aftermath of natural disasters. For example, when the earthquake of May AD 526 destroyed Antioch there was lament in Constantinople. The emperor participated in liturgical celebrations without his crown or the purple robe, while the people were dressed in dark colours as a sign of mourning.[26]

---

[20] See the discussion of emotion cultures in Hochschild (1979), (1983). See also Floris Bernard and Jan R. Stenger in this volume.

[21] Ignatios, *Life of Tarasios* 57, ed. and trans. Efthymiadis (1998) 149, 199.

[22] Ignatios, *Life of Tarasios* 64.3–4, ed. and trans. Efthymiadis (1998) 158, 203.

[23] Ignatios, *Life of Tarasios* 64.12–15, ed. and trans. Efthymiadis (1998) 158–9, 203.

[24] *Typikon*, ed. Mateos (1962–3) 240.

[25] οὗτος ὁ ἐν ἁγίοις πατὴρ ἡμῶν ἐγένετο τῆς Κωνσταντινουπόλεως καὶ γέννημα καὶ θρέμμα, τὴν ἀξίαν πρωτασηκρῆτις (*Synaxarion*, 25 February, ed. Delehaye (1902) 487–8).

[26] The event is described in a variety of sources (see discussion in Ambraseys (2009) 184–9). Theophanes the Confessor refers to collective lamentation but with no reference to the barefoot emperor: 'the most pious emperor Justin was so greatly grieved in his soul that he took off both the diadem from his head and the purple and mourned in sackcloth for many days, so that when he went to church on a feast day he refused to wear the crown or the chlamys, but went dressed very plainly in a purple mantle and wept in the presence of the whole Senate. Everybody wept and wore mourning like him' (trans. Mango and Scott (1997) 264; Theophanes, *Chronographia* AM 6019, ed. de Boor (1980 [1883]) 173.1–7). The lament in Constantinople is also mentioned in Malalas, *Chronographia* 17.16, ed. Thurn (2000) 346–50; trans. Jeffreys et al. (1986) 238–40.

366   *Vicky Manolopoulou*

Emotions relating to mourning and supplication were closely associated. For example, Photios, in his Homily 3, a sermon following the Russian attack on Constantinople (in AD 860 and commemorated annually) that was possibly delivered in Hagia Sophia, notes that lamenting past misfortunes and supplicating for God's mercy should be done before a disaster; 'Not to attend vigils now, and run to litanies, and beat the breast and sigh deeply, and raise the arms, and bend the knees, and weep mournfully, and look dejected when the pricks of death are sharpened against us: we should have done these things long ago.'[27] The reason for this is that there was a perceived link between demonstrating *metanoia* (repentance)[28] and God's *philanthrōpia* (love of humankind). Repentance was essential for salvation: 'For in so acting now, indeed before a Judge who is, above all righteous, and whose heart is not overly inclined to pardon, it is not to pity, I think, that we are moving God, but we make ourselves the fierce accusers of the sins which were by us committed.'[29] Demonstrating collective repentance is also highlighted in Photios' homily on the departure of the Russians:[30]

When, moreover, as the whole city was carrying with me her raiment for the repulse of the besiegers and the protection of the besieged, we offered freely our prayers and performed the litany, thereupon with ineffable compassion she spoke out in motherly intercession: God was moved. His anger was averted, and the Lord took pity of His Inheritance.[31]

Similarly, John of Nikiu refers to the event and the lament in Constantinople and notes that the emperor participated in processions barefoot (John of Nikiu, *Chronicle* 90.30–4, trans. Charles (1916) 136–7). George Kedrenos is the only source that refers to seven-day processions at Hebdomon as part of the lamentations: ἀγγελθέντος δὲ τοῦ πάθους ὁ μὲν βασιλεὺς μεγάλως ἤλγησε τὴν ψυχήν, καὶ ῥίψας τὸ διάδημα καὶ τὴν πορφύραν ἐπένθει ἐν σάκκῳ καὶ σποδῷ ἡμέρας πολλάς, καὶ ἐν τῇ ἑορτῇ δὲ λιτὸς εἰσῆλθεν εἰς τὴν ἐκκλησίαν, μὴ καταδεξάμενος φορέσαι σήμαντρον βασιλικὸν τὸ οἱονοῦν. ἀλλὰ καὶ πάντες οἱ ἐν τῇ πόλει φαιὰν στολὴν ἐνδυσάμενοι πανδημεὶ εἰς τὸ πρὸ τῆς πόλεως πεδίον ἑπτὰ σημείοις ἀπέχον ἐλιτάνευον ἐπὶ ἑπτὰ ἡμέραις νηστεύοντες (George Kedrenos, *Historiarum compendium* 400.1, ed. Tartaglia (2016) 622.10–16).

[27] Trans. Mango (1958) 86; Photios, *Homilies* 3.1, ed. Laourdas (1959) 31–2: οὐ νῦν παννυχίζειν καὶ λιταῖς προστρέχειν καὶ στήθη τύπτειν καὶ βαθὺ στενάζειν καὶ χεῖρας ἐπαίρειν καὶ γόνατα κάμπτειν καὶ γοερὰ δακρύειν καὶ στυγνὸν προσβλέπειν, ὅτε τοῦ θανάτου τὰ κέντρα ἠκονημένα ἥκει καθ' ἡμῶν· πάλαι προσήκει ταῦτα ποιεῖν.

[28] 'normally regarded as sorrow for sin, a feeling of guilt, a sense of grief and horror at the wounds we have inflicted on others and ourselves' Ware (1980) 140, cited in Hunt (2004) 32. For a discussion of the literature on repentance see Torrance (2012) 1–24.

[29] Trans. Mango (1958) 86; Photios, *Homilies* 3.1, ed. Laourdas (1959) 32: ἐν ᾧ γὰρ ταῦτα πράττομεν νυνί, παρά γε δικαίῳ μάλιστα κριτῇ καὶ μὴ παρὰ πολὺ τὴν γνώμην πρὸς τὴν συγγνώμην ἐπιρρεπῶς ἔχοντι, οὐκ εἰς ἔλεον, οἶμαι, κινοῦμεν τὸν Θεόν, ἀλλὰ τῶν ὑπηργμένων ἡμῖν ἁμαρτημάτων κατήγοροι καθιστάμεθα πικροί.

[30] Eshel (2018) 72.

[31] Trans. Mango (1958) 102; Photios, *Homilies* 4.4, ed. Laourdas (1959) 45: ἧς καὶ τὴν περιβολὴν εἰς ἀναστολὴν μὲν τῶν πολιορκούντων, φυλακὴν δὲ τῶν πολιορκουμένων σὺν ἐμοὶ πᾶσα ἡ πόλις ἐπιφερόμενοι τὰς ἱκεσίας ἐκουσιαζόμεθα, τὴν λιτανείαν ἐποιούμεθα, ἐφ' οἷς ἀφάτῳ φιλανθρωπίᾳ, μητρικῆς παρρησιασαμένης ἐντεύξεως, καὶ τὸ θεῖον ἐπεκλίθη καὶ ὁ θυμὸς ἀπεστράφη καὶ ἠλέησε Κύριος τὴν κληρονομίαν αὐτοῦ. Also cited in Eshel (2018) 75.

14. Visualizing and Enacting Emotions 367

Photios makes a clear link between collective repentance demonstrated during processions and the ceasing of the calamity:

Repentance stopped the destruction: let us not stir it up with negligence. His anger was softened by the streams of our tears: let us not kindle it again with outbursts of incontinent laughter, with addiction to theatrical plays. The sword sharpened against us has been sheathed, withdrawn by our litanies and prayers.[32]

One way of demonstrating repentance collectively was through commemorative processions. A good example is a supplicatory procession that was triggered after the cinders from a volcanic eruption reached Constantinople in AD 472 during the reign of Emperor Leo I. One of the illuminations in the *Menologion* of Basil II shows people looking at the sky, observing the phenomenon, and others in despair, covering their faces (Fig. 14.2).[33] The event passed into the liturgical calendar and was commemorated annually on 6 November. The day is dedicated to the memory of the fallen ash.[34] According to the sources recording this event, fiery clouds appeared in the sky, and soon cinders fell, burning the city. There was the belief that the *philanthrōpia* of God had become ashes to burn everyone. People found refuge in the churches of the city, shivering from fear, participating in supplicatory processions (*litai*), crying for God's mercy, so that they and their city would not be burned.[35] Seeing people's penitence, God rained only cinders, which covered the entire city, instead of fire.[36] The annual commemoration in-

---

[32] Trans. Mango (1958) 105–6; Photios, *Homilies* 4.5, ed. Laourdas (1959) 48: ἔστη ἡ θραῦσις τῇ μετανοίᾳ, μὴ κινήσωμεν αὐτὴν τῇ ἀμελείᾳ· κατεπραΰνθη ὁ θυμὸς αὐτοῦ τοῖς τῶν δακρύων ἡμῶν ὀχετοῖς, μὴ ἀνάψωμεν πάλιν αὐτὸν βρασμῷ γέλωτος ἀκρατοῦς καὶ θυμελικῶν ἀθυρμάτων ἐνδελεχισμοῖς· ἡ καθ' ἡμῶν ἠκονημένη συνεστάλη ῥομφαία, λιταῖς καὶ δεήσεσιν ὑποχωρήσασα.

[33] The *Menologion* of Basil II, which dates to the late tenth or early eleventh century, contains information on the saints' lives and events that are commemorated on each day of the liturgical year. The manuscript is incomplete, as it covers only the first six months starting from 1 September. Each folio is dedicated to one feast, and is accompanied by an illumination made by eight different painters; see Ševčenko (1962b), (1991). For the liturgical use of imperial *Menologia* see Ševčenko (1993) 59. For the text, see *Menologium Basilianum, PG* 117 cols 19–614.

[34] τῇ αὐτῇ ἡμέρᾳ ἡ ἀνάμνησις τῆς πεσούσης ἐκ τοῦ οὐρανοῦ κόνεως ἤτοι τέφρας ἢ στακτῆς (*Menologium Basilianum, PG* 117 cols. 147–8). The *Typikon* notes that the day is dedicated to 'the memory of the ash brought down through the *philanthrōpia* of God, during the reign of Leo the Bessian the great emperor' (τῇ αὐτῇ ἡμέρᾳ, μνήμη τῆς μετὰ φιλανθρωπίας κατενεχθείσης κόνεως, ἐπὶ Λέοντος τοῦ μεγάλου βασιλέως τοῦ Βέσσου, *Typikon*, ed. Mateos (1962–3) 90–3).

[35] Tears are a sign of repentance. For a discussion on tears in Byzantine literature see Hinterberger (2006b), (2017b).

[36] ἐπὶ δὲ τῆς αὐτοῦ βασιλείας ἔβρεξεν ἐν Κωνσταντινουπόλει κονίαν ἀντὶ βροχῆς καὶ ἐπὶ παλαιστῇ ὕψους ἔστηκεν εἰς τοὺς κεράμους ἡ κονία· καὶ πάντες ἔτρεμον λιτανεύοντες καὶ λέγοντες, ὅτι "πῦρ ἦν καὶ ἐσβέσθη καὶ εὑρέθη κονία τοῦ θεοῦ φιλανθρωπευσαμένου", Malalas, *Chronographia* 14.42, ed. Thurn (2000) 295; trans. Jeffreys et. al. (1986) 205–6. See also Theodoros Anagnostes, *Historia ecclesiastica* 2.398, ed. Hansen (1971) 111 and a reference to the established commemorative procession for the event in 4.508, ed. Hansen (1971) 144. Cf. *Chronicon Paschale* 598.10–14, ed. Dindorf (1832), trans. Whitby and Whitby (1989) 90–1; Theophanes,

368 Vicky Manolopoulou

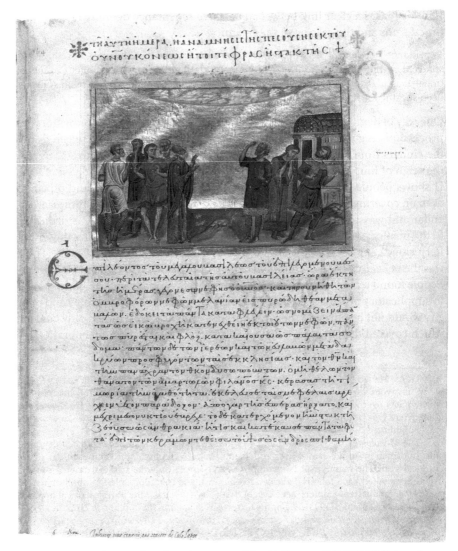

Figure 14.2. *Menologion* of Basil II, Vat. gr. 1613, fol. 164. Source: © [2022] Biblioteca Apostolica Vaticana, by permission of Biblioteca Apostolica Vaticana, all rights reserved.

14. Visualizing and Enacting Emotions

cluded a procession that, along with the patriarch, exited the Great Church very early in the morning, before moving to the Forum of Constantine and then to the church of Saints Peter and Paul at the Triconch. At the Forum, the following *troparion* was sung to show penitence: 'Lord, we sinned, and we acted lawlessly, we prostrate ourselves, have mercy on us.'[37] The message that the *troparion* of the day was highlighting was that it was people's sins and lawless actions that had caused the divine wrath, and only through repentance could they be saved. Participating in the procession and singing the *troparion* of the *litē* was a collective confession of sin, demonstration of repentance, and supplication for mercy.

Another example is the commemoration of a terrible earthquake that shook Constantinople on 26 January AD 447.[38] According to the *Menologion* of Basil II, the earthquake was the worst the city had ever seen. It seems that the aftershock activity of this earthquake lasted for a long time and that other cities also suffered. Theodosios II, Patriarch Anatolios, and the populace of Constantinople were singing the following *troparion* during a procession outside the city walls, at Hebdomon, praying for deliverance from the earthquake: 'through our repentance deliver us from your just wrath and our faults. For you shattered the earth due to our sins, terrifying us, so that we glorify you as the sole good one and lover of mankind.'[39] The *troparion* communicates the idea that the earthquake is a manifestation of God's wrath, and so just, since it was people's sins that caused it. The emperor participated in the procession barefoot as an act of humility and repentance. Then the text concludes: 'since then, this commemoration is celebrated'. The earthquake of AD 447 was celebrated annually on 26 January at the Great Church. Following the *orthros* in the patriarch's presence and after the blessing of the *Trisagion*, the psalmists started the *troparion*: 'Lord, you rose the day when you justly punished us, so we all prostrate ourselves to you in fear saying: Holy Lord, our Saviour have mercy on us.'[40] This *troparion* is also a supplication for God's mercy. It is very similar to the one that, according to the *Menologion*, the people were singing at Hebdomon while on a procession praying for deliverance from the earthquake. As in the *troparion* sung on 6 November discussed above, the punishment was recognized as justly falling

---

Chronographia AM 5966, ed. de Boor (1980 [1883]) 119.29–33; trans. Mango and Scott (1997) 186.

[37] Κύριε, ἡμάρτομεν καὶ ἠνομήσαμεν, προσπίπτομεν, ἐλέησον ἡμᾶς, *Typikon*, ed. Mateos (1962–3) 90–3.

[38] Grumel (1958) 77; Croke (1981).

[39] ῥῦσαι ἡμᾶς Κύριε τῆς δικαίας σου ὀργῆς, καὶ τῶν παραπτωμάτων ἡμῶν διὰ τῆς μετανοίας· ἐσάλευσας γὰρ τὴν γῆν συνετάραξας διὰ τὰς ἁμαρτίας ἡμῶν· ἐμβάλλων φόβον εἰς τὰς καρδίας ἡμῶν, τοῦ δοξάζειν σε τὸν μόνον ἀγαθὸν καὶ φιλάνθρωπον· ἔκτοτε οὖν ἑορτάζεται ἡ τοιαύτη ἀνάμνησις (Vat. gr. 1613, fol. 350, *PG* 117 cols. 279–80).

[40] *Typikon*, ed. Mateos (1962–3) 21: 2ἀνέτειλας, Κύριε, τὴν ἡμέραν ἐν ᾗ δικαίως ἐπαίδευσας ἡμᾶς, καὶ μετὰ φόβου πάντες σοι προσπίπτομεν λέγοντες· Ἅγιε Δέσποτα Σωτὴρ ἡμῶν, ἐλέησον ἡμᾶς.

370   *Vicky Manolopoulou*

upon the sinful people, who therefore prayed in fear for forgiveness. A similar message comes from a *troparion* sung during the annual commemoration of the earthquake of AD 557 celebrated on 14 December: 'Lord, we sinned, and we acted lawlessly, we prostrate ourselves, have mercy on us.'[41] These *troparia* express the belief that demonstrating repentance is critical for deliverance and link the emotions of fear of God[42] and love for humankind (*philanthrōpia*) to a progression from sin to salvation.[43]

Fear is highlighted in the *troparia* that were supposedly sung during the processions taking place at the actual events but also in the *troparia* commemorating these events – fearing for one's life during or just after a catastrophe is undoubtedly different from a reference to fear during a commemoration of a distressful moment. Such commemorations enabled the community to make sense of the disaster or similar threats to the community and affected how people responded to future disasters. Participants in such commemorations might have experienced the event commemorated or a similar event, and thus commemorations were a way to mitigate trauma. Tangible cultural memory (e.g. inscriptions after wall repairs) but also intangible cultural memory (e.g. annual commemorations of disasters) served as mechanisms for the community to be informed about past disasters and to prepare for recurrent hazards such as earthquakes.[44] Photios, for example, highlights the importance of commemorations:

> But if we cling to our former sins, which God forbid (Oh, that there be not one amongst us so insensitive and incorrigible as to disregard such great vexation sent by God!), if then we pollute ourselves with these same passions and stain ourselves with the mire of pleasures instead of expiating past calamities with persevering repentance, and using bygone ills to guard our future life, into what ruin, alas, are we casting ourselves again, of what disasters are we digging a pit, how great a storm of evils are we, in our mad folly, raising against ourselves![45]

He also notes the importance of remembering past disasters to prevent new ones afflicting the community: 'So let none of us be forgetful of these things; let no one ruin these promises with oblivion, for oblivion of them can kindle God's

---

[41] *Typikon*, ed. Mateos (1962–3) 130–2.

[42] On fear of God and holy love, fear of the day of judgement, fear in connection to tears, and holy love see Hunt (2004).

[43] On grief for sin see also Hunt (2004) 17–25.

[44] On commemorations after disaster see Eyre (2007).

[45] Trans. Mango (1958) 105; Photios, *Homily* 4.5, ed. Laourdas (1959) 47–8: ἐὰν δὲ τοῖς ἔμπροσθεν ἡμῶν ἁμαρτήμασιν, ὃ μὴ γένοιτο, προστηκώμεθα (μηδὲ γὰρ μηδ' εἴη τις ἐν ἡμῖν οὕτως ἀνάλγητος καὶ ἀδιόρθωτος, ὡς ἀλογῆσαι τοσαύτης καὶ τηλικαύτης θεηλάτου ἀγανακτήσεως), ἂν οὖν τούτοις αὐτοῖς ἐμμολυνώμεθα τοῖς πάθεσι καὶ τῷ βορβόρῳ τῶν ἡδονῶν ἰλυσπώμεθα καὶ μὴ τῇ ἐπιμονῇ τῆς μετανοίας τὰ φθάσαντα ἐξιλασώμεθα, μηδὲ φυλακὴν τοῦ μέλλοντος βίου τῶν λυπηρῶν τὰ παρῳχηκότα ποιησώμεθα, φεῦ, εἰς οἶον πάλιν ἑαυτοὺς ἐπιρρίπτομεν ὄλεθρον, οἵων συμφορῶν ἀνορύσσομεν βόθυνον, ἡλίκων κακῶν χειμῶνα καθ' ἑαυτῶν ἀγριαίνοντες ἐπεγείρομεν.

14. Visualizing and Enacting Emotions

wrath.[46] He warns of what happens if people forget past disasters and how they were delivered from them: 'we were delivered from evils which often had held us; we should have been thankful but showed no gratitude. We were saved, and remained heedless; we were protected, and were contemptuous. For these things punishment was to be feared ... We forgot to be grateful when the benefit had gone by.'[47] Expressing gratitude was also essential, and processions were a way of demonstrating and communicating ideas about emotions relevant to gratitude.

The idea that commemorations of past disasters were expressions of gratitude that aimed to prevent future calamities is also present in liturgical books. For example, the commemoration of the earthquake of AD 740 celebrated annually on 26 October in the *Menologion* of Basil II is stated as an expression of gratitude and prayer for future protection: 'So since then in commemoration of this distress, we gratefully celebrate this feast annually, praying that this threat won't befall us.'[48] People performed litanies in their present, remembering their past for their future, and ideas about emotions of wrath, fear, and *metanoia* were entangled with joy and hope for the supplication to be accepted and hence hope for salvation and protection. The *litē* became a procession in time[49] when people processed through the streets united with their ancestors, the whole body of the *ekklēsia* (past and present). Thus, the *litē* shaped an emotional community that dwelt in the place where a similar one dwelt in the past and another one was going to dwell in the future. These communities all met in the minds of the faithful in an eternal moment that was fulfilled during participation in the liturgy.[50]

Commemorative processions were not only a form of prayer as a gesture of gratitude for deliverance and supplications for future protection but also a public demonstration of piety that was linked to the idea that processions were a way of preventing future calamities. They were also a way of communicating ideas about imperial piety and humility – virtues of an emperor linked to military victory. Pious emperors of the past were remembered as showing repentance and pleading for salvation. Emperors participating in the processions were linked with their predecessors, the protagonists of the events that were being commem-

---

[46] On the occasion of the departing of the Russians. Trans. Mango (1958) 104; Photios, *Homily* 4.5, ed. Laourdas (1959) 46–7: μηδεὶς οὖν ἡμῶν τούτων ἀμνημονείτω· μηδεὶς τὰς τοιαύτας ὑποσχέσεις λήθη λυμηνάσθω· ἡ γὰρ τούτων λήθη ὀργὴν οἶδεν ἀνάπτειν Θεοῦ.

[47] Trans. Mango (1958) 83; Photios, *Homily* 3.1, ed. Laourdas (1959) 20–30: ἐρρύσθημεν κακῶν, οἷς πολλάκις συνεσχέθημεν· δέον εὐχαριστεῖν, οὐκ εὐγνωμονήσαμεν· ἐσώθημεν, ἠμελήσαμεν· ἐφρουρήθημεν, κατεφρονήσαμεν ἐφ' οἷς δέος ἦν τιμωρίαν ὑποσχεῖν ... οὐκ ἐμνήσθημεν τῆς εὐχαριστίας, παρελθούσης τῆς εὐεργεσίας.

[48] ἐκ τότε οὖν μεμνημένοι τῆς τοιαύτης ἀνάγκης, εὐχαρίστως ἑορτάζομεν ἐτησίως τὴν παροῦσαν ἑορτήν, εὐχόμενοι μὴ τοιαύτη περιπεσεῖν ἀπειλῇ (Vat. gr. 1613, fol. 142, *PG* 117 cols. 129–30).

[49] See Louth (2013a) 122–40.

[50] Gador-Whyte (2017) 147–92.

372   *Vicky Manolopoulou*

orated. Experiencing this atmosphere[51] and participating in this emotional community formed social identities, as people became attuned to the notions of the City and the Church.

References to emotion were central in the way past events were remembered and explained. Thus, such commemorations were critical to the way ideas about human and divine emotion were communicated during these processions. For example, as mentioned above, the commemoration of the earthquake of AD 740 celebrated annually on 26 October was an expression of gratitude and prayer for future protection. Emotion was central to this understanding. For the same day, the *Typikon* starts by stating that the day is dedicated to 'memory of the great menace of the earthquake that befell us with *philanthrōpia*'.[52] The *troparion* of the day enabled people to attune to the reality of the past disaster: 'You who look upon the earth and make it tremble, deliver us from the fearful menace of the earthquake, Oh Christ our God, and by the intercessions of the Theotokos, send down upon us your rich mercies as the sole *Philanthrōpos*.'[53] The *troparion* was chanted at the Great Church, where the celebration started with the patriarch's participation. The procession moved to the Forum, where there was a station, and then to the church of Theotokos Blachernae, where the same *troparion* was sung once more. Similarly, other *troparia* chanted during commemorative processions linked divine love and wrath to past disasters and reflect the idea that the punishment is just and not vindictive.[54] Therefore, the annual commemoration of disasters, including the performance and experience of such *troparia*, also had a cathartic role, since remembering the event was a way of remembering and celebrating God's *philanthrōpia*.

This idea is also reflected in the writings of important figures of the Church; Theodore Studites (AD 759–826), for example, links disaster with chastisement: 'now civil war was about to take place which like other God-send disasters, earthquakes and famines, flood and fire was sent for our chastisement because of his just judgement'.[55] The disaster, therefore, was seen as a form of discipline

---

[51] Harris and Sørensen (2010) 153 define atmosphere as 'the emotional experience engendered by being in a particular place and situation'. Atmosphere comes to light at the junction of people, places, and things and usually involves architecture and the use of the properties of material things. Different atmospheres can emerge at the same place, as they are outcomes of the affective fields. They can also be produced through practice to create new affective fields: Harris and Sørensen (2010) 152. See also Manolopoulou (2013).

[52] *Typikon*, ed. Mateos (1962–3) 78–80: καὶ τῇ αὐτῇ ἡμέρᾳ, μνήμη τῆς μετὰ φιλανθρωπίας ἐπενεχθείσης φοβερᾶς ἀπειλῆς τοῦ σεισμοῦ.

[53] *Typikon*, ed. Mateos (1962–3) 78–80: ὁ ἐπιβλέπων ἐπὶ τὴν γῆν καὶ ποιῶν αὐτὴν τρέμειν, ῥῦσαι ἡμᾶς τῆς φοβερᾶς τοῦ σεισμοῦ ἀπειλῆς, Χριστὲ ὁ Θεὸς ἡμῶν, καὶ κατάπεμψον ἡμῖν πλούσια τὰ ἐλέη σου, πρεσβείαις τῆς Θεοτόκου, ὡς μόνος Φιλάνθρωπος.

[54] Manolopoulou (2016) 173–89.

[55] Theodore Studites, *Epistles* 478.28–30, ed. Fatouros (1992) 696: νυνὶ δὲ ἐμφύλιος πόλεμος πρόκειται, ὅς, ὥσπερ αἱ ἄλλαι θεομηνίαι, σεισμοί τε καὶ λιμοί, καταποντισμοὶ καὶ ἐμπρήσεις, παρὰ θεοῦ πρὸς σωφρονισμὸν ἡμῶν δικαίᾳ κρίσει ἀνερριπίσθη.

14. Visualizing and Enacting Emotions 373

to help people overcome a sinful way of life. This idea is also reflected in the writings of later authors commenting on feasts and commemorations of the year. For example, Neophytos the Recluse (AD 1134–*ca.* 1220) connects disaster with chastisement: 'For this reason, therefore, in various times terrible earthquakes were sent from God who leads people towards repentance and faith.'[56] The divine emotion of love for humankind (*philanthrōpia*) refers to both the disaster and the salvation: God's love for humankind was the underlying reason for the menace, but it was also the same emotion coined as the reason the disaster past. For Neophytos the acts and fate of the individual were inextricably linked to the community.[57] This idea was already present much earlier, evidenced in Justinian's *Novella* 77, which is linked to the earthquakes of the sixth century:[58]

We exhort these, too, to take to heart the fear of God and the coming judgement, and to abstain from such acts of diabolical, unacceptable licentiousness, in order that their cities as well, along with their inhabitants, may not be found being destroyed under God's righteous anger, by reason of such impious doings; we are taught by the holy scriptures that as a result of such impious practices, cities and their inhabitants have actually been destroyed together ... [I]t is because of offences such as these that famines, earthquakes and plagues occur ... and to inflict on them the most extreme punishments, so that both the city and our realm may not be found to suffer for such impious practices.[59]

Divine wrath would endanger the lives of many, so laws ensured the ongoing survival and prosperity of the community. Thus, the ideas communicated during processions about human and divine emotion had an eschatological or soteriological notion that is also present in other spheres of life. Thus, processions as part of the intangible cultural memory of disasters served also as a way of legitimizing power, since the dynamic of fear of God/fear of wrath and *philanthrōpia* was communicated annually during these processions.

---

[56] Neophytos, *Panegyrike* A, 16.33–5, ed. Giagkou and Papatriantafyllou-Theodoridi (1999) 328: διὰ τοῦτο γὰρ καὶ κατὰ διαφόρους καιροὺς σεισμοὶ φοβεροὶ ἐπηνέχθησαν πρὸς Θεοῦ πρὸς πίστιν καὶ μετάνοιαν ἄγων τοὺς ἀνθρώπους. See also Galatariotou (1991) 249.

[57] Galatariotou (1991) 249.

[58] Crompton (2006) 146–7.

[59] Trans. Miller and Sarris (2019) 539–40; Justinian, *Novella* 77, ed. Kroll and Schöll (1968 [1895]), 381–3, τούτοις παρεγγυῶμεν λαβεῖν κατὰ νοῦν τὸν τοῦ θεοῦ φόβον καὶ τὴν μέλλουσαν κρίσιν καὶ ἀπέχεσθαι τῶν τοιούτων διαβολικῶν καὶ ἀτόπων ἀσελγειῶν, ἵνα μὴ διὰ τῶν τοιούτων ἀσεβῶν πράξεων ὑπὸ τῆς τοῦ θεοῦ δικαίας ὀργῆς εὑρεθῶσι καὶ αἱ πόλεις μετὰ τῶν οἰκούντων ἐν αὐταῖς ἀπολλύμεναι. διδασκόμεθα γὰρ διὰ τῶν ἁγίων γραφῶν, ὅτι ἐκ τῶν τοιούτων ἀσεβῶν πράξεων καὶ πόλεις τοῖς ἀνθρώποις συναπώλοντο ... διὰ γὰρ τὰ τοιαῦτα πλημμελήματα καὶ λιμοὶ καὶ σεισμοὶ καὶ λοιμοὶ γίνονται ... ἵνα μὴ ἐκ τοῦ παραβλέπειν τὰς τοιαύτας ἁμαρτίας εὑρεθῇ καὶ ἡ πόλις καὶ ἡ πολιτεία διὰ τῶν τοιούτων ἀσεβῶν πράξεων ἀδικουμένη. Also Bailey (1955) 73–4.

14.2. Prayer and evoking the right emotions

Processions were, therefore, a mobile form of prayer of the city in the city, where the people aimed to collectively display emotions associated with repentance to attract God's mercy and forgiveness. Private and collective prayer was believed to be very effective.[60] The miracle during the reign of Theodosios the Great at the Church of Saint Anastasia in Constantinople where the prayers of the faithful brought a dead woman back to life,[61] and the processions led by Theodore of Sykeon that saved villagers from multiple threats[62] are just examples of the power that collective prayer had had in the minds of the faithful since Late Antiquity. But for the prayer to be effective, it needed to be performed in the right way. For example, when Antioch suffered terrible earthquakes, Symeon the Younger (*ca.* AD 592) ordered people to sing during processions *troparia* that had been divinely revealed to him, for the earthquake to cease.[63] A famous example of the perception of the power of hymns and collective prayer was the story of the divine revelation of the *Trisagion* commemorated on 24 September.[64] The hymn was divinely revealed to a child during a procession for the earthquake that shook Constantinople in AD 438 during the reign of Theodosius II (AD 408–50).[65] People had gathered at Hebdomon, performing processions and praying collectively for the earthquake to cease. It was only when the people sang the correct version of the *Trisagion* that the tremor stopped.[66] Singing the hymn during the procession was linked to attracting God's mercy and was a demonstration of Orthodoxy.

It is worth noting that, although processions created emotional communities, this does not mean that everyone was able to attune to these communities. Hence, when one is discussing processions and emotions, one should take into consid-

---

[60] For more on how prayer was practised see Taft (2006) 100–3 and Bitton-Askelony and Krueger (2016).

[61] Symeon Logothetes, *Chronicon* 95.7, ed. Wahlgren (2006) 121: κοινῆς ὑπὸ τῶν ὀρθοδόξων γενομένης εὐχῆς ἀναστῆναι τὴν τελευτήσασαν ('a pregnant woman who fell down there and died, yet was resurrected by the collective prayer of the orthodox', trans. Wahlgren (2019) 92). Logothetes' Chronicle was compiled sometime between 959 and 969 (Neville (2018) 118–23). For a further sources and discussion of this miracle see Snee (1998).

[62] E.g. *Life of Theodore of Sykeon* 36, ed. Festugière (1970) 32. The *Life of Theodore of Sykeon* was written sometime in the early seventh century by Eleusios-Georgios and contains a number of references that connect collective prayer and miracles.

[63] *Life of Simeon Stylites the Younger* 104–7, ed. Van den Ven (1962) 81–8.

[64] 'Holy God, Holy Strong, Holy Immortal, have mercy on us' (Ἅγιος ὁ Θεός, Ἅγιος ἰσχυρός, Ἅγιος ἀθάνατος, ἐλέησον ἡμᾶς). For the development of the hymn see Ginter (2017) 43–5.

[65] There is confusion as to whether this earthquake occurred in AD 437 or 438. For example, both Ambraseys (2009) 163–5 and Baldovin (1993) 30–1 give AD 437 as the date. For discussion on whether the earthquake took place in AD 437 or 438 see Croke (1981) 126–31.

[66] *Synaxarion*, ed. Delehaye (1902) 77–80. The hymn went through various modifications that relate to Trinitarian controversies. The way it was commemorated in the tenth century related to the fact that the Council of Trullo (AD 692) forbade any modification to the hymn (Canon 81).

eration that these were prescribed ritualized actions. This does not mean that we cannot talk about the effect that participation had on the individual. Even if it is impossible to pinpoint the exact emotions that individuals experienced, there is no evidence that they were not able to attune to these communities, and it is always possible to discuss emotion by exploring what could give rise to emotion.

14.3. *Sunaisthēsis* and emotion

Praying in the right fashion was also about evoking the right emotions. In the sixth century, Justinian's legislation ordered hitherto silent parts of the liturgy to be heard by the congregation, to achieve greater compunction (*katanuxis*), which was inextricably linked to *metanoia* and salvation.[67] The church's architecture, decoration, and furnishings all contributed to experiencing the church as a sacred space.[68] Decorum, gestures, clothing, but also objects such as processional crosses, lectionaries, torches, censers, and relics, were part of the *litai* and engaged the senses,[69] and their affective properties contributed to the creation and experience of a specific atmosphere that was designed to present the whole landscape as a church.[70] This atmosphere was created as a means of arousing emotions and creating a link to the divine either in terms of presence or in terms of communication.[71]

Incense, for example, was a symbol of prayer and of divine presence.[72] Using incense during processions engaged more than one sense:[73] the sight and smell of the smoke coming off the censer and the sound the censer made as the deacon swung it. The motion of the smoke rising to the air was also connected with another moment during the liturgical day experienced when the vesperal psalmody was heard: 'Let my prayer rise like incense before you, a lifting up of my hand as an evening sacrifice' (Ps. 140:2).[74]

Processional torches (*phatlia*) made of wax and olive oil were also affective, as they emitted a very sweet and pleasant odour that is associated with paradise.[75]

---

[67] Justinian, *Novella* 137.6, ed. Kroll and Schöll (1968 [1895]), 699; trans. Miller and Sarris (2019) 918–19. Hunt (2004) 42–3, 68; Krueger (2014) 106–19. For earlier examples of regulations in relation to emotional responses, see Chaniotis (2013c) 170–1. For a discussion on silence see also Haines-Eitzen (2017).

[68] Caseau (2013); Louth (2013b).

[69] See also James (2004); Pentcheva (2006).

[70] Regarding the landscape being a church see also Baldovin (1987) 268.

[71] Chaniotis (2013c) 173. For the role of the senses in experiencing the sacred during the liturgy see Caseau (1999), (2013), (2014).

[72] Caseau (1999) 107.

[73] For *sunaisthēsis* ('joint perception') see Caseau (2014) 90–1.

[74] Taft and Kazhdan (1991b); Krueger (2014) 68–9. For the relationship between image and word see also Webb (2017).

[75] Taft and Kazhdan (1991a). See also Ashbrook Harvey (2017a).

376 *Vicky Manolopoulou*

They contributed to making processions awe-inspiring spectacles, as the city would be transformed – in the words of John Chrysostom – into a 'river of fire': 'one wouldn't be wrong in calling this sea also a river of fire. So throughout the night the lamps packed tightly together in a continuous line stretching as far as this martyrium supplied a vision of a fiery river to those watching.'[76] The light they produced was also in a dialectic relationship not only with the space where they were lit but also with the timing of the procession, as their effect would be different indoors and outdoors and at other times of the day, given processions could take place under a range of different natural lighting conditions. Seeing the light produced by the processional torches was also affective because of its soteriological meaning:

We command that those who want to exalt themselves, do that spiritually in the holy churches, that is by praying, by reading, by singing psalms, and by giving alms. Rejoice all of you in doing so, as true Christians, as servants of Christ, as children of the light, as heirs of the kingdom of heaven; perform litanies from the house of the Lord to the house of God, rejoice while you are walking and praying, loving each other beaming through the virtues like the sun.[77]

Participants are called 'children of light', God's 'children' that reflect 'the virtues like the sun'; with Christ being the very true light that disperses the spiritual darkness and lights up the way towards salvation. The words 'Light – Life'[78] that often appear on personal objects or as part of architectural decorations are used as a reference to Christ. This formula appears also as part of procession-al cross bases; crosses were also a symbol of Christ.[79] Thus, people carrying the processional torches who followed a processional cross in a way were following Christ. The change between darkness and light, as well as the physical action of following the cross, enabled people to experience the words of Christ heard at

---

[76] The homily was delivered between AD 400 and 402 during a procession at Drypia, a suburb outside Constantinople (Mayer and Allen (2000) 85–6): John Chrysostom, *Homilia dicta postquam reliquiae martyrum*, PG 63 cols 467–72, οὐκ ἄν τις ἁμάρτοι τὴν θάλατταν ταύτην καὶ ποταμὸν πυρὸς προσειπών· οὕτως αἱ λαμπάδες αἱ διὰ τῆς νυκτὸς αἱ πυκναὶ καὶ συνεχεῖς μέχρι τοῦ μαρτυρίου τούτου διαπαντὸς ἐκταθεῖσαι, πυρίνου ποταμοῦ φαντασίαν παρεῖχον τοῖς ὁρῶσι. Also cited in Baldovin (1987) 183. It is possible that apart from processional torches lanterns were also used in processions; see Bouras and Parani (2008) 5, 21.

[77] Trans. Berger (2006) 432–3 (adapted); Pseudo-Gregentios, *Nomoi* 285–90, ed. Berger (2006): προστάττομεν τοὺς βουλομένους μετεωρίζεσθαι πνευματικῶς τοῦτο γίνεσθαι ἐν ταῖς ἁγίαις ἐκκλησίαις, οἷον διὰ προσευχῆς, διὰ ἀναγνωσμάτων, διὰ ψαλμῳδίας καί δι' ἐλεημοσύνης. ἐν τούτοις εὐφραίνεσθε ἅπαντες ὡς ἐπ' ἀληθὲς χριστιανοί, ὡς δοῦλοι Χριστοῦ, ὡς τέκνα φωτός, ὡς κληρονόμοι τῆς βασιλείας τῶν οὐρανῶν· λιτανεύετε ἐξ οἴκου κυρίου ἐπὶ οἶκον θεοῦ πορευόμενοι καὶ προσευχόμενοι εὐφραίνεσθε, ἀγαπῶντες ἀλλήλους ἀπαστράπτοντες ταῖς ἀρεταῖς ὡς ὁ ἥλιος. This passage was intended for Negra but was written in Constantinople (Berger (2006) 41) reflecting perceptions of processions taking place in the capital.

[78] ΦΩΣ – ΖΩΗ; for a discussion on objects bearing this Greek-cross inscription and its meaning see Bouras and Parani (2008) 26–7.

[79] For a discussion on the processional cross base see Cotsonis (1994) 110.

14. Visualizing and Enacting Emotions

moments during the liturgical celebration of the day: 'I am the light of the world, the one that follows me will not walk in darkness but will have the light of life' (John 8:12).[80] By following Christ, people demonstrated that they were part of his flock. Thus, walking was an enactment of faith and hope. 'I am the way, and the truth and the life; nobody comes towards the father except through me' (John 14:6).[81] Processions aimed to create the right atmosphere for people to attune to a notion of one united body of 'real Christians'. The body of the individual was also a vital part of another 'body': that of the *ekklēsia*. As one body, it is characterized by unity: it is the flock of God, the 'body' of Christ.[82] The assembly of individual bodies framed the body of the procession. During *litai*, the faithful were able to demonstrate their Orthodoxy and rejoice in the hope of salvation, as promised by the Resurrection of Christ, and in the expectation of the Second Coming and the Resurrection of the dead.

Processional crosses were the heart of a procession.[83] They were decorated or jewelled and were often inscribed with prayers and votive dedications or contained relics. A good example is a processional cross inscribed with the *Trisagion* hymn; as discussed above, this hymn was believed to have been miraculously revealed at the Campus at the Hebdomon, outside the city walls (Fig. 14.3).[84] The vision of the cross during a procession therefore engaged not only one sense – vision – but also hearing, as it was also in a dialectic relationship with the hymns and the readings. Hymns, as in the case of the *Trisagion* and other divinely revealed hymns, had similar properties to relics. The affective properties of the cross were related not only to its soteriological significance as a banner of faith and hope,[85] but also to the belief that it sanctified the landscape.

The cross was followed by an archdeacon who carried a Gospel. The cover was often decorated with precious materials, as it covered the priceless meaning of the Word and was a symbol of Christ, the incarnate Word of God.[86] As with the sight of the cross or the light from the torches,[87] the Gospel also contributed to the image of people following Christ and so shaped the creation of a sacred atmosphere. Seeing the Gospel was also in a dialectic relationship with hearing the readings. The account of the fourth-century pilgrim, Egeria, describing the emotional reactions of hearing the Gospel, is fairly typical in this respect: 'to each of the readings and prayers there is such emotion and lamentation from all the

---

[80] ἐγώ εἰμι τὸ φῶς τοῦ κόσμου· ὁ ἀκολουθῶν ἐμοὶ οὐ μὴ περιπατήσῃ ἐν τῇ σκοτίᾳ ἀλλ᾽ ἕξει τὸ φῶς τῆς ζωῆς.

[81] ἐγώ εἰμι ἡ ὁδὸς καὶ ἡ ἀλήθεια καὶ ἡ ζωή· οὐδεὶς ἔρχεται πρὸς τὸν πατέρα εἰ μὴ δι᾽ ἐμοῦ.

[82] 1 Cor. 12:12–27.

[83] Cotsonis (1994) 19.

[84] A marble cross that was found at Hebdomon and is currently at the archaeological museum in Istanbul also had the same inscription. Downey (1954).

[85] Taft (2006) 53.

[86] Taft (2006) 45, 53, 144. Christ as the Word in John 1:1, 1:14.

[87] See also Hunter-Crawley (2013) for the 'Cross of Light' and the senses.

Figure 14.3. Processional cross with the *Trisagion* hymn, sixth century, Accession Number 50.5.3, Metropolitan Museum of Art. Public domain.

people that is astonishing; for there is no one, either older or younger who on that day in those three hours does not bewail more than can be reckoned that the Lord had suffered those things for us'.[88]

Hearing was not passive: the faithful participated by repeating short, easily remembered refrains.[89] The *troparia* of the day, also discussed above, communicated the text of the hymn that highlighted divine presence, confession of sin, divine emotion, and divine intervention, amongst other things. Apart from hearing, they also engaged the senses in another way, as they were in a dialectic

---

[88] Egeria, *Travels*, 37:7, ed. and trans. Bradshaw and McGowan (2020) 82–3. Also cited in Taft (2006) 76. For discussion on hearing in Byzantium see Ashbrook Harvey and Mullett (2017) 67–122.

[89] For a discussion on the literacy level of the people hearing these hymns and their understanding see Taft (2006) 129–31.

14. Visualizing and Enacting Emotions 379

relationship with the affective aspects of the space in which they were performed.[90] A good example of this is a processional *troparion* addressing the Theotokos as the wall of the city: 'Virgin Theotokos, you are an invincible wall for us the Christians; by turning to you for refuge, we stay invulnerable, and when we sin again, we have you to intercede. That is why we cry to you in thanksgiving; rejoice *highly favoured one*, the Lord, is with you.'[91] The *troparion* was sung on 9 July at the Pege Gate,[92] 7 August at the Pteron Gate,[93] and 16 August from the Attalos Gate to the Golden Gate, at the Golden Gate, and at the Theotokos Jerusalem.[94] Calling the Theotokos the wall of the city at the walls of the city not only reinforces the idea that the city is under the protection of its *poliouchos*, the Theotokos, but also that *She* becomes the symbol of the city, since the walls were symbols of a city.[95] Site-specificity[96] becomes a rhetorical device in a dialectic relationship with the message communicated by the *troparion*. The physicality of that space also engaged more than one sense: vision, smell, and touch. Similarly, the psalms, hymns, and *troparia* include homophone words that, when performed, could create powerful imagery: for example, words such as *eleos* (mercy) and *elaion* (oil) – the oil that burns in the candles and lamps used in prayer.[97]

Being outside also had affective properties. This was due to the lighting conditions and site-specificity as discussed above, but also because during processions all dwelling places participated in the networks of affective relationships between people and God.

The idea that processions sanctify the landscape is present already in Late Antiquity and stays the same throughout the Byzantine period. Carrying around sacred objects and singing hymns was done not only to transform the whole city into a church by creating an atmosphere, but also because they could sanctify and purify the landscape by its coming into contact with them.[98] A good example

---

[90] For a discussion of the way hearing is involved in experiencing space mentally see Webb (2017) 264–5.

[91] *Typikon*, ed. Mateos (1962) 334, 362, 374: τεῖχος ἀκαταμάχητον ἡμῶν τῶν χριστιανῶν ὑπάρχεις, Θεοτόκε Παρθένε· πρὸς σὲ γὰρ καταφεύγοντες ἄτρωτοι διαμένομεν, καὶ πάλιν ἁμαρτάνοντες ἔχομέν σε πρεσβεύουσαν. διὸ εὐχαριστοῦντες βοῶμέν σοι· χαῖρε, κεχαριτωμένη, ὁ Κύριος μετὰ σοῦ.

[92] The *Typikon* actually specifies that the *troparion* starts to be sung when the procession is close to the wall. *Typikon*, ed. Mateos (1962–3) 334.

[93] The text notes that the *troparion* is sung when the procession is at the Pteron Gate. *Typikon*, ed. Mateos (1962–3) 362.

[94] The *troparion* starts before reaching the Golden Gate and again when the procession reaches the Golden Gate and after the *litē* has entered Theotokos Jerusalem, a church close to the Golden Gate. *Typikon*, ed. Mateos (1962–3) 374.

[95] See also Cameron (1978) and Mango (2000).

[96] This term often refers to a work of art or performance designed for a specific site that is in a dialectic relationship. Bennett and Polito (2014).

[97] Krueger (2010) 135.

[98] Similarly, on earlier examples that relate to theatricality, emotion, and divine presence, see Chaniotis (2013c) 174–6.

380   *Vicky Manolopoulou*

that demonstrates this dual attribute of a procession as an expression of repentance and also a way of purifying the landscape is the procession due to a drought described in John Skylitzes' *Chronicle* (eleventh century).

> Because there was a drought and for six whole months no rain had fallen, the emperor's brothers held a procession, John carrying the holy Mandylion, the Great Domestikos the Letter of Christ to Abgar, the *prōtovestiarios* George the holy Swaddling Bands. They travelled on foot from the Great Palace to the church of the exceedingly holy Mother of God at Blachernae. The patriarch and the clergy made another procession, and not only did it not rain but a massive hail-storm was unleashed which broke down trees and shattered the roof tiles of the city.[99]

Skylitzes refers to a procession taking place in AD 1037; after six months of drought, Emperor Michael IV and his brothers (George, John, Constantine, and Niketas) with the patriarch Alexios led a supplicatory procession. The procession started from the Great Palace and terminated at the church of the Theotokos at Blachernae. George (*Prōtovestiarios*) carried the Holy Swaddling Bands (τὰ ἅγια σπάργανα), John (Orphanotrophos) carried the Mandylion (τὸ ἅγιον μανδύλιον), Constantine (Great Domestikos) carried the letter of Christ to Abgar (τὴν πρὸς Αὔγαρον ἐπιστολὴν τοῦ Χριστοῦ). The procession was successful, as it caused, according to Skylitzes, a massive hailstorm.[100] Using relics during processions, processions welcoming relics, but also processions as part of liturgical commemorations that were associated with relics, were also affective because they highlighted the idea that the city is protected by the presence of these relics in the city. This idea was also communicated throughout the liturgical year with hymns either dedicated to relics or dedicated to saints, with references to their relics and their efficacy. The churches that hosted the relics also contributed to this sacred atmosphere. The presence of both relics and churches created an atmosphere that proclaimed a continuous holy presence or expectance of presence in the city. This atmosphere was created and experienced throughout the liturgical year and especially during processions.

All these objects and conditions were used, as mentioned above, to create a sacred atmosphere and enhance emotional responses. Processions were very popular, and the image that we have as to how they were experienced is far from one that reflects compunction. For example, the Trier ivory (Fig. 14.4) displays

---

[99] Trans. Wortley (2010) 377–8; John Skylitzes, *Synopsis historion* 400.39–44, ed. Thurn (1973). Skylitzes was a member of the imperial court in Constantinople during the reign of Alexios Komnenos (1081–1118). For a discussion on the illumination that depicts this procession see Tsamakda (2002) 235–6.

[100] The idea that processions are effective against harmful physical phenomena is present already in Late Antiquity and stays the same throughout the Byzantine period. This can be attested by a plethora of references to such processions in hagiographical and historical accounts but also to the prayers that can be found in *euchologia* that are to be chanted during processions that are a response to these events.

Figure 14.4. *Litē* for a relic in Constantinople, ivory panel, Trier, Cathedral Treasury. Source: Hohe Domkirche Trier, Domschatz; Photo: Ann Münchow.

a crowded street with people standing both within and in front of a porticoed building, burning incense and watching the arrival of a procession, while others are on or in the process of climbing on to the roof of a church. Two figures holding a reliquary are depicted sitting on a cart pulled by two equines headed towards the church. Although a static carving made of ivory, the image is multi-sensory and full of motion: the censers depicted can be imagined being swung back and forth, producing fragrant smoke that combined with the other smells from the street through which the cart was moving. The sound of the chains of the censers would have mixed with people's voices together with the sound of the horses leading the cart to the church where the relic was meant to be deposited.[101]

A similar image is depicted by the Constantinopolitan Christopher of Mytilene in a satirical poem, composed sometime between AD 1000 and 1050 (*Poem* 1) that describes a procession in honour of Saint Thomas. Saint Thomas's feast day was on 6 October with a procession starting from the Great Church, stopping at the Forum, and then reaching the church of the saint at the Amantiou quarter.[102]

The thing was more a brawl than a festival:

> Everyone running in the midst of the porticoes,
> everyone running in the midst of the passages,
> looking around for cover in the corners,
> or gravely wounded with many injuries,

---

[101] Holum and Vikan (1979). See also Brubaker (1999).
[102] *Typikon*, ed. Mateos (1962–3) 60–3.

382 *Vicky Manolopoulou*

taken aback by the unusual events.
One of them lay in front of the avenue,
another ran, stumbled over the stones and fell,
another one was half burned by the torches,
another's hair was scorched by dripping candles,
and others got their beards consumed by fire.
Somebody else walked by, holding a torch,
and, hit by heavy hands right in the navel.
he threw the torch away to clutch his belly.[103]

Christopher of Mytilene describes the crowds flocking around buildings and streets in the city, creating a sensuous and vivid image of a procession similar to the one shown on the Trier ivory. Tarasios' funerary procession discussed above was also such a busy and noisy event that the emperor ordered military intervention to prevent people from being hurt.[104]

Concluding remarks

Processions, as part of the Byzantine ritual, shaped an understanding of the interrelationship between the earthly and heavenly realms, and emotion was central to this process; this was not only because ideas about emotion were shaped and communicated during processions but also because the way they were organized and performed aimed to create an emotional response in the participants but also enabled them to participate in emotional communities. Targeting collective emotion did not necessarily mean a shared emotional experience for all individuals; rather, it aimed to create an emotional community where the affective relationship networks from which emotions emerge could be forged. Emotions such as fear, terror, grief that are linked to disasters were associated with sin and repentance but also divine emotion such as wrath and *philanthrōpia*, the love for humankind.[105] These emotions related to the way people made sense of both their world and its challenges and relationship with God, the Theotokos, and the saints.

---

[103] Christopher of Mytilene, *Poem* 1.5–18, ed. and trans. Bernard and Livanos (2018) 2–4, 3–5.

[104] Ignatios, *Life of Tarasios* 64.12–15, ed. and trans. Efthymiadis (1998) 158–9, 203.

[105] Similarly, for Antiquity, Chaniotis (2013c) 171 observes: 'Fear and hope dominate every encounter of humans with the gods, during a ritual and beyond that.'

15

Evoking Fear through the Image of the Last Judgement[*]

Galina Fingarova

Introduction

In an effort to bring the impact of Byzantine images closer to modern viewers, Leslie Brubaker has suggested an association with contemporary advertising, despite the fundamental differences between the societies that created and used these media. For both, of prime importance is the message; it is promoted to the audience through easily recognizable pictures charged with 'a huge variety of cultural codes and deep interpretations'.[1] They are interconnected with words which decipher the pictures, but at the same time are verified by them. The beholder is expected to respond emotionally to the message, to 'complete' the image, and even to become part of it.[2] Based on these considerations, this study of the Byzantine image of the Last Judgement, which first appeared during the eighth or ninth century, will investigate the modes it used to evoke emotions and will corroborate the account found in textual sources by showing that its main aim was to induce fear in the viewer.[3]

Fear is one of the basic emotions, but also a concept with complex and multi-dimensional characteristics and categories. In spite of its universality, fear, like most other emotions, shows distinct shapes, expressions, evaluations, and even sensations in different cultures and periods.[4] The *Oxford Dictionary of English* defines fear as 'an unpleasant emotion caused by the threat of danger, pain, or

---

[*] This chapter was initiated and developed when I became part of the Emotions through Time project as an external contributor. I am extremely grateful to all network members for inspiring discussions and helpful suggestions as well as to both anonymous reviewers for their constructive feedback and advice with regard to content and references.

[1] Brubaker (1989b) 81.

[2] Brubaker (1989b) 80–2.

[3] The most important study on the image of the Last Judgement is still Brenk (1966); see further Milošević (1963); Brenk (1964), (1972); Velmans (1984); Garidis (1985); Drakopoulou (2000), with focus on the fear of punishments; Christe (2001); Angheben (2002); Angheben and Pace (2006); Ševčenko (2009).

[4] Scott and Kosso (2002) xii–xiii; Hinterberger (2010a) 123; Rosenwein (2017) 63. On fear from historical and interdisciplinary perspectives, see Laffan and Weiss (2012); Plamper and Lazier (2012).

384 *Galina Fingarova*

harm'.[5] Like us, the Greeks and Romans perceived most categories of fear as negative and inhibiting, including physical or natural fears and particularly the fear of death and the gods.[6] As Anne Scott and Cynthia Kosso have shown, they attempted to control, avoid, or overcome them and promoted instead social fear and especially fear of loss of honour.[7]

Contrary to Greek and Roman as well as to modern attitudes, in Byzantium fear was valued positively and, like other emotions, was closely related to Christian religion and to the values of the Byzantine state.[8] The positive attitude in Byzantium towards fear is best exemplified by its role in evoking κατάνυξις. This is a form of mourning on the part of the faithful, above all of monks, over their own sins and those of mankind. The tears shed cleansed the soul and prepared it for paradise. Thoughts that were considered suitable to bring tears were those evoking fear.[9] Perfectly appropriate to raise fear and hope among Christians was the Last Judgement, which became an article of faith early on because it was the main event of the Second Coming of Christ, when He will judge humans in accordance with their sins and virtues: the sinners will be condemned to eternal suffering while the righteous will enjoy eternal bliss.[10] The contrasting juxtaposition of punishment and reward, of hell and paradise, which is clearly emphasized in the parable of the separation of the sheep and goats at Matthew 25:31–46, was used by Early Christian authors in order to educate Christian communities and motivate them towards ethical behaviour. In this context, fear of hell and punishment was treated with varying degrees of intensity, but always in a positive sense.[11] It was extensively used by John Chrysostom, who em-

---

[5] Stevenson (2010) 638; see also the *Cambridge English Dictionary*, https://dictionary.cambridge.org/dictionary/english/fear (accessed 3 December 2017).

[6] Scott and Kosso (2002) xiii–xix.

[7] Scott and Kosso (2002) xix. This statement is best exemplified by the particular perception of fear in ancient Sparta, where the personification of Fear was worshiped as a god with the aim of instigating fear in the enemy. The Spartans themselves were not afraid of war and death, but of their mothers, who before battle gave them a shield with the instruction 'with it, or on it', meaning that either the shield would be brought back or the corpse would be brought back on it; see Chaniotis (2017b) 20; see also Patera (2013).

[8] Nemesios of Emesa and John of Damascus ranked fear (φόβος) together with lust (ἡδονή), pain (λύπη), and rage (θυμός) among the four basic emotions and subdivided it further into six categories: ὄκνος, 'hesitation or fear of future actions'; αἰδώς, 'fear of blame'; αἰσχύνη, 'shame or fear of having acted dishonestly'; κατάπληξις, 'consternation at the sight of a great imaginary apparition'; ἔκπληξις, 'terror caused by an unusual apparition'; and ἀγωνία, 'anguish or fear of failure': Nemesios, *De nat. hom.* 17–21, esp. 20; John of Damascus, *Expo. fid.* 27–30, esp. 29; on fear in Byzantium see Kazhdan (1991) 780–1; Hinterberger (2010a) 128–30, 133.

[9] Hinterberger (2006) 33–8; (2010) 130.

[10] On the idea of the afterlife and Last Judgement in ancient religions and in Christianity, Brenk (1966) 19–36; Brandon (1967); Griffiths (1991); Podskalsky and Cutler (1991); Marinis (2017).

[11] Alexandre (2000) treats the use of fear in the Homilies of Gregory of Nyssa; Henning (2014) offers an extensive study of the use of fear of hell and punishments in Early Christian education, which begins with a discussion of the Classical period.

15. Evoking Fear through the Image of the Last Judgement 385

phasized 'its edifying consequences in an educational context but also its power to maintain civic peace and order'.[12] Maximus the Confessor evaluated the fear of God's Judgement as an appropriate emotion because of its beneficial aspects in inspiring faith and love, deterring sins and vices, and guiding the faithful towards salvation.[13]

Because of its positive evaluation, fear of the Last Judgement was used as a crucial argument to convert people to Christianity. Such conversion was first implied in the New Testament as, for example, John 3:18 says: 'Whoever believes in Him is not condemned, but whoever does not believe has already been condemned, because he has not believed in the name of God's uniquely existing Son.' Although the use of fear of the Last Judgement for conversion to Christianity sparked criticism among pagans during Early Christian times,[14] it became a *topos* in the following centuries.[15]

15.1. Textual evidence of conversion to Christianity effected by an image

Two passages, one in a speech against the Iconoclast emperor Constantine V from around AD 770 and the other in the Chronicle of *Theophanes Continuatus* written approximately 170 years later, are regarded as outstanding examples that narrate such a conversion – in the first case of one who has deviated from the Orthodox doctrine, and in the second of a non-Christian. However, in both stories the *topos* was modified because the conversion was effected by an image.[16]

The passage in the *Oratio adversus Constantinum Cabalinum* from *ca.* 770 is regarded as one of the earliest references to an image of the Last Judgement. In the sections in question, this polemical treatise deals with the value and educational function of images. It explains that sacred images possess the power to open up the human spirit. The anonymous author addresses his opponent, the Iconoclast emperor Constantine V, with the question:

ἐπεὶ, εἰπέ μοι, ἐὰν ἴδῃς διὰ εἰκονικῆς τυπώσεως τὴν δευτέραν Χριστοῦ τοῦ Θεοῦ ἡμῶν παρουσίαν, πῶς μετὰ δόξης ἔρχεται, καὶ τὰς τῶν ἀγγέλων μυριάδας ἔμπροσθεν τοῦ θρόνου αὐτοῦ παρεστώσας μετὰ φόβου καὶ τρόμου· ποταμὸν δὲ ἐκπορευόμενον πύρινον ἐκ τοῦ θρόνου αὐτοῦ κατεσθίοντα τοὺς ἁμαρτωλούς· πάλιν δὲ ὅταν θεάσῃ ἐκ δεξιῶν αὐτοῦ τῶν δικαίων τὴν χαρὰν καὶ εὐφροσύνην, καὶ πῶς ἀγάλλονται ἔμπροσθεν τοῦ Νυμφίου·

---

[12] Papadogiannakis (2018) 352. The use of fear of hell and punishment in the works of John Chrysostom was extensively treated by Brändle (1979); see also Henning (2014) 218–20; and lastly Papadogiannakis (2018).

[13] On fear according to Maximus the Confessor see most recently Papadogiannakis (2017a).

[14] Jörg (2007).

[15] Brenk (1964) 112–14; (1966) 28.

[16] Brenk (1964) 110–14.

386   *Galina Fingarova*

εἰπέ μοι, οἷος σκληρὸς καὶ ἀμείλικτος τὸν νοῦν καὶ τὴν καρδίαν ὑπάρχει, οὐ μὴ κατανυ-
γῇ ἡ καρδία ἐκ τῆς φοβερᾶς ἐκείνης ὥρας·

If you look at a representation of the Second Coming of Christ you would see how He comes in his glory, and (you would see) the myriad crowd of angels standing before His throne with fear and trembling, the river of fire that flows from his throne and consumes the sinners; if you then see the joy and gladness of the righteous on the right hand of Christ, and how they rejoice before the Bridegroom, tell me who could then in mind and in heart remain so hard and stubborn, that his heart will not be pierced by that fearsome hour?[17]

In the Chronicle of *Theophanes Continuatus* from the tenth century the image of the Last Judgement is again used, in order to emphasize its impact on the pagan ruler of Bulgaria, Khan Boris, and his subsequent conversion to Christianity. The starting point of the story is the desire of the ruler to decorate one of his residences with hunting scenes as 'delights of his eyes'. He commissioned a Byzantine painter, a monk named Methodios, to execute the desired representation, but when the painter stood in front of him Boris changed his mind and

ἔκ τινος θείας προνοίας οὐ τὰς ἐν πολέμῳ ἀνδροκτασίας ἢ τὰς ζῴων καὶ θηρίων ἐπικελεῦ-
σαι γράψειν σφαγάς, ἀλλ᾽ ἃ βούλοιτο, τοῦτο μόνον ἐπειπὼν ὡς εἰς φόβον τοὺς ὁρῶντας
ἐκ τῆς θέας ἐνάγεσθαι βούλοιτο καὶ ἅμα παρακαλεῖσθαι πρὸς ἔκπληξιν ἀπὸ τῆς γραφῆς.
μηδὲν γοῦν οὗτος πρὸς φόβον ἕτερον ἐνάγειν ἢ τὴν τοῦ θεοῦ δευτέραν εἰδὼς παρουσίαν, ταύτην ἐκεῖσε καθυπέγραψεν, καὶ τοὺς δικαίους ἐντεῦθεν τὰ βραβεῖα τῶν πόνων
ἀπολαμβάνοντας, ἐκεῖθεν δὲ τοὺς πεπλημμεληκότας τοὺς τῶν βεβιωμένων δρεπομένους
καρποὺς καὶ πρὸς τὴν ἀπειλημένην κόλασιν ἀπελαυνομένους τε καὶ ἀποπεμπομένους
σφοδρῶς. ταῦτ᾽ οὖν, ἐπειδὴ πέρας ἔσχεν ἡ γραφή, κατιδών, καὶ δι᾽ αὐτῶν τὸν τοῦ θεοῦ
φόβον ἐν ἑαυτῷ συλλαβὼν καὶ κατηχηθεὶς τὰ καθ᾽ ἡμᾶς θεῖα μυστήρια, νυκτῶν ἀωρὶ
τοῦ θείου μεταλαγχάνει βαπτίσματος.

by some divine providence, he commanded him to depict not the slaughter of men in battle or killing of animals and wild beasts, but whatever he wanted, adding only that he wanted those who beheld to be frightened at the sight and brought to consternation by the depiction. The monk, then, knowing of nothing else than the Second Coming to excite fear, depicted this there, with the Righteous on one side receiving the rewards of their toils, and on the other side those who had sinned, reaping the fruits of what they had done during their lives and being driven off and dispatched harshly to the threatened punishment. Seeing this, when the depiction was finished, Bogoris [Boris] thereby conceived within himself the fear of God and was instructed in our divine Mysteries, and at dead of night he partook of divine baptism.[18]

In contrast to earlier texts which emphasize fear as an affective reaction to the Last Judgement, both passages imply fear through the description of the view-

---

[17] Trans. Ševčenko (2009) 258 (with a few modifications); *Oratio adv. Constantinum Cabalinum*, PG 95.309–44, here 324 (with a few adaptations).

[18] *Theophanes Continuatus* 4.15, ed. and trans. Featherstone and Signes Codoñer (2015) 232–5 (translation slightly adapted); cf. trans. Ševčenko (2009) 259.

15.2. Byzantine depictions of the Last Judgement

er's emotional response to the depicted image of the Last Judgement. This fear is evoked by contrasting the rewards and joy of the righteous with the punishments and fear of sinners on both sides of the frightening image of the Judge in glory.

As neither text can be connected with any known image, Beat Brenk posed the unanswered question: were the descriptions of the texts based on real images, or did they use this device to intensify the visualization of the salvific reality?[19]

15.2. Byzantine depictions of the Last Judgement

There are no known Byzantine images of the Last Judgement from the time before the end of the Iconoclasm in 843, although their existence is strongly suggested. The earliest surviving depictions are normally thought to be the frescoes in the narthex of St Stephen's in Kastoria, in north-western Greece, dated to the ninth or to the tenth century,[20] and in some churches in the province of Cappadocia, in modern central-eastern Turkey, from the first half of the tenth century.[21] Taken together these examples contain all the elements that belong to the standard repertory of a typical Byzantine Last Judgement composition. However, in these early depictions the elements either occur separately or are arranged in markedly different configurations which lead to a variety of compositional formats.[22]

The evolution and standardization of the iconography of the Last Judgement was essentially complete by the eleventh century, when the image appears in the narthex of the Panagia ton Chalkeon church in Thessaloniki, painted shortly after 1028 (Fig. 15.7) and on folios 51^v and 93^v of a Gospel book (cod. gr. 74) in the Bibliothèque nationale in Paris produced in the second half of the eleventh century at the monastery of St John of Stoudios in Constantinople. Additional representative examples are two icons kept in St Catherine's monastery on Mount Sinai, one from the end of the eleventh or twelfth century (no. 150) and the other slightly later from the twelfth century (no. 151, Fig. 15.6);[23] the mosaics on the west wall in the Cathedral of Santa Maria Assunta in Torcello executed by Byzantine artists in the eleventh century (Fig. 15.1); and an ivory panel in the Victoria and Albert Museum in London, an Italo-Byzantine work of the twelfth

---

[19] Brenk (1964) 114.

[20] Brenk (1966) 80–2 dates the frescoes in Kastoria before 1040 and regarded them as the earliest surviving version of the Last Judgement; Siomkos (2005) 33 dated the Last Judgement frescoes to the tenth century; Angheben and Pace (2006) 34–5: *ca.* 900; Ševčenko (2009) 259–60: ninth century.

[21] For example, the church of St John or Ayvalı Kilise in Güllü dere, 913–20; church no. 2 in Göreme, tenth century; Yılanlı Kilise (Church of the Serpents), tenth century; see Christe (2001) 21–4; Jolivet-Lévy (2006) with further bibliography.

[22] Angheben and Pace (2006) 34–6.

[23] Numbering according to Soteriou and Soteriou (1956–8), vol. 1, pls 150–1; vol. 2, 128–31.

388   *Galina Fingarova*

century. Although marked by slight differences in arrangement, all these examples show a similar multipartite composition which became canonical for the
Orthodox world and was maintained – in church decoration and in the minor
arts – until the post-Byzantine period, with only minor modifications.[24]

15.3. Description of a representative Last Judgement image

As a basis for illustrating a typical Last Judgement image we shall use the mosaic
panel in Torcello (Fig. 15.1) because of its precise articulation, which facilitates
legibility.[25] The composition is clearly separated into four horizontal and three
vertical registers. In the centre of the uppermost register appears Christ the Judge
in a *mandorla* with two fiery wheels underneath flanked by a seraphim. On both
sides stand the intercessors of humankind, the Virgin Mary and John the Baptist,
in the so-called *deēsis*. Laterally are seated the twelve Apostles separated into
two groups, each headed by an archangel, whereas a host of angels fills the background. On the central axis, below Christ is represented the so-called *hetoimasia*,
the prepared throne with the instruments of Christ's Passion and the closed
Book with seven seals. It is guarded by angels and adored by the first sinners,
Adam and Eve. To the left of the empty throne an angel is rolling up the scroll of
heaven, suggesting that the events depicted are taking place at the end of time.
Next to the angel two further angels trumpet to wake the dead in the sea, which
is personified by a female naked figure riding on a marine monster. The monster and other sea creatures disgorge parts of naked human bodies, illustrating
the sea giving back the dead it had devoured. To the right of the *hetoimasia* is
depicted the counterpart to this scene – the resurrection of the dead on earth.
Instead of sea creatures, various wild animals and birds disgorge the devoured
human bodies in response to the trumpeting of the angels; additionally, the
dead wrapped in shrouds rise from their tombs in a gesture of supplication. In
the middle of the register below is placed the *psuchostasia*, consisting of an angel
with a scale meant to weigh the deeds of the judged and of two devils who try
to influence the scale to their advantage. The central axis ends with the image of
the Virgin orans in the *tumpanon* over the door. The lateral depictions of both
lowermost registers show the extreme contrast between the condemned on the
left side of Christ and the saved on his right. The domain of Hades is shown as a

---

[24] For example, during the Late Byzantine period the typical Last Judgement composition
was enriched by depictions of punishments of individual sins, although some scattered scenes
were depicted already in the church of St Stephen in Kastoria and in some tenth-century
churches in Cappadocia, Mouriki (1975–6) 157–64; Garidis (1982); (1985) 86–91; Dekazou
(1998); Drakopoulou (2000); Kalopissi-Verti (2012) 144–8.

[25] Andreescu (1972); (1976), esp. 245–76; Polacco (1984); Kartsonis (1986) 159–61, 221–3; Angheben and Pace (2006) 58–60.

Figure 15.1. Cathedral of Santa Maria Assunta, Torcello, eleventh century, mosaic on the west wall: Last Judgement, Anastasis, and Crucifixion. Christie (2001) fig. 11.

390 *Galina Fingarova*

lake of fire supplied by the fiery current which starts its flow from under Christ's *mandorla*. The dark blue figure of Hades sits enthroned on a monster, holds on his lap a youth embodying a condemned soul,[26] and welcomes with his raised right hand the sinners who are pushed into the lake of fire by two fiery angels. While the flames have already consumed the bodies of the sinners, still visible are their heads with insignia emphasizing their secular and religious status. The disorder of the flames is enhanced by the addition of small naked devils in dark blue who fly around and torment the sinners. The register below shows the collective punishments of the eternally damned arranged in six rectangular fields: naked figures in eternal flames headed by the Rich Man who was condemned to eternal thirst because he had refused to give water to the poor Lazarus (Luke 16:19–31); naked full-length figures in eternal darkness; the outer darkness; skulls devoured by multiple worms; heads in eternal flames; and parts of human bodies in deep darkness. The prominent right side of Christ is occupied in the upper register by the choirs of the elect. Like the sinners in the lake of fire, their social and religious status is clearly distinguishable through their clothes and headgear, but they are arranged in orderly groups and raise their arms in a pious gesture of supplication. Below is paradise, the gate of which is guarded by a fiery angel. St Peter accompanied by an angel approaches it. Within the garden of paradise planted with green trees reside the Good Thief Dismas holding a cross, the Mother of God as orans, and the Old Testament patriarch Abraham with the soul of an innocent, probably the poor Lazarus, on his lap, flanked by the souls of innocent children.

15.4. Pre- and Early Christian representations of afterlife and judgement

As has been pointed out many times, the elements of the composition of the Last Judgement cannot be attributed to a single text, but derive from a variety of biblical and apocryphal sources as well as from patristic literature.[27] Equally, the iconographic motifs used to present the texts in visual form have a variety of origins, some of them dating back to the Early Christian period,[28] and even to ancient, pre-Christian times.[29] Thus, the image has been identified as a compilation which developed by stages between the eighth and the tenth centuries.[30] Although it does not have direct prototypes it is reasonable, be-

---

[26] The youth has been identified either as Judas: Garidis (1985) 63; Angheben (2002) 124; Angheben and Pace (2006) 55; Ševčenko (2009) 253–4; or as the Antichrist: Polacco (1984) 67; Christe (2001) 28, 30.

[27] Brenk (1964) 108–9; (1966) 90–3; Garidis (1985) 23–4; Christe (2001) 33; Angheben (2002); Angheben and Pace (2006) 12–17; Ševčenko (2009) 254–5.

[28] For example, Christ flanked by Apostles and the *hetoimasia*.

[29] As, for example, the *psuchostasia*.

[30] Brenk (1966) 80; Angheben and Pace (2006) 35.

15. Evoking Fear through the Image of the Last Judgement   391

fore proceeding to the investigation of the iconography and the impact of the image on the viewer, to look at representations of judgement and afterlife from preceding periods in order to evaluate its peculiarities.

As a representative example from the pre-Christian period can be taken the so-called sarcophagus of Velletri from the second century AD (Figs 15.2, 15.3),[31] because it displays a complete and clearly composed image of the eschatological ideas, desires, and hopes of its patron, which according to Bernard Andreae reflect the mentality of an entire era.[32]

The decoration spreads over all four sides and is subdivided into three hierar-chically arranged registers. The centre of the front (Fig. 15.2) accentuates the rulers of Hades, Pluto and Proserpina, who have assumed the role of judges over the deceased because, in contrast to ancient Greek, Roman funerary art did not represent the judges of the dead, Minos, Rhadamanthys, and Aeacus, known from Greek and Roman mythology.[33] The enthroned couple are flanked by the standing figures of Jupiter and Neptune. In this way side by side appear the three sons of Saturn as rulers of the main areas of the world – earth, sea, and under-world. On both sides are two scenes of deliverance from Hades – that of Alcestis and of Protesilaus. They are interpreted as evidence of the immortality of pious humans. The lower register of the front is devoted to the Rape of Proserpina be-cause of its clear allegory of death. Proserpina had to go to Hades in order to bring new life which gives hope of cosmic renewal. The upper register on the remaining three sides (Fig. 15.3) represents the labours of Hercules, which are interpreted as a model life on earth despite his efforts and combats; such life is rewarded with joy in the other world. Particularly emphasized in the centre of the left side is the scene of Hercules dragging Cerberus out of the Gate of Hades, which depicts a mortal as a victor over death and gives hope of salvation. The middle scene on the right side and the register below, showing *pietas* towards the older generation and the gods through offerings, reiterate that the requirement of salvation is *pietas*. Finally, the small strip of the lower register of the back presents a coherent whole of the other world: the voyage there with the ship of Charon, the Garden of the Hesperides or the Isles of the Blessed on the left, and the pun-ishments of the great sinners – Sisyphus, Tantalus, and the Danaides on the right.

The decoration of the Velletri sarcophagus has been interpreted as 'an en-cyclopaedic compendium of motifs and images' combined to advance the moral statement that the achievement of a desired afterlife depends on good behaviour on earth. Its patron invoked 'all the divine assistance, all the possible mythological

---

[31] On the Velletri sarcophagus, see Bartoccini (1958); Andreae (1963); Lawrence (1965); An-dreae (2005).

[32] Andreae (1963) 87.

[33] Andreae (1963) 30.

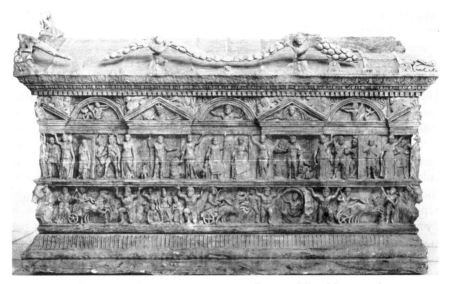

Figure 15.2. Velletri sarcophagus, Museo Civico, Velletri, middle of the second century AD, front side, upper register: Pluto and Proserpina, flanked by Jupiter and Neptune, on the sides deliverance from Hades of Alkestis and of Protesilaos; lower register: rape of Proserpina. Andreae (1963) pl. 1.

Figure 15.3. Velletri sarcophagus, Museo Civico, Velletri, middle of the second century AD, back side, upper register: labours of Hercules; lower register: Garden of the Hesperides, ship of Charon, punishments of Sisyphus, Tantalus, and the Danaides. Andreae (1963) pl. 3.

Figure 15.4. Lid of a Roman sarcophagus, Metropolitan Museum of Art, New York, *ca*. 300 AD, Separation of the sheep from the goats. Christie (2001) fig. 2.

models to avoid the ultimate condemnation to Hades' and to mitigate the apparent finality of death by allowing the latent possibility of hope.[34]

In a similar way, Early Christian funerary art attaches particular importance to the hope of redemption and the fate of the individuals after death and ignores the idea of a universal judgement with its rewards and punishments.[35] There are only two preserved images from the Early Christian period that hint at the idea of the Last Judgement by depicting the parable of the separation of the sheep from the goats (Matt. 25:31–46) – a lid of a Roman sarcophagus in the Metropolitan Museum of Art in New York from around AD 300 and a mosaic panel in Sant'Apollinare Nuovo in Ravenna from the first half of the sixth century.[36]

The lid of the sarcophagus (Fig. 15.4) shows Christ sitting in a bucolic landscape with eight sheep to his right and five goats to the left. His head is turned towards the sheep and his right hand is laid on the head of the first of them. This is the so-called gesture of *impositio manus*, expressing acceptance, favour, and protection. The palm of his raised left arm is, however, turned towards the goats in a gesture of rejection, and it seems that the first goat reacts to this gesture. Christ is additionally separated from the goats by a bundle of scrolls. The image clearly contrasts the disorder and reluctance on the left side of Christ, and his rejection of the goats, with the order and unity on his right side and his affectionate acceptance.[37]

The panel in Ravenna (Fig. 15.5) is located on the northern clerestory of the basilica and constitutes a part of a cycle of Christ's miracles. The composition is again symmetrical, with three sheep on Christ's right and three goats on his left. His open right hand with stretched thumb points to the sheep, which indicates

---

[34] Brilliant (1999) 148. On the interpretation of the decoration, Andreae (1963) 26–87; Lawrence (1965) 220–1.

[35] The emphasis on redemption is best exemplified by the preference given to representations of Jonah's salvation in Early Christian art: Brenk (1966) 74–5.

[36] The parable was also represented in the apse of the basilica in Fundi, but in a symbolic-allegorical way. As the representation is not preserved, its reconstruction is based on a description by Paulinus of Nola (*Ep.* 32.17), Ihm (1960) 80–3, cat. no. XXXVII, 181–2; Brenk (1966) 39–41; Christe (2001) 15–16; Angheben and Pace (2006) 21–3.

[37] Brenk (1966) 38–9; Christe (2001) 15.

Figure 15.5. Sant'Apollinare Nuovo, Ravenna, first half of the sixth century, mosaic panel on the northern clerestory: Separation of the sheep from the goats. Angheben and Pace (2006) fig. on p. 20.

welcoming and acceptance. His left hand is hidden beneath the cloak, thus giving the goats the brush-off. New in this image are the angels behind the animals. The interpretation by Engelbert Kirschbaum that they embody the good and the fallen angels is broadly accepted in the literature.[38] While the goal of the image in Sant'Apollinare Nuovo was to show that, as in the other miracle scenes, Christ will meet the obligation of his divine mission at the Last Judgement as he did during his earthly life, the relief on the sarcophagus, which takes up the Roman tradition of bucolic representation, was meant to give hope to the deceased.

Both images (Figs 15.4, 15.5) use a symmetrical composition with Christ on the central axis as a divider between two contrasting categories – the elect and the condemned – but do not depict the manner of the punishments and rewards. In describing the Last Judgement in a paradigmatic and metaphorical way they adopt the attitude of the Roman sarcophagus in Velletri (Figs 15.2, 15.3) and differ sharply from the images of the Last Judgement that appeared in the eighth or ninth century.[39]

---

[38] Kirschbaum (1940). On the representation, Brenk (1966) 38–9; Deichmann (1974) 169–70; Christe (2001) 16; Angheben and Pace (2006) 20–2.

[39] Brenk (1966) 212–13.

15.5. Interpretation of the Last Judgement iconography

As Brenk has pointed out, the eighth/ninth-century images laid emphasis on legal and emotional aspects of the Last Judgement and included the human being as God's instrument in the representation of the salvific history. The Last Judgement thus became 'eine der ersten Szenen in der Geschichte der christlichen Ikonographie, welche dem Menschen als Betrachter seinen Platz vor dem Angesicht des Allmächtigen einräumt'.[40] It gave pictorial expression to the thoughts and emotions of the faithful by introducing crucial novelties such as the depiction of the insurmountable polarity between good and bad, and the sharp contrast between divine omnipotence and human nothingness.[41] Thus, the terms 'polarity' and 'contrast' correspond to the main substance of the image, and according to Angheben this is the great originality of the Last Judgement in comparison to other biblical scenes.[42] Furthermore, the Last Judgement depicts a vast number of protagonists, emphasizing in this manner its universality, and depicts simultaneously several successive events, thus depriving the composition of temporal and spatial coherence.[43] At first sight, this multiplicity of actors and events overwhelms the conceptual ability of the viewer, but a closer observation reveals some principles of symmetry and hierarchy similar to those used for the Early Christian images and the sarcophagus of Velletri discussed above, and these help us understand the composition (Figs 15.1–6). In its oversimplified form it consists of the judging Christ with his heavenly court over the elect on his prominent right side and the condemned on his left, which recalls the images described in the texts discussed above. Christ is no longer the good shepherd sitting in the middle of his flock or the youthful son of God meeting the obligation of his divine mission from the Early Christian depictions of the parable of the separation of the sheep from the goats, but the almighty ruler of the world who reappeared in his glory and with his celestial court to judge the living and the dead. The majesty and dignity of Christ is represented by his frontality and immobility. Though he stretches his arms to show the wounds or makes the gesture of acceptance and rejection, he is totally confined into the *mandorla* of light as a sign of his inaccessible divinity. The surrounding figures react to the divine presence with proper and moderate movements, thus indicating the harmonious order prevailing in the celestial realm.[44]

Such order characterizes the privileged right side of Christ as the area of the elect. The righteous who wait to enter paradise are arranged in neat groups; they,

---

[40] Brenk (1966) 212: 'one of the first scenes in the history of Christian iconography, which gives the human being as beholder his/her place in front of the Almighty' (author's translation).

[41] Brenk (1966) 51, 212–13.

[42] Angheben and Pace (2006) 9.

[43] Angheben and Pace (2006) 9–12, 17; Ševčenko (2009) 255–8.

[44] On immobility and gesticulation in Byzantium, Brubaker (2009). The rule is 'the more holy the figure, the less active', Brubaker (2009) 46.

396   Galina Fingarova

as well as the prominent inhabitants of paradise, are almost immobile, with only slight movements of their gaze and arms raised in gestures of prayer.[45] Paradise itself is a light-flooded, cultivated garden, which implies the Byzantine interpretation of the garden as a place of order, harmony, and safety that represents the civilized world.[46]

In sharp contrast, hell is dominated by fire and darkness, disorder and chaos. Its ruler appears as the antipode of Christ – almost naked, dark-skinned, with white, dishevelled hair and beard, using a monster as a throne. His servants – dark demons – are shown in hectic motion. The tortured damned are naked or dismembered, and their facial expressions and gestures are often uncontrolled and contorted, indicating the pain they suffer and the fear that they are feeling. As Eunice Dauterman and Henry Maguire have shown, such uncontrolled movements, expressions of inappropriate emotions, fierce and monstrous creatures, as well as nude and contorted human beings and dismembered bodies, were not only explicitly condemned by the teachings of the Church, but were also considered to be 'liable to possession by invisible forces'.[47] They belonged to the realm of disorder (ἀταξία), which was regarded as distinctive of heretics and barbarians and abhorred and feared by the Byzantines.[48]

Thus, the image of the Last Judgement uses the depiction of disorder to evoke fear in the faithful, and juxtaposes it with harmonious order to show them the desired destination. In contrast to the clear representation of the fear and hope evoked by the sight of the events in hell and paradise, the visual language is vague about the effect on the beholder of the portrayal of the supreme Judge with his assembly. The scene is remotely placed at the very top and Christ's divinity is additionally isolated by the *mandorla*, which makes it impossible to approach him. The only access is provided by the images of the Mother of God and John the Baptist, who intercede on behalf of humankind.

15.6. Textual explanation of the visual language

The visual language is unambiguously clarified by three epigrams composed in 1293–4 by the scholar and monk Maximus Planudes for an icon of the Last Judgement which has not survived,[49] but may have resembled slightly earlier

---

[45] See n. 44.

[46] On the idea of the garden as a representation of the civilized world of Byzantium, Nilsson (2013), esp. 15–24; on earthly paradise in Byzantium, Maguire (2002).

[47] Maguire and Maguire (2007) 160.

[48] Maguire and Maguire (2007) 11–28 (on hybrids and monsters), 97–134 (on nakedness), 135–45 (on disorderly movements), 153–6 (on representation of heads).

[49] Drpić (2016) 18–21, with references. The epigrams are to be found in Planudes, *Epist.* 73.112.8–23.

15. Evoking Fear through the Image of the Last Judgement   397

(Fig. 15.6) and near-contemporary icons preserved at Mount Sinai that show a typical Byzantine composition.[50]

The first epigram addresses the upper part of the image, laying emphasis on the terrifying vision of the eschatological tribunal and its presider. This arouses the viewer's fear and forces him or her to follow a God-pleasing life.

> ὦ κρίσις, ὦ στάσις, ὦ φοβερώτατον αὖ τὸ θέατρον,
> ἔνθα θεὸς προκάθηται, ὃς ἔργματα πάντα δικάζει.
> οὐ φρίξεις ὁρόων; οὐ δάκρυα θερμὰ κατάξεις;
> οὐ ῥυθμιεῖς, ἄνθρωπε, τεὸν βίον; ὧδε γὰρ ἥξει.

> Judgement! Assembly! This most frightening spectacle! Here presides God who judges every deed. Will you not shudder while gazing <at him>? Will you not shed hot tears? Man, will you not set your life straight? For this is how it will happen.[51]

The second epigram was meant for the lower part of the icon, to the left of Christ, where the punishments of the sinners are represented. The viewer is again gripped by fear at the mere sight of the depicted torments.

> οἵας μοι κολάσεις ἐπταικότι, σῶτερ, ἀπειλεῖς;
> αἵ με καταπλήττουσι καὶ ἐν πινάκεσσι γραφεῖσαι·
> ὧν πεῖραν τρομέω γάρ, τῶνδε δέδοικα καὶ ὄψιν.

> With what kind of punishments, O Savior, do you threaten me, the sinner? Even the ones painted on panels terrify me. I tremble at the prospect of experiencing them; the very sight of them frightens me.[52]

In the third epigram the viewer appeals to the choirs of saints and the inhabitants of paradise, the Mother of God, Abraham, and the Good Thief, who are represented to the right of Christ, and expresses his wish to join them.

> μή ποτε μή τι γένοιτο, τὸ δή με δυνήσεται οἰκτρῶς,
> λήξιος ὑμετέρης, ἁγίων ἀγέλη, διορίσσαι.
> χαίροις, ὦ βασίλεια, καὶ σύ, πάτερ Ἀβραάμ, αὕτως·
> καὶ τὸν μειλίχιον λῃστὴν λέγω, εἰ θέμις ἐστί·
> δέξασθ᾽ ἐνναέτην με παρ᾽ ἐσχατιαῖς παραδείσου.

> May nothing ever happen to separate me lamentably from your lot, O flock of saints! Rejoice, O Queen [i.e. Virgin], and you, father Abraham, and I also address the meek thief: if it is right, allow me to inhabit the farthest quarters of Paradise.[53]

---

[50] The icons date from the end of the eleventh to the thirteenth century: Soteriou and Soteriou (1956–8), vol. 1, pls 150–1; vol. 2, 128–31; Parpulov (2010) 383, 385, 389, nos XII.75.6, XII.118.2, XIII.69, fig. 118, with references.

[51] After Drpić (2016) 19.

[52] After Drpić (2016) 19.

[53] After Drpić (2016) 21.

Figure 15.6. Icon of the Last Judgement, Monastery of St Catherine, Mount Sinai, twelfth century. By permission of St Catherine's Monastery, Sinai, Egypt. Photograph courtesy of Michigan-Princeton-Alexandria Expeditions to Mount Sinai.

15. Evoking Fear through the Image of the Last Judgement

In emphasizing the emotions of the viewer at the sight of the three main parts of the icon, the epigrams not only clarify the visual language, but also increase its effect and even generate emotions themselves.

The importance of texts for interpretation of images and of the emotional response of the beholder has recently been illustrated by Anna Sitz, who drew attention to the late ninth- or early tenth-century apse decoration of Pancarlık Kilise near Ürgüp in Cappadocia, which features a representation of Christ in glory. The base of Christ's throne bears an inscription stating: μικρὸς ὁ τύπος· μέγας ὁ φόβος· ὁρῶν τὸν τύπον, τίμα τὸν τόπον ('Small is the image, great is the fear; seeing the image, honour the place').[54] Sitz compared this epigraph to inscriptions found in two other churches in Cappadocia – a funerary chapel now known as the Eğri Taş Kilisesi in the Ihlara Valley, dated to 921-7, and the Bezirhane Kilisesi in Avcılar, only a few kilometres from Pancarlık, from the tenth or eleventh century. Both inscriptions accompany a cross and contain the same text: ὁρῶν τὸν τύπον, τίμα τὸν τόπον· μικρὸς ὁ τύπος μεγάλη δόξα· διὰ τοῦ τύπου τούτου σῴζεται κόσμος ('Seeing the image, honour the place; small is the image, great is the glory. Through this image the world is saved').[55] On the assumption that these two inscriptions are rooted in a local, oral tradition, Sitz explains the transformations undertaken in the Pancarlık epigraph as an attempt to intensify the impact on the viewer, which she identifies as 'great fear'. The emotional response is additionally enhanced by the portrayal of Christ in glory instead of the Cross, and by the fact that both inscription and image are experienced in an architectural setting.[56]

15.7. The depiction of the Last Judgement in an architectural setting

A similar escalation in the experience of the beholder characterizes the composition of the Last Judgement as well, when it is depicted in a three-dimensional space. Three examples of the Last Judgement in its usual architectural setting will be briefly discussed to illustrate this.

As a starting point we shall take the already discussed eleventh-century mosaic in the Cathedral of Santa Maria Assunta in Torcello. This extends over the west wall of the basilica, below the images of the Crucifixion and the Anastasis (Fig. 15.1). Whereas for a variety of reasons the west wall of churches was very often decorated with the composition of the Last Judgement, the decision in this

---

[54] On the inscription with different readings, Sitz (2017) 23, figs 1-3.

[55] On the inscriptions with different readings, Sitz (2017) 25-6, figs 15-16.

[56] Sitz (2017); cf. the fear evoked by the image of Christ in the dome of Panagia Theotokos church in Trikomo, Cyprus, in interconnection with inscription and architectural setting. See Binning (2018).

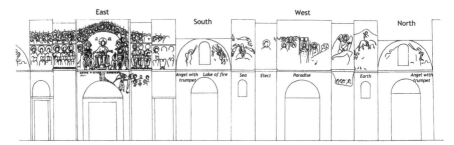

Figure 15.7. Church of Panagia ton Chalkeon, Thessaloniki, shortly after 1028, drawing of the disposition of the Last Judgement in the narthex. After Papadopoulos (1966) drawing 5, with modifications by the author.

case was additionally affected by the door at the end of the vertical axis leading into the baptistery.[57] According to Anna Kartsonis, the scenes represented above the door allude to 'the process and aims of baptism by illustrating the events typified by it. Here the Crucifixion illustrates the cause and the Anastasis, together with the Last Judgment, the result.'[58] Noticeable in this context is the disposition of the contrasting representations of rewards in paradise and punishments in hell on either side of the door. These are the only images placed on the beholder's eye level, inviting him or her to make the choice – eternal blessing through baptism or eternal punishments in the dark caves of the sinners.

In the church of Panagia ton Chalkeon in Thessaloniki the Last Judgement, painted shortly after 1028, decorates the narthex (Fig. 15.7). This architectural unit connects the outside secular world with the naos, which is designated symbolically as heaven on earth. The narthex is the most visited place of a church and has a variety of functions, both liturgical and practical. For many reasons, the narthex became the usual architectural unit for the depiction of the Last Judgement, whose set of paintings reminds the faithful of the transience of all earthly things and prepares them for the experience of the sacred space of the naos. In Panagia ton Chalkeon the faithful who enter the narthex from the outside world first confront the judging Christ with his tribunal and heavenly court. The fiery river flows down over the central arch and the sinners are pushed into it by an angel. The inscription over the arch, quoting Matthew 25:34, is merciless: 'Depart from me, ye cursed, into the everlasting fire prepared for the devil and the angels.'

In contrast, as the faithful come from the naos, where they have experienced the sacred, and as they are about to leave the church, they encounter the representation of paradise over the exit. The images of trumpeting angels in

---

[57] Esp. Kartsonis (1986) 159–61, 221–3.
[58] Kartsonis (1986) 222.

the south and north lunettes function as a link between the representations of the east and west parts.[59] In this way, when entering the church, the faithful are gripped by fear at the sight of the judging tribunal and of hell, but leave it full of hope for eternity.

In Kariye Camii in Istanbul, the former main church of the Chora monastery, the Last Judgement was assigned to the *parekklēsion*. This was built between 1316 and 1321 to the south of the church in order to serve as the mortuary chapel of the donor, Theodore Metochites, and his associates (Fig. 15.8).[60] Due to its eschatological significance the Last Judgement was especially appropriate for the decoration of spaces with funerary function. In the particular case of the *parekklēsion* at Chora its scenes and elements are spread over the domical vault and its pendentives and lunettes of the eastern bay in close thematic relationship to the redemptive scenes of Anastasis and two resurrection miracles of Christ in the conch of the apse and the arch of the bema.[61] Paul Underwood considers the composition to be unique because it masterfully uses the domical vault to depict 'the celestial character of the apparition of "the Son of man in heaven"', thus converting it into a 'dome of heaven'.[62] Instead, the pendentives and lunettes are used to depict the scenes and elements that are not directly connected to the vision of the Second Coming (such as the land and sea giving up their dead, Lazarus in Abraham's bosom and the Rich Man in hell, the torments of the damned and the elect in paradise). Striking in this context is the fact that the representation of the torments of the damned in hell in the eastern half of the southern lunette takes relatively little space in comparison to the scene in paradise which spreads over the entire opposite lunette.[63] Furthermore, due to the existence of a window next to the torments their image is dim and hardly visible, whereas the paradise is suffused with light by this same window. In this way more emphasis is laid on the rewards of the elect in a way that is closely connected to the primary aim of the iconographic programme – to give hope of salvation to the deceased donor and his associates buried in the *arcosolia* tombs along the lateral walls, who thus became part of the depicted events.[64]

---

[59] Papadopoulos (1966) 57–70; Brenk (1966) 82–4; Baun (2007) 156–62.

[60] The frescoes of the *parekklēsion* are regarded as one of the latest stages in the decoration of the church, executed in 1320–1 after the mosaics of the naos and the narthexes: Underwood (1966) 15–16, 188; Der Nersessian (1975) 305.

[61] On the Last Judgement as part of the decorative programme of the *parekklēsion*, see Underwood (1966) 187–212; Der Nersessian (1975) 305–49; Ousterhout (1995); (2002) 70–88, 110–17; on the interplay of the iconographic programme and the ritual function of the *parekklēsion*, see Akyürek (2001).

[62] Underwood (1966) 200–1. See also Ousterhout (1995) 72; (2002) 113. A further allusion to the idea that the events are taking place in heaven is made by the clouds that support the choirs of the elect: Der Nersessian (1975) 327.

[63] Der Nersessian (1975) 331.

[64] Ousterhout (1995) 72–5; (2002) 114–17.

Figure 15.8. Parekklesion of the Chora monastery (Kariye Camii), Istanbul, 1316–21, view to the east: Anastasis in the apse and scenes of the Last Judgement spread over the domical vault, pendentives, and lunettes of the eastern bay. Photo: author.

15.8. Donor portraits connected to the image of the Last Judgement

Such participation is very often realized by placing donor portraits in close proximity to the image of the Last Judgement as, for example, in the church of Panagia Phorbiotissa in Asinou on Cyprus, where about ten donors – monks and laypersons – are depicted in the narthex underneath the composition of the Last Judgement, which dates from the fourteenth century (Fig. 15.9). Strikingly enough, monks – with only one exception – take pride of place close to the Virgin Phorbiotissa and the *deēsis* on the east wall and to the area of the elect in the northern part of the narthex, while laypersons are depicted in the southern part, which contains the scenes of the damned. However, the laypersons enjoy protection, as they stand next to their patron saints with arms raised in prayer; the female donors are even depicted within the frame of the saint.[65] Such a treatment clearly reflects the emotional perception of the images by the donor – fear of the proximity of hell and desire to reach paradise. This attitude finds its visual culmination in two miniatures – one from the eleventh century on fol. 93[v] of the Gospel book (cod. gr. 74) in the Bibliothèque nationale in Paris, and the other from the fourteenth century on fol. 124[r] of the Gospels of Tsar Ivan Alexander (BL Add. 39627) in the British Library in London (Fig. 15.10) – where the figures of contemporary persons are boldly placed within the representation of paradise – in the first case a group of monks and the abbot of the monastery where the manuscript was produced, and in the second the ruler of Bulgaria, Tsar Ivan Alexander, who commissioned the book.[66]

That the representation of human portraits close to or within images was meant to depict the emotional response of the viewers to them finds confirmation in an epigram written to accompany the portrait of a certain Basil Serblias that was painted on the reverse of an icon of Christ Peribleptos. As the verses make clear, the donor's reason for depicting himself on the back was fear even at the sight of the image of Christ:

> ὃν γὰρ Χερουβὶμ οὐ στέγοντα προσβλέπειν
> πρόσωπον κρύπτει τοῖς πτέρυξιν ἐν τρόμῳ,
> πῶς οὐχ ὁρᾶν ἂν καὶ γεγραμμένος τρέμω;
> ὀπισθογραφῶν τοιγαροῦν μου τὸν τύπον
> κἂν τῇ γραφῇ σήμαντρα τοῦ φόβου φέρω.

How would I not tremble, even as a depiction, while gazing at the One upon whom the cherubim do not dare to look, but hide their faces with their wings in terror? Therefore, by painting my portrait on the back, I express my fear as well in the picture.[67]

---

[65] Kalopissi-Verti (2012) 179–90, esp. 180.
[66] Ševčenko (2009) 262–4, figs 14.4, 14.6.
[67] *Anthologia Marciana*, no. 219 (B56), Greek text and trans. after Drpić (2016) 375–7.

Figure 15.9. Church of Panagia Phorbiotissa, Asinou, Cyprus, narthex, fourteenth century, donor portraits underneath the Last Judgement. Photo: author.

НАНОУАСѢ · НИКѢТОЖЕНЕВѢСТѢ · ННАПѤ
ЛНИЖЕСѪТѢНАНБСЕХѢ · НИСНѢТѢ
КЛЮШЦѢ · БЛНДѢТЕСАНБДНТЕ·НАНО
ЛНТЕА · НЕВѢѢСТЕБСОКОГДАВРѢ АЛАНРІ
НДЕТѢ :

ρме

Figure 15.10. Gospels of Tsar Ivan Alexander (BL Add. 39627), British Library, London, fourteenth century, fol. 124ʳ: Last Judgement; Tsar Ivan Alexander is represented in the Paradise. Shivkova (1977) pl. XXVII, p. 124, fig. 155.

406 *Galina Fingarova*

This explanation reminds us of the epigram written by Maximus Planudes to accompany the punishments of the sinners in hell, which says that 'even the ones painted on panels terrify' the viewer, as well as of texts from the eighth and ninth century that tell of conversion to Christianity because of fear at the sight of an image of the Last Judgement.

Conclusion

In all probability, the way the Byzantines experienced the visual was different from our own[68] – we are not gripped by fear at the sight of the judging Christ or the torments in hell; to us the intended impact of the image of the Last Judgement is fully comprehensible only in connection with the texts. But can we trust the texts? Leslie Brubaker gives a positive answer to this question.[69] She argues that the viewer's emotional response to images gained increasing significance in texts of the ninth century. Between the fourth and the ninth centuries a process of transformation in the Byzantine perception of the visual took place which culminated in the debates concerning images and their relationship to texts during the Iconoclastic controversy. The perception of the images was highly affected by the concept of the Iconophiles who emerged as winners from the debates: they point to the equality and even to the superiority of images over texts and use them to authenticate and identify the historical truth of the latter. This status was credited to images by virtue of their ability to evoke emotions, a case in point being the opening paragraphs of the Council of 787, which justify the sanctity of images with reference to the tears they induce in the viewer.[70] This concept is best reflected in the image of the Last Judgement, which, starting in the eighth or ninth century, developed as a tool *par excellence* to evoke fear in the viewer; this emotional aspect was enhanced in a variety of ways in order to reveal the way to salvation.

---

[68] Emphasized by Brubaker (1989a) 19–20.
[69] Brubaker (1989a), (1989b).
[70] Mansi (1759–98), vol. 13, pp. 9, 12, 32; see also Brubaker (1989a) 25.

16

The Terrible Power in Giving Birth

Images of Motherhood from Antiquity to Byzantium

Viktoria Räuchle

Introduction

In Modern Western culture, the love of a mother is regarded as a natural imperative: innate, insuperable, and inextricably linked to the body. Deeply rooted in the nature/culture dichotomy, the conception of maternal love as a pre-discursive elemental law has shaped the cultural ideals of motherhood and therefore also their artistic representations. In literature and visual arts alike, the perfect mother–child relation is characterized by physical intimacy and closeness. The act of breastfeeding in particular epitomizes good (i. e. devoted and selfless) maternal behaviour.[1] The nexus between female corporeality and maternal affection can also be found in ancient discourses: numerous sources from the Classical to the early Christian period (and beyond) suggest that maternal affection stems from the maternal body and its reproductive functions. However, this basic idea of a natural maternal disposition does not automatically entail the same ideals of motherhood and maternal emotionality.

This essay explores the visual codification of motherhood from the Graeco-Roman period to the early Byzantine era. It seeks to elaborate on the questions when and why images (and texts) emphasize the corporeal rather than the sociocultural aspects of motherhood – and whether and how these different modes of representation convey emotional content. In order to tackle these issues without drowning in the ocean of maternal imagery from various periods, contexts, and media, the study will focus on written and visual representations of maternal figures with infants and toddlers.[2] Special emphasis will be laid on the figure type of the so-called kourotrophos ('child-rearer'), which shows a (usually female)

---

[1] On continuities and changes in the image of the ideal mother in (Early) Modern Western cultures see e. g. Badinter (1980); Wilson (1984); Wall (2001); Opitz (2002); Räuchle (2017) 18–20.

[2] Naturally, this focus covers only a fraction of the complex discourses on ideal motherhood and maternal affection. For a more comprehensive study on maternal feeling rules in Classical Athens see Räuchle (2017).

408 *Viktoria Räuchle*

figure holding a child in her arms or on her lap. This extremely long-lasting figure type encompasses an enormous variety of subtypes – from rigidly enthroned, representative goddesses to tenderly breastfeeding mothers – and also occurs in manifold media, settings, and functions, thus allowing for a diachronic survey concerning the interrelation of female physicality and maternal emotionality.

16.1. Framing mothers

The ancient terms *ēthos* and *pathos* will form the conceptual framework for my considerations, for two reasons: first, they refer to internal properties and/or experiences, which are (albeit loosely) associated with the spheres of culture/ mind and nature/body, respectively. Secondly, these concepts can be applied to the representational modes of ancient imagery. *Ēthos* as a philosophical concept is usually translated as 'character' and refers to personal attitudes and behavioural dispositions, be they good or bad. Although rooted in a person's nature, it can be shaped and altered by habituation. It is thus a result of deliberate choices to act in certain ways. Therefore, a person's reputation depends on whether his/her *ēthos* is in accordance with the norms and ideals of the community.[3] Throughout Antiquity and Byzantine times, the ideal of moderation and self-restraint (Greek *sōphrosunē*, Latin *continentia* or *moderatio*) forms an essential element in the conception of good *ēthos*. A key concern in this discourse is the ability to control one's *pathē* ('passions', 'affects', 'emotions').

Apart from the literal translation of *pathos*, 'suffering' or 'experience', there is no clear definition of the term in the ancient writings nor a consistent array of affective phenomena to be categorized as such.[4] However, most ancient authors would agree that the pathē, although largely contingent on judgements and beliefs, have a strong physiological dimension and an aspect of immediacy: they are experienced with and through the body, as acute and often involuntary reactions to internal or external stimuli.[5]

The differentiation of *ēthos* and *pathos* has a long tradition in the interpretation of ancient images.[6] Visual art conveys a figure's *internal* properties (e.g. character traits and emotional states) through *external* schemata (e.g. physiognomy, language, facial expressions, and gestures).[7] Previous studies dif-

---

[3] Cf. Calboli Montefusco (1998) 166.

[4] On ancient definitions and catalogues of emotion see Rapp (2002) 545–52; Krajczynski and Rapp (2009); cf. Konstan (2006b) 3–40.

[5] On embodiment see Cairns, Introduction A and B in this volume.

[6] The distinction can be traced back to as early as the fourth century BC, when the terms are used to discuss the representation of human character and human emotion in works of art: Pollitt (1974) 194–200; cf. Pollitt (1976).

[7] The ancient term *schēma* (lit. 'form', 'shape', but also 'appearance', 'manner', etc.) was introduced by Maria Luisa Catoni as a tool for the analysis of ancient imagery: Catoni (2008).

16. The Terrible Power in Giving Birth 409

ferentiate between calm, restrained schemata, which illustrate a figure's state of mind or character (*ēthos*), and schemata of an intense expressiveness and/ or corporeality, which are associated with involuntary affects or acute emotions (*pathos*).[8] It is widely accepted that the ideal of (emotional) self-restraint traceable in ancient literary discourses also shaped the visual language to a great extent: ancient art has a predilection to convey a figure's *ēthos* rather than their *pathos*.[9]

Of course, there is no clear-cut distinction between schemata of *pathos* and schemata of *ēthos* – just as the underlying concepts are not always easy to discern.[10] Yet the antithesis, simplified though it is, does serve to identify general tendencies in the conception and representation of ideal motherhood and helps trace the seemingly universal interrelation of maternal emotions and the female body through antiquity and early Byzantium

16.2. Greek mothers

In the written sources of Classical Athens, maternal love is perceived as being a law of nature and repeatedly connected to the reproductive functions of the female body: pregnancy, giving birth, and breastfeeding. Amongst the tragic poets of the fifth century BC, it is especially Euripides who frequently exploits maternal *pathos* in order to indulge in the human frailty of his stage characters and thus to intensify the emotional reaction of the audience. His play *Suppliants* is all about the excessive grief of mothers who lost their sons in war, while the chorus of *Phoenician Women* describe their 'childloving' disposition (φιλότε-κνόν) as 'awe-inspiring' or 'terrible' (δεινὸν) and connect it to the pains of labour (αἱ δι' ὠδίνων γοναί).[11] The term δεινόν is also used by Sophocles' Clytaemnestra to deplore the 'terrible power in giving birth', which does not allow her to feel

---

[8] See e.g. Neumann (1965) 106–8; Pollitt (1972) 43–54; Franzoni (2006), esp. 245; Prioux (2011) 142–4. Gerhard Neumann differentiates between momentary, extensive movements, which convey emotions – 'pathetic' gestures – and habitual, contemplative postures that convey a figure's state of character – 'noetic' gestures. Jeremy Pollitt discusses Polygnotus' Ilioupersis and Nekyia, where 'it is clear that some were represented with a calm, contemplative mien in which their ethos was revealed, while others where representations of pathos emanating from suffering'. Claudio Franzoni builds upon Aby Warburg's famous classification of certain emotionally charged visual tropes as '*pathos* formulas' and introduces a second category called '*ēthos* formulas', which translate a figure's character and attitude into bodily schemata.

[9] Franzoni (2006) 63–8; Prioux (2011) 137. The scepticism towards the expression of emotion is particularly apparent in the relatively calm and motionless features predominating in Graeco-Roman and Byzantine imagery. They can be understood as idealized manifestations of actual behavioural norms and display rules. From Classical Antiquity through Byzantine times, visual art primarily communicates via gestures and postures.

[10] For the differentiation of these terms in the Byzantine discourse see MacDougall in this volume.

[11] Trans. Coleridge (1938); Eur. *Phoen.* 355–6: δεινὸν γυναιξὶν αἱ δι' ὠδίνων γοναί, καὶ / φι-λότεκνόν πως πᾶν γυναικεῖον γένος.

hatred towards her offspring.[12] The tragedians repeatedly describe the love of a mother as a powerful force – even or especially in moments where the female protagonist makes decisions that are diametrically opposed to it. In a fragment from the *Erechtheus*, the title character's wife Praxithea reasons over her decision to sacrifice her own daughter in order to save the city of Athens from its demise. In her extensive monologue she leaves no doubt about her deep affection for her child and also alludes several times to the act of giving birth.[13] The programmatic emphasis on Praxithea's maternal instincts intensifies the tragic potential of her action and thus makes her a true heroine, ready to surrender her own interests to those of the community.[14]

Aristotle, too, gives a detailed account of maternal love: in the eighth and ninth books of his *Nicomachean Ethics*, he reflects on the nature of *philia* and repeatedly talks about the love of parents and especially mothers towards their offspring – again linking the maternal emotion to the physical act of giving birth.[15] These statements are not isolated cases, but reflect the general view of the interrelation between female corporeality and maternal affection at that time. The written sources on maternal affection stress its bodily dimension and its uncontrollability, thus not only rooting it in the female nature but also following the stereotype of women as being particularly vulnerable to the power of *pathos*.

Against this background, we would also expect the visual evidence to highlight the corporeal aspects of motherhood and her physical connection with the child, yet here we find a decisively anti-physical characterization of maternity – if any. On Athenian vase paintings of the Classical period, only a few examples of so-called *gynaikōnitis* scenes (idealized depictions of the women's quarters) characterize the lady of the house as a mother through the addition of an infant; it is almost always a nurse or female attendant who carries the child around, while the mother is either paying no attention at all or communicating with it via eye contact and gestures.[16] Instead of emphasizing the natural bond between mother and child, these images stress the social role of mothers. Athenian grave reliefs of the late Classical era usually follow the same model: erected along the streets outside the city walls, these monuments depict the deceased amidst their surviving relatives and thus visualize the family bonds even beyond

---

[12] Trans. Jebb (1894); Soph. *El.* 770–1: δεινὸν τὸ τίκτειν ἐστίν· οὐδὲ γὰρ κακῶς / πάσχοντι μῖσος ὧν τέκη προσγίγνεται.

[13] Eur. fr. 358; 359; 360a.

[14] About two generations later, the Athenian orator Lycurgus quotes Praxithea's statement as an example of exemplary patriotism. See Lycurg. 1, 98–101, esp. 101. On the background story see *LGPN* 2 s. v. Leokrates (3).

[15] Arist. *Eth. Nic.* 1168a24–6: διὰ ταῦτα δὲ καὶ αἱ μητέρες φιλοτεκνότεραι· ἐπιπονωτέρα γὰρ ἡ γέννησις, καὶ μᾶλλον ἴσασιν ὅτι αὑτῶν ('This is why mothers love their children more than fathers, because parenthood costs the mother more trouble (and the mother is more certain that the child is her own)', trans. Rackham (1926)).

[16] On the iconography of early childcare (*trophē*) in Greek vase painting: Lewis (2002) 81–3; Sommer and Sommer (2015) 45–51; Räuchle (2017) 77–98 (with further references).

Figure 16.1. Grave stele of Phylonoe, *ca.* 370–360 BC, Athens NM inv. no. 3790.
Source: Athens, National Archaeological Museum; photo: K. Xenikakis.

death. Several steles characterize the deceased woman as a young mother by adding a swaddled infant to the scene.[17] Again, the infant is usually carried by a nurse while the mother engages with other family members. It therefore serves merely as an attribute to denote the deceased's status as a *gynē*. Only few monuments contain homeopathic doses of maternal affection: on the grave relief of Phylonoe, the deceased woman is depicted elegantly reclining on a chair and gazing at a small infant offered to her by a female companion. While the child leans forward and desperately stretches out its arm towards the mother, she remains in her calm, pensive pose (Fig. 16.1).[18] The emotions are there, hidden in the

---

[17] This figure type denotes the newborn and thus might also be read as a sign that the mother died during (or soon after) giving birth; cf. Räuchle (2017) 102–3, 109–10.

[18] Grave stele of Phylonoe, *ca.* 370–360 BC, Athens NM inv. no. 3790; CAT 2.780; Räuchle (2017) cat. no. G75; Bergemann (1997) cat. no. 123.

412 *Viktoria Räuchle*

dyadic composition, the longing gesture of the child and the maternal gaze – but they are filtered through the behavioural norms and artistic conventions of the time. The deceased's emotional restraint in the image resonates in the accompanying epigram, which praises her moral virtues: 'Here rests Phylonoe, daughter of ..., prudent, reasonable, and gifted with every virtue.'[19] Feeling rules and iconographic tradition work as a double coding of emotion expression.

The physical aspects of motherhood – so often addressed in literary sources – are almost absent in the visual accounts. About a dozen Athenian grave reliefs dating to the late Classical period refer to the grave owner's tragic cause of death in childbirth by subtly alluding to the pains of labour: the deceased mother sits on her stool in a more than usually reclined position, her head sometimes bowed under the strains of giving birth, while a female attendant supports her from the back.[20] Yet another handful of grave steles, all of them non-Athenian, depict women in the act of breastfeeding.[21]

Late Hellenistic funerary art exploits the maternal *pathos* in a slightly more dramatic manner. The painted stele for Hediste from Thessaly dating to the second century BC is a particularly touching funerary monument for a woman, who died in childbirth, as it combines references to parturition *and* breastfeeding (Fig. 16.2).[22] In the painted picture zone, the woman is lying on a bed, with her eyes closed and her breasts exposed, which in this context is a clear sign of her fatal vulnerability. A beardless young man (arguably her husband) watches her from the edge of the bed, while two female attendants appear in the background of the scene, one of them holding an infant in her arms. The grave epigram below the picture frame not only tells the reader that both mother and child died from the hardships of birth but also laments her tragic fate as she should never be able to 'moisten the lips of her new-born child at her breast'.[23] By explicitly referring to

---

[19] *IG* II² 12963 (own translation): ἐνθάδε Φυλονόη κεῖται θυγάτηρ σώφρων, εὐσύνετος, πᾶσαν ἔχο[υσ᾽ ἀρετήν].

[20] For parturition scenes on Athenian grave reliefs of the classical era see Vedder (1988); Catoni (2005); Räuchle (2017) 56–63. Cf. an Athenian votive relief dedicated to a kourotrophic deity on the occasion of a successful delivery, *ca.* 410 BC, New York MMA inv. no. 24.97.92; Reeder (1995) 334–5 no. 103; Dierichs (2002) 86 fig. 47; Vikela (2015) cat. no. Ar15.

[21] For nursing scenes on non-Athenian grave reliefs see Bosnakis (2012). Cf. the dedicatory inscription for a (now lost) bronze statue of Euanthis who was represented with a child on her lap, breastfeeding: marble base belonging to the monument of Protogenes, early third century BC, from Kaunos; Marek (2006) 243–4.

[22] Grave stele of Hediste, *ca.* 200 BC, Volos Archaeological Museum inv. no. L1; Pollitt (1986) 4–5, fig. 3; Vedder (1988) 183–4; Liston and Papadopoulos (2004) 31, fig. 15.

[23] Cf. Peek (1960) 100–1 no. 142: λυπρὸν ἐφ᾽ Ἡδίστηι Μοῖραι τότε νῆμα ἀπ᾽ ἀτράκτων / κλῶσαν, ὅτε ὠδῖνος νύμφη ἀπηντίασεν· / σχετλίη· οὐ γὰρ ἔμελλε τὸ νήπιον ἀνκαλιεῖσθαι / μαστῶι τε ἀρδεύσειν χεῖλος ἑοῖο βρέφους· / ἐν γὰρ ἐσεῖδε φάος, καὶ ἀπήγαγεν εἰς ἕνα τύμβον / τοὺς δισσοὺς ἀκρίτως τοῖσδε μολοῦσα Τύχη ('A painful thread for Hediste did the Fates weave from their spindles when, / as a young wife she came to the throes of childbirth. / Ah wretched one! For it was not fated that she should cradle the infant in / her arms, nor moisten the lips of her new-

Figure 16.2. Grave stele of Hediste, *ca.* 200 BC, Volos Archaeological Museum inv. no. L1. After Arvanitopoulos (1928) pl. II; painting by Emile Gillieron père.

the act of breastfeeding, the epigram conjures the natural bond between mother and child and thus intensifies the emotive power of the monument.

A passage in Pliny's *Natural History* confirms the peculiar affect-enhancing potential of the nursing mother through the description of a painting by Aristides of Thebes, an artist active during the second half of the fourth century BC:

He [Aristides] was the first of all painters who depicted the mind and expressed the feelings of a human being, what the Greeks term *ēthē*, and also the emotions; he was a little too hard in his colours. His works include ... on the capture of a town, showing an

born child at her breast. / One light looks upon both and Fortune has brought both to a single tomb, / making no distinction when she came upon them', trans. Pollitt (1986) 4).

infant creeping to the breast of its mother who is dying of a wound; it is felt that mother is aware of the child and is afraid that as her milk is exhausted by death it may suck blood.[24]

Pliny subsumes *animus* ('mind', 'soul', 'consciousness', etc.) and *sensus* ('feeling', 'sentiment', 'perception', etc.) under the Greek term *ēthos* and separately lists the *perturbationes* ('commotions', 'passions', 'emotions'), the closest equivalent to the Greek *pathē*.[25] The passage thus corroborates the traditional distinction between *ēthos* and *pathos*, but at the same time demonstrates that the dividing line between these concepts in terms of emotional content is often blurred.[26] With regard to the emotive power, on the other hand, Aristides' rendition of the maternal body is nothing but pure *pathos*.[27] According to Erwin Panofsky it is a prime example for 'the rise of that emotional subjectivism and that new emphasis on *pathos*' which constitutes the visual arts during the second half of the fourth century BC.[28]

Literature had discovered the affective radiance of the breastfeeding motif long before: in Homer's *Iliad* (22.82–6), Hecuba sheds tears, loosens the folds of her robe and shows her bare breast to her adult son Hector in order to convince him to stay away from the deadly battlefield. Euripides' Andromache utters similar laments when she faces the impending death of her beloved son, Astyanax (cf. Euripides, *Trojan Women* 758–9). In these cases, the juxtaposition with the life-giving act of lactation enhances the traumatic effect of the child's imminent death and thereby evokes sympathy in the audience.[29] Although or perhaps precisely because the breastfeeding motif is so strongly associated with maternal *pathos*, it is rarely used to characterize an ideal mortal woman in her maternal qualities, but first and foremost serves as a rhetorical device to amplify the emotional experience of the recipient.[30]

---

[24] Trans. Rackham (1984); Plin. *HN* 35.98: 'is omnium primus animum pinxit et sensus hominis expressit, quae vocant graeci ἤθη, item perturbationes, durior paulo in coloribus. huius opera ... oppido capto ad matris morientis ex volnere mammam adrepens infans, intelligiturque sentire mater et timere, ne emortuo e lacte sanguinem lambat.' Cf. Füssli and Füssli (1810) 28; Prioux (2011) 156.

[25] Pollitt (1972) 44.

[26] Cf. Prioux (2011) 156: 'Of course, such a topic clearly involved pathos but also characterization: Pliny remarks that the dying mother seems to perceive her baby's attempt to drink and appears to fear that she provides him with blood instead of milk. Motherly instinct is thus preserved at the doorsteps of death and gives rise to a specific fear.'

[27] On the dying or dead mother as a Pathosformel in the Warburgian sense from Aristides to modern art: Schütze (2002–3); Frank (2018).

[28] Panofsky (1960) 115.

[29] Even mothers who face their own death can invoke the selfless act of breastfeeding in order to escape their fatal lot. See Aesch. *Cho.* 896–8, cf. 527–34.

[30] On the maternal breast as a harbinger of tragic events see Bonfante (1997) 175: 'The horror to come is underscored by the private, moving scene of the mother nursing the child, an image of vulnerability not normally shown, and therefore special'; cf. Salzman-Mitchell (2012), esp. 158; Räuchle (2017) 73–4.

16. The Terrible Power in Giving Birth

Figure 16.3. Terracotta statuette of kourotrophic deity, fifth century BC, Berlin SMPK inv. no. TC 5891. Source: Munich, Museum für Abgüsse Klassischer Bildwerke, Photothek.

Even in the context of religion and cultic veneration, the (mainland) Greeks were hesitant to include the image of nursing in their repertoire. Terracotta statuettes of divine kourotrophoi usually take on the form of a standing or sitting woman holding an infant in her arms; but unlike the examples from Italy and Magna Graecia, which we will address in a moment, these divine caretakers from mainland Greece rarely nurture their fosterlings (Fig. 16.3).[31] Since even male

---

[31] Terracotta statuette of a divine kourotrophos (possibly Eileithyia) holding a child in her right arm, fifth century BC, from Athens, Berlin SMPK inv. no. TC 5891; Winter (1903) 76, no. 1; 144, no. 5; Hadzisteliou Price (1978) 56, no. 623, fig. 46. For Greek kourotrophos types: Winter (1903) 139–55; Hadzisteliou Price (1978), esp. 32–3 cat. nos 232–7.

416   *Viktoria Räuchle*

figures and animals can appear as kourotrophoi, these statuettes do not embody the maternal principle in its biological aspects but the sociocultural dimension of childcare.[32] Kourotrophic terracotta figurines were often dedicated by mothers and families to divinities concerned with birth and child-rearing. Ironically, Artemis and Eileithyia, two virgins who had never experienced motherhood themselves, were among the most important kourotrophic deities to be invoked for a happy delivery, a healthy baby, or a safe upbringing. This reluctance to stress the corporeal aspects of maternity in their divine and mythological caretakers is deeply rooted in the Greek conception of their pantheon: 'The gods are aristocratic, civilized – they hand their divine babies over to nurses of a lower social order than their goddess mothers.'[33] The social role in upbringing was thus completely detached from the natural role in procreation.

So, although the written accounts leave no doubt that maternal affection was perceived as a natural quality connected to the reproductive functions of the female body, the Athenian community did not perceive their ideal woman as a mere 'creature of instinct'. On the contrary, the desirable maternal disposition was conveyed through calm gestures and postures as well as a rather distant attitude towards the child: a well-tempered affection, shaped according to the feeling rules of Classical Greek society and filtered through artistic conventions. The representation of maternal physicality, on the other hand, had an affect-enhancing quality of alarming intensity and vehemence and was therefore primarily implemented as an emotive device. This is not to say that the reproductive power of the female body was perceived as negative per se – it was considered as a law of nature after all. But its uninhibited expression resided at the limits of appropriateness and thus implied the notion of transgression.

16.3. Etrusco-Roman mothers

While the pictorial traditions and strategies in Greece favour the role of women as socializing figures over their biological properties, the Etruscan and Italic traditions take a different approach by idolizing the maternal body and worshiping Great Goddesses. This finds its most apparent iconographic manifestation in the corpulent kourotrophos types predominant in Italy and Sicily from the eighth century BC onwards. As in the case of Greek kourotrophoi, these figures are not necessarily congruent with a biological mother but first and foremost have to be understood as divine nurturers. But unlike their Greek counterparts, the Italian ones are often shown breastfeeding and thus emphasize the

---

[32] On male and zoomorphic kourotrophoi: Hadzisteliou Price (1978) 71–7.
[33] Bonfante (1997) 185.

16. The Terrible Power in Giving Birth   417

Figure 16.4. Limestone statue of a female figure nursing twins, mid-sixth century BC, Syracuse Museo Nazionale Paolo Orsi inv. no. 53524. Photo: T. Keßler.

reproductive functions of the female body.[34] Even the Greek settlers in Sicily and Southern Italy could not escape the power of these nurturing creatures and incorporated them in their imagery. A limestone statue found in the necropolis of Megara Hyblaea and dated to the mid-sixth century BC shows a majestically

---

[34] Cf. Bonfante (1997) 185: 'The [nursing] motif appears on cult statues, votive statuettes, funerary images, bronze instruments, and horse trappings; on objects dating from the eighth century to the first century BC and beyond; on monuments from Etruria, Latium, Sicily, Magna Graecia, and other regions of Italy, where different languages were spoken, but where Great Goddesses were worshipped.' On the Italian kourotrophoi see Hadzisteliou Price (1978) 166–86; Bonfante (1989); (1997) 177–84; (2013) 436–9.

418   *Viktoria Räuchle*

enthroned, full-bodied woman nursing two babies (Fig. 16.4).[35] Her maternal corporeality becomes particularly apparent through the large breasts that bulge out from the slits in her dress. In the cultural context of (Southern) Italy, the kourotrophos represents the archetype of the life-giving female. Furthermore, the motif of breastfeeding alludes to the apotropaic functions of maternal milk within the magico-religious framework of fertility cults.[36] In this respect, the (Southern) Italian religion and ritual practices differ significantly from those in Greece.[37]

The cultic veneration of the maternal principle and the strong focus on its physical aspects survived well into the religious imagery (and ritual practices) of Republican and Imperial Rome. The Italic goddesses were granted a seat in the Roman pantheon, which was now and again complemented by imported newcomers from the East – for example the Egyptian goddess Isis, who was venerated throughout the Empire in her role as divine nurturer.[38] Especially during the Augustan period, the divine circle was enlarged by creating new personifications.[39] One of the most famous examples can be found on the so-called Tellus panel from the Ara Pacis Augustae, which shows a female divinity (her identity is debated) sitting amidst a scenery abundant with visual codes for fertility and prosperity.[40] She is not breastfeeding but the allusion is clearly made by the position of the two infants longing for her breasts, which are additionally emphasized by the suggestive draping of her dress. Although now rendered in the sublime style of Classical Greece, these deities maintained their decisively corporeal qualities.[41] By combining attributes and symbols of various mother goddesses, the figure presents a prime example of the eclectic, at times formulistic iconography of the new deities who entered Roman religion in early Imperi-

---

[35] Limestone statue of a female figure nursing twins, mid-sixth century BC, from the necropolis at Megara Hyblaea, Syracuse Museo Nazionale Paolo Orsi inv. no. 53524; Bonfante (1989) 87 pl. XXXV; Shepherd (2012) 215–16, fig. 16.1. On the iconography cf. Ridgway (1977) 135: 'The figure is so different from any Greek work that it must represent indigenous art.' Ross Holloway suggests that the statue group might represent Night with the twins Sleep and Death in her arms; see Holloway (1991) 82–3. However, the function of this and similar statues as well as the identity of the female figure remain disputed; see Shepherd (2012) 16–17.

[36] Bonfante (1997) 187.

[37] Bonfante (2013) 437: 'The importance in Italy in the art of all periods of the figure of the female kourotrophos contrasts with its absence in the official religion of the Greeks ... and its occurrence in Italy constitutes the most visible and remarkable difference between this imagery and that of mainland Greece.'

[38] For the imagery of Isis lactans see Tran Tam Tinh (1973). Augustus never included Oriental gods such as Isis and Magna Mater in his official state religion: see Zanker (1990) 114–15.

[39] Zanker (1990) 178. On the Roman practice of translating abstract concepts and political principles into personifications, allegories, and symbols see Hölscher (1980) 273–9.

[40] So-called Tellus panel, east front of the outer face of the Ara Pacis Augustae, 13–9 BC, Rome; Zanker (1990) 175, fig. 135; Pollini (2012) 232, fig. V. 22.

[41] As Larissa Bonfante aptly notes, this life-giving goddess 'belongs in the context of Italian art, though expressed in a Greek style and form'; see Bonfante (1997) 183.

16. The Terrible Power in Giving Birth   419

al times.[42] Whoever she may be, this kourotrophic deity does not convey ideas about maternal love and devotion but serves as an allegory for fertility and prosperity visualizing the *beneficia* of Augustus, the Golden Age of the Pax Romana.

Besides maternal goddesses and divine nurturers, only barbarian women and servants are regularly portrayed in schemata of unvarnished maternal corporeality. A statue group found near San Lorenzo in Rome, completely indebted to the Greek tradition and probably belonging to a victory monument from the second century BC, depicts a foreign woman clad in a simple dress taking care of two children, one of whom is greedily sucking milk from her exposed breast.[43] Thanks to iconographic parallels with terracotta statuettes of foreign nurses, it is safe to say that this is not a 'civilized' mother watching over her children: she is either a female servant tending her mistress's offspring or a barbarian mother showcasing her primitive nature.[44] On the column of Marcus Aurelius featuring the emperor's victory over the Dacians, one scene shows a line of women who are again characterized as barbarians by deviant physiognomies, dishevelled hair, foreign dresses, expressive gestures, and not least an extreme physical closeness to their children.[45] The emphasis on the women's maternal qualities is just one of many pictorial strategies to depict them as victims of their own passions and thus to mark them 'as socially, politically, and legally deficient'.[46]

Images of Roman women, on the other hand, usually avoid these unrestrained schemata of pathos in favour of a more decorous characterization. Most honorific and funerary statues for women stress their status as matrons rather than their role as caring mothers. This can be exemplified by a funerary statue of a Roman matron with her little daughter from the late Republican period (Fig. 16.5).[47] Lacking any interaction with her child, the mother gazes to her right while elegantly raising her left hand to the neckline. With her voluminous mantle tightly wrapped around the body and pulled over the back of her head, she is represented in the Pudicitia type – a schema designed to praise a woman's chastity and ethical behaviour.[48] The little girl, too, has decently covered her body

---

[42] Cf. Zanker (1990) 172–7.

[43] Statue group of woman with two children, second century BC, Rome Centrale Montemartini inv. no. 1712; Bertoletti et al. (1999) 48; Bertoletti et al. (2006) 31, fig. 21.

[44] A barbarian woman nursing her infant might have been among the group of dying Gauls in the Greater Attalid Dedication; see Coarelli (1995); Prioux (2011) 168 n. 60. Cf. Plin. *HN* 35.98 for a similar topic.

[45] Scene CIV, column of Marcus Aurelius, Rome, AD 176–92; Diddle Uzzi (2007) 65–6, fig. 3.3; Beckmann (2011) 19–36.

[46] Diddle Uzzi (2007) 79. On stylistic, formal, and iconographic elements as a means of social distinction see Hölscher (1987), esp. 58.

[47] Statue group of mother and daughter, mid-first century BC, Rome Musei Capitolini inv. no. 2176; Fittschen and Zanker (1983) no. 42, pl. 54. The matron's head rotation suggests that the statue group was paired up with a togatus (Fittschen and Zanker (1983) 39); the ensemble most probably served as a funerary monument for a Roman family.

[48] On the semantics of the Pudicitia see Alexandridis (2004) 60–1.

Figure 16.5. Statue group of mother and daughter, mid-first century BC, Rome Musei Capitolini inv. no. 2176. Source: DAI Rome, neg. no. 2001.2102, http://arachne.uni-koeln.de/item/marbilder/7240385 (accessed 6 August 2021).

and displays a modest demeanour, with her arms close to the body and a slightly bowed head. The dresses and postures of mother and daughter can be interpreted as schemata of *ēthos*, as signifiers for female virtues. Similar tendencies can be found in Republican laudations and Imperial grave inscriptions: here, women are primarily honoured for their *pudicitia* ('modesty'), *castitas* ('chastity'), *pietas* ('prudence'), *gravitas* ('dignity'), *pulchritudo* ('beauty'), *modestia* ('humility'), and *fides* ('fidelity') to name just a few.[49] The mention of *fecunditas*

---

[49] Von Hesberg-Tonn (1983) 212–37; Alexandridis (2004) 14, 29–31; Murer (2017) 8.

Figure 16.6. Roman child sarcophagus of the late Antonine period, Rome Villa Doria Pamphili. Source: DAI Rome, neg. no. 8332, http://arachne.uni-koeln.de/item/marbilder /3791742 (accessed 6 August 2021).

('fertility') often complements but is never prioritized over the catalogue of virtues just cited.[50]

Starting in the late second century, a few images from a more 'private' sphere convey the notion of mother–child bonding through enhanced physicality. On a child sarcophagus at the Villa Doria Pamphili in Rome, a nursing scene is placed in the centre of the main side (Fig. 16.6).[51] Although the identity of the breastfeeding woman is not entirely certain, her noble features, fine dress, and not least her prominent position justify interpreting her as the mother.[52] The rendition of the motif differs drastically from representations of divine nurses in that it puts the nursing woman in a setting of 'everyday life' and further emphasizes the close bond between her and the child through eye contact and gentle gestures. This development towards a slightly more physical *and* emotional iconography of motherhood seems to have resonated with the taste of early Christians in Rome, too: A mid-third-century wall painting in the Priscilla catacomb shows a woman gently cradling a child, with a bearded man pointing to a star. It is traditionally interpreted as the earliest representation of Mary

---

[50] Cf. Alexandridis (2004) 30.

[51] Roman child sarcophagus, late Antonine period, Villa Doria Pamphili; Amedick (1991) cat. no. 236, pl. 55.2; Huskinson (1996) cat. no. 1.33; Dimas (1998) cat. no. 394, pl. 2.3.

[52] This interpretation is also supported by a similar scene on the sarcophagus of Marcus Cornelius Statius, where the breastfeeding woman's head is executed as a portrait and thus leaves no doubt that it is indeed the mother herself who nourishes the child: Roman child sarcophagus, ca. AD 150, Paris Louvre inv. no. Ma 659; Amedick (1991) cat. no. 114; Huskinson (1996) cat. no. 1.23; Dimas (1998) cat. no. 386. Inscription on lower rim of the coffin: M(arco) CORNELIO M(arci) F(ilio) PAL(atina tribu) STATIO ....FECER(unt)....

422 *Viktoria Räuchle*

holding Christ, probably in the presence of a prophet (Fig. 16.7).[53] While later representations from the fourth century onwards emphasize the queen-like status of Mary, by showing an enthroned lady holding a rigidly sitting boy on her lap, the scene stresses the close physical and emotional bond between mother and child: although the woman's breast is covered by her dress, the infant's position and gestures clearly evoke the act of nursing.[54]

At least for the Roman upper class, there is ample evidence that mothers delegated the task of breastfeeding to wet nurses. As in Classical Greece, early childcare was outsourced to professional caretakers and female household slaves, while mothers started to play a substantial role in their children's upbringing only in later years.[55] The prevalence of the practiceof wet-nursing is apparent in a number of advisory texts but also in some authors harshly criticizing it as going against norm and nature.[56] Gellius, for instance, passes down the radical position of the philosopher Favorinus:

> For what kind of unnatural, imperfect and half-motherhood is it to bear a child and at once send it away from her? To have nourished in her womb with her own blood something which she could not see, and not to feed with her own milk what she sees, now alive, now human, now calling for a mother's care? (Gell. *NA* 12.1, trans. Rolfe (1927))

The Platonist Plutarch, too, seems to be a keen advocate for mothers breastfeeding their children themselves when he points out that mothers would 'feed (their children) with livelier affection and greater care', while nurses would only 'love for pay'.[57] The nexus between the bodily aspects of motherhood (i. e. giving birth and lactation) and maternal love is already attested in the Greek sources; what is new, however, is the resulting moral (and natural!) obligation for mothers to breastfeed.

Despite this 'pro-lactation' discourse of male moralists, representations of tenderly caring mothers remained the exception from the rule. While the nursing motif only appears twice on *Vita Romana* sarcophagi for children, the more

---

[53] Wall painting with nursing mother, Cripta della Madonna, Priscilla catacomb, Rome, mid-third century AD; Paterson Corrington (1989) 411, pl. 6 (above); Bisconti (1996); Dresken-Weiland (2012) 210. Contrast Parlby (2008) 48, who has challenged the interpretation as Mary and Christ and suggests that the scene 'may be nothing more than a poignant funerary portrait of a dead mother and child'.

[54] Bisconti (2006) 31 correctly observes that the iconography of the *virgo lactans* stands in the tradition of earlier (and contemporary) pagan imagery yet he overrates the prevalence of the breastfeeding motif in scenes of everyday life.

[55] Cf. Dixon (1988), esp. 120–35; Dasen (2010) 307–10.

[56] For the choice of a wet nurse see Sor. *Gyn.* 2.32; Oreib. 32.5–7. Further passages are listed in: Braams (1913); Dixon (1988), esp. 120–9; Pedrucci (2013) 240–8; (2015) 37–43.

[57] Trans. Babbitt (1927); Plut. *Mor.* 3c (*De lib. educ.* 5): περὶ δὲ τροφῆς ἐχόμενον ἂν εἴν λέγειν. δεῖ δέ, ὡς ἐγὼ ἂν φαίην, αὐτὰς τὰς μητέρας τὰ τέκνα τρέφειν καὶ τούτοις τοὺς μαστοὺς ὑπέχειν. συμπαθέστερόν τε γὰρ θρέφουσι καὶ διὰ πλείονος ἐπιμελείας, ὡς ἂν ἔνδοθεν καὶ τὸ δὴ λεγόμενον ἐξ ὀνύχων ἀγαπῶσαι τὰ τέκνα. αἱ τίτθαι δὲ καὶ αἱ τροφοὶ τὴν εὔνοιαν ὑποβολιμαίαν καὶ παρέγγραπτον ἔχουσιν, ἅτε μισθοῦ φιλοῦσαι.

Figure 16.7. Wall painting with nursing mother, mid-third century, Rome Priscilla catacomb. After Wilpert (1903) pl. 22.

canonical scene to document the earliest stage of life is the infant's first bath, as is shown, for instance, on the left side of the above-mentioned sarcophagus at the Villa Doria Pamphili (Fig. 16.6).[58] The interpretation of this motif as a visual marker for 'birth' is justified by a closer look at the figure of the mother: slightly leaning back on a simple stool and supporting herself with her right arm, she assumes a posture similar to those in Greek images of parturient women. The act of birthing is again implied in an idealized form and thus adapted to the cultural norms of moderation and restraint.[59] Besides this subtle reference to maternal physicality, the scene first and foremost captures the matron's privileged position in the domestic hierarchy: the nurse, characterized by coarse features and a simple dress, bends forward to lift the newborn out of the bathing tub; the boy stretches out his arms towards his mother, who makes no effort to return his signs of affection. The composition thus follows the general pattern of early childcare we already observed in Greek images.[60] This ideal of maternal countenance is also well attested in the written sources: instead of indulging in her natural inclination to maternal affects, the exemplary matron was expected to display emotional self-restraint by assuming a stern, ethical attitude towards her children.[61]

In conclusion, the imagery of the Republican and Imperial period reveals certain contradictions with regard to ideal motherhood and its connection to *pathos* and *ēthos*: in the religious sphere, the Romans continue to worship the maternal principle in the shape of Great Goddesses and divine nursing figures, thus venerating the life-giving powers of the female body. In the iconography of Roman matrons, however, maternal qualities only play a subordinate role in the symphony of female virtues. They are rarely characterized as caring mothers, let alone as mothers offering their breast in an act of selfless devotion, but instead are portrayed as moral role models.

---

[58] The motif of the first bath enters Roman art in the first century for the birth of Dionysus; see Bowersock (2012), esp. 4. In early Christian and Byzantine art, it would be adopted for the nativity of Jesus; see Bowersock (2012) 11–12; Moraw (2012) 250–1.

[59] Cf. Schulze (1998) 57. A funerary relief from Ostia depicts the act in all its drastic physicality: the parturient sits on a birthing stool while the midwife crouching on the floor is aiding with delivery. The inscription names the professional midwife Scribonia Attica as the grave owner; terracotta relief, Hadrianic-Antonine period, Ostia Museo Ostiense inv. no. 5204; Kampen (1981) cat. no. 611g.

[60] Consequently, the first bath can also appear on adult sarcophagi to praise a woman; cf. Dimas (1998) 66–7; e.g. lid of the Portonaccio sarcophagus with scenes of a woman's life, ca. AD 290, Rome Palazzo Massimo inv. no. 112327; Amedick (1991) 151, cat. no. 179.

[61] E.g. Tac. *Dial.* 28; cf. Dixon (1988) 131.On tenderness and affection between mother and child in Roman imagery see Huskinson (2010) 535–6.

16. The Terrible Power in Giving Birth

16.4. Early Christian mothers (of God)

In the early Christian and Byzantine periods, it becomes increasingly difficult to trace iconographic traditions, as visual art takes a deliberately anti-Classical path in its formal, rigid style and its renunciation of a 'naturalistic' body concept. Furthermore, while many visual motifs and themes are clearly adopted from ancient iconography, their semantic content is often transformed and charged with religious symbolism containing various layers of meaning – a development that Jaś Elsner has aptly termed a transformation 'from literal to symbolic'.[62] Thirdly, the functions and purposes of maternal images (and visual media in general), as well as their context of reception, change drastically: the lion's share of maternal images feature the Mother of God herself; mortal women, in contrast, are rarely depicted as mothers holding their children.[63] These changes in terms of style, vocabulary, and function often make it difficult to keep an eye on potential continuities when it comes to the characterization of motherhood.

The motif of Maria lactans ('nursing Mary') or the Galaktotrophousa ('she who nourishes with milk') as she is called in the East, only plays a minor role in early Christian art. Before the twelfth century, the nursing subject appears almost exclusively in Coptic Egypt,[64] especially in the context of male monasteries.[65] On a wall painting decorating a monk's cell in the friary of St Jeremiah in Saqqara, for instance, the mother sits in frontal position and puts her breast in the mouth of the child, who in turn clasps her wrist in order to pull her closer to its lips (Fig. 16.8).[66] In terms of form and style, the Coptic Galaktotrophousa

---

[62] Elsner (1995) 190.

[63] For images of children (with their mothers) in Byzantium see Hennessy (2008) 83–110. For the iconography of matrons in late antique portraiture see Schade (2003) 95–151.

[64] Apart from the example in the Priscilla catacomb, there is a marble krater with Mary nursing Christ in the presence of the three Magi: Rome Museo delle Terme inv. no. 67629. The dating and provenance of this piece are disputed; Hans-Georg Severin argues that it was created in Constantinople under the reign of Valens or Theodosius I; Severin (1970). Less convincingly, Lucia Langener favours an urban Roman provenance and regards this piece as the 'missing link' between the Alexandrian Isis lactans and the Christian Maria lactans; see Langener (1996) 207–34.

[65] Six of the thirteen representations that Elizabeth Bolman lists in her catalogue of Coptic Galaktotrophousae are preserved on wall paintings in Coptic friaries; five of them can be dated to the sixth and seventh centuries AD and are preserved in monk's cells (monasteries of St Jeremiah in Saqqara and St Apollo in Bawit); the one in the Monastery of the Virgin Mary adorned the *khurus* (chancel) and is of a slightly later date (seventh to tenth century AD); see Bolman (2005) 13 n. 3, nos 4–9. A further five representations appear in illuminated manuscripts created in Coptic *scriptoria*: Bolman (2005) 13 n. 3, nos 10–14. A more comprehensive list (including Late Byzantine representations) is offered by Langener (1996) cat. nos KN 244–50 (for profane representations of nursing women) and KN 251–64 (for sacral representations of the Galaktotrophousa).

[66] Secco wall painting, Cell A, Monastery of St Jeremiah, Saqqara, sixth to seventh century AD, Cairo Coptic Museum inv. no. 8014; Quibell (1908) pl. XL; Bolman (2005) 13 n. 3, no. 4.

Figure 16.8. Wall painting with Galaktotrophousa, sixth to seventh century, Cairo Coptic Museum inv. no. 8014. After Quibell (1908) pl. XLI.

16. The Terrible Power in Giving Birth 427

is the direct descendant of Isis lactans, the Egyptian goddess nourishing the child Horus. It thus forms the 'last in an exceptionally long tradition of similar depictions from Pagan Egypt'.[67]

The strong dependence on pagan practices is particularly obvious in the context of funerary art – to the extent that the identification of the nursing woman is anything but certain: on a grave stele from Fayyum dating to the fourth or fifth century, a female figure sits in frontal position on a folding stool and offers her breast to an infant in her arms (Fig. 16.9).[68] While the relief shows many formal similarities with Graeco-Roman representations of Isis lactans, the divine donor of eternal life, the crosses on both sides of the woman substantiate a Christian context and have led some interpreters to believe that the stele features one of the earliest depictions of the Virgin nursing the Child.[69] However, the stele bears traces of a painted Greek inscription that clearly confirms its function as a tombstone: consisting of the deceased's personal dates and a farewell, it repeats a typical formula already established in funerary epitaphs of the Imperial time and thereby testifies to the syncretic practice in Coptic Egypt of merging pagan and Christian traditions.[70] Against this background, it is more plausible to interpret the image on our stele from Fayyum as a funerary portrait of the deceased woman as a 'Christianized' Isis lactans.[71]

The meaning of the Coptic Galaktotrophousa is hotly debated among scholars. Earlier contributions have interpreted it as a visual sign for maternal devotion and tenderness and, therefore, as a manifestation of Christ's human nature.[72] Elizabeth Bolman dismisses this reading as being obscured by a tendency 'to impose on the pre-modern image associations of mother and child bonding, su-

---

[67] Bolman (2005) 18.

[68] Grave stele from Fayyum, fourth to fifth century AD, Berlin Skulpturensammlung und Museum für Byzantinische Kunst inv. no. 4726; Tran Tam Tinh (1973) pl. 77, fig. 202; Hadzisteliou Price (1978) fig. 26; Paterson Corrington (1989) pl. 5; Langener (1996) cat. no. KN 244; Bolman (2005) 13 n. 3, no. 1. A second limestone stele with a nursing woman presents similar difficulties: Limestone stele with nursing woman, maybe from Fayyum; maybe seventh century AD; Cairo Coptic Museum inv. no. 8006; Bolman (2005) 13 n. 3, no. 2.

[69] See Wessel (1964), (1978); further references in Langener (1996) 153 n. 30.

[70] The inscription on the left side can be reconstructed as: '... 21 (or 41) years old. Nobody is immortal.' On the right side of the figure, there are traces of a 'final greeting': 'Farewell, good woman'; see Effenberger (1977) 163–7. On the epigraphic tradition behind these lines see Lefebvre (1907) *passim*; Effenberger (1977) 165–6.

[71] See Tran Tam Tinh (1973) 45; Effenberger and Severin (1992) 154.

[72] Klaus Wessel even argued for a dyophysite provenance of the Coptic Galaktotrophousa in order to explain the 'strong emphasis on humaneness', Wessel (1964) 234: 'Die sehr starke Betonung des Menschlichen, die sowohl in der Stillung des Kindes wie in dessen spielerischer Zärtlichkeit der Mutter gegenüber zum Ausdruck kommt, läßt sich m. E. nur auf dem Boden dyophysitischen Christentums recht gut verstehen, also als ein hart betonter Ausdruck der Lehre von der vollen Entfaltung der menschlichen Natur in dem Gottmenschen.' See rebuttals in Langener (1996) 148–61; Bolman (2005) *passim*.

Figure 16.9. Nursing mother on a grave stele from Fayyum, fourth to fifth century, Berlin Skulpturensammlung und Museum für Byzantinische Kunst inv. no. 4726. Source: bpk/ Skulpturensammlung und Museum für Byzantinische Kunst, SMB/Antje Voigt.

The Terrible Power in Giving Birth   429

preme maternal responsibility and love'.[73] And indeed, the iconographic origins and display contexts of the early Galaktotrophousa speak in her favour: the image type (and its qualities as an object of devotion) continue the long tradition of Isis lactans, an icon of immortality and resurrection rather than maternal affection. Furthermore, more than half of the images of Mary nursing Christ were found in Coptic friaries most probably adhering to monophysitism, a doctrine that emphasized the divine aspect of Christ's manifestation rather than his human nature.[74] Finally, Byzantine sources on actual rearing practices suggest that the image of a breastfeeding woman did not automatically evoke the association of maternal tenderness and affection. A couple of Egyptian papyri from the early Byzantine period (fourth to seventh century) confirm that, at least in upper-class households, the menial tasks of early childcare, including breastfeeding, were still delegated to professional nurses.[75] Admittedly, other sources suggest that breastfeeding was perceived as a mother's moral obligation: several hagiographies from the early Christian period chronicle that the future saint was nursed by his or her mother.[76] However, these stories are intended to portray the saints' extraordinary strength of faith as they renounce the comfort of a loving family and prefer the ascetic life in the service of God. In the literary genre of hagiography, the narrative of the affectionate and caring mother serves to increase the venerability of the saints and their voluntary sacrifices.

Against this background, it is more convincing to interpret the image of the Galaktotrophousa as a metaphor, with Mary's milk symbolizing the divine *logos* that has to be imbibed in order to reach the Kingdom of God.[77] Early Christian authors provide plenty of evidence for this reading; already in the second century, Clement of Alexandria talks extensively about the symbolism of lactation and describes the milk in Mary's breast as the 'drink of immortality', which originates directly from God:

But the Lord Christ, the fruit of the Virgin, did not pronounce the breasts of women blessed, nor selected them to give nourishment; but when the kind and loving Father had rained down the Word, Himself became spiritual nourishment to the good. O mystic marvel! The universal Father is one, and one the universal Word; and the Holy Spirit is one and the same everywhere, and one is the only virgin mother. I love to call her the Church. This mother, when alone, had not milk, because alone she was not a woman. But she is once virgin and mother – pure as a virgin, loving as a mother.[78]

---

[73] Bolman (2005) 13.

[74] Bolman (2005) 15.

[75] Cf. Paterson Corrington (1989) 406; Ariantzi (2012) 80.

[76] Cf. Ariantzi (2012) 81–6.

[77] Cf. Bolman (2005) 19: 'The Coptic Galaktotrophousa) is not about human frailty but about life after death, and shows one of the principal means of attaining this state – drinking the Logos.'

[78] Trans. Wilson (1867); Clem. Al. *Paed.* 1.6.39.2–42.1: ὁ δὲ κύριος ὁ Χριστὸς ὁ τῆς παρθέ-νου καρπὸς οὐκ ἐμαχάρισεν τοὺς γυναικείους μαστοὺς οὐδὲ ἔκρινεν αὐτοὺς τροφεῖς, ἀλλὰ τοῦ

430 *Viktoria Räuchle*

The metaphorical implications of the divine milk as 'liquid of wisdom' and 'drink of immortality' can already be found in the cult of Isis and the philosophical schools of Graeco-Roman Alexandria.[79] In the Christian era, however, the symbolism is taken one step further by radically detaching the act of lactation from the maternal principle: it has become a signifier of the 'spiritual nourishment' imparted by the Father, while Mary serves as a mere vehicle. Mary does not simply embody the female qualities of fertility and childbirth so important in pagan cults but is, in Clement's words, 'once virgin and mother'. It almost seems as if in the type of Maria lactans the traits of the Greek virgin kourotrophoi and of the fertility goddesses of early Italy and (Graeco-Roman) Egypt are merged: being enthroned in a frontal pose and offering her breast to the newborn, she follows a long iconographic tradition that was established to praise the life-giving qualities of the female body – but her status as a virgin immediately counteracts these associations, as it reduces her to a mere transmitter of the life-giving power of God.[80] To paraphrase Elsner, the meaning of the breastfeeding motif has shifted 'from literal to symbolic'. So again, the nursing motif does not primarily aim to convey maternal qualities but first and foremost works as a symbol for the promise of salvation offered by Mary and her magic milk.

Mary's maternal qualities and emotional involvement, however, are scarcely ever addressed in the images before the ninth century. Throughout the Byzantine Empire, she is mostly represented as the dignified Theotokos ('bearer of God'), as the Council of Ephesus had defined her in AD 431: a majestically enthroned queen in a rigid, frontal posture, holding the child on her lap and thus presenting it to the world.[81] This transcendent image of the Theotokos is in sharp contrast with her characterization in contemporary Byzantine literature: already in the fourth and fifth centuries, hymns and homilies exploit the emotive effect of Mary's suffering as a mortal mother in order to portray the Passions of Christ in the most dramatic forms possible.[82] Just like the mothers of heroes in Athenian

---

φιλοστόργου καὶ φιλαντρώπου πατρὸς ἐπομβρήσαντος τὸν λόγον αὐτὸς ἤδη τροφὴ γέγονεν πνευματικὴ τοῖς σώφροσιν. ὦ θαύματος μυστικοῦ· εἷς μὲν ὁ ὅλων πατήρ, εἷς δὲ καὶ ὁ τῶν ὅλων λόγος, καὶ τὸ πνεῦμα τὸ ἅγιον ἓν καὶ τὸ αὐτὸ πανταχοῦ, μία δὲ μόνη γίνεται μήτηρ παρθένος· ἐκκλησίαν ἐμοὶ φίλον αὐτὴν καλεῖν. γάλα οὐκ ἔσχεν ἡ μήτηρ αὕτη μόνη, ὅτι μόνη μὴ γέγονεν γυνή, παρθένος δὲ ἅμα καὶ μήτηρ ἐστίν, ἀκήρατος μὲν ὡς παρθένος, ἀγαπητικὴ δὲ ὡς μήτηρ. The fifth-century author Cyril of Alexandria (*Discourse on the Virgin Mary*, BMO 6782, fol. 32b1–2) follows a similar notion when he states that God inserted the milk 'from the heavens' in Mary's breasts; cf. the 'breasts of the Father' in *Odes of Solomon* 19. For more references see Ene D-Vasilescu (2018) 15–33.

[79] Cf. Paterson Corrington (1989) 398–404.

[80] On the paradoxical union of virginity and maternity in the Mother of God see Möbius (1996); Schade (2003) 164–5.

[81] Kalavrezou (2000) 41. For the manifold iconographic origins of early icons of Mary with Christ see Belting (1990), esp. 70–2.

[82] Kalavrezou (2005) 105. On the adoption of *pathos* formulas from poetry to the visual arts see Belting (1990) 43–4.

tragedies, the Mother of God serves as an emotional catalyst for the audience.[83] The visual arts lag behind for a couple of hundred years; only in the post-Iconoclastic era, i. e. in the ninth and tenth centuries, do they start to put a programmatic emphasis on the 'human, all too human' agonies of Christ. This leads to the formation of new image types and narrative contexts that try to convey the personal emotions and feelings of the Holy Family through enhanced physicality and expressiveness. Mary's maternal qualities play a decisive role in this development: 'Accepting motherhood with its emotive powers, in turn extended the pictorial language of religious imagery into human expression, a territory not found before in Christian art.'[84] Nevertheless, the images continue to express maternal *pathos* in a moderate manner, which abstains from unvarnished representations of corporality – even as Eleousa, the Mother of God maintains her *ēthos*.[85]

Conclusion

This chapter has traced the emotional implications of maternal imagery in Greek, Roman, and Byzantine contexts. Contrary to modern expectations, references to maternal corporeality do not necessarily convey ideas of tenderness and affection but bear various meanings that are at times completely detached from the concept of maternal love. The image of nursing proved particularly suited to demonstrate this phenomenon: in the Greek culture of the Classical and Hellenistic era, the breastfeeding motif was rarely implemented to characterize a woman as an ideal mother but served as a means of intensifying the emotional reaction of the recipient. The Etrusco-Roman culture followed a different line by venerating the maternal body in the form of corpulent female figures nursing infants at their breasts; but again, these images were not designed to convey the ideal of maternal affection and instead served as a metaphor for fertility and prosperity. Early Byzantine art was generally not interested in highlighting the corporeal aspects of motherhood. Only in Coptic Egypt do we find a series of images that portray the Mother of God as Galaktotrophousa, a figure type with strong symbolic implications. Throughout Antiquity, the *pathos* formula of breastfeeding appears in various contexts but is rarely associated with the love of a mother as a desirable and explicitly positive female quality.

---

[83] For the spectacular orchestration of Mary's suffering and its roots in the Classical Greek tradition see Mullett in this volume.

[84] Kalavrezou (2000) 44.

[85] Cf. Serafimova (2010) 176, analysing Nativity scenes with regard to the representation of motherhood and maternal emotion: 'The common feature of all the models is the rendition of motherhood as an emotional symptom imbued by a restrained expressiveness which is ... in compliance with the Byzantine aesthetics of the sublime.'

Representations of ideal motherhood and maternal affection, on the other hand, portray the mother–child bond in rather moderate forms that only subtly hint at its physical dimensions. The ideal Greek mother is depicted as a mental attachment figure for her child and primarily engages with it through communicative gestures and eye contact. Representations of (mortal) Roman mothers concentrate on their status as dignified matrons. Despite the strong emphasis on the maternal principle in the religious realm, the role of Roman women as mothers is hardly ever represented in schemata of unvarnished corporeality. Early Byzantine art shows Mary as a queen-like figure holding the divine Child in her arms or on her lap, a sublime 'bearer of God' transcending the rigours of human emotionality. From Classical Greece to Early Byzantium, the exemplary mother is portrayed in a restrained manner that is in line with the virtues of moderation and self-restraint. Ideal maternal affection is conveyed in schemata of *ēthos* – with just a little dash of corporeality and just a pinch of *pathos*.

Afterword

David Konstan

Did something, or some things, change in the conception of the emotions between the Classical period of Greece and the Byzantine world? The question is itself problematic in several ways. First of all, there was no single concept of emotion, or the emotions, in Classical Greece and Rome. Aristotle's view of the *pathē*, to the extent that it is consistent over his various writings, differs from that of the Stoics; as for Plato and Epicurus, it is not clear that they have a specific term that corresponds even loosely with what we think of as emotion, although they identify and discuss several particular affects that we readily recognize, such as anger and pity.[1] Certainly, Aristotle's treatment of the *pathē* in the *Rhetoric* comes closest to including under that label the kinds of affects that are commonly regarded as emotions today, and it is fair to assume that the Stoics were heavily influenced by his list, even if their classification and account of the *pathē* differed. Even so, Aristotle's lists have some peculiar properties that may call into question whether he in fact understood emotions in quite the way we might suppose.

It is by now customary to think of Aristotle's conception of the *pathē* as highly cognitive in nature, or at least containing a strong cognitive element: emotions involve judgements, and are defined in the *Rhetoric* as causing a change in our judgements, provided that they are accompanied by pleasure and pain (2.1, 1378a20–3). But what kind of judgements are these? It is clear that, for Aristotle, the *pathē* generally involve evaluations of an ethical nature: we pity people who suffer undeservedly, just as we are indignant when people prosper unjustly. We are angry when we are treated in a way that is incommensurate with our social standing, and we like or hate others on the basis of their virtues and vices. Shame is evidently moral, since we experience it when our actions reveal a defect in our character, and even envy is felt specifically when our social equals fare better than we ourselves do – a notion of rank and propriety motivates this passion. Fear too depends on an assessment of relative strength, and if it is not precisely ethical, in that it arises when we anticipate a danger to ourselves, irrespective of whether we deserve it (it is the most self-centred of the *pathē*), in practice we often bring

---

[1] For an overview, see Konstan (2006a).

434   *David Konstan*

such threats upon ourselves by failing to calculate properly the balance of forces and yield to a certain arrogance or over-confidence.

I mention all this because I have come to think, or rather simply to suspect, that, in drawing up his inventory of the *pathē* in the *Rhetoric*, Aristotle may properly be regarded as the inventor of the very concept of emotion – no one had quite assembled under a single heading a set of affects so similar to what we consider the passions – and yet his motivation in selecting just these items, or what he felt they most had in common, may not have corresponded very closely at all to the feeling of a surge, a hormonal welling up, that for us is central to the idea of an emotion. To put it differently, Aristotle's assortment is right but for the wrong reasons: ethical and social values played a primary role in his conception of the *pathē* in a way that they do not in modern theories. We only see him as the *prōtos heuretēs* of the idea of emotion because we read him in the light of the modern conception and treat the social and moral aspects as ancillary.[2]

Later writers, even when they were massively under the influence of Aristotle's analyses, did not necessarily follow him in this connection. I am thinking here especially of Aspasius, whose commentary on the *Nicomachean Ethics* is the earliest surviving commentary on any of the master's treatises (it dates to the mid-second century AD; some parts of the commentary, however, are lost). In his treatment of the *pathē* in particular, Aspasius both documents a controversy among earlier exponents of the school (in particular, Andronicus of Rhodes (first century BC) and Boethus, a disciple of Andronicus), and offers an original interpretation of the emotions (if we persist in calling them such) in his own right. In broad outline, Aspasius divides the *pathē* into two broad *genera*, pleasure and pain, under one or the other of which the various specific *pathē*, including the homonymous species of pleasure and pain, which he treats as *pathē*, may be subsumed (conceivably he was influenced in this latter respect by Epicurean terminology). These *pathē* may arise prior to any supposition or *hupolēpsis*, directly from perception or an impression – in this respect he sets his face squarely against the Stoic view – or else a supposition may indeed come first, in line, it would seem, with Aristotle's own conception.[3] Either way, the pleasure and pain that are the generic features of any *pathos*, whatever the *differentiae* that distinguish the several species, take the form of motions in the non-rational or *alogon* part of the soul, and such a change is accompanied in turn by a corresponding motion in the body. Although appetite or *epithumia* is to a degree problematic because it may seem to partake of both pleasure and pain and thus require a higher genus under which all *pathē* fall, in fact, Aspasius concludes, desires or *orexeis* are either pleasant or painful: anger is offered as an example of

---

[2] Cf. Konstan 2020.

[3] Aristotle too speaks of the *pathē* as responding to a *phantasia*, but they always involve a judgement or evaluation of the nature of the stimulus.

Afterword 435

the latter kind (appetite or *epithumia*, according to Aspasius, can also arise either with or without supposition). This is not the place to enter into detail about Aspasius' theory, which I have discussed elsewhere;[4] I mention it only to show that even among professed Aristotelians emotions might be regarded in quite distinct ways. More particularly, when the largely rhetorical context for the discussion of emotions began to recede into the background, thinkers seem to have moved away from the emphasis on merit and social position and looked more to the way emotions feel. As they did so, the so-called valence of emotions, their positive or negative quality, came to the fore as their primary feature, as it often is in modern theories, and the element of judgement or supposition, with its accompanying moral and social appraisals, was at least partly obscured.

If Aspasius' view is any clue to a transformation that was beginning to take place in the structure of feeling, to use Raymond Williams' term, or in the emotional community, in the phrase coined by Barbara Rosenwein, of Late Antiquity, then we may perhaps find here some intimation or anticipation of how Byzantine thinkers regarded the emotions. In this connection, I would like to examine a curious moment, as it seems to me, in one of the novelistic stories recounted by Symeon Metaphrastes in his *Menologion*, specifically the tale of Ioustina and Kyprianos. I do not suppose I need to inform readers of the outline of the plot, but simply to set the context, let me recall that Ioustina as a young woman converted to Christianity and decided to remain a virgin for life, conceiving of herself as married to Jesus. Unlike in such martyr tales as the *Passion of Perpetua and Felicitas*, Ioustina, or rather Iousta as she was called until rebaptized, as it were, by Kyprianos, convinced both her mother and her father of the superiority of her faith over the worship of the pagan gods, and so they did not constitute the obstacle to her devotion. This came rather in the form of an unwelcome suitor named Aglaïdas, who, prompted by the Evil One (ὁ Πονηρός), sought first to seduce her and then, his passion frustrated, asked for her hand in marriage, which of course Ioustina rejected outright. Aglaïdas then resorted to carrying her off by force, but a band of tough locals put the brigands to flight. Even so, Aglaïdas did not give up but fought still to restrain her, since, as Symeon writes, 'One thing was for him worse than death itself: losing Ioustina' (13).[5] This display of daring and contempt of life on the part of a dissolute character is itself worthy of further comment, but let me turn rather to Aglaïdas' next move, which is to seek the help of Kyprianos, a native of Carthage who was renowned as an expert in magic. Kyprianos agrees and summons up one of the evil spirits (ἐν τῶν πονηρῶν πνευμάτων, 17) to carry out the assault on Ioustina's will. The spirit is a boastful sort, and expresses himself in terms that are conveniently catalogu-

---

[4] See Konstan (2019a).
[5] Trans. Papaioannou (2017c) 15. Unless otherwise noted, all translations of this work are by Papaioannou.

436 *David Konstan*

ed and analysed in the chapter by Martin Hinterberger in the present volume: the task will be easy, he says, for one like him, who has torn down cities, roused a son to slay his father, instilled hatred between brothers and spouses, corrupted virgins, and caused seasoned monks to lust after the flesh. The demon gives Aglaïdas a drug and orders him to sprinkle it round Ioustina's house, assuring him that she will immediately yield to his wishes. Now, she did in fact awaken with what Symeon calls 'an inflammation in her kidneys' (19; the Greek is διεθερμαίνετο τοὺς νεφρούς),[6] but she resisted in prayer and brandished the cross and so she 'drove away the demon who covered himself with shame and much fright' (αἰσχύνη καλυψάμενον σὺν πολλῷ τῷ δέει).

Kyprianos thereupon invokes a second demon, who again fails and returns shamefaced (μετ'αἰσχύνης, 21) to Kyprianos. Finally, 'the father and ruler of the demons' (ὁ πατὴρ τε καὶ ἄρχων τῶν δαιμόνων) makes an appearance, complaining about the poor help nowadays, 'for among the demons arrogance and haughtiness (τὸ ἀλαζονικὸν καὶ μεγάλαυχον) exceed the other evils (κακῶν)' (my translation); it is unclear here whether these are the words of the chief demon himself and part of his reproach at the poor technique of his underlings or Symeon's own comment on the faults of devils generally, but they are of a piece with the vice of *alazoneia*, which is, as Martin Hinterberger shows, that overvaluation of one's abilities that often arises from past successes. This demon, in any case, attempts the subtler strategy of disguising himself as a Christian woman, who works herself into Ioustina's confidence and then proceeds to raise arguments against the ideal of virginity. But Ioustina resists even this sly attempt on her virtue, and so, as this devil 'swaggered with more boastfulness than the rest, he was subject also to greater shame' (πλείονα ... τὴν αἰσχύνην ἔχων, 24), and he returns to Kyprianos humbly (ταπεινός) for all his bluster, 'bearing on his face clear signs of his defeat'.

What especially interests me here is the nature of the shame that all three demons experience. The question has several aspects. First, ought devils to be capable of shame at all? Juanita Feros Ruys has investigated the evolution of views concerning the emotional capacities of demons.[7] She cites the example of the autobiographical essay, *Monodiae*, by the monk Guibert of Nogent, written in 1115, and writes:

> Guibert appears to accept unquestioningly a cultural landscape that contains both angels and demons who interact with humans, whether in waking life or through dreams. Yet in a new development, the devils and demons in Guibert's world are not just disinterested opportunistic tempters, although they are quite often that as well, but are also more often personally and maliciously involved in their hostile attacks upon pious humans.

---

[6] For the localization of passions in bodily organs, see the chapters in this volume by Stavroula Constantinou and by Douglas Cairns (especially on the *thumos* and *kradiē* in Homer).

[7] Feros Ruys (2012) 184–209, cited hereafter by page number; see also Feros Ruys (2015) and (2017).

Afterword 437

On the one hand, Guibert depicts demons as

taking advantage of excessive human emotions as a first point of attack, as is evinced in the account of the nocturnal demonic assault upon his mother: 'In the dead of a dark night, as she lay awake in her bed filled with this unbearable anxiety, the Devil, whose custom it is to attack those who are weakened by grief, the Adversary himself, appeared all of a sudden and lay upon her, crushing her with his tremendous weight until she was almost dead.'

But in addition, the demons themselves are given a rich emotional life. As Ruys says, 'Guibert notes that demons are "more violently embittered" (*vehementius ... acerbari*) against recent converts or those who constantly maintain their monastic profession', and he 'relates a story of how the devil stalked through a monastery dormitory one night before stopping at the foot of the bed of a particularly pious young man, declaring: "This one irritates me [*me vexat*] more than all the others who are sleeping here."' Ruys quotes Guibert as affirming that

without a doubt it is a matter of faith that the enemies of humankind, with a most bitter envy [*acerbissima invidentia*] of those who are changing for the better, are saddened [*tristari*] by their escape ... It must be believed how grievously [*quam gravissime*] that sudden movement of will towards good gnaws at diabolical hearts. Nor should we wonder if the sudden and fragile emotional reaction of any penitent should grieve [*doleat*] the Devil.

And Ruys comments: 'This marks a new conception of the emotional investment of demons and the devil in the fate of humankind.' There is good reason for the belatedness, moreover, of this conception of demonic emotions: for if demons are evil *pneumata*, as Symeon Metaphrastes indeed calls them in the story we are considering, then as spirits they have no bodies, and it is hard to imagine that strictly incorporeal entities would feel emotions at all – after all, even the saintly Ioustina experiences passion in her kidneys. But supposing that they do, as the later sources testify, we may nevertheless note that, in the various passions that Ruys finds ascribed to devils, shame seems not to figure at all.

Once more, there is a good reason for this absence. Aristotle had defined shame as follows: 'Let *aiskhunē*, then, be a pain or disturbance concerning those ills, either present, past, or future, that are perceived to lead to disgrace, while shamelessness is a disregard or impassivity concerning these same things' (*Rhetoric* 2.6, 1383b12–14). Aristotle goes on to observe:

If shame is as we have defined it, then it follows that we feel shame for those kinds of ills that seem disgraceful, either for ourselves or those we care about. Such are all those actions that arise out of vice, for example throwing away one's shield or fleeing; for they come from cowardice. Also confiscating a deposit, or wronging someone; for they come from unjustness. And sleeping with the wrong people, or those who are related to the wrong people, or at the wrong time; for they come from sensuality.

Other examples of vices that Aristotle enumerates include wrongful gain, il-liberality or servility, effeminacy, small-mindedness, meekness, and conceitedness. Each of these defects is manifested in visible outward behaviour, for example making a profit off the poor, lack of generosity, flattery, lack of endurance, and blowing one's own horn. These behaviours reveal the vice in question, and so lead to disgrace (*adoxia*), that is, a loss of reputation and social standing. Now, if the motive for shame is behaviour that makes manifest a vice, it would appear to be contradictory, or at the very least odd, for demons to experience this particular emotion. They are, after all, the bearers of vice *par excellence*. If the demons or evil spirits feel ashamed of their failure to deter Ioustina from her profession of virginity, it must be because they have not lived up to the standard of achievement that is expected of them and which they expect of themselves, which consists precisely in their ability to foment sin and corruption in the world. They observe, as it were, a mirror-image set of values, the opposite of the virtues: they represent a kind of anti-matter of the soul, according to which the kinds of defects for which they feel ashamed include insufficient deceit and the incapacity to do evil. I believe that there is no clear precedent for this conception in Classical Antiquity, since there was not the radical opposition between forces of absolute good and evil such as we find in the Judaeo-Christian tradition, each the counter-image of the other with its own standards and way of life, like the two angels, 'one of righteousness and one of wickedness', described in the *Shepherd of Hermas* (6.1.36), to which Petra von Gemünden calls attention in her chapter in this volume (personifications of Virtue and Vice, such as we find in the allegory of Hercules' choice recounted by Xenophon and related allegories, rely on argument rather than on affect). This conception had the effect, among other things, of bunching all bad behaviour under the single category of sinfulness, thereby shifting the focus of attention from the moral quality of individual emotions to the more general condition of the self.[8]

In another way, this change of emphasis may be seen too as a consequence or working out of Aspasius' conception of emotions as reactions to events that do not necessarily require supposition or *hupolēpsis*, thereby reducing drastically the cognitive aspect of the *pathē* and rendering them more like what the Stoics regarded as pre- or proto-emotions, that is, *propatheiai*, to which even the sage is susceptible and which do not depend on assent or ethical values.[9] From this point of view, in which all the emotions are regarded as subsets of pain and

---

[8] As Galina Fingarova shows in her chapter in the present volume, representations of the Last Judgement exhibit a stark opposition between those who are saved and those who are condemned, one group on the left of Jesus, the other on his right (ἐντεῦθεν vs ἐκεῖθεν in the account of the Second Coming of *Theophanes Continuatus* 4.15); this contrast between despondency and suffering on the one side and exaltation on the other is not documented in Late Antique representations, as Fingarova shows, and evidently begins with the Byzantine period.

[9] Maternal love, which Viktoria Räuchle discusses in her chapter in the present volume, is instinctive in animals as well as in human beings (Aristotle describes it as φύσει, 'by nature'), and as such is a pre-emotion rather than a full-fledged *pathos* according to the Stoic classification.

Afterword 439

pleasure, one may feel shame simply at the failure or incapacity to carry out one's plans, whatever their nature: the devils feel ashamed simply because they were shown to be not very good at devilry.

I would like to suggest, rather tentatively, that the morally neutral view of the emotions, by which one can feel shame, or a kind of proto-shame, even at the failure to perform vicious acts, may have gone hand in hand with another development in the Byzantine approach to the emotions, one that has been pointed out by several contributors to this volume. I am referring to the new attention that is paid to such trans-emotional experiences as wonder and awe (*thauma*, *sebas*, and the like), and with these to interpersonal sympathy based solely on what we may call fellow-feeling. Divna Manolova (this volume) quotes Theodore Metochites' stirring evocation of the pleasure of gazing at the heavens, 'and how, when the sky is clear, each sight everywhere brings not only wonder (*thauma*) but also joy (*terpsis*) to the roaming eyes, not only inspiration (*to theiasmon*) but also a mood (*diathesis*) that gladdens and sweetens the heart' (*Sententious Remarks* 43: *That It Is Very Pleasant to Behold the Sky and the Heavenly Bodies* 1.1, ed. and trans. Hult (2016)). In a poem, Theodore Metochites declares: 'Sometimes, the very thought of Athanasius (how can I say it?) converts me into a Bacchant, bounding with joy. My expressions of joy reveal that my heart leaps within as well, full of indescribable pleasure (ἀφάτῳ τερπωλῇ)' (5.65, trans. Polemis (2014)). These transcendent states, often either ineffable in themselves or responding to some experience beyond words, like Gregory of Nazianzus' account, mentioned by Byron MacDougall, of what must be 'marvelled at for its incomprehensibility (τῷ δὲ ἀλήπτῳ θαυμάζηται)' (*Oration* 38.7 Moreschini), take pride of place, it seems, in the affective discourse of Byzantine writers, and are of a piece with the emphasis on sympathy or loss of self. In this same spirit, Floris Bernard cites Symeon the New Theologian's description: 'Whoever has inside the light of the most holy Spirit, cannot endure to see it and falls head-on on the ground. He shouts and yells in amazement (ἐκπλήξει) and fear by seeing and experiencing a thing that is beyond nature, word, or thought' (*Theological and Practical Chapters* 3.21).[10]

There is a precedent for this kind of transcendental enthusiasm in Neoplatonism, captured most vividly in Plotinus' essay on beauty, in which he intones that a vision of ideal beauty must induce 'wonderment (θάμβος) and a delicious trouble (ἔκπληξιν ἡδεῖαν, better rendered as a 'pleasant shock'), longing and love and a trembling that is all delight' (trans. MacKenna and Page (1957)), a sense of inspiration that Andrea Capra (this volume) traces back to Plato's image, in the *Ion*, of a magnetic chain of poetic enthusiasm and forward to Michael Psellos' praise of Gregory of Nazianzus, in which he imagines Gregory as having 'seized

---

[10] Cf. also Procopius, *De aedificiis* 1.1.27 on the 'ineffable beauty' of the Hagia Sophia, and Paulus Silentiarius, *Descriptio Sanctae Sophiae* 442 on the 'wonder' it inspires.

440   *David Konstan*

the beauty and power of his discourse in an ineffable way from some heavenly source' (*Discourse Improvised ... about the Style of the Theologian*, 27–45).[11] One of the way stations along the route from Plotinus to Psellos was Philoponus, the Christian commentator on Aristotle who held that 'the affections (*pathē*) are given to the soul as it descends <into the domain of> becoming' (*In De anima* 52.4–7), a notion that problematizes the attribution of emotions to immaterial demons. Indeed, if the final recipient of the emotional inspiration that comes from God is not the poet, philosopher, or orator but the audience who hears or reads their works, then we may see in John Chrysostom's ability to rouse the passions of his public, as Jan Stenger documents, the final link in the chain of transmission; but even in John's preaching, the emotions in question are very often the elevated moods of wonder and awe, for example in relation to the miracle of the Eucharist, that anticipate the predominant affections of Byzantine rhetoric. One might even include under such manifestations of exaltation, as opposed to the ordinary emotions elicited by specific stimuli that are analysed by Classical writers, those extremes of rage labelled *oxucholia* in the *Shepherd of Hermas* (see Petra von Gemünden's analysis in this volume) and identified in the anonymous Byzantine *War of Troy* by a variety of terms such as *thumos, orgē*, and *kholē* and magnified to ultimate proportions in expressions such as χολιαστικὸς εἰς ἄκρον (2080), χολιαστιώτατος (2093), and ὀργισθικός (2096; cited by Stavroula Constantinou, this volume).

Let me be clear about the suggestion I am making: I do not for a moment wish to minimize the awareness, on the part of the Byzantine writers, of the individual emotions and their significance in daily life. Apart from all else, they were steeped in the Classical tradition, and as Douglas Cairns shows (this volume), commentators like Eustathius had a profound understanding of Homeric psychology from which modern scholars have much to learn. John Sikeliotes knew his Hermogenes equally well, as Aglae Pizzone reminds us. And yet, when it came to listing the primary emotions, he selected, at least in one passage, *to lupēron, to thaumastikon, to skhetliastikon*, and *to thrēnētikon*, which sound like states or moods rather than the kind of *pathē* that Aristotle and his followers identified.[12] I am proposing, then, that there did indeed occur a change in the discourse

---

[11] Trans. Papaioannou (2013) 72; cf. Michael Psellos' *Encomium on Michael Kroustoulas* (*Orationes minores* 37), cited by Niels Gaul (this volume) for the shock (ἔκπληξις), exaltation (ἐπανηρόμην), and bewitchment (κατέθελγε, κατεκήλει) that are produced by great preaching in the church; also Ioannes Lazaropoulos, *Dossier on Saint Eugenios of Trebizond* 15–64 for 'the wonderful things that happened in connection with the miracle', etc. (also cited by Gaul).

[12] Compare the central role of grief and threnody in the *Christos Paschon*, summarized in Margaret Mullett (this volume) and the contrasting sentiment of *thauma* at the Resurrection; also the emphasis on grief or pain (vs awe) in Ignatius' *Life of Tarasios* 62–4, cited by Vicky Manolopoulou (this volume). Compare also Makres' account of an icon in his *Ekphrasis of the Martyrdom of Saint Demetrios* 167.26–168.30, cited by Sarah Teetor in her contributions to the network's Vienna workshop and Cyprus conference. The contrast between despondency

concerning emotions in the Byzantine period, in respect to the Classical, whatever individuals in either epoch actually experienced in daily life, and that this alteration, while it had roots to some extent in Neoplatonic and other semi-mystical philosophical traditions, owed a primary inspiration to a new form of religious exaltation associated not just with the arrival of Christianity but more especially with the rise of a particular monastic variety of faith, with its emphasis on the vision of ineffable glories and the aspiration to a transformation of self inspired by a new sense of wonder, awe, and transcendent beauty. It seems to me that all the essays collected in the present volume testify, in one way or another, to this new inflection of the primary affects, and that, taken together, they document what can be said to constitute a distinct stage in the transformation of emotions through time.

---

and elation is a central theme of the Passion of Christ and all who suffered martyrdom in imitation of it.

Bibliography

Abelson, R. P. (1981) 'Psychological status of the script concept', *American Psychologist* 36, 715–29.

Acerbi, F. (2020) 'Logistic, arithmetic, harmonic theory, geometry, metrology, optics and mechanics', in S. Lazaris (ed.), *Companion to Byzantine Science* (Leiden) 105–59.

Adkins, A. W. H. (1970) *From the Many to the One* (London).

Adler, A. (ed.) (1928–38) *Suidae Lexicon*, 5 vols (Leipzig).

Aerts, W. J. (ed.) (1990) *Michaelis Pselli Historia syntomos* (Corpus Fontium Historiae Byzantinae 30) (Berlin).

Agapitos, P. A. (1998a) 'Narrative, rhetoric and "drama" rediscovered: scholars and poets in Byzantium interpret Heliodorus', in R. Hunter (ed.), *Studies in Heliodorus* (Cambridge Philological Society Supplement 21) (Cambridge) 125–56.

Agapitos, P. A. (1998b) 'Teacher, pupils and imperial power in eleventh-century Byzantium', in Y. L. Too and N. Livingstone (eds), *Pedagogy and Power: Rhetorics of Classical Learning* (Ideas in Context 50) (Cambridge) 170–91.

Agapitos, P. A. (2003) 'Ancient models and novel mixtures: the concept of genre in Byzantine funerary literature from Photios to Eustathios of Thessalonike', in G. Nagy and A. Stavrakopoulou (eds), *Modern Greek Literature: Critical Essays* (London) 5–22.

Agapitos, P. A. (2017) 'John Tzetzes and the blemish examiners: a Byzantine teacher on schedography, everyday language and writerly disposition', *Medioevo greco* 17, 1–57.

Agapitos, P. A. (ed.) (2006) *Αφήγησις Λιβίστρου και Ροδάμνης: κριτική έκδοση της Διασκευής α* (Βυζαντινή και Νεοελληνική Βιβλιοθήκη 9) (Athens).

Akyürek, E. (2001) 'Funeral ritual in the Parekklesion of the Chora Church', in N. Necipoğlu (ed.), *Byzantine Constantinople: Monuments, Topography and Everyday Life* (Leiden) 89–104.

Aland, K. and Aland, B. (1989) *Der Text des Neuen Testaments: Einführung in die wissenschaftlichen Ausgaben sowie in Theorie und Praxis der modernen Textkritik*, 2nd edn (Stuttgart).

Alden, M. (2005) 'Lions in paradise: lion similes in the *Iliad* and the lion cubs of *Il.* 18.318–22', *Classical Quarterly* 55, 335–42.

Alexander, J. C. (2006) 'Cultural pragmatics: social performance between ritual and strategy', in J. C. Alexander, B. Giesen, and J. L. Mast (eds), *Social Performance: Symbolic Action, Cultural Pragmatics, and Ritual* (Cambridge) 29–90.

Alexandre, M. (2000) 'Perspectives eschatologiques dans les "Homélies sur les Béatitudes" de Grégoire de Nysse', in H. R. Drobner and A. Viciano (eds), *Gregory of Nyssa, Homilies on the Beatitudes: an English Version with Commentary and Supporting Studies. Proceedings of the Eight International Colloquium on Gregory of Nyssa, Paderborn, 14–18 September 1998* (Leiden) 257–91.

444 *Bibliography*

Alexandridis, A. (2004) *Die Frauen des römischen Kaiserhauses: eine Untersuchung ihrer bildlichen Darstellung von Livia bis Iulia Domna* (Mainz).

Alexiou, M. (1974) *The Ritual Lament in Greek Tradition* (Cambridge).

Alexiou, M. (1975) 'The Lament of the Virgin in Byzantine literature and modern Greek folk-song', *Byzantine and Modern Greek Studies* 1, 111–40.

Alexiou, M. (2002 [1974]), *The Ritual Lament in Greek Tradition*, 2nd edn, revised by D. Yatromanolakis and P. Roilos (Lanham, MD).

Alexiou, M. and Cairns, D. L. (eds) (2017) *Greek Laughter and Tears: Antiquity and After* (Edinburgh).

Alexopoulou, M. (2013) '*Christus patiens* and the reception of Euripides' *Bacchae* in Byzantium', in A. Bakogianni (ed.), *Dialogues with the Past*, vol. 1, *Classical Reception: Theory and Practice* (London) 123–37.

Alpers, K. (2013) *Untersuchungen zu Iohannes Sardianos und seinem Kommentar zu den Progymnasmata des Aphthonios*, 2nd edn (Braunschweig).

Amato, E. (2012) 'Procopio di Gaza modello dell'*Ekphrasis* di Filagato da Cerami sulla Cappella Palatina di Palermo', *Byzantion* 82, 1–16.

Amato, E.,with Corcella, A. and Ventrella, G. (eds) and Maréchaux, P. (trans.) (2014) *Procope de Gaza: discours et fragments* (Paris).

Ambraseys, N. (2009) *Earthquakes in the Eastern Mediterranean and the Middle East: a Multidisciplinary Study of Seismicity up to 1900* (Cambridge).

Amedick, R. (1991) *Vita Privata: die Sarkophage mit Darstellungen aus dem Menschenleben* (Die antike Sarkophagreliefs 1.4) (Berlin).

Amstutz, J. (1968) *ΑΠΛΟΤΗΣ: eine begriffsgeschichtliche Studie zum jüdisch-christlichen Griechisch* (Theophaneia 19) (Bonn).

Anderson, H. (1985) '4 Maccabees', in J. H. Charlesworth (ed.), *The Old Testament Pseudepigrapha* (Garden City, KS) 531–64.

Andreae, B. (1963) *Studien zur römischen Grabkunst* (Heidelberg).

Andreae, B. (2005) 'Il grande sarcofago di Velletri a cinquant'anni dalla sua scoperta', in M. Angle, A. Germano, and F. Zevi (eds), *Museo e territorio: atti del IV convegno, Velletri 7–8 maggio 2004* (Rome) 31–6.

Andreescu, I. (1972) 'Torcello I. Le Christ inconnu. II. Anastasis et Judgement dernier: têtes vraies, têtes fausses', *Dumbarton Oaks Papers* 26, 185–223.

Andreescu, I. (1976) 'Torcello III. La chronologie relative des mosaiques parietales', *Dumbarton Oaks Papers* 30, 245–345.

Angheben, M. (2002) 'Les Jugements derniers byzantins des XIe–XIIe siècles et l'iconographie du jugement immédiat', *Cahiers archéologiques* 50, 105–34.

Angheben, M. (text) and Pace, V. (ed.) (2006), *Alfa e Omega: il Giudizio universale tra Oriente e Occidente* (Castel Bolognese).

Angold, M. (2016) 'Mesarites as a source: then and now', *Byzantine and Modern Greek Studies* 40.1, 55–68.

Annas, J. (1989) 'Epicurean emotions', *Greek, Roman, and Byzantine Studies* 30, 145–64.

Annas, J. (1992) *Hellenistic Philosophy of Mind* (Berkeley).

Anrich, G. (ed.) (1913) *Hagios Nikolaos: der Heilige Nikolaos in der griechischen Kirche. Texte und Untersuchungen*, vol. 1 (Berlin).

Arabatzis, G. (2012) 'Michael of Ephesus and the philosophy of living things (*In De partibus animalium*, 22.25–23.9)', in K. Ierodiakonou and B. Bydén (eds), *The Many Faces of Byzantine Philosophy* (Athens) 51–78.

Bibliography 445

Ariantzi, D. (2012) *Kindheit in Byzanz: emotionale, geistige und materielle Entwicklung im familiären Umfeld vom 6. bis zum 11. Jahrhundert* (Berlin).

Armstrong, D. (2008) '"Be angry and sin not": Philodemus versus the Stoics on natural bites and natural emotions', in J. T. Fitzgerald (ed.), *Passions and Moral Progress in Graeco-Roman Thought* (London) 79–121.

Arvanitopoulos, A. S. (1928) *Γραπταὶ στῆλαι Δημητριάδος-Παγασῶν* (Athens).

Aschermann, H. (1955) *Die paränetischen Formen der 'Testamente der zwölf Patriarchen' und ihr Nachwirken in der frühchristlichen Mahnung: eine formgeschichtliche Untersuchung* (Ph.D. Diss. Berlin).

Ashbrook Harvey, S. (2009) 'Holy impudence, sacred desire: the women of Matthew 1:1–16 in Syriac tradition', in G. Kalantzis and T. F. Martin (eds), *Studies on Patristic Texts and Archaeology: If These Stones Could Speak ... Essays in Honor of Dennis Edward Groh* (New York) 29–50.

Ashbrook Harvey, S. (2017a) 'Fragrant matter: the work of holy oil', in S. Ashbrook Harvey and M. Mullett (eds), *Knowing Bodies, Passionate Souls: Sense Perceptions in Byzantium* (Washington, DC) 153–68.

Ashbrook Harvey, S. (2017b) 'Guiding grief: liturgical poetry and ritual lamentation in early Byzantium', in M. Alexiou and D. Cairns (eds), *Greek Laughter and Tears: Antiquity and After* (Edinburgh) 199–218.

Ashbrook Harvey, S. and Mullett, M. (2017) (eds) *Knowing Bodies, Passionate Souls: Sense Perceptions in Byzantium* (Washington, DC).

Asmis, E. (1992) 'Plato on poetic creativity', in R. Kraut (ed.), *The Cambridge Companion to Plato* (Cambridge) 338–64.

Auguet, R. (1972) *Cruelty and Civilization: the Roman Games* (London).

Aujac, G. (ed.) (1988) *Denys d'Halicarnasse: opuscules rhétoriques*, vol. 2, *Démosthène* (Paris).

Austin, J. L. (1979) 'Other minds', in J. O. Urmson and G. J. Warnock (eds), *Philosophical Papers* (Oxford), 76–116. First published in *Proceedings of the Aristotelian Society* Supplement 20 (1946), 148–87.

Averill, J. A. (1980) 'On the paucity of positive emotions', in K. R. Blankstein, P. Pliner, and J. Polivy (eds), *Assessment and Modification of Emotional Behavior* (New York) 7–45.

Babbitt, F. C. (ed. and trans.) (1927) *Plutarch's Moralia*, vol. 1 (Loeb Classical Library 197) (London).

Babiniotis, G. D. (2002) *Λεξικό της Νέας Ελληνικής γλώσσας*, 2nd edn (Athens).

Badinter, E. (1980) *L'amour en plus: histoire de l'amour maternel* (Paris).

Bailey, S. D. (1955) *Homosexuality and the Western Christian Tradition* (London).

Bailly, A. (1950) *Dictionnaire grec–français* (Paris).

Baldovin, J. (1987) *The Urban Character of Christian Worship: the Origins, Development and Meaning of Stational Liturgy* (Rome).

Baldovin, J. (1993) 'A note on the liturgical processions in the Menologion of Basil II', in E. Carr, S. Parenti, A. Thiermeyer, and R. F. Taft (eds), *Eulogema: Studies in Honor of R. Taft* (Rome) 25–39.

Barber, C. (2007) *Contesting the Logic of Painting: Art and Understanding in Eleventh-Century Byzantium* (Leiden).

Barber, C. and Papaioannou, S. (eds) (2017) *Michael Psellos on Literature and Art: a Byzantine Perspective on Aesthetics* (Notre Dame, IN).

Barclay, K. (2020) *The History of Emotions: a Student Guide to Methods and Sources* (London).

446 *Bibliography*

Barclay, K., Crozier-de Rosa, S., and Stearns, P. (2020) *Sources for the History of Emotions: a Guide* (London).

Barkhuizen, J. H. (2007) 'Romanos Melodos, "On the massacre of the Holy Innocents": a perspective on *ekphrasis* as a method of patristic exegesis', *Acta Classica* 50, 29–50.

Barnard, L. W. (1966) 'Hermas, the church, and judaism', in L. W. Barnard, *Studies in the Apostolic Fathers and Their Background* (Oxford) 151–63.

Barnes, J. (ed.) (1984), *The Complete Works of Aristotle* (Princeton).

Barrett, L. F. (2004) 'Feelings or words? Understanding the content in self-report ratings of emotional experience', *Journal of Personality and Social Psychology* 87, 266–81.

Barrett, L. F. (2005) 'Feeling is perceiving: core affect and conceptualization in the experience of emotion', in L. F. Barrett, P. M. Niedenthal, and P. Winkielman (eds), *Emotion and Consciousness* (New York) 255–84.

Barrett, L. F. (2006a) 'Solving the emotion paradox: categorization and the experience of emotion', *Personality and Social Psychology Review* 10, 20–46.

Barrett, L. F. (2006b) 'Valence as a basic building block of emotional life', *Journal of Research in Personality* 40, 35–55.

Barrett, L. F. (2009) 'Variety is the spice of life: a psychological construction approach to understanding variability in emotion', *Cognition and Emotion* 23.7, 1284–1306.

Barrett, L. F. (2017) *How Emotions Are Made: the Secret Life of the Brain* (New York).

Bartelink, G. J. M. (1952) *Lexicologisch-semantische studie over de taal van de apostolische vaders: bijdrage tot de studie van de groeptaal der Griekse christenen* (Utrecht).

Bartoccini, R. (1958) *Il sarcofago di Velletri* (Rome).

Basson, A. (2009) 'A few metaphorical source domains for emotions in the Old Testament', *Scriptura* 100, 121–8.

Batson, C. D. (2009) 'These things called empathy: eight related but distinct phenomena', in J. Decety and W. Ickes (eds), *The Social Neuroscience of Empathy* (Cambridge, MA).

Bauer, J. B. and Felber, A. (1988) 'Herz', *Realexikon für Antike und Christentum*, vol. 14 (Stuttgart) 1093–131.

Bauer, W. (1988) *Griechisch–deutsches Wörterbuch zu den Schriften des Neuen Testaments und der frühchristlichen Literatur*, ed. K. Aland and B. Aland, 6th edn (Berlin).

Baumeister, R. F., Vohs, K. D., DeWall, C. N., and Zhang, L. (2007) 'How emotion shapes behavior: feedback, anticipation, and reflection, rather than direct causation', *Personality and Social Psychology Review* 11, 167–203.

Baumgärtel, F. (2000) 'καρδία. A. Im Alten Testament', in *Theologisches Wörterbuch zum Neuen Testament*, vol. 3 (Stuttgart) 609–11.

Baumgartner, E. (ed.) (1998) *Benoit de Sainte Maure, Le Roman de Troie* (Paris).

Baun, J. R. (2000) 'Middle Byzantine "tours of Hell": outsider theodicy?', in D. C. Smythe (ed.), *Strangers to Themselves: the Byzantine Outsider* (Aldershot) 47–60.

Baun, J. R. (2007) *Tales from Another Byzantium: Celestial Journey and Local Community in the Medieval Greek Apocrypha* (Cambridge).

Beagon, M. (2011) 'The curious eye of the Elder Pliny', in R. K. Gibson and R. Morello (eds), *Pliny the Elder: Themes and Contexts* (Leiden) 71–88.

Beaton, R. (1996) *The Medieval Greek Romance*, 2nd edn (London).

Becker, J. (1970) *Untersuchungen zur Entstehungsgeschichte der Testamente der zwölf Patriarchen* (Arbeiten zur Geschichte des antiken Judentums und des Urchristentums 8) (Leiden).

Becker, J. (1980) *Die Testamente der zwölf Patriarchen* (Jüdische Schriften aus hellenistisch-römischer Zeit 3.1) (Gütersloh).

Beckmann, M. (2011) *The Column of Marcus Aurelius: the Genesis and Meaning of a Roman Imperial Monument* (Chapel Hill).

Beekes, R. (2009) *Etymological Dictionary of Greek* (Leiden).

Beeley, C. (2008) *Gregory of Nazianzus on the Trinity and the Knowledge of God: in Your Light We Shall See Light* (Oxford).

Behm, J. (2000) 'καρδία. B–D', in *Theologisches Wörterbuch zum Neuen Testament*, vol. 3 (Stuttgart) 611–16.

Bekker, I. (ed.) (1837) *Aristotelis opera*, vol. 6 (Oxford).

Belfiore, E. S. (1992) *Tragic Pleasures: Aristotle on Plot and Emotion* (Princeton).

Belting, H. (1990) *Bild und Kult: eine Geschichte des Bildes vor dem Zeitalter der Kunst* (Munich).

Belting, H. (1994) *Likeness and Presence: a History of the Image before the Era of Art*, trans. E. Jephcott (Chicago).

Beneker, J. and Gibson, C.A. (ed. and trans.) (2016) *The Rhetorical Exercises of Nikephoros Basilakes: Progymnasmata from Twelfth-Century Byzantium* (Dumbarton Oaks Medieval Library 43) (Cambridge, MA).

Bennett, S. and Polito, M. (2014) *Performing Environments: Site-Specificity in Medieval and Early Modern English Drama* (New York).

Berg, B. van den (2018) 'Homer and the good ruler in the "Age of Rhetoric": Eustathios of Thessalonike on excellent oratory', in J. Klooster and B. van den Berg (eds), *Homer and the Good Ruler in Antiquity and Beyond* (Leiden) 219–38.

Berg, B. van den and Manolova, D. (forthcoming) 'Byzantine commentaries on ancient texts: introduction', in B. van den Berg, D. Manolova, and P. Marciniak (eds), *Byzantine Commentaries on Ancient Greek Texts (12th–15th C)* (Cambridge).

Bergemann, J. (1997) *Demos und Thanatos: Untersuchungen zum Wertsystem der Polis im Spiegel der attischen Grabreliefs des 4. Jahrhunderts v. Chr. und zur Funktion der gleichzeitigen Grabbauten* (Munich).

Berger, A. (2006) *Life and Works of Saint Gregentios, Archbishop of Taphar: Introduction, Critical Edition and Translation* (Berlin).

Berger, K. (1989) *Die Weisheitsschrift aus der Kairoer Geniza: Erstedition, Kommentar und Übersetzung* (Texte und Arbeiten zum neutestamentlichen Zeitalter 1) (Tübingen).

Berger, K. (1991) *Historische Psychologie des Neuen Testaments* (Stuttgarter Bibel Studien 146.147) (Stuttgart).

Bericat, E. (2016) 'The sociology of emotions: four decades of progress', *Current Sociology* 64, 491–513.

Bernard, F. (2013) '*Asteiotes* and the ideal of the urbane intellectual in the Byzantine eleventh century', *Frühmittelalterliche Studien* 47, 129–42.

Bernard, F. (2014) *Writing and Reading Byzantine Secular Poetry 1025–1081* (Oxford).

Bernard, F. (2015) 'Humor in Byzantine letters of the tenth to twelfth centuries: some preliminary remarks', *Dumbarton Oaks Papers* 69, 179–95.

Bernard, F. (2017) 'Educational networks in the letters of Michael Psellos', in M. Jeffreys and M. Lauxtermann (eds), *The Letters of Psellos: Cultural Networks and Historical Realities* (Oxford) 13–41.

Bernard, F. (forthcoming), 'Poetry in emotion: the case of anger', in M. Mullet and S. Ashbrook Harvey (eds), *Managing Emotion: Passion, Emotions, Affects, and Imaginings in Byzantium* (Abingdon).

Bernard, F. and Livanos, C. (2018) *The Poems of Christopher of Mytilene and John Mauropous* (Cambridge, MA).

Bernardi, J. (ed.) (1978) *Grégoire de Nazianze, Discours 1–3* (Paris).

Bernardi, J. (ed.) (1992) *Grégoire de Nazianze, Discours 42–43* (Paris).

Bernier-Farella, H. (2015) 'Ritual voices and social silence: funerary lamentations in Byzantium', in I. R. Kleiman (ed.), *Voice and Voicelessness in Medieval Europe* (Basingstoke) 47–63.

Berryman, S. (2009) *The Mechanical Hypothesis in Ancient Greek Natural Philosophy* (Cambridge).

Betancourt, R. (2015) 'A Byzantine liturgical commentary in verse: introduction and translation', *Orientalia Christiana Periodica* 81, 433–72.

Bertoletti, M. (1999) *Sculture di Roma antica: collezioni dei Musei Capitolini alla Centrale Montemartini* (Milan).

Bertoletti, M., Cima, M., and Talamo, E. (2006) *Centrale Montemartini: Musei Capitolini* (Milan).

Betancourt, R. (2016) 'Why sight is not touch: reconsidering the tactility of vision in Byzantium', *Dumbarton Oaks Papers* 70, 1–24.

Betancourt, R. (2018) *Sight, Touch, and Imagination in Byzantium* (Cambridge).

Bettenworth, A. and Hammerstaedt, J. (eds) (2020) *Writing Order and Emotion: Affect and the Structures of Power in Greek and Latin Authors* (Hildesheim).

Bianchi, N. (2005) 'Tempesta nello stretto ovvero Filagato da Cerami lettore di Alcifrone', *Bollettino dei Classici* 26, 91–7.

Bianchi, N. (ed.) (2009) 'Frammento omiletico inedito per la Vergine: Filagato da Cerami, hom. LXXXVI', *Bollettino della Badia greca di Grottaferrata* 6, 307–11.

Bianchi, N. (2011a) 'Filagato da Cerami lettore del De domo ovvero Luciano in Italia meridionale', in N. Bianchi (ed.), *La tradizione dei testi greci in Italia meridionale: Filagato da Cerami philosophos e didaskalos – copisti, lettori, eruditi in Puglia tra XII e XVI secolo* (Bari) 39–52.

Bianchi, N. (2011b) 'Filagato da Cerami lettore di Eliodoro (e di Luciano e Alcifrone)', in N. Bianchi (ed.), *Romanzi greci ritrovati: tradizione e riscoperta dalla tarda antichità al Cinquecento* (Bari) 29–46.

Binning, R. S. (2018) 'Christ's all-seeing eye in the dome', in B. Pentcheva (ed.), *Aural Architecture in Byzantium: Music, Acoustics, and Ritual* (London) 101–26.

Bischof-Köhler, D. (2012) 'Empathy and self-recognition in phylogenetic and ontogenetic perspective', *Emotion Review* 4.1, 40–8.

Bisconti, F. (1996) 'La madonna di Priscilla: interventi di restauro ed ipotesi sulla dinamica decorativa', *Rivista di archeologia cristiana* 72.1–2, 7–34.

Bitton-Askelony, B. and Krueger, D. (2016) *Prayer and Worship in Eastern Christianities, 5th to 11th Centuries* (London).

Blass, F., Debrunner, A., and Rehkopf, F. (2001) *Grammatik des neutestamentlichen Griechisch*, 18th edn (Göttingen).

Blondell, R. (2002) *The Play of Characters in Plato's Dialogues* (Cambridge).

Blowers, P. M. (2010) 'Pity, empathy, and the tragic spectacle of human suffering: exploring the emotional culture of compassion in late ancient Christianity', *Journal of Early Christian Studies* 18, 1–27.

Bobou, O. (2013) 'Emotionality in Greek art', in A. Chaniotis and P. Ducrey (eds), *Unveiling Emotions II. Emotions in Greece and Rome: Texts, Images, Material Culture* (Stuttgart) 273–311.

Boddice, R. (2018) *The History of Emotions* (Manchester).

Bodin, H. and Hedlund, R. (eds) (2013) *Byzantine Gardens and Beyond* (Uppsala).

Bibliography 449

Bodnár, I. (2011) 'The Pseudo-Aristotelian Mechanics: the attribution to Strato', in M.-L. Desclos and W. Fortenbaugh (eds), *Strato of Lampsacus: Text, Translation and Discussion* (New Brunswick) 443–55.

Boegehold, A.L. (1999) *When a Gesture Was Expected: a Selection of Examples from Archaic and Classical Greek Literature* (Princeton).

Boehm, I., Ferrary, J.-L., and Franchet d'Espèrey, S. (eds) (2016) *L'Homme et ses passions: actes du XVIIe Congrès international de l'Association Guillaume Budé organisé à Lyon du 26 au 29 août 2013* (Paris).

Boersma, H. (2014) '"Numbed with grief": Gregory of Nyssa on bereavement and hope', *Journal of Spiritual Formation and Soul Care* 7, 46–59.

Bolman, E.S. (2005) 'The enigmatic Coptic Galaktotrophousa and the cult of the Virgin in Egypt', in M. Vassilaki (ed.), *Images of the Mother of God: Perceptions of the Theotokos in Byzantium* (Aldershot) 13–22.

Bonfante, L. (1989) 'Iconografia delle madri: Etruria a Italia antica', in A. Rallo (ed.), *Le donne in Etruria* (Rome) 85–106.

Bonfante, L. (1997) 'Nursing mothers in Classical art', in A. O. Koloski-Ostrow and C. L. Lyons (eds), *Naked Truths: Women, Sexuality and Gender in Classical Art and Archaeology* (London) 174–96.

Bonfante, L. (2013) 'Mothers and children', in J. MacIntosh Turfa (ed.), *The Etruscan World* (London) 426–46.

Boor, C. de (ed.) (1980 [1883]), *Theophanis Chronographia* (Leipzig).

Boquet, D. and Nagy, P. (eds) (2016) *Histoire intellectuelle des émotions, de l'antiquité à nos jours* (L'atelier du Centre de recherches historiques 16) (Paris).

Borges, J.L. (1935) 'Etcétera', in *Historia universal de la infamia* (Buenos Aires).

Boroditsky, L. (2012) 'How the languages we speak shape the ways we think: the FAQs', in M. J. Spivey, K. McRae, and M. F. Joanisse (eds), *The Cambridge Handbook of Psycho-linguistics* (Cambridge) 615–32.

Boroditsky, L., Schmidt, L.A., and Phillips, W. (2003) 'Sex, syntax, and semantics' in D. Gentner and S. Goldin-Meadow (eds), *Language in Mind: Advances in the Study of Language and Thought* (Cambridge, MA) 61–79.

Bosnakis, D. (2012) 'Ἐπιτύμβια ανάγλυφη στήλη με παράσταση θηλάζουσας από την Κάλυμνο', *Αρχαιολογικόν δελτίον* 58–64 (2003–9), 377–90.

Bouras, L. and Parani, M.G. (2008) *Lighting in Early Byzantium* (Washington, DC).

Bouras-Vallianatos, P. (2015) 'Galen's reception in Byzantium: Symeon Seth and his refutation of Galenic theories on human physiology', *Greek, Roman, and Byzantine Studies* 55, 431–69.

Bouras-Vallianatos, P. (2016) 'A new witness to Michael Psellos' poem "On Medicine" ("De medicina")', *Jahrbuch der österreichischen Byzantinistik* 65, 9–12.

Bourbou, C. (2013) 'The imprint of emotions surrounding the death of children in Antiquity', in A. Chaniotis and P. Ducrey (eds), *Unveiling Emotions II. Emotions in Greece and Rome: Texts, Images, Material Culture* (Stuttgart) 331–50.

Bourbouhakis, E.C. (2010) 'Rhetoric and performance', in P. Stephenson (ed.), *The Byzantine World* (London) 175–87.

Bourdieu, P. (1972) *Esquisse d'une théorie de la pratique* (Geneva).

Bowersock, G.W. (2012) 'Infant gods and heroes in Late Antiquity: Dionysos' first bath', in R. Schlesier (ed.), *A Different God? Dionysos and Ancient Polytheism* (Berlin) 3–12.

Boyd, B. (2009) *On the Origin of Stories: Evolution, Cognition, and Fiction* (Cambridge, MA).

450   *Bibliography*

Braams, W. (1913) *Zur Geschichte des Ammenwesens im klassischen Altertum* (Jenaer Medizin-historische Beiträge 5) (Jena).

Bradshaw, P. F. and McGowan, A. (eds) (2020) *Egeria, Journey to the Holy Land* (Brepols Library of Christian Sources 1) (Turnhout).

Brague, R. (1980) 'De la disposition: à propos de *diathesis* chez Aristote', in P. Aubenque (ed.), *Concepts et catégories dans la pensée antique* (Paris) 285–307.

Braithwaite, G. (1984) 'Romano-British face pots and head pots', *Britannia* 15, 99–131.

Brambs, J. G. (ed.) (1885) *Christus Patiens: Tragoedia quae inscribi solet CHRISTOS PASCHON Gregorio Nazianzeno falso attributa* (Leipzig).

Brändle, R. (1979) *Matth. 25,31–46 im Werk des Johannes Chrysostomos: ein Beitrag zur Auslegungsgeschichte und zur Erforschung der Ethik der griechischen Kirche um die Wende vom 4. zum 5. Jahrhundert* (Tübingen).

Brandon, S. G. F. (1967) *The Judgment of the Dead: an Historical and Comparative Study of the Idea of a Post-Mortem Judgement in the Major Religions* (London).

Braund, S. M. and Gill, C. (eds) (1997) *The Passions in Roman Thought and Literature* (Cambridge).

Braund, S. M. and Most, G. W. (eds) (2003a) *Ancient Anger: Perspectives from Homer to Galen* (Yale Classical Studies 32) (Cambridge).

Braund, S. M. and Most, G. W. (2003b) 'Introduction', in S. M. Braund and G. W. Most (eds) *Ancient Anger: Perspectives from Homer to Galen* (Yale Classical Studies 32) (Cambridge) 1–10.

Breithaupt, F. A. (2015a) 'Empathy for empathy's sake: aesthetics and empathic sadism', in A. Assmann and I. Detmers (eds) *Empathy and Its Limits* (London) 151–65.

Breithaupt, F. A. (2015b) 'Empathic sadism: how readers get implicated', in L. Zunshine (ed.), *The Oxford Handbook of Cognitive Literary Studies* (Oxford) 440–60.

Bremmer, J. N. (1983) *The Early Greek Concept of the Soul* (Princeton).

Bremmer, J. N. and Roodenburg, H. (eds) (1991), *A Cultural History of Gesture: from Antiquity to the Present Day* (London).

Brenk, B. (1964) 'Die Anfänge der byzantinischen Weltgerichtsdarstellung', *Byzantinische Zeitschrift* 57, 106–26.

Brenk, B. (1966) *Tradition und Neuerung in der christlichen Kunst des ersten Jahrtausends: Studien zur Geschichte des Weltgerichtsbildes* (Vienna).

Brenk, B. (1972) 'Weltgericht', in *Lexikon der christlichen Ikonographie*, vol. 4, *Allgemeine Ikonographie*, 513–23.

Brilliant, R. (1999) '"What is death, that I should fear it?": aspects of the Roman response', in N. Blanc and A. Buisson (eds), *Imago antiquitatis: religions et iconographie du monde romain* (Paris) 145–8.

Brisson, L. (ed.) (1998) *Platon: Le banquet* (Paris).

Broderson, K. (ed.) (2010) *Theano: Briefe einer antiken Philosophin. Griechisch/Deutsch* (Stuttgart).

Broomhall, S. and Lynch, A. (eds) (2019) *The Routledge History of Emotions in Europe, 1100–1700* (London).

Brouwer, R. (2015) 'Stoic sympathy', in E. Schliesser (ed.), *Sympathy: a History* (Oxford) 15–35.

Brown, A. (2012) 'Performance and reception of Greek tragedy in the early medieval Mediterranean', in S. L. Hathaway and D. W. Kim (eds), *Intercultural Transmission in the Medieval Mediterranean* (London) 146–62.

Brown, P. and Levinson, S. C. (1987) *Politeness: Some Universals in Language Usage* (Cambridge).

Browning, R. (1963) 'A Byzantine treatise on tragedy', in L. Varcl and R. F. Willetts (eds), *Γέρας: Studies Presented to G. Thomson on the Occasion of His 60th Birthday* (Acta Universitatis Carolinae, Philosophica et Historica 1) (Prague) 67–81.

Browning, R. (1975) 'Homer in Byzantium', *Viator* 6, 15–37.

Brox, N. (1991) *Der Hirt des Hermas, übersetzt und erklärt* (Kommentar zu den apostolischen Vätern 7) (Göttingen).

Brubaker, L. (1989a) 'Perception and conception: art, theory and culture in ninth-century Byzantium', *Word and Image* 5, 19–32.

Brubaker, L. (1989b) 'Byzantine art in the ninth century: theory, practice and culture', *Byzantine and Modern Greek Studies* 13, 23–93.

Brubaker, L. (1999) 'The Chalke gate, the construction of the past, and the Trier ivory', *Byzantine and Modern Greek Studies* 23, 258–85.

Brubaker, L. (2009) 'Gesture in Byzantium', in M. J. Braddick (ed.), *The Politics of Gesture: Historical Perspectives* (*Past and Present* Supplement 4) (Oxford) 36–56.

Brubaker, L. and Wickham, C. (2021) 'Processions, power, and community identity: East and West', in R. Kramer and W. Pohl (eds), *Empires and Communities in the Post-Roman and Islamic World, c. 400–1000 CE* (Oxford) 121–87.

Brügger, C. (2016) *Homers Ilias, Gesamtkommentar: Sechzehnter Gesang (Π). Kommentar* (Basler Kommentar 9.2) (Berlin).

Bruner, J. (1986) *Actual Minds, Possible Worlds* (Cambridge, MA).

Bruner, J. (1991) 'The narrative construction of reality', *Critical Inquiry* 18.1, 1–21.

Bryant Davies, R. (2017) 'The figure of Mary Mother of God in *Christus patiens*: fragmentary tragic myth and passion narrative in a Byzantine appropriation of Euripidean tragedy', *Journal of Hellenic Studies* 137, 1–25.

Burgess, G. S. and Kelly, D. (trans.) (2017) *The Roman de Troie by Benoît de Sainte-Maure* (Cambridge).

Burnet, J. (ed.) (1967 [1900]), *Platonis opera*, vol. 1 (Oxford).

Burrows, M. (1958) *More Light on the Dead Sea Scrolls: New Scrolls and New Interpretations with Translations of Important Recent Discoveries* (New York).

Burrus, V. (2008) *Saving Shame: Martyrs, Saints and Other Abject Subjects* (Philadelphia).

Buxton, R. (2006) 'Similes and other likenesses', in R. Fowler (ed.), *The Cambridge Companion to Homer* (Cambridge) 139–55.

Bydén, B. (2002) '"To every argument there is a counter-argument": Theodore Metochites' defence of scepticism (*Semeiosis* 61)', in K. Ierodiakonou (ed.), *Byzantine Philosophy and Its Ancient Sources* (Oxford) 183–217.

Bydén, B. (2003) *Theodore Metochites' Stoicheiosis Astronomike and the Study of Natural Philosophy and Mathematics in Early Palaiologan Byzantium* (Studia Graeca et Latina Gothoburgensia 66) (Göteborg).

Cairns, D. L. (1993) *Aidōs: the Psychology and Ethics of Honour and Shame in Ancient Greek Literature* (Oxford).

Cairns, D. L. (1996a) '*Hybris*, dishonour, and thinking big', *Journal of Hellenic Studies* 116, 1–32.

Cairns, D. L. (1996b) '"Off with her αἰδώς": Herodotus 1.8.3–4', *Classical Quarterly* 46, 78–83.

Cairns, D. L. (1996c) 'Veiling, αἰδώς, and a red-figure amphora by Phintias', *Journal of Hellenic Studies* 116, 152–8.

452   *Bibliography*

Cairns, D. L. (2003) 'Ethics, ethology, terminology: Iliadic anger and the cross-cultural study of emotion', in S. M. Braund and G. W. Most (eds), *Ancient Anger: Perspectives from Homer to Galen* (Yale Classical Studies 32) (Cambridge), 11–49.

Cairns, D. L. (ed.) (2005) *Body Language in the Greek and Roman Worlds* (Swansea).

Cairns, D. L. (2008) 'Look both ways: studying emotion in ancient Greek', *Critical Quarterly* 50.4, 43–62.

Cairns, D. L. (2013a) 'A short history of shudders', in A. Chaniotis and P. Ducrey (eds), *Unveiling Emotions II. Emotions in Greece and Rome: Texts, Images, and Material Culture* (Stuttgart) 85–107.

Cairns, D. L. (2013b) 'The imagery of *erôs* in Plato's *Phaedrus*', in E. Sanders, C. Thumiger, C. Carey, and N. Lowe (eds), *Erôs in Ancient Greece* (Oxford) 233–50.

Cairns, D. L. (2014a) 'Exemplarity and narrative in the Greek tradition', in D. L. Cairns and R. Scodel (eds), *Defining Greek Narrative* (Edinburgh) 103–36.

Cairns, D. L. (2014b) 'Ψυχή, θυμός, and metaphor in Homer and Plato', *Études platoniciennes* 11. http://etudesplatoniciennes.revues.org/566.

Cairns, D. L. (2016a) 'Clothed in shamelessness, shrouded in grief: the role of "garment" metaphors in ancient Greek concepts of emotion', in G. Fanfani, M. Harlow, and M.-L. Nosch (eds), *Spinning Fates and the Song of the Loom: the Use of Textiles, Clothing and Cloth Production as Metaphor, Symbol and Narrative Device in Greek and Latin Literature* (Oxford) 25–41.

Cairns, D. L. (2016b) 'Metaphors for hope in Archaic and Classical Greek poetry', in R. R. Caston and R. A. Kaster (eds), *Hope, Joy and Affection in the Classical World* (Oxford) 13–44.

Cairns, D. L. (2016c) 'Mind, body, and metaphor in ancient Greek concepts of emotion', *L'atelier du Centre de recherche historique* 16. http://acrh.revues.org/7416.

Cairns, D. L. (2017a) 'Emotions', *Encyclopaedia of Ancient History*, 23 June 2017. https://onlinelibrary.wiley.com/doi/abs/10.1002/9781444338386.wbeah30086.

Cairns, D. L. (2017b) 'Horror, pity, and the visual in Ancient Greek aesthetics', in D. L. Cairns and D. Nelis (eds), *Emotions in the Classical World: Methods, Approaches, and Directions* (Heidelberger althistorische Beiträge und epigraphische Studien 59) (Stuttgart) 53–77.

Cairns, D. L. (2017c) 'Mind, metaphor, and emotion in Euripides (*Hippolytus*) and Seneca (*Phaedra*)', in D. L. Cairns and D. P. Nelis (eds), *Seneca's Tragic Passions* (*Maia* 69.2), 247–67.

Cairns, D. L. (2017d) 'The tripartite soul as metaphor', in P. Destrée and R. G. Edmonds (eds), *Plato and the Power of Images* (Leiden) 219–38.

Cairns, D. L. (2018) 'Introduction: distributed cognition and the classics', in M. Anderson, D. L. Cairns, and M. Sprevak (eds), *Distributed Cognition in Classical Antiquity* (Edinburgh) 18–36.

Cairns, D. L. (ed.) (2019a) *A Cultural History of the Emotions in Antiquity* (London).

Cairns, D. L. (2019b) 'Introduction: emotion history and the Classics', in D. L. Cairns (ed.), *A Cultural History of the Emotions in Antiquity* (London) 1–15.

Cairns, D. L. (2019c) 'Thymos', *Oxford Classical Dictionary Online* (Oxford). doi: http://dx.doi.org/10.1093/acrefore/9780199381135.013.8180.

Cairns, D. L. (2020a) 'Emotion and the communicability of suffering: Richard Gaskin's *Tragedy and Redress*', *British Journal of Aesthetics* 60.3, 351–7.

Cairns, D.L. (2020b) 'Phaedra's fantasy other: phenomenology and the enactive mind in Euripides' *Hippolytus*', in M. Liatsi (ed.), *Ethics in Ancient Greek Literature: from Homer to Epicurus* (Berlin) 117–28.

Cairns, D.L. (2021) 'The dynamics of emotion in Euripides' *Medea*', *Greece and Rome* 68, 8–26.

Cairns, D.L. (2022) 'Forms of pride in ancient Greek culture', in R. Barth, M. Fritz, and H. Schulz (eds), *Stolz und Demut: zur emotionalen Ambivalenz religiöser Positionierungen* (Berlin).

Cairns, D.L. (forthcoming) 'Vision, visualization, and emotional contagion: some conceptual and methodological issues', in F. Budelmann and K. Earnshaw (eds), *Cognitive Visions*.

Cairns, D.L. and Fulkerson, L.F. (eds) (2015) *Emotions between Greece and Rome* (*Bulletin of the Institute of Classical Studies* Supplement 125) (London).

Cairns, D.L. and Nelis, D. (eds) (2017) *Emotions in the Classical World: Methods, Approaches, and Directions* (Heidelberger althistorische Beiträge und epigraphische Studien 59) (Stuttgart).

Cairns, D.L. and Virág, C. (eds) (forthcoming) *In the Mind, in the Body, and in the World: Emotions in Early China and Ancient Greece* (New York).

Calbi, M., Siri, F., Heimann, K., Barratt, D., Gallese, V., Kolesnikov, A., and Umiltà, M. A. (2019) 'How context influences the interpretation of facial expressions: a source localization high-density EEG study on the "Kuleshov effect"', *Nature: Scientific Reports* 9.2107. https://www.nature.com/articles/s41598-018-37786-y.pdf.

Calboli Montefusco, L. (1998) 'Ethos', *Der Neue Pauly* 4, 166–7.

Callahan, J.F. (ed.) (1992) Gregory of Nyssa, *De beatitudinibus, Gregorii Nysseni opera*, vol. 7.2 (Leiden) 75–170.

Calvet-Sebasti, M.-A. (ed.) (1995) *Grégoire de Nazianze, Discours 6–12* (Sources chrétiennes 405) (Paris).

Cameron, A. (1978) 'The Theotokos in sixth-century Constantinople: a city finds its symbol', *Journal of Theological Studies* 29.1, 79–108.

Cameron, A. (1991) *Christianity and the Rhetoric of Empire: the Development of Christian Discourse* (Berkeley).

Campeggiani, P. (2013) *Le ragioni dell'ira: potere e riconoscimento nell'antica Grecia* (Rome).

Cancik, H. (1998) 'The end of the world, of history, and of the individual in Greek and Roman Antiquity', in J.J. Collins (ed.), *The Encyclopedia of Apocalypticism*, vol. 1, *The Origins of Apocalypticism in Judaism and Christianity* (New York) 84–125.

Candiotto, L. (2015) 'Aporetic state and extended emotions: the shameful recognition contradictions in the Socratic elenchus', *Ethics and Politics* 17, 233–48.

Candiotto, L. and Renaut, O. (eds) (2020) *Emotions in Plato* (Leiden).

Canevaro, L.G. (2018) *Women of Substance in Homeric Epic: Objects, Gender, Agency* (Oxford).

Canevaro, L.G. (2019) 'Materiality and Classics: (re)turning to the material', *Journal of Hellenic Studies* 139, 222–32.

Cánovas, C.P. (2011) 'The genesis of the arrows of love: diachronic conceptual integration in Greek mythology', *American Journal of Philology* 132, 553–79.

Capano, A. (2013) 'La μελέτη come fenomeno teatrale pubblico nell'età imperiale', in M. Reig and X. Riu (eds), *Drama, Philosophy, Politics in Ancient Greece: Contexts and Receptions* (Barcelona) 207–19.

454 *Bibliography*

Capra, A. (2010), 'Plato's Hesiod and the will of Zeus: philosophical rhapsody in the *Timaeus* and the *Critias*', in G. Boys-Stones and J. Haubold (eds), *Plato and Hesiod* (Oxford) 200–18.

Capra, A. (2014) *Plato's Four Muses: the Phaedrus and the Poetics of Philosophy* (Washington, DC).

Capra, A. (2017) 'Seeing through Plato's looking glass: *muthos* and *mimesis* from *Republic* to *Poetics*', *Aisthesis* 10, 75–86.

Capra, A. (2018) 'Aristophanes' iconic Socrates', in A. Stavru and C. Moore (eds), *Socrates and the Socratic Dialogue* (Leiden) 64–83.

Capra, A. (2020) 'Aristotle's *Poetics* and the anatomy of tragedy', in P. Destrée, M. Heath, and D. Munteanu (eds), *The Poetics in Its Aristotelian Context* (London) 183–205.

Capra, A. and Martinelli Tempesta, S. (2011) 'Riding from Elea to Athens (via Syracuse). The *Parmenides* and the early reception of eleatism: Epicharmus, Cratinus and Plato', *Méthexis* 24, 153–93.

Caquot, A. and Philonenko, M. (1987) 'Introduction générale', in A. Dupont-Sommer and M. Philonenko (eds), *Ecrits intertestamentaires* (Bibliothèque de la Pléiade) (Paris) xv–cxlvi.

Carmignac, J. (1957) *Le docteur de justice et Jésus-Christ* (Paris).

Carroll, N. (2001) 'Art, narrative and emotion', in N. Carroll, *Beyond Aesthetics: Philosophical Essays* (Cambridge) 215–34.

Carroll, N. (2011) 'On some affective relations between audiences and the characters in popular fictions', in A. Coplan and P. Goldie (eds), *Empathy: Philosophical and Psychological Perspectives* (Oxford) 162–84.

Carroll, N. (2015) 'Theater and the emotions', in L. Zunshine (ed.), *The Oxford Handbook of Cognitive Literary Studies* (Oxford) 313–26.

Caruso, S. (ed.) (1974) 'Le tre omelie inedite "Per la Domenica delle Palme" di Filagato da Cerami', Ἐπετηρὶς Ἑταιρείας Βυζαντινῶν Σπουδῶν 41, 109–27.

Casasanto, D. (2008) 'Who's afraid of the big bad Whorf? Crosslinguistic differences in temporal language and thought', *Language Learning* 58, Supplement 1, 63–79.

Casasanto, D. (2016) 'Linguistic relativity', in N. Riemer (ed.), *Routledge Handbook of Semantics* (New York) 158–74.

Casasanto, D. (2017) 'Relationships between language and cognition', in B. Dancygier (ed.), *Cambridge Handbook of Cognitive Linguistics* (Cambridge) 19–37.

Caseau, B. (1999) 'Christian bodies: the senses and Early Byzantine Christianity', in L. James (ed.), *Desire and Denial in Byzantium: Papers from the 31st Spring Symposium of Byzantine Studies, University of Sussex, Brighton, March 1997* (Aldershot) 101–9.

Caseau, B. (2013) 'Experiencing the sacred', in C. Nesbitt and M. Jackson (eds), *Experiencing Byzantium: Papers from the 44th Spring Symposium of Byzantine Studies, Newcastle and Durham, April 2011* (Farnham) 59–77.

Caseau, B. (2014) 'Cultural history of the senses: religion and the senses', in R. Newhauser (ed.), *A Cultural History of the Senses in the Middle Ages* (Oxford) 89–109.

Castelli, E.A. (2000) 'Asterius of Amasea: *ekphrasis* on the holy martyr Euphemia', in R. Valantasis, *Religions of Late Antiquity in Practice* (Princeton).

Castelli, E.A. (2005) 'Persecution and spectacle: cultural appropriation in the Christian commemoration of martyrdom', *Archiv für Religionsgeschichte* 7, 102–36.

Caston, R.R. and Kaster, R.A. (eds) (2016) *Hope, Joy, and Affection in the Classical World* (New York).

Caswell, C. (1990) *A Study of Thumos in Early Greek Epic* (Leiden).

Bibliography 455

Catoni, M. L. (2005) 'Le regole del vivere, le regole del morire: su alcune stele attiche per donne morte di parto', *Revue archéologique* 39, 27–53.

Catoni, M. L. (2008) *La comunicazione non verbale nella Grecia antica: gli schemata nella danza, nell'arte, nella vita* (Turin).

Cavallo, G. (2007) 'Places of public reading in Late Antiquity', in T. Derda, T. Markiewicz, and E. Wipszycka (eds), *Alexandria: the Auditoria of Kom el-Dikka and Late Antique Education (Journal of Juristic Papyrology* Supplement 8) (Warsaw) 151–6.

Cave, T. (2016) *Thinking with Literature: towards a Cognitive Criticism* (Oxford).

Celentano, M. S. (2016) 'Giovanni Crisostomo, *Sulle statue* 2: omelia e/o orazione politica?', in P. Derron (ed.), *La rhétorique du pouvoir: une exploration de l'art oratoire délibératif grec* (Vandœuvres) 343–68.

Cerri, G. (1991) *Platone sociologo della comunicazione* (Milan).

Certeau, M. de (1975) *The Writing of History* (New York).

Chaniotis, A. (2011) 'Emotional community through ritual: initiates, citizens, and pilgrims as emotional communities in the Greek world', in A. Chaniotis (ed.), *Ritual Dynamics in the Ancient Mediterranean: Agency, Emotion, Gender, Representation* (Stuttgart) 263–90.

Chaniotis, A. (2012a) 'Constructing the fear of the gods: epigraphic evidence from Greece and Asia Minor', in A. Chaniotis (ed.), *Unveiling Emotions: Sources and Methods for the Study of Emotions in the Greek World* (Stuttgart) 205–34.

Chaniotis, A. (2012b) 'Moving stones: the study of emotions in Greek inscriptions', in A. Chaniotis (ed.), *Unveiling Emotions: Sources and Methods for the Study of Emotions in the Greek World* (Stuttgart) 91–130.

Chaniotis, A. (2012c) 'Unveiling emotions in the Greek world: introduction', in A. Chaniotis (ed.), *Unveiling Emotions: Sources and Methods for the Study of Emotions in the Greek World* (Stuttgart) 11–36.

Chaniotis, A. (ed.) (2012d) *Unveiling Emotions: Sources and Methods for the Study of Emotions in the Greek World* (Stuttgart).

Chaniotis, A. (2013a) 'Empathy, emotional display, theatricality, and illusion in Hellenistic historiography', in A. Chaniotis and P. Ducrey (eds), *Unveiling Emotions II. Emotions in Greece and Rome: Texts, Images, Material Culture* (Stuttgart) 53–84.

Chaniotis, A. (2013b) 'Processions in Hellenistic cities: contemporary discourses and ritual dynamics', in R. Alston, O. M. van Nijf, and C. G. Williamson (eds), *Cults, Creeds and Contests* (Louvain) 21–47.

Chaniotis, A. (2013c) 'Staging and feeling the presence of god: emotion and theatricality in religious celebrations in the Roman East', in L. Bricault and C. Bonnet (eds), *Panthée: Religious Transformations in the Roman Empire* (Leiden) 169–89.

Chaniotis, A. (2015) 'Affective diplomacy: emotional scripts between Greek communities and Roman authorities', in D. L. Cairns and L. Fulkerson (eds), *Emotions between Greece and Rome* (London) 87–103.

Chaniotis, A. (2017a) 'The life of statues: emotion and agency', in D. L. Cairns and D. P. Nelis (eds), *Emotions in the Classical World: Methods, Approaches, and Directions* (Heidelberger althistorische Beiträge und epigraphische Studien 59) (Stuttgart) 143–58.

Chaniotis, A. (2017b) 'A world of emotions – why should we care?', in A. Chaniotis, N. Kaltsas, and I. Mylonopoulos (eds), *A World of Emotions: Ancient Greece, 700 BC–200 AD* (New York) 16–25.

Chaniotis, A. (ed.) (2021) *Unveiling Emotions III: Arousal, Display, and Performance of Emotions in the Greek World* (Stuttgart).

456   Bibliography

Chaniotis, A. and Ducrey, P. (eds) (2013) *Unveiling Emotions II. Emotions in Greece and Rome: Texts, Images, Material Culture* (Stuttgart).

Chaniotis, A. and Steel, C. (2019) 'Emotions in public: collectivities and polities', in D. L. Cairns (ed.), *A Cultural History of the Emotions in Antiquity* (London) 147–61.

Charles, R. H. (1908) *The Greek Versions of the Testaments of the Twelve Patriarchs* (Oxford).

Charles, R. H. (1916) *The Chronicle of John (c. 690 A.D.), Coptic Bishop of Nikiu: Translated from Hermann Zotenberg's Ethiopic Text* (London).

Chiesa, M. C. (1991) 'Le problème du langage intérieur chez les Stoïciens', *Revue internationale de philosophie* 178, 301–21.

Chiron, P. (2007) 'The *Rhetoric to Alexander*', in I. Worthington (ed.), *A Companion to Greek Rhetoric* (Oxford) 90–106.

Christe, Y. (2001) *Das Jüngste Gericht* (Regensburg).

Chryssavgis, J. (1989) *Ascent to Heaven: the Theology of the Human Person According to Saint John of the Ladder* (Brookline, MA).

Clarke, M. (1995) 'Between lions and men: images of the hero in the *Iliad*', *Greek, Roman, and Byzantine Studies* 36.2, 137–59.

Clarke, M. (1999) *Flesh and Spirit in the Songs of Homer: a Study of Words and Myths* (Oxford).

Clarke, M. (2004) 'Manhood and heroism', in R. Fowler (ed.) *The Cambridge Companion to Homer* (Cambridge) 11–30.

Coarelli, F. (1995) *Da Pergamo a Roma: i Galati nella città degli Attalidi* (Rome).

Coleridge, E. P. (1938) 'Phoenissae', in W. J. Oates and E. O'Neill, Jr (eds), *Euripides: the Complete Greek Drama*, vol. 2 (New York).

Collingwood, R. G. (1938) *The Principles of Art* (Oxford).

Collins, T. (1971) 'The physiology of tears in the Old Testament: Part 1', *Catholic Biblical Quarterly* 33, 18–38.

Colombetti, G. (2009) 'What language does to feelings', *Journal of Consciousness Studies* 16.9, 4–26.

Colombetti, G. (2014) *The Feeling Body: Affective Science Meets the Enactive Mind* (Cambridge, MA).

Conca, F. (ed.) (1983) *Pseudo-Nilus of Ancyra, Narrationes septem de monachis in Sina* (Leipzig).

Conley, T. M. (2002–3) 'Demosthenes dethroned: Gregory Nazianzus in Sikeliotes' scholia on Hermogenes' Περὶ ἰδεῶν', *Illinois Classical Studies* 27/8, 145–52.

Connolly, J. (2001) 'Reclaiming the theatrical in the Second Sophistic', *Helios* 28.1, 75–96.

Constantinou, S. (2010) 'Grotesque bodies in hagiographical tales: the monstrous and the uncanny in Byzantine collections of miracle stories', *Dumbarton Oaks Papers* 64, 43–54.

Constantinou, S. (2013) 'Retelling the tale: the Byzantine rewriting of *Floire and Blancheflor*', in J. Eming and M. Baisch (ed.), *Hybridität und Spiel: der europäische Liebes- und Abenteuerroman von der Antike zur Frühen Neuzeit* (Berlin) 227–42.

Constantinou, S. (2019a) 'Gendered emotions and affective genders: a response', in S. Constantinou and M. Meyer (eds), *Emotions and Gender in Byzantine Culture* (London) 283–315.

Constantinou, S. (2019b) 'Homosocial desire in *The War of Troy*: between (wo)men', in A. J. Goldwyn and I. Nilsson (eds), *The Late Byzantine Romance: a Handbook* (Cambridge) 254–71.

Bibliography 457

Constantinou, S. (2021) '*Metaphrasis*: mapping premodern rewriting', in S. Constantinou and C. Høgel (eds), *Metaphrasis: a Byzantine Concept of Rewriting and Its Hagiographical Products* (Leiden) 1–57.

Constantinou, S. and Meyer, M. (eds) (2019), *Emotions and Gender in Byzantine Culture* (London).

Cooper, C. (2004) 'Demosthenes actor on the political and forensic stage', in C. J. Mackie (ed.), *Oral Performance and Its Context* (Leiden).

Cooper, J. M. (1996) 'An Aristotelian theory of the emotions', in A. O. Rorty (ed.), *Essays on Aristotle's Rhetoric* (Berkeley) 238–57.

Cooper, J. M. (1998) 'Posidonius on emotions', in J. Sihvola and T. Engberg-Pedersen (eds), *The Emotions in Hellenistic Philosophy* (Stuttgart) 71–112.

Coplan, A. (2011) 'Will the real empathy please stand up? A case for a narrow conceptualization', *Southern Journal of Philosophy* 49, 40–65.

Coplan, A. and Goldie, P. (eds) (2011), *Empathy: Philosophical and Psychological Perspectives* (Oxford).

Corcella, A. (2009) 'Note a Filippo il Filosofo (Filagato da Cerami)', *Medioevo greco* 9, 47–9.

Corcella, A. (2010) 'Echi del romanzo e di Procopio di Gaza in Filagato Cerameo', *Byzantinische Zeitschrift* 103, 25–38.

Corcella, A. (2011a) 'Riuso e reimpiego dell'antico in Filagato', in N. Bianchi (ed.), *La tradizione dei testi greci in Italia meridionale: Filagato da Cerami philosophos e didaskalos – copisti, lettori, eruditi in Puglia tra XII e XVI secolo* (Bari) 12–19.

Corcella, A. (2011b) 'Tre nuovi testi di Procopio di Gaza: una dialexis inedita e due monodie già attribuite a Coricio', *Revue des études tardo-antiques* 1, 1–14.

Cornford, F. M. (1934) *The Origin of Attic Comedy* (Cambridge).

Costa, A., Foucart, A., Arnon, I., Aparici, M., and Apesteguia, J. (2014), '"Piensa" twice: on the foreign language effect in decision making', *Cognition* 130.2, 236–54.

Cotsonis, J. A. (1994) *Byzantine Figural Processional Crosses* (Washington, DC).

Cova, F. and Deonna, J. A. (2014) 'Being moved', *Philosophical Studies* 169.3, 444–66.

Cox Miller, P. (2012) *The Corporeal Imagination: Signifying the Holy in Late Ancient Christianity*, 2nd edn (Philadelphia).

Cramer, J. A. (1836) *Anecdota Graeca e codd. manuscriptis bibliothecarum Oxoniensium*, vol. 3 (Oxford, repr. Amsterdam, 1963).

Cribiore, R. (2001a) 'The grammarian's choice: the popularity of Euripides' *Phoenissae* in Hellenistic and Roman Education', in Y. L. Too (ed.) *Education in Greek and Roman Antiquity* (Leiden) 241–59.

Cribiore, R. (2001b) *Gymnastics of the Mind: Greek Education in Hellenistic and Roman Egypt* (Princeton).

Cribiore, R. (2009) *The School of Libanius in Late Antique Antioch* (Princeton).

Crislip, A. (2011) 'Envy and anger at the world's creation and destruction in the "Treatise without title 'On the origin of the world'"' (NHC II,5)', *Vigiliae christianae* 65, 285–310.

Crislip, A. (2013) *Thorns in the Flesh: Illness and Sanctity in Late Ancient Christianity* (Philadelphia).

Croke, B. (1981) 'Two early Byzantine earthquakes and their liturgical commemoration', *Byzantion* 51, 122–47.

Crompton, L. (2006) *Homosexuality and Civilization* (Cambridge, MA).

Crotty, K. (1994) *The Poetics of Supplication: Homer's Iliad and Odyssey* (Ithaca, NY).

Crotty, K. (2009) *The Philosopher's Song: the Poets' Influence on Plato* (Lanham, MD).

458 Bibliography

Cuff, B. M. P., Brown, S. J., Taylor, L., and Howatt, D. J. (2016), 'Empathy: a review of the concept', *Emotion Review* 8, 144–53.

Cullhed, E. (ed.) (2016) *Eustathios of Thessalonike: Commentary on Homer's Odyssey*, vol. 1, *On Rhapsodies α–β* (Studia Byzantina Upsaliensia 17) (Uppsala).

Cullhed, E. (2020) 'What evokes *being moved*?' *Emotion Review* 12.2, 111–17.

Cullhed, S. S. (2015) *Proba the Prophet: the Christian Virgilian Cento of Faltonia Betitia Proba (Mnemosyne* Supplement 378) (Leiden).

Cullyer, H. (2008) 'Chrysippus on Achilles: the evidence of Galen *De placitis Hippocratis et Platonis* 4.6–7', *Classical Quarterly* 58, 537–46.

Cummings, M. (2017) 'The interaction of emotions in the Greek novels', in M. P. Futre Pinheiro, D. Konstan, and B. D. MacQueen (eds), *Cultural Crossroads in the Ancient Novel* (Berlin) 315–26.

Cunningham, M. (1995) 'Innovation or mimesis in Byzantine sermons?', in A. R. Littlewood (ed.), *Originality in Byzantine Literature, Art and Music* (Oxford) 67–80.

Cunningham, M. (1998) 'Andrew of Crete: a high-style preacher of the eighth century', in M. Cunningham and P. Allen (eds), *Preacher and Audience: Studies in Early Christian and Byzantine Homiletics* (Leiden) 267–93.

Cunningham, M. (2003) 'Dramatic device or didactic tool? The function of dialogue in Byzantine preaching', in E. Jeffreys (ed.), *Rhetoric in Byzantium* (London) 101–13.

Cuomo, S. (2002), 'The machine and the city: Hero of Alexandria's *Belopoeica*', in C. J. Tuplin, T. E. Rihll, and L. Wolpert (eds), *Science and Mathematics in Ancient Greek Culture* (Oxford) 165–77.

Cupane, C. (2011) 'Στήλη τῆς ἀστειότητος: Byzantinische Vorstellungen weltlicher Vollkommenheit in Realität und Fiktion', *Frühmittelalterliche Studien* 45, 193–209.

Cupane, C. (2014) 'Other worlds, other voices: form and function of the marvelous in Late Byzantine fiction', in P. Roilos (ed.), *Medieval Greek Storytelling: Fictionality and Narrative in Byzantium* (Wiesbaden) 183–202.

Curtis, R. and Koch, G. (eds) (2009) *Einfühlung: zur Geschichte und Gegenwart eines ästhetischen Konzepts* (Paderborn).

Dagron, G. (ed.) (1978) *Vie et miracles de sainte Thècle* (Subsidia Hagiographica 62) (Paris).

Dahl, N. A. (2000) 'Kleidungsmetaphern: der alte und der neue Mensch', in D. Hellholm (ed.), *Studies in Ephesians: Introductory Questions, Text- and Edition-Critical Issues, Interpretation of Texts and Themes* (Wissenschaftliche Untersuchungen zum Neuen Testament 131) (Tübingen).

Daley, B. E. (1998) *On the Dormition of Mary: Early Patristic Homilies* (Crestwood, NY).

Daley, B. E. (2006) *Gregory of Nazianzus* (London).

Damasio, A. R. (1994) *Descartes' Error: Emotion, Reason, and the Human Brain* (New York).

Damasio, A. R. (1999) *The Feeling of What Happens: Body and Emotion in the Making of Consciousness* (New York).

Damon, C. (2017) 'Emotions as a historiographical dilemma', in D. L. Cairns and D. P. Nelis (eds), *Emotions in the Classical World: Methods, Approaches, and Directions* (Heidelberger althistorische Beiträge und epigraphische Studien 59) (Stuttgart) 177–94.

Daniélou, J. (1957) *Les manuscrits de la Mer Morte et les origines du christianisme* (Livre de vie 121) (Paris).

Darrouzès, J. (1957) *Syméon le Nouveau Théologien: chapitres théologiques, gnostiques et pratiques* (Sources chrétiennes 51) (Paris).

Bibliography 459

Dasen, V. (2010) 'Childbirth and infancy in Greek and Roman antiquity', in B. Rawson (ed.) *A Companion to Families in the Greek and Roman Worlds* (Malden, MA) 291–314.

Dassmann, E. (1991) 'Hiob', *Reallexikon für Antike und Christentum* 15, 366–442.

Daston, L., and Park, K. (1998) *Wonders and the Order of Nature, 1150–1750* (Cambridge, MA).

Datema, C. (ed.) (1970) *Asterius of Amasea, Homilies I–XIV: Text, Introduction and Notes* (Leiden).

Davies, G. M. (1994) 'The language of gesture in Greek art: gender and status on grave stelai', *Apollo* 140.389, 6–11.

Davies, G. M. (2005) 'On being seated: gender and body language in Hellenistic and Roman art', in D. L. Cairns (ed.), *Body Language in the Greek and Roman Worlds* (Swansea) 215–38.

Davis, J. and Hinterberger, M. (eds) (forthcoming) *The Metaphrasis of Niketas Choniates' Chronike Diegesis* (Byzantinisches Archiv) (Berlin).

Dawes, E. A. (1928) *Anna Comnena (Komnene): The Alexiad* (London).

De Lacy, P. (1996) 'Galen and the Greek poets', *Greek, Roman, and Byzantine Studies* 7, 259–66.

De Lacy, P. (ed. and trans.) (2005) *Galen: On the Doctrines of Hippocrates and Plato* (Corpus Medicorum Graecorum 5.4.1.2) (Berlin).

De Sousa, R. (1987) *The Rationality of Emotion* (Cambridge, MA).

De Sousa, R. (1990) 'Emotions, education, and time', *Metaphilosophy* 21, 434–46.

Deichmann, F. W. (1974) *Ravenna: Hauptstadt des spätantiken Abendlandes*, vol. 2.1 (Wiesbaden).

Dekazou, A. (1998) 'Οι ατομικές τιμωρίες των αμαρτωλών στην παράσταση της Δευτέρας Παρουσίας στη βυζαντινή και μεταβυζαντινή μνημειακή ζωγραφική', Master's thesis, Athens.

Delehaye, H. (ed.) (1902) *Synaxarium Ecclesiae Constantinopolitanae* (Brussels).

Demetracopoulos, J. A. (2005) 'Christian scepticism: the reception of Xenophanes' B34 in heathen and Chistian Antiquity and its sequel in Byzantine thought', in A. Frazier and P. Nold (eds), *Essays in Renaissance Thought and Letters in Honor of John Monfasani* (Leiden) 243–445.

Dennis, G. T. (2001) 'Death in Byzantium', *Dumbarton Oaks Papers* 55, 1–7.

Deonna, J. A. (2011) 'Etre ému', in C. Tappolet, F. Teroni, and A. Konzelman Ziv (eds), *Les ombres de l'âme: penser les emotions negatives* (Geneva) 111–28.

Der Nersessian, S. (1975) 'Program and iconography of the frescoes of the parecclesion', in P. A. Underwood (ed.), *The Kariye Djami*, vol. 4, *Studies in the Art of Kariye Djami* (Princeton), 305–49.

Derderian, K. (2001) *Leaving Words to Remember: Greek Mourning and the Advent of Literacy* (Leiden).

Destrée, P. (2012) 'The speech of Alcibiades (212c4–222b7)', in C. Horn (ed.), *Platon: Symposion* (Berlin) 191–205.

Deutscher, G. (2010) *Through the Language Glass: Why the World Looks Different in Other Languages* (New York).

Dewey, J. (1895) 'The theory of emotion II: the significance of emotions', *Psychological Review* 2, 13–32.

Dhorme, E. (1923) *L'emploi métaphorique des noms de parties du corps en hébreu et en akkadien* (Paris).

460   *Bibliography*

Dibelius, M. (1923) *Die Apostolischen Väter*, vol. 4, *Der Hirt des Hermas* (Handbuch zum Neuen Testament Ergänzungsband) (Tübingen).

Dibelius, M. (1992) '"Hirt" des Hermas', in F. X. Funk, K. Bihlmeyer, and M. Whittaker (eds), *Die Apostolischen Väter: griechisch–deutsche Parallelausgabe* (Tübingen) 325–555.

Dickey, E. (2007) *Ancient Greek Scholarship: a Guide to Finding, Reading, and Understanding Scholia, Commentaries, Lexica, and Grammatical Treatises, from Their Beginnings to the Byzantine Period* (Oxford).

Diddle Uzzi, J. (2007) 'The power of parenthood in official Roman art', in A. Cohen and J. B. Rutter (eds), *Constructions of Childhood in Ancient Greece and Italy* (*Hesperia* Supplement 41) (Princeton) 61–81.

Dierichs, A. (2002) *Von der Götter Geburt und der Frauen Niederkunft* (Mainz).

Dieten, J.-L. van (ed.) (1975) *Nicetae Choniatae Historia* (Corpus Fontium Historiae Byzantinae 11) (Berlin).

Dilley, P.C. (2017) *Monasteries and the Care of Souls in Late Antique Christianity: Cognition and Discipline* (Cambridge).

Dimas, S. (1998) *Untersuchungen zur Themenwahl und Bildgestaltung auf römischen Kindersarkosphagen* (Münster).

Dindorf, L. (ed.) (1832) *Chronicon Paschale* (Bonn).

Dixon, S. (1988) *The Roman Mother* (London).

Dodds, E.R. (ed.) (1944) *Euripides, Bacchae: Edited with Introduction and Commentary* (Oxford).

Dostálová, R. (1982) 'Die byzantinische Theorie des Dramas und die Tragödie *Christos Paschon*', *Jahrbuch der österreichischen Byzantinistik* 32, 73–82.

Dow, J. (2015) *Passions and Persuasion in Aristotle's Rhetoric* (Oxford).

Dowden, K. (1996) 'Heliodorus: serious intentions', *Classsical Quarterly* 46, 267–85.

Downey, G. (1954) 'A processional cross', *Metropolitan Museum of Art Bulletin* 12.9, 276–80.

Downey, G. (ed. and trans.) (1957) 'Nikolaos Mesarites: description of the Church of the Holy Apostles at Constantinople', *Transactions of the American Philosophical Society* n.s. 47.6, 855–924.

Drakopoulou, E. (2000) 'Ο φόβος της τιμωρίας στη βυζαντινή και μεταβυζαντινή ζωγραφική', in E. Grammatikopoulou (ed.), *Οι συλλογικοί φόβοι στην ιστορία* (Athens), 93–110.

Dresken-Weiland, J. (2012) *Immagine e parola: alle origini dell'iconografia Cristiana* (Vatican).

Driver, S.R. (1908) *The Book of the Prophet Jeremiah: a Revised Translation with Introductions and Short Explanations*, 2nd edn (London).

Dronke, P. (ed.) (1994) *Verses pascales de tres Maries*, in *Nine Medieval Latin Plays* (Cambridge Medieval Classics 1) (Cambridge), 92–100.

Drpić, I. (2016) *Epigram, Art and Devotion in Later Byzantium* (Cambridge).

Dübner, F. (1846) *Christus patiens, Ezechieli et christianorum poetarum reliquiae dramaticae* (Paris).

Dué, C. (2002) *Homeric Variations on a Lament by Briseis* (Lanham, MD).

Dué, C. (2006) *The Captive Woman's Lament in Greek Tragedy* (Austin, TX).

Dufour, M. and Wartelle, A. (eds) (1973) *Aristote, Rhétorique Livre III* (Paris).

Duluş, M. (2011) 'Philagathos of Cerami and the monastic renewal in the twelfth-century Norman kingdom: preaching and persuasion', in N. Bianchi (ed.), *La tradizione dei testi greci in Italia meridionale: Filagato da Cerami philosophos e didaskalos – copisti, lettori, eruditi in Puglia tra XII e XVI secolo* (Bari) 52–63.

Duluş, M. (2018) 'Rhetoric, exegesis and florilegic structure in Philagathos of Cerami: an investigation of the homilies and of the allegorical exegesis of Heliodorus' *Aethiopika*' (Ph.D. Diss. Budapest).

Duluş, M. (2020) 'Philagathos of Cerami, Procopius of Gaza, and the rhetoric of appropriation', *Greek, Roman, and Byzantine Studies* 60, 472–9.

Duluş, M. (2021) 'From rhetorical appropriation to spiritual transposition: the homilies of Philagathos of Cerami and the ancient novels', *Byzantion* 91, 111–54.

Duncan, A. (2006) *Performance and Identity in the Classical World* (Cambridge).

Durand, M. G. de (1993) 'La colère chez S. Jean Chrysostome', *Revue des sciences religieuses* 67, 61–77.

Durkheim, É. (2001 [1912]) *The Elementary Forms of Religious Life*, trans. C. Cosman (Oxford).

Dyck, A. R. (1986) 'Michael Psellos, On Euripides and George of Pisidia', in *The Essays on Euripides and George of Pisidia and on Heliodorus and Achilles Tatius* (Byzantina Vindobonensia 16) (Vienna).

Dyson, M. E. (2006) *Pride: the Seven Deadly Sins* (Oxford).

Easterling, P. (1999) 'Actors and voices: reading between the lines in Aeschines and Demosthenes', in S. Goldhill and R. Osborne (eds), *Performance Culture and Athenian Democracy* (Cambridge) 154–66..

Eastmond, A. (2008) 'Art and the periphery', in R. Cormack, J. F. Haldon, and E. Jeffreys (eds), *The Oxford Handbook of Byzantine Studies* (Oxford) 771–6.

Eco, U. (1995) 'On the impossibility of drawing a map of the Empire on a scale of 1:1', in *How to Travel with a Salmon: and Other Essays* (San Diego) 95–106.

Edsall, M. (2002) 'Religious narratives and religious themes in the novels of Achilles Tatius and Heliodorus', *Ancient Narrative* 1, 114–33.

Edwards, L. H. (2013) 'A brief conceptual history of *Einfühlung*: 18th-century Germany to post-World War II U. S. Psychology', *History of Psychology* 16.4, 269–81.

Edwards, M. (trans.) (2000) *Neoplatonic Saints: the Lives of Plotinus and Proclus by Their Students* (Liverpool).

Edwards, M. (2007) 'Alcidamas', in I. Worthington (ed.), *Companion to Greek Rhetoric* (Oxford) 47–57.

Effenberger, A. (1977) 'Die Grabstele aus Medinet el-Fajum: zum Bild der stillenden Gottesmutter in der koptischen Kunst', *Forschungen und Berichte* 18, 158–68.

Effenberger, A. and Severin, H.-G. (1992) *Staatliche Museen zu Berlin: das Museum für spätantike und byzantinische Kunst* (Mainz).

Efthymiadis, S. (ed.) (1998) *The Life of the Patriarch Tarasios by Ignatios Deacon (BHG 1698)* (Birmingham Byzantine and Ottoman Monographs 4) (Aldershot).

Ehrman, B. D. (2003) *The Apostolic Fathers*, vol. 2, *Epistle of Barnabas, Papias and Quadratus, Epistle to Diognetus, The Shepherd of Hermas* (Cambridge, MA).

Eijk, P. van der (2008) 'Therapeutics', in R. J. Hankinson (ed.), *The Cambridge Companion to Galen* (Cambridge) 283–303.

Ekman, P. (2003) *Emotions Revealed: Understanding Faces and Feelings* (London).

Elgvin, T. (1997) '"To master his own vessel": 1 Thess 4:4 in light of new Qumran evidence', *New Testament Studies* 43, 604–19.

462   Bibliography

Elm, S. (2012) *Sons of Hellenism, Fathers of the Church: Emperor Julian, Gregory of Nazianzus, and the Vision of Rome* (Transformation of the Classical Heritage 49) (Berkeley).

Elmer, D. (2008) 'Heliodoros's "sources": intertextuality, paternity, and the Nile River in the *Aithiopika*', *Transactions of the American Philological Association* 138, 411–50.

Elsner, J. (1995) *Art and the Roman Viewer: the Transformation of Art from the Pagan World to Christianity* (Cambridge).

Ene D-Vasilescu, E. (2018) *Heavenly Sustenance in Patristic Texts and Byzantine Iconography: Nourished by the Word* (Oxford).

Engberg-Pedersen, T. (2017), *John and Philosophy: a New Reading of the Fourth Gospel* (Oxford).

Engelen, E.-M. and Röttger-Rössler, B. (2012), 'Current disciplinary and interdisciplinary debates on empathy', *Emotion Review* 4, 3–8.

Engels, J. (1998) *Funerum sepulchrorumque magnificentia: Begräbnis- und Grabluxusgesetze in der griechisch-römischen Welt mit einigen Ausblicken auf Einschränkungen des funeralen und sepulkralen Luxus im Mittelalter und in der Neuzeit* (Stuttgart).

Eppel, R. (1930) *Le piétisme juif dans les Testaments des douze Patriarches* (Paris).

Erffa, C.E. von (1937) Αἰδώς *und verwandte Begriffe in ihrer Entwicklung von Homer bis Demokrit* (*Philologus* Supplement 30.2) (Leipzig).

Erler, M. (2011) 'The happiness of bees: affect and virtue in the *Phaedo* and in the *Republic*', in M. Migliori, L. M. Napolitano Valditara, and A. Fermani (eds), *Inner Life and Soul: Psychē in Plato* (Sankt Augustin) 59–71.

Eshel, S. (2018) *The Concept of the Elect Nation in Byzantium* (Leiden).

Evans, J. and Carman, C.C. (2013) 'Mechanical astronomy: a route to the ancient discovery of epicycles and eccentrics', in N. Sidoli and G. van Brummelen (eds), *From Alexandria, through Baghdad: Surveys and Studies in the Ancient Greek and Medieval Islamic Mathematical Sciences* (Heidelberg) 145–74..

Eyre, A. (2007) 'Remembering: community commemoration after disaster', in H. Rodriguez, E. Quarantelli, and R. Dynes (eds), *Handbook of Disaster Research* (New York) 441–55.

Fatouros, G. (ed.) (1992) *Theodori Studitae Epistulae*, vol. 2 (Corpus Fontium Historiae Byzantinae, Series Berolinensis 31) (Berlin).

Feagin, S. L. (1996) *Reading with Feeling* (Ithaca, NY).

Featherstone, J. and Signes Codoñer, J. (ed. and trans.) (2015) *Chronographiae quae Theophanis Continuati nomine fertur libri I–IV* (Berlin).

Fehr, B. and Russell, J.A. (1984) 'Concept of emotion viewed from a prototype perspective', *Journal of Experimental Psychology: General* 113.3, 464–86.

Feke, J. (2014) 'Meta-mathematical rhetoric: Hero and Ptolemy against the philosophers', *Historia Mathematica* 41, 261–76.

Ferguson, E. (2009) *Baptism in the Early Church* (Grand Rapids).

Ferneyhough, C. (2016) *The Voices Within: the History and Science of How We Talk to Ourselves* (London).

Feros Ruys, J. (2012) 'Sensitive spirits: changing depictions of demonic emotions in the twelfth and thirteenth centuries', *Digital Philology: a Journal of Medieval Cultures* 1, 184–209..

Feros Ruys, J. (2015) 'Tears such as angels weep: the evolution of sadness in demons', in M. Champion and A. Lynch (eds), *Understanding Emotions in Early Europe* (Turnhout) 51–71.

Feros Ruys, J. (2017) *Demons in the Middle Ages* (Kalamazoo).

Festugière, A. J. (ed.) (1970) *Vie de Théodore de Sykéon* (Subsidia Hagiographica 48) (Brussels).

Fischer, A. H. (1991) *Emotion Scripts: a Study of the Social and Cognitive Facets of Emotion* (Leiden).

Fish, S. (1970) 'Literature in the reader: affective stylistics', *New Literary History* 2.1, 123–62.

Fisher, E. A. (1994) *Michaelis Pselli Orationes hagiographicae* (Leipzig).

Fiske, A. P. (2019) *Kama Muta: Discovering the Connecting Emotion* (London).

Fittschen, K. and Zanker, P. (1983) *Kaiserinnen- und Prinzessinnenporträts* (Katalog der römischen Porträts in den Capitolinischen Museen und den anderen kommunalen Sammlungen der Stadt Rom 3) (Mainz).

Fitzgerald, J. T. (ed.) (2008) *Passions and Moral Progress in Graeco-Roman Thought* (London).

Fögen, T. (2001) 'Ancient theorizing on non-verbal communication' in R. M. Brend, A. Lommel, and A. Melby (eds), *Speaking and Comprehending: Papers of the 27th Forum of the Linguistic Association of Canada and the United States* (*LACUS* Forum 27) (Los Angeles) 203–16.

Fögen, T. (ed.) (2009) *Tears in the Graeco-Roman World* (Berlin).

Follieri, E. (1991/2) 'Ancora una nota sul "Christus Patiens"', *Byzantinische Zeitschrift* 84/5, 255–7.

Fontaine, J. R. J. (2009) 'Shame', in D. Sander and K. R. Scherer (eds), *Oxford Companion to Emotion and the Affective Sciences* (Oxford) 367–8.

Fortenbaugh, W. W. (2002 [1975]) *Aristotle on Emotion*, 2nd edn (London).

Fortenbaugh, W. W. (2017) 'The Pseudo-Aristotelian *Problems* on sympathy', in D. L. Cairns and D. P. Nelis (eds), *Emotions in the Classical World: Methods, Approaches, and Directions* (Heidelberger althistorische Beiträge und epigraphische Studien 59) (Stuttgart) 125–42.

Fowler, D. P. (1997) 'Epicurean anger' in S. M. Braund and C. Gill (eds), *The Passions in Roman Thought and Literature* (Cambridge) 16–35.

Foxhall, L. (2019) 'In private: the individual and the domestic community' in D. L. Cairns (ed.), *A Cultural History of the Emotions in Antiquity* (London) 125–45.

Frank, S. K. (2018) 'Pathosformel "tote Mutter" zwischen Bild und Text', in S. K. Frank (ed.), *Bildformeln: Visuelle Erinnerungskulturen in Osteuropa* (Bielefeld) 269–303.

Frankfurter, D. (2021) 'Desperation and the magic of appeal: representation of women's emotion in magical spells and ritual figurines', in A. Chaniotis (ed.), *Unveiling Emotions III: Arousal, Display, and Performance of Emotions in the Greek World* (Stuttgart) 517–36.

Franzoni, C. (2006) *Tirannia dello sguardo: corpo, gesto, espressione nell'arte greca* (Turin).

Fredal, J. (2006) *Rhetorical Action in Ancient Athens: Persuasive Artistry from Solon to Demosthenes* (Carbondale).

Frede, D. (1996) 'Mixed feelings in Aristotle's *Rhetoric*', in A. O. Rorty (ed.), *Essays on Aristotle's Rhetoric* (Berkeley) 258–85.

Freese, J. H. (trans.), revised by Striker, G. (2020) *Aristotle: Art of Rhetoric* (Loeb Classical Library 193) (Cambridge, MA).

French, D. R. (1998) 'Rhetoric and the rebellion of A.D. 387 in Antioch', *Historia* 47, 468–84.

Frevert, U. (2009) 'Was haben Gefühle in der Geschichte zu suchen?', *Geschichte und Gesellschaft* 35, 183–208.

Frevert, U. (2011) *Emotions in History: Lost and Found* (Budapest).

Frey, J. (1997) 'Different patterns of dualistic thought in the Qumran library: reflections on their background and history' in M. Bernstein, F. García Martínez, and J. Kampen (eds), *Legal Texts and Legal Issues: Proceedings of the Second Meeting of the International Organization for Qumran Studies, Published in Honour of J. M. Baumgarten* (Studies on the Texts of the Desert of Judah 23) (Leiden) 275–335.

Frey, J. (2001) 'Die Bedeutung der Qumranfunde für das Neue Testament', in M. Fieger, K. Schmid, and P. Schwagmeier (eds), *Qumran: die Schriftrollen vom Toten Meer. Vorträge des St. Galler Qumran-Symposiums vom 2./3. Juli 1999* (Novum Testamentum et Orbis Antiquus 47) (Fribourg) 129–208.

Fuchs, E. (1931) *Glaube und Tat in den Mandata des Hirten des Hermas* (Ph.D. Diss. Marburg).

Fulkerson, L. (2013) *No Regrets: Remorse in Classical Antiquity* (Oxford).

Fusillo, M. (1986) '"Mythos" aristotelico e "récit" narratologico', *Strumenti Critici* 52, 381–92.

Fusillo, M. (1999) 'The conflict of emotions: a *topos* in the Greek erotic novel', in S. Swain (ed.), *Oxford Readings in the Greek Novel* (Oxford) 60–82 (first published as 'Le conflit des émotions: un topos du roman grec érotique', *Museum Helveticum* 47 (1990), 201–21).

Füssli, J. R. and Füssli, J. H. (1810) *Allgemeines Künstlerlexikon, oder: Kurze Nachricht von dem Leben und den Werken der Maler, Bildhauer, Baumeister, Kupferstecher, Kunstgießer, Stahlschneider etc.*, vol. 1 (Zurich).

Gador-Whyte, S. (2017) *Theology and Poetry in Early Byzantium: the Kontakia of Romanos the Melodist* (Cambridge).

Galatariotou, C. (1991) *The Making of a Saint: the Life, Times and Sanctification of Neophytos the Recluse* (New York).

Galinier, M. (2012) 'Domi forisque: les vêtements romains de la Vertu', in F. Gherchanoc and V. Huet (eds), *Vêtements antiques: s'habiller, se déshabiller dans les mondes anciens. Actes du colloque ANHIMA 2009* (Paris) 189–208.

Gallagher, S. (2005) *How the Body Shapes the Mind* (Oxford).

Gallagher, S. (2012) *Phenomenology* (London).

Gallagher, S. (2020) *Action and Interaction* (Oxford).

Gallagher, S. and Hutto, D. D. (2008) 'Understanding others through primary interaction and narrative practice', in J. Zlatev, T. Racine, C. Sinha, and E. Itkonen (eds), *The Shared Mind: Perspectives on Intersubjectivity* (Amsterdam) 17–38.

Gallagher, S. and Zahavi, D. (2008) *The Phenomenological Mind: an Introduction to Philosophy of Mind and Cognitive Science* (London).

Garidis, M. (1982) 'Les punitions collectives et individuelles des damnés dans le Jugement Dernier (du XIIe au XIVe siècle)', *Zbornik za Likovne Umetnosti* 18, 1–18.

Garidis, M. (1985) *Études sur le jugement dernier post-byzantin du XVe à la fin du XIXe siècle: iconographie, esthétique* (Thessaloniki).

Garland, L. (1997) 'Morality versus politics at the Byzantine court: the charges against Marie of Antioch and Euphrosyne', *Byzantinische Forschungen* 24, 286–93.

Garland, R. (1985) *The Greek Way of Death* (London).

Garzya, A. (1984) 'Per la cronologia del *Christus Patiens*', in *Studi in onore di Adelmo Barigazzi*, vol. 1 (Rome) 237–40.

Garzya, A. (1989) 'Ancora per la cronologia del *Christus Patiens*', *Byzantinische Zeitschrift* 82, 110–13.

Bibliography 465

Gaskin, R. (2018) *Tragedy and Redress in Western Literature: a Philosophical Perspective* (London).

Gaul, N. (2011) *Thomas Magistros und die spätbyzantinische Sophistik: Studien zum Humanismus urbaner Eliten in der frühen Palaiologenzeit* (Wiesbaden).

Gaul, N. (2014) 'Rising elites and institutionalization – *ēthos/mores* – "debts" and drafts: three concluding steps towards comparing networks of learning in Byzantium and the 'Latin' West, *c.*1000–1200', in S. Steckel, N. Gaul, and M. Grünbart (eds), *Networks of Learning: Perspectives on Scholars in Byzantine East and Latin West, c.1000–1200* (Berlin) 235–80.

Gaul, N. (2018) 'Performative reading in the Late Byzantine *theatron*', in I. Toth and T. Shawcross (eds), *Reading in the Byzantine Empire* (Cambridge) 215–33.

Gaul, N. (2020) 'The letter in the *theatron*: epistolary voice, character, soul, and their audience', in A. Riehle (ed.), *A Companion to Byzantine Epistolography* (Leiden) 353–73.

Gaul, N. (forthcoming) 'Shivers of excitement: *ekplēxis* in performative contexts', in M. Mullett and A. White (eds), *Performing Byzantium*.

Gautier, P. (1978) 'Monodies inédites de Michel Psellos', *Revue des études byzantines* 36, 82–151.

Geeraerts, D. (2015) 'Four guidelines for diachronic metaphor research', in J. E. Díaz Vera (ed.) *Metaphor and Metonymy across Time and Cultures: Perspectives on the Sociohistorical Linguistics of Figurative Language* (Cognitive Linguistics Research 52) (Berlin) 15–27.

Geffcken, J. (1908) *Christliche Apokryphen* (Religionsgeschichtliche Volksbücher 1.15) (Tübingen).

Géhin, P., Guillaumont, C., and Guillaumont, A. (eds) (1998) *Évagre le Pontique, Sur les pensées* (Sources chrétiennes 438) (Paris).

Geiger, M. (1911) 'Über das Wesen und die Bedeutung der Einfühlung', *Bericht über den Kongress der deutschen Gesellschaft für Psychologie* 4, 29–73.

Gemünden, P. von (2007) 'Affekte und Affektkontrolle im antiken Judentum und Urchristentum', in G. Theissen and P. von Gemünden (eds), *Erkennen und Erleben: Beiträge zur psychologischen Erforschung des frühen Christentums* (Gütersloh) 249–69.

Gemünden, P. von (2009) 'Methodische Überlegungen zur Historischen Psychologie exemplifiziert am Themenkomplex der Trauer in der Bibel und ihrer Umwelt', in *Affekt und Glaube: Studien zur Historischen Psychologie des Frühjudentums und Urchristentums* (Novum Testamentum et Orbis Antiquus 73) (Göttingen) 13–33.

Gendron, M., Lindquist, K. A., Barsalou, L., and Barrett, L. F. (2012), 'Emotion words shape emotion percepts', *Emotion* 12, 314–25.

Gerstel, S. E. J. (2019) 'Images in churches in Late Byzantium: reflections and directions', in S. Brodbeck and A. O. Poilpré with M. Stavrou (eds), *Visibilité et presence de l'image dans l'espace ecclesial: Byzance et Moyen Âge occidental* (Paris) 93–120.

Gesenius, W. (1915) *Hebräisches und Aramäisches Handwörterbuch über das Alte Testament* (Leipzig).

Giagkou, T. and Papatriantafyllou-Theodoridi, N. (eds) (1999) 'Πανηγυρική Βίβλος Α.', in I. Karabidopoulos, C. Oikonomou, D. G. Tsames, and N. Zacharopoulos (eds), Ἁγίου Νεοφύτου τοῦ Ἐγκλείστου Συγγράμματα, vol. 3 (Paphos).

Giannouli, A. (2009) 'Die Tränen der Zerknirschung: zur katanyktischen Kirchendichtung als Heilmittel', in P. Odorico, P. Agapitos, and M. Hinterberger (eds), '*Doux remède ...*': *poésie et poétique à Byzance. Actes du IVe Colloque international philologique 'Hermeneia', Paris, 23–24–25 février 2006* (Dossiers byzantins 9) (Paris) 141–55.

466 *Bibliography*

Giannouli, A. (2013) 'Catanyctic religious poetry: a survey', in A. Rigo, P. Ermilov, and M. Trizio (eds), *Theologica minora: the Minor Genres of Byzantine Theological Literatur* (Turnhout) 86–109.

Gibson, C.A. (2008) *Libanius's Progymnasmata: Model Exercises in Greek Prose Composition and Rhetoric* (Atlanta).

Gill, C. (1984) 'The *ēthos/pathos* distinction in rhetorical and literary criticism', *Classical Quarterly* 34, 149–66.

Gill, C. (1996) *Personality in Greek Epic, Tragedy, and Philosophy* (Oxford).

Gill, C. (1998) 'Did Galen understand Platonic and Stoic thinking on emotions?', in J. Sihvola and T. Engberg-Pedersen (eds), *The Emotions in Hellenistic Philosophy* (Dordrecht) 138–48.

Gill, C. (2007) 'Galen and the Stoics: mortal enemies or blood brothers?', *Phronesis* 52, 88–120.

Gill, C. (2010a) *Naturalistic Psychology in Galen and Stoicism* (Oxford).

Gill, C. (2010b) 'Stoicism and Epicureanism', in P. Goldie (ed.), *The Oxford Handbook of Philosophy of Emotion* (Oxford) 143–65.

Ginter, K. (2017) 'The Trisagion riots (512) as an example of interaction between politics and liturgy', *Studia Ceranea* 7, 41–57.

Giuliano, F. M. (2005) *Platone e la poesia: teoria della composizione e prassi della Ricezione* (Sankt Augustin).

Glasson, T. F. (1961) *Greek Influence in Jewish Eschatology* (London).

Gleason, M. (1995) *Making Men: Sophists and Self-Presentation in Ancient Rome* (Princeton).

Goffman, E. (1967) *Interaction Ritual: Essays in Face-to-Face Behavior* (New York).

Gokey, F. X. (1961) *The Terminology for the Devil and Evil Spirits in the Apostolic Fathers: a Dissertation* (Washington, DC).

Goldie, P. (1999) 'How we think of others' emotions', *Mind and Language* 14, 394–423.

Goldie, P. (2002) *The Emotions: a Philosophical Exploration* (Oxford).

Goldie, P. (2011), 'Anti-empathy', in A. Coplan and P. Goldie (eds), *Empathy: Philosophical and Psychological Perspectives* (Oxford) 302–17.

Goldie, P. (2012) *The Mess Inside: Narrative, Emotion, and the Mind* (Oxford).

Goldin-Meadow, S. (2003) *Hearing Gesture: How Our Hands Help Us Think* (Cambridge, MA).

Goldstein, B. R. (1997) 'Saving the phenomena: the background to Ptolemy's planetary theory', *Journal for the History of Astronomy* 28, 1–12.

Goldwyn, A. J. (2015) 'John Malalas and the origins of the allegorical and novelistic traditions of the Trojan War in Byzantium', *Troianalexandrina* 15, 23–49.

Goldwyn, A. J. (2018) *Byzantine Ecocriticism: Women, Nature, and Power in the Medieval Greek Romance* (London).

Goldwyn, A. J. and Nilsson, I. (eds) (2019) *The Late Byzantine Romance: a Handbook* (Cambridge).

Golitzin, A. (2013) *Mystagogy: a Monastic Reading of Dionysius Areopagita* (Collegeville).

Gordon, S. L. (1981) 'The sociology of sentiments and emotions', in M. Rosenberg and R. H. Turner (eds), *Social Psychology: Sociological Perspectives* (New York), 562–9.

Graf, F. (1991) 'Gestures and conventions: the gestures of Roman actors and orators', in J. Bremmer and H. Roodenburg (eds), *A Cultural History of Gesture* (Ithaca, NY) 36–58.

Graver, M. (2007) *Stoicism and Emotion* (Chicago).

Griffiths, J.G. (1991) *The Divine Verdict: a Study of Divine Judgement in the Ancient Religions* (Leiden).

Griffiths, P. (1997) *What Emotions Really Are: the Problem of Psychological Categories* (Chicago).

Groote, M. de (2012) *Christophori Mitylenaii Versuum variorum collectio Cryptensis* (Corpus Christianorum, Series Graeca 74) (Turnhout).

Grosdidier de Matons, J. (ed.) (1967) *Romanos le Mélode, Hymnes: Introduction, Texte Critique, Traduction et Notes*, vol. 4 (Sources chrétiennes 128) (Paris) 380–420.

Grumel, V. (1958) *Traité d'études byzantines*, vol. 1, *La chronologie* (Paris).

Grünbart, M. (forthcoming) 'Die Macht des Klangs: akustische Dimensionen des griechischen Mittelalters', in N. Jaspert and H. Müller (eds), *Klangräume des Mittelalters* (Vorträge und Forschungen 88) (Konstanz).

Grünbart, M., Kislinger, E., Muthesius, A. (eds) (2007) *Material Culture and Well-Being in Byzantium* (Vienna).

Guillaumont, A. and Guillaumont, C. (eds) (1971) *Évagre le Pontique: Traité pratique ou Le moine* (Sources chrétiennes 170 and 171) (Paris).

Gunderson, E. (2000) *Staging Masculinity: the Rhetoric of Performance in the Roman World* (Ann Arbor).

Gutsell, J.N. and Inzlicht, M. (2010) 'Empathy constrained: prejudice predicts reduced mental simulation of actions during observation of out-groups', *Journal of Experimental Social Psychology* 46.5, 841–5.

Guy, J.-C. (ed.) (1993–2005) *Les apophthegmes des pères, collection systématique* (Sources chrétiennes 387, 474, and 498) (Paris).

Hadzisteliou Price, T. (1978) *Kourotrophos: Cults and Representations of the Greek Nursing Deities* (Leiden).

Hahnemann, G.M. (1992) *The Muratorian Fragment and the Development of the Canon* (Oxford Theological Monographs 47.3) (Oxford).

Haines-Eitzen, K. (2017) 'Geographies of silence in Late Antiquity' in S. Ashbrook Harvey and M. Mullett (eds), *Knowing Bodies, Passionate Souls: Sense Perception in Byzantium* (Washington, DC) 111–22.

Halkin, F. (ed.) (1989) *Hagiographica inedita decem* (Corpus Christianorum, Series Graeca 21) (Turnhout).

Hall, E. (1995) 'Lawcourt dramas: the power of performance in Greek forensic oratory', *Bulletin of the Institute of Classical Studies* 40, 39–58.

Hall, E. (2004) 'Introduction: why Greek tragedy in the late twentieth century?', in E. Hall, F. Macintosh, and A. Wrigley (eds), *Dionysus since 69: Greek Tragedy at the Dawn of the Third Millennium* (Oxford) 1–46.

Hall, J. (2004) 'Cicero and Quintilian on the oratorical use of hand gestures', *Classical Quarterly* 54, 143–60.

Hall, J. (2007) 'Oratorical delivery and the emotions: theory and practice', in W. Dominik and J. Hall (eds), *A Companion to Roman Rhetoric* (Oxford) 218–34.

Hall, S.G. (trans.) (2000) 'On the beatitudes', in H. R. Drobner and A. Viciano (eds), *Gregory of Nyssa, Homilies on the Beatitudes: an English Version with Supporting Studies. Proceedings of the Eighth International Colloquium on Gregory of Nyssa* (Leiden) 21–90.

Halliwell, S. (1990) 'Traditional Greek conceptions of character', in C. B. R. Pelling (ed.), *Characterization and Individuality in Greek Literature* (Oxford) 32–59.

Halliwell, S. (2002) *The Aesthetics of Mimesis: Ancient Texts and Modern Problems* (Princeton).

468   *Bibliography*

Halliwell, S. (2008) *Greek Laughter: a Study of Cultural Psychology from Homer to Early Christianity* (Cambridge).

Halliwell, S. (2017) 'The poetics of emotional expression: some problems of ancient theory', in D. L. Cairns and D. P. Nelis (eds), *Emotions in the Classical World: Methods, Approaches and Directions* (Heidelberger althistorische Beiträge und epigraphische Studien 59) (Stuttgart) 105–23.

Halperin, D. (1992), 'Plato and the erotics of narrativity', *Oxford Studies in Ancient Philosophy* Supplement 2 (Oxford) 93–129.

Hankinson, R. J. (ed.) (2008) *The Cambridge Companion to Galen* (Cambridge).

Hansen, G. H. (ed.) (1971) *Theodoros Anagnostes Kirchengeschichte* (Berlin).

Hansen, T., Olkkonen, M., Walter, S., and Gegenfurtner, K. R. (2006) 'Memory modulates color appearance', in *Nature Neuroscience* 9.11, 1367–8.

Harré, R. (ed.) (1986) *The Social Construction of Emotions* (Oxford).

Harré, T. and Finlay-Jones, R. (1986) 'Emotion talk across times', in R. Harré (ed.) *The Social Construction of Emotions* (Oxford) 220–33.

Harris, E. (2017) 'How to "act" in an Athenian court: emotions and forensic performance', in S. Papaioannou, A. Serafim, and B. da Vela (eds), *The Theatre of Justice: Aspects of Performance in Greco-Roman Oratory and Rhetoric* (Leiden) 223–42.

Harris, O. and Sørensen, T. (2010) 'Rethinking emotion and material culture', *Archaeological Dialogues* 17.2, 145–63.

Harris, W. V. (2001) *Restraining Rage: the Ideology of Anger Control in Classical Antiquity* (Cambridge, MA).

Harrison, N. V. (2006) 'Gregory Nazianzen's festal spirituality: anamnesis and mimesis', *Philosophy and Theology* 18, 27–51.

Hatch, E. and Redpath, H. (2005) *A Concordance to the Septuagint and the Other Greek Versions of the Old Testament: Including the Apocryphal Books* (Grand Rapids).

Hausherr, I. (1944) *Penthos: la doctrine de la componction dans l'Orient chrétien* (Rome).

Hausrath, A. and Hunger, H. (eds) (1959–70) *Corpus fabularum Aesopicarum* (Leipzig).

Havelock, E. A. (1963) *Preface to Plato* (Oxford).

Hayakawa, S., Costa, A., Foucart, A., and Keysar, B. (2016) 'Using a foreign language changes our choices', *Trends in Cognitive Sciences* 20.11, 791–3.

Heath, J. (1999) 'The serpent and the sparrows: Homer and the parodos of Aeschylus' Agamemnon', *Classical Quarterly* 49, 396–407.

Heath, J. (2005) *The Talking Greeks: Speech, Animals, and the Other in Homer, Aeschylus, and Plato* (Cambridge).

Heath, M. (1987) *The Poetics of Greek Tragedy* (London).

Heisenberg, A. and Wirth, P. (eds) (1978) *Georgii Acropolitae opera* (Stuttgart).

Hellholm, D. (2009) 'Der Hirt des Hermas', in W. Pratscher (ed.), *Die Apostolischen Väter: eine Einleitung* (Göttingen) 227–53.

Hennessy, C. (2008) *Images of Children in Byzantium* (Burlington).

Henning, M. (2014) *Educating Early Christians through the Rhetoric of Hell: 'Weeping and Gnashing of Teeth' as Paideia in Matthew and the Early Church* (Tübingen).

Hense, O. and Wachsmuth, C. (eds) (1894) *Ioannis Stobaei Anthologium*, vol. 3 (Berlin).

Hershkowitz, D. (1998) *The Madness of Epic* (Oxford).

Hesberg-Tonn, B. von (1983) *Coniunx Carissima: Untersuchungen zum Normcharakter im Erscheinungsbild der römischen Frau* (Ph.D. Diss. Stuttgart).

Bibliography 469

Hess, U., Houde, S., and Fischer, A. (2014) 'Do we mimic what we see or what we know?', in C. von Scheve and M. Salmela (eds), *Collective Emotions: Perspectives from Psychology, Philosophy, and Sociology* (Oxford) 94–107.

Hilberg, I.H. (1886) 'Kann Theodoros Prodromos der Verfasser des Χριστὸς Πάσχων sein?', *Wiener Studien* 8, 282–314.

Hilhorst, A. (1976) *Sémitismes et latinismes dans le Pasteur d'Hermas* (Graecitas Christianorum Primaeva 5) (Nijmegen).

Hill, B. (1997) 'Imperial women and the ideology of womanhood in the eleventh and twelfth centuries', in L. James (ed.), *Women, Men, and Eunuchs: Gender in Byzantium* (London) 76–99.

Hill, R. (trans.) (2008) *Cyril of Alexandria, Commentary on the Twelve Prophets* (Washington, DC).

Hinterberger, M. (1999) *Autobiographische Traditionen in Byzanz* (Wiener byzantinistische Studien 22) (Vienna).

Hinterberger, M. (2003) "Φόβῳ κατασεισθείς": τα πάθη του ανθρώπου και της αυτοκρατορίας στον Μιχαήλ Ατταλειάτη. Το αιτιολογικό σύστημα ενος ιστοριογράφου του ΙΙου αιώνα', in V. N. Vlysidou (ed.), *Η αυτοκρατορία σε κρίση(;): το Βυζάντιο τον ΙΙο αιώνα (1025–1081)* (Athens) 155–67.

Hinterberger, M. (2006a) 'Panel V. 3. Emotions' in E. Jeffreys (ed.), *Proceedings of the International Congress of Byzantine Studies, London 21–26 August 2006*, vol. 2 (Aldershot) 165–9.

Hinterberger, M. (2006b) 'Tränen in der byzantinischen Literatur: ein Beitrag zur Geschichte der Emotionen', *Jahrbuch der österreichischen Byzantinistik* 56, 27–51.

Hinterberger, M. (2010a) 'Emotions in Byzantium', in L. James (ed.), *A Companion to Byzantium* (Chichester) 123–34.

Hinterberger, M. (2010b) 'Envy and Nemesis in the Vita Basilii and Leo the Deacon: literary mimesis or something more?', in R. Macrides (ed.), *History as Literature in Byzantium: Papers from the Fortieth Spring Symposium of Byzantine Studies, University of Birmingham, April 2007* (Farnham) 187–203.

Hinterberger, M. (2012) 'Ein Editor und sein Autor: Niketas Stethatos und Symeon Neos Theologos', in P. Odorico (ed.), *La face cachée de la littérature byzantine: le texte en tant que message immédiat* (Paris) 247–64.

Hinterberger, M. (2013a) *Phthonos: Missgunst, Neid und Eifersucht in der byzantinischer Literatur* (Serta graeca: Beiträge zur Erforschung griechischer Texte 29) (Wiesbaden).

Hinterberger, M. (2013b) 'Phthonos: a pagan relic in Byzantine imperial acclamations', in A. Beihammer, M. Parani, and S. Konstantinou (eds), *Court Ceremonies and Ritual Power in the Medieval Mediterranean* (Leiden) 51–65.

Hinterberger, M. (2014a) 'Between simplification and elaboration: Byzantine Metaphraseis in comparison', in J. Signes Codoñer and I. Pérez Martín (eds), *Textual Transmission in Byzantium: between Textual Criticism and Quellenforschung* (Lectio 2) (Turnhout) 33–60.

Hinterberger, M. (2014b) 'Ο τελχίν στη βυζαντινή λογοτεχνία: βάσκανος δαίμων και φθονερός άνθρωπος', in T. G. Kolias and K. G. Pitsakis (eds), *Aureus, Τόμος αφιερωμένος στον καθηγητή Ε. Κ. Χρυσό* (Athens) 225–42.

Hinterberger, M. (2017a) 'Basil of Caesarea and Gregory of Nazianzus speaking about anger and envy: some remarks on the Fathers' methodology of treating emotions and modern emotion studies', in M. Vinzent and Y. Papadogiannakis (eds), *Studia Patris-*

tica 83: *Papers Presented at the Seventeenth International Conference on Patristic Studies Held in Oxford 2015*, vol. 9, *Emotions* (Leuven) 313–41.

Hinterberger, M. (2017b) '"Messages of the soul": tears, smiles, laughter and emotions expressed by them in Byzantine literature', in M. Alexiou and D. Cairns (eds) *Greek Laughter and Tears: Antiquity and After* (Edinburgh) 125–45.

Hinterberger, M. (2017c) 'The vocabulary of Byzantine classicizing and literary koine texts: a database of correspondences', in A. Gagatsis (ed.), *The A. G. Leventis Research Projects 2000–2016: Final Reports* (Nicosia) 217–29.

Hinterberger, M. (2022) 'The rose and the dung beetle: Theodore Laskaris on "friendship" and "envy"', in L. James, O. Nicholson, and R. Scott (eds), *After the Text: Byzantine Enquiries in Honour of Margaret Mullett* (Abingdon) 191–204.

Hitzer, B. (2011) 'Emotionsgeschichte: ein Anfang mit Folgen', *H-Soz-Kult* 23 November 2011. https://www.hsozkult.de/literaturereview/id/forschungsberichte-1221.

Hochschild, A. R. (1979) 'Emotion work, feeling rules, and social structure', *American Journal of Sociology* 85, 551–75.

Hochschild, A. R. (1983) *The Managed Heart: the Commercialization of Human Feeling* (Berkeley).

Hock, R. F. and O'Neill, E. N. (2002) *The Chreia and Ancient Rhetoric: Classroom Exercises* (Atlanta).

Hofer, A. P. (2013) *Christ in the Life and Teachings of Gregory of Nazianzus* (Oxford).

Hoffman, M. L. (1977) 'Empathy: its development and prosocial implications', in H. Howe and C. Keasy (eds), *Nebraska Symposium on Motivation* 25 (Lincoln) 169–217.

Hoffman, M. L. (2011), 'Empathy, justice, and the law', in A. Coplan and P. Goldie (eds) *Empathy: Philosophical and Psychological Perspectives* (Oxford) 230–54.

Hollander, H. W. and de Jonge, M. (1985) *The Testaments of the Twelve Patriarchs: a Commentary* (Studia in Veteris Testamenti Pseudepigrapha 6) (Leiden).

Holloway, R. (1991) *The Archaeology of Ancient Sicily* (London).

Holmes, M. W. (2007), *Apostolic Fathers: Greek Texts and English Translations*, 3rd edn (Grand Rapids).

Hölscher, T. (1980) 'Die Geschichtsauffassung in der römischen Repräsentationskunst', *Jahrbuch des Deutschen Archäologischen Instituts* 95, 265–321.

Hölscher, T. (1987) *Römische Bildsprache als semantisches System: vorgetragen am 16. Juni 1984* (Heidelberg).

Holst-Warhaft, G. (1992) *Dangerous Voices: Women's Laments and Greek Literature* (London).

Holum, K. G. and Vikan, G. (1979) 'The Trier Ivory, "adventus" ceremonial, and the relics of St. Stephen', *Dumbarton Oaks Papers* 33, 113–33.

Honigsbaum, M. (2020) *The Pandemic Century: a History of Global Contagion from the Spanish Flu to Covid-19* (London).

Hook, L. van (1919) 'Alcidamas versus Isocrates: the spoken versus the written word', *Classical Weekly* 12, 89–94.

Hörandner, W. (ed.) (1974) *Theodoros Prodromos: Historische Gedichte* (Wiener byzantinistische Studien 11) (Vienna).

Hörandner, W. (1988) 'Lexikalische Beobachtungen zum Christos Paschon', in E. Trapp, J. Diethart, G. Fatouros, A. Steiner, and W. Hörandner (eds), *Studien zur byzantinischen Lexikographie* (Byzantina Vindobonensia 18) (Vienna) 183–202.

Horden, P. and Hsu, E. (eds) (2013) *The Body in Balance: Humoral Medicines in Practice* (New York).

Horn, F. (2016a) '"Bitter-sweet love": a cognitive linguistic view of Sappho's ἔρος γλυκύπικρος (Frg. 130 Voigt)', *Poetica* 48, 1–21.

Horn, F. (2016b) '"Building in the deep": notes on a metaphor for mental activity and the metaphorical concept of mind in early Greek epic', *Greece and Rome* 63, 163–74.

Horn, F. (2018) 'Dying is hard to describe: metonymies and metaphors of death in the *Iliad*', *Classical Quarterly* 68, 359–83.

Horna, K. (1929) 'Der Verfasser der Christus patiens', *Hermes* 64, 429–31.

Huber, I. (2001) *Die Ikonographie der Trauer in der griechischen Kunst* (Mannheim).

Huchet, J.-C. (1989) 'The romances of antiquity', in D. Hollier (ed.), *A New History of French Literature* (Cambridge, MA) 36–41.

Huitink, L. (2019) '*Enargeia*, enactivism and the ancient readerly imagination', in M. Anderson, D. Cairns, and M. Sprevak (eds), *Distributed Cognition in Classical Antiquity* (Edinburgh) 169–89.

Hult, K. (ed. and trans.) (2002), *Theodore Metochites on Ancient Authors and Philosophy: Semeioseis gnomikai 1–26 & 71. A Critical Edition with Introduction, Translation, Notes, and Indexes* (Studia Graeca et Latina Gothoburgensia 65) (Göteborg).

Hult, K. (ed. and trans.) (2016) *Theodore Metochites on the Human Condition and the Decline of Rome: Semeioseis gnomikai 27–60. A Critical Edition with Introduction, Translation, Notes, and Indexes* (Studia Graeca et Latina Gothoburgensia 70) (Göteborg).

Hunger, H. (1968a) *Die byzantinische Literatur der Komnenenzeit: Versuch einer Neubewertung* (Anzeiger der philosophisch-historischen Klasse der Österreichischen Akademie der Wissenschaften) (Vienna).

Hunger, H. (ed.) (1968b) *Der byzantinische Katz-Mäuse-Krieg* (Byzantina Vindobonensia 3) (Vienna).

Hunger, H. (ed.) (1981) *Anonyme Metaphrase zu Anna Komnene, Alexias XI–XIII: ein Beitrag zur Erschließung der byzantinischen Umgangssprache* (Wiener byzantinistische Studien 15) (Vienna).

Hunt, E. L. (1961) 'Plato and Aristotle on rhetoric and rhetoricians', in R. F. Howes (ed.), *Historical Studies on Rhetoric and Rhetoricians* (Ithaca, NY) 19–70.

Hunt, H. (2004) *Joy-bearing Grief: Tears of Contrition in the Writings of the Early Syrian and Byzantine Fathers* (Leiden).

Hunt, H. (2015) *A Guide to St. Symeon the New Theologian* (Eugene, OR).

Hunter-Crawley, H. (2013) 'The Cross of Light: experiencing divine presence in Byzantine Syria', in C. Nesbitt and M. Jackson (eds), *Experiencing Byzantium: Papers from the 44th Spring Symposium of Byzantine Studies, Newcastle and Durham, April 2011* (Farnham) 175–93.

Hurley, E. (2010) *Theatre and Feeling* (Basingstoke).

Huskinson, J. (1996) *Roman Children's Sarcophagi: Their Decoration and Social Significance* (Oxford).

Huskinson, J. (2010) 'Picturing the Roman family', in B. Rawson (ed.) *A Companion to Families in the Greek and Roman Worlds* (Malden, MA) 521–41.

Hutto, D. D. (2008) *Folk Psychological Narratives: the Sociocultural Basis of Understanding Reasons* (Cambridge, MA).

Hutto, D. D. (2011) 'Understanding fictional minds without Theory of Mind!', *Style* 45.2, 276–82, 415.

Ideler, J. L. (ed.) (1841) *Physici et medici Graeci minores*, vol. 1 (Berlin, repr. Amsterdam, 1963).

472   *Bibliography*

Ihm, C. (1960) *Die Programme der christlichen Apsismalerei vom vierten Jahrhundert bis zur Mitte des achten Jahrhunderts* (Wiesbaden).

Inselmann, A. (2012) *Die Freude im Lukasevangelium: ein Beitrag zur psychologischen Exegese* (Wissenschaftliche Untersuchungen zum Neuen Testament 2.322) (Tübingen).

Iser, W. (1976) *The Act of Reading: a Theory of Aesthetic Response* (Baltimore).

Ivaz, L., Costa, A., and Duñabeitia, J.A. (2016) 'The emotional impact of being myself: emotions and foreign-language processing', *Journal of Experimental Psychology: Learning, Memory, and Cognition* 42.3, 489–96.

Jackson, L. (2016) 'Greater than *logos*? Kinaesthetic empathy and mass persuasion in the choruses of Plato's *Laws*', in E. Sanders and M. Johncock (eds), *Emotion and Persuasion in Classical Antiquity* (Stuttgart) 147–61.

Jacob, C. (2010) *Das geistige Theater: Ästhetik und Moral bei Johannes Chrysostomus* (Münster).

Jahn, T. (1987) *Zum Wortfeld 'Seele-Geist' in der Sprache Homers* (Munich).

James, L. (2003) 'Color and meaning in Byzantium', *Journal of Early Christian Studies* 11, 223–33.

James, L. (2004) 'Senses and sensibility in Byzantium', *Art History* 27, 523–37.

James, L. and Webb, R. (1991) '"To understand ultimate things and enter secret places": *ekphrasis* and art in Byzantium', *Art History* 14, 1–17.

James, W. (1884) 'What is an emotion?', *Mind* 9, 188–205.

James, W. (1890) *The Principles of Psychology*, vol. 2 (New York).

James, W. (1894) 'The physical basis of emotion', *Psychological Review* 1, 516–29.

Janeras, S. (1986) 'I vangeli domenicali della resurrezione nelle tradizioni liturgiche agiopolita e bizantina', in G. Farnedi (ed.), *Paschale Mysterium: studi in memoria dell'Abate prof. Salvatore Marsili (1910–1983)* (Rome) 55–69.

Jebb, R.C. (ed.) (1894) *The Electra of Sophocles* (Cambridge).

Jeffreys, E. (1993) 'Place as a factor in the edition of early demotic texts', in N. Panagiotakis (ed.), *Origini della letteratura neogreca*, vol. 2 (Venice) 310–24.

Jeffreys, E. (2007) 'Fantasy and the medieval Greek *War of Troy*', in M. Kokoszko (ed.), *Byzantina Europeaea* (Łodz) 199–208.

Jeffreys, E. (trans.) (2012) *Four Byzantine Novels: Theodoros Prodromos, Rhodanthe and Dosikles, Eumathios Makrembolites, Hysmine and Hysminias, Constantinos Manasses, Aristandros and Kallithea, Niketas Eugenianos, Drosilla and Charikles* (Translated Texts for Byzantinists 1) (Liverpool).

Jeffreys, E. (2013) 'Byzantine romances: Eastern or Western?', in *Renaissance Encounters: Greek East and Latin West*, ed. M. Brownlee and D. Gondicas (Princeton) 221–37.

Jeffreys, E. (2014) 'We need to talk about Byzantium: or, Byzantium, its reception of the classical world as discussed in current scholarship, and should Classicists pay attention?', *Classical Receptions Journal* 6.1, 158–74.

Jeffreys, E. (2016) 'A date and context for the *War of Troy*', in U. Moennig (ed.), '... ΩΣ ΑΘΥΡΜΑΤΑ ΠΑΙΔΑΣ': *Festschrift für Hans Eideneier* (Berlin) 85–93.

Jeffreys, E. (2019) 'From Herakles to Erkoulios, or the place of the *War of Troy* in the late Byzantine romance movement', in A. J. Goldwyn and I. Nilsson (eds) *The Late Byzantine Romance: a Handbook* (Cambridge) 166–87.

Jeffreys, E. and Jeffreys, M. (2015) 'A Constantinopolitan poet views Frankish Antioch', *Crusades* 14, 49–151.

Jeffreys, E., Jeffreys, M., and Scott, R. (eds) (1986) *The Chronicle of John Malalas* (Melbourne).

Bibliography

473

Jeffreys, M. and Lauxtermann, M. (2017) *The Letters of Psellos: Cultural Networks and Historical Realities* (Oxford).

Jehl, R. (2005) 'Acedia and burnout syndrome: from an occupational vice of the early monks to a psychological concept in secularized professional life', in R. Newhauser (ed.), *In the Garden of Evil: the Vices and Culture in the Middle Ages* (Toronto) 455–76.

Jenkins, D. (2017) 'Michael Psellos', in A. Kaldellis and N. Siniossoglou (eds), *The Cambridge Intellectual History of Byzantium* (Cambridge) 447–61.

Jolivet-Lévy, C. (2006) 'Prime rappresentazioni del Giudizio universale nella Cappadocia bizantina (X secolo)', in M. Angheben and V. Pace (eds), *Alfa e Omega: il Giudizio universale tra Oriente e Occidente* (Castel Bolognese) 47–51.

Joly, R. (1968) *Hermas, Le Pasteur: introduction, texte critique, traduction et notes*, 2nd edn (Sources chretiennes 53[bis]) (Paris).

Jonge, M. de (1960) 'Christian influence in the Testaments of the Twelve Patriarchs', *Novum Testamentum* 4.3, 182–235.

Jonge, M. de (1962) 'Once more: Christian influence in the Testaments of the Twelve Patriarchs', *Novum Testamentum* 5, 311–19.

Jonge, M. de (1975 [1953]), *The Testaments of the Twelve Patriarchs: a Study of Their Text, Composition and Origin*, 2nd edn (Assen).

Jonge, M. de (1978) *The Testaments of the Twelve Patriarchs: a Critical Edition of the Greek Text* (Pseudepigrapha Veteris Testamenti Graece) (Leiden).

Jörg, U. (2007) 'Angstmacherei: Beobachtungen zu einem polemischen Einwand gegen das junge Christentum und zur Auseinandersetzung mit ihm in der apologetischen Literatur', in F. R. Prostmeier (ed.), *Frühchristentum und Kultur* (Freiburg im Breisgau), 111–26.

Jouanna, J. (2012) *Greek Medicine from Hippocrates to Galen: Selected Papers*, trans. N. Allies (Studies in Ancient Medicine 40) (Leiden).

Jowett, B. (1892) *The Dialogues of Plato, Translated into English with Analyses and Introductions*, vol. 1, 3rd revised and corrected edn, Oxford.

Jugie, M. (1944) *La mort et la assomption de la Saint Vierge, étude historico-doctrinale* (Vatican City).

Kagan, J. (2007) *What Is Emotion? History, Measures, and Meanings* (New Haven).

Kalamakis, D. C. (ed.) (1992) Λεξικὰ τῶν ἐπῶν Γρηγορίου τοῦ Θεολόγου μετὰ γενικῆς θεωρήσεως τῆς Πατερικῆς λεξικογραφίας (Athens).

Kalavrezou, I. (2000) 'The maternal side of the Virgin', in M. Vassilaki (ed.), *Mother of God: Representations of the Virgin in Byzantine Art* (Milan) 41–5.

Kalavrezou, I. (2005) 'Exchanging embrace: the body of salvation', in M. Vassilaki (ed.), *Images of the Mother of God: Perceptions of the Theotokos in Byzantium* (Aldershot) 103–15.

Kalimtzis, K. (2012) *Taming Anger: the Hellenic Approach to the Limitations of Reason* (London).

Kalopissi-Verti, S. (2012) 'The murals of the narthex: the paintings of the late thirteenth and fourteenth centuries', in A. Weyl Carr and A. Nicolaïdès (eds), *Asinou across Time: Studies in the Architecture and Murals of the Panagia Phorbiotissa, Cyprus* (Washington, DC) 115–208.

Kambylis, A. and Reinsch, D. R. (eds) (2001) *Annae Comnenae Alexias* (Corpus Fontium Historiae Byzantinae, Series Berolinensis 40.1) (Berlin).

Kamesar, A. (2004) 'The *logos endiathetos* and the *logos prophorikos* in allegorical interpretation: Philo and the D-scholia to the *Iliad*', *Greek, Roman, and Byzantine Studies* 44, 163–81.

Kampen, N. (1981) *Image and Status: Roman Working Women in Ostia* (Berlin).

Kanavou, N. (2013) '"Negative" emotions and Greek names', in A. Chaniotis and P. Ducrey (eds), *Unveiling Emotions II. Emotions in Greece and Rome: Texts, Images, Material Culture* (Stuttgart) 167–89.

Karamanolis, G. (2019) 'Review of M. Trizio, *Il neoplatonismo di Eustrazio di Nicea*, Bari 2016, Edizioni di Pagina', *Jahrbuch der österreichischen Byzantinistik* 69, 355–7.

Karpozilos, A. (1990), *The Letters of Ioannes Mauropus, Metropolitan of Euchaita: Greek Text, Translation, and Commentary* (Thessaloniki).

Karpozilos, A. (1997) Βυζαντινοὶ ἱστορικοὶ καὶ χρονογράφοι, τόμος Α΄ (4ος-7ος αἰ.) (Athens).

Kartsonis, A. (1986) *Anastasis: the Making of an Image* (Princeton).

Kassel, R. (1976) *Aristotelis Ars rhetorica* (Berlin).

Kaster, R. A. (2005) *Emotion, Restraint, and Community in Ancient Rome* (Oxford).

Kazantzidis, G. and Spatharas, D. (eds) (2018) *Hope in Ancient Literature, History, and Art* (Berlin).

Kazhdan, A. (1991a) 'Fear', in *The Oxford Dictionary of Byzantium*, vol. 2 (Oxford) 780–1.

Kazhdan, A. (ed.) (1991b) *The Oxford Dictionary of Byzantium* (Oxford).

Kazhdan, A. P. and Epstein, A. W. (1985) *Change in Byzantine Culture in the Eleventh and Twelfth Centuries* (The Transformation of the Classical Heritage 7) (Berkeley).

Kee, H. C. (1983) 'Testaments of the Twelve Patriarchs', in J. H. Charlesworth (ed.), *The Old Testament Pseudepigrapha*, vol. 1 (Garden City, NY) 775–828.

Keen, S. (2013) 'Narrative empathy', in *The Living Handbook of Narratology*. https://www.lhn.uni-ham burg.de/node/42.html.

Kehl, A. (1984) 'Gewand = Person?', in E. Dassmann and K. Thraede (eds), *Vivarium, Festschrift Th. Klauser* (*Jahrbuch für Antike und Christentum* Supplement 11) (Münster) 213–19.

Kelly, H. A. (1985) *The Devil at Baptism: Ritual, Theology, and Drama* (Ithaca, NY).

Kelly, H. A. (2006) *Satan: a Biography* (Cambridge).

Keltner, D. and Haidt, J. (2003) 'Approaching awe, a moral, spiritual, and aesthetic emotion', *Cognition and Emotion* 17, 297–314.

Kennedy, G. (1994) *A New History of Classical Rhetoric* (Princeton).

Kennedy, G. (2003) *Progymnasmata: Greek Textbooks of Prose Composition and Rhetoric* (Atlanta).

Kennedy, G. (trans.) (2007) *Aristotle, On Rhetoric: a Theory of Civic Discourse* (New York).

Kenner, H. (1960) *Weinen und Lachen in der griechischen Kunst* (Abhandlungen der Österreichischen Akademie der Wissenschaften: philosophisch-historische Klasse 234.2) (Vienna).

Keydell, R. (ed.) (1967) *Agathiae Myrnaei historiarum libri quinque* (Corpus Fontium Historiae Byzantinae 2) (Berlin).

Keysar, B., Hayakawa, S. L., and An, S. G. (2012) 'The foreign-language effect: thinking in a foreign tongue reduces decision biases', *Psychological Science* 20.10, 1–8.

King, H. (2013) 'Female fluids in the Hippocratic corpus: how solid was the humoral body?', in P. Horden and E. Hsu (eds) *The Body in Balance: Humoral Medicines in Practice* (New York) 25–52.

Kipfer, S. (ed.) (2017) *Visualizing Emotions in the Ancient Near East* (Fribourg).

Kirschbaum, E. (1940) 'L'angelo rosso e l'angelo turchino', *Rivista di archeologia cristiana* 17, 210–48.

Knuuttila, S. (2004) *Emotions in Ancient and Medieval Philosophy* (Oxford).

Koder, J. (2011) *Die Hymnen Symeons, des Neos Theologos: Überlegungen zur literarischen Einordnung und zu den Intentionen des Autors* (Munich).

Koder, J. and Paramelle, J. (1969) *Syméon le Nouveau Théologien, Hymnes* (Sources chrétiennes 156, 174, and 196) (Paris).

Konstan, D. (1991) 'The tragic emotions', *Comparative Drama* 33.1, 1–21.

Konstan, D. (2001) *Pity Transformed* (London).

Konstan, D. (2003) 'Aristotle on anger and the emotions: the strategies of status', in S. M. Braund and G. W. Most (eds) *Ancient Anger: Perspectives from Homer to Galen* (Yale Classical Studies 32) (Cambridge) 99–120.

Konstan, D. (2006a) 'The concept of "emotion" from Plato to Cicero', *Méthexis* 19, 139–51.

Konstan, D. (2006b) *The Emotions of the Ancient Greeks: Studies in Aristotle and Classical Literature* (Toronto).

Konstan, D. (2007) 'Rhetoric and emotion', in I. Worthington (ed.), *A Companion to Greek Rhetoric* (Malden, MA) 411–25.

Konstan, D. (2010a) 'The passions of Achilles: translating Greece into Rome', in R. Deist (ed.), *The Passions of Achilles: Reflections on the Classical and Medieval Epic* (*Electronic Antiquity* 14.1) 7–22.

Konstan, D. (2010b) *Before Forgiveness: the Origins of a Moral Idea* (New York).

Konstan, D. (2019a) 'Aspasius on *pathē*', in F. Masi, S. Maso, and C. Viano (eds), *Ēthikē Theōria: studi sull'Etica Nicomachea in onore di Carlo Natali*, vol. 2 (Rome) 271–86.

Konstan, D. (2019b) 'Drama', in D. L. Cairns (ed.), *A Cultural History of the Emotions in Antiquity* (London) 63–81.

Konstan, D. (2020) 'Afterword: the invention of emotion?', in L. Candiotto and O. Renaut (eds), *Emotions in Plato* (Leiden) 372–81.

Konstan, D. (forthcoming) *Emotions across Cultures: China and Greece* (Berlin).

Konstan, D. and Rutter, K. (eds) (2003) *Envy, Spite and Jealousy: the Rivalrous Emotions in Ancient Greece* (Edinburgh Leventis Studies 2) (Edinburgh).

Korenjak, M. (2000) *Publikum und Redner: ihre Interaktion in der sophistischen Rhetorik der Kaiserzeit* (Munich).

Kotsifou, C. (2012a) 'A glimpse into the world of petitions: the case of Aurelia Artemis and her orphaned children', in A. Chaniotis (ed.), *Unveiling Emotions: Sources and Methods for the Study of Emotions in the Greek World* (Stuttgart) 317–27.

Kotsifou, C. (2012b) '"Being unable to come to you and lament and weep with you": grief and condolence letters on Papyrus', in A. Chaniotis (ed.), *Unveiling Emotions: Sources and Methods for the Study of Emotions in the Greek World* (Stuttgart) 389–412.

Kotsifou, C. (2012c) 'Emotions and papyri: insights into the theatre of human experience', in A. Chaniotis (ed.), *Unveiling Emotions: Sources and Methods for the Study of Emotions in the Greek World* (Stuttgart) 39–90.

Kotter, P. B. (ed.) (1973) *Die Schriften des Johannes von Damaskos*, vol. 2, Ἔκδοσις ἀκριβῆς τῆς ὀρθοδόξου πίστεως, *Expositio fidei* (Patristische Texte und Studien 12) (Berlin).

Kövecses, Z. (2003) *Metaphor and Emotion: Language, Culture, and Body in Human Feeling* (Cambridge).

Kövecses, Z. (2008) 'Universality and variation in the use of metaphor', in N.-L. Johannesson and D. C. Minugh (eds), *Selected Papers from the 2006 and 2007 Stockholm Metaphor Festivals* (Stockholm) 56–74.

476 *Bibliography*

Koziak, B. (1999) 'Homeric *thumos*: the early history of gender, emotion, and politics', *The Journal of Politics* 61, 1068–91.

Koziak, B. (2000) *Retrieving Political Emotion: Thumos, Aristotle and Gender* (University Park, PA).

Krajczynski, J. and Rapp, C. (2009) 'Emotionen in der antiken Philosophie: Definitionen und Kataloge', in M. Harbsmeier and S. Möckel (eds), *Pathos, Affekt, Emotion: Transformationen der Antike* (Frankfurt am Main) 47–78.

Krewet, M. (2011) *Die Theorie der Gefühle bei Aristoteles* (Heidelberg).

Krewet, M. (2013) *Die stoische Theorie der Gefühle: ihre Aporien, ihre Wirkmacht* (Heidelberg).

Kriaras, E. (1967–) *Λεξικό της μεσαιωνικής Ελληνικής δημώδους γραμματείας* (Thessaloniki).

Krivochéine, B. (1963–5) *Syméon le Nouveau Théologien, Catéchèses* (Sources chrétiennes 96, 104, and 113) (Paris).

Kroll, G. and Schöll, R. (eds) (1968 [1895]) *Novellae, Corpus Iuris Civilis* (Berlin).

Krueger, D. (2010) *Byzantine Christianity* (Minneapolis).

Krueger, D. (2014) *Liturgical Subjects: Christian Ritual, Biblical Narrative, and the Formation of the Self in Byzantium* (Philadelphia).

Krueger, D. (2017) 'The transmission of liturgical joy in Byzantine hymns for Easter', in B. Bytton-Ashkelony and D. Krueger (eds), *Prayer and Worship in Eastern Christianities: 5th to 11th Centuries* (London) 133–50.

Krueger, D. (forthcoming) 'Joy and complexity in a hymn of Romanos the Melodist', in M. Mullett and S. Ashbrook Harvey (eds), *Managing Emotion: Passions, Affects, Imaginings* (Abingdon).

Kruger, P.A. (2009) 'Gefühle und Gefühlsäußerungen im Alten Testament: einige einführende Bemerkungen', in B. Janowski and K. Liess (eds), *Der Mensch im Alten Israel: neue Forschungen zur alttestamentlichen Anthropologie* (Herders biblische Studien 59) (Freiburg im Breisgau) 243–62.

Küchler, M. (1979) *Frühjüdische Weisheitstraditionen: zum Fortgang weisheitlichen Denkens im Bereich des frühjüdischen Jahweglaubens* (Orbis Biblicus Orientalis 26) (Fribourg).

Kühn, C. G. (ed.) (1821–33) *Claudii Galeni opera omnia*, vols 1–19 (Leipzig, repr. Hildesheim 1965).

Kulhánková, M. (2014) 'Der bestrafte Mönch: ein erster Einblick in die Analyse der Erzähltechnik in den byzantinischen erbaulichen Diegeseis', *Jahrbuch der österreichischen Byzantinistik* 64, 139–53.

Kustas G. L. (1973), *Studies in Byzantine Rhetoric* (Thessaloniki).

Lachenaud, G. (2013) *Les routes de la voix: l'antiquité grecque et le mystère de la voix* (Paris).

Lada, I. (1993) '"Empathetic understanding": emotion and cognition in Classical dramatic audience-response', *Proceedings of the Cambridge Philological Society* 39, 94–140.

Lada, I. (1996) 'Emotion and meaning on the Athenian tragic stage', in M. Silk (ed.) *Tragedy and the Tragic: Greek Theatre and Beyond* (Oxford) 397–413.

Laffan, M. and Weiss, M. (eds) (2012) *Facing Fear: the History of an Emotion in Global Perspective* (Princeton).

Lagarde, P. (1882) *Iohannis Euchaitorum Metropolitae quae in codice Vaticano graeco 676 supersunt* (Göttingen).

Laird, J. D. (2007) *Feelings: the Perception of Self* (Oxford).

Bibliography 477

Laird, R. (2012) *Mindset, Moral Choice and Sin in the Anthropology of John Chrysostom* (Strathfield, NSW).

Lake, K. (1970) *The Apostolic Fathers*, vol. 2, *The Shepherd of Hermas, The Martyrdom of Polycarp, The Epistle of Diognetus* (Cambridge, MA).

Lakoff, G. (1987) *Women, Fire, and Dangerous Things: What Categories Reveal about the Mind* (Chicago).

Lampe, G. W. H. (1961), *A Patristic Greek Lexicon* (Oxford).

Lanata, G. (1963) *Poetica preplatonica* (Florence).

Lanfranchi, P. (2016) 'L'usage des émotions dans la polémique anti-juive: l'exemple des discours contre les Juifs de Jean Chrysostome', in M.-A. Vannier (ed.), *Judaïsme et christianisme chez les Pères* (Turnhout) 237–52.

Lang, M. (2014) 'Wermut', *Das Wissenschaftliche Bibellexikon im Internet*. www.wibilex.de.

Lange, A. (1995) *Weisheit und Prädestination: weisheitliche Urordnung und Prädestination in den Textfunden von Qumran* (Studies on the Texts of the Desert of Judah 18) (Leiden).

Langener, L. (1996) *Isis lactans – Maria lactans: Untersuchungen zur koptischen Ikonographie* (Altenberge).

Lankila, T. (2017) 'A crypto-pagan reading of the figure of Hierotheus and the 'Dormition' passage in the Corpus Areopagiticum', in D. Butorac and D. Layne (eds), *Proclus and His Legacy* (Berlin) 175–82.

Lanzoni, S. (2018) *Empathy: a History* (New Haven).

Laourdas, V. (ed.) (1959) Φωτίου Ὁμιλίαι (Ἑλληνικά Supplement 12) (Thessaloniki).

Lasater, P. M. (2017) '"The emotions" in biblical anthropology? A genealogy and case study with "ירא"', *Harvard Theological Review* 110.4, 520–40.

Lateiner, D. (1995) *Sardonic Smile: Nonverbal Behavior in Homeric Epic* (Ann Arbor).

Lateiner, D. and Spatharas, D. (eds) (2017) *The Ancient Emotion of Disgust* (Oxford).

Lauha, R. (1983) *Psychophysischer Sprachgebrauch im Alten Testament: eine struktursemantische Analyse von נפש, לב und רוח* (Annales Academiae Scientiarum Fennicae, Dissertationes humanarum litterarum 35) (Helsinki).

Lauritzen, F. (2013) *The Depiction of Character in the Chronographia of Michael Psellos* (Byzantios: Studies in Byzantine History and Civilization 7) (Turnhout).

Lauxtermann, M. (2002) 'Byzantine poetry and the paradox of Basil II's reign', in P. Magdalino (ed.), *Byzantium in the Year 1000* (Leiden) 233–70.

Lawrence, M. (1965) 'The Velletri Sarcophagus', *American Journal of Archaeology* 69, 207–22.

Leeuwen, J. van (2016) *The Aristotelian Mechanics: Text and Diagrams* (Boston Studies in the Philosophy and History of Science 316) (Cham).

Lefebvre, G. (1907) *Recueil des inscriptions grecques-chrétiennes d'Égypte* (Cairo).

Leidl, C. G. (2003) 'Metaphor and literary criticism', in G. Boys-Stones (ed.), *Metaphor, Allegory, and the Classical Tradition: Ancient Thought and Modern Revisions* (Oxford) 31–54.

Leighton, S. R. (1996) 'Aristotle and the emotions', in A. O. Rorty (ed.), *Essays on Aristotle's Rhetoric* (Berkeley) 206–37.

Lelord, F. and André, C. (2001) *La force des émotions: amour, colère, joie* (Paris).

Lentari, T. (2014) 'Gazes in love scenes and glances at their depiction: notes on *The War of Troy*', in E. Camateros, T. Kaplanis, and J. Pye (eds) *"His Words Were Nourishment and His Counsel Food": a Festschrift for David W. Holton* (Newcastle) 7–22.

Leone, P. L. (ed.) (1982) *Nicephori Gregorae epistulae*, 2 vols (Matino).

Lesêtre, H. (1988) 'Foie', *Dictionnaire de la Bible*, vol. 2 (Paris) cols 2297–8.

478   *Bibliography*

Leutzsch, M. (1998) 'Hirt des Hermas', in U. Körtner and M. Leutzsch, *Papiasfragmente, Hirt des Hermas* (Schriften des Urchristentums 3) (Darmstadt) 105–497.

Lev Kenaan, V. (2011) '*Thauma idesthai*: the mythical origins of philosophical wonder', in H. Kenaan and I. Ferber (eds), *Philosophy's Moods: the Affective Grounds of Thinking* (Contributions to Phenomenology 63) (Dordrecht) 13–26.

Levy, P. (ed.) (1912) *Michael Psellus: De Gregorii Theologi charactere iudicium, accedit eiusdem de Ioannis Chrisostomi charactere iudicium ineditum* (Leipzig).

Lewis, C. S. (1960) *The Four Loves* (London).

Lewis, M. (2000) 'Self-conscious emotions: embarrassment, pride, shame, and guilt', in M. Lewis and J. M. Haviland-Jones (eds), *Handbook of Emotions*, 2nd edn (New York) 623–36.

Lewis, S. (2002) *The Athenian Woman: an Iconographic Handbook* (London).

Leyerle, B. (2001) *Theatrical Shows and Ascetic Lives: John Chrysostom's Attack on Spiritual Marriage* (Berkeley).

Leyerle, B. (2015) 'The etiology of sorrow and its therapeutic benefits in the preaching of John Chrysostom', *Journal of Late Antiquity* 8, 368–85.

Leyerle, B. (2020) *The Narrative Shape of Emotion in the Preaching of John Chrysostom* (Oakland).

Linardou, K. (2016) 'Imperial impersonations: disguised portraits of a Komnenian prince and his father', in A. Bucossi and A. Rodriguez Suarez (eds), *John II Komnenos, Emperor of Byzantium: in the Shadow of Father and Son* (London) 155–82.

Lindquist, K. A. and Barrett, L. F. (2008) 'Constructing emotion: the experience of fear as a conceptual act', *Psychological Science* 19, 898–903.

Lindquist, K. A., Barrett, L. F., Bliss-Moreau, E., and Russell, J. A. (2006) 'Language and the perception of emotion', *Emotion* 6, 125–38.

Lindquist, K. A., Gendron, M., and Satpute, A. B. (2016) 'Language and emotion: putting words into feelings and feelings into words', in L. F. Barrett, M. Lewis, and J. M. Haviland-Jones (eds) *Handbook of Emotions*, 4th edn (New York) 579–94.

Lipps, T. (1903) *Leitfaden der Psychologie* (Leipzig).

Liston, M. A. and Papadopoulos, J. K. (2004) 'The "Rich Athenian Lady" was pregnant: the anthropology of a Geometric tomb reconsidered', *Hesperia* 73, 7–38.

Littlewood, A. R. (ed.) (1985) *Michaelis Pselli oratoria minora* (Leipzig).

Littlewood, A. R. (1999) 'The Byzantine letter of consolation in the Macedonian and Komnenian periods', *Dumbarton Oaks Papers* 53, 19–41.

Ljubarskij, J. (1978) *Михаил Пселл. Личность и творчество: к истории византийского предгуманизма* (Moscow).

Ljubarskij, J. N. (1992) 'Man in Byzantine historiography from John Malalas to Michael Psellos', *Dumbarton Oaks Papers* 46, 177–86.

Llewellyn-Jones, L. (2003) *Aphrodite's Tortoise: the Veiled Woman of Ancient Greece* (Swansea).

Lloyd-Jones, H. (ed. and trans.) (1994) *Sophocles*, vol. 2, *Antigone. The Women of Trachis. Philoctetes. Oedipus at Colonus* (Loeb Classial Library 21) (Cambridge, MA).

Löhr, H. (2016) 'Person und strukturiertes Selbst im frühesten Christentum: drei Erkundungsgänge', in S. Beyerle (ed.), *Die Erfindung des Menschen: Person und Persönlichkeit in ihren lebensweltlichen Kontexten* (Theologie – Kultur – Hermeneutik 21) (Leipzig) 285–303.

Lombardo, S. (1997) *Homer, Iliad* (Indianapolis).

Loraux, N. (1990) *Les mères en deuil* (Paris).

Bibliography

Loraux, N. (1998) *Mothers in Mourning*, trans. C. Pache (Ithaca, NY).

Lossau, M. (1971) 'μοχθηρία τῶν πολιτειῶν und ὑπόκρισις. Zu Arist. Rhet. 3,1,1403b34 f.', *Rheinisches Museum* 114, 146–58.

Lourié, B. (2010) 'Peter the Iberian and Dionysius the Areopagite: Honigmann–van Esbroeck's thesis revisited', *Scrinium* 6, 143–212.

Louth, A. (2013a) *Introducing Eastern Orthodox Theology* (London).

Louth, A. (2013b) 'Experiencing the liturgy in Byzantium', in C. Nesbitt and M. Jackson (eds), *Experiencing Byzantium: Papers from the 44th Spring Symposium of Byzantine Studies, Newcastle and Durham, April 2011* (Farnham) 79–88.

Lovato, V. F. (2017) 'Portrait de héros, portrait d'érudit: Jean Tzetzès et la tradition des *eikonismoi*', *Medioevo greco* 17, 137–56.

Lugaresi, L. (2017) 'Rhetoric against theatre and theatre by means of rhetoric in John Chrysostom', in A. J. Quiroga Puertas (ed.), *Rhetorical Strategies in Late Antique Literature: Images, Metatexts and Interpretation* (Leiden).

Luibheid, C. (trans.) and Rorem, P. (ed.) (1987) *Pseudo-Dionysius: the Complete Works* (New York).

Lumb, T. W. and Rattenbury, R. M. (eds) (1960) *Héliodore, Les Éthiopiques (Théagène et Chariclée)* (Paris).

Lupyan, G., Rahman, R. A., Boroditsky, L., and Clark, A. (2020) 'Effects of language on visual perception', *Trends in Cognitive Sciences* 24.11, 930–44.

Luther, S. (2015) *Sprachethik im Neuen Testament: Analyse des frühchristlichen Diskurses im Matthäusevangelium, im Jakobusbrief und im 1 Petrusbrief* (Wissenschaftliche Untersuchungen zum Neuen Testament 2.394) (Tübingen).

Lutz, C. A. (1988) *Unnatural Emotions: Everyday Sentiments on a Micronesian Atoll and Their Challenge to Western Theory* (Chicago).

MacKenna, S. (trans.), revised by Page, B. S. (1957) *Plotinus, The Enneads* (London).

MacMullen, R. (2003) *Feelings in History, Ancient and Modern* (Claremont, CA).

Macrides, R. (2020) 'The logos of Nicholas Mesarites', in M. Mullett and R. Ousterhout (eds), *The Holy Apostles: a Lost Monument, a Forgotten Project, and the Presentness of the Past* (Washington, DC) 175–91.

Magdalino, P. (1984) 'Byzantine snobbery', in M. Angold (ed.), *The Byzantine Aristocracy, IX to XIII Centuries* (British Archeological Reports International Series 221) (Oxford) 58–78.

Magdalino, P. (1989) 'Honour among Romaioi: the framework of social values in the world of Digenes Akrites and Kekaumenos', *Byzantine and Modern Greek Studies* 13, 183–218.

Magdalino, P. (1993) *The Empire of Manuel I Komnenos, 1143–1180* (Cambridge).

Magoulias, H. J. (1984) *O City of Byzantium, Annals of Niketas Choniatēs* (Detroit).

Maguire, E. D. and Maguire, H. (2007) *Other Icons: Art and Power in Byzantine Secular Culture* (Princeton).

Maguire, H. (1974) 'Truth and convention in Byzantine descriptions of works of art', *Dumbarton Oaks Papers* 28, 113–40.

Maguire, H. (1977) 'The depiction of sorrow in Middle Byzantine Art', *Dumbarton Oaks Papers* 31, 123–74.

Maguire, H. (1981) *Art and Eloquence in Byzantium* (Princeton).

Maguire, H. (1996) *The Icons of Their Bodies: Saints and Their Images in Byzantium* (Princeton).

Maguire, H. (2002) 'Paradise withdrawn', in A. Littlewood, H. Maguire, and J. Wolschke-Bulmahn (eds), *Byzantine Garden Culture* (Washington, DC) 23–35..

480 *Bibliography*

Maguire, H. (2003) 'Byzantine rhetoric, Latin drama and the portrayal of the New Testament', in E. Jeffreys (ed.), *Rhetoric in Byzantium* (Aldershot) 215–33.

Maguire, H. (2007a) 'The good life', in R. Hoffman (ed.), *Late Antique and Medieval Art of the Mediterranean World* (Oxford) 63–84.

Maguire, H. (2007b) 'Medieval art in southern Italy: Latin drama and the Greek literary imagination', in H. Maguire (ed.), *Image and Imagination in Byzantine Art* (Aldershot) 219–39.

Maguire, H. (2017) 'The asymmetry of text and image in Byzantium', *Perspectives médiévales*. doi: 10.4000/peme.12218.

Mahr, A.C. (ed.) (1947) *The Cyprus Passion Cycle* (Publications in Medieval Studies 9) (Notre Dame, IN).

Malingrey, A.-M. (ed.) (1972) *Jean Chrysostome, Sur la vaine gloire et l´éducation des enfants* (Sources chrétiennes 188) (Paris).

Mandler, J.M. (1984) *Stories, Scripts, and Scenes: Aspects of Schema Theory* (Hillsdale, NJ).

Mango, C. (1958) *The Homilies of Photius Patriarch of Constantinople* (Cambridge, MA).

Mango, C. (2000) 'Constantinople as Theotokoupolis', in M. Vasilaki (ed.), *Mother of God: Representations of the Virgin in Byzantine Art* (Athens) 17–25.

Mango, C.A. and Scott, R. (1997) *The Chronicle of Theophanes Confessor: Byzantine and Near Eastern History AD 284–813* (Oxford).

Manolopoulou, V. (2013) 'Processing emotion: litanies in Byzantine Constantinople', in C. Nesbitt and M. Jackson (eds), *Experiencing Byzantium: Papers from the 44th Spring Symposium of Byzantine Studies, Newcastle and Durham, April 2011* (Farnham) 153–72.

Manolopoulou, V. (2016) 'Processing Constantinople: understanding the role of *litē* in creating the sacred character of the landscape' (Ph.D. Diss. Newcastle).

Manolopoulou, V. (2019) 'Processing time and space in Byzantine Constantinople', in C. Morris, G. Papantoniou, and A. Vionis (eds), *Unlocking Sacred Landscapes* (Nicosia) 155–67.

Manolova, D. (2017) 'The student becomes the teacher: Nikephoros Gregoras' *Hortatory Letter Concerning Astronomy*', in A. M. Cuomo and E. Trapp (eds), *Toward a Historical Sociolinguistic Poetics of Medieval Greek* (Byzantios: Studies in Byzantine History and Civilization 12) (Turnhout) 143–60.

Mansi, J.D. (1759–98), *Sacrorum Conciliorum nova et amplissima collectio*, 31 vols (Florence).

Maraval, P. (1971) *Gregory of Nyssa, Vita sanctae Macrinae* (Sources chrétiennes 178) (Paris).

Marciniak, P. (2004) *Greek Drama in Byzantine Times* (Katowice).

Marciniak, P. (2007) 'Byzantine *theatron*: a place for performance?', in M. Grünbart (ed.), *Theatron: rhetorische Kultur im Spätantike und Mittelalter* (Berlin) 277–85.

Marciniak, P. (2022) 'Sophocles, Euripides and the unusual cento', in L. James, O. Nicholson and R. Scott (eds), *After the Text: Byzantine Enquiries in Honour of Margaret Mullett* (Abingdon) 167–75

Marcovich, M. (ed.) (1992) *Theodori Prodromi de Rhodanthes et Dosiclis amoribus libri IX* (Stuttgart).

Marek, C. (2006) *Die Inschriften von Kaunos* (Munich).

Marinis, V. (2014) *Architecture and Ritual in the Churches of Constantinople: Ninth to Fifteenth Centuries* (New York).

Marinis, V. (2017) *Death and the Afterlife in Byzantium: the Fate of the Soul in Theology, Liturgy, and Art* (New York).

Bibliography 481

Mariß, R. (2002) *Alkidamas: über diejenigen, die schriftliche Reden schreiben, oder über die Sophisten. Eine Sophistenrede aus dem 4. Jahrhundert eingeleitet und kommentiert* (Münster).

Markopoulos, A. (2008) *Τέσσερα κείμενα για την ποίηση του Συμεών του Νέου Θεολόγου* (Athens).

Markopoulos, T. (2019) 'Linguistic contacts in the Late Byzantine romances: where cultural influence meets language interference', in A. J. Goldwyn and I. Nilsson (eds), *The Late Byzantine Romance: a Handbook* (Cambridge) 144–65.

Markschies, C. (2006) 'Hermas, Hermae Pastor', in H. Cancik and H. Schneider (eds), *Brill's New Pauly: Antiquity.* http://dx.doi.org/10.1163/1574-9347_bnp_e509970.

Marsden, E. W. (ed.) (1971) *Greek and Roman Artillery: Technical Treatises* (Oxford).

Martin, V. and Budé, G. de (1927) *Eschine: Discours*, vol. 1, *Contre Timarque* (Paris).

Martzavou, P. (2012a) 'Dream, narrative, and the construction of hope in the "healing miracles" of Epidauros', in A. Chaniotis (ed.), *Unveiling Emotions: Sources and Methods for the Study of Emotions in the Greek World* (Stuttgart) 177–204.

Martzavou, P. (2012b) 'Isis aretalogies, initiations, and emotions: the Isis aretalogies as a source for the study of emotions', in A. Chaniotis (ed.), *Unveiling Emotions: Sources and Methods for the Study of Emotions in the Greek World* (Stuttgart) 267–92.

Maslov, B. (2012) 'The limits of Platonism: Gregory of Nazianzus and the invention of *theōsis*', *Greek, Roman, and Byzantine Studies* 52, 440–68.

Masséglia, J. (2012a) 'Emotions and archaeological sources: a methodological introduction', in A. Chaniotis (ed.), *Unveiling Emotions: Sources and Methods for the Study of Emotions in the Greek World* (Stuttgart) 131–50.

Masséglia, J. (2012b) 'Make or break decisions: the archaeology of allegiance in Ephesos', in A. Chaniotis (ed.), *Unveiling Emotions: Sources and Methods for the Study of Emotions in the Greek World* (Stuttgart) 329–55.

Masséglia, J. (2012c) '"Reasons to be cheerful": conflicting emotions in the Drunken Old Women of Munich and Rome', in A. Chaniotis (ed.), *Unveiling Emotions: Sources and Methods for the Study of Emotions in the Greek World* (Stuttgart) 413–30.

Masséglia, J. (2013) 'Feeling low: social status and emotional display in Hellenistic art', in A. Chaniotis and P. Ducrey (eds), *Unveiling Emotions II. Emotions in Greece and Rome: Texts, Images, Material Culture* (Stuttgart) 313–30.

Masséglia, J. (2015) *Body Language in Hellenistic Art and Society* (Oxford).

Matelli, E. (1992) 'ENDIATHETOS e PROPHORIKOS LOGOS: note sulla origine della formula e della nozione', *Aevum* 66, 43–70.

Matelli, E. (2016) 'Theophrastus on catharsis and the need for release from evils due to emotions', *Skenè: Journal of Theatre and Drama Studies* 2.1, 69–103.

Mateos, J. (ed.) (1962–3) *Le Typicon de la Grande Église*, 2 vols (Rome).

Matt, S. J. (2011) 'Current emotion research in history: or doing history from the inside out', *Emotion Review* 3, 117–24.

Matt, S. J. (2014) 'Recovering the invisible: methods for the historical study of the emotions', in S. J. Matt and P. Stearns (eds), *Doing Emotions History* (Urbana) 41–53.

Matt, S. J. and Stearns, P. N. (eds) (2014) *Doing Emotions History* (Urbana).

Maurer, C. (1990) 'σκεῦος', in *Theologisches Wörterbuch zum Neuen Testament*, vol. 7 (Stuttgart) 359–68.

Maxwell, J. (2006) *Christianization and Communication in Late Antiquity: John Chrysostom and His Congregation in Antioch* (Cambridge).

Mayer, W. (2015) 'Shaping the sick soul: reshaping the identity of John Chrysostom', in G. D. Dunn and W. Mayer (eds), *Christians Shaping Identity from the Roman Empire to Byzantium: Studies Inspired by Pauline Allen* (Leiden) 140–64.

Mayer, W. and Allen, P. (2000) *John Chrysostom* (London).

Mazzucchi, C. M. (1990) 'Longino in Giovanni di Sicilia: con un inedito di storia, epigrafia e toponomastica di Cosma Manasse dal cod. Laurenziano 57. 5', *Aevum* 64.2, 183–98.

Mazzucchi, C. M. (2006) 'Damascio, autore del *Corpus Dionysiacum* e il dialogo *ΠΕΡΙ ΠΟΛΙΤΙΚΗΣ ΕΠΙΣΤΗΜΗΣ*', *Aevum* 80, 299–334.

McCormick, M. (1986) *Eternal Victory: Triumphal Rulership in Late Antiquity, Byzantium, and the Early Medieval West* (Cambridge).

McFee, G. (2011) 'Empathy: interpersonal vs artistic?', in A. Coplan and P. Goldie (eds), *Empathy: Philosophical and Psychological Perspectives* (Oxford) 185–210.

McGill, S. (2005) *Virgil Recomposed: the Mythological and Secular Centos in Antiquity* (American Classical Studies 48) (Oxford).

McGuckin, J. A. (1996) 'Symeon the New Theologian (d. 1022) and Byzantine monasticism', in A. Bryer and M. Cunningham (eds), *Mount Athos and Byzantine Monasticism: Papers from the Twenty-eighth Spring Symposium of Byzantine Studies, Birmingham, March 1994* (Aldershot) 17–35.

McLaughlin, P. (2013) 'The question of the authenticity of the *Mechanical Problems*'. http://www.philosophie.uni-hd.de/md/philsem/personal/mclaughlin_authenticity_2013_2.pdf.

McLynn, N. (2006) 'Among the hellenists: Gregory and the sophists', in J. Børtnes and T. Hägg (eds), *Gregory of Nazianzus: Images and Reflections* (Copenhagen) 213–38.

McNiven, T. (1982) 'Gestures in Attic vase-painting: use and meaning 550–450 BC' (Ph.D. Diss. Michigan).

McNiven, T. (2000a) 'Behaving like an other: gender-specific gestures in Athenian vase painting', in B. Cohen (ed.), *Not the Classical Ideal: Athens and the Construction of the Other in Greek Art* (Leiden) 71–97.

McNiven, T. (2000b) 'Fear and gender in Greek art', in A. E. Rautman (ed.), *Reading the Body: Representations and Remains in the Archaeological Record* (Philadelphia) 124–31.

Mead, G. H. (1964) 'The mechanism of social consciousness', *Selected Writings* (Indianapolis) 134–41 (first published in *Journal of Philosophy, Psychology and Scientific Methods* 9 (1912) 401–6).

Meineck, P. (2018) *Theatrocracy: Greek Drama, Cognition, and the Imperative for Theatre* (Abingdon).

Mellas, A. (2017) 'Tears of compunction in St John Chrysostom's *On Eutropius*', in M. Vinzent and Y. Papadogiannakis (eds), *Studia Patristica LXXXIII: Papers Presented at the Seventeenth International Conference on Patristic Studies Held in Oxford 2015*, Vol. 9, *Emotions* (Leuven) 159–72.

Mellas, A. (2018) 'Dreaming liturgically: Andrew of Crete's *Great Kanon* as a mystical Vision', in N. Bronwen and E. Anagnostou-Laoutides (eds), *Dreams, Memory and Imagination in Byzantium* (Leiden) 293–314.

Mellas, A. (2020) *Liturgy and the Emotions in Byzantium* (Cambridge).

Mendonça, D. (2019) 'What a difference depth makes', *Revista de Filosofia: Aurora, Curitiba* 31.54, 671–94.

Menge, H. (1984) *Großwörterbuch Griechisch–Deutsch*, 25th edn (Berlin).

Menninghaus, W., Wagner, V., Hanich, J., Wassiliwizky, E., Kuehnast, M., and Jacobsen, T. (2015) 'Towards a psychological construct of being moved', *PLoS One* 10.6, 1–33.

Bibliography 483

Merleau-Ponty, M. (2012) *The Phenomenology of Perception*, ed. and trans. D. A. Landes (London).

Messis, C. and Nilsson, I. (2019) 'Eros as passion, affection and nature: gendered perceptions of erotic emotion in Byzantium', in S. Constantinou and M. Meyer (eds), *Emotions and Gender in Byzantine Culture* (New Approaches to Byzantine History and Culture) (Stuttgart) 159–90.

Messis, C. and Papaioannou, S. (2013) 'Histoires "gothiques" à Byzance: le saint, le soldat et le Miracle de l'Euphemie et du Goth (BHG 739)', *Dumbarton Oaks Papers* 67, 15–48.

Messis, C. and Papaioannou, S. (2021) 'Orality and textuality', in S. Papaioannou (ed.), *The Oxford Handbook of Byzantine Literature* (Oxford), 241–72.

Metzger, B. (1987) 'Muratorian Canon', in *The Canon of the New Testament: Its Origin, Development and Significance* (Oxford) 191–201.

Mewaldt, J. (ed.) (1914) *Galeni in Hippocratis de natura hominis commentaria tria* (Corpus Medicorum Graecorum 5.9.1) (Leipzig).

Michel, H. J. (1973) *Die Abschiedsrede des Paulus an die Kirche, Apg 20,17–38: Motiv-geschichte und theologische Bedeutung* (Studien zum Alten und Neuen Testament 35) (Munich).

Milik, J. T. (1955) 'Le Testament de Lévi en araméen', *Revue biblique* 62, 39–406.

Miller, D. J. D and Sarris, P. (2019) *The Novels of Justinian: a Complete Annotated English Translation* (Cambridge).

Miller, P. C. (2005) 'Relics, rhetoric, and mental spectacles in Late Ancient Christianity', in G. de Nie, K. F. Morrison, M. Mostert (eds), *Seeing the Invisible in Late Antiquity and the Early Middle Ages: Papers from 'Verbal and Pictorial Imaging: Representing and Accessing Experience of the Invisible, 400–1000' (Utrecht, 11–13 December 2003)* (Turnhout) 25–52.

Miller, W. I. (1997) *The Anatomy of Disgust* (Cambridge, MA).

Milobenski, E. (1964) *Der Neid in der griechischen Philosophie* (Wiesbaden).

Milošević, D. (1963) *Das Jüngste Gericht* (Recklinghausen).

Mitchell, M. M. (2000) *The Heavenly Trumpet: John Chrysostom and the Art of Pauline Interpretation* (Tübingen).

Möbius, H. (1996) 'Mutterbilder: die Gottesmutter und ihr Sohn', in R. Möhrmann (ed.), *Verklärt, verkitscht, vergessen: die Mutter als ästhetische Figur* (Stuttgart) 21–38.

Mondzain, M.-J. (2005) *Image, Icon, Economy: the Byzantine Origins of the Contemporary Imaginary*, trans. R. Franses (Stanford).

Montanari, F. (2015) *The Brill Dictionary of Ancient Greek* (Leiden).

Montiglio, S. (2010) '"My soul, consider what you should do": psychological conflicts and moral goodness in the Greek novels', *Ancient Narrative* 8, 25–58.

Morani, M. (ed.) (1935) *Nemesius, De natura hominis* (Leipzig).

Morani, M. (ed.) (1987) *Nemesii Emeseni De natura hominis* (Leipzig).

Moraw, S. (2012) 'Visual differences: Dionysos in ancient art', in R. Schlesier (ed.), *A Different God? Dionysos and Ancient Polytheism* (Berlin) 233–52.

Morel, P.-M. (2016) 'La physiologie des passions dans le *De motu animalium* d'Aristote', in I. Boehm, J.-L. Ferrary, and S. Franchet d'Espèrey (eds), *L'homme et ses passions: actes du XVIIe Congrès international de l'Association Guillaume Budé organisé à Lyon du 26 au 29 août 2013* (Paris) 291–301.

Moreschini, C. (ed.) and Gallay, P. (trans.) (1990) *Grégoire de Nazianze, Discours 38–41* (Paris).

Moreschini, C. and Norelli, E. (2000) *Histoire de la littérature chrétienne antique grecque et latine*, vol. 1, *De Paul à l'ère de Constantin* (Geneva).

Morgan, J. R. (1989) 'The story of Knemon in Heliodorus' *Aithiopika*', *Journal of Hellenic Studies* 109, 99–113.

Most, G. W. (2003) 'Anger and pity in Homer's *Illiad*', in S. M. Braund and G. W. Most (eds) *Ancient Anger: Perspectives from Homer to Galen* (Yale Classical Studies 32) (Cambridge) 50–75.

Mouriki, D. (1975–6) 'An unusual representation of the Last Judgment in a thirteenth century fresco at St. George near Kouvaras in Attica', Δελτίον τῆς Χριστιανικῆς Ἀρχαιολογικῆς Ἑταιρείας 6.8, 145–71.

Mras, K. (ed.) (1954–6), *Eusebius Werke*, vol. 8, *Die Praeparatio evangelica* (Die griechischen christlichen Schriftsteller 43.1 and 43.2) (Berlin).

Mueller, M. (2016) *Objects as Actors: Props and the Poetics of Performance in Greek Tragedy* (Chicago).

Mühlenberg, E. (ed.) (1996) *Gregory of Nyssa, Oratio Catechetica* (Leiden).

Muellner, L. (1996) *The Anger of Achilles: Mênis in Greek Epic* (Ithaca, NY).

Mühl, M. (1962) 'Der λόγος ἐνδιάθετος und προφορικός von der älteren Stoa bis zur Synode von Sirmium 351', *Archiv für Begriffsgeschichte* 7, 7–56.

Mullett, M. (1981) 'The Classical tradition in the Byzantine letter', in M. Mullett and R. Scott (eds), *Byzantium and the Classical Tradition* (Birmingham) 75–93.

Mullett, M. (1984) 'Aristocracy and patronage in the literary circles of Comnenian Constantinople', in M. J. Angold (ed.), *The Byzantine Aristocracy: IX to XIII Centuries* (BAR International Series 221) (Oxford) 173–201.

Mullett, M. (1999) 'From Byzantium with love', in L. James (ed.), *Desire and Denial in Byzantium: Papers from the 31st Spring Symposium of Byzantine Studies, Brighton, March 1997* (Society for the Promotion of Byzantine Studies 7) (Aldershot) 1–22.

Mullett, M. (2006) 'Novelisation in Byzantium: narrative after the revival of fiction', in J. Burke (ed.), *Byzantine Narrative: Papers in Honour of Roger Scott* (Byzantina Australiensia 16) (Melbourne) 1–28.

Mullett, M. (2020) 'Contexts for the *Christos Paschon*', in A. Olsen Lam and R. Schroeder (eds), *The Eloquence of Art: Studies in Honour of Henry Maguire* (Abingdon) 204–17.

Mullett, M. (2021) 'Spoiling the Hellenes: intertextuality, appropriation, embedment. The case of the Christos Paschon', in I. Jevtic and I. Nilsson (eds), *Spoliation as Translation: Medieval Worlds in the Eastern Mediterranean* (Convivium Supplementum 2021.2) (Brno) 99–115.

Mullett, M. (forthcoming a) 'Performability, lament, and the tragedy *Christos Paschon*', in N. Tsironi (ed.) *Lament as Performance in Byzantium* (Abingdon).

Mullett, M. (forthcoming b) 'Painting and polyphony: the *Christos Paschon* as commentary', in B. van den Berg, P. Marciniak, and D. Manolova (eds), *Preserving, Commenting, Adapting: Byzantine Commentaries on Ancient Texts in the Twelfth Century and Beyond* (Cambridge).

Mullett, M. (forthcoming c) 'Performance issues in the *Christos Paschon*', in N. Tsironi (ed.) *Essays in Memory of P. Sherrard*.

Mullett, M. and Ashbrook Harvey, S. (forthcoming) *Managing Emotion: Passions, Affects and Imaginings* (Washington, DC).

Munteanu, D. L. (2009) '*Qualis tandem misericordia in rebus fictis?* Aesthetic and ordinary emotion', *Helios* 36, 117–47.

Munteanu, D. L. (ed.) (2011) *Emotion, Genre, and Gender in Classical Antiquity* (London).

Bibliography 485

Munteanu, D. L. (2012) *Tragic Pathos: Pity and Fear in Greek Philosophy and Tragedy* (Cambridge).

Munteanu, D. L. (2017) 'Grief: the power and shortcomings of Greek tragic consolation', in D. L. Cairns and D. P. Nelis (eds), *Emotions in the Classical World: Methods, Approaches, and Directions* (Heidelberger althistorische Beiträge und epigraphische Studien 59) (Stuttgart) 79–103.

Muraoka, T. (2009) *A Greek–English Lexicon of the Septuagint* (Leuven).

Murer, C. (2017) *Stadtraum und Bürgerin: Aufstellungsorte kaiserzeitlicher Ehrenstatuen in Italien und Nordafrika* (Berlin).

Murray, A. T. (ed. and trans.), revised by Wyatt, W. F. (1999 [1924]) *Homer, Iliad* (Loeb Classical Library 170 and 171) (Cambridge, MA).

Murray, P. (1996) *Plato on Poetry: Ion, Republic 376e–398b, Republic 595–608b* (Cambridge).

Murray, P. (1999) 'What is a *muthos* for Plato?', in R. Buxton (ed.), *From Myth to Reason? Studies in the Development of Greek Thought* (Oxford) 251–62.

Nagel, T. (1974) 'What is it like to be a bat?', *Philosophical Review* 83.4, 435–50.

Nagy, G. (2002) *Plato's Rhapsody and Homer's Music: the Poetics of the Panathenaic Festival in Classical Athens* (Washington, DC).

Naiden, F. S. (2019) 'Religion and spirituality', in D. L. Cairns (ed.), *A Cultural History of the Emotions in Antiquity* (London) 35–45.

Nelson, R. (1989) 'The discourse of icons, then and now', *Art History* 12, 144–57.

Nelson, R. (2000) 'To say and to see: *ekphrasis* and vision in Byzantium', in R. Nelson (ed.), *Visuality before and beyond the Renaissance: Seeing as Others Saw* (Cambridge) 143–68.

Nelson, R. (2005) 'Byzantine art vs Western medieval art', in P. Pagès, M. Balard, E. Malamut and J. M. Spieser (eds), *Byzance et le monde extérieur: contacts, relations, échanges* (Paris) 255–70.

Nelson, R. (2007) 'Image and inscription: pleas for salvation in spaces of devotion', in E. James (ed.), *Art and Text in Byzantine Culture* (New York) 100–19.

Nesbitt, C. and Jackson, M. (eds) (2013) *Experiencing Byzantium* (Farnham).

Neumann, G. (1965) *Gesten und Gebärden in der griechischen Kunst* (Berlin).

Neville, L. (2018) *Guide to Byzantine Historical Writing* (Cambridge).

Neville, L. (2019) 'Pity and lamentation in the authorial personae of John Kaminiates and Anna Komnene', in S. Constantinou and M. Meyer (eds), *Emotion and Gender in Byzantine Culture* (London) 65–92.

Niebuhr, K.-W. (1987) *Gesetz und Paränese: Katechismusartige Weisungsreihen in der frühjüdischen Literatur* (Wissenschaftliche Untersuchungen zum Neuen Testament 2.28) (Tübingen).

Niedenthal, P. M., Winkielman, P., Mondillon, L., and Vermeulen, N. (2009) 'Embodiment of emotion concepts', *Journal of Personality and Social Psychology* 96.6, 1120–36.

Niedenthal, P. M., Wood, A., and Rychlowska, M. (2014) 'Embodied emotion concepts', in L. Shapiro (ed.), *The Routledge Handbook of Embodied Cognition* (London) 240–9.

Nightingale, A. W. (1995) *Genres in Dialogue: Plato and the Construct of Philosophy* (Cambridge).

Nightingale, A. W. (2001) 'On wandering and wondering: *theôria* in Greek philosophy and culture', *Arion* 9, 23–58.

Nightingale, A. W. (2004) *Spectacles of Truth in Classical Greek Philosophy: Theoria in Its Cultural Context* (Cambridge).

486 Bibliography

Nikolaou. T. (1969) *Der Neid bei Ioannes Chrysostomus, unter Berücksichtigung der Griechischen Philosophie* (Bonn)..

Nilsson, I. (2004) 'From Homer to Hermoniakos: some considerations of Troy matter in Byzantine literature', *Troianalexandrina* 4, 8–34.

Nilsson, I. (2013) 'Nature controlled by artistry: the poetics of the literary garden in Byzantium', in H. Bodin and R. Hedlund (eds), *Byzantine Gardens and Beyond* (Uppsala) 15–29.

Noë, A. (2004) *Action in Perception* (Cambridge, MA).

Noret, J. (1983) 'Grégoire de Nazianze, l'auteur le plus cité, après la Bible, dans la littérature ecclésiastique byzantine', in J. Mossay (ed.), *II. Symposium Nazianzenum: Louvain-la-Neuve, 25–28 août 1981* (Paderborn) 259–66.

Norlin, G. (trans.) (1928) *Isocrates. To Demonicus. To Nicocles. Nicocles or the Cyprians. Panegyricus. To Philip. Archidamus* (Loeb Classical Library 209) (Cambridge, MA).

Norris, F. (1991) *Faith Gives Fullness to Reasoning: the Five Theological Orations of Gregory Nazianzen* (Leiden).

Nünlist, R. (2012) 'Homer as a blueprint for speechwriters: Eustathius' commentaries and rhetoric', *Greek, Roman, and Byzantine Studies* 52, 493–509.

Nürnberger, A. (2019) *Zweifelskonzepte im Frühchristentum: Dipsychia und Oligopistia im Rahmen menschlicher Dissonanz- und Einheitsvorstellungen in der Antike* (Novum Testamentum et Orbis Antiquus 122) (Göttingen).

Nussbaum, M. C. (1994) *The Therapy of Desire: Theory and Practice in Hellenistic Ethics* (Princeton).

Nussbaum, M. C. (1996) 'Aristotle on emotions and rational persuasion', in A. O. Rorty (ed.), *Essays on Aristotle's Rhetoric* (Berkeley) 303–21.

Nussbaum, M. C. (2001) *Upheavals of Thought: the Intelligence of Emotions* (Cambridge).

Nutton, V. (2007) 'Galen in Byzantium', in M. Grünbart, E. Kislinger, and A. Muthesius (eds), *Material Culture and Well-Being in Byzantium* (Vienna) 171–76.

Nutton, V. (2008) 'The fortunes of Galen', in R. J. Hankinson (ed.), *The Cambridge Companion to Galen* (Cambridge) 355–90.

Oakley, J. H. (2004) *Picturing Death in Classical Athens: the Evidence of the White Lekythoi* (Cambridge).

Oatley, K. (2011) *Such Stuff as Dreams: the Psychology of Fiction* (Malden, MA).

Oatley, K. (2012) *The Passionate Muse: Exploring Emotion in Stories* (Oxford).

Oberhaus, M. (1991) *Gregor von Nazianz, Gegen den Zorn (Carmen 1,2,25): Einleitung und Kommentar* (Paderborn).

Oberhelman, S. (2015) 'Toward a typology of Byzantine and Post-Byzantine healing texts', *Athens Journal of Health* 2.2, 133–46.

Odorico, P. (1990) 'La cultura della συλλογή', *Byzantinische Zeitschrift* 83, 1–21.

Odorico, P. (2011) 'Cadre d'exposition/cadre de pensée: la culture du recueil', in P. van Deun and C. Mace (eds), *Encyclopaedic Trends in Byzantium?* (Leuven) 89–108.

Oepke, A. (1935) 'Wortfeld δύω', *Theologisches Wörterbuch zum Neuen Testament*, vol. 2 (Stuttgart) 318–21.

O'Meara, D. (2017) 'Conceptions of science in Byzantium', in A. Kaldellis and N. Siniossoglou (eds), *The Cambridge Intellectual History of Byzantium* (Cambridge) 169–82.

Onians, R. B. (1954) *The Origins of European Thought about the Body, the Mind, the Soul, the World, Time, and Fate*, 2nd edn (Cambridge).

Bibliography 487

Opitz, C. (2002) 'Pflicht-Gefühl: zur Codierung von Mutterliebe zwischen Renaissance und Aufklärung', in I. Kasten (ed.), *Kulturen der Gefühle in Mittelalter und Früher Neuzeit* (Stuttgart) 154–70.

Osiek, C. (1999) *Shepherd of Hermas: a Commentary*, ed. H. Koester (Hermeneia) (Minneapolis).

Osiek, C. (2000) 'Hirt des Hermas', in *Religion in Geschichte und Gegenwart*, 4th edn, vol. 3 (Tübingen) cols 1788–90.

O'Sullivan, J. N. (2010) 'χόλος', *Lexikon des frühgriechischen Epos* (Göttingen) cols 1227–33.

Ousterhout, R. (1995) 'Temporal structuring in the Chora parekklesion', *Gesta* 34, 63–76.

Ousterhout, R. (2002) *The Art of the Kariye Camii* (London).

Ousterhout, R. (2013) 'Women at tombs: narrative, theatricality, and the contemplative mode', in A. Eastmond and E. James (eds), *Wonderful Things: Byzantium through Its Art* (Society for the Promotion of Byzantine Studies 16) (Farnham) 229–46.

Pace, C. (2010) 'Tragedia, *ekplēxis* e *apatē* nell'anonima *Vita di Eschilo*', *Seminari romani di cultura greca* 11, 229–54.

Padel, R. (1992) *In and Out of the Mind: Greek Images of the Tragic Self* (Princeton).

Pagani, L. (2017) 'Eustathius' use of ancient scholarship in his *Commentary on the Iliad*: some remarks', in F. Pontani, V. Katsaros, and V. Sarris (eds), *Reading Eustathios of Thessalonike* (*Trends in Classics* Supplement 46) (Berlin) 79–110.

Pais, A. (2016) 'Re-affecting the stage: affective assonance as the function of the audience', *Humanities* 5, 79.

Palme, B. (2021) 'Emotional strategies in petitions of Dioskoros of Aphrodito', in A. Chaniotis (ed.), *Unveiling Emotions III: Arousal, Display, and Performance of Emotions in the Greek World* (Stuttgart) 321–42.

Palmer, G. E. H., Sherrard, P., and Ware, K. (ed. and trans.) (1981) *The Philokalia: the Complete Text Compiled by St Nikodimos of the Holy Mountain and St Makarios of Corinth*, vol. 2 (London).

Panaccio, C. (1999) *Le discours intérieur: de Platon à Guillaume d'Ockam* (Paris).

Panaccio, C. (2017) *Mental Language from Plato to Ockham*, trans. J. P. Hochschild and M. K. Ziebart (New York).

Panofsky, E. (1960) *Renaissance and Renascences in Western Art* (Stockholm).

Papadogiannakis, I. (2017a) 'Dialogical pedagogy and the structuring of emotions in *Liber Asceticus*', in A. Cameron and N. Gaul (eds), *Dialogues and Debates from Late Antiquity to Late Byzantium* (London) 94–104.

Papadogiannakis, Y. [= I.] (2017b) 'Introduction', in M. Vinzent and Y. Papadogiannakis (eds), *Studia Patristica LXXXIII: Papers Presented at the Seventeenth International Conference on Patristic Studies Held in Oxford 2015*, vol. 9, *Emotions* (Leuven) 1–18.

Papadogiannakis, I. (2018) 'Prescribing emotions, constructing emotional community in John Chrysostom's Antioch', in S.-P. Bergjan and S. Elm (eds), *Antioch II. The Many Faces of Antioch: Intellectual Exchange and Religious Diversity, CE 350–450* (Tübingen) 339–60.

Papadogiannakis, I. (2019) 'Homiletics and the history of emotions: the case of John Chrysostom', in C. de Wet and W. Mayer (eds), *Revisioning John Chrysostom: New Approaches, New Perspectives* (Leiden) 300–33.

Papadopoulos, K. (1966) *Die Wandmalereien des XI. Jahrhunderts in der Kirche Παναγία τῶν Χαλκέων in Thessaloniki* (Graz).

488 *Bibliography*

Papaioannou, S. (2006) 'Gregory and the constraint of sameness', in J. Børtnes and T. Hägg (eds), *Gregory of Nazianzus: Images and Reflections* (Copenhagen) 59–81.

Papaioannou, S. (2011) 'Byzantine *enargeia* and theories of representation', *Byzantinoslavica: Revue international des études byzantines* 69, 48–60.

Papaioannou, S. (2013) *Michael Psellos: Rhetoric and Authorship in Byzantium* (Cambridge).

Papaioannou, S. (2015) 'Sicily, Constantinople, Miletos: the life of a eunuch and the history of Byzantine humanism', in T. Antonopoulou, M. Loukai, and S. Kotzabassi (eds), *Myriobiblos: Essays on Byzantine Literature and Culture* (Berlin) 261–84.

Papaioannou, S. (2017a) 'Encomium for the monk Ioannes Kroustoulas who read aloud at the Holy Soros', in C. Barber and S. Papaioannou (eds), *Michael Psellos on Literature and Art: a Byzantine Perspective on Aesthetics* (Notre Dame, IN) 218–44.

Papaioannou, S. (2017b) 'An encomium of Gregory of Nazianzos' style', in C. Barber and S. Papaioannou (eds), *Michael Psellos on Literature and Art: a Byzantine Perspective on Aesthetics* (Notre Dame, IN) 118–48.

Papaioannou, S. (ed. and trans.) (2017c) *Christian Novels from the Menologion of Symeon Metaphrastes* (Cambridge, MA).

Papaioannou, S. (2019a), 'Ioannes Sikeliotes (and Ioannes Geometres) revisited with an appendix: edition of Sikeliotes' scholia on Aelius Aristides', in A. Binggelli and V. Déroche (eds), *Mélanges Bernard Flusin* (Travaux et mémoires 23.1) (Paris) 659–92.

Papaioannou, S. (ed.) (2019b) *Michael Psellus, Epistulae* (Berlin).

Papaioannou, S. (2021) 'Theory of literature', in S. Papaioannou (ed.), *The Oxford Handbook of Byzantine Literature* (Oxford) 76–109.

Papathomopoulos, M. and Jeffreys, E. (eds) (1996) Ὁ Πόλεμος τῆς Τρωάδος *(The War of Troy)* (Athens).

Pape, W. (1954) *Griechisch–deutsches Handwörterbuch*, 3rd edn (Graz).

Parlby, G. (2008) 'The origins of Marian art in the catacombs and the problems of identification', in C. Maunder (ed.), *The Origins of the Cult of Virgin Mary* (London) 41–56.

Parpulov, G. R. (2010) 'Mural and icon painting at Sinai in the thirteenth century', in S. E. J. Gerstel and R. S. Nelson (eds), *Approaching the Holy Mountain: Art and Liturgy at St Catherine's Monastery in the Sinai* (Turnhout) 345–414.

Paschos, E. A. and Simelidis, C. (ed. and trans.) (2017) *Introduction to Astronomy by Theodore Metochites (Stoicheiosis Astronomike 1.5–30)* (Hackensack, NJ).

Passingham, R. (2016) *Cognitive Neuroscience: a Very Short Introduction* (Oxford).

Passow, F. (2008) *Handwörterbuch der griechischen Sprache*, vol. 2.2 (Darmstadt).

Patera, M. (2013) 'Reflections on the discourse of fear in Greek sources', in A. Chaniotis and P. Ducrey (eds), *Unveiling Emotions II. Emotions in Greece and Rome: Texts, Images, Material Culture* (Stuttgart) 109–34.

Paterson Corrington, G. (1989) 'The milk of salvation: redemption by the Mother in Late Antiquity and Early Christianity', *Harvard Theological Review* 82, 393–420.

Patillon, M. (1988) *La théorie du discours chez Hermogène le rhéteur, essai sur la structure de la rhétorique ancienne* (Paris).

Patillon, M. (ed.) (1997) *Aelius Théon, Progymnasmata* (Paris).

Patillon, M. (ed.) (2012) *Hermogène, Les catégories stylistiques du discours (De ideiis); Synopses des exposés sur les IDEAI* (Paris).

Paverd, F. van de (1991) *St. John Chrysostom, the Homilies on the Statues: an Introduction* (Rome).

Pavlenko, A. (2012) 'Affective processing in bilingual speakers: disembodied cognition?', *International Journal of Psychology* 47.6, 405–28.

Pedrick, V. (1982) 'Supplication in the *Iliad* and the *Odyssey*', *Transactions of the American Philological Association* 112, 125–40.

Pedrucci, G. (2013) *L'allattamento nella Grecia di epoca arcaica e classica* (Rome).

Pedrucci, G. (2015) 'Baliatico, αἰδώς e malocchio: capire l'allattamento nella Grecia di epoca arcaica e classica anche con l'aiuto delle fonti romane', *Eugesta (Journal of Gender Studies in Antiquity)* 5, 27–53.

Peek, W. (1960) *Griechische Grabgedichte: griechisch und deutsch* (Berlin).

Peers, G. (2015) 'Modernism's Byzantium, Byzantium's Modernism', in R. Betancourt and M. Taroutina (eds), *Byzantium/Modernism: the Byzantine as Method in Modernity* (Leiden) 15–36.

Peers, G. (2020) *Animism, Materiality, and Museums: How Do Byzantine Things Feel?* (Leeds).

Pelliccia, H. (1995) *Mind, Body, and Speech in Homer and Pindar* (Göttingen).

Pentcheva, B.V. (2006) 'The performative icon', *Art Bulletin* 88, 631–55.

Pentcheva, B.V. (2010) *The Sensual Icon: Space, Ritual and the Senses in Byzantium* (Philadelphia).

Pepe, C. (2018) 'The rhetorical commentary in Late Antiquity', *Aion* 40, 86–108.

Perczel, I. (2009) 'The earliest Syriac reception of Dionysius', in S. Coakley and C. Stang (eds) *Re-thinking Dionysius the Areopagite* (Chichester) 27–41.

Perczel, I. (2012) 'Pseudo-Dionysius the Areopagite and the Pseudo-Dormition of the Holy Virgin', *Le Muséon* 125, 55–97.

Pérez Martín, I. (ed.) (2002) *Miguel Ataliates, Historia: introducción, edición, traducción y commentario* (Nueva Roma 15) (Madrid).

Perria, L. (1982) 'La clausola ritmica nella prosa di Filagato da Cerami', *Jahrbuch der österreichischen Byzantinistik* 32, 365–73.

Pessoa, L. (2013) *The Cognitive-Emotional Brain: from Interactions to Integration* (Cambridge, MA).

Peterson, E. (1959) 'Kritische Analyse der fünften Vision des Hermas', in E. Peterson, *Frühkirche, Judentum und Gnosis: Studien und Untersuchungen* (Rome) 271–84.

Peterson, E. (1965) 'Giudaismo e cristianesimo: culto giudaico e culto cristiano', *Rivista di letteratura e storia religiosa* 1, 367–91.

Pfister, M. (1988) *The Theory and Analysis of Drama*, trans. J. Halliday (Cambridge).

Phelan, J. (1996) *Narrative as Rhetoric: Techniques, Audiences, Ethics* (Columbus, OH).

Philonenko, M. (1960) *Les interpolations chrétiennes des Testaments des Douze Patriarches et les manuscrits de Qoumrân* (Cahiers de la Revue d'histoire et de philosophie religieuses 35) (Paris).

Pickard-Cambridge, A.W. (1968) *The Dramatic Festivals at Athens*, 2nd edn, revised by J. Gould and D. M. Lewis (Oxford).

Pietersma, A. and Wright, B.G. (2007) *A New English Translation of the Septuagint and Other Greek Translations Traditionally Included under That Title* (New York).

Pizzocaro, M. (1994) *Il triangolo amoroso: la nozione di 'gelosia' nella cultura e nella lingua greca arcaica* (Bari).

Pizzone, A. (2011) 'Late-Antique ΦΑΝΤΑΣΙΑ and the Greek Fathers: a survey', in D. Hernandez de la Fuente (ed.), *New Perspectives on Late Antiquity* (Newcastle upon Tyne).

490   *Bibliography*

Pizzone, A. (2014) 'Anonymity, dispossession and reappropriation in the *Prolog* of Nikephoros Basilakes', in A. Pizzone (ed.), *The Author in Middle Byzantine Literature* (Byzantinisches Archiv 28) (Berlin) 225–43.

Pizzone, A. (2016) 'Emotions and audiences in Eustathios of Thessalonike's commentaries on Homer', *Dumbarton Oaks Papers* 70, 225–44.

Pizzone, A. (2021) '"A hand of ivory": moving objects in Psellos' oration for his daughter Styliane. A case-study', *Emotion Review* 13, 289–98.

Pizzone, A. (2022) 'Tzetzes and the *prokatastasis*: a tale of people, manuscripts, and performances', in E. Prodi (ed.), *TZETZIKAI EPEYNAI* (Bologna) 19–74.

Plamper, J. (2012) *Geschichte und Gefühl: Grundlagen der Emotionsgeschichte* (Munich).

Plamper, J. (2015) *The History of Emotions: an Introduction* (Oxford).

Plamper, J. and Lazier, B. (eds) (2012) *Fear across Disciplines* (Pittsburgh).

Plümacher, E. (1992 [1978]) 'σκεῦος, ους, τό', *Exegetisches Wörterbuch zum Neuen Testament*, 2nd edn, vol. 3 (Stuttgart) cols 597–9.

Podskalsky, G. and Cutler, A. (1991) 'Last Judgment', *The Oxford Dictionary of Byzantium*, vol. 2 (Oxford) 1181–2.

Polacco, R. (1984) *La Cattedrale di Torcello* (Venice).

Polemis, I. (ed.) (2014) *Michaelis Pselli Orationes funebres* (Berlin).

Polemis, I. (2015) 'Funeral oration for the most blessed patriarch *kyr* Ioannes Xiphilinos', in A. Kaldellos and I. Polemis (eds) *Psellos and the Patriarchs: Letters and Funeral Orations for Keroullarios, Leichoudes and Xiphilinos* (Notre Dame, IN) 177–228.

Pollini, J. (2012) *From Republic to Empire: Rhetoric, Religion, and Power in the Visual Culture of Ancient Rome* (Norman).

Pollitt, J. J. (1972) *Art and Experience in Classical Greece* (Cambridge).

Pollitt, J. J. (1974) *The Ancient View of Greek Art: Criticism, History and Terminology* (New Haven).

Pollitt, J. J. (1976) 'The ethos of Polygnotos and Aristeides', in L. Bonfante (ed.), *Essays in Archaeology and the Humanities: in memoriam Otto J. Brendel* (Mainz) 49–54.

Pollitt, J. J. (1986) *Art in the Hellenistic Age* (Cambridge).

Pollmann, K. (1997) 'Jesus Christus und Dionysus', *Jahrbuch der österreichischen Byzantinistik* 47, 87–106.

Pontani, F. (2005) *Sguardi su Ulisse: la tradizione esegetica greca all' Odissea* (Rome).

Pontani, F. (2006) 'The first Byzantine commentary on the *Iliad*: Isaac Porphyrogenitus and his scholia', *Byzantinische Zeitschrift* 99, 551–96.

Pontani, F., Katsaros, V., and Sarris, V. (eds) (2017) *Reading Eustathios of Thessalonike* (*Trends in Classics* Supplement 46) (Berlin).

Pradel, F. (1907) *Griechische und süditalienische Gebete, Beschwörungen und Rezepte des Mittelalters* (Giessen).

Pralon, D. (2015) 'Les personnages d'Homère selon Isaac Comnène Porphyrogénète: les portraits d'Agamemnon et de Ménélas', in S. Dubel, A.-M. Favreau-Linder, and E. Oudot (eds), *À l'école d'Homère* (Études de littérature ancienne 24) (Paris) 230–46..

Pratscher, W. (2011) 'Apostolische Väter, als Sammlung', *Das Wissenschaftliche Bibellexikon im Internet*. www.wibilex.de.

Preston, S. D. and De Waal, F. (2002) 'Empathy: its ultimate and proximate bases', *Behavioral and Brain Sciences* 25.1, 1–75.

Price, A. W. (1995) *Mental Conflict* (London).

Prinz, J. (2004) *Gut Reactions: a Perceptual Theory of Emotion* (New York).

Bibliography 491

Prioux, É. (2011) 'Emotions in ekphrasis and art criticism', in D. LaCourse Munteanu (ed.), *Emotion, Genre and Gender in Classical Antiquity* (Bristol) 135–74.

Procopé, J. F. (1998) 'Epicureans on anger', in J. Sihvola and T. Engberg-Pedersen (eds), *The Emotions in Hellenistic Philosophy* (Dordrecht) 171–96.

Pucci, J. (1998) *The Full-Knowing Reader: Allusion and the Power of the Reader in the Western Literary Tradition* (New Haven).

Puchner, W. assisted by Walker White, A. (2017) *Greek Theatre between Antiquity and Independence: a History of Reinvention from the Third Century BC to 1830* (Cambridge).

Pusey, P. E. (ed.) (1868) *Cyril of Alexandria, Commentarius in XII prophetas minores* (Oxford).

Qimron, E. and Charlesworth, J. H. (1994) 'Rule of the Community (1QS)', in J. H. Charlesworth (ed.), *The Dead Sea Scrolls: Hebrew, Aramaic, and Greek Texts with English Translations*, vol. 1 (Tübingen) 1–51.

Quibell, J. E. (1908) *Excavations at Saqqara 1906–07*, vol. 2 (Cairo).

Rabe, H. (ed.) (1896) *Commentaria in Aristotelem graeca*, vol. 21.2 (Berlin).

Rabe, H. (ed.) (1913) *Hermogenes* (Leipzig).

Rabe, H. (ed.) (1926) *Aphthonios, Progymnasmata* (Leipzig).

Rabe, H. (ed.) (1927) *Ioannis Sardiani Commentarium in Aphthonii Progymnasmata* (Leipzig).

Rabinowitz, P. (1998) *Before Reading: Narrative Conventions and the Politics of Interpretation* (Columbus, OH).

Rackham, H. (trans.) (1926) *Aristotle, Nicomachean Ethics* (Loeb Classical Library 73) (London).

Rackham, H. (trans.) (1984) *Pliny, Natural History*, vol. 9 (Loeb Classical Library 394) (London).

Rapp, C. (2002) *Aristoteles, Rhetorik*, vol. 2 (Berlin).

Rapp, C. (2008) 'Aristoteles: Bausteine für eine Theorie der Emotionen', in U. Renz and H. Landweer (eds), *Klassische Emotionstheorien: von Platon bis Wittgenstein* (Berlin) 45–68.

Räuchle, V. (2017) *Die Mütter Athens und ihre Kinder: Verhaltens- und Gefühlsideale in klassischer Zeit* (Berlin).

Räuchle, V. (2019) 'The visual arts', in D. L. Cairns (ed.), *A Cultural History of the Emotions in Antiquity* (London) 83–108.

Read, H. (2019) 'A typology of empathy and its many moral forms', *Philosophy Compass* 14.10, e12623. https://onlinelibrary.wiley.com/doi/10.1111/phc3.12623.

Ready, J. L. (2011) *Character, Narrator and Simile in the Iliad* (Cambridge).

Reardon B. P. (ed.) (1989) *Collected Ancient Greek Novels* (Berkeley).

Reddy, W. M. (1997) 'Against constructionism: the historical ethnography of emotions', *Current Anthropology* 38.3, 327–51.

Reddy, W. M. (2001) *The Navigation of Feeling: a Framework for the History of Emotions* (Cambridge).

Reeder, E. D. (ed.) (1995) *Pandora: Women in Classical Greece* (Baltimore).

Reeve, C. D. C. (trans.) (2017) *Aristotle, De anima* (Indianapolis).

Regnault, L. and De Préville, J. (eds) (2001) *Dorothée de Gaza: œuvres spirituelles* (Sources chrétiennes 92) (Paris).

Rehkopf, F. (1989) *Septuaginta-Vokabular* (Göttingen).

Reik, T. (1936) *Surprise and the Psycho-Analyst: on the Conjecture and Comprehension of Unconscious Processes* (London).

492 *Bibliography*

Reilly, J. and Seibert, L. (2003) 'Language and emotion', in R. J. Davidson, K. R. Scherer, and H. H. Goldsmith (eds), *Handbook of Affective Sciences* (Oxford) 535–59.

Reinsch, D. R. (ed.) (1996) *Alexias, Anna Komnene* (Cologne).

Reinsch, D. R. (2000) 'Women's literature in Byzantium? The case of Anna Komnene', in T. Gouma-Peterson (ed.), *Anna Komnene and Her Times* (New York) 83–106.

Reinsch, D. R. (ed.) (2014) *Michaelis Pselli Chronographia* (Millennium-Studien 51) (Berlin).

Reinsch, D. R. (ed.) (2015) *Michael Psellos: Leben der byzantinischen Kaiser 976–1075* (Berlin).

Reinsch, D. R. and Kambylis, A. (eds) (2001) *Annae Comnenae Alexias* (Corpus Fontium Historiae Byzantinae 40) (Berlin).

Repath, I. (2007) 'Emotional conflict and Platonic psychology in the Greek novel', in J. R. Morgan and M. Jones (eds), *Philosophical Presences in the Ancient Novel* (Groningen) 53–84.

Ribbeck, O. (1882) *Alazon: ein Beitrag zur antiken Ethologie und zur Kenntniss der griechisch-römischen Komödie nebst Übersetzung des Plautinischen Miles Gloriosus* (Leipzig).

Richter, I. (1967) 'Das Kopfgefäß: zur Typologie einer Gefäßform' (MA thesis, Cologne).

Riddell, J. F. (2000) *The Clyde: the Making of a River* (Edinburgh).

Rider, J. (2011) 'The inner life of women in medieval romance literature', in J. Rider and J. Friedman (eds), *The Inner Life of Women in Medieval Romance Literature: Grief, Guilt, and Hypocrisy* (London) 1–25.

Ridgway, B. S. (1977) *The Archaic Style in Greek Sculpture* (Princeton).

Ritoók, Z. (1991) 'Alkidamas über die Sophisten', *Philologus* 185, 157–63.

Roberts, R. C. (2003) *Emotions: an Essay in Aid of Moral Psychology* (Cambridge).

Röhricht, F. (2015) '"Body schema", "body image", and bodily experience: concept formation, definitions, and clinical relevance in diagnostics and therapy', in G. Malock and H. Weiss (eds), *The Handbook of Body Psychotherapy and Somatic Psychology* (Berkeley) 237–47.

Roilos, P. (2014) '*Phantasia* and the ethics of fictionality in Byzantium: a cognitive anthropological perspective', in P. Roilos (ed.), *Medieval Greek Storytelling: Fictionality and Narrative in Byzantium* (Wiesbaden) 9–30.

Roilos, P. (2018) 'Ancient Greek rhetorical theory and Byzantine discursive politics: John Sikeliotes on Hermogenes', in T. Shawcross and I. Toth (eds), *Reading in the Byzantine Empire and Beyond* (Cambridge) 159–84.

Roisman, J. (2007) 'Rhetoric, manliness, and contest', in I. Worthington (ed.), *A Companion to Greek Rhetoric* (Oxford) 393–410.

Rolfe, J. C. (trans.) (1927) *The Attic Nights of Aulus Gellius* (Loeb Classical Library 195, 200, and 212) (London).

Roose, H. (2005) 'The fall of the "great harlot" and the fate of the aging prostitute: an iconographic approach to Revelation 18', in A. Weissenrieder, F. Wendt, and P. von Gemünden (eds), *Picturing the New Testament: Studies in Ancient Visual Images* (Wissenschaftliche Untersuchungen zum Neuen Testament 2.193) (Tübingen) 228–52.

Rorem, P. (1993) *Pseudo-Dionysius: a Commentary on the Texts and an Introduction to Their Influence* (New York).

Rorem, P. and Lamoreaux, J. (1998) *John of Scythopolis and the Dionysian Corpus: Annotating the Areopagite* (Oxford).

Bibliography 493

Rosch, E. (1978) 'Principles of categorization' in E. Rosch and B. B. Lloyd (eds), *Cognition and Categorization* (Hillsdale, NJ) 27–48.

Rosenwein, B. H. (2002) 'Worrying about emotions in History', *American Historical Review* 107, 821–45.

Rosenwein, B. H. (2006) *Emotional Communities in the Early Middle Ages* (Ithaca, NY).

Rosenwein, B. H. (2017) 'History of emotions and emotions in history: the ambiguous smile', in A. Chaniotis, N. Kaltsas, and I. Mylonopoulos (eds), *A World of Emotions: Ancient Greece, 700 BC–200 AD* (New York) 62–71.

Rosenwein, B. H. and Cristiani, R. (2018) *What Is the History of Emotions?* (Cambridge).

Ross, W. D. (ed.) (1970 [1924]), *Aristotle's Metaphysics*, 2 vols, repr. of 1953 corr. edn (Oxford).

Rossi-Taibbi, G. (ed.) (1969) *Filagato da Cerami. Omelie per i vangeli domenicali e le feste di tutto l'anno. Omelie per le feste fisse* (Palermo).

Rothstein, D. (2007) 'From metaphor to legal idiom: the depiction of women as "vessels" in antiquity and its implications for 4Q416', *Zeitschrift für altorientalische und biblische Rechtsgeschichte* 13, 56–78.

Ruffell, I. (2008) 'Audience and emotion in the reception of Greek drama', in M. Revermann and P. Wilson (eds), *Performance, Iconography, Reception: Studies in Honour of O. Taplin* (Oxford) 37–58.

Russell, D. A. (trans.) (2002) *Quintilian. The Orator's Education, Volume V: Books 11–12* (Loeb Classical Library 494) (Cambridge, MA).

Russell, D. A. and Wilson, N. G. (ed. and trans.) (1981) *Menander Rhetor, On Epideictic* (Oxford).

Russell, J. A. (1991a) 'Culture and the categorization of emotions', *Psychological Bulletin* 110, 426–50.

Russell, J. A. (1991b) 'In defense of a prototype approach to emotion concepts', *Journal of Personality and Social Psychology* 60, 37–47.

Russell, J. A. (2003) 'Core affect and the psychological construction of emotion', *Psychological Review* 110, 145–72.

Russell, J. A. (2005) 'Emotion in human consciousness is built on core affect', *Journal of Consciousness Studies* 12, 26–42.

Russell, J. A. (2009) 'Emotion, core affect, and psychological construction', *Cognition and Emotion* 23.7, 1259–83.

Russell, J. A. (2017) 'Mixed emotions viewed from the psychological constructionist perspective', *Emotion Review* 9.2, 111–17.

Russell, J. A. and Barrett, L. F. (1999) 'Core affect, prototypical emotional episodes, and other things called emotion: dissecting the elephant', *Journal of Personality and Social Psychology* 76, 805–19.

Russell, J. A. and Barrett, L. F. (2009) 'Core affect', in D. Sander and K. Scherer (eds), *Oxford Companion to Emotion and the Affective Sciences* (New York) 104.

Russo, J. (2012) 'Re-thinking Homeric psychology: Snell, Dodds and their critics', *Quaderni urbinati di cultura classica* 101, 11–28.

Rylaarsdam, D. (2014) *John Chrysostom on Divine Pedagogy: the Coherence of His Theology and Preaching* (Oxford).

Sagnard, F. (ed.) (1970) *Clemens Alexandrinus, Extraits de Théodote* (Sources chrétiennes, Série annexe de textes non chrétiens 23) (Paris).

Sahas, D. J. (1986) *Icon and Logos: Sources in Eighth-Century Iconoclasm* (Toronto).

Salvo, I. (2012) 'Sweet revenge: emotional factors in "Prayers for Justice"', in A. Chaniotis (ed.), *Unveiling Emotions: Sources and Methods for the Study of Emotions in the Greek World* (Stuttgart) 235–66.

Salvo, I. (2016) 'Emotion, persuasion and gender in Greek erotic curses', in E. Sanders and M. Johncock (eds), *Emotion and Persuasion in Classical Antiquity* (Stuttgart) 263–79.

Salzman-Mitchell, P. (2012) 'Tenderness and taboo: images of breast-feeding mothers in Greek and Latin literature', in L. Hackworth Peterson and P. Salzman-Mitchell (eds), *Mothering and Motherhood in Ancient Greece and Rome* (Austin, TX) 141–64.

Sander, D., Grandjean, D., and Scherer, K. R. (2018) 'An appraisal-driven componential approach to the emotional brain', *Emotion Review* 10.3, 219–31.

Sanders, E. (2012) 'Beyond the usual suspects: literary sources and the historian of emotions', in A. Chaniotis (ed.), *Unveiling Emotions: Sources and Methods for the Study of Emotions in the Greek World* (Heidelberger althistorische Beiträge und epigraphische Studien 52) (Stuttgart) 151–73.

Sanders, E. (2014) *Envy and Jealousy in Classical Athens: a Socio-Psychological Approach* (Oxford).

Sanders, E. and Johncock, M. (eds) (2015) *Emotion and Persuasion in Classical Antiquity* (Stuttgart).

Sanders, E., Thumiger, C., Carey, C., and Lowe, N. J. (eds) (2013), *Erôs in Ancient Greece* (Oxford).

Sargologos, É. (ed.) (1964) *La vie de Saint Cyrille le Philéote moine byzantin (†1110)* (Subsidia hagiographica 39) (Brussels).

Sargologos, É. (ed.) (1990) *Un traité de vie spirituelle et morale du XIe siècle: le florilège sacro-profane du manuscrit 6 de Patmos. Introduction, texte critique, notes et tables* (Thessaloniki).

Sauer, G. (2004 [1971]) 'קשׁף qṣp zornig sein', in *Theologisches Handwörterbuch zum Alten Testament*, vol. 2, 6th edn (Gütersloh) 663–6.

Scarantino, A. (2016) 'The philosophy of emotions and its impact on affective science', in L. F. Barrett, M. Lewis, and J. M. Haviland-Jones (eds), *Handbook of Emotions*, 4th edn (New York) 3–48.

Schachter, S. and Singer, J. E. (1962) 'Cognitive, social, and physiological determinants of emotional state', *Psychological Review* 69, 379–99.

Schade, K. (2003) *Frauen in der Spätantike – Status und Repräsentation: eine Untersuchung zur römischen und frühbyzantinischen Bildniskunst* (Mainz).

Schank, R. C. and Abelson, R. P. (1977) *Scripts, Plans, Goals and Understanding: an Inquiry into Human Knowledge Structures* (Hillsdale, NJ).

Schargel, D. and Prinz, J. J. (2017) 'An enactivist theory of emotional content', in H. Naar and F. Teroni (eds), *The Ontology of Emotions* (Cambridge) 110–29.

Schauer, M. (2002) *Tragisches Klagen: Form und Funktion der Klagedarstellung bei Aischylus, Sophokles und Euripides* (Munich).

Scheer, M. (2012) 'Are emotions a kind of practice (and is that what makes them have a history)? A Bourdieuian approach to understanding emotion', *History and Theory* 51.2, 193–220.

Schein, S. L. (1984) *The Mortal Hero: an Introduction to Homer's Iliad* (Berkeley).

Scheler, M. (1973) *Wesen und Formen der Sympathie* (Gesammelte Werke 7) (Munich).

Schellenberg, A. (2007) 'Vernunft/Verstand (AT)', *Das Wissenschaftliche Bibellexikon im Internet*. www.wibilex.de.

Schenk, R. (1886) *Zum ethischen Lehrbegriff des Hirten des Hermas* (Aschersleben).

Scherer, K. R. (1984) 'On the nature and function of emotion: a component process approach', in K. R. Scherer and P. Ekman (eds), *Approaches to Emotion* (Hillsdale, NJ) 293–318.

Scherer, K. R. (2001) 'Appraisal considered as a process of multilevel sequential processing', in K. R. Scherer, A. Schorr, and T. Johnstone (eds), *Appraisal Processes in Emotion: Theory, Methods, Research* (New York) 92–120.

Scherer, K. R. (2005) 'What are emotions? And how can they be measured?', *Social Science Information* 44, 695–729.

Scherer, K. R. (2009) 'The dynamic architecture of emotion: evidence for the component process model', *Cognition and Emotion* 23.7, 1307–51.

Scherer, K. R. and Brosch, T. (2009) 'Culture-specific appraisal biases contribute to emotion dispositions', *European Journal of Personality* 23, 265–88.

Schiefsky, M. (2012) 'Galen and the tripartite soul', in R. Barney, T. Brennan, and C. Brittain (eds) *Plato and the Divided Self* (Cambridge) 331–49.

Schilder, P. (1923) *Das Körperschema: ein Beitrag zur Lehre vom Bewusstsein des eigenen Körpers* (Berlin).

Schilder, P. (1950) *The Image and Appearence of the Human Body: Studies in the Constructive Energies of the Psyche* (New York).

Schironi, F. (2018) *The Best of the Grammarians: Aristarchus of Samothrace on the Iliad* (Ann Arbor).

Schloßberger, M. (2020) 'Max Scheler', in T. Szanto and H. Landweer (eds), *The Routledge Handbook of Phenomenology of Emotion* (Abingdon) 72–86.

Schmidt, O. J. (1997) 'Das Normannenbild im Geschichtswerk des Niketas Choniates', *Jahrbuch der österreichischen Byzantinistik* 47, 157–77.

Schmidt, W. (ed.) (1976) *Heronis Alexandrini opera quae supersunt omnia*, vol. 1 (Stuttgart) 1–333.

Schmitz, T. A. (1997) *Bildung und Macht: zur sozialen und politischen Funktion der zweiten Sophistik in der griechischen Welt der Kaiserzeit* (Munich).

Schmitz, T. A. (2017) 'Professionals of paideia? The sophists as performers', in W. A. Johnson and D. S. Richter (eds), *The Oxford Handbook of the Second Sophistic* (Oxford) 169–180.

Schnapp, F. (1884) *Die Testamente der zwölf Patriarchen* (Halle).

Schnell, R. (2015) *Haben Gefühle eine Geschichte? Aporien einer History of Emotions* (Göttingen).

Schönberger, O. (ed.) (2001) *Physiologus: griechisch/deutsch* (Reclams Universal-Bibliothek altgriechisch) (Stuttgart).

Schouler, B. (1987) 'Les sophistes et le théâtre au temps des empereurs', in P. Ghiron-Bistagne and B. Schouler (eds), *Anthropologie et théâtre antique: actes du Colloque international, Montpellier 6–8 mars 1986* (Cahiers de Gita 3) (Montpellier) 273–94.

Schreiber, S. (2014) *Der erste Brief an die Thessalonicher* (Ökumenischer Taschenbuch-Kommentar Neues Testament 13.1) (Gütersloh).

Schroer, S. and Staubli, T. (1998) *Die Körpersymbolik der Bibel* (Darmstadt).

Schulz, V. (2013) *Die Stimme in der antiken Rhetorik* (Göttingen).

Schulze, H. (1998) *Ammen und Pädagogen: Sklavinnen und Sklaven als Erzieher in der antiken Kunst und Gesellschaft* (Mainz).

Schütze, S. (2002–3) 'Die sterbende Mutter des Aristeides: ein Archetypus abendländischer Affektdarstellung und seine Restitution durch Cesare Francanzano', *Jahrbuch des Kunsthistorischen Museums Wien* 4–5, 164–89.

Scodel, R. and Caston, R. R. (2019) 'Literature', in D. L. Cairns (ed.), *A Cultural History of the Emotions in Antiquity* (London) 109–24.

Scott, A. and Kosso, C. (2002) 'Introduction', in A. Scott and C. Kosso (eds), *Fear and Its Representations in the Middle Ages and Renaissance* (Turnhout) xi–xxxvii.

Scrutton, A. P. (2011) *Thinking through Feeling: God, Emotion and Passibility* (New York).

Seaford, R. (1994) *Reciprocity and Ritual: Homer and Tragedy in the Developing City-State* (Oxford).

Serafim, A. (2017) *Attic Oratory and Performance* (Abingdon).

Serafimova, A. (2010) 'Пикторалната семиотика на мајчинствотово византиските слики на Христовото раѓање: Развојни фази и модели', *Patrimonium* 3.7–8, 263–76.

Ševčenko, I. (1956) 'The definition of philosophy in the Life of Saint Constantine', in M. Halle, H. Glunt, H. McLean, and C. H. van Schooneveld (eds), *For Roman Jakobson: Essays on the Occasion of His Sixtieth Birthday, 11 October, 1956* (The Hague) 449–57, reprinted in I. Ševčenko (1991) *Byzantium and the Slavs* (Cambridge) 93–106.

Ševčenko, I. (1962a) *Études sur la polémique entre Théodore Métochite et Nicéphore Choumnos* (Brussels).

Ševčenko, I. (1962b) 'The illuminators of the *Menologium* of Basil II', *Dumbarton Oaks Papers* 16, 248–76.

Ševčenko, N. P. (1991) '*Menologion* of Basil II', in A. P. Kazhdan, A.-M. Talbot, A. Cutler, T. E. Gregory, and N. P. Ševčenko (eds), *The Oxford Dictionary of Byzantium* (Oxford) 1341–2.

Ševčenko, N. P. (1993) 'The Walters "Imperial" *Menologion*', *Journal of the Walters Art Gallery* 51, 43–64.

Ševčenko, N. P. (2009) 'Images of the Second Coming and the fate of the soul in Middle Byzantine art', in R. J. Daly (ed.), *Apocalyptic Thought in Early Christianity* (Grand Rapids) 250–72.

Ševčenko, N. P. (2011) 'The service of the Virgin's lament revisited', in L. Brubaker and M. B. Cunningham (eds), *The Cult of the Mother of God in Byzantium* (Birmingham Byzantine and Ottoman Studies 11) (Farnham) 247–77.

Severin, H.-G. (1970) 'Oströmische Plastik unter Valens und Theodosius I', *Jahrbuch der Berliner Museen* 12, 211–52.

Sewter, E. R. A. (trans.) (1969) *The Alexiad of Anna Comnena* (Baltimore).

Shapiro, H. A. (1991) 'The iconography of mourning in Athenian art', *American Journal of Archaeology* 95, 629–56.

Sharples, R. W. and Van der Eijk, P. J. (2008) *Nemesius: On the Nature of Man* (Translated Texts for Historians 49) (Liverpool).

Shaver, P., Schwartz, J., Kirson, D., and O'Connor, C. (1987) 'Emotion knowledge: further exploration of a prototype approach', *Journal of Personality and Social Psychology* 52.6, 1061–86.

Shawcross, T. (2003) 'Re-inventing the homeland in the historiography of Frankish Greece: the Fourth Crusade and the legend of the Trojan War', *Byzantine and Modern Greek Studies* 27, 129–52.

Shay, J. (2002) *Odysseus in America: Combat Trauma and the Trials of Homecoming* (New York).

Shay, J. (2003 [1994]) *Achilles in Vietnam: Combat Trauma and the Undoing of Character* (New York).

Sheldon-Williams, I. P. (1966) 'The ps.-Dionysius and the Holy Hierotheus', *Studia Patristica* 8, 108–17.

Bibliography

Shepherd, G. (2012) 'Women in Magna Graecia', in S. L. James and S. Dillon (eds), *A Companion to Women in the Ancient World* (Chichester) 215–28.

Scheve, C. von and Ismer, S. (2013) 'Towards a theory of collective emotions', *Emotion Review* 5, 406–13.

Shin, H. I. and Kim, J. (2017) 'Foreign language effect and psychological distance', *Journal of Psycholinguistic Research* 46.6, 1339–52.

Shivkova, L. (1977) *Das Tetraevangeliar des Zaren Ivan Alexander* (Recklinghausen).

Shoemaker, S. (2003) *Ancient Traditions of the Virgin Mary's Dormition and Assumption* (Oxford).

Shorey, P. (trans.) (1930) *Plato, The Republic: Books I–V* (Loeb Classical Library 237) (Cambridge, MA).

Signes Codoñer, J. (2014a) *The Emperor Theophilos and the East, 829–842: Court and Frontier in Byzantium during the Last Phase of Iconoclasm* (Farnham).

Signes Codoñer, J. (2014b) 'Towards a vocabulary for rewriting in Byzantium', in J. Signes Codoñer and I. Pérez Martín (eds), *Textual Transmission in Byzantium: between Textual Criticism and Quellenforschung* (Lectio 2) (Turnhout) 61–90.

Sihvola, J. and Engberg-Pedersen, T. (eds) (1998) *The Emotions in Hellenistic Philosophy* (Dordrecht).

Simons, D. J. and Chabris, C. F. (1999) 'Gorillas in our midst: sustained inattentional blindness for dynamic events', *Perception* 28.9, 1059–74.

Singer, P. N. (2017) 'The essence of rage: Galen on emotional disturbances and their physical correlates', in R. Seaford, J. Wilkins and M. Wright (eds), *Selfhood and the Soul: Essays on Ancient Thought and Literature in Honour of Christopher Gill* (Oxford) 161–96.

Siomkos, N. (2005) *L'église Saint-Etienne à Kastoria: étude des différentes phases du décor peint (Xe–XIVe siècles)* (Thessaloniki).

Sissa, G. (2018) *Jealousy: a Forbidden Passion* (Cambridge).

Sittl, C. (1890) *Die Gebärden der Griechen und Römer* (Leipzig).

Sitz, A. (2017) '"Great fear": epigraphy and orality in a Byzantine apse in Cappadocia', *Gesta* 56, 5–26.

Slingerland, H. D. (1977) *The Testaments of the Twelve Patriarchs: a Critical History of Research* (Society of Biblical Literature Monograph Series 21) (Missoula, MT).

Slings, S. R. (ed.) (2003) *Platonis Respublica* (Oxford).

Smith, J. (2001) 'Another look at 4Q416 2 ii.21, a critical parallel to First Thessalonians 4:4', *Catholic Biblical Quarterly* 63, 499–504.

Smith, M. S. (2009) 'Herz und Innereien in israelitischen Gefühlsäußerungen', in A. Wagner (ed.), *Anthropologische Aufbrüche: Alttestamentliche und interdisziplinäre Zugänge zur historischen Anthropologie* (Forschungen zur Religion und Literatur des Alten und Neuen Testaments 232) (Göttingen) 171–81.

Smith, T. (2021) 'Complexes of emotions in *Joseph and Aseneth*', *Journal for the Study of the Pseudepigrapha* 30, 133–55.

Snee, R. (1998) 'Gregory Nazianzen's Anastasia church: Arianism, the Goths, and hagiography', *Dumbarton Oaks Papers* 52, 157–86.

Snell, B. (1953) *The Discovery of the Mind*, trans. T. G. Rosenmeyer (Oxford).

Snyder, G. F. (1968) *The Shepherd of Hermas: a New Translation and Commentary* (The Apostolic Fathers 6) (Camden).

Solmsen, F. (1938) 'Aristotle and Cicero on the orator's playing upon the feelings', *Classical Philology* 33, 390–404.

Solmsen, F. (1941) 'The Aristotelian tradition in ancient rhetoric', *American Journal of Philology* 62.2, 169–90.

Solomon, R.C. (2007) *True to Our Feelings: What Our Emotions Are Really Telling Us* (New York).

Soltic, J. (2014) 'ΓΝΩΡΙΖΕ in the Greek *War of Troy*: a peremptory command or just a filled pause?', *Byzantion* 84, 329–55.

Sommer, M. and Sommer, D. (2015) *Care, Socialization, and Play in Ancient Attica: a Developmental Childhood Archaeological Approach* (Aarhus).

Sorabji, R. (2000) *Emotion and Peace of Mind: from Stoic Agitation to Christian Temptation* (Oxford).

Soteriou, G. and Soteriou, M. (1956–8), Εἰκόνες τῆς μονῆς Σινᾶ, 2 vols (Athens).

Spanneut, M. (1976) 'Geduld', *Realexikon für Antike und Christentum*, vol. 9 (Stuttgart) cols 234–94.

Spatharas, D. (2019) *Emotions, Persuasion, and Public Discourse in Classical Athens* (Berlin).

Spaulding, S. (2017) 'Cognitive Empathy', in H. Maibom (ed.), *The Routledge Handbook of Philosophy of Empathy* (London), 13–21.

Spencer, S.J. (2017) 'Like a raging lion: Richard the Lionheart's anger during the Third Crusade in Medieval and Modern historiography', *English Historical Review* 132.556, 495–532.

Spinney, L. (2017) *Pale Rider: the Spanish Flu of 1918 and How It Changed the World* (London).

Staden, H. von (2000) 'Body, soul, and nerves: Epicurus, Herophilus, Erasistratus, the Stoics and Galen', in J. P. Wright and P. Potter (eds), *Psyche and Soma: Physicians and Metaphysicians on the Mind–Body Problem from Antiquity to Enlightenment* (Oxford) 79–116.

Stanford, W.B. (1983) *Greek Tragedy and the Emotions* (London).

Stang, C. (2012) *Apophasis and Pseudonymity in Dionysius the Areopagite: 'No Longer I'* (Oxford).

Staubli, T. (2015) 'Ikonographische Quellen als Grundlagenmaterial für die Rekonstruktion anthropologischer Themen der Südlevante', in J. van Ooerschot and A. Wagner (eds), *Anthropologie(n) des Alten Testaments* (Veröffentlichungen der Wissenschaftlichen Gesellschaft für Theologie 42) (Leipzig) 241–64.

Stearns, P.N. (1989) *Jealousy: the Evolution of an Emotion in American History* (New York).

Stearns, P.N. (2000) 'History of emotions: issues of change and impact', in M. Lewis and J. M. Haviland-Jones (eds), *Handbook of Emotions*, 2nd edn (New York) 16–29.

Stearns, P.N. and Stearns, C.Z. (1985) 'Emotionology: clarifying the history of emotions and emotional standards', *American Historical Review* 90, 813–36.

Stearns, P.N. and Stearns, C.Z. (1986) *Anger: the Struggle for Emotional Control in America's History* (Chicago).

Stefec, R. (ed.) (2016) *Flavii Philostrati Vitas sophistarum* (Oxford).

Stegemann, H. (1988) 'Zu *Textbestand* und Grundgedanken von 1QS III,13–IV,26', *Revue de Qumrān* 13, 95–131.

Stenger, J. (2015) 'John Chrysostom and the power of literary imagination', in J. Stenger (ed.), *Spätantike Konzeptionen von Literatur* (Heidelberg) 207–26.

Stenger, J. (2017) 'Staging laughter and tears: Libanius, Chrysostom and the Riot of the Statues', in M. Alexiou and D. L. Cairns (eds), *Greek Laughter and Tears: Antiquity and After* (Edinburgh) 166–86.

Bibliography 499

Stenger, J. (2018) 'Healing place or abode of the demons? Libanius's and Chrysostom's rewriting of the Apollo sanctuary at Daphne', in S.-P. Bergjan and S. Elm (eds), *Antioch II. The Many Faces of Antioch: Intellectual Exchange and Religious Diversity, CE 350–450* (Tübingen) 193–220.

Stenger, J. (2019) *Johannes Chrysostomos und die Christianisierung der Polis: 'Damit die Städte Städte werden'* (Tübingen).

Sternberg, R. H. (ed.) (2005) *Pity and Power in Ancient Athens* (Cambridge).

Sternberg, R. H. (2006) *Tragedy Offstage: Suffering and Sympathy in Ancient Athens* (Austin, TX).

Stevenson, A. (ed.) (2010) *Oxford Dictionary of English*, 3rd edn (Oxford).

Stewart, C. (2000) 'Evagrius Ponticus on Prayer and Anger', in R. Valantasis (ed.), *Religions of Late Antiquity and Practice* (Princeton) 65–81.

Stolz, F. (2004), 'לב leb, Herz', *Theologisches Handwörterbuch zum Alten Testament*, vol. 1, 6th edn (Gütersloh) cols 861–7.

Strack, H. L. and Billerbeck, P. (1922–56) *Kommentar zum Neuen Testament aus Talmud und Midrasch* 1–5 (Munich).

Striker, G. (1996) 'Emotions in context: Aristotle's treatment of the passions in the *Rhetoric* and his moral psychology', in A. O. Rorty (ed.), *Essays on Aristotle's Rhetoric* (Berkeley) 286–302.

Struck, P. T. (2016) *Divination and Human Nature: a Cognitive History of Intuition in Classical Antiquity* (Princeton).

Stueber, K. R. (2006), *Rediscovering Empathy: Agency, Folk Psychology, and the Human Sciences* (Cambridge, MA).

Stueber, K. R. (2012) 'Varieties of empathy, neuroscience and the narrativist challenge to the contemporary theory of mind debate', *Emotion Review* 4, 55–63.

Sturz, F. G. (1818) *Etymologicum graecae linguae Gudianum* (Leipzig).

Suchla, B. R. (ed.) (1990) *Corpus Dionysiacum*, vol. 1, *Pseudo-Dionysius Areopagita, De divinis nominibus* (Berlin).

Sullivan, S. D. (1995) *Psychological and Ethical Ideas: What Early Greeks Say* (Leiden).

Susemihl, F. (ed.) (1967 [1884]), *Aristotelis Ethica Eudemia* (Amsterdam) 1–123.

Suter, A. (ed.) (2008) *Lament: Studies in the Ancient Mediterranean and Beyond* (New York).

Swearingen, C. J. (1994) '*Ethos*: imitation, impersonation, and voice', in J. S. Baumlin and T. French Baumlin (eds), *Ethos: New Essays in Rhetorical and Critical Theory* (Dallas) 115–48.

Switek, G. (1972) 'Discretio spirituum: ein Beitrag zur Geschichte der Spiritualität', *Theologie und Philosophie* 47, 36–76.

Taft, R. F. (1991) 'Trisagion', in A. P. Kazhdan, A.-M. Talbot, A. Cutler, T. E. Gregory, and N. P. Ševčenko (eds), *The Oxford Dictionary of Byzantium* (Oxford) 2121.

Taft, R. F. (1992) *The Byzantine Rite: a Short History* (Collegeville, PA).

Taft, R. F. (2006) *Through Their Own Eyes: Liturgy as the Byzantines Saw It* (Berkeley).

Taft, R. F. and Kazhdan, A. (1991a) 'Candles', in A. P. Kazhdan, A.-M. Talbot, A. Cutler, T. E. Gregory, and N. P. Ševčenko (eds), *The Oxford Dictionary of Byzantium* (Oxford) 371–2.

Taft, R. F. and Kazhdan, A. (1991b) 'Incense', in A. P. Kazhdan, A.-M. Talbot, A. Cutler, T. E. Gregory, and N. P. Ševčenko (eds), *The Oxford Dictionary of Byzantium* (Oxford) 991.

500 *Bibliography*

Tait, J. (2021) 'Examining the exploitation of the emotion in Demotic Egyptian letter-writing' in A. Chaniotis (ed.), *Unveiling Emotions III: Arousal, Display, and Performance of Emotions in the Greek World* (Stuttgart) 231–42.

Taplin, O. (1978) *Greek Tragedy in Action* (London).

Taplin, O. (1986) 'Fifth-century tragedy and comedy: a *synkrisis*', *Journal of Hellenic Studies* 106, 163–74.

Taplin, O. and Billings, J. (2010) 'What does tragedy do for people?' (podcast, Oxford) http://writersinspire.podcasts.ox.ac.uk/content/what-does-tragedy-do-people.

Tartaglia, L. (ed.) (2016) *Georgii Cedreni Historiarum compendium* (*Bollettino dei Classici* Supplement 30) (Rome).

Thein, K. (2014) 'Aristotle on Why Study Lower Animals (*De Partibus Animalium*, I, 5, 644b22–645a36)', *EIRENE* 50, 208–29.

Theißen, G. (2007) *Erleben und Verhalten der ersten Christen: eine Psychologie des Urchristentums* (Gütersloh).

Theodoridis, C. (ed.) (1982–2013) *Photii Patriarchae Lexicon* (Berlin).

Thomas, E. (2017) 'Performance space', in W. A. Johnson and D. S. Richter (eds), *The Oxford Handbook of the Second Sophistic* (Oxford) 181–201.

Thumiger, C. (2017) *A History of the Mind and Mental Health in Classical Greek Medical Thought* (Cambridge).

Thurn, H. (ed.) (1973) *Ioannis Scylitzae Synopsis historiarum* (Corpus Fontium Historiae Byzantinae 5) (Berlin).

Thurn, H. (ed.) (2000) *Ioannis Malalae Chronographia* (Corpus Fontium Historiae Byzantinae 35) (Berlin).

Tieleman, T. (1996) *Galen and Chrysippus on the Soul: Argument and Refutation in the De Placitis, Books II–III* (Leiden).

Tieleman, T. (2003) *Chrysippus' On Affections: Reconstruction and Interpretation* (Leiden).

Tieleman, T. (2008) 'Methodology', in R. J. Hankinson (ed.), *The Cambridge Companion to Galen* (Cambridge) 49–65.

Tiemersma, D. (1989) *Body Schema and Body Image: an Interdisciplinary and Philosophical Study* (Amsterdam).

Tittmann, I. A. H. (ed.) (1808) *Ioannis Zonarae Lexicon* (Leipzig).

Tollefsen, T. (2006) '*Theosis* according to Gregory', in J. Børtnes and T. Hägg (eds), *Gregory of Nazianzus: Images and Reflections* (Copenhagen) 257–70.

Tomaryn Bruckner, M. (2010) 'Between prophecy and *plainte* in the *Roman de Troie*', in R. Deist (ed.), *The Passions of Achilles: Reflections on the Classical and Medieval Epic* (*Electronic Antiquity* 14.1) (Blacksburg, VA)127–49.

Tomkins, S. S. (1984) 'Affect Theory', in K. R. Scherer and P. Ekman (eds), *Approaches to Emotion* (Hillsdale, NJ) 163–95.

Tomkins, S. S. (1987) 'Script Theory', in J. Arnoff, A. I. Rabin, and R. A. Zucker (eds), *The Emergence of Personality* (New York) 147–216.

Torrance, A. C. (2012) *Repentance in Late Antiquity: Eastern Asceticism and the Framing of the Christian Life c. 400–650* (Oxford).

Torre, C. (2008) 'Un intellettuale greco di epoca normanna: Filagato da Cerami e il *De mundo* di Aristotele', *Miscellanea di studi storici* 15, 63–119.

Torre, C. (2011) 'Su alcune presunte riprese classiche in Filagato da Cerami', in N. Bianchi (ed.), *La tradizione dei testi greci in Italia meridionale: Filagato da Cerami philosophos e didaskalos – copisti, lettori, eruditi in Puglia tra XII e XVI secolo* (Bari) 21–39.

Bibliography 501

Torre, C. (ed.) (2012) 'Inediti di Filagato Karameus dall' Ambros. C 100 sup. (Omelie LVI e LVIII Rossi Taibbi)', *Bizantinistica* 14, 105–51.

Trabattoni, F. (2020) 'L'ira in Platone', in L. Neri (ed.), *Forme di una passione: la rappresentazione dell'ira tra letteratura, teatro e filosofia* (Rome) 43–54.

Tran Tam Tinh, V. (1973) *Isis lactans: corpus des monuments greco-romains d'Isis allaitant Harpocrate* (Leiden).

Trapp, E. (1994–2017) *Lexikon der Byzantinischen Gräzität, besonders des 9.–12. Jahrhunderts* (Veröffentlichungen zur Byzanzforschung 6) (Vienna).

Trevisan, P. (ed.) (1939) *San Basilio, Commento al profeta Isaia* (Turin).

Trim, R. (2015) 'The interface between synchronic and diachronic conceptual metaphor: the role of embodiment, culture and semantic field', in J. E. Díaz Vera (ed.), *Metaphor and Metonymy across Time and Cultures: Perspectives on the Sociohistorical Linguistics of Figurative Language* (Cognitive Linguistics Research 52) (Berlin) 94–120.

Trizio, M. (2016), *Il neoplatonismo di Eustrazio di Nicea* (Bari).

Troianos, S. N. (ed.) (2007) *Οἱ νεαρές Λέοντος ΣΤ΄ τοῦ Σοφοῦ* (Athens).

Troscianko, E. T. (2014) *Kafka's Cognitive Realism* (New York).

Tsakaridou, C. A. (2013) *Icons in Time, Persons in Eternity: Orthodox Theology and the Aesthetics of the Christian Image* (Farnham).

Tsamakda, V. (2002) *The Illustrated Chronicle of Ioannes Skylitzes in Madrid* (Leiden).

Tsironis [= Tsironi], N. (1998) 'Historicity and poetry in ninth-century homiletics: the homilies of Patriarch Photios and George of Nicomedia', in M. Cunningham and P. Allen (eds), *Preacher and Audience: Studies in Early Christian and Byzantine Homiletics* (Leiden) 295–316.

Tsironi, N. (2011) 'Emotions and the senses in Marian Homilies of the Middle Byzantine period', in L. Brubaker and M. B. Cunningham (eds), *The Cult of the Mother of God in Byzantium: Texts and Images* (Farnham) 179–96.

Tsironi, N. (forthcoming) 'Gendered emotions: the case of *storge*', in M. Mullett and S. Ashbrook Harvey (eds), *Managing Emotion: Passions, Affects and Imaginings* (Washington, DC).

Tsolakes, E. T. (ed.) (1959) *Μιχαὴλ Γλυκᾶ στίχοι οὓς ἔγραψε καθ' ὃν κατεσχέθη καιρόν* (Ἐπιστημονικὴ Ἐπετηρὶς Φιλοσοφικῆς Σχολῆς Supplement 3) (Thessaloniki).

Tuilier, A. (ed.) (1969) *La passion du Christ: tragédie. Grégoire de Nazianze. Introduction, texte critique, traduction, notes et index* (Sources chrétiennes 149) (Paris).

Tulli, M. and Erler, M. (eds) (2016), *Plato in Symposium: Selected Papers from the Tenth Symposium Platonicum* (Sankt Augustin).

Turner, H. J. M. (1990) *St. Symeon the New Theologian and Spiritual Fatherhood* (Leiden).

Turyn, A. (1957) *The Byzantine Manuscript Tradition of the Tragedies of Euripides* (Illinois Studies in Language and Literature 43) (Champaign–Urbana).

Tybjerg, K. (2003) 'Wonder-making and philosophical wonder in Hero of Alexandria', *Studies in History and Philosophy of Science Part A* 34, 443–66.

Ulrich, J. (2007) 'Angstmacherei: Beobachtungen zu einem polemischen Einwand gegen das frühe Christentum und zur Auseinandersetzung mit ihm in der apologetischen Literatur', in F. R. Prostmeier (ed.), *Frühchristentum und Kultur* (Freiburg im Breisgau) 111–26.

Underwood, P. A. (1966) *The Kariye Djami*, vol. 1, *Historical Introduction and Description of the Mosaics and Frescoes* (New York).

Unger, R. W. (2007) *Beer in the Middle Ages and the Renaissance* (Philadelphia).

502 *Bibliography*

Usher, M. D. (1998) *Homeric Stitchings: the Homeric Centos of the Empress Eudocia* (Greek Studies: Interdisciplinary Approaches) (Lanham, MD).

Usher, S. (1974) *Dionysius of Halicarnassus: Critical Essays*, vol. 1 (Cambride, MA).

Valiavitcharska, V. (2013) *Rhetoric and Rhythm in Byzantium: the Sound of Persuasion* (Cambridge).

Valiavitcharska, V. (2020) 'The advanced study of rhetoric between the seventh and the ninth century', *Jahrbuch der Österreichischen Byzantinistik* 70, 487–508.

Valiavitcharska V. (2021) 'Rhetorical figures', in S. Papaioannou (ed.), *The Oxford Handbook of Byzantine Literature* (Oxford) 316–35.

Vedder, U. (1988) 'Frauentod, Kriegertod im Spiegel der attischen Grabkunst des 4. Jhs. v. Chr.', *Mitteilungen des Deutschen Archäologischen Instituts (Athen. Abt.)* 103, 161–91.

Velmans, T. (ed.) (1984) *Contribution à l'étude du jugement dernier dans l'art byzantin et post-byzantin* (Paris).

Ven, P. van den (1962) *La Vie ancienne de S. Syméon Stylite le Jeune (521–592)* (Subsidia Hagiographica 32) (Brussels).

Vermeule, E. T. (1979) *Aspects of Death in Early Greek Art and Poetry* (Berkeley).

Vetter, P. and Newen, A. (2014) 'Varieties of cognitive penetration in visual perception', *Consciousness and Cognition* 27, 62–75.

Vielhauer, P. (1975) *Geschichte der urchristlichen Literatur: Einleitung in das Neue Testament, die Apokryphen und die Apostolischen Väter* (Berlin).

Vignemont, F. and Singer, T. (2006) 'The empathetic brain: how, when, and why?', *Trends in Cognitive Sciences* 10, 435–41.

Vikela, E. (2015) *Apollo, Artemis, Leto: eine Untersuchung zur Typologie, Ikonographie und Hermeneutik der drei Gottheiten auf griechischen Weihreliefs* (Athenaia 7) (Munich).

Vilborg, E. (ed.) (1955) *Achilles Tatius, Leucippe and Clitophon* (Stockholm).

Vinzent, M. and Papadogiannakis, Y. (eds) (2017) *Studia Patristica LXXXIII: Papers Presented at the Seventeenth International Conference on Patristic Studies Held in Oxford 2015*, vol. 9, *Emotions* (Leuven).

Vogiatzi, M. (2019) *Byzantine Commentaries on Aristotle's Rhetoric: Anonymous and Stephanus, In Artem rhetoricam commentaria* (Commentaria in Aristotelem graeca et byzantina 8) (Berlin).

Vogt, S. (2008) 'Drugs and pharmacology', in R. J. Hankinson (ed.), *The Cambridge Companion to Galen* (Cambridge) 304–22.

Voss, C. (2004) *Narrative Emotionen: eine Untersuchung über Möglichkeiten und Grenzen philosophischer Emotionstheorien* (Berlin).

Vries-van der Velden, E. de (1999) 'Les amitiés dangereuses: Psellos et Léon Paraspondylos', *Byzantinoslavica* 60, 315–50.

Waal, F. de (2009) *The Age of Empathy: Nature's Lessons for a Kinder Society* (New York).

Wagner, A. (2006a) 'Gefühle, in Sprache geronnen: die historische Relativität von Gefühlen am Beispiel von "Hass"', in *Emotionen, Gefühle und Sprache im Alten Testament: vier Studien* (Kleine Untersuchungen zur Sprache des Alten Testaments und seiner Umwelt 7) (Waltrop) 49–74.

Wagner, A. (2006b) 'Eifern und eifersüchtig sein: zur sprachlichen Konzeptualisierung von Emotionen im Deutschen und Hebräischen', in *Emotionen, Gefühle und Sprache im Alten Testament: vier Studien* (Kleine Untersuchungen zur Sprache des Alten Testaments und seiner Umwelt 7) (Waltrop) 75–100.

Wahlgren, S. (ed.) (2006) *Symeonis Magistri et Logothetae Chronicon* (Corpus Fontium Historiae Byzantinae 44) (Berlin).

Wahlgren, S. (ed. and trans.) (2018), *Theodore Metochites' Sententious Notes, Semeioseis gnomikai 61–70 and 72–81: a Critical Edition with Introduction, Translation, Notes, and Indexes* (Studia Graeca et Latina Gothoburgensia 71) (Göteborg).

Wahlgren, S. (2019) *The Chronicle of the Logothete* (Liverpool).

Wall, G. (2001) 'Moral constructions of motherhood in breastfeeding discourse', *Gender and Society* 15, 592–610.

Walsh, T.R. (2005) *Fighting Words and Feuding Words: Anger and the Homeric Poems* (Lanham, MD).

Walz, C. (ed.) (1832–6) *Rhetores graeci*, 9 vols (Stuttgart).

Ware, K.T. (1980) 'The Orthodox experience of repentance', *Sobornost: Eastern Churches Review*, 18–28.

Warren Smith, J. (2001) 'Macrina, tamer of horses and healer of souls: grief and the therapy of hope in Gregory of Nyssa's *De anima et resurrectione*', *Journal of Theological Studies* 52, 37–60.

Waterfield, R. (trans.) (2018) *Aristotle: The Art of Rhetoric* (Oxford).

Way, A.S. (trans.) (1959) *Euripides*, vol. 1 (Loeb Classical Library 12) (Cambridge, MA).

Webb, R. (1997a) 'Imagination and the arousal of the emotions in Greco-Roman rhetoric', in S. M. Braund and C. Gill (eds), *The Passions in Roman Thought and Literature* (Cambridge) 112–27.

Webb, R. (1997b) 'Salome's sisters: the rhetoric and realities of dance in Late Antiquity and Byzantium', in L. James (ed.), *Women, Men and Eunuchs: Gender in Byzantium* (London) 119–48.

Webb, R. (2009) *Ekphrasis, Imagination and Persuasion in Ancient Rhetorical Theory and Practice* (Farnham).

Webb, R. (2017) 'Virtual sensations and inner visions: words and the senses in Late Antiquity and Byzantium', in S. Ashbrook Harvey and M. Mullett (eds), *Knowing Bodies, Passionate Souls: Sense Perception in Byzantium* (Washington, DC) 261–70.

Wehrle, J. and Kampling, R. (1995) 'Herz', *Neues Bibel-Lexikon*, vol. 2 (Ostfildern) 137–41.

Weinel, H. (1899) *Die Wirkungen des Geistes und der Geister im nachapostolischen Zeitalter bis auf Irenäus* (Freiburg im Breisgau).

Weinel, H. (1924 [1904]) 'Der Hirt des Hermas', in E. Hennecke (ed.), *Neutestamentliche Apokryphen*, 2nd edn (Tübingen).

Weinrich, H. (1976) *Sprache in Texten* (Stuttgart).

Weiss, J. (1910) *Der erste Korintherbrief*, 9th edn (Kritisch-exegetischer Kommentar über das Neue Testament) (Göttingen).

Wenger, A. (ed.) (1970) *Jean Chrysostome, huit catéchèses baptismales inédites: introduction, texte critique, traduction et notes* (Paris).

Wessel, K. (1964) 'Zur Ikonographie der koptischen Kunst', in K. Wessel (ed.), *Christentum am Nil: Internationale Arbeitstagung zur Ausstellung 'Koptische Kunst', Essen, Villa Hügel, 23.25. Juli 1963* (Recklinghausen) 233–9.

Wessel, K. (1978) 'Die stillende Gottesmutter', *Studien zur altägyptischen Kultur* 6, 185–200.

Whitby, M. and Whitby, M. (1989) *Chronicon Paschale 284–628* (Liverpool).

White, A.W. (2015) *Performing Orthodox Ritual in Byzantium* (Cambridge).

White, S. D. (1998) 'The politics of anger', in B. H. Rosenwein (ed.), *Anger's Past: the Social Uses of an Emotion in the Middle Ages* (Ithaca, NY) 127–52.

Whitman, C. H. (1958) *Homer and the Heroic Tradition* (Cambridge, MA).

Whitman, C. H. (1964) *Aristophanes and the Comic Hero* (Cambridge, MA).

504 *Bibliography*

Whitmarsh, T. (2005) *The Second Sophistic* (*Greece and Rome* New Surveys in the Classics 35) (Oxford).

Wiater, N. (2011) *The Ideology of Classicism: Language, History, and Identity in Dionysius of Halicarnassus* (Berlin).

Wierzbicka, A. (1999) *Emotions across Languages and Cultures: Diversity and Universals* (Cambridge).

Williams, B. (1993) *Shame and Necessity* (Berkeley).

Wilpert, J. (1903) *Die Malereien der Katakomben Roms: Tafeln* (Freiburg).

Wilson, N. (1996) *Scholars of Byzantium*, 2nd edn (London).

Wilson, S. (1984) 'The myth of motherhood a myth: the historical view of European child-rearing', *Social History* 9, 181–98.

Wilson, W. (1867) *The Writings of Clement of Alexandria* (Edinburgh).

Winawer, J., Witthoft, N., Frank, M. C., Wu, L., Wade, A. R., and Boroditsky, L. (2007) 'Russian blues reveal effects of language on color discrimination', *Proceedings of the National Academy of Sciences of the United States of America* 104.19, 7780–5.

Winter, F. (1903) *Die Typen der figürlichen Terrakotten*, vol. 1 (Berlin).

Winter, T. N. (2007) *The Mechanical Problems in the Corpus of Aristotle* (University of Nebraska, Lincoln Faculty Publications, Classics and Religious Studies Department 68). https://bit.ly/38Kg9Ub.

Wisse, J. (1989) *Ethos and Pathos from Aristotle to Cicero* (Amsterdam).

Wittgenstein, L. (1967) *Zettel*, ed. G. H. von Wright and G. E. M. Anscombe, trans. G. E. M. Anscombe (Oxford).

Wittgenstein, L. (2009) *Philosophische Untersuchungen/Philosophical Investigations*, 4th edn, trans. G. E. M. Anscombe, P. M. S. Hacker, and J. Schulter (Oxford).

Wojciehowski, H. C. and Gallese, V. (2011) 'How stories make us feel: toward an embodied narratology', *California Italian Studies* 2.1. https://escholarship.org/uc/item/3jg726c2.

Wolff, H.-W. (2010) *Anthropologie des Alten Testaments* (Gütersloh).

Woods, M. C. (2019) *Weeping for Dido: the Classics in the Medieval Classroom* (Princeton).

Worthington, I. (2017) 'Audience reaction, performance and the exploitation of delivery in the courts and assembly', in S. Papaioannou, A. Serafim, and B. da Vela (eds), *The Theatre of Justice: Aspects of Performance in Greco-Roman Oratory and Rhetoric* (Leiden) 13–25.

Wortley, J. (trans.) (2010) *John Skylitzes, A Synopsis of Byzantine History 811–1057* (Cambridge).

Wright, J. (2015) 'Between despondency and the demon: diagnosing and treating spiritual disorders in John Chrysostom's *Letter to Stageirios*', *Journal of Late Antiquity* 8, 352–67.

Wright, W. C. (trans.) (1921) *Philostratus, Lives of the Sophists. Eunapius, Lives of Philosophers* (Loeb Classical Library 134) (Cambridge, MA).

Wrzol, L. (1923) 'Die Hauptsündenlehre des Johannes Cassianus und ihre historischen Quellen', *Divus Thomas* 3.37, 385–404.

Zaborowski, R. (2002) *La crainte et le courage dans l'Iliade et l'Odyssée: contribution lexicographique à la psychologie homérique des sentiments* (Warsaw).

Zaccagni, G. (1998) 'La πάρεργος ἀφήγησις in Filagato da Cerami: una particolare tecnica narrativa', *Rivista di studi bizantini e neoellenici* 35, 47–65.

Zaccagni, G. (ed.) (2011) 'Filagato, hom. XLI. Edizione e traduzione', in N. Bianchi (ed.), *La tradizione dei testi greci in Italia meridionale: Filagato da Cerami philosophos e didaskalos – copisti, lettori, eruditi in Puglia tra XII e XVI secolo* (Bari) 149–63.

Zahavi, D. (2010) 'Empathy, embodiment and interpersonal understanding: from Lipps to Schutz', *Inquiry* 53.3, 285–306.

Zanker, A. T. (2019) *Metaphor in Homer: Time, Speech, and Thought* (Cambridge).

Zanker, P. (1989) *Die trunkene Alte: das Lachen der Verhöhnten* (Frankfurt am Main).

Zanker, P. (1990) *The Power of Images in the Age of Augustus* (Ann Arbor).

Zanker, P. (1995) *The Mask of Socrates: the Image of the Intellectual in Antiquity* (Berkeley).

Zeimbekis, J. and Raftopoulos, A. (eds) (2015) *The Cognitive Penetrability of Perception: New Philosophical Perspectives* (Oxford).

Zeller, D. (1992) 'ἀφροσύνη, ης, ἡ', *Exegetisches Wörterbuch zum Neuen Testament*, vol. 1, 2nd edn (Stuttgart) cols 444–6.

Zhang, L. and Lin, W. (2013) *Selective Visual Attention: Computational Models and Applications* (Oxford).

Zhmud, L. (2006) *The Origin of the History of Science in Classical Antiquity*, trans. A. Chernoglazov (Berlin).

Zickfeld, J. H., Schubert, T. W., Seibt, B., Blomster, J. K., Arriaga, P., Basabe, N., Fiske, A. P. (2019) 'Kama Muta: conceptualizing and measuring the experience often labelled being moved across 19 nations and 15 languages', *Emotion* 19, 402–24.

Zimmermann, B. (2009) 'Zum Begriff Muthos in der griechischen Literatur', in B. Zimmermann (ed.), *Mythische Wiederkehr: der Ödipus- und Medea-Muthos im Wandel der Zeiten* (Freiburg) 11–16.

Zuntz, G. (1965) *An Inquiry into the Transmission of the Plays of Euripides* (Cambridge).

Index locorum

1QS (*The Community Rule*) (anon.)
3:13–4:26   108

Agathias Scholasticus
Histories
2.10.4   309

Alexander (son of Numenius)
On Figures
xii.7–14   153

Andrew of Crete
On the Dormition of Mary (*PG*)
97.1088B   134–5

Anthologia Marciana
219 (B56)   403

Aristeides, Ailios
Hieros Logos
5   211–12

Aristotle
Metaphysics
1, 982b11–21   77–9

Nicomachean Ethics
2, 1108a20–3   307–8
5.11, 1138b5–13   239

On the Soul
1.1, 403a29–403b3   354
1.4, 408b13–15   239

Rhetoric
2.1, 1378a20–3   433–4
2.2, 1378a30–1378b2
        342
2.6, 1383b12–14   437–8

3, 1408a19–23   123
3.1, 1403b15–1404a8
        202–3

[Aristotle]
Mechanics
847a10–18   81–2

Asterius of Amasea
Homilies
11.4.2–4   251–2

Attaleiates, Michael
History
171.17–23   312–13

Augustine of Hippo
Confessions
3.2   250

Basil of Caesarea
Regulae brevius tractatae (*PG*)
31.1117B   310

Basil of Seleucia
Oratio XVIII in Herodiadem (*PG*)
85.226D–236C   269

Cedrenos/Kedrenos, George
Historiarum compendium
281   305

Choniates, Niketas
History
35.39–36.49   314

508   *Index locorum*

136.58–61	328
153.26–32	317
171.52–5	319–20
204.91–5	315–16
243.24–31	327–8
252.81–253.85	315
275.12–276.19	329
301.17–302.37	320–1
365.65–8	317–18
435.53–61	314
460.86–7	329–30
483.36–489.30	330–1
489.47–51	315
507.60–508.66	331–2
519.39–520.57	316
575.59–66	321

Christopher of Mytilene

Poems
1.5–18	381–2

Christos Paschon (anon.)
292–357	300
731–837	295–6
847–931	296–7
1427–45	299
1453–6	299–300

Chrysostom, John

Catech. bapt.
4.30	247

Homilia dicta postquam reliquiae martyrum (*PG*)
63.467–72	376

Homilies on First Corinthians (*PG*)
61.115.42–3	197

Homilies on the Gospel of John (*PG*)
59.119–20	270

Homilies on the Gospel of St Matthew (*PG*)
57.200–1	182–3
57.236.38–238.12	194–6

Homilies on the Statues (*PG*)
2.1 (*PG* 49.33.38–35.1	
	184–5
2.1 (*PG* 49.35.17–26)	
	187–8

49.36	186
49.135.48–50	190
49.137.43–138.12	191–2
49.139.38–46	192
49.141.4–14	193

Clement of Alexandria

Paedagogus
1.6.39.2–42.1	429–30

Commentary on Aristotle's Rhetoric (anon.) (Rabe 1896)
159.5–25	215–16

Commentary on Hermogenes (anon.) (Walz 1832–6)
vii.2.883.15–884.7	151–2

Cyril of Alexandria

Commentary on the 12 Prophets
1.640.8–11	257
1.645.14–19	257

Demosthenes

Orationes
18.287–91	209

Dionysios of Halikarnassos/Dionysius of Halicarnassus

On Demosthenes
21.3–22.2	124–7
53–4	210–11

Dorotheos of Gaza

Didaskaliai
2.31–2	311

Doxapatres, John

Commentary on Aphthonios' Progymnasmata
xiv.89.26–90.8	149–50

Egeria

Travels
37.7	377–8

Index locorum

Euripides

Erechtheus
frr. 358, 359, 360a 410

Hippolytus
565–600 296

Phoenician Women
355–6 409

Eustathius

Ad Iliadem
4.391.28 239
4.553.9–554.2 241–2
4.583.6–13 243
4.585.3–7 242
4.588.16–20 242–3
4.634.23–635.4 242

Ad Odysseam
2.223–4 244–5
3.222.6–15 240–1
3.223.6–9 241

Galen

A Method of Medicine to Glaucon
11.62.7–11 355

On the Differences of Fevers
8.283.7–9 354

On the Doctrines of Hippocrates and Plato
3.3.21–2 238
8.4.21.23–4 353

On the Hippocratic Epidemics
259–260.4 355

On the Preservation of Health
6.138.6–8 352–3

[Galen]

On Humours
19.488.11–13 347

Gellius, Aulus

Attic Nights
12.1 422

Gregoras, Nikephoros

Letters
34.45–61 85–6

Gregory of Nazianzos/Nazianzus

Orationes
1.4–5 136–7
6.18 128
38.7 137–8
39.1 138
39.2.3–4 145–6
39.7 137
39.11 121, 138–9
39.14 130–1
43.67 127–8, 138

Gregory of Nyssa

De deitate filii et spiritus sancto et In Abraham (PG)
46.572c 255–6

Heliodorus

Aethiopica
2.22.4 264
7.7.5 265
10.13.1–3 277–8
10.38.4 276

Hermogenes

On Types of Style
2.7.11–12 144

Hero of Alexandria

Belopoeica
71.1–73.11 82

Pneumatics (Schmidt 1976)
1 82

Homer

Iliad
2.311–320 264
9.646 354
10.455–7 254
13.455–9 230

510 Index locorum

16.203 101
18.107–110 40
22.82–6 414
22.98–130 232–3
22.376–88 231–2

Odyssey
9.294–306 229–30
20.5–43 233–6

Ignatios/Ignatius

Life of the Patriarch Tarasios
57 365
62.1–2 364
64.3–15 364–5, 382

Inscriptions (anon.)
100–1 no. 142 (Peek)
412–13
IG II² 12963 412

Isocrates/Isokrates

To Philip
25–7 208–9

John of Damascus

Exposition of the Orthodox Faith
13.91–8 150–1

John of Sardis

*Commentary on the Progymnasmata
of Aphthonius*
200.18 127
206.26–207.3 126–7

Justinian

Novellae
77 373

Klimakos, John (*PG*)
88 310

Komnene, Anna
1.13.3–4 334–5
10.10.6 319
11.12.5–6 318

12.3.2–4 332–3
15.9.1 335

Marinus of Neapolis

Vita Procli
3 72

Mauropous, John

Poems
54.64–7 170

Maximus the Confessor

De caritate (*PG*)
90.1036B 311

Menologium Basilianum (anon.) (*PG*)
117.129–30 371
117.279–80 369

Metaphrastes, Symeon

Menologion
13–24 435–6

Metochites, Theodore

Introduction to Astronomy (Paschos
and Simelidis 2017)
1.5 91

Orationes
14.27.1–11 221

Poems
5.65 439

Sententious Remarks
13.2.1–8 88–9
31.1.1–5 86–8
42.1.2–2.4 90–1
43.1.1–3 92, 439
43.2.7 93
60.6.2 93

Nemesios/Nemesius of Emesa

On the Nature of Man
20.81.2–3 346
21.81.19–82.3 326

Index locorum

Neophytos the Recluse

Panegyrike A
6.33–5   373

New Testament

John
8:12   145–6, 377

Matthew
25:31–46   384–5, 393, 393, 394

Oratio adversus Constantinum Cabalinum
(anon.) (*PG*)
95.309–44   385–6

Philagathos of Cerami

Homilies
6.1–16   260–8
17   270–1
22.8–9   271–3
24.6–24.11   252–5, 257–9
27   275–6
31.30–1   274–5
34   276–8
35.5   273–4
35.8   268--9
51.7   256

Philoponus

In Aristotelis libros De anima
52.4–7   440

Philostratos

Vitae Sophistarum (Stefec 2016)
488   212–13
509   210
519–20   213
537   212
542–3   213
569   214
614   206

Photios/Photius

Homilies (Laourdas 1959)
3.1   366, 371
4.4   366
4.5   367, 370–1
8.1   135–6

Planudes, Maximus

Epistles
73.112.8–23   396–7, 399, 406

Plato

Ion
530b–536c   62–4

Laws
816b–c   61

Meno
79e–80c   68

Phaedo
94c–e   236

Phaedrus
267c7–d3   207

Republic
378e–379a   61
441b–c   237–8
605c9–d4   124, 129

Symposium
215a–216b   65–8

Theaetetus
155d1–5   77

Pliny the Elder

Natural History
35.98   413–14

Plotinus
1.6.4   69–70

Plutarch

De liberis educandis
5   422

Porphyrius

Vita Plotini
1   71

Proclus

In Platonis Rempublicam commentarii
1.16.2–13   70

512   *Index locorum*

Psellos, Michael

Chronographia (Reinsch 2014)
1.35.4	323
6a.7	166–7

Discourse Improvised to the Bestarches Pothos
27–45	72–3, 129, 439–40
46–59	222–3
308–14	215

Historia Syntomos (Aerts 1990)
46.30.14–23	305, 311–12

Letters (Papaioannou 2019)
43.68–72	168
175.32–7	168–9

Orationes
3 (Polemis 2014)
9.5–15	217–18

3 (Gautier 1978)
25–7	162

4 (Polemis 2014)
3.10–18	163–4
7.13–24	164–5

7 (Fisher 1994)
140–6	166

8 (Polemis 2014)
1.23–30	160–1
3.14–23	161–2

9 (Polemis 2014)
3.16–21	162–3

10 (Polemis 2014)
26.1–4	165–6

37 (Littlewood 1985)
37.61–9	219
37.147–56	219–20
37.157–64	218
37.274–81	220–1

Pseudo-Dionysius the Areopagite

On Divine Names
3.2, 141.4–14	131–4

Pseudo-Gregentios

Nomoi
285–90	376

Pseudo-Nilus of Ancyra

Narrations
6.1.11–12	262

Quintilian

Institutio Oratoria
11.3.184	211

Shepherd of Hermas (anon.)

Mandata
3.3–4	111–12
4.1	112
4.3.1–2	98
5.1.2–3	106
5.2.2–4	102
5.2.6–8	105, 106, 107
6.1.2–6	104–5
6.2.1–9	112–15, 117n209

Visiones
1.1–9	110–11
1.2.4	111

Sikeliotes, John

Commentary on Hermogenes' On Types of Style (Walz 1832–6)
vi.120.14–121.13	153–5
vi.139.14–140.2	152–3
vi.306.18–308.2	144–6
vi.419.17–420.19	146–9
vi.422.22–423.26	149

Skylitzes, John

Synopsis historion
400.39–44	380

Sophocles/Sophokles

Electra
770–1	409–10

Stephanos Skylitzes

Commentary on Aristotle's Rhetoric (Rabe 1896)
309.12–25	216
310.35–311.4	216–17

Index locorum

Studites, Theodore

Epistles

478.28–30	372–3

Symeon the New Theologian

Theological and Practical Chapters

1.17	171
1.32	172–3
1.85	171
3.12	172
3.21	173, 439
3.31–3	172

Hymns (Koder & Paramelle 1969)

4.1–16	175–6

Sermons (Krivochéine 1963-5)

4.586–650	175
29.218–42	174–5

Tatius, Achilles

Leukippe and Kleitophon

3.2.8	263
5.24.3	274

Theophanes Continuatus (anon.)

4.15	386–7, 438n8

Thucydides

1.23.6	23

Typikon of the Great Church (anon.)
(Mateos 1962–3)

21	369–70
78–80	372
90–3	369
130–2	370
334, 362, 374	379

War of Troy (anon.)

15–16	340
98–9	340
734–7	340
1182–3	343
1976–2013	343
2086–93	341–2
3280–3	349
6708–11	356–7
6947–53	355
9477–9485	357–8
10889	352

Index rerum

Achilles 40, 232, 342, 344, 352, 354, 357–8
Aemilian (Emperor) 305, 311–12
affective fields 44, 362, 372n. 51
aidōs 28–9, 68n. 25, 161, 243, 303–4, 325–7, 329–38, 384n. 8; *see also* shame
Aischines 205, 206, 207–8, 209, 210
aischunē 68n. 25, 303–4, 325–9, 330, 331, 336–8, 436–8, 439; *see also* shame
alazoneia (arrogance) 303–9, 311–25, 336–8, 436
Alcestis 258–9, 391, *392*
Alciphron 269, 272
Aldouinos (Baldwin of Sicily) 317–18
Andromache 258, 285, 356, 414
Andronikos I Komnenos 315, 329
angels 108, 111, 112–13, 115, 117, 438
anger 20–1, 30–1
 – Christian analysis of 97, 100-4, 106-9, 117
 – of God 110–11, 289, 369, 371, 372–3, 382
 – of orators 181, 182, 196–7
 – of warriors 40, 339–58
 – philosophical analysis of 342, 343, 345, 346, 347, 349–50, 354, 434–5
 – physiology of 346–7, 352–3, 354–8
Antiochos of Aigai 213–14
apatheia 161, 167, 171–2, 176, 285
apocalypse *see* eschatology
architecture, affectivity of 375, 399–402, *400*, *402*
Aristides (painter) 413–14
Ariston 308
Aristophanes 207, 307
Aristotle 35, 147, 239, 307–8, 437–8, 410, 433–4
 – on anger 342–3, 345, 347, 349–50, 354
 – on emotional persuasion 123, 125, 182, 202–3, 204

 – on wonder 77–9, 81–2, 83–4, 85
arrogance *see alazoneia*
ascetics 73, 128, 138–9, 173, 179, 259, 429
Aspasius 434–5, 438
atmosphere 44, 287, 300, 362, 372, 375, 377, 379, 380

baptism 98, 107, 117, 173, 400; *see also* Epiphany
Barrett, Lisa Feldman 10–12, 14, 17, 21
Basilakes, Nikephoros 293–4
Basil of Caesarea 46, 127–8, 138, 262, 310, 354n. 51
blushing 196, 197, 332, 336
Boris I (ruler of Bulgaria) 386–7
Botaneiates, Michael 312
breastfeeding 409, 412–14, *413*, 416–18, *417*, 419, 421–2, *421*, *423*, 429, 431; *see also* Isis; Mary, Galaktotrophousa

charis (grace, elegance) 161, 162, 164, 165, 167, 169, 176
cheerfulness 107, 161–2, 163, 165, 168–9, 170
childbirth 409–10, 412, 416, *421*, 424
cholē 97, 99–100, 117, 346–8, 349, 350, 351; *see also* anger
cholos 31, 40, 97, 101, 293, 346, 358; *see also* anger
Choniates, Niketas 303, 316–18, 319–22, 323–5, 327–32, 333n. 120, 336, 337
Choumnos, Nikephoros 221
Christopher of Mytilene,169, 381–2
Chrysippus 238, 353
Chrysostom, John 46, 73, 179–99, 247, 270, 309–10, 376, 384–5, 440
Cicero 125, 126n. 18
commemoration *see* memory

Index rerum

compunction 42, 146, 172–5, 176, 375, 384

Constantine IX Monomachos 165

constructionism, psychological 10–15

conversion *see* repentance

core affect 10–15

dancing 65, 136, 268–9, 270, 272

deliberation, phenomenology of 227–46

delivery, rhetorical 187, 201–2, 204, 206–223; *see also* gestures; posture; voice

demons 108, 270–1, 310, 396, 435–8, 440

Demosthenes 124–5, 126, 206, 209–11

desire, sexual 99, 110-11, 117, 268–73

Devil, the 41, 108, 109, 110, 247, 310, 437; *see also* demons

Dio Chrysostom 212–13

Dionysius of Halicarnassus 124–7, 128, 135, 139, 210–11

Doctrine of the Two Spirits 108–10

dress 40, 166, 191, 212, 310, 418, 419, 420, 421

Eirene (Empress, wife of Alexios I) 332–33

ekphrasis 128, 190, 247–79, 294

ekplēxis 66, 69–70, 92, 173, 293, 439

ekstasis (ecstasy) 66, 70, 71, 133, 136

embodied appraisal 20–1

emotional communities 6n. 12, 43, 157–77, 189, 198, 199, 345, 358, 362–4, 365, 371–2, 374, 382

emotion history 3-8, 14, 19, 32–3

emotion labels 12–13, 26–31, 157

enargeia 128, 190–1, 252, 279

entropē 325, 326–7, 330, 333, 336, 337; *see also* shame

Epiphany (Orthodox) 130–1, 136, 138–9

eschatology

- Christian 43, 95, 96, 99, 108, 115–16, 117, 279, 373, 383–90, *389*, 393–406, *393*, *394*, *398*, *402*, *404*, *405*
- pagan 391, *392*, *393*

ēthopoiïa 134n. 40, 205, 214, 244, 248, 259, 265–6, 293, 294

Euphrosyne (Empress, wife of Alexios III) 315, 316, 329–31, 333

Euripides 30–1, 258–9, 281–302, 409–10, 414

Eustratius of Nicaea 82–3

Evagrios of Pontos 171, 310

eyebrows 176, 312, 315–16, 321, 322–3, 337

facial expressions 16, 158, 163, 170, 175, 177, 183, 209, 222, 304, 342, 355–6, 396, 408; *see also* blushing; eyebrows; gaze; laughter; smiles; sullenness; tears

fear 20–1, 22, 23, 340, 350, 384, 433–4

- and transcendence 137–9, 146, 155, 156, 173, 278, 439
- of God 111, 137, 367, 369–71, 372–3, 382
- of Hell/Last Judgement 189, 195, 384–5, 386–7, 396–7, 399, 401, 403, 406
- rhetorical arousal of 63, 137–9, 155, 182, 188, 190–2, 193–4, 199

florilegia 46, 249, 261, 311

funerary art

- mothers 410–13, *411*, *413*, *420*, 421, *421*, 424, 427, *428*
- afterlife 391–3, *392*, *393*

Galen 238, 346–7, 352–3, 354, 355, 356

gall bladder 99–102, 114, 117

gaze 316, 322, 396, 412, 419, 421, 432

gestures 39, 190–1, 257, 262, 269, 272, 375

- in art 38, 41, 156, 388, 390, 393, 395, 396, 409n. 8, 410, 412, 416, 419, 421, 422, 432
- of orator 183, 204–5, 207–8, 209–11, 212–13, 214–15, 219–21, 223

God *see* anger, of God; fear, of God; *philanthropia; theōsis*

Gorgias 182

Great Goddesses 416, *417*, 424

Gregory of Nazianzus 72-3, 127–31, 136–9, 145–6, 156, 215, 222–3, 330, 439

Gregory of Nyssa 253, 254, 255–6, 261, 266

grief 161, 183–9, 252–68, 293, 364–6; *see also* compunction; laments

Guibert of Nogent 436–7

516   *Index rerum*

habitus 158, 222
heart
– and anger 102, 111, 112, 113–15, 346, 353, 354, 355
– cognitive-affective organ 151, 227, 234–9, 243–4, 436
Hector 232–3, 242–3, 298, 344, 349, 351, 355–7
Hecuba 341n. 7, 414
Heliodorus 264, 265, 269, 272–3, 276, 277–8
Heraclitus 85
Herakleides 206
Hercules 391, *392*, 438
Hermogenes 141–2, 144, 146, 153, 215,
Herod 255, 257, 268–9, 273–4
Herodotus 309
Holy Spirit 103–4, 105, 106, 107, 109, 110, 116–17, 173
Homer 61–4, 201, 227–46, 254, 264, 341, 347, 350, 353, 354, 358, 414
hubris 306, 307, 308–9
humours, theory of 157, 346–7, 352–3, 355–6
huperēphania 307, 308, 309–11, 316, 322, 323, 337

images, emotional response to 255–6, 385–7, 396–7, 399, 403, 406;
   see also ekphrasis
icons 251–2, 255–6, 257, 396–7, *398*, 399, 403, 406
intersubjectivity 8–9, 12–14, 15, 16. 19
Isis 418, 427, 429, 430
Isocrates 124–5, 126, 127, 208–9
Ivan Alexander (Tsar of Bulgaria) 403, *405*

James, William 10, 20–1
Job 184–5, 187
John of Damascus 150–1, 326, 346, 354, 384n. 8
Justinian 373, 375

Kariye Camii church (Istanbul) 401, *402*
katanuxis see compunction
kenodoxia (vanity) 307, 309–11, 313, 337
Kleon 207, 208

Komnene, Anna 303, 313, 318–19, 322, 332-5, 336, 337
Komnene, Theodora 315–16
Komnenos, John 314
kourotrophoi 415–19, *415*, *417*, 424, 430
Kroustoulas, Ioannes 218–21

laments 186–7, 198, 253, 257–9, 261–2, 266, 283, 284–5, 286–7, 288–90, 293, 296–7, 299–300
language and affective processing 9–10, 12–13, 15, 27–9, 157
Latin liturgical drama 249, 275
Latins/Westerners 317–21, 337
laughter 68, 161–2, 165, 169, 171;
   see also smiles
liver 99–102, 114, 347
Livistros and Rodamne 350

Magdalene, Mary 276–8, 291–2, 298
makrothumia 97, 103–5, 107, 108–9, 111, 113
Manuel I Komnenos 336
Mary, mother of God
– and Christ child 421–2, *423*, 429, 430, 432
– emotions of 284–92, 294, 295–300, 379
– Galaktotrophousa (Coptic) 425-6, *426*, 427, 429–30, 431
Mauropous, John 168, 169–70, 177
Maximus the Confessor 311 385
Medea 30–1, 238, 295–6, 297, 300
memory
– ritual commemoration 361, 364–7, 369–72
– liturgical recollection 130, 190, 250, 259, 290; *see also ekphrasis*
Menander Rhetor 186–7, 261, 262
Menelaus 201, 343
Menologium Basilianum (anon.), 367, *368* 369, 371
Mesarites, Nicholas 294
Mesopotamites, Konstantinos 315, 330, 331
metanoia see repentance
metaphor 39–40, 61, 71, 85, 103–7, 109, 114–15, 116–17, 185, 228, 234–5, 236,

Index rerum

239, 246, 318, 336, 337, 349–51, 355–6, 429–30

Metaphrastes, Symeon 166, 435–6, 437

Metochites, Theodore 86–93, 94, 221, 401, 439

metonymy 39, 117, 228, 233–4, 236, 292, 322, 337, 352

mimesis 59, 60, 136–9, 250, 261, 294, 301

mothers
- emotions 257–9, 261–8, 341n.7, 409–10, 412–14, *413*, 416, 419, 421–2, *423*, 431; *see also* Mary, mother of God, emotions
- *ēthos* 410–12, *411*, 416, 419–21, *420*, 424, 431–2

Nain, Son of the Widow of 259, 260–8

necks 321, 322, 323–4, 337

Nemanja, Stephen 328

Neoplatonism 69–72, 73, 85, 439

Nestor 201, 352

Niobe 258–9

objects, affectivity of 375–82

Odysseus 201, 212, 229–30, 233–9, 240–1, 244–5, 340

orators
- *ēthos* of 126–9, 196–7, 208–9; *see also* *ēthopoiïa*; sincerity; sympathy
- *pathē* of 123–4, 126–9, 180–1, 184–6, 196–8, 260; *see also* sincerity; sympathy
- emotive techniques 186–8, 189–91, 194–5, 198–9; *see also* delivery, rhetorical; *ekphrasis*; *ēthopoiïa*

orgē 31, 97, 101, 195, 236, 289, 293, 347–8; *see also* anger

Panagia Phorbiotissa church (Asinou) 403, *404*

Panagia ton Chalkeon church (Thessaloniki) 387, 400–1, *400*

Paraspondylos, Leo 166–7

Paschal Kanon 42, 47

Passion of Christ, emotions of 274–5, 275–6, 276–8, 284–94, 430–1

patience *see makrothumia*

Peleus 340

Perikles 207

phantasia 86–8, 94, 128

philanthrōpia 366–7, 370, 372–3, 382

phrenes 227, 228, 231, 233, 239

phrikē 139, 292

phthonos 41, 206, 286, 287, 289, 292, 293, 294, 299, 308n.25, 320n.72

physiognomy 177, 251, 408–9, 419; *see also* facial expressions; posture

Plato 60–9, 70, 71, 73, 77, 79, 91,124, 129, 137, 203, 207, 236, 237–9, 250, 303–4, 307, 324, 433

Plotinus 69–70, 71, 439–40

Plutarch 207, 308, 422

Pluto 391, *392*

Polemo 212, 213

Porphyrius 71

posture 16–17, 39, 158, 170, 175–6, 177, 190–1, 204, 218, 219, 409n.8, 416, 420, 430; *see also* dancing, necks, walking

prefocusing (priming) 131, 139, 187, 204, 213–14

Priam 343

pride 29–30; *see also alazoneia*; *huperēphania*

Proserpina 391, *392*

Psellos, Michael 59, 71–3, 129, 147n.31, 159–69, 176–7, 215, 217–21, 222–3, 305, 311–12, 323, 439–40

Ptolemy, Claudius 83, 84

purification, emotional 98, 104, 106, 109, 137–9, 146, 173, 379; *see also* baptism

Pyrrhus 340, 352

Pythagoras 88

Quintilian 204, 211, 260

radiance 71, 73, 92, 414

repentance (conversion) 95, 98, 107, 109, 111, 117, 366–7, 369–70, 371, 373–4, 375, 385–7, 406

rhetoric *see* delivery, rhetorical; orators; rhetoric, Christian; sincerity, rhetorical; sympathy, rhetorical

rhetoric, Christian
- and icons 43, 155–6, 249–52, 255–6, 257, 279, 301
- and theatre 183, 205–6, 249–51, 259, 301–2
- theorization of 141–56

518 *Index rerum*

Roman de Troie 339–40, 342, 343, 345, 348
Russell, James A. 10, 11, 14, 17, 21, 23

Salome 268–70
Santa Maria Assunta cathedral (Torcello) 387, 388–90, 399–400, *389*
Satan *see* Devil, the
Schnell, Rüdiger 3–8, 13n. 52, 16, 24
scripts 7, 18n. 76, 19, 21, 22–3, 29–30, 32, 68n. 32, 157–77, 180–1, 187, 313
Second Sophistic 205, 210–14, 221
senses, and emotions 85–93, 190–1, 199, 253–4, 257–8, 259, 260, 262, 375–82; *see also ekphrasis, enargeia*
shame 28–9, 59, 68, 193, 194–8, 199, 273–4, 293, 296, 303–4, 325–38, 343, 433, 436–9
Sikeliotes, John 141–156, 440
simile 234, 244, 264, 348, 351–2
sincerity, rhetorical 144–6, 148–9, 155–6, 164, 209
skuthrōpos see sullenness
smiles 162, 166, 168–9, 176; *see also* laughter
Socrates 59, 60, 65–8, 69, 70, 71, 73
Sopater 144
Sophokles 207, 215, 409–10
Stoics/ Stoicism 143–4, 238–9, 326, 337, 353, 438
Stylites, Symeon 374
sullenness 163, 164–5, 166, 169, 170 175, 176
Symeon the New Theologian 170–7, 439
sympathy, rhetorical 62–4, 65–6, 73–4, 121–39, 181–94

Tamar 271–3
Tarasios, Saint 364–5, 382
tears 63, 66, 187, 220, 255, 263, 266, 293–4, 355–6, 406
– and compunction 42, 172–5, 176, 384
– of orator 184, 204n. 16, 209, 222, 260
Testaments of the Twelve Patriarchs 108–9
theatre 183, 205–6, 249–50, 301
Theodosius I 183–4, 374
Theodosius II 369, 374
Theophrastus 204, 308
theōria 78–84, 90–1, 133, 137–8
theōsis 136–9, 279
Theotokos, the *see* Mary, mother of God
thumos
– anger 31, 195, 239–40, 291, 293, 314, 46, 347–8, 349, 350–1, 358
– cognitive-affective organ 227–36, 238–43
Trisagion 369, 374, 377, *378*

vanity *see kenodoxia*
voice, of orator 183, 201, 202–3, 204–5, 207–9, 210–11, 213, 215–20

walking 166, 176, 315, 322, 377
wonder (τὸ θαυμάζειν) 39, 75–94, 173, 267, 78, 439–40, 441

Xerxes 309
Xiphilinos, Ioannes 217–18,

zēlotupia (jealousy) 30–1